The Elusive Executive

Discovering Statistical Patterns in the Presidency

Gary King
Harvard University

Lyn Ragsdale
University of Arizona

A Division of Congressional Quarterly Inc.
1414 22nd Street, N.W., Washington, D.C. 20037

Printed in the United States of America

Library of Congress Cataloging-in-Publication Data

King, Gary.
    The elusive executive : discovering statistical patterns in the presidency / Gary King and Lyn Ragsdale.
        p.   cm.
    Bibliography: p.
    Includes index.
    ISBN 0-87187-443-1   ISBN 0-87187-432-6 (pbk.)
    1. Presidents—United States.   I. Ragsdale, Lyn, 1954-
II. Title.
JK516.K46   1988
353.03′1—dc19   87-33015
                                                                CIP

To our families

E.R., E.L., A.K., M.K., M.D., C.D.
J.R., C.R., T.R.

Contents

Contents

Tables and Figures

TABLES

FIGURES

Tables and Figures

Acknowledgments

This book has been a total collaboration: the "Ts" written by one author were crossed by the other (and then sometimes erased by the first). We did much of the data collection, coding, and computer analysis jointly. In data collection, coding, and management we were also aided by several talented individuals, including Andrea Az, John Fobanjong, Uri Maimon, and Charles Pearson. Our special thanks to Jo Andrews and Kerry Gardner, who provided helpful suggestions and unflaggingly and meticulously got the job done. We are indebted to Sally Garnatt, William Lockwood, and George P. Sharrard for their computer expertise and to Mary Sue Passe and Kelli-Cheyenne Waldron for their expert secretarial assistance. Everett Carll Ladd, Marilyn Potter, John Barry, and others at the Roper Center for Public Opinion Research at the University of Connecticut, Storrs, assisted us in acquiring the Gallup data for our analyses in Chapter 6. For their helpful advice, comments, and suggestions throughout various phases and title changes, we sincerely thank Steven Brams, Leon Epstein, Barbara Hinckley, Bryan London, Tracy Ragsdale, Elizabeth Rosenthal, Jerrold Rusk, and Graham Wilson. Jeffrey Cohen and Karen Hult thoroughly reviewed the manuscript and offered valuable comments.

We owe a special debt of gratitude to Joanne D. Daniels, Kerry V. Kern, Ellen Kresky, Nancy A. Lammers, John L. Moore, Marcia Brubeck, and Kathryn C. Suárez at Congressional Quarterly for masterful production, marketing, and editorial assistance. We also gratefully acknowledge a New York University Research Challenge Award and a New York University Academic Computing Facility Grant both made to Gary King and a University of Arizona Social and Behavioral Sciences Faculty Grant made to Lyn Ragsdale. Lyn Ragsdale also wishes to thank the Russell Sage Foundation for a year as a postdoctoral fellow, during which time both authors were in New York and conceived the original idea for the book. Finally, we thank the many academic researchers who have graciously supplied us with data for analysis in this book and those who have requested our data and analyses.

The following individuals and publishers have graciously extended permission to reprint copyrighted material from the sources indicated:

The Academy of Political Science: from Roger Brown, "Party and Bureaucracy: From Kennedy to Reagan," *Political Science Quarterly* 97 (Summer 1982):285, Table 2.

Herbert Alexander and Lexington Books, D. C. Heath: from Herbert Alexander, *Financing the 1968 Election* and *Financing the 1972 Election;* copyright © 1971, 1976.

American Enterprise Institute for Public Policy Research: from *Public Opinion,* March/May 1979, 29; October/November 1979, 24; February/March 1981, 38; April/May 1983, 36; October/November 1984, 38-40, 48-49; April/May 1985, 8; February/March 1986, Table 6.1; Summer 1986, 28, 32; September-October 1986, Table 6.20; copyright © the American Enterprise Institute for Public Policy Research, Washington, D.C.; and from Eric Davis, "Congressional Liaison: The People and the Institutions," in *Both Ends of the Avenue,* ed. Anthony King, 67, Table 3-1, and 68, Table 3-2; copyright © 1983 the American Enterprise Institute for Public Policy Research, Washington, D.C.

The American Political Science Association: from Robert Axelrod, "Presidential Election Coalitions in 1984," *American Political Science Review* 80 (March 1986):282-283; and from Jack Holmes and Robert Elder, Jr., "Our Best and Our Worst Presidents: Some Possible Reasons for Perceived Performance," paper presented at the annual meeting of the American Political Science Association, 1986.

Citizens' Research Foundation: from Herbert Alexander, *Financing the 1960 Election* and *Financing the 1964 Election;* copyright © 1962, 1966.

Congressional Quarterly: from Herbert Alexander, *Financing the 1976 Election;* from *Congressional Quarterly Weekly Report,* July 31, 1976, 2036; January 17, 1981, 138; August 4, 1984, 1924; September 7, 1985, 1760; April 5, 1986, 771; May 10, 1986, 1027; from *Congressional Quarterly Almanac,* 1976, 969; from *Congressional Quarterly Guide to Current American Government,* 1986, 72; from *Congressional Quarterly's Guide to U.S. Elections,* 1985; from *Congressional Quarterly's Guide to 1976 Elections: A Supplement to CQ's Guide to U.S. Elections,* 1977; *Congressional Quarterly's Guide to the U.S. Supreme Court,* 1979, 946-948; and from *The Washington Lobby,* 3d ed., 1979, 29.

Thomas Cronin, William Keech, and Little, Brown and Co.: from William Keech, "Selecting and Electing Presidents, 1936-1980," in

Rethinking the Presidency, 2d ed., ed. Thomas Cronin, 32, Table 1; copyright © Thomas E. Cronin.

The Gallup Organization, Inc.: from *Gallup Opinion Index,* Report 182, October/November 1980, 13-59; and from *Gallup Report,* February 1983, 12; March 1983, 15; September 1983, 10, 11, 13, 14; April 1984, 18-20; July 1984, 21; August/September 1984, 13; October 1984, 22; December 1984, 4-5.

Sheldon Goldman: from his "Reorganizing the Judiciary: The First Term Appointments," *Judicature* 68 (April-May 1985): Tables 1, 2, and 3.

Holmes and Meier Publishers, Inc.: from Philip H. Burch, Jr., *Elites in American History,* vol. 3, Tables 11, 12, 13, 14, and 15; copyright © 1980 by Philip H. Burch, Jr.

Institute for the Study of Human Issues: from Stephen Wayne, "Expectations of the President," in *The President and the Public,* ed. D. Graber, 31.

Johns Hopkins University Press: from Paul Light, *The President's Agenda,* Tables 2, 3, 5, 6, 7.

Little, Brown and Co.: from Thomas E. Cronin, *The State of the Presidency,* 2d ed., 386; copyright © 1980 by Thomas E. Cronin.

Plenum Publishing Corp. and Dean Simonton: from Dean Simonton, "Presidential Greatness: The Historical Consensus and Its Psychological Significance," *Political Psychology* 7 (June 1986):281.

Praeger Publishers, a division of Greenwood Press: from Lawrence Margolis, *Executive Agreements and Presidential Power in Foreign Policy,* 101-105, Table 1; copyright © 1986 Praeger Publishers.

Princeton University Press: from Steven J. Rosenstone, Roy L. Behr, and Edward H. Lazarus, *Third Parties in America: Citizen Response to Major Party Failure;* copyright © 1984 by Princeton University Press.

University of Nebraska Press: from Richard Hansen, *The Year We Had No President;* copyright © 1962 by the University of Nebraska Press.

University of North Carolina Press: from Alexander Heard, *The Costs of Democracy;* copyright © 1960 The University of North Carolina Press.

University of Tennessee Press: from Martha Kumar, "Presidential Libraries: Gold Mine, Booby Trap, or Both?" in *Studying the Presidency,* ed. George Edwards and Stephen Wayne, 201, Table 8.1.

University of Texas Press and John H. Kessel: from John H. Kessel, "The Structure of the Carter White House," *American Journal of Political Science* 27 (August 1983):456, Table 7; and from John H. Kessel, "The Structure of the Reagan White House," *American Journal of Political Science* 28 (May 1984):247, 248, 250, Tables 7, 8, 9, 10.

The Elusive Executive

Introduction:
Information and Meaning
in the Study of the Presidency

The modern American presidency is the most scrutinized political institution in the world. Fully 20 percent of all American national news concerns the president directly; an additional 20 percent relates to the cabinet or other administration officials (Sigal 1973). Up-to-the-minute information on the radio and television, summaries and analyses published the following day or week by newspapers, magazines, and other periodicals, and nearly three thousand works published since the mid-1930s (see Greenstein, Berman, and Felzenberg 1977) all focus enormous attention on presidents and the presidency. Myriad polling organizations interview thousands of Americans each year to determine the president's public image and persuasive impact, and much of this information becomes publicly available.

Some forty-eight research centers, foundations, and private institutions are concerned, at least in part, with presidential activities (Goehlert and Martin 1985). Presidential election statistics from every voting district in the nation are collected and printed. The U.S. Government Printing Office publishes massive documents containing every bill that crosses the president's desk, every treaty negotiated, and every executive order promulgated.

Presidential libraries scattered around the country house thousands of presidential documents, including many personal papers, written correspondence by and to the president and his top aides, position and briefing papers, daily schedules, appointment calendars, oral histories, and telephone logs. Almost every word the president utters is recorded and published. (Table I.1 summarizes the holdings of the libraries of presidents from Herbert Hoover to Gerald Ford.) In addition, biographies of every White House employee and lists of White House expenditures are also available. Reporters, government

1

officials, academics, and ordinary citizens consume large parts of this immense body of electronic and print material.[1]

As if such opportunities to glean information were not enough, the White House provides daily recorded messages about the president's precise schedule (see Table I.2). To find out if a bill has passed a particular house of Congress or if it has been vetoed or signed by the president, a caller can ask the office of the White House clerk. Or a toll-free number can be dialed to hear a daily message excerpted from the president's most recent public speech. Although ordinary citizens cannot reach the president directly, they can easily write him a letter or speak with a member of his staff.

Information and Meaning

In short, we have more information about presidents and the presidency than about any other elected official or office in any country at any time. But *information is not meaning.* Murray Edelman explained that "meaning is basically different from information and incompatible with it. Meaning is associated with order—with a patterned cognitive structure that permits anticipation of future developments. . . . Information involves complexity or lack of order: inability to foresee" (1971, 31). Despite the mass of information, or perhaps because of it, scholars and others have rarely discerned meaning. Thus, the essential character of the American executive remains elusive.

We believe that scholars must concentrate on two important steps to understand the American presidency more fully. First, scholars must move from anecdotal observation to systematic description. The need to do so too often passes unrecognized in social science research. The wealth of anecdotal observation available on the presidency must be synthesized so that comparison and evaluation are as easy as possible. Systematic description reduces the information overload that precludes meaningful understanding and paves the way for the next important step: the move from systematic description to explanation.

Scholars, journalists, politicians, and interested citizens spend much time assessing a president's accomplishments and speculating about the ways in which he will address national policy issues, cope with an errant appointee, react to the latest public opinion poll, or calculate the probability of reelection. Unfortunately, such speculations about a president may reflect anecdotal evidence and reminiscences rather than data systematically acquired and analyzed.

Anecdotal observation has at least three negative consequences. First, it leads observers to make misinformed judgments and state-

Table I.1: Holdings of Presidential Libraries

Item	Hoover	Roosevelt	Truman	Eisenhower
Manuscripts				
Pages	5,769,492	16,402,774	12,824,047	18,645,343
Audiovisual				
Still photos	24,577	126,663	73,964	108,000
Film	133,464	303,424	301,906	597,775
Video tape	3	10	175	29
Audio tape	199	934	246	804
Oral history				
Pages	9,578	2,917	36,800	21,923
Museum objects	4,168	22,104	18,518	26,630
Printed materials				
Books	22,998	45,109	44,109	44,352
Serials	23,972	32,259	66,939	29,498
Other	615	86,961	73,243	22,484
Daily calendar				
Size (pages)	unknown	unknown	15,200	8,000

	Kennedy	Johnson	Nixon	Ford
Manuscripts				
Pages	28,860,592	34,775,043	45,865,312	14,961,627
Audiovisual				
Still photos	116,270	556,905	435,000	310,026
Film	6,022,281	803,743	2,220,000	700,000
Video tape	166	4,660	3,900	882
Audio tape	3,124	10,457	1,490	872
Oral history				
Pages	29,640	35,395	2,200	0
Museum objects	13,920	37,716	21,750	6,857
Printed materials				
Books	20,909	24,883	23,174	9,000
Serials	23,498	2,427	0	33
Other	5,069	4,585	0	3,117
Daily calendar				
Size (reels)	10	13	secret	secret

Source: An updated and expanded version of Kumar (1983, Table 8-1).

Table I.2 White House Phone Numbers

Purpose	Recorded?	Number
President's schedule	Yes	202-456-2343
First Lady's schedule	Yes	202-456-6269
Status of legislation	No	202-456-2226
President's daily message	Yes	800-424-9090
		202-456-7198
Counsel to the President	No	202-456-2632
Chief of staff	No	202-456-6797
Press secretary	No	202-456-2100
Legislative affairs	No	202-456-6620
Public liaison	No	202-456-2270
Personnel	No	202-456-7060
All others	No	202-456-1414

Note: The president or any of his staff can also be written in care of the Executive Office of the President, 1600 Pennsylvania Avenue, N.W., Washington, D.C. 20500.

ments. For example, the 1980 and 1984 elections, particularly the latter, are widely perceived as two of the largest presidential election victories ever. Accordingly, Democrats and Republicans alike believe that the American public supported President Ronald Reagan's policies wholeheartedly. Although his 1984 victory was a substantial electoral college win, fully one-third of all election victories in this century were decided by *larger* popular vote margins (see Chapter 7). Moreover, two-thirds of all presidential elections in this century were decided by larger popular vote margins than Reagan's 1980 victory.[2]

Second, anecdotal observation leaves citizens and scholars without a reliable basis for comparison and analysis. Presidential behavior, reporters' comments, newspaper editorials, presidents' biographies and autobiographies, as well as political arguments by members of Congress or the administration are impossible to evaluate adequately without knowledge of comparable situations and statistics. For example, commentators often overstated Ronald Reagan's popularity and reporters talked of Reagan as a "Teflon" president, his personal popularity seemingly untouched by the relative unpopularity of his political positions. Such an erroneous evaluation could be avoided by systematic analysis of the evidence. Chapter 6 makes clear that at many times during his tenure Reagan has been one of the least popular presidents on record. In addition, anecdotal observation leads presidency scholarship to be too incumbent-specific. This situation prompted Hugh Heclo (1977) to argue:

> The lessons emphasized in the literature . . . change with the latest judgments about the merits and demerits of what "he" is doing to "us." This may be a good recipe for writing trenchant interpretations of current events, but it does not provide in-depth empirical information about what is actually happening in the presidency as an institution. (28)

Finally, anecdotal observation has produced a situation in which much "academic writing has been highly derivative of . . . secondary sources, often accepting their unsubstantiated generalizations at face value" (Heclo 1977, 22). Presidency watchers of all kinds have an interest in eliminating anecdotal observation and thus reducing the chasm between information and meaning.

Statistical Patterns in the Presidency

This book offers a systematic statistical description of presidential politics, primarily from the 1950s to the 1980s. It attempts to transform the mass of information on the American presidency into an easily available, more meaningful, and somewhat more digestible form. In so doing it seeks to provide a better foundation for explanations of presidents and the presidency. The statistics presented here have never before appeared in one volume. Many have never before been published, and most have been reanalyzed and reorganized into formats intended to be more meaningful and more useful to the reader. Experts may be surprised that many of the data even exist.

The statistics encompass presidents' legislative initiatives and successes, executive orders and agreements, White House staffs and other federal appointees, public appearances, elections, and the public approval of presidential performances. We culled material principally from original archival sources that do not usually offer such data in meaningful and easily retrievable forms. Here they have been integrated with other data from a variety of sources to give the reader a longitudinal and institutional look at the American presidency. This material makes possible systematic comparisons that may suggest statistical patterns across presidential terms. Students can evaluate the decisions of any president relative to the actions of other presidents. The data also permit generalizations about change and continuity in the presidency as an institution as well as about the reactions of other institutions and the public to the presidency. In the text of this book we discuss many of these generalizations and patterns for the first time but many others await discovery in the data we present.

This volume bears a cousinly resemblance to Ornstein, Mann, Malbin, Shick, and Bibby's book, *Vital Statistics on Congress.* Ornstein and others sought to create an "easy-to-use handbook containing information on all aspects of Congress" (1984, xvii). These scholars were able to compile the bulk of their tables and figures directly from a well-developed quantitative literature, but we were not so fortunate. The quantitative literature on the presidency is not so mature.

Indeed, the synthesis of *existing* systematic information on the presidency is only one purpose of this book. We had two other primary goals: to create a large body of *original* systematic data on the American presidency and to redirect scholarly priorities in presidency research. We hope that this book will help initiate a turning point for analysis in the field. Judging from recent trends in this area of American politics and older trends in others, research on the presidency is becoming progressively more comparative and more systematic. As a result, scholars will be called upon to create and develop new statistics for systematic analysis. To be sure, other important approaches to the presidency do not lend themselves to statistical treatment. George and George (1964), for example, have written an excellent presidential psychobiography. This thorough, nonquantitative study and others like it make important contributions to the presidency literature that are not considered here.

Our theoretical approach to the presidency emphasizes the institutional and plural character of the executive. This contrasts with the focus in much of the presidency literature on specific actions taken by particular individuals and on the image of presidents as independent, singularly powerful decision makers. Instead, the presidency should be understood as if it were another Congress—a complex organization of many individuals with diverse goals. The president is but one of the individuals in the executive. Like Congress, the presidency has established areas of specialization, institutional loyalty, coalitions of competing interests, autonomous individuals, and a representative link to the American people. Our "plural presidency" approach involves not only an examination of the enormous complexity and diversity within the White House but also the discovery of patterns that emerge from this complex configuration. The intricacies define the institution of the presidency—an ongoing set of behaviors displayed by presidents and other political actors that have come to be expected. Often the term *institution* is used simply to designate the organization of the executive branch; we use this term more broadly to include many types of persisting patterns in observable behavior across presidential administrations.

In Chapter 1, we identify four patterns that characterize the plural presidency: program complexity, group diversity, organizational diffusion, and incumbent strategy. These patterns of the plural presidency result from several aspects of the office that have emerged since its inception: policy making by presidents, the use of the administrative apparatus to manage policy decisions, the public connection between presidents and the citizenry, the electoral dynamics that shape and are shaped by the office, and the constraints imposed by separation of powers.

Chapter 2 considers legislative action as one of the primary ways in which presidents attempt to make policy and as one of the principal indicators of their success. We analyze the presidents' agendas, the frequency and proportion with which presidential positions are taken on House and Senate roll calls, presidential success with regard to legislation, presidential vetoes, and congressional overrides from 1953 to 1984.

Chapter 3 surveys the increasingly large set of independent presidential actions, including executive orders and executive agreements, of every president since Washington. We also analyze other policy devices used by presidents such as presidential waivers, transfers of foreign assistance funds, use of the "drawdown authority," and budget requests and approvals. Such devices offer presidents more flexibility but also less publicity as policy makers.

One of the consequences of presidential policy-making responsibility has been the growth in and institutionalization of the White House staff since 1921. Chapter 4 examines the expansion of personnel, the increases in operating budgets for the executive office, and the changes in staff organization. We also analyze information on presidential appointments to departments, independent agencies, diplomatic posts, and the federal courts since the Eisenhower administration.

Chapter 5 explores another aspect of the presidency by discussing the public appearances of each president, beginning with Harry Truman. When frustrated in their efforts to bargain directly with other political elites on policy matters, presidents may attempt to gain support from the American public by making appeals directly to the nation or to smaller interest groups. Chapter 5 presents summaries of major national televised addresses, news conferences, public appearances in and out of Washington, and the days of presidential travel outside the United States.

As a companion to Chapter 5, Chapter 6 considers the presidency from the perspective of the public rather than the president. We consider approval of the current president as expressed by the public as a whole and by certain subgroups within the population. With previously unanalyzed opinion data from the Gallup Polling Organization, the subgroups are identified by the disaggregation or joint disaggregation of party identification, race, gender, education, occupation, and many other demographic variables. Public approval of presidential actions on more specific issues, such as foreign policy and the economy, together with a variety of other measures are also summarized. We present measures of public tolerance of certain presidential behaviors and of minority candidates for president.

Chapter 7 addresses the election and reelection prospects of presidents, both within their own parties and in competition with opposing parties. Primary results, political convention votes, and popular and electoral college votes all appear by state in more convenient formats than have previously been offered. We analyze information on voter turnout, electoral mandates, and the group composition of presidential electoral coalitions as well as election anomalies, third-party bids, and campaign financing. We also outline the incumbent party's success in congressional elections.

Chapter 8 evaluates the growing literature on the reputations of individual presidents. Our findings suggest that the most successful presidential analyses are likely to focus on the plural aspects of the institution rather than on the idiosyncratic attributes of individual incumbents. We also summarize our conceptual and methodological arguments.

Notes

1. Between 1939 and 1982, 915 unpublished M.A. theses and Ph.D. dissertations were written on presidents and the presidency. Nearly all dissertations are about individual presidents. No dissertations were undertaken on William Henry Harrison, Zachary Taylor, Franklin Pierce, or Chester Arthur (see University Microfilms International 1983).
2. For arguments about public opinion and electoral mandates, popular votes are more relevant than electoral college results.

1

The Plural Presidency

An obscure photograph hangs on a wall among several hundred pictures at the Henry Ford Museum in Dearborn, Michigan. Taken in the summer of 1921, it shows four men—Henry Ford, Thomas Edison, Harvey Firestone, and Warren Harding—all of them dressed in white trousers and three of them wearing straw hats. If the photo reflects its times in America, one may well ask which of the four was viewed as most important, most powerful, most accomplished, and most revered. Each could claim to have exercised a significant impact on American life. Ford had invented the automobile, Edison had developed the electric light bulb, and Firestone had pioneered research on the production of rubber. Warren Harding was then president of the United States.

Although the question might give a casual observer pause, it would not long bemuse scholars of the presidency who often comment on the prominence of chief executives, including Harding, as central political actors and legendary figures in American culture. The researchers would further suggest that this public prominence is unlikely to be rivaled. Presidents are key symbols of American unity and serve as convenient cognitive aids (Greenstein 1974). People respond to them, more than to other politicians, as benevolent but powerful guardians of the nation (Sigel 1966; Tannenhaus and Foley 1981). Perhaps as a consequence, citizens hold the chief executive responsible for the good and bad times the country encounters, whether or not he influenced the situation or could have done so (Mueller 1973; Kernell 1978). In short, Ford, Edison, and Firestone simply could not have generated the exceptional fascination that is associated with America's presidents.[1]

Still, the attention paid to the chief executive by the public, the media, and scholars treats presidents exclusively as individuals and fails to consider them within the institution of the presidency. They are viewed from a political-actor perspective, which analyzes the players in the game, their roles, their resources, and their personalities. March and Olsen (1984), critical of studies that consider political actors at the expense of political institutions, summarize this point of view:

> The first presumption is that a political system consists of a number (often a large number) of elementary actors. . . . The second presumption is that collective behavior is best understood as stemming from the (possibly intricate) interweaving of behavior understandable at a lower level of aggregation. . . . The central faith is that outcomes at the collective level depend only on the intricacies of the interactions among individual actors. (March and Olsen 1984, 735-736)

From the political-actor perspective, institutions are nothing more than the sum total of the behavior of individual participants.

In contrast, an institutional perspective treats institutions as "political actors in their own right" (March and Olsen 1984, 738). Individual behavior does not indicate the whole character of the institution; instead, the institution illuminates the individuals' actions. Institutions, in other words, are collections of regularly occurring patterns of behavior that help explain the conduct of individual actors. The organizational characteristics of the institution as an institution encompass specific constraints and advantages that affect the human actors. Furthermore, the institution attaches a particular character to agenda items, to the types of policies that are ultimately made, and to their implementation. The institutional structures and patterns are often more important for an understanding of policy making than the behavior of the policy makers. Viewed within this context, a president becomes only one of many actors within the presidency as it interacts with other political institutions.

Our treatment of the presidency as an institution transcends a description of the administrative offices that surround presidents in the Executive Office of the President (EOP; see Chapter 4). Often the terms *presidency* and *institution* are used simply to mean the agencies and offices within the White House, ranging from the special trade representative to the Office of Management and Budget (OMB). Here we treat the organization of the White House as only one aspect of the institution. We are also concerned with the patterns that characterize the presidency and shape its relations with other institutions, such as Congress. Unlike early institutional approaches (Corwin 1957), ours addresses the way in which the *behavior* of individual officeholders is predicated upon and interrelates with the dynamic *institution* within which they act.

Singular Images, Plural Institution

Within the political-actor perspective, presidents are depicted as central and unitary figures. This conception of them reflects early decisions of the Constitutional Convention in 1787, which rejected the idea of a plural executive advocated by the New Jersey Plan and instead accepted the notion of a single executive set forth in the Virginia Plan. During their deliberations, the framers debated whether, in Edmund Randolph's words, "the great requisites for the Executive Department, vigor, dispatch, [independence], and responsibility could not be found in three men, as well as in one man" (Farrand 1913, 1: 66). In concluding its discussion the convention agreed with James Wilson of Pennsylvania that a single executive would "not so soon introduce a monarchy or despotism, as a complex one" (Farrand 1913, 1: 71). Ultimately the framers were satisfied that a single executive would be more likely to bring energy and safety to a republican scheme. In Federalist No. 70, Alexander Hamilton wrote:

> The ingredients which constitute energy in the executive are unity; duration; an adequate provision for its support; and competent powers. The ingredients which constitute safety in the republican sense are a due dependence on the people, and a due responsibility.... That unity is conducive to energy will not be disputed. Decision, activity, secrecy, and dispatch will generally characterize the proceedings of one man in a much more eminent degree than the proceedings of any greater number. (Hamilton, Madison, and Jay 1961, 424)

Although Hamilton's view describes the presidency as it was originally conceived, the description does not fit the office as it has developed since. Hamilton overemphasized the autonomy of individual presidents and prompted researchers to do so as well by examining the ways in which successive incumbents make policy decisions and present themselves to the nation. Such an approach makes an understanding of the office contingent on a comparison of its various occupants. This view not only suggests that the executive operates alone but also stresses the uniqueness and idiosyncrasies of each officeholder. Similarly, researchers often discuss presidents' relations with political institutions, including the political parties, the bureaucracy, the media, the courts, and Congress. In each instance, an individual president is depicted as interacting in different ways with a multitude of other politicians.

A more appropriate emphasis is the plural nature of the presidency, its policy environment, and the demands placed upon the institution by different groups and nations. It is not that three persons are president rather than one; instead, different and often conflicting demands are placed on the presidency, as though, at any one time, the office had several occupants who frequently disagreed with each other. Hamilton's words "unity," "decisions," "activity," "secrecy," "dispatch," and "duration" have given way to "collectivity," "inchoateness," "activity," "secrecy," "delay," and "tension." Although secrecy and breadth of activity characterize the presidency to an even greater extent now than before, the office is not the single entity that the framers proposed and that people emphasize in describing it. The plural presidency exhibits four components: (1) program complexity—the interplay of various interests that do not form a coherent whole, (2) group diversity—the demands and opinions voiced by different groups within the citizenry, (3) organizational diffusion—the methods of organization that make the institution a collection of offices rather than a single unit, and (4) incumbents' strategies and interests. Each can be examined to determine how (and how much) the office described by Hamilton has changed.

Program Complexity

The concept of a plural presidency originates in presidents' *activity* in proposing, establishing, and dismantling programs in disparate policy areas. Although early conceptions of the office presumed that the executive would take steps to develop a coherent foreign policy, the notion of positive government, first articulated in the early twentieth century, pushed presidents into many other realms. A positive intervention by government in people's lives began in such areas as business regulations, wages and hours, social welfare, and health. This reduced the coherence of the president's programs across and even within such areas as trade, foreign aid, agriculture, natural resources, defense, social welfare, and the economy. The office now does "more of any one thing," does "more things" in total, and has a "larger cumulative presence" in the government and society than ever before (Heclo 1981, 3-4). Consequently presidents spend considerable time preparing agendas, taking positions on legislation (as we will see in Chapter 2), issuing executive orders, and negotiating treaties and executive agreements (see Chapter 3). Yet these types of activities cross many policy arenas, may be largely incompatible, and may well produce inconsistent program proposals and outcomes.

Such complexity also enlarges the institution and in so doing removes presidents from its direct control. Presidents take on greater areas of responsibility but have less ability to supervise the decisions of the office directly. Ultimately actions of the institution are *inchoate* because the breadth of the institution's activities and the constraints imposed by separation of powers prevent presidents from controlling the policy-making process firmly. Presidents may take the first step in creating programs, but these steps may bear no resemblance to the measures finally enacted. President Jimmy Carter, for example, developed a comprehensive energy program during his first four months in office that was subsequently dissected and differently reassembled by Congress over the next year. The institution may also exhibit *delay* because of the volume of activity, the often preliminary nature of the decisions, and the size of the apparatus involved in the decision making. President John F. Kennedy, to take another example, ordered U.S. missiles removed from Turkey but discovered during the Cuban missile crisis that they had not been removed.

Group Diversity

The program complexity facing the presidency is heightened by the demands and benefits presented by various groups and nations. Typically, interest-group politics is assumed to take its most vigorous forms in the legislature. Yet the presidency also appeals to and reflects group interests and opinions that characterize American politics more broadly. The various groups seek a number of public and private goals and are in many cases insulated from one another, so that they can consistently win public policy programs that favor their demands. One example of how American presidents have recognized and encouraged this plurality by appealing to particular groups and regions was Ronald Reagan's support of antiabortion activists. Reagan backed an antiabortion amendment to the Constitution, met with key antiabortion groups at the White House and in other forums, and remained the electoral choice of these groups.

Although presidents have the image of being solitary, central figures who are the only elected officials to act on behalf of the entire nation, the imagery belies the selective attention that presidents accord key demographic groups, regions, and organized interests. Recently scholars have begun to use the phrase "presidential parties" with reference to the identifiable groups who support a president for election and who maintain the alliance during the incumbent's tenure in office. These presidential parties shape and reshape the national parties that have always looked to the White House for direction in bringing together supporters (see Chapters 6 and 7). The groups' demands cross several policy areas and may present inconsistent programmatic requests that result in national policy stalemates.

We want to emphasize here our strong reservations about use of the term *pluralism* to describe this aspect of the plural presidency. An enormous literature has proposed and debated theories of pluralism. Although few scholars have objected to David Truman's (1951) essentially empirical assertion that American politics can best be understood as the interaction of groups, many have protested normative pluralist arguments (Dahl 1956, 1961) that view group competition as a prerequisite for democracy. Scholars continue to discuss groups as important to the understanding of American politics, but they often stress groups' dominance while simultaneously raising questions about their legitimacy or fairness (Schattschneider 1975; Lowi 1979). We opt to remain at a largely Madisonian level, describing the groups as sometimes competing and sometimes dominant factions that give a particular but not necessarily positive cast to government relations. We therefore do not use the word "pluralism" in the context of group politics.

Organizational Diffusion

To accommodate the programmatic and group demands, presidents have established increasingly elaborate organizational structures within the White House. Many observers regard Congress as a decentralized body with diffused organizational units, and the presidency can be viewed in similar terms. Presidents have adopted many strategies for obtaining information for decision making and for administering programs once they have been established. Presidents can call on an immediate circle of advisers, a much larger and more distant White House staff that houses its own bureaucracy, and appointees to departments and agencies who have interests and goals not necessarily in line with those of the chief executive (these approaches are discussed in Chapter 4). As both a decision-making and an administrative body, the presidency is supposed to speak with one voice but often does not. Presidents attempt to centralize executive decision making in the White House in order to have the final say, but decisions are made in various layers of the organization, with limited coordination or control possible from the top. As a result, decisions attributed directly to a president are often made with only minimal presidential knowledge or supervision.

Executive organization is a *collective* apparatus that involves numerous units, each with its own norms and standard operating procedures that are likely to differ from those of other units. These units have discernible boundaries, so fragmentation occurs. The institution defines the way decisions are made through diffused patterns of communication, various organizational units, and spheres of influence, which are limited for any individual actor, even the president.

> In action after action, responsibility for decision is fluid and restless as quicksilver, and there seems to be neither a person nor an organization on whom it can be fixed. At times the point of decision seems to have escaped into the labyrinth of governmental machinery, beyond layers and layers of bureaucracy. (Roger Hilsman, quoted in Johnson 1984, 56)

Moreover, the organizational component ties in with various interest groups that are seeking to satisfy their needs. As Lowi writes,

> Administration gives each basic interest an institutional core, renders each interest less capable of being absorbed or neutralized, gives each interest the capacity to articulate goals, integrate members, provide for leadership and succession, in short to perpetuate itself. (Lowi 1979, 33)

The plural office ties together programmatic concerns across varied policy areas with distinct administrative approaches and staffs.

Incumbent Strategy

Presidents often vary in the program interests and political strategies that they are most likely to emphasize. Lyndon B. Johnson advanced social welfare proposals through a predominantly legislative strategy; Ronald Reagan advanced his budget-cutting goals through public, legislative, and administrative means. Beyond their individual interests, presidents also promote, with varying degrees of intensity, partisan approaches to policy decisions. These personal and partisan endeavors are handled through the increasingly complex network of policy areas, personnel, and precedents established in the institution. The Office of Management and Budget, for example, now regularly oversees the creation of presidents' legislative programs by examining proposals from the White House and throughout the executive bureaucracy to determine whether they are "in accordance" with the president's program. In addition incumbents use *secrecy* to protect their own discretion and to achieve some flexibility within the institution. Secrecy may help presidents to wrest control from the ongoing administrative organization in specific situations.

Past research has tended to focus on the differences among presidents in politics, programs, and performance. In so doing, such research perpetuates the image of singularity and fails to take the institution into account as a context within which individual presidents act. Here we recognize that individual goals and strategies of incumbents form part of the institution of the presidency. A *tension* is thus displayed between the ongoing units and procedures of the institution and the transient, temporary course of presidents as actors within the institution. The image of a solitary president is reinforced by this tension. Still, the president is only one participant in the presidency.

The four components of the presidency—programmatic complexity, group diversity, organizational diffusion, and incumbents' strategies—make plain that this is a plural institution rather than a singular one. The presidency involves many programs that cross policy areas, disparate approaches to the various issues at hand, different groups that communicate with the White House, myriad participants who work in the White House, and individual emphases that reflect the particular incumbent in office. The plural nature of the presidency makes it difficult for presidents to maintain any of the characteristics that the framers identified as necessary—energy, vigor, dispatch, and independence. In the context of separation of powers, these four qualities merge in a tableau that may be complex and inconsistent. The plural presidency places single executives at a disadvantage by confronting them with greater demands from different groups and policy areas and yet extending greater opportunities to satisfy these demands through an ever-larger administrative organization and a broad list of responsibilities sanctioned by statute. Presidents meet only some of the demands and thereby minimize the influence they achieve over political outcomes.

Origins of the Plural Presidency

In order to understand more clearly the development of the four interrelated patterns that compose the plural presidency, we will now consider five central origins of the plural executive: policy stewardship, electoral dependence, public representation, administrative assistance, and separation of powers. The interrelationship of these origins provides the impetus for the patterns of the plural presidency. The first two emerged from the Constitutional Convention. Debate in Philadelphia hinged on two sources of argument. First, would a single executive gain too much power—would it be, according to Edmund Randolph, "a foetus of monarchy?" (Farrand 1913, 1: 66). Second, could a nonelected national executive serve representative government? As Gouverneur Morris argued, "The executive . . . ought to be so constituted as to be the great protector of the Mass of the people. . . . If he is to be the Guardian of the people let him be appointed by the people" (Farrand 1913, 2: 52-53). This debate was resolved in favor of a single executive capable of strength yet restrained by bonds with the citizenry. James Madison, writing to Thomas Jefferson in October 1787, during the first months of ratification, stated that the president, as conceived, would "unite a proper energy in the Executive . . . with the essential characters of Republican Government" (Hutchinson and Rachal 1962, 10: 207-208). Thus the framers linked two primary aspects of the presidency that were seen as a necessity for policy strength (energy and competent powers) and popular consent (expressed through indirect elections).

A third origin, closely tied to the policy energy and electoral dependence of the office, arose a short time later as the presidency became an office that was continuously public rather than public only during elections. Thomas Jefferson commented on this development: "In a government like ours, it is the duty of the Chief Magistrate, in order to enable himself to do all the good which his station requires, . . . to unite in himself the confidence of the whole people. This alone, in any case, where the energy of the nation is required, can produce a union of the powers of the whole, and point them in a single direction, as if all constituted by one body and one mind" (Ford 1892-1899, 8: 26).[2] Jefferson's remarks suggest that throughout their terms presidents act as the sole representative of the nation. This notion extends the links between policy and electoral origins that were mentioned by the framers. The framers sought to use the president's electoral dependence on the people to temper presidential power, but Jefferson viewed ongoing public representation as a way to enlarge the president's role in setting policy. His vision makes the office seem more popular than it was originally conceived, but it also serves, as Jefferson noted, to advance policy initiatives taken by presidents as the people's representatives.

These three origins would appear to promote executive unity. Instead, however, because of subsequent developments they promote only the illusion of unity. To judge from the origins, presidents should properly act as popular policy makers. Standing at the center of government, presidents are supposed to serve the best interests of the nation. Thus presidents' behavior moves well beyond the actions of officials who do "nothing more than . . . carry the will of the Legislature into effect" (Roger Sherman, quoted in Farrand 1913, 1: 65). They become responsible for numerous activities of government for which they often have no direct constitutional responsibility. Presidential ability to influence other policy institutions and political actors depends largely on the opinions of varied groups. The central irony of the American executive is that the image of singularity creates the plural presidency.

The policy energy of the office led to a fourth component of the presidency—the need for administrative assistance in the form of advisers and counselors to the president. During the early republic, this group was seen as an "aristocracy of talent and virtue" to help the president make policy decisions on behalf of the people. Hamilton observed:

> The administration of government, in its most precise signification, is limited to executive details, and falls peculiarly within the province of the executive department. . . . The persons, therefore, to whose immediate management these different matters are committed ought to be considered as the assistants or deputies of the Chief Magistrate, on this account they ought derive their offices from his appointment. (Hamilton, Madison, and Jay 1961, 435-436)

Yet the expansion of this administrative component heightens the plural elite institution: presidents become one of many officials within the presidency, and although staff members are employed to assist presidents, chief executives may not be readily able to control their numbers and interests.

Each of these four roots of the plural presidency—policy stewardship, electoral dependence, public representation, and administrative assistance—rests within the context of a fifth origin, separation of powers. This origin, viewed in relation to the others, has most troubled presidents and those who observe them. The first four lead to the assumption that the presidency is preeminent in American government; the fifth suggests that the preeminence is always constrained within the limitations imposed by other constitutionally and legally established institutions. Too often, writers on the American presidency have extrapolated from the image of a solitary executive to propose a notion of presidential government. This concept involves, quite simply, "the idea that the president, backed by the people, is or can be in charge of the country" (Heclo 1981, 1). Yet the concept of presidential government is not woven into the broader picture of shared powers dictated by the Constitution. When separation of powers is overlooked, the image of a single executive, with this individual at the center of national politics and policy making, assumes exaggerated importance.

The fifth origin, that of constitutional constraints, creates a conflict at the center of the presidency: the president tends to assume power while at the same time being restricted in his ability to do so.

Presidents must confront Congress as they attempt to be preeminent policy makers. They seek to exercise greater control of policy making by expanding the presidency as an institution and by attempting to assume greater control of the bureaucracy, yet bureaucratic departments and agencies pursue their own courses and in some ways are often more responsive to Congress. Presidents may attempt to overcome these problems of shared power by seeking the approval of the public, but they have no assurance that such public contact will be beneficial. Presidents rely on the image of unity while nevertheless working within an institution with various program goals, organizational schemes, and political roles. This contradiction becomes the essence of the plural presidency.

We now examine in turn each of the four origins as it exists in contradiction with the fifth. In subsequent chapters, the plural presidency is systematically analyzed through a comprehensive compilation of empirical material relevant to the origins of the executive.

The Policy Steward

In its earliest form, the policy role of the presidency can be traced back to Washington, who insisted that the president be predominant in foreign affairs. He demonstrated this attitude in both his executive proclamation of U.S. neutrality with regard to an impending war in Europe in 1793 and his negotiation of Jay's Treaty with Great Britain in 1794, which placed the Senate in the position of ratifying diplomatic initiatives rather than actively involving itself in them. By developing economic and legislative proposals, Jefferson made presidents more important in policy matters as well as in directing foreign diplomacy. Jefferson realized that he faced a practical dilemma in balancing the desire to pursue policy directions actively with the public's belief at the time that presidents should not visibly appear to guide the congressional course of events:

> If we recommend measures in a public message, it may be said that members [of Congress] are not sent here ... to register the edicts of a sovereign. If we express opinions in conversation, we have then our ... back-door counsellors. If we say nothing, "we have no opinions, no plans, no cabinet." (Quoted in Ketcham 1984, 109)

Resolving the conflict, Jefferson carefully but quietly developed policy strategies by funneling proposals, including draft legislation, to supportive members of Congress, asking them to exercise their best judgment about whether or not to introduce his presidential measures.

Despite precedents set by Jefferson and by his successors, most notably Jackson, Polk, and Lincoln, the presidency did not firmly establish itself as the cornerstone of policy making in the nineteenth century. Although presidents' positions on policy matters were sought, their views were seen as advisory in some cases and incidental to congressional efforts in most others. During the first hundred years of the office, presidents were chief executives less than they were the principal patronage officers of their parties. They spent considerable time dealing, in Grover Cleveland's words, with "this dreadful, damnable office-seeking [which] hangs over me and surrounds me—and makes me feel like resigning" (quoted in Tourtellot 1964, 166). Policy initiatives by the government depended on Congress, whose members depended on presidents only to make the proper appointments of party office seekers from their states. Nineteenth-century American government was congressional government, acting much as the framers had supposed it would (see Wilson 1973).

Theodore Roosevelt was the first president to assert himself as a policy initiator after the turn of the century. He demanded that the president act as "a steward of the people bound actively and affirmatively to do all he could for the people ... unless such action was forbidden by the Constitution or by the laws" (Roosevelt 1913, 389). According to this view, as Roosevelt bluntly stated, he did not usurp power but "greatly broadened it" (1913, 389). Roosevelt thus provided an expanded, creative view of presidential policy activities by extending the constitutional powers of presidents beyond the explicit language of the document and the specific powers enumerated to encompass any activity not expressly prohibited by current interpretations of the Constitution. This constitutional reading gave presidents an affirmative ability to act whenever and however they could, short of violating a direct constitutional or legislative prohibition. Jefferson's edict of one hundred years before was thus formalized: it is the "duty of the Chief Magistrate ... to do all the good his station requires."

The enlarged notion of the constitutional powers of the presidency was coupled with broader theories regarding the role of government that were advanced after the turn of the century. Progressives pushed for the regulation of an increasingly powerful industrialized and centralized economy. A quarter century later, as part of the New Deal, government's redistributive actions helped people who would not survive otherwise in a marketplace economy.[3] This intervention of government into the lives of the citizenry permanently revised the concept of the presidency. Franklin Roosevelt went beyond his cousin

Theodore in expanding the types and numbers of policy initiatives that could come from the White House.

Congress further promoted the intertwining of government activism and presidential responsibility. In contrast to its role in the earlier period as "the predominant and controlling force, the centre and source of all motive and all regulative power" (Wilson 1973, 31), Congress first somewhat inadvertently, but then in successive legislation much more completely and intentionally, gave presidents greater control in economic, domestic, and foreign policy. In passing the Budget and Accounting Act of 1921, Congress established the Bureau of the Budget, originally intended to introduce order into Congress's own chaotic budget process. The bureau did so increasingly by focusing power in the White House, until it was actually moved in 1939 from the Treasury Department, where it had initially been placed, to the Executive Office of the President (Berman 1979). The bureau took on the job of coordinating into a unified package the plethora of legislation sought by departments that Congress no longer wished to examine piecemeal. By trying to base coordination of legislation in the executive branch, Congress also lost some control over its initiation.

In addition, Congress in the 1940s passed a series of bills giving control of policy to the White House. The Full Employment Act of 1946 charged the president with responsibility for developing a plan to maintain full national employment. The Taft-Hartley Act of 1947 required presidents to intervene in emergencies created by labor strikes. The National Security Act of 1947 held presidents responsible for integrating foreign and domestic military policies. The Atomic Energy Act of 1947 required chief executives to oversee the development and use of atomic weapons. Single instances in which presidents acted as Rooseveltian stewards were institutionalized and then codified into law. These efforts indicate a new method of governing within the American system by centralizing policy responsibility in the presidency. Congress obviously maintains some dominion in delegating the authority, but it less firmly controls the operating authority itself.

By convention, presidents also added to their supervision of national policy by submitting annual legislative programs to Congress in their State of the Union messages. Harry S Truman first designed and adopted this innovation to enhance his capacity to control and lead the national policy process. Although Dwight D. Eisenhower had no desire to follow Truman's precedent, he reluctantly did so after being soundly criticized by members of his own party in Congress for failing to submit a set of proposals (Moe 1985, 251). Truman's precedent became presidential routine. All subsequent presidents have developed and delivered to Congress their programs for national prosperity, security, and stability.

Together, the president, as a constitutionally mandated steward, and the national government, as a positive state, provide an important basis for the image of presidents as singular political actors. The increasing activism of the government becomes attached to the president as "the representative of no constituency, but of the whole people," and presidents thereby become the initiators of policy change (Wilson 1908, 68). Simultaneously, however, stewardship and positive government lead to a plural institution. The institution then formalizes efforts by individual incumbents to accommodate broadening policy spheres and to address growing demands for various types of actions, ranging from legislative messages to budget proposals. These institutional patterns, developed across a complex of policy types and activities, remain as presidents come and go.

The singular image and the plural institution also confront the policy efforts of other governmental institutions specified by separation of powers. The role of the president as policy steward, as Richard Neustadt aptly observed, "does not signify that all the rest of government is at his feet. It merely signifies that other men [sic] have found it practically impossible to do *their* jobs without assurance of initiatives from him. . . . They find his actions useful in their business" (1960, 74). Indeed, the presidency may be little more than a convenient stage upon which to dramatize key national issues and upon which to rest the overall responsibility for national problem solving. Congress and the bureaucracy continue to promote the interests of attentive constituents and clients, regardless of presidential proposals. In many of the policy arenas entered by chief executives, other politicians may serve longer and better. Presidents are unlikely to be able to act with the energy and dispatch desired by the framers or with the consistency and clarity that the unified concept of a single executive implies.

Administrative Assistance

"The president needs help." So began the report of the Brownlow Committee on Administrative Management in 1936, and so began the concerted growth of a formal organization in the White House designed to aid presidents in coordinating and managing the departments and activities of the government. The increasing involvement of the executive office in policy required a larger staff to administer and manage the programs that presidents were asked to propose and oversee. The Hoover Commission on the Organization of the Executive

Branch of the Government in 1947 echoed the call for administrative assistance. The White House Office increased in size by sevenfold from 37 staff members in 1937 to 248 by 1953 and has remained at roughly 400 employees since 1979 despite the "reduction in forces" ordered by the Reagan administration for other government agencies. The key premise upon which both the Brownlow Committee and the Hoover Commission based their recommendations was that "the American Executive must be regarded as one of the very greatest contributions by our Nation to the development of modern democracy" (*Report of the President's Committee on Administrative Management* 1937, iv). This concept of administration closely mirrors the view of presidents as policy makers. Both ideas assume that presidents are strong, single executives, and both support the correlate thesis that the presidency should preside over the national government.

The image of singularity and the notion of presidential government had three administrative consequences. First, the White House staff became a permanent, reasonably specialized, and highly expandable institution. Its growth, which included the formation of the Office of Management and Budget (reorganized from the Bureau of the Budget during the Nixon administration), the Council of Economic Advisers, and the National Security Council, occurred in tandem with a fundamental revision of practices surrounding the presidential support staff. Although a small personal staff remained, it was aided by an increasingly bureaucratic organization that made decisions with or without the president and continued intact as successive presidents came and went. An administrative presidency arose, with various organizational bases diffused across scores of offices and staffs, from the Council on Environmental Quality to the Office of Drug Abuse Policy. Each vied for the attention and favor of the presidents themselves.

Second, the demands placed on presidents as policy makers increased the importance of appointments to the rest of the federal bureaucracy; by making such appointments presidents could attempt to control the administration of national programs. Presidents have long lamented a problem on which Harry Truman commented: "I thought I was the president, but when it comes to these bureaucrats, I can't do a damn thing" (quoted in Nathan 1983, 2). Through their appointments, contemporary presidents have tried to increase bureaucratic attentiveness to the White House with varying degrees of success. Most recently, the Reagan administration has displayed keen interest in making middle- and lower-level subcabinet appointments on the basis of ideological commitment and has enjoyed some success. Officials are chosen who are ideologically in step with Reagan and who are encouraged to advance these views in their policy decisions. In some instances, these individuals' doctrines have so disheartened other agency staffers with opposing views that the latter have voluntarily left government. When philosophy and budgets changed drastically within the Environmental Protection Agency, for example, an estimated twenty-five hundred full-time employees asked to leave the agency (Nathan 1983, 79). Such vacancies were then filled by still other loyalists, so that receptivity to presidential requests increased.

As a third way of supervising the federal bureaucracy, presidents attempt to adapt their administrations to take on a management role. Lyndon B. Johnson, and more notably Richard Nixon, tried to use the relative smallness and loyalty of the executive office to overcome the size and the perceived disloyalty to the president of federal departments and agencies (Nathan 1983). To some extent the expansion of the executive office has thus been designed to control the larger bureaucracy.

These three efforts reveal that presidents as administrators have principally sought to create "political responsiveness" rather than the "neutral competence" often considered desirable in large organizations (Kaufman 1956). Management tasks should be carried out by loyalists, whether partisan, personal, or ideological. Overall coordination should be kept in the White House and among those advisers closest to the president, who will carefully pursue presidential interests. This arrangement is designed to create sufficient organizational capacity for presidents to perform their diverse policy roles.

Unintended consequences have nevertheless accompanied the pursuit of political responsiveness. In Nixon's efforts to control the executive branch more firmly, he essentially made his executive staff into a "counterbureaucracy," with the result that coordination of the presidency from within became difficult. Two aides of President Carter were critical:

> The EOP [Executive Office of the President] has suffered for a decade from serious weaknesses. It has become too big, containing too many staffs and advisors peripheral to its central functions. It has always been structured in a confusing manner, inviting internal conflicts over decision-making, advice-giving, and coordinating authority. Its operating procedures have been haphazard, unfair, and easily "gamed." (Quoted in Nathan 1983, 70)

This approach encouraged attempts during Ronald Reagan's first term to control the now-bureaucratic White House by centralizing administration still further toward the president's immediate advisers and by asserting a new, invigorated role for the OMB in the review of regulatory agencies' proposals. "This process of regulatory review allowed the OMB to venture into territory long regarded as the rightful domain of the established bureaucracy and to act as the president's agent in screening and shaping decisions that would otherwise be lost to the permanent government" (Moe 1985, 262).

The centralization, however, invites consideration of "White House competence" that now must be achieved not only to promote policy-making decisions but also to coordinate the information and influence necessary to implement and administer the decisions (Moe 1985, 245). The concept of presidential government presupposes that a sizable, loyal administrative apparatus attends to presidential business. This business, however, suggests that bureaucratic decision making, whether in the executive office or in executive departments and agencies, may well constrain, if not redefine, presidential initiatives. In the first instance the executive office may become too large to be effective; in the second, the departmental units may pay less heed to presidents than to Congress, with its jurisdictional similarities and oversight capacity. Here, too, the paradox of presidents' institutional staff support vis-à-vis separation of powers becomes apparent. Although the illusion that they function as solitary individuals drives presidents first to seek policy control and then to enlarge administrative organizations in an effort to gain it, presidents are often unable to surmount the constraints of coequal branches of Congress and the bureaucracy. The image ultimately fosters a plural institution that has trouble commanding both policy and administrative matters. The more presidents attempt to gain control of policy-making initiatives by creating larger staffs and increasing supervision of the bureaucracy, the more they risk losing control. The presidency's administrative roots offer the chief executive less flexibility and discretion in choosing among policy options rather than more. As a result, the plural presidency emerges—pervaded by organizational diffuseness in numerous staff units with independent goals and programmatic interests.

Public Representation

Presidents' ability to influence policy outcomes depends to a significant extent on their ability to garner public approval (for the most persuasive account, see Neustadt 1960). Although presidential efforts to achieve bureaucratic responsiveness are difficult, attempts to secure public responsiveness may be less problematic. Contemporary presidents continually seek occasions when they can prevail upon the public as their popular support rises and falls (Kernell 1986). In so doing, they rely on, and in turn reinforce, the image of the single executive. Chief executives cultivate a mediated intimacy with their audiences through frequent public appearances. In addition, chief executives advance the notion of presidential government by justifying their decisions on the basis of ties to a national community. Jimmy Carter, for example, created an emotional bond between himself and the American people by declaring, "I promised you a President who is not isolated from the people, who feels your pain, and who shares your dreams and who draws his strength and wisdom from you" (*Public Papers of the Presidents, Jimmy Carter, 1979,* 1235). This concern of the presidency—the conversion of public support into policy success—is so constant from one president to the next and is so much taken for granted today that its origins are often forgotten.

The idea of the public presidency is founded on a conception of the office as an institution of the citizenry rather than an institution of the citizenry *through* party. This view predominated during the early republic among presidents from George Washington to John Quincy Adams but was replaced by a more party-oriented conception of the office by Andrew Jackson and Martin Van Buren (see the account in Ketcham 1984). A shift away from the party model began after the turn of the century by innovations of Theodore Roosevelt. Roosevelt reacted against the narrow party functionary role defined by most of his predecessors. He proposed in its place a more direct connection between the presidency and the citizenry: "I want to make a good president . . . [who will] follow policies external and internal which shall be for the real and ultimate benefit of our people as a whole, and all party considerations will be absolutely secondary" (quoted in Tourtellot 1964, 52). He dramatized his actions and opened the presidential office to scrutiny by the press. Roosevelt's initiative was reinforced by technological advances in print and telecommunications that produced telephones, telegraphs, and newspapers with mass circulation and made news coverage ever more current. Presidents became capable of dominating national political news as both a source of information and a subject of interest (Rubin 1981).

The increased public visibility of the presidency offered the opportunity for its occupant to mold, if not to create, public opinion in a way that would work to the advantage of the president's policy concerns. Roosevelt, with characteristic wit, remarked, "People used to say of me that I . . . divined what the people were going to think. I did not 'divine' I simply made up my mind what they ought to think, and then did my best to get them to think it" (quoted in Edwards 1983, 38).

Woodrow Wilson, who like Roosevelt perceived the presidency as the office of the people, commented on the president's ability to gain not only public attention but also, concomitantly, public approval. As Wilson noted, the public's "instinct is for unified action, and it craves a single leader" (Wilson 1908, 68). If he succeeds in this imagery, he then becomes, according to Wilson, "irresistible" because his views are considered to be in the best interest of the nation. Thus a president's success at manipulating or forming public opinion rests on his ability to make a partisan or ideologically based set of interests appear to be in the public interest. Essentially, Wilson argued that presidents are able to achieve this feat by portraying themselves as symbols of (or as the embodiment of) the nation. Issues of party debate are thus transformed into matters of patriotism and national consensus, allowing presidents to claim public support.

Wilson and Roosevelt thus placed the office at the center not only of American government but also of national public attention. Regardless of whether future presidents aspired to the policy activism associated with these two presidents, twentieth-century presidents nevertheless became the focus of public scrutiny and curiosity. The public celebration of the presidency transcends any one holder of the office. Although the original idea of the public presidency was tentative and incumbent specific, it is today a permanent fixture of the office and of national politics. Calvin Coolidge, no less than Franklin Roosevelt, acted as the most prominent citizen in the country when he received demands for public appearances. Coolidge complained, "When others are enjoying a holiday, he [the president] is expected to make a public appearance in order to entertain and instruct by a formal address" (Coolidge 1929, 219).

The increasing demand for public appearances by presidents, and presidents' exploitation of them, directly link the president and the citizenry. Television in particular makes the contact between the president and his audience seem immediate and continuous. Although citizens rarely meet presidents personally, the public knows chief executives as they daily enter peoples' living rooms through television. In addition, public opinion polls give presidents increasing familiarity with the public. The direct relationship between presidents and citizens, shaped by advanced technology, heightens the public foundation of presidential government. The extent to which leadership is conveyed is likely to be as crucial as the positions taken in determining whether presidents will be able to stay afloat in public opinion polls and thereby to claim the support of a popular constituency in advancing policy initiatives. With the advent of this public dimension the image of a president operating solo is thus fully woven into the fabric of the office.

Yet while public strategies may depend on and advance the image of a solitary figure, plurality results. Although presidents may wish to present themselves as unifying symbols of the nation, public response is typically far from unified. Groups within the nation may respond with varying degrees of support to various personal qualities, performance skills, and policy efforts of presidents (Wayne 1982b). Then, too, chief executives may well place greatest emphasis on their own ideological and policy agendas, identifying them as serving a single national interest, and may thereby add to the plurality of responses. As one instance of this group diversity, consider Reagan's courting of groups that favor public school prayer. Although Reagan has publicly stated that he approves of school prayer, he has not worked very hard to change the law, nor has he succeeded in doing so. His inaction has antagonized many groups in favor of school prayer who feel that he has not been supportive enough. He has also angered groups opposed to school prayer and similar requirements.

Finally, although presidents make many types of appearances, from airport speeches to televised addresses, they are never fully sure which attempts will prove effective with which groups. Presidents behave much like campaigners for office who are never quite certain to what extent bumper stickers, billboards, and television advertisements are persuasive but are willing to try virtually anything in the hopes that one or more methods will pay off and that none will backfire. Presidents may assume that by engaging in a variety of activities at reasonable levels they will only increase their ability to influence others. Yet some activities may dissuade rather than persuade groups and others may have no effect at all. The combination of different audiences and different techniques creates opportunities for diverse public images of the president rather than a single one. Group diversity in the presidency is born when the image of a single executive is beamed across the spectrum of interests in the American populace.

Electoral Dependence

The study of elections and campaigns bears on the study of governing from the White House. The electoral process defines the types of people who will and will not be elected president and the resources and perspectives they bring to the office. Presidential candidates of the nineteenth century were chosen from negotiations among political machines within the two parties largely on the criterion of how well the candidates could award patronage to major local elements of the party. Often those with strong national reputations aspiring to the office were passed over because the state parties feared loss of control. Thus the elections were frequently battles between relatively weak or unknown candidates who, once in office, served the patronage needs of state parties, not the policy needs of the nation. Weak candidates became weak presidents who could be controlled by strong state party organizations. The electoral arrangements by which the person entered office were not suited to producing a chief executive who would assume a policy-making role and would enjoy significant public prestige.

In the first half of the twentieth century, bargaining at party conventions often determined which party nominees would be selected. The bargaining took place among party leaders, who then served as campaign managers for the candidate, putting together a coalition of party loyalists to win the election. Bargaining also figured importantly in the politics that confronted presidents in office. Attempts to keep together the New Deal Democratic coalition characterized the 1930s and 1940s.

The electoral process and the presidency itself have changed, however. The cumulative effects of a series of events spanning the last thirty years reveal that "coalition building proceeds less through mediating organizations and elite negotiation and more through the direct mobilization of national constituencies" (Kernell 1986, 38). The number of states holding presidential primaries increased from thirteen in 1940 to thirty-four in 1984 (see Chapter 7). Pledged delegates, bound to vote for a particular candidate on the first convention ballot, totaled 71 percent of all Democratic delegates and 69 percent of all Republican delegates in 1980. In contrast, pledged delegates constituted fewer than 15 percent of Republican and Democratic delegates to the 1952 conventions (see Chapter 7). Beginning with Eisenhower, presidential candidates have increasingly chosen to establish their own campaign committees and organizations (the most infamous being Richard Nixon's Committee to Reelect the President, or CREEP, in 1972) separate from their parties' national committees (see the discussion in Lowi 1985, 71-79). Signs of eroding party strength in the electorate have been found in the increase in split-ticket voting and the rise in numbers of people who consider themselves independents, unaffiliated with either party (Burnham 1982).

These factors and others contribute to a focus on presidential candidates in a "multiphased popularity contest" and eliminate the conditions that party elites once imposed (Kernell 1986, 40). Candidates come directly before the electorate or, more accurately, directly before the television cameras that show the campaign to the electorate. The media events of candidates' campaigns, like incumbent presidents' public activities, take candidates directly before the public. Walter Mondale, discussing the requirements of presidential campaigns, stated, "Modern politics requires television.... I don't believe it's possible anymore to run for president without the capacity to build confidence and communications every night. It's got to be done that way" (quoted in Kernell 1986, 42).

We do not mean to imply that American political parties are languishing. Instead they are assuming new and interesting forms. In presidential politics, the "nucleus" (Schlesinger 1985) that serves as a cynosure for political ambition is the presidential campaign organization, not the formal political party apparatus. These "presidential parties" are the new organizations that were once under the control of national and local political parties. They are not temporary, one-time collections of individuals, however, but include evolving coalitions from past campaigns. In this way, American politics reproduces itself and traditional parties impose some degree of structure on the process. After all, in every election nearly all the presidential parties may easily be sorted into Democratic or Republican camps. Yet even here the plural nature of the presidency is evident from the wide-ranging interests and the diverse citizens who make up the emerging presidential parties. Program complexity and group diversity characterize campaigns for the presidency as much as they do the operations of the presidency.

Presidential Plurality without Power

The significance of candidate-centered campaigns and presidential parties brings together the five central origins of the modern presidency. Just as candidates are judged on the basis of public appearance, so are presidents. The ability to communicate after the inauguration is as important as it is during the campaign. Part of the White House bureaucracy becomes a well-adapted and expanded office for press relations. Presidents may deploy public support gained from their appearances to command or challenge prevailing positions in Congress, but members of Congress have their own bases of public support and policy preferences. The types of programs offered by presidents may well change because of the direct link between the president and the people. Solutions may become simplified, personalized, and often short term, bypassing more far-reaching entanglements and avoiding complex situational factors. Thus in foreign affairs there emerge simple black-and-white conflicts involving quick military interventions that can effect easy victories and minimize the use of slower diplomatic channels, never likely to bring about clear-cut victories.

In domestic affairs, the president, working with Congress, may arrive at similarly direct and oversimplified actions. Congress, also constrained by shared constitutional powers, has a "penchant for the blunt simple action—the national debt limit, the minimum wage, the price rollback, the 10 percent across-the-board budget slash, the amendment cutting off aid to Communist countries" (Mayhew 1974, 138). The close affiliation of both institutions with the public leads to "the ability of mass publics to prescribe means as well as ends" in policy making (1974, 139). The public often looks for quick action and immediate results.

The White House may seek to develop these kinds of policies with clear immediate payoffs in the public arena. In the short term such policies reflect the image of singularity and thereby satisfy most citizens' overly simplified view of the presidency in American government. The policies may also temporarily minimize problems defined by separation of powers as presidents engage in quick, independent-looking actions and as Congress seeks quick, easy-looking solutions. By the same token, in the short term these policies may circumvent problems of plurality: policy interconnections are avoided, and the administrative apparatus is not brought into play. In the longer term, however, presidents cannot avoid the dilemma of plurality. Programs are in and of themselves complex and are tied to other policy decisions and nondecisions that may dissolve complexity into incoherence. Factions within the nation will not long stay united behind quick solutions to intricate and possibly intractable problems. Finally, although presidents publicly espouse quick fixes, the administrative organization, coupled with key departments and agencies, pursues a number of independent answers and obscures the issue of responsibility for actions taken.

Hamilton wrote in Federalist No. 71 about the pitfalls of plurality in the executive.

> There is always danger of difference of opinion.... Whenever these [differences] happen, they lessen the respectability, weaken the authority and distract the plans and operations of those whom they divide. If ... the supreme executive magistracy of a country, consist[ed] of a plurality of persons, they might impede or frustrate the most important measures of the government. (Hamilton, Madison, and Jay 1961, 425-426)

Beyond the variations in opinion, Hamilton indicated that one of the

> weightiest objections to a plurality in the executive ... is that it tends to conceal faults and destroy responsibility.... The circumstances which may have led to any national miscarriage or misfortune are sometimes so complicated that where there are a number of actors who may have had different degrees and kinds of agency, though we may clearly see upon the whole that there has been mismanagement, yet it may be impracticable to pronounce to whose account the evil which may have been incurred is truly chargeable. (427-428)

Hamilton's words fit the contemporary plural presidency. The framers' fears about a plural executive have become central features of the modern presidency. The vastness of the administration designated to aid in managing the obligation allows individuals to deny responsibility. Reagan's problems regarding the Iran-contra connection make plain the plurality. Policy demands on the office lead to bizarre links connecting Iranian arms sales, American hostages, Israeli diplomacy with Islam, and Nicaraguan contra rebels. The broad expanse of other, unrelated policy claims on the presidency allows the president to deny knowledge of the deal. Because of his proclaimed preoccupation with other pressing policy matters, Reagan's denial of involvement acquires at least a moderate air of plausibility. The fact that there are many individuals involved in the president's policy planning *other than the president* allows each one to deny involvement in any or all aspects of the sales and transfers.

The central consequence of the plural presidency becomes clear. Presidents do not firmly control the presidency and other actors within it, but, more importantly, the American citizenry loses control of the presidency as it follows its own course, and responsibility for that course vanishes internally. Indeed, Hamilton commented that "the plurality of the executive tends to deprive the people of the two greatest securities they can have for the faithful exercise of any delegated power, first, the restraints of public opinion, which lose their efficacy," because of the number of people involved and uncertainty of who is to blame, and second, the opportunity to discover, not only who was involved, but what the nature of the misconduct was "in order either to [secure] their removal from office or to [administer] their actual punishment in cases which admit of it" (428-429).

The image of singularity is ultimately hollow. It reflects an attempt to centralize as well as to isolate government responsibility for problem solving in the presidency. The executive acquired its authority because it was the people's office. Presidents and presidential candidates have proclaimed themselves the people's officers and have shouldered greater and greater responsibility for more and more aspects of American government and life. Although the singular imagery suggests that a democratic leader wields the power in the system, the existing plurality suggests that the president's power is dissipated by its own scope and the power held by others. Such a leader has responsibility but not necessarily influence over the problems of the nation. The executive office may be considerably less democratic than is commonly believed.

Notes

1. The studies that detail the preeminence of presidents, especially as viewed by the American public, also include Kernell (1986), Light (1982), Wayne (1982b), and Edwards (1983).
2. Letter to William Giles, March 23, 1801, in Ford (1892-1899, 26). Jefferson's thought presaged the views of twentieth-century presidents who worked to make presidents formally important as creators of policy and as public representatives. Theodore Roosevelt maintained that "the President could do anything that the needs of the Nation demanded unless such action was forbidden by the Constitution or by the laws" (Roosevelt 1913, 389). In even stronger language, Woodrow Wilson stated: "His [the president's] position takes the imagination of the country. He is the representative of no constituency, but of the whole people. . . . If he rightly interprets the national thought and boldly insists upon it, he is irresistible. . . . [The country's] instinct is for unified action and it craves a single leader" (Wilson 1908, 68).
3. Regulatory legislation after the turn of the century included three key statutes promulgated in 1906: the Pure Food and Drug Act, the Meat Inspection Act, and the Hepburn Act on railroad regulation. During the New Deal, Congress and the president created the Federal Deposit Insurance Corporation (1933), the Federal Housing Administration (1934), and Social Security (1935) while continuing to widen the regulatory scope of government with the Securities Exchange Act (1934), the National Labor Relations Act (1935), and the Fair Labor Standards Act (1938). For a discussion of regulatory and redistributive legislation of the New Deal, see Lowi (1985, 44-48).

2

Legislative Decisions in the Presidency

In his eight years as president of the United States, George Washington publicly expressed an opinion on only 5 pieces of congressional legislation. He recommended bills concerning the militia, the army, and a temporary commission to negotiate with the Indians; he vetoed an apportionment bill on constitutional grounds and a bill on the military because it was poorly drafted. Washington's three recommendations were approved, and his two vetoes went unchallenged. Nearly two hundred years later, Ronald Reagan in his first four years as president took positions on 341 pieces of legislation, signed into law more than 1,600 bills passed by Congress, and vetoed 39 others. The nineteenth-century norm was to minimize presidential involvement in legislative politics; the twentieth-century norm is to expect it. "The presentation of an annual program to Congress, the coordination of that program within the executive branch, the drafting of legislation, and the submission of special messages are now standard fare" (Wayne 1982a, 45).

In considering presidential involvement in legislative affairs, studies generally focus on presidents as *individual policy makers* rather than on the actions of the presidency as a *policy-making institution*. Presidents are depicted as "proximate policy makers" (Lindblom 1968, 30n), as "policy actors," or as lone figures who try to impose a broad, national policy focus upon a parochial and wayward, if not annoying, congressional body. The image suggests that each president acts anew, asserting new legislative priorities, facing unique challenges presented by Congress, and adopting individual strategies to establish his priorities before the group.

This view denies that institutional relations exist between the two branches of government. Although presidents may individually engage in certain activities, the efforts are neither new nor unique. All presidents now display a considerable degree of institutionalized behavior in their relations with Congress. Presidents annually present policy proposals to Congress in State of the Union messages or announce a legislative program for congressional debate. Each year, too, presidents submit the federal budget, as required by the Budget and Accounting Act of 1921. Although these actions are undertaken by individual executives, the expectations upon which they rest relate to the institution of the presidency.

Furthermore, many of the actions that presidents appear to undertake single-handedly are ultimately executed by a well-developed organization in the Executive Office of the President. The Office of Management and Budget monitors incoming requests for legislation, outgoing legislative proposals, and final bills from Congress. The legislative decisions of the presidency must thus weather the conflict between an image of presidents as "chief legislators" and the institution of the presidency as one participant in the legislative process but not the dominant participant.

To what degree can presidents live up to their image as "chief legislators" within the confines of the institution? The answer to this question depends on the answers to four others: On what type of organizational workings do presidents rely in dealing with Congress? How are policy proposals initiated by presidents? Across how many policy areas do the presidents' proposals and positions extend? How successful are presidents in the positions they take in Congress? In this chapter we examine these four questions in light of the central components of the plural presidency—policy complexity, group diversity, organizational diffusion, and incumbent strategies.

The Organization of Relations with Congress

The organizational structures of the White House reveal the plurality involved in presidents' relations with Congress. During the post-World War II period, legislative and executive staffs have grown enormously. Interactions between the branches of government at all levels have expanded. In recent years, these trends have accelerated. Nelson Polsby writes that, only five decades ago,

> the executive office was a few clerks and assistants, and Congress made do with comparably small professional staffs. Now both institutions are burgeoning establishments, capable of waging titanic battles employing bales of memoranda, sophisticated word-processors, and all the other weaponry of modern bureaucratic warfare. (1983, 19)

Organizational units within the White House undertake two key congressional roles: legislative liaison efforts that sell presidential proposals to Congress and legislative management that supervises the flow of legislation, legislative requests, and budget proposals to and from the White House.

As staff and resources have increased, the formal congressional liaison staff has expanded. Since the days of George Washington personnel in the executive branch have sporadically helped presidents communicate with Congress. Herbert Hoover tentatively formalized such assistance by relying on one staff member to supervise congressional liaison. Harry Truman, who wanted help in pursuing annual legislative programs, introduced a staff with official legislative liaison responsibilities. Yet the two junior presidential assistants assigned the task were primarily messengers who could not speak for the president (Holtzman 1970, 231-234). Not until Dwight Eisenhower was the Office of Congressional Relations finally established. Since then the office has become increasingly institutionalized. In addition, cabinet members and other staff officials serve as presidential agents to Congress. To some extent, presidents' own liaison work is also institutionalized as the precedents set by one officeholder become the expected and established techniques of his successors.

Tables 2.1 and 2.2 provide a systematic look at formal legislative liaison staffs. Table 2.1 summarizes the pre-White House experience of the staffs of President Kennedy through President Reagan. The professionalization and institutionalization of this office are highlighted by the fact that sixty-one of the sixty-five people represented in the table had national governmental experience. Most White House staff members have experience as either members of congressional staffs or lobbyists. A declining number of staff aides have prior experience with the national political parties. Liaison staff members are now essential to a president's success; they are usually able to speak for the president and can sometimes even make modest changes in proposed legislation on the spot. Table 2.2 shows that, after their stints as liaison, presidential aides are much more likely to become lobbyists than to pursue any other occupation. White House experience makes these people valuable to a large number of potential employers because of their institutional experience and because of the possibility that they enjoyed personal access to presidents.

The task of legislative management involves two processes that are handled within the Office of Management and Budget: the processes involved in legislative clearance and in the handling of enrolled bills, depicted in Figures 2.1. and 2.2. The first process begins with proposals and recommendations drafted by executive departments and agencies that become part of a president's annual legislative program or are introduced separately. As part of its legislative clearance role, OMB sets priorities among the departmental requests, determines whether they are "in accordance" with the president's program, and integrates those considered to be so with other central requests that represent the president's own personal priorities. These are then submitted to Congress. A classic instance of the legislative clearance process at work, and its detachment from presidents' own involvement, took place on August 9, 1974, when Richard Nixon announced his resignation. A congressional staff member called a high-ranking White House official during the day to inquire as to whether a minor piece of legislation was "in accordance with the president's program" (as reported by Heclo 1981, 3). Neither a president nor a presidential program existed in those hours, but the institution of the presidency continued to operate.

The second process involving OMB concerns "enrolled" bills—those passed by the House and Senate that await presidential signature. Except in the case of particularly visible legislation or items they initiate, presidents are unlikely to keep tabs on legislation passed on Capitol Hill. The Office of Management and Budget steps in again with procedures to determine whether the president should sign or veto a bill. After gathering recommendations from relevant departments and agencies, it presents its own recommendations, which presidents typically adopt (Wayne, Cole, and Hyde 1979).

The organizational patterns within which incumbents' actions are fixed provide an initial sense of the plural nature of the presidency in its relations with Congress. The tasks of legislative liaison and management have become sufficiently elaborate that presidents exert less than full control over their processes or content. The use of proposals made by the executive bureaucracy that are channeled by the OMB, itself a large bureaucratic unit, and advocated by an enlarged liaison staff diffuses the presidential policy process and increases the potential for incoherence. Presidents are policy actors in their own legislative clearance and enrolled bill processes, but they hardly appear to be chief policy makers.

Presidential Priorities and Position Taking

Through their staffs and their own activities, presidents attempt to communicate their preferences to Congress. The communication takes two forms—the direct submission of policy proposals to Congress and the positions taken by presidents on legislation. The policy proposals serve as policy focal points in Congress. Although presidents are often described as policy initiators, the proposals are not necessarily original or crafted in the White House. Instead, ideas for legislation come from a variety of sources—from the media, the campaign trail, private citizens, interest groups, the White House, and Capitol Hill. Determining exactly who deserves the original credit for a policy idea is difficult because it is typically a product of many peoples' contributions across several years, well before legislation is drafted (Kingdon 1984). Studies that have grappled with the question of policy initiation show a high degree of congressional involvement (Chamberlain 1946; Moe and Teel 1970). Presidents may thus behave less as policy initiators than as policy dramatists; they offer dramatic declarations of the need for legislation. They can also increase momentum by making pleas for quick congressional action and citizen support.

The proposals reveal differences that exist among presidents but also show the institutional parameters within which the variations occur. The most formal method presidents use is the State of the Union message. Many of the proposals discussed during these addresses are the results of the legislative clearance process. The analysis presented in Table 2.3 demonstrates that all presidents since Kennedy have made the bulk of their domestic policy requests in their first year in office. In later years, new requests always decline, and repeated requests uniformly increase (Light 1982, 41). As Table 2.4 indicates, the majority of domestic policy requests during the first year of a president's tenure occur in his first six months. Indeed, except in Nixon's first term, the most first-year requests occur beween January and March.

Two generalizations emerge from these observations. First, policy change is likely to occur with a change in presidents. This point is only implied in Table 2.4, because the substance of the proposals is not indicated. Nevertheless, more new requests are likely to accompany a new president than one who has been around for a while. Second, not only is the presidential cliché about "hitting the ground running" good advice to the president-elect, but all presidents from Kennedy to Carter have come into office with a list of urgent requests. These lists require presidents to act immediately upon entering office and also indicate that presidents may well stumble as they hit the ground. Although the lists show their stated priorities, presidents find it difficult to monitor and devote concerted attention to each of the twenty or more proposals. As a result presidents operate under a time constraint, and their reliance on the White House organization to construct proposals and line up legislative support increases.

The intended benefits of these requests are evident in Table 2.5. Reelection was the dominant incentive for all staffs but that of Lyndon Johnson. For all presidents, "concern with history" and being a "great president" were the least important motivations for most domestic program requests.

The substance of presidents' domestic policy requests can be measured by the statistics provided in Tables 2.6 and 2.7. Light's (1982) interviews and records from the Office of Management and Budget suggest that presidents have very different priorities, as Table 2.6 shows. Presidents' domestic programs also vary considerably (Table 2.7).[1] These tables offer strong evidence that presidential policy change is most likely to occur with a change in incumbents. As shown in Table 2.6, for example, the Kennedy administration was particularly interested in education programs, whereas education was a much less dominant concern for any of the other four presidents represented in the table. Table 2.7, in another example, reveals the considerable attention given to energy programs beginning with Nixon's second term that was absent in prior administrations.

Valerie Bunce argues that presidential succession should be studied as an explanatory variable. She criticizes those who have "reduced succession to the status of a dependent variable, a process that needs to be described and explained rather than one which acts on the political environment" (1981, 14) and offers evidence for her argument that, measured by budgetary priorities, "new leaders mean new policies and old leaders mean the continuation of old priorities" (255). Bunce's data and conclusions are more controversial than they appear. Brunk and Minehart (1984) have strongly challenged her methods and findings. (A good summary of the controversy appears in Bunce and Roeder 1986.) Whether or not Bunce's argument is specifically convincing for budget items, Tables 2.6 and 2.7 make clear that it applies to various aspects of presidents' preferences and performances.

Presidential succession substantially affects congressional politics. With a new president comes the dramatization of a new set of priorities, a new partisan dividing line in the congressional policy battle, and a new round of partisan conflict. Whether presidents can claim any degree of success in determining the outcome of the congressional debate is another matter. They may establish some of the key issues to be discussed but may exercise little control over their results. (Presidential success will be thoroughly examined in the section "Calibrating the Pendulum of Power," below.) Generational effects occur both in Congress directly and as a congressional response to new constituents and their preferences. Kesselman's roll call studies

(1961, 1965) provided the first systematic evidence of this type of effect. Kesselman observed two cohorts of representatives for each of two sessions of Congress—one before and one immediately following a party change in the White House. He found that representatives who were members of the president's party were more likely to vote for the "internationalist" position on relevant roll calls. Similarly, the opposition party members tended to display more "isolationist" voting patterns (see also Clausen 1973, 199). Both patterns are true regardless of the party to which the president belongs.

Richard Bensel (1980) offers another interesting example about the degree to which representatives support the "Rule of [statutory] Law" standard—the tendency to rely on specific statutes in governance rather than on bureaucratic and executive discretion, as the theories of Hayek (1944, 1960) and Lowi (1979) suggest. The typical president, possessing the normal degree of institutional loyalty, *regardless of party affiliation,* would oppose such a standard, and in fact Bensel provides evidence that presidents favor executive discretion. Of greater interest, however, he finds that representatives who belong to the president's party supported the Rule of Law standard less frequently than did opposition party members. Bensel (1980) writes, "It seems that members of Congress pursue similar substantive policy goals regardless of partisan control of the presidency but that these goals take a different statutory form" (740).

Although these examples do not demonstrate presidential influence on congressional decisions, they do emphasize that presidential successions impose predictable patterns on the congressional process that are neither partisan nor specific to an individual incumbent. One of the central features of the interinstitutional exchange between the presidency and Congress is that new presidents change the partisan battle lines and the context of the congressional debate.

Certain forms of continuity from one administration to the next, however, can be seen in Table 2.7. Responding to national and international events associated with the supply of oil, individual presidents, beginning with Nixon, paid concerted attention to energy. Confronted with public pressure to save the environment, presidents from Kennedy to Nixon expressed increasing commitment to policies protecting natural resources. When pressure faded in the 1970s, so too did the issue emphases of Presidents Ford and Carter. Some policy change that appears to coincide with the arrival of new presidents thus may be due just to changes in the political environment; perhaps any new president would have changed priorities in a similar manner. Sorting out these difficult issues is one of the principal problems of presidential analysis.

Table 2.7 also reveals that certain issues are not major priorities for any president: agriculture, transportation, and, somewhat surprisingly, civil rights.[2] Furthermore, it shows that at least one issue area— health—is a modest priority for all the presidents studied. Thus although these tables present convincing evidence that a change in executive branch policy is most likely to occur with a change in incumbents, the tables also emphasize that considerable policy stability exists across administrations. Certain institutional and political constraints may minimize differences among presidents on these policy issues.

Another method of evaluating presidential priorities is to observe the preferences that presidents reveal in the positions they take on congressional legislation. Position taking not only measures responses to congressional legislation in which presidents were not fully involved but also takes into account presidents' own initiatives and desires. Once they have taken positions, presidents are in no way guaranteed success in Congress, but they are virtually always assured of consideration. Table 2.8 reports the total number of House roll call votes and the number of votes on which presidents have taken public positions from 1957 to 1984. The editors of *Congressional Quarterly Weekly Report* have monitored the position taken by each president on House and Senate legislation since 1957.[3] Their specific rules for determining whether a president took a public stand are given by the following statement:

> *Presidential Issues.* CQ tries to determine what the president personally, as distinct from other administration officials, does and does not want in the way of legislative action by analyzing his messages to Congress, press conference remarks and other public statements and documents. Members must be aware of the position when the vote is taken.
> *Borderline Cases.* By the time an issue reaches a vote, it may differ from the original form in which the president expressed himself. In such cases, CQ analyzes the measure to determine whether, on balance, the features favored by the president outweigh those he opposed or vice versa. Only then is the vote classified. . . .
> *Changed Position.* . . . the position of the president [is determined] at the time of a vote, even though that position may be different from an earlier position, or may have been reversed after the vote was taken.

For each of the 9,689 roll call votes taken in the House of Representatives from 1957 to 1984, we consulted the *Congressional Quarterly Almanac* to determine whether the president took a position. Presidents took positions on 2,517 of these roll call votes (about 26 percent). We then individually recorded, checked for accuracy and consistency, and classified each presidential position into one of the seven policy areas discussed in the next section. We also assessed congressional members' roll call support of presidents' positions.

The data in this volume do not include presidential positions taken on Senate roll call votes. We imposed some constraints on the data we were to collect and thus decided not to include these Senate data. We do not mean to imply that the Senate is any less important than the House. Indeed, this chapter reflects a troubling tendency in the literature on Congress and the presidency to focus on only one branch of Congress. We must remember, therefore, that the results we discuss here for the House of Representatives do not necessarily apply to the Senate. Data must be collected and analyzed separately before such inferences can reliably be drawn.[4]

The most dramatic trend in Table 2.8 is the sharp drop in position taking after Lyndon Johnson's tenure as president. This immediate change is not surprising; we would expect the large Democratic majorities under Johnson to produce more legislation on which the president would feel comfortable taking a position than when Republican Richard Nixon was in the White House. Still, the change lasted. Even Democrat Jimmy Carter did not approach the pre-Nixon percentage of position taking. Whereas Presidents Eisenhower, Kennedy, and Johnson took positions on between 43 percent and 61 percent of congressional roll call votes, Presidents Nixon, Ford, Carter, and Reagan took positions on only between 5 percent and 31 percent of roll call votes in their administrations. The change may be partly explained by the sheer number of congressional roll call votes since the 1960s, but this explanation is not totally convincing.

Why the sharp break in the trend after 1968? Presidents, wary of an increasingly independent-minded congressional membership, may have recommended legislation only when it was of particular importance to them in an attempt to minimize defeat. This course of action offers a viable strategy for Republican presidents Nixon, Ford, and Reagan, who faced a House controlled by the Democrats. For Carter, who was perceived as a Washington outsider by many congressional members, even within the Democratic party, this too may have been a way of establishing priorities. Furthermore, in many ways Carter behaved as if he were a Republican (Browning 1986, 126).

A second point of interest in Table 2.8 is that, for most presidents, position taking on congressional roll calls drops in election years. Several factors seem to account for this trend. First, the entire House of

Representatives is up for reelection during these years, so that the number of presidentially relevant pieces of legislation is likely to be somewhat smaller. Controversial bills are probably also kept to a minimum. Second, a president up for reelection is likely to have less time to push his proposals through Congress. As a result, fewer relevant bills reach the floor of the House, and the president has less reason to take public positions. Finally, when a president is not running for reelection, as with Johnson in 1968 or Eisenhower in 1960, presidential influence, and perhaps effort, decline. A president in this position prefers to be viewed as a senior statesman and keeps more than ever out of the partisan fray. These factors may all result in fewer opportunities for public position taking in election years.

Policy Complexity in Position Taking

The policy areas of legislation on which presidents take positions are as diverse as presidents' programmatic interests. Table 2.9 reports the number of bills on which positions were taken in seven policy categories—foreign trade, foreign aid, defense, social welfare and civil rights, government and economic management, energy and natural resources, and agriculture and farm policy—during the last seven presidencies. Kessel, using content analyses of State of the Union messages (1974) and presidential campaign platforms and speeches (1977), and Clausen (1973), using congressional roll call votes, find similar policy categories that seem to be appropriate for American politics. Our categories differ in two ways from those in previous research. First, because of a paucity of votes, we combined civil rights in the social welfare category. Substantively and empirically, civil rights has more in common with social welfare than with any of the other categories; both areas involve a strong liberal-conservative dimension. Many of the same groups—women, minorities, the poor, the children—are affected by social welfare and civil rights programs. Second, specialists in international relations and foreign policy (for example, Hughes 1978) prefer the three-category presentation of foreign policy used here to the single category suggested by Clausen and Kessel.

The substantive differences among these seven issue areas highlight the policy complexity with which the presidency must deal. Each of the policy types introduces different demands, different incentives, and different chances of success for presidents in Congress. Presidents are not likely to be able to act as central policy makers in each of these fields. As a consequence, little consistency may exist across these policy types. Although the possibility of policy change may be offered with the inauguration of a new president, the policy complexity facing all presidents may well limit their ability to secure congressional outcomes to their liking.

As one example of this policy complexity, one can compare agricultural issues with issues concerning the environment and natural resources. Agriculture, as an area of activity supporting farm programs and price subsidies, has occupied presidents' attention since the early years of the republic. The demands placed on the presidency in this policy area come from a narrow, readily identified group with minimal organization. Incentives to take stands on agriculture, especially for recent presidents who find the proportion of the population working on farms declining, are low. Presidents may be embarrassed by farmers, but large-scale victories or defeats are unlikely. With narrow demands and low incentives, presidents are not likely to make numerous policy initiatives in this area of distributive policy. As Table 2.9 shows, presidents take positions on agriculture less often than on any of the other policy areas. Instead, this type of policy creates potent demands on legislators representing the geographic regions with agricultural bases. The specialization and reciprocity of actions inside Congress suggest that the positions taken by these members will have greater importance than those taken by presidents. Thus success for presidents may well be lower in this area than in some others, as representatives bend to the wishes of their colleagues from farm states. We consider the veracity of this hypothesis below.

By comparison, the area of natural resources places intense and conflicting demands on the institutions from environmentalists and conservationists who wish to protect land, water, air, and minerals and from businesses and industries that see such protection as inhibiting their right of "free" enterprise. Furthermore, the policies adopted not only affect the interested groups on both sides but are likely to have immediate, noticeable effects on the entire population.[5] Hence presidents will find it difficult to avoid taking positions. Incentives are also high for presidents to accommodate the demands made by one or both sides if the proponents are relatively well organized and may extend or withhold reelection support. It is not surprising, then, as Table 2.9 shows, that presidents, especially since Johnson, take numerous stands on resource issues, in numbers that exceed those in the area of agriculture. Presidents' success in this policy area may well be higher than in some other areas, including agriculture, because the presidency as an institution has greater ability to command congressional attention on a nationally based regulatory policy that is not fully subject to congressional logrolling.

Although agriculture and natural resources are only two of the seven policy categories, the comparison offers an indication of the heterogeneous policy environment within which the presidency and Congress interact. If we consider the possible combinations when the five other policy areas are added, the complexity becomes acute. Presidents take fair numbers of positions in each of the policy categories. Table 2.9 indicates that, in addition to resource policy, presidents are most apt to take positions on issues relating to social welfare and government and economic management.

The strategies and emphases of individual incumbents are also evident in responses to the different types of policy. The preferences of presidents as revealed through positions taken on House roll call votes (Table 2.9) concur with the perceptions of presidents' staff about the most important domestic programs (Table 2.6). The top concerns of all five of President Kennedy's staff members fall into the categories of social welfare and government and economic management, and these are the categories of roll calls on which President Kennedy took the largest number of public positions. The situation is virtually the same for Lyndon Johnson, even though the particular programs that interested the two presidents differed. Indeed, although Richard Nixon had program preferences that differed dramatically from those of his two predecessors, his activities also most often fell into the areas of social welfare and government and economic management. Ford and Carter were also interested in government and economic management, but their presidencies had a distinctive and sustained emphasis on energy policy. Reagan's 30 percent tax cut and his general economic policy appear in the 1981 figure under government and economic management. Also noticeable is the increasing interest in defense policy over the first three years of Reagan's administration; 1983 was the only year since 1957 when a president took more positions on defense policy than on any other policy matter. This reveals how the policy complexity that all presidents face is interconnected with more specific program strategies that each pursues.

Calibrating the Pendulum of Power

Research on the relationship between presidents and Congress has long spoken of a pendulum of power swinging between the two branches of government. The first swing toward the presidency is usually seen as having occurred when Andrew Jackson was in the White House. The pendulum is said to have swung slowly but surely back toward Congress over most of the rest of the 1800s. Observers suggested that Abraham Lincoln enjoyed a swing in favor of the White House during the Civil War, but by 1865, and certainly after his assassination, Congress regained its advantage. The presidency fought back during the early part of Woodrow Wilson's presidency, but by the time of the League of Nations debate, the pendulum was swinging toward Congress. Historians typically argue that the presidency did not regain its relative strength again until Franklin Roosevelt's first term. Lyndon Johnson is then seen as having enjoyed a brief favorable swing in 1965-1966, but not until the administration of Ronald Reagan in 1981 do analysts mark a resurgence in the modern presidency.

Yet how valuable are discussions of the timing, direction, and duration of pendulum swings? The analyses rely on the political actor perspective and concentrate on the unique situations of individual presidents. They overlook the ongoing patterns of an institution-to-institution exchange and the many outcomes within a given time period that may not clearly favor either branch. Even Lincoln was subject to several congressional committees that acted as overseers of his war efforts.

It is perhaps more useful to think about a continuum regarding the influence of the presidency and Congress on policy. The continuum ranges from the "presidential end," at which researchers suggest that presidents do have or should have strong influence, to the "congressional end," at which scholars argue that Congress dominates the policy process. In viewing the extreme positions and those in between, the pendulum becomes more valuable in explaining disagreements among scholars than the intricacies of relations between presidents and Congress.

Research regarding presidential dominance versus congressional dominance includes the full range of plausible positions. On the presidential end of this debate is the argument that, because presidents set the agenda in Congress, they take the primary initiative and have profound influence. Huntington writes, for example, "If Congress legislates, it subordinates itself to the president. If it refuses to legislate, it alienates itself from public opinion. Congress can assert its power or it can pass laws; but it cannot do both" (1965, 6). Others take a step toward Congress and place the party leaders between presidents and Congress. Jackson's (1974) results "suggest that there is a considerable amount of presidential influence, but it is exerted through the formal party structure" (71, see also Truman 1959, 289-308; de Grazia 1965). Next, there are three general middle positions. The first is held by Sundquist (1968), who identifies two wholly separate systems of public policy, one emanating from the executive and one from the legislative branch, each with its own strengths and weaknesses. Friedrich's (1937) "Rule of Anticipated Reactions," which holds that a president proposes only what he anticipates will stand a reasonable chance of success in Congress, is also a middle ground. Another middle position rests on the high rate of congressional turnover since 1972, the increase in the power and number of subcommittees, and the declining influence of the committee chairs (Smith and Deering 1984). It suggests that "because there are fewer members who can influence large numbers of their colleagues, the number of points at which presidents must attempt to influence the Congress is . . . that much more" (Davis 1979). Thus although presidents' influence is seen as declining, the influence of particular members of Congress is not concomitantly increasing. Congress is unconsciously following the strategy of *divide or be conquered*. Greater decentralization has allowed Congress to forestall efforts by presidents to gain the upper hand in legislation. Finally, several scholars stand at the congressional end of this influence-on-policy continuum. Hinckley (1978) is a good example of this extreme:

> It is commonplace to observe that the president has become the twentieth century Chief Legislator. However, with the proliferation of the federal bureaucracy far beyond the scope of a single executive's sight, in some areas congressional committees have become the chief executive. (138-139)

Such are the stories told and the positions taken about the relative influence of Congress and presidents on national policy. Many points on the continuum have been carefully documented in qualitative and historical retrospectives and in a smaller, but growing, number of quantitative analyses. There is still a problem, however, in systematically comparing different presidents and assessing their relative influence on and success in Congress. To estimate presidential influence in Congress adequately, systematic and comparative measures of presidential behavior and of the president's resulting success in Congress are needed.[6]

A common way of judging presidential success in Congress is Congressional Quarterly's "presidential boxscores." The boxscores are summary measures resulting from classification of presidential proposals and observation to determine whether they are approved by Congress and enacted into law. Conceptually, this is an ideal data set. Empirically, it has two severe problems. First, it is not clear what counts as a proposal. Suppose the president says that solving the unemployment problem requires a seven-point plan, with many subpoints. Is the plan one, seven, or many more policy proposals? Even if this issue was resolved, how could we know precisely when a presidential proposal has passed? What if only the Senate approves the bill? These difficult questions seem to have no easy or uniform answer. Congressional Quarterly stopped calculating the boxscores in 1975 because of what it called their "dubious quality." It was wisely decided that the measure had too little validity to justify its continuance (see Peterson 1985, and Shull 1983, for other problems with and uses of the measure).

Another indicator of presidential success is based on Congressional Quarterly's "key votes," a set of about fifteen roll call votes selected each year by the editors as the most important. Although key votes represent an improvement over the boxscores, they too have several inherent problems. Key votes necessarily disregard the vast majority of floor votes in Congress. They are also chosen by a changing group of Congressional Quarterly editors with a reasonable, but not replicable, set of decision rules. Most importantly, however, this approach is likely to overrepresent controversial (as distinct from "important") roll call votes (see King 1986a).[7]

Our use of presidents' positions does not alleviate all these problems. One of the problems that cannot readily be solved is that some important legislation may be killed in committee or subcommittee before it reaches the floor for a roll call vote. Calculation of congressional support of a president's position, however, constitutes an improvement in both replicability and reliability. Every roll call vote on which a president takes a position is included. Presidents do not usually take positions on trivial legislation, so the problem of variation in the importance of roll call votes is partly solved. Because all the roll call votes are used, the problem of selection bias is reduced. Furthermore, we average percentages, rather than raw numbers, thus controlling for differing participation levels; the tables also report average participation levels.[8]

Consider first the overall percentage of representatives who vote in support of presidents' positions. These figures, provided in Table 2.10, suggest several generalizations. First, as one would expect, Democratic presidents are more successful in the Democratic House than Republican presidents. The results are not completely uniform, however. Although congressional support for Jimmy Carter was generally higher than for the Republican presidents, it was consistently lower than for Presidents Kennedy and Johnson. Furthermore, during one year each for President Nixon and Ford, congressional support was higher than it was any year under any Democratic president. In addition, Republican presidents received more support in three other years than Carter did in any year of his four-year term.

Second, President Reagan's seemingly magical legislative success during the 1981 Congress was not exceptional in comparison with the records of other presidents. The president's major tax and budget victories were offset by other matters that year. *Indeed, contrary to reports in the popular press, this systematic comparison indicates that in not one of his first four years did Reagan reach the success rate of the Carter administration.* The Carter years, moreover, were not especially successful ones. In short, a pendulum, real or imagined, did not swing as much in the president's favor during Reagan's first term as is often assumed.

Finally, and more generally, Table 2.10 makes clear that there is no pendulum for any of the presidents observed; rather, shifts occur within the middle range of the continuum. Support for the legislative positions of our last seven presidents has remained within a fairly narrow band. Among all members, presidential support rarely dips below the 50 percent mark (except for Reagan in 1983 and 1984) and only infrequently exceeds 70 percent. The implication is that the institutions of the presidency and Congress shape individual presidents' success in Congress. Congressional decentralization, committee strength, and policy interests with regard to clientele place a ceiling on presidential support, whereas party loyalty, regularized liaison efforts, and strategic veto threats prevent this support from dropping too low. The congressional and executive institutions place constraints on and provide resources for actors within them, thereby narrowing the degree of difference and the variation in feasible behavior.

The Partisan Connection

The political party system is one of the primary institutional connections between Congress and the presidency. It helps to reconcile some of the differences and provides a basis of communication between the two institutions. This function should come as no surprise, given the simultaneous, similar, and interconnected development of political parties in these two institutions. Richard P. McCormick (1975) makes the point quite clearly:

> The constitutional arrangements for electing a president encouraged co-operation among political leaders throughout the nation on behalf of particular candidates. In quite a different way, the election of members of the House of Representatives by popular vote served to relate state and national politics. As parties were delineated on this national basis, the same alignments became operative in contests for state and even local offices. (94)

Two hundred years later, political party alignments still help to explain congressional support for presidents. Party, region, and their overlap present many groups of congressional members with whom presidents may fail or succeed. Table 2.10 presents measures of aggregate support for the incumbent's party and the opposition party. It also shows the average number of representatives voting on bills—a measure of the operative size of the congressional body. In all but one year, presidents received more support from their party in Congress than from the opposition party. The one exception occurred in the first months of Ford's term in 1974, when few roll call votes were taken and when Ford took a public position on fewer still. Kennedy and Johnson received strong support from their party, surpassing the Democrat's support for Carter and the Republican's support for Eisenhower, Nixon, Ford, and Reagan. In line with the analysis of Cooper and Bombardier (1968), we see that Lyndon Johnson was not noticeably more successful than John Kennedy either among all House members or among only Democrats. Johnson's advantage over his predecessor was achieved by a much larger Democratic majority and somewhat more support from opposition Republicans.

Midterm congressional elections are well known for reducing the percentage of in-party members in Congress. Table 2.10 reveals for the first time that the newly enlarged out party tends to support the incumbent president at an even lower rate after the midterm election, thus exaggerating the midterm election losses. Except perhaps for Johnson after the 1966 midterm election, the increase in size does not yield less partisan cohesiveness. Instead, the out party may be buoyed by a successful recent election, and its congressional members may be encouraged to identify more with their party label and programs. The measures in Table 2.10 can also be used to assess the extent to which presidents influenced congressional members in partisan terms. Although President Reagan's program received relatively bipartisan support during his first two years in office, for example, opposition party support for Reagan during his next two years was among the lowest ever for an incumbent president.

Presidents, Policies, and Parties

The policy complexity of the presidency suggests that presidential success in Congress will vary by policy area. Presidency researchers have developed two hypotheses about such policy-specific success. First, conventional wisdom has long held that presidents are more influential in foreign policy than in domestic policy. Descriptions of this "two presidencies" thesis pervade American government text-books and scholarly literature (Wildavsky 1966; Cronin 1980). Second, what might be called the "bipartisan foreign policy hypothesis" posits a pre-Vietnam period in which foreign policy is more bipartisan than domestic policy (Bliss and Johnson 1975; Jordan and Taylor 1981). For the post-1965 period, many scholars argue that, if it has not disappeared entirely, the magnitude of this bipartisanship difference has dropped substantially. One representative statement of the commonly perceived differences between foreign and domestic policy making appears in a textbook by Murphy and Danielson:

> Historically, . . . Congress has not restricted presidential power in foreign policy nearly as much or as consistently as in domestic affairs. The needs for secrecy and speed in international relations, although often exaggerated, are real; and Congress finds it difficult to act with dispatch and impossible to keep secrets. Moreover, constituents are apt to put far less pressure on legislators to intervene in foreign than in domestic affairs. (1977, 334-335)

Other reasons often given for greater bipartisanship and congressional support of the president in foreign policy include a tendency toward more presidential effort in foreign policy making, fewer competing interest groups in foreign policy, the president's formal constitutional powers, the military-industrial complex, and an apparent greater issue complexity in foreign affairs. Unfortunately, the systematic evidence in support of the two presidencies and bipartisanship hypotheses is conflictual and inconsistent. The partial evidence bearing on the bipartisan hypothesis indicates that foreign policy politics may actually be *more* partisan than domestic policy. Clausen (1973), for example, found that, among his policy dimensions of congressional roll call votes (one foreign and four domestic), only on the international involvement dimension did members of both parties respond to a change in the party of the president. Holsti and Rosenau (1984) reach similar conclusions in a study of leaders randomly selected from *Who's Who in America*. They conclude that "American foreign policy is in disarray" and that "American leaders are strikingly divided on a broad range of foreign policy questions."

The situation for the two presidencies thesis is almost equally troubling. Wildavsky (1966) and LeLoup and Shull (1979) find supporting evidence, but Sigelman (1980) questions their data and, in a reanalysis, finds evidence against the hypothesis. LeLoup and Shull (1979), however, find reasons to question Sigelman's data. In another reanalysis based on different data, King (1986b) finds that members of the House of Representatives support the president about as often on domestic policies as on foreign but that the party leaders of the House clearly fit both the two presidencies and the bipartisan foreign policy conceptions of American politics. King hypothesized that the conventional wisdom reflected observations about the more visible congressional party leaders and had mistakenly been applied to the congressional membership.

This confusing empirical situation cannot easily be resolved, but the issue seems to be an important normative consideration for many scholars. A range of proposals, for example, advocate supporting the president more on foreign policy and on making foreign policy more bipartisan by creating ad hoc bipartisan groups in Congress to follow important foreign policy issues (Hamilton et al. 1978), increasing congressional expertise (Rourke 1977), establishing committees composed of members from the president's cabinet and Congress (Manning 1977), increasing politically responsible behavior from America's political leaders (Bax 1977), and having the president act in ways that would encourage congressional party leaders to work together, avoiding conflict on foreign policy issues (Frye and Rogers 1979).

Inconsistencies and disagreements in research exist regarding the current extent of bipartisanship and congressional support for presidents on matters of foreign policy. There are also disagreements about what should be done to improve the situation—if indeed the situation needs improving. We cannot resolve this controversy here, but a more complete presentation of the measures of presidential support in different policy categories will contribute toward more informed understanding of these matters.

Table 2.11 presents aggregate support for the president on House roll call votes for seven policy categories, three foreign and four domestic. Because the number of roll calls for each category differs, care must be taken in interpreting these figures. As a result, we have greater confidence in some of these measures than in others (see Table 2.9 for the total number of roll call votes in each category).[9] This table bears directly on the two presidencies hypothesis. Although there is some general tendency for presidential support to be higher among members of Congress in the three foreign policy categories than in the four domestic policies, the variation within these two broad areas is immense. For sixteen of the twenty-eight years represented in Table 2.11, support for the president is highest in one of the three foreign policy areas. Even among these sixteen years, however, the second highest category of support for the president is in one of the domestic policy areas (almost 40 percent of the time). The results also indicate some similarities across presidents within specific policy areas. Presi-

53

dents consistently appear to do well in matters of foreign trade and defense. From 1957 to 1984, they receive support from 66.5 percent of the House membership on trade and 62.1 percent on defense. The seven presidents studied also gain reasonably strong support on resource and government management issues (59 percent and 58 percent support, respectively). Presidential success in foreign aid, social welfare, and agriculture varies more. The findings do not suggest two presidencies distinguished by the content of the issues. Instead, they indicate multiple policy presidencies that rest on the intermixing of content with institutional advantages and limitations. Presidents are constitutionally mandated to act in the areas of defense and diplomacy, and statutes (the Budget and Accounting Act of 1921 and the Full Employment Act of 1946) give them a dominant role in economic policy. With these constitutional and statutory bases for action, presidents may commit greater resources to legislative efforts in these areas, and congressional members may be more willing to support presidential positions. In contrast, the remaining areas are characterized more by changing political stakes than by stable institutional attributes.

Table 2.11 also reveals a considerable amount of other information. The failure of Carter's energy policy, for example, is evident from his quite average congressional support in the natural resources category. In none of his four years did he receive his highest level of support in this area. The dramatic erosion of President Nixon's support is also quite apparent. Support on defense issues dropped during the Vietnam War from a high of 86 percent in 1969 to only 44 percent in 1973 and 49 percent in 1974. Nixon's foreign aid support dropped a remarkable twenty-three percentage points from 1973 to 1974. Also apparent is a decline in levels of presidential support that continued after Nixon's resignation. The highest levels of support received by Presidents Ford through Reagan are not as high as those for Presidents Eisenhower to Nixon (in his first term). Greater institutional cleavages between Congress and the presidency may occur as party ties between the two institutions weakened and as respect for the presidency declined after Watergate. Additional evidence to support this statement appears in Table 2.12, in which support from members of the president's own party also seems to have diminished since Nixon's second term.

The results set forth in Tables 2.12 and 2.13 offer mixed evidence on the bipartisan foreign policy hypothesis. Again, broad contours of support can be found for this hypothesis but only in the most general sense. For most years, in-party support is greater across the seven policy areas than out-party support. In most years, however, this gap in support between the two parties is only marginally smaller on foreign policy roll call votes than on domestic. Furthermore, the disparity between foreign and domestic policy support for the president did not noticeably differ in either party. The exceptions are quite numerous, however, and the variations within foreign and domestic policy areas are large.

These data are a rich source of information relevant to many other hypotheses. As might be expected, for example, opposition party support for Reagan's conservative social welfare legislation was abysmal, lower than the social welfare support given to any president except Gerald Ford. To take another example, support for President Reagan's tax plan was apparently not as bipartisan as was originally thought. Reagan received nearly unanimous support among his partisans (91.95 percent), but on average, less than one-third of the Democratic representatives were supportive across the twenty-one government management roll call votes taken in 1981. Ronald Reagan's success on his tax and budget plan can be compared with Jimmy Carter's failure on energy policy. Carter had relatively low support from Republicans on his energy proposals, but he obtained support from his own party members at only slightly higher rates. Reagan's party was in the minority, but his success, to a considerable extent, was still forged on a partisan base, so that he drew votes from virtually all Republicans. In this case, partisan support made it possible for a presidential proposal to succeed.

The Democratic party has always had a somewhat schizophrenic personality. The liberal northerners and conservative southerners have voted as differently as if they had been two separate political parties. Therefore, when analyzing measures of presidential success in Congress, it pays to heed regional differences.[10] The overall figures, presented in Table 2.14, demonstrate that Democratic presidents do universally better in Congress among the northern Democrats than among the southern Democrats.[11] Carter did not do as well among either the northern establishment or the southern one (his base) as did Kennedy and Johnson. The differences between northern and southern Democratic support for Nixon and Ford were much more even, with the advantage shifting back and forth. In fact, Nixon's southern electoral strategy seemed to pay off most clearly for the Republican party in House roll call votes under Ronald Reagan; this partisan president lost considerably more among the northern Democrats than among his southern ideological compatriots. More detailed accounts of regional levels of presidential support from the Democratic party appear in Tables 2.15 and 2.16 by policy category.

In total, the analyses of presidents' positions and legislative support across seven policy areas detract from the two presidencies hypotheses and support the thesis of multiple policy presidencies that shape the success of individual incumbents, and order the ways in which the institutions of presidency and Congress interact. Presidents must accommodate these policy variations in building strategies and coalitions in Congress. As we discuss in Chapter 4, the institution has responded by creating increasingly specialized units to match this multiplicity.

Presidents, Legislation, and Group Interests

Observers of presidents' legislative activities seldom consider how they may be viewed by interest groups that are also very much a part of the legislative process. Indeed, politicians, journalists, and many others pay considerable attention to the efforts of interest groups in the legislative process, but their focus is only on groups' dealings with members of Congress. Scholars write detailed accounts of "iron triangles" to account for the communication and influence patterns manifested by a specific interest group, a congressional committee, and an executive department or agency. So much time is spent drawing the triangles that presidents are usually treated as irrelevant to interest groups within the halls of Congress. These groups are presumed to enjoy the access and support they need as clients of the committees and executive departments, neither of which presidents can easily control.

Nevertheless, presidents do pay attention to interest groups, and interest groups do pay attention to presidents. Of greatest importance in understanding the attention given by interest groups to presidents is the concept of intergroup variation. Just as congressional members differ by party and region in their support of presidential positions on legislation, so too do interest groups vary in their opinions of presidents' legislative positions. Furthermore, these group assessments are likely to change across a president's term.

The data in Table 2.17 offer a first opportunity to explore group ratings of presidents' positions on roll call votes. Congressional scholars are familiar with the ideological scores given members of Congress by key interest group associations. The groups we have chosen represent a small cross-section of available groups: the Americans for Democratic Action (ADA), considered a barometer of liberal thinking; the Committee on Political Education (COPE), a group associated with the AFL-CIO that monitors the positions members of Congress take on labor legislation; the Americans for Constitutional Action (ACA), the

ADA's conservative counterpart; and the Chamber of Commerce of the United States (CCUS), a probusiness group. Until now, these organizations have not assigned interest group scores to presidents. They can, however, be reconstructed for presidents from the positions they take on the same legislation used by interest groups to compile their congressional rankings. We have calculated the presidential interest group ratings for each roll call vote in each year from 1960 to the present.

Table 2.17 displays a liberal-conservative continuum for the seven presidents studied. It ranges from Lyndon Johnson, who received the highest ADA scores (liberal), to Ronald Reagan, who received the lowest ADA scores and very high ACA and CCUS (conservative) scores. Within the terms of the seven presidents, Johnson is conspicuous for the consistency that characterized his five years in office. Nixon and Reagan varied much more over their terms. Variation across groups can also be seen. Although Reagan, for example, was rated very low by the ADA, he received slightly higher marks from labor (COPE), and he was perceived to be less conservative by the conservative ACA than by the liberal ADA. This difference may show that Reagan was indeed not conservative enough to suit right-wing groups.

A similar pattern can be noted for Carter, who was perceived to be less liberal by the liberal ADA organization than by the conservative ACA organization. His scores for labor (COPE) and business (CCUS) also suggest a more moderate presidency than the ADA and ACA scores. The Reagan and Carter results indicate the diversity of groups encountered by presidents. Presidents have a difficult time satisfying groups even within a narrow liberal or conservative band along the ideological continuum. The plural presidency encompasses differences among these groups in addition to differences within the congressional membership and across issue areas.

Vetoes and Congressional Overrides

In his classic book, *Congressional Government*, Woodrow Wilson wrote that a president's "power of veto . . . is, of course, beyond all comparison, his most formidable prerogative" (1973, 53). It is "the president's ultimate legislative weapon in that it gives him the weight of two-thirds of the members of each house of Congress" (Watson and Thomas 1983, 257). It is also a "weapon" that is understood in notably institutional terms. It is exercised infrequently and overridden rarely. Indeed, overuse of the veto power is sometimes identified as a sign of presidential weakness. For every president from Washington to Reagan, we recorded from government documents, checked for errors, classified into policy areas, aggregated, and analyzed each presidential veto and congressional attempt to override.

Table 2.18 summarizes these data. Presidents Ulysses Grant, Grover Cleveland, Theodore Roosevelt, Franklin Roosevelt, Harry Truman, and Gerald Ford used the veto most often; Presidents Franklin Pierce, Andrew Johnson, Harry Truman, and Gerald Ford saw their vetoes overridden most frequently. Table 2.18 also reveals that the expansion of legislative activity by the presidency in the twentieth century has produced a concomitant increase in vetoes. Even if we include Cleveland, nineteenth-century presidents averaged some thirty-two vetoes during their terms (only fourteen vetoes per term if Cleveland is not considered); twentieth-century presidents beginning with Theodore Roosevelt averaged ninety-eight vetoes per term.

Presidential vetoes and congressional override attempts have long been of interest, but like so many areas of presidential research, they have only recently seen systematic empirical analysis. The state of the art in this research indicates that the use of the veto "varies according to the resources of the president and the character of the political environment" (Rohde and Simon 1985, 410). Policy areas are also important in explaining congressional overrides.

From our original data collection, we were able to produce the more detailed set of veto measures in Table 2.19. (Totals appear in the first two columns of Table 2.20.) Table 2.19 shows a dramatic decline in the number of private bills vetoed after Eisenhower.[12] Apparently presidents no longer saw such minor matters as worthy of presidential attention. Policy complexity as a part of the plural presidency can be observed in other categories. The largest number of vetoes appears in the social welfare, government and economic management, and energy and natural resources categories, the areas in which presidents take their greatest numbers of positions (Table 2.9). Among the other areas from 1946 to 1984, there was not one veto by any president of foreign aid legislation and only scattered vetoes in foreign trade. Defense policy vetoes occurred about as frequently as vetoes in some of the domestic policy areas. Moreover, very few vetoes on agricultural matters are present. These patterns again suggest the role that multiple policy presidencies play in Congress.

Within categories and across presidents, the variation is striking. During the entire Kennedy and Johnson administrations, for example, there was only one veto of a defense bill. Indeed, in the midst of the Vietnam War, even the first three years of the Nixon administration saw no defense vetoes. On the other hand, Harry Truman was not so lucky. During his years in office, there was an average of nearly 2.5 defense vetoes per year. Some (but not all) of the variation in veto behavior can be explained by the partisan division of Congress. Indeed, variation in this policy area is so dramatic and of such a different nature for different presidencies that Rohde and Simon's (1985) analysis of all veto decisions is unlikely to apply as well in different policy areas.[13]

Annual numbers of congressional attempts to override presidential vetoes, along with the total number of vetoes, appear in Table 2.20. The variation here is also apparent. Note that Kennedy and Johnson were never challenged by either house of Congress. Carter won two challenges and lost two others, whereas Reagan won three and lost four congressional challenges. Tables 2.21 and 2.22 give more of the flavor of congressional challenges, showing every instance of successful and unsuccessful challenges from 1946 to 1984. There we can see that vetoes of private bills are virtually never challenged. Many types of legislation can also be responsible for instigating presidential-congressional conflict; the lists include bills in six of the seven policy areas, at every level of apparent importance and potential impact on the American public and for dozens of individual and specialized pieces of legislation.

Presidents as Chief Legislators?

After all the political speeches are said and the congressional votes are done, presidents are apparently *not* "chief legislators" who "guide Congress in much of its lawmaking activity" (Rossiter 1960, 26). Congress has never been organized as a tight, efficient institution that clearly states priorities and expeditiously acts upon them. Congress has always been a decentralized, somewhat inefficient institution that nevertheless asserts priorities and acts upon them in a slower, consensus-seeking fashion. The results in this chapter indicate that presidents do present a variety of policy proposals to Congress. Perhaps their most important role in the national policy-making process is to highlight certain problems and solutions to the exclusion of others. In acting as policy dramatists, they appear to be chief legislators and chief policy makers, but results reported in this chapter suggest that this appearance is deceptive.

The image of a single executive initiating legislation conflicts with that of a plural presidency confronting individual presidents with diverse tasks in various policy areas affecting different groups. Many of the efforts are handled by a well-developed set of organizations within the White House. Presidents may be expected to perform as policy initiators, but the institutional relations between the presidency and Congress severely restrict the success of their performance on any one occasion. Congressional support of presidential positions is not overly high and differs markedly from one issue to another and across party and regional breakdowns among members. Moreover, presidents must grapple with not one but two diffuse, reluctant institutions, Congress and the presidency. That presidents' congressional successes are often only nominal reflects in part difficulties in the coordination of legislative proposals, legislative liaison work, and strategies to achieve legislative success within the White House and on Capitol Hill.

In sum, three points should be kept in mind about presidential relations with Congress. First, the presidency, not the officeholder, is the "policy actor" to watch. Second, the impact of the institution is likely to vary widely across the various policy areas and groups. Finally, incumbents construct strategies within the confines of the institutional plurality. They may be able to emphasize, and succeed in, one area more than another, but they must recognize each area and act within the channels established by them.

Although the Constitution specified a role for presidents in signing and vetoing legislation, the framers never anticipated the public and vigorous role that presidents now play in drafting legislation and lobbying to build coalitions of members of Congress for its passage. Presidents as individual incumbents are now evaluated by the citizenry for the proposals they send to Congress and their ability to obtain successful results. Ironically, however, these evaluations reflect an anachronistic image that no longer describes the presidency's behavior in policy making. Instead, the institution involves plural points of authority and plural avenues of responsibility that can be asserted, shared, or hidden. This plurality is one that the framers would not have foreseen and of which most Americans remain unaware.

Notes

1. These are tallied from the legislative clearance records of the Office of Management and Budget and from State of the Union messages. The counts involve items that had cleared "in accordance" with the president's program by OMB and had been mentioned in at least one State of the Union message.
2. A distinction should be noted here between the number of proposals submitted to Congress by the White House and the importance attached to

any one proposal. The frequency with which proposals are submitted within a policy area provides one indication of the breadth of attention given the issue category by a president, but a single proposal may be viewed as a major priority by the chief executive. Although Johnson did not submit numerous proposals on civil rights, for instance, a few central measures showed concerted attention to this policy area.

3. Congressional Quarterly has kept track of presidential positions since 1953. The editors changed the decision rules and methods of recording positions in 1957, however, so that the data from 1953-1956 may not be comparable with those after 1957 (see below as well as the 1956 and 1957 editions of the *Congressional Quarterly Almanac*).

4. It is our intention to provide comparable Senate data in future editions of this volume.

5. Farm policies also affect the entire population as market prices rise or fall, in some instances because of policy decisions, but these citizen effects are always more difficult to trace to governmental decisions because various intermediary factors, including production costs, inflation, and distribution expenses, are also involved. Natural resources are much more nearly public goods.

6. Hammond and Fraser (1984) and Edwards (1985) make a number of explicit and useful proposals about measuring presidential success, but their wide-ranging aggregate approaches are not always sufficient to reveal the breadth of congressional responses to presidential preferences. Edwards (1985), in particular, creates a number of dubious indexes. His "nonunanimous support" index is likely to have severe selection bias (Achen 1986), and his "single-vote support" index seems quite biased because it includes some important roll calls and omits a large variety of others (see King 1986a).

7. Other scholars use Congressional Quarterly's "Presidential Support Score." This measure is based on the proportion of times each member of Congress votes with the incumbent president. The scores have been used successfully in many studies, but they were mainly intended for use in analyzing patterns of individual members of Congress. Although they can be quite useful, our goal is to view Congress from the president's perspective.

8. Percentages become more reliable when they are based on larger numbers of members. For some purposes, these data should therefore be weighted by the average number of members participating. See the discussion of sampling variance in Chapter 6 for details.

9. See Chapter 6 for a discussion of sampling variance. The discussion also applies here, as basing a percentage on more interviews or more roll calls increases our confidence in the number in both cases. The position-taking counts in Tables 2.8 and 2.9 can be used to weight (and thus to increase validity and reduce statistical problems such as heteroskedasticity and measurement error).

10. Roll call tables based on regional variables are available only as far back as 1962 because this is the year when Congressional Quarterly began to record roll call statistics by region.

11. Some combine the southern Democrats with the Republicans into a "conservative coalition." These measures could be obtained by taking a weighted average of the appropriate columns in Tables 2.10 and 2.14.

12. Private bills specifically provide relief for a named individual or individuals. The relief includes granting immigration rights to individuals or providing citizens with certain tax breaks or other financial advantages.
13. Indeed, our preliminary statistical analyses indicate that the parameter estimates in their model vary enormously across policy areas. Some of this variation may reflect increased sampling variation because there are fewer vetoes to analyze, but some is surely due to the complexities across policy areas.

Table 2.1 Number of Congressional Liaison Aides to the President Ranked by Aides' Pre-White House Experience, Kennedy to Reagan

Aides' Experience	Kennedy	Johnson	Nixon	Ford	Carter	Reagan	Total
Congress	3	0	9	3	5	4	24
Lobbying	0	1	2	0	2	2	7
Party	2	1	2	0	1	0	6
Congress and lobbying	0	0	4	5	2	4	15
Congress and party	1	0	2	0	0	1	4
Lobbying and party	0	3	0	0	0	0	3
Congress, lobbying, and party	0	1	1	0	0	0	2
None	0	0	0	0	2	2	4
Total	6	6	20	8	12	13	65

Sources: Pika (1979); Congressional Quarterly (1979); Davis (1983).

Table 2.2 Number of Congressional Liaison Aides to the President Ranked by Aides' Post-White House Experience, Kennedy to Ford

Experience	Kennedy	Johnson	Nixon	Ford	Total
Lobbying	4	2	13	3	22
Congress	0	2	3	3	8
Other [a]	2	2	3	2	9
Unknown	0	0	1	0	1
Total	6	6	20	8	40

[a] Included in this category are lawyers and political consultants who may have lobbied on occasion.

Sources: Pika (1979); Davis (1983).

Figure 2.1   The Legislative Clearance Process

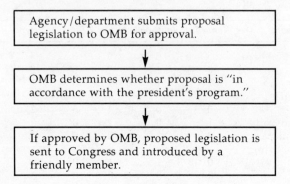

Figure 2.2   The Enrolled Bill Process

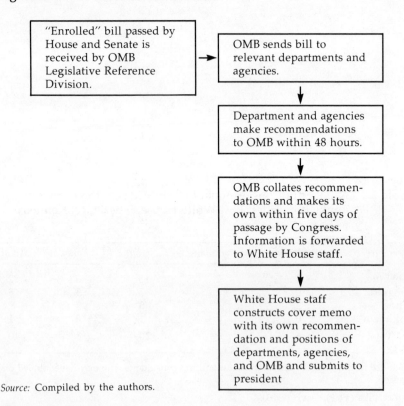

Source: Compiled by the authors.

Table 2.3 Number of Presidential Requests of Congress in State of the Union Messages

	First-time requests	Repeat requests
Kennedy		
1961	25	0
1962	16	8
1963	6	12
Johnson, I		
1964	6	11
Johnson, II		
1965	34	4
1966	24	7
1967	19	8
1968	14	12
Nixon, I		
1969	17	0
1970	12	9
1971	8	12
1972	3	14
Nixon, II		
1973	20	3
1974	5	11
Ford		
1975	10	3
1976	6	7
Carter		
1977	21	0
1978	8	3
1979	8	5
1980	4	7

Source: OMB Legislative Reference Division clearance record in Light (1982, 42).

Table 2.4 Requests for Legislation, First Year (percent)

	January–March	April–June	July–September	October–December	Total
Kennedy 1961	76	24	0	0	100
Johnson 1965	94	6	0	0	100
Nixon 1969	12	41	41	6	100
Nixon 1973	40	30	15	15	100
Carter 1977	33	57	10	0	100

Source: OMB Legislative Reference Division clearance record in Light (1982, 45).

Table 2.5 Benefits Sought in Domestic Programs (percent)

President	Benefit		
	Electoral [a]	Historical [b]	Programmatic [c]
Kennedy	54	25	42
Johnson	44	37	52
Nixon	70	43	22
Ford	60	22	44
Carter	57	23	39

Note: A total of 126 White House staff members were asked to name the benefits they hoped for in the selection of the top domestic programs of their respective administrations. Only the first two programs for each presidency were pursued. The percentages for each administration total more than one hundred because respondents could give more than one reply.

[a] Programs intended to aid in the president's reelection efforts.
[b] Programs intended to influence the way future historians will view the current president and presidency.
[c] Programs that especially accord with the president's ideological orientation or personal beliefs.

Source: Light (1982, 72).

Table 2.6 President's Most Important Domestic Programs

President	Program	*Percentage of staff mentioning program*
Kennedy	Aid to education	91
	Medicare	77
	Unemployment	45
	Area redevelopment	18
	Civil rights	18
Johnson	Poverty	86
	Civil rights	79
	Medicare	64
	Aid to education	32
	Model cities	29
	Wilderness preservation	11
	Environmental protection	4
Nixon	Welfare reform	75
	Revenue sharing	65
	Crime	40
	Energy	35
	Environmental protection	15
Ford	Energy	79
	Inflation	50
	Regulatory reform	8
Carter	Energy	84
	Inflation	63
	Welfare reform	59
	Hospital cost containment	28
	Economic stimulus	19
	Reorganization	9

Note: Paul Light asked 126 White House staff members to name the most important domestic programs of their respective administrations. Respondents could give more than one reply.

Source: Light (1982, 70).

Table 2.7 Percentage of Domestic Programs by Issue Area, Kennedy to Carter

Program	Kennedy/ Johnson	Johnson	Nixon, I	Nixon, II	Ford	Carter
Agriculture	4	2	3	0	0	2
Civil rights	7	4	3	0	0	0
Consumer affairs	4	10	5	4	0	10
Crime	4	9	13	4	19	0
Education	19	13	8	4	0	4
Energy	0	0	0	40	31	24
Government affairs	4	10	18	8	6	15
Health [a]	9	8	13	12	12	13
Labor/employment	19	5	5	0	6	9
Natural resources	13	17	18	20	6	7
Transportation	4	7	8	0	0	5
Urban affairs/welfare	17	18	10	8	19	11

[a] Includes medical education, for example, nurses' training, medical school construction.

Source: OMB Legislative Reference Division clearance record in Light (1982, 85).

Table 2.8 Presidential Position Taking on House Roll Calls, 1957-1984

	Total roll calls	Positions [a]	Dollar positions [b]	Positions as percentage of roll calls [c]
Eisenhower, II				
1957	100	54	0	54.0
1958	93	48	0	51.6
1959	87	53	0	60.9
1960	91	41	0	45.1
Kennedy				
1961	113	65	0	57.5
1962	124	60	0	48.4
1963	119	71	0	59.7
Johnson, I				
1964	113	52	0	46.0
Johnson, II				
1965	201	112	0	55.7
1966	193	102	0	52.8
1967	245	126	0	51.4
1968	233	101	0	43.3
Nixon, I				
1969	177	47	0	26.6
1970	266	64	0	24.1
1971	320	61	0	19.1
1972	329	37	0	11.2
Nixon, II				
1973	541	125	26	27.9
1974	476	107	22	27.1
Ford				
1974	61	0	3	4.9
1975	612	89	27	19.0
1976	661	49	27	11.5
Carter				
1977	706	75	23	13.9
1978	834	115	27	17.0
1979	672	143	16	23.7
1980	604	114	20	22.2

(Table continues)

Table 2.8   (continued)

	Total roll calls	*Positions* [a]	*Dollar positions* [b]	*Positions as percentage of roll calls* [c]
Reagan				
1981	353	75	16	25.8
1982	459	75	19	20.5
1983	498	80	23	20.7
1984	408	111	16	31.1

[a] Number of House roll calls on which the president took a clear public position.
[b] Number of House roll calls on which the president took a clear public position and the House responded by approving a different dollar amount from the one the president had preferred. These were not separately recorded by *Congressional Quarterly* until 1973.
[c] Total number of positions presidents have taken as a percentage of the total number of House roll calls.

Source: Each roll call was individually coded by the authors from the *Congressional Quarterly Almanac* (annual volumes). The data were also checked for inconsistencies, aggregated, and analyzed by the authors.

Table 2.9 Presidential Position Taking in the House by Issue Area, 1957-1984

	Foreign trade	Foreign aid	Defense	Social welfare	Government	Resources	Agriculture
Eisenhower, II							
1957	2	6	4	18	9	10	5
1958	5	4	9	13	7	8	2
1959	1	7	3	9	11	15	7
1960	3	7	1	15	6	5	4
Kennedy							
1961	5	10	5	12	18	9	6
1962	3	10	6	10	19	8	4
1963	3	9	8	14	23	9	5
Johnson, I							
1964	4	9	5	14	9	10	1
Johnson, II							
1965	5	10	10	36	30	16	5
1966	7	13	4	24	36	18	0
1967	5	12	9	42	43	11	4
1968	5	10	7	29	28	18	4
Nixon, I							
1969	1	4	2	18	18	2	2
1970	1	5	2	21	20	13	2
1971	9	2	9	25	9	7	0
1972	3	3	7	8	11	5	0
Nixon, II							
1973	10	3	15	20	36	26	15
1974	2	11	15	23	35	21	0

(Table continues)

Table 2.9 (continued)

	Foreign trade	Foreign aid	Defense	Social welfare	Government	Resources	Agriculture
Ford							
1974	0	0	0	0	0	0	0
1975	7	4	10	14	22	27	5
1976	3	1	5	11	10	19	0
Carter							
1977	4	9	11	10	15	25	1
1978	13	19	20	11	31	20	1
1979	32	21	14	31	17	28	0
1980	10	19	11	14	31	22	7
Reagan							
1981	4	1	15	4	21	15	15
1982	3	4	22	6	15	20	5
1983	5	6	27	20	8	9	5
1984	19	1	20	26	19	22	4

Note: For this table and those that follow, the following definitions hold: Foreign trade = foreign trade, diplomacy, or immigration. Foreign aid = foreign aid. Defense = military, defense, veterans' issues. Social welfare = social welfare, civil rights, Indian affairs, and education. Government = government and economic management, income tax issues. Resources = energy, natural resources, environment, and transportation. Agriculture = agriculture and farm policy. The figures in the table are the number of House roll calls in which the president took a position in each issue area.

Source: Each roll call was individually coded by the authors from the *Congressional Quarterly Almanac* (annual volumes). The data were also checked for inconsistencies, aggregated, and analyzed by the authors.

Table 2.10 Average Annual Roll Call Support for the President by Members of the House, 1957-1984

	All members		Out party		In party	
	Voting	% with president	Voting	% with president	Voting	% with president
Eisenhower, II						
1957	386.39	56.01	208.20	53.68	178.19	59.28
1958	374.71	64.36	199.46	63.11	175.25	65.62
1959	395.43	57.28	257.85	46.69	137.58	77.02
1960	391.76	53.29	250.78	47.46	140.98	63.60
Kennedy						
1961	391.37	65.16	156.86	40.84	234.51	81.36
1962	381.97	68.52	154.65	47.70	227.32	82.63
1963	376.82	65.16	156.66	36.50	220.15	85.43
Johnson, I						
1964	382.58	67.38	160.83	43.18	221.75	84.84
Johnson, II						
1965	384.34	71.31	124.46	46.37	259.88	83.09
1966	342.57	69.81	114.24	46.27	228.33	81.58
1967	379.75	67.61	167.15	51.83	212.60	79.81
1968	362.98	69.92	161.43	59.96	201.55	77.89
Nixon, I						
1969	376.49	59.75	210.47	56.14	166.02	64.39
1970	358.64	71.44	201.05	66.06	157.58	78.34
1971	385.93	64.20	223.72	53.12	162.11	79.52
1972	366.35	64.03	214.54	56.40	152.89	74.52
Nixon, II						
1973	395.27	51.61	218.93	39.07	176.34	67.28
1974	380.51	55.80	214.34	48.82	166.18	64.77
Ford						
1974	368.67	72.40	207.00	76.36	161.67	67.41
1975	406.35	50.23	269.93	40.75	136.42	69.01
1976	389.49	48.11	258.90	37.31	130.59	69.53
Carter						
1977	393.87	60.73	132.45	43.63	261.41	69.43
1978	384.19	58.90	130.26	39.73	253.93	68.74
1979	399.06	58.55	146.35	36.67	252.71	71.25
1980	387.06	60.51	143.28	44.36	243.78	70.12

(Table continues)

Table 2.10 (continued)

	All members		Out party		In party	
	Voting	% with president	Voting	% with president	Voting	% with president
Reagan						
1981	403.99	56.98	223.77	45.32	180.21	71.40
1982	392.71	55.37	217.73	43.78	174.84	69.89
1983	409.95	46.59	251.01	29.90	158.94	72.94
1984	401.59	47.71	246.05	37.17	155.53	64.33

Source: Each roll call was individually coded by the authors from the *Congressional Quarterly Almanac* (annual volumes). The data were also checked for inconsistencies, aggregated, and analyzed by the authors.

Table 2.11 Percentage of Support for the President on House Roll Calls by Issue Area, 1957-1984

	Foreign trade	Foreign aid	Defense	Social welfare	Government	Resources	Agriculture
Eisenhower, II							
1957	70.10	54.36	50.56	56.86	56.37	55.44	54.13
1958	70.10	60.01	80.62	63.23	62.79	51.42	50.25
1959	99.46	70.30	49.36	55.15	68.96	45.95	50.27
1960	56.05	58.34	0.25	55.57	34.81	55.15	72.48
Kennedy							
1961	84.17	71.60	85.06	70.14	55.75	51.90	60.11
1962	71.70	61.67	83.07	78.79	69.97	58.30	49.23
1963	69.59	54.51	71.30	74.93	62.71	65.60	54.97
Johnson, I							
1964	74.31	64.54	49.40	65.37	62.98	84.56	50.97
Johnson, II							
1965	81.45	68.87	68.73	72.67	66.64	81.71	56.01
1966	75.45	69.88	53.12	69.46	67.14	77.07	—
1967	59.72	58.65	79.48	69.90	68.02	62.67	62.75
1968	68.60	69.97	77.18	72.50	61.71	75.44	72.54
Nixon, I							
1969	85.86	56.15	86.08	59.29	59.88	45.62	44.63
1970	76.29	64.75	68.18	58.14	82.80	80.53	55.96
1971	66.10	51.20	65.55	61.72	73.45	60.68	—
1972	80.07	65.16	68.00	55.94	61.76	66.15	—
Nixon, II							
1973	51.33	72.51	44.18	47.56	57.51	50.50	48.22
1974	55.33	49.35	48.59	54.86	57.69	67.02	—

(Table continues)

Table 2.11 (continued)

	Foreign trade	Foreign aid	Defense	Social welfare	Government	Resources	Agriculture
Ford							
1975	69.86	61.83	52.73	30.47	49.01	52.45	57.15
1976	52.47	60.25	56.46	45.18	43.05	48.94	—
Carter							
1977	67.68	49.21	61.51	73.56	56.02	60.53	75.66
1978	54.97	52.82	54.91	58.52	64.32	62.78	64.11
1979	60.69	53.92	64.77	59.85	57.95	55.40	—
1980	72.79	50.76	55.39	66.20	59.87	59.33	72.67
Reagan							
1981	54.72	31.66	55.62	52.33	59.08	73.04	42.87
1982	67.70	61.59	65.84	47.55	41.05	56.05	46.59
1983	43.32	57.50	57.82	38.78	39.77	30.67	46.95
1984	56.48	50.60	55.54	38.68	47.39	41.15	62.53

Source: Each roll call was individually coded by the authors from the *Congressional Quarterly Almanac* (annual volumes). The data were also checked for inconsistencies, aggregated, and analyzed by the authors.

Table 2.12 Percentage of In-party Support for the President on House Roll Calls by Issue Area, 1957-1984

	Foreign trade	Foreign aid	Defense	Social welfare	Government	Resources	Agriculture
Eisenhower, II							
1957	70.34	55.91	56.07	47.73	67.52	69.99	66.83
1958	59.12	59.21	93.11	58.11	62.85	52.44	82.37
1959	100.00	65.11	81.57	70.08	83.80	74.66	87.03
1960	63.01	63.24	0.69	60.32	50.84	79.17	92.36
Kennedy							
1961	93.50	81.17	87.11	86.86	78.81	71.88	77.67
1962	96.08	76.94	91.98	82.71	85.08	76.06	74.04
1963	88.92	80.67	85.91	84.26	87.04	86.21	85.60
Johnson, I							
1964	89.35	82.75	66.15	85.11	84.31	94.34	84.81
Johnson, II							
1965	85.39	83.49	79.98	85.91	77.86	89.61	76.58
1966	83.97	80.82	66.18	81.19	81.72	84.89	—
1967	65.75	76.57	76.43	80.96	83.75	75.97	70.93
1968	80.04	78.14	93.17	78.23	68.37	85.16	79.36
Nixon, I							
1969	99.42	40.12	92.87	63.29	69.92	51.07	40.45
1970	71.01	63.37	92.79	73.10	88.35	79.75	50.75
1971	85.30	59.04	80.61	82.89	82.10	61.17	—
1972	77.15	58.81	91.39	68.86	76.43	63.61	—
Nixon, II							
1973	56.32	75.89	65.34	56.71	81.37	63.06	62.40
1974	78.34	52.05	60.14	59.39	68.11	74.55	—

Table 2.12 (continued)

	Foreign trade	Foreign aid	Defense	Social welfare	Government	Resources	Agriculture
Ford							
1975	59.89	73.07	67.30	50.64	73.29	76.13	76.06
1976	67.41	86.67	81.22	65.06	59.92	73.54	—
Carter							
1977	67.13	58.46	71.73	85.53	59.87	71.13	92.39
1978	63.72	58.13	65.30	68.21	77.43	72.27	70.70
1979	78.35	68.62	68.95	72.95	68.70	65.94	—
1980	81.22	64.98	53.50	75.58	74.22	66.18	77.65
Reagan							
1981	66.36	21.91	68.68	76.68	91.95	76.18	43.80
1982	94.08	72.83	80.47	62.95	57.12	68.36	59.22
1983	71.31	51.31	87.66	69.34	64.05	65.76	62.53
1984	69.85	71.60	84.89	56.69	54.71	52.75	92.58

Source: Each roll call was individually coded by the authors from the *Congressional Quarterly Almanac* (annual volumes). The data were also checked for inconsistencies, aggregated, and analyzed by the authors.

Table 2.13 Percentage of Out-party Support for the President on House Roll Calls by Issue Area, 1957-1984

	Foreign trade	Foreign aid	Defense	Social welfare	Government	Resources	Agriculture
Eisenhower, II							
1957	70.19	53.30	46.33	65.19	46.74	44.37	43.13
1958	79.55	60.65	69.77	67.62	62.67	50.21	20.70
1959	99.18	73.23	31.79	47.60	61.11	30.49	29.89
1960	52.23	55.54	0.00	52.91	25.87	41.16	61.41
Kennedy							
1961	70.95	56.02	81.34	45.20	21.40	22.35	34.09
1962	37.18	39.44	69.63	73.14	47.48	31.86	12.38
1963	42.84	17.02	50.33	61.64	28.02	37.62	12.33
Johnson, I							
1964	54.09	39.42	26.89	37.81	32.67	71.08	5.65
Johnson, II							
1965	73.57	38.14	45.12	44.43	43.35	64.64	11.76
1966	58.00	47.99	28.57	45.42	38.00	62.10	—
1967	52.42	35.24	83.34	55.51	47.64	46.11	52.17
1968	54.26	59.69	58.27	65.17	53.38	63.27	63.95
Nixon, I							
1969	75.00	69.13	80.53	56.01	52.20	41.18	47.87
1970	80.81	65.70	47.92	46.45	78.37	81.51	60.07
1971	52.20	45.63	54.38	46.45	67.20	60.53	—
1972	82.23	69.84	51.24	45.85	51.36	68.05	—
Nixon, II							
1973	47.60	69.93	27.20	40.11	38.50	40.41	36.76
1974	37.46	47.43	40.01	51.29	49.55	60.88	—

(Table continues)

Table 2.13 (continued)

	Foreign trade	Foreign aid	Defense	Social welfare	Government	Resources	Agriculture
Ford							
1975	74.90	56.29	45.30	20.35	36.58	40.60	47.71
1976	44.74	46.79	43.94	35.32	34.44	36.55	—
Carter							
1977	69.59	31.22	41.44	50.39	48.57	39.24	43.36
1978	37.99	42.80	33.85	39.59	39.27	44.03	51.72
1979	30.38	28.43	57.56	37.24	39.21	37.41	—
1980	58.73	26.83	58.60	50.23	35.88	47.78	64.07
Reagan							
1981	45.43	39.55	45.20	32.62	32.65	70.30	41.95
1982	47.05	52.57	54.05	35.52	28.24	46.28	36.15
1983	25.32	61.50	38.81	19.33	24.68	8.82	36.93
1984	48.15	37.25	36.79	27.29	42.42	33.92	44.08

Source: Each roll call was individually coded by the authors from the *Congressional Quarterly Almanac* (annual volumes). The data were also checked for inconsistencies, aggregated, and analyzed by the authors.

Table 2.14 Democratic Roll Call Support for the President in the House by Region, 1962-1984

	Northern Democrats		Southern Democrats	
	Average voting	Percentage with president	Average voting	Percentage with president
Kennedy				
1962	133.43	91.94	93.88	69.40
1963	130.54	94.61	89.62	72.04
Johnson, I				
1964	131.25	94.16	90.50	71.21
Johnson, II				
1965	172.12	92.11	87.76	65.25
1966	153.12	89.28	75.22	65.68
1967	134.29	89.02	78.31	64.03
1968	126.38	86.95	75.18	62.90
Nixon, I				
1969	135.51	56.43	75.32	55.45
1970	127.33	66.64	73.73	64.91
1971	149.33	45.34	74.49	68.44
1972	142.97	54.75	70.49	59.35
Nixon, II				
1973	143.45	33.64	75.46	49.49
1974	142.08	44.45	72.36	57.46
Ford				
1974	135.00	80.59	72.00	68.86
1975	186.92	36.97	83.01	49.14
1976	179.86	30.47	79.04	52.80
Carter				
1977	179.36	75.11	82.05	57.02
1978	174.00	74.83	77.20	55.20
1979	173.16	76.65	79.55	59.45
1980	166.05	73.48	77.73	62.99
Reagan				
1981	150.56	38.38	73.21	59.47
1982	146.39	38.18	71.35	55.34
1983	166.14	22.54	84.88	44.16
1984	164.14	32.22	81.91	47.28

Source: Each roll call was individually coded by the authors from the *Congressional Quarterly Almanac* (annual volumes). The data were also checked for inconsistencies, aggregated, and analyzed by the authors.

Table 2.15 Percentage of Northern Democratic Support for the President in the House by Issue Area, 1962-1984

	Foreign trade	Foreign aid	Defense	Social welfare	Government	Resources	Agriculture
Kennedy							
1962	97.10	94.29	96.45	89.37	95.24	85.98	78.08
1963	95.90	94.35	93.27	97.64	96.33	90.76	86.97
Johnson, I							
1964	90.33	96.10	69.76	98.71	96.08	99.26	81.88
Johnson, II							
1965	96.91	95.26	82.74	97.19	88.66	93.40	79.62
1966	92.43	89.78	73.00	94.41	87.83	87.37	—
1967	73.84	91.69	75.30	94.25	91.47	81.06	71.55
1968	93.55	93.32	95.68	89.94	78.92	89.71	69.49
Nixon, I							
1969	62.24	88.49	71.37	58.82	50.23	42.50	22.58
1970	97.67	77.02	44.44	49.07	77.08	79.87	41.54
1971	34.36	49.41	38.72	41.28	62.89	58.75	—
1972	88.42	84.40	34.18	46.27	48.65	72.54	—
Nixon, II							
1973	54.30	69.14	15.47	38.73	28.29	35.33	34.06
1974	23.77	52.55	33.23	46.37	46.43	55.14	—
Ford							
1975	83.11	55.80	39.46	18.54	30.72	33.16	51.95
1976	41.90	30.22	32.45	33.75	30.39	26.31	—

Carter							
1977	64.48	64.32	81.88	93.21	59.36	79.02	97.87
1978	70.57	63.65	72.71	73.02	82.83	78.35	86.02
1979	85.75	79.47	73.15	76.28	73.49	68.24	—
1980	82.80	75.65	47.90	80.17	77.89	68.99	75.74
Reagan							
1981	40.94	53.02	35.56	25.86	21.43	62.36	42.63
1982	40.79	51.26	40.97	33.77	26.79	43.29	32.95
1983	20.57	65.30	22.63	13.54	21.16	5.75	41.23
1984	43.84	25.43	21.68	24.21	42.08	32.96	32.51

Source: Each roll call was individually coded by the authors from the *Congressional Quarterly Almanac* (annual volumes). The data were also checked for inconsistencies, aggregated, and analyzed by the authors.

Table 2.16 Percentage of Southern Democratic Support for the President in the House by Issue Area, 1962-1984

	Foreign trade	Foreign aid	Defense	Social welfare	Government	Resources	Agriculture
Kennedy							
1962	94.93	51.61	85.93	73.14	70.84	62.11	68.35
1963	79.73	60.20	75.19	64.51	73.76	79.40	83.66
Johnson, I							
1964	87.66	62.66	61.34	65.66	67.10	86.95	88.89
Johnson, II							
1965	62.22	60.21	74.37	63.80	56.14	82.29	70.66
1966	67.56	61.84	53.17	53.62	68.91	80.10	—
1967	51.45	49.91	78.34	58.49	70.40	67.55	69.87
1968	56.59	52.71	89.11	58.78	51.04	77.89	95.93
Nixon, I							
1969	100.00	31.87	97.59	51.36	55.68	38.89	89.50
1970	49.28	46.15	54.08	41.96	80.25	84.38	91.33
1971	86.46	41.23	85.39	57.09	75.57	62.59	—
1972	68.55	38.78	86.92	43.68	56.40	59.14	—
Nixon, II							
1973	36.26	71.46	49.62	42.78	57.90	50.11	41.47
1974	65.17	37.80	52.87	60.95	56.05	72.06	—
Ford							
1975	56.17	57.22	57.81	24.42	49.60	57.33	38.44
1976	51.88	83.13	70.88	39.12	43.90	59.20	—

Carter							
1977	73.01	46.18	49.83	68.94	60.86	53.52	80.68
1978	49.40	45.36	48.64	57.18	65.32	58.97	37.93
1979	62.39	44.80	59.34	65.51	58.41	61.07	—
1980	77.93	42.16	65.83	65.85	66.41	60.04	82.19
Reagan							
1981	54.74	11.27	65.04	46.40	55.80	86.20	40.28
1982	59.46	55.19	81.71	38.95	31.10	52.11	42.22
1983	35.12	53.90	70.08	30.73	31.63	14.67	28.38
1984	56.62	62.20	67.94	33.41	43.19	36.04	67.19

Source: Each roll call was individually coded by the authors from the *Congressional Quarterly Almanac* (annual volumes). The data were also checked for inconsistencies, aggregated, and analyzed by the authors.

Table 2.17 Reconstructed Interest Group Ratings of the President

Year	Percentage of agreement				N of roll calls				Percentage of positions			
	ADA	COPE	ACA	CCUS	ADA	COPE	ACA	CCUS	ADA	COPE	ACA	CCUS
Eisenhower												
1960	42.86	—	—	—	9	—	—	—	77.78	—	—	—
Kennedy												
1961	88.89	—	—	—	10	—	—	—	90.00	—	—	—
1963	100.00	—	—	—	12	—	—	—	83.33	—	—	—
Johnson												
1964	100.00	—	—	—	13	—	—	—	84.62	—	—	—
1965	100.00	—	—	—	19	—	—	—	52.63	—	—	—
1966	90.00	—	—	—	17	—	—	—	58.82	—	—	—
1967	90.00	—	—	—	15	—	—	—	66.67	—	—	—
1968	100.00	—	—	—	12	—	—	—	66.67	—	—	—
Nixon												
1969	20.00	—	—	—	15	—	—	—	33.33	—	—	—
1970	50.00	—	—	—	14	—	—	—	28.57	—	—	—
1971	8.33	—	—	—	37	—	—	—	32.43	—	—	—
1972	33.33	—	—	—	16	—	—	—	37.50	—	—	—
1973	11.11	0.00	81.82	—	25	11	27	—	36.00	63.64	40.74	—
1974	12.50	0.00	60.00	—	23	11	15	—	34.78	9.09	33.33	—
Ford												
1975	28.57	11.11	75.00	90.91	18	23	28	17	38.89	39.13	42.86	64.71
1976	0.00	12.50	100.00	100.00	20	23	28	16	25.00	34.78	35.71	37.50

Carter											
1977	66.67	85.71	25.00	28.57	21	23	26	17	42.86	30.43	65.38	41.18
1978	77.78	100.00	18.18	16.67	20	20	27	18	45.00	25.00	40.74	33.33
1979	72.73	57.14	11.11	33.33	20	20	26	17	55.00	35.00	34.62	52.94
1980	72.73	83.33	11.76	58.82	17	11	21	34	64.71	54.55	66.67	50.00
Reagan											
1981	0.00	22.22	80.00	93.75	20	15	24	19	60.00	60.00	62.50	84.21
1982	11.11	22.22	100.00	88.89	20	20	23	22	45.00	45.00	47.83	40.91
1983	7.69	0.00	89.47	88.89	20	17	28	20	65.00	29.41	67.86	45.00
1984	0.00	0.00	83.33	85.71	20	13	21	16	45.00	23.08	57.14	43.75

Note: ADA = Americans for Democratic Action. COPE = Committee on Political Education (AFL-CIO). ACA = Americans for Constitutional Action. CCUS = Chamber of Commerce of the United States.

Source: Calculated by the authors.

Table 2.18 Number of Vetoes by President, 1789-1985

Years	President	Regular	Pocket	Overridden
1789-1797	George Washington	2	0	0
1797-1801	John Adams	0	0	0
1801-1809	Thomas Jefferson	0	0	0
1809-1817	James Madison	5	2	0
1817-1825	James Monroe	1	0	0
1825-1829	John Quincy Adams	0	0	0
1829-1837	Andrew Jackson	5	7	0
1837-1841	Martin Van Buren	0	1	0
1841-1841	William H. Harrison	0	0	0
1841-1845	John Tyler	6	4	1
1845-1849	James K. Polk	2	1	0
1849-1850	Zachary Taylor	0	0	0
1850-1853	Millard Fillmore	0	0	0
1853-1857	Franklin Pierce	9	0	5
1857-1861	James Buchanan	4	3	0
1861-1865	Abraham Lincoln	2	5	0
1865-1869	Andrew Johnson	21	8	15
1869-1877	Ulysses S. Grant	45	48	4
1877-1881	Rutherford B. Hayes	12	1	1
1881-1881	James A. Garfield	0	0	0
1881-1885	Chester A. Arthur	4	8	1
1885-1889	Grover Cleveland	304	110	2
1889-1893	Benjamin Harrison	19	25	1
1893-1897	Grover Cleveland	42	128	5
1897-1901	William McKinley	6	36	0
1901-1909	Theodore Roosevelt	42	40	1
1909-1913	William H. Taft	30	9	1
1913-1921	Woodrow Wilson	33	11	6
1921-1923	Warren G. Harding	5	1	0
1923-1929	Calvin Coolidge	20	30	4
1929-1933	Herbert Hoover	21	16	3
1933-1945	Franklin D. Roosevelt	372	263	9
1945-1953	Harry S Truman	180	70	12
1953-1961	Dwight D. Eisenhower	73	108	2
1961-1963	John F. Kennedy	12	9	0
1963-1969	Lyndon B. Johnson	16	14	0
1969-1974	Richard M. Nixon	26	17	7
1974-1977	Gerald R. Ford	48	18	12
1977-1981	Jimmy Carter	13	18	2
1981-1985	Ronald Reagan	18	21	4

Sources: Calculated by the authors from *Presidential Vetoes* (1978, 1985).

Table 2.19 Annual Number of Presidential Vetoes by Issue Area, 1946-1984

	Private	Foreign trade	Foreign aid	Defense	Social welfare	Government	Resources	Agriculture
Truman, I								
1946	36	0	0	3	2	4	4	0
1947	16	0	0	2	2	8	3	1
1948	29	0	0	1	3	5	5	0
Truman, II								
1949	22	0	0	2	1	2	5	0
1950	34	1	0	4	1	3	2	1
1951	10	0	0	4	0	1	0	0
1952	1	2	0	1	0	2	2	0
Eisenhower, I								
1953	8	0	0	0	0	1	1	0
1954	25	2	0	2	2	8	3	0
1955	4	0	0	1	0	4	2	0
1956	9	0	0	1	1	3	8	1
Eisenhower, II								
1957	8	0	0	1	0	2	1	0
1958	27	0	0	3	1	5	2	1
1959	9	0	0	0	3	2	4	2
1960	11	1	0	0	2	8	2	0
Kennedy								
1961	3	0	0	0	1	3	1	0
1962	8	1	0	0	0	2	1	0
1963	2	1	0	0	0	0	0	0

(Table continues)

Table 2.19 (continued)

	Private	Foreign trade	Foreign aid	Defense	Social welfare	Government	Resources	Agriculture
Johnson, I								
1964	6	0	0	0	0	0	0	0
Johnson, II								
1965	4	0	0	1	1	0	1	0
1966	2	0	0	0	1	2	2	0
1967	1	1	0	0	1	0	0	0
1968	2	1	0	0	0	0	1	1
Nixon, I								
1969	0	0	0	0	0	0	0	0
1970	2	0	0	0	2	5	0	0
1971	0	0	0	0	2	2	1	0
1972	1	0	0	2	7	2	5	0
Nixon, II								
1973	0	0	0	2	2	4	2	2
1974	3	1	0	0	2	7	4	2
Ford								
1974	0	1	0	0	1	3	3	2
1975	0	2	0	1	3	4	4	2
1976	2	2	0	2	4	7	4	2
Carter								
1977	0	0	0	0	0	0	1	1
1978	1	2	0	3	0	7	4	0
1979	0	0	0	0	0	0	0	0
1980	2	0	0	1	1	4	4	0

Reagan	Private	Foreign trade	Defense	Government	Social welfare	Energy	Farm
1981	0	0	0	0	2	0	0
1982	1	0	0	0	7	3	0
1983	0	1	2	2	2	2	2
1984	4	0	2	2	6	5	0

Note: For this table and the others reporting presidential vetoes, the following definitions apply: Private = private bills (all other categories include only public bills). Foreign trade = foreign trade, diplomacy, or immigration. Defense = military, defense, veterans issues. Social welfare = social welfare, civil rights, Indian affairs, and education. Government = government and economic management, income tax issues. Energy = energy, natural resources, environment, and transportation. Farm = agriculture and farm policy.

Sources: Calculated by the authors from *Presidential Vetoes* (1978, 1985).

Table 2.20 Congressional Challenges to Presidential Vetoes, 1946-1984

	Vetoes			Veto challenges		Percentage to override [d]	
	Total [a]	Pocket [b]	No challenge [c]	Sustained	Successful	House	Senate
Truman, I							
1946	49	16	30	3	0	60.38	—
1947	32	19	10	2	1	73.25	67.20
1948	43	14	23	1	5	78.64	80.04
Truman, II							
1949	32	2	29	0	1	86.65	88.24
1950	46	6	35	3	2	88.53	70.44
1951	15	5	7	1	2	83.71	86.71
1952	8	4	3	0	1	71.28	68.67
Eisenhower, I							
1953	10	6	4	0	0	—	—
1954	42	25	17	0	0	—	—
1955	11	8	2	1	0	—	58.06
1956	23	14	8	1	0	48.91	—
Eisenhower, II							
1957	12	9	3	0	0	—	—
1958	39	24	14	1	0	52.88	77.53
1959	20	10	5	4	1	67.31	66.05
1960	24	12	9	2	1	72.44	65.38
Kennedy							
1961	8	2	6	0	0	—	—
1962	12	7	5	0	0	—	—
1963	3	2	1	0	0	—	—

Johnson, I							
1964	6	2	4	0	0	—	—
Johnson, II							
1965	7	0	7	0	0	—	—
1966	7	4	3	0	0	—	—
1967	3	1	2	0	0	—	—
1968	5	5	0	0	0	—	—
Nixon, I							
1969	0	0	0	0	0	—	—
1970	9	3	0	4	2	62.51	71.35
1971	5	2	1	2	0	—	60.00
1972	17	13	1	1	2	78.27	88.28
Nixon, II							
1973	10	1	0	8	1	60.70	69.48
1974	19	2	8	5	4	80.19	84.27
Ford							
1974	10	9	1	0	0	—	—
1975	16	0	5	7	4	73.72	68.53
1976	23	7	6	6	4	73.42	65.57
Carter							
1977	2	0	2	0	0	—	—
1978	17	13	2	2	0	51.11	—
1979	0	0	0	0	0	—	—
1980	12	5	5	0	2	94.97	93.87
Reagan							
1981	2	1	1	0	0	—	—
1982	11	3	3	3	2	68.92	72.92
1983	9	3	5	0	1	70.38	100.00
1984	17	14	2	0	1	79.23	87.76

(Notes follow)

Table 2.20 (continued)

[a] Total number of vetoes of all types: public, private, pocket, and regular.

[b] There is no possibility of a congressional challenge for pocket vetoes. Once in 1970, and again in 1973, Sen. Edward M. Kennedy (D-Mass.), successfully challenged the president's right to pocket veto a bill during the usual short congressional recess. An additional pocket veto was challenged in 1983, but this case is still awaiting a verdict from the Supreme Court (see *Barnes v. Carmen*, 106 S.Ct. 1258). In this table, all three bills are counted as having been pocket vetoed and not challenged by Congress.

[c] Number of bills not challenged among those that might have been challenged.

[d] Average percentage of the members of the House and Senate who vote to override on veto challenge motions; dashes indicate no challenges.

Sources: Calculated by the authors from *Presidential Vetoes* (1978, 1985).

Table 2.21 Unsuccessful Attempts to Override Presidential Vetoes, 1945–1984

Date[a]	Bill	House vote Percentage to override	House vote Total	Senate vote Percentage to override	Senate vote Total	Description
Truman, I						
1946: June 11	H.R.4908	65.38	390	—	—	Appoints board to investigate labor disputes[b]
1946: June 29	H.R.6042	54.92	315	—	—	Amends Emergency Price Control Act and Stabilization Act of 1942
1946: August 1	H.J.225	59.40	234	—	—	Quiets titles of states to lands beneath tidewaters and navigable waters within their boundaries[b]
1947: June 16	H.R.1	66.17	405	—	—	Reduces individual income tax payments
1947: July 18	H.R.3950	73.46	407	61.29	93	Reduces individual income tax payments
1948: May 15	S.1004	—	—	61.84	76	Amends the Atomic Energy Act of 1946, requiring FBI investigation before appointment
Truman, II						
1950: June 30	H.R.87	74.74	285	62.34	77	Promotes veterans of World War II in field service of the Post Office Department
1950: August 21	S.3906	—	—	43.48	69	Amends the War Contractors Relief Act[b]
1950: September 9	H.J.238	95.64	321	—	—	Amends the Nationality Act of 1940; all immigrants with legal right to permanent residence may become naturalized citizens of the United States

(Table continues)

Table 2.21 (continued)

Date[a]	Bill	House vote — Percentage to override	House vote — Total	Senate vote — Percentage to override	Senate vote — Total	Description
1951: May 15	H.R.3096	82.11	380	—	—	Allows acquisition and disposition of land and interest in land by the Army, Navy, Air Force, and Federal Civil Defense Administration
Eisenhower, I						
1955: May 19	S.1	—	—	58.06	93	Increases the rates of compensation of officers and employees in the field service of the Post Office Department
1956: April 16	H.R.12	48.91	413	—	—	Amends the Agricultural Act of 1949 for price supports for basic commodities and milk[b]
Eisenhower, II						
1958: August 4	S.2266	52.88	382	77.53	89	Regulates wage rates for employees of Portsmouth, N.H., Naval Shipyard
1959: April 27	S.144	65.73	426	68.82	93	Amends Reorganization Plan, the Rural Electrification Administration
1959: July 7	S.57	—	—	57.89	95	Extends and amends Housing Act of 1959; provides and improves housing; and provides for the renewal of urban communities[b]
1959: August 26	H.R.7509	66.50	412	—	—	Appropriates funds for civil functions administered by the Army, Interior, and the Tennessee Valley Authority

Date	Bill					Description
1959: September 3	S.2539	—	—	61.70	94	Extends and amends laws for providing and improving housing and for the renewal of urban communities[b]
1960: February 22	H.R.3610	61.33	406	—	—	Amends the Federal Water Pollution Act to increase funds for sewage treatment works and establishes the Office of Water Pollution Control[b]
1960: May 13	S.722	—	—	53.57	84	Establishes Area Redevelopment Program to alleviate unemployment and underemployment in certain economically depressed areas
Kennedy[c]						
Johnson, I[c]						
Johnson, II[c]						
Nixon, I						
1970: January 26	H.R.13111	54.20	417	—	—	Appropriates funds for Department of Labor and HEW and related agencies[b]
1970: August 11	H.R.17548	51.01	398	—	—	Appropriates funds for sundry parts of the Department of Housing and Urban Development
1970: October 12	S.3637	—	—	63.04	92	Revises the Communications Act of 1934 on political broadcasting
1970: December 16	S.3867	—	—	57.83	83	Assures opportunities for employment and training to unemployed and underdeveloped persons through state and local assistance
1971: June 29	S.575	—	—	61.29	93	Appropriates funds for Appalachian Development Act of 1965, as amended

(Table continues)

Table 2.21 (continued)

Date[a]	Bill	House vote		Senate vote		Description
		Percentage to override	Total	Percentage to override	Total	
1971: December 9	S.2007	—	—	58.62	87	Continues programs authorized under the Economic Opportunity Act of 1964
1972: August 16	H.R.15417	54.28	374	—	—	Appropriates funds for Departments of Labor, HEW and related agencies
Nixon, II						
1973: March 27	S.7	—	—	62.50	96	Amends Vocational Rehabilitation Act to extend and revise the authorization funds to states for vocational rehabilitation services
1973: April 5	H.R.3298	54.35	414	—	—	Restores the rural water and sewer grant program under the Consolidated Farm and Rural Development Act
1973: May 18	S.518	57.00	414	73.81	84	Abolishes offices of director and deputy director of OMB, establishes the Office of Director, Office of Management and Budget, and transfers certain functions thereto
1973: June 27	H.R.7447	58.21	414	—	—	Appropriates supplemental funds for the fiscal year[b]
1973: August 1	S.504	65.47	417	82.80	93	Amends Public Health Service Act to provide assistance and encouragement for the development of comprehensive emergency medical service system

Date	Bill					Description
1973: September 6	H.R.7935	61.23	423	—	—	Amends Fair Labor Standards Act of 1938 to increase the minimum wage rates [b]
1973: September 22	S.1672	—	—	62.11	95	Amends Small Business Act
1973: October 23	S.1317	—	—	56.25	96	Authorizes funds for the U.S. Information Agency
1974: March 6	S.2589	—	—	59.18	98	Authorizes the president and state and local governments to develop contingency plans for reducing oil consumption and assuring the continuation of public services in the event of emergency fuel shortages
Ford						
1974: October 14	H.J.1131	62.29	358	—	—	Appropriates additional funds for the fiscal year 1975
1974: October 17	H.J.1163	65.98	244	—	—	Appropriates additional funds for the fiscal year 1975
1974: October 29	H.R.6624	59.15	399	—	—	Provides relief for Alvin W. Burt, Jr., Eileen Wallace Kennedy Pope, and David Douglas Kennedy, a minor
1974: November 26	H.R.6191	62.41	399	—	—	Amends Tariff Schedules of the United States to provide that certain forms of zinc be admitted free of duty
1975: May 1	H.R.4296	57.38	427	—	—	Adjusts target prices and loan and purchase levels on 1975 crops of cotton, corn, wheat, and soybeans, and for milk price supports at 85 percent of parity
1975: May 20	H.R.25	66.03	421	—	—	Provides for the cooperation between the Secretary of the Interior and states for regulation and reclamation of surface coal mining operations

(Table continues)

Table 2.21 (continued)

Date[a]	Bill	House vote Percentage to override	House vote Total	Senate vote Percentage to override	Senate vote Total	Description
1975: May 28	H.R.4481	65.64	422	—	—	Passes Emergency Employment Appropriations Act
1975: June 24	H.R.4485	63.06	425	—	—	Provides for greater home ownership opportunities for middle income families and to encourage more efficient use of land and energy resources
1975: September 9	S.1849	—	—	61	100	Extends the Emergency Petroleum Allocation Act
1975: December 17	H.R.5559	62.80	422	—	—	Amends Internal Revenue Code for exclusion of income from the temporary rental of railroad rolling stock by foreign corporations
1975: December 31	S.2350	—	—	18.18	88	Amends the National Security Act of 1947, to include the Secretary of the Treasury as National Security Council member
1976: January 30	S.J.121	—	—	42.05	88	Provides for quarterly adjustments in milk price supports
1976: February 13	H.R.5247	76.50	417	64.29	98	Authorizes a local public works capital development and investment program
1976: April 6	H.R.9803	74.88	402	63.83	94	Postpones for six months the requirement that a day care center meet the standards to qualify for federal payment for services under the Social Security Act

1976: April 12	H.R.8617	60.30	403	—	—	Restores to the federal civilian and postal service employees their rights to participate voluntarily, as private citizens, in the political process of the nation[b]
1976: July 2	H.R.12384	67.33	401	54.84	93	Authorizes certain construction at military installations
1976: September 24	H.R.13655	74.18	395	53.95	76	Establishes a five-year research and development program leading to advanced automobile propulsion systems
Carter						
1978: August 17	H.R.10929	48.11	397	—	—	Provides procurement for Department of Defense Appropriation Authorization Act 1979
1978: October 5	H.R.12928	54.00	413	—	—	Passes Energy and Water Development Appropriation Act
Reagan						
1982: March 20	S.1503	—	—	61.70	94	Implements Standby Petroleum Allocation Act
1982: June 24	H.R.5922	62.62	404	—	—	Provides urgent supplemental appropriations and rescinds certain budget authority
1982: June 25	H.R.6682	58.88	411	—	—	Provides urgent supplemental appropriations

Note: This table includes every instance in which there was at least one unsuccessful attempt by one congressional chamber to override a presidential veto. Dashes indicate no vote to override in that chamber.

[a] Date of veto.
[b] And for other purposes.
[c] No vetoes during this presidency.

Source: Calculated by the authors from *Presidential Vetoes* (1978, 1985).

Table 2.22 Congressional Overrides of Presidential Vetoes, 1945-1984

Date [a]	Bill	House vote		Senate vote		Description
		Percentage to override	Total	Percentage to override	Total	
Truman, I						
1947: June 20	H.R.3020	79.95	414	73.12	93	Passes Taft-Hartley Act, 1947
1948: April 1	H.R.4790	77.94	399	88.51	87	Reduces individual income-tax payments
1948: April 5	H.R.5052	91.67	336	91.67	84	Excludes newspaper vendors from provisions of social security and IRS code
1948: June 10	S.110	74.44	399	71.59	88	Amends Interstate Commerce Act
1948: June 14	H.R.6355	71.46	403	80.90	89	Provides supplemental appropriations for Federal Security Agency [b]
1948: June 14	H.J.296	79.89	373	84.42	77	Provides for employment taxes and social security pending congressional action
Truman, II						
1949: April 21	H.R.1036	86.65	367	88.24	51	Provides for the relief of R. C. Owen, Jr., and Ray Owen
1950: September 6	H.R.6217	96.40	333	95.08	61	Provides for veterans of Spanish-American War, Boxer Rebellion, and Philippine Insurrection
1950: September 22	H.R.9490	85.63	334	85.07	67	Requires registration of Communist organizations in Internal Security Act [b]
1951: August 6	H.R.3193	87.60	363	88.46	78	Establishes a rate of pension under part III of Veteran's Regulation No. I (a)
1951: October 18	S.1864	80.80	276	84.62	65	Authorizes purchase of automobiles by disabled WWII veterans
1952: June 25	H.R.5678	71.28	390	68.67	83	Revises the laws relating to immigration, naturalization, and nationality

President / Year: Date	Bill	%	Vote	%	Vote	Description
Eisenhower, I[c]						
Eisenhower, II						
1959: September 9	H.R.9105	69.83	401	75.79	95	Appropriates funds for civil functions for the Army, Interior, and the Tennessee Valley Authority
1960: June 30	H.R.9883	83.33	414	75.51	98	Adjusts compensation of employees of federal government[b]
Kennedy[c]						
Johnson, I[c]						
Johnson, II[c]						
Nixon, I[d]						
1970: June 22	H.R.11102	74.01	377	80.00	95	Amends Public Health Service Act for modernization of medical facilities
1970: August 11	H.R.16916	71.71	403	82.80	93	Appropriates funds for the Office of Education
1972: October 4	H.R.15927	92.41	382	93.83	81	Amends Railroad Retirement Act of 1937 to provide a temporary increase in pay[b]
1972: October 17	S.2770	91.48	270	81.25	64	Amends the Federal Water Pollution Control Act
Nixon, II[d]						
1973: October 24	H.J.542	67.78	419	80.65	93	Concerns the war powers of Congress
Ford						
1974: October 12	H.R.15301	96.77	372	98.63	73	Amends the Railroad Retirement Act of 1937
1974: October 17	H.R.12471	92.29	402	70.65	92	Amends the Freedom of Information Act
1974: October 29	H.R.14225	98.27	405	98.90	91	Extends the Rehabilitation Act of 1973 for one additional year

(Table continues)

Table 2.22 (continued)

Date[a]	Bill	House vote		Senate vote		Description
		Percentage to override	Total	Percentage to override	Total	
1974: November 26	H.R.12628	97.52	404	98.90	91	Increases funds for vocational rehabilitation and education allowances for veterans[b]
1975: July 25	H.R.5901	90.24	420	88.00	100	Appropriates funds for Education Divisions and related agencies
1975: July 26	S.66	89.93	427	81.71	82	Amends Public Health Service Act to revise and extend funds for nurse training and health services
1975: October 3	H.R.4222	95.66	415	85.87	92	Amends National School Lunch and Child Nutrition acts
1975: December 19	H.R.8069	73.29	423	74.47	94	Appropriates funds for Departments of Labor, HEW, and related agencies
1976: July 3	S.391	78.80	401	81.52	92	Amends the Mineral Leasing Act of 1920[b]
1976: July 6	S.3201	76.35	406	75.26	97	Amends Public Works and Economic Development Act of 1965, to help fight recession.
1976: September 13	H.R.8800	75.25	408	72.60	73	Appropriates funds for Energy Research and Development Administration for electric vehicles
1976: September 29	H.R.14232	77.04	405	81.71	82	Appropriates funds for the Department of Labor and HEW

Carter						
1980: June 5	H.R.7428	90.79	369	87.18	78	Extends public debt limit through June 30, 1980
1980: August 22	H.R.7102	98.77	406	100.00	85	Provides for recruitment and retention of personnel in Department of Medicine and Surgery in Veterans Administration
Reagan						
1982: July 8	H.R.6198	82.65	392	90.32	93	Amends the manufacturing clause of the Copyright Law
1982: August 28	H.R.6863	72.01	418	66.67	90	Appropriates supplemental funds for the fiscal year
1983: October 19	H.R.1062	70.38	422	100.00	95	Authorizes secretary of interior to convey certain lands in Lane County, Oregon
1984: February 21	S.684	79.23	390	87.76	98	Authorizes an ongoing program of water resources research

Note: HEW = Health, Education, and Welfare.

[a] Date of veto.

[b] And for other purposes.

[c] No vetoes during this presidency.

[d] Once in 1970 and again in 1973, Sen. Edward M. Kennedy (D-Mass.) successfully challenged President Nixon's right to pocket veto a bill during the usual short congressional recess. An additional pocket veto was challenged in 1983, but this case is still awaiting a verdict from the Supreme Court (see *Barnes v. Carmen*, 106 S.Ct. 1258). Although these bills were technically overridden, no action was taken by either house of Congress. Therefore, in this table none of the three bills is listed as having been overridden.

Source: Calculated by the authors from *Presidential Vetoes* (1978, 1985).

3

"Independent" Executive Actions

On September 24, 1957, Dwight Eisenhower issued Executive Order No. 10730, directing the secretary of defense to order the Arkansas National Guard into the service of the United States. The Guard was to protect nine black teenagers who were attempting to attend Central High School in Little Rock but were being resisted by mobs of angry whites and the recalcitrant governor of the state, Orval Faubus. President Eisenhower acted to enforce a school desegregation order handed down by the U.S. District Court in Arkansas and, in so doing, carried out the requirements of U.S. law. In a far different case, Lyndon Johnson, under authority of the Tariff Act of 1930, enacted Executive Order No. 11377 on October 23, 1967, authorizing the U.S. Tariff Commission to monitor the annual consumption of whisk brooms in America, noting the types, numbers, and uses made of these brooms. Pursuing the Agricultural Trade Development and Assistance Act (7 U.S.C. 1701), which authorizes the president "to negotiate and carry out agreements with friendly countries to provide for the sale of agricultural commodities," the Carter administration on August 28, 1979, entered into an executive agreement with Morocco. Under the agreement, the United States sold wheat and wheat flour to Morocco while the Moroccan government developed self-help measures to improve its agricultural production.

In these three instances, each president acted literally as chief executive, faithfully carrying out the law of the land. So that they may do so, Congress has granted presidents considerable discretion (and hence considerable autonomy) in the issuing of orders, agreements, and other pronouncements. Although the chief executive acts under authority granted him in the Constitution and in congressional statutes, he is not bound by any specific instructions of Congress.

Eisenhower, Johnson, and Carter acted unilaterally, without immediate congressional approval and without any coordinate decisions by Congress. These executive orders, executive agreements, and other presidential efforts technically constitute execution of the law of the land, but in many instances they more genuinely amount to creation of it. The president acts as a substitute legislative policy maker, identifying a problem, establishing a procedure or program to solve it, and allocating resources and personnel to put the program into operation. The chief executive thus moves well beyond the actions designated by the framers to carry out the intent of the legislature.

At first glance these forms of policy making appear to give presidents—as independent political actors—greater latitude and flexibility than efforts that involve the checks and balances of the legislature. Such greater freedom seemingly extends not only to the negotiation of treaties and executive agreements and the issuance of executive orders but also to the transfer, commitment, and rescission of allocated monies. If Hamilton's qualities of decision, energy, and dispatch are to be found anywhere in the chief executive, they should be associated with those activities in which presidents are most nearly independent of Congress.

As we shall see in this chapter, such "independent" executive decisions, like the legislative efforts of the executive, reflect a plural institution. Presidents, forced by the numbers and varying types of decisions that span national and international policy spheres to depend upon the ongoing executive apparatus, are in many instances only vaguely aware of the details of many decisions ultimately made. Johnson signed, but undoubtedly did not ponder, the whisk broom order. Negotiations in the Moroccan case were handled by the interim U.S. chargé d'affaires, a State Department official; in this instance and in many others, the president did not even sign the executive agreement.[1]

The executive organization (which we will thoroughly examine in Chapter 4) often works in conjunction with departments of the federal bureaucracy, so that the decisions are even less independent and more routine. Furthermore, presidents are not entirely free of institutional relations with Congress itself. At times, Congress requires notification about the various types of executive decisions and restricts their scope.

Once again, the plural presidency undermines the image of presidents as unitary political actors. We examine the contours of the plural presidency as they appear in three sets of presidents' executive actions: (1) international agreements, (2) executive orders, and (3) discretionary funding decisions.

Treaties and Executive Agreements

Historically, the negotiation of treaties has been a purely executive matter. When the Senate rebuked George Washington for attempting personal consultation on an Indian treaty, the presidency assumed the position of chief treaty negotiator. Justice Sutherland wrote in *United States* v. *Curtiss-Wright Export* (299 U.S. 304, 1936), "he [the President] alone negotiates. Into the field of negotiation the Senate cannot intrude." Sutherland also reiterated words that John Marshall had used when he called the president "the sole organ of the nation" in foreign affairs. Judging from these views, presidents are singular political actors in matters of diplomacy, unencumbered by pressures from Congress and only slightly impeded by the advise and consent procedures set forth in the Constitution.

Presidents also enter into executive agreements. The primary distinction between treaties and executive agreements is not the substance of policies proposed but rather the process through which the proposals do or do not go. Although treaties require the consent of the Senate, by a two-thirds vote as prescribed in the Constitution, executive agreements do not. Some of the executive agreements rest on the constitutional authority of presidents as commanders in chief or on their authority in foreign relations. Others have statutory authorization. Often presidents refer to no specific authority but instead claim the ability to act in a very global fashion, "by virtue of the authority vested in me by the Constitution and the statutes and as president of the United States."

Executive agreements are often used for relatively routine matters, for example to enable nations to exchange postal services and to fix the tax status of foreign nationals in the United States and of American citizens abroad. Other sorts of executive agreements are far more important, however, and significantly shape American foreign policy. The actions effected by such executive orders have included the annexation of Texas and Hawaii, initiatives taken by the United States prior to the bombing of Pearl Harbor in World War II, the initiation and termination of U.S. involvement in the Korean War, and key escalations during the Vietnam War (Margolis 1986). The Supreme Court maintained in *United States* v. *Pink* that executive agreements have the same force in law as treaties (315 U.S. 203, 1942). Presidents' discretion and autonomy in making executive agreements seem even greater than in making treaties.

Despite apparently substantial executive autonomy, presidential independence in diplomacy is restricted. First, important treaties in modern times usually evolve through informal consultations with members of the Senate that help ensure ratification but may also require significant presidential compromises. Second, despite Sutherland's statement that "he alone negotiates," in actuality the State Department and the Executive Office of the President together negotiate many treaties and executive agreements, with presidents often entering the process near the end, if at all. Third, although scholars often regard foreign policy as one broad, homogeneous category of presidential involvement, foreign policy takes many forms, and the nations targeted by U.S. foreign policy are widely dissimilar in regional outlook and regime type. Complexity and diversity exercise a restraining influence on the presidency because they must be accommodated over long periods of time.

We trace the development of the plural presidency in foreign affairs along four dimensions: (1) the expansion of foreign policy activity, by sheer numbers and different types; (2) the relationship among different types of activities; (3) the multiplicity of policy areas within which these activities take place; and (4) the nations involved in these international negotiations.

Activity Expansion

As noted in Chapter 1, the complexity of policy making in the modern presidency has been fostered in part by the sheer volume of presidential actions and by the diversity of those actions. Presidents' efforts in foreign affairs illustrate the expansion of presidential activity and the resulting complexity. To measure foreign policy actions, we recorded and aggregated all international agreements from 1789 to the present and classified those since 1949 by policy, president, party, nation, region, and regime type. These international agreements include executive agreements, conventions, protocols, and treaties. Conventions, protocols, and treaties are different names for the same thing, and all are often classified as "treaties." For example, a convention with Mexico established the International Commission for Scientific Investigation of Tuna (July 18, 1950); a protocol provided for cooperation in the civil uses of Atomic Energy with Canada (April 23, 1980); and a treaty between the United States and the Soviet Union dealt with antiballistic missiles (May 26, 1972). Whether a document is termed a convention, a protocol, or a treaty, it must be submitted to the Senate for ratification.[2]

Tables 3.1 and 3.2 show the total number of international agreements. In Table 3.1, the column marked "treaties" includes protocols and conventions. Table 3.2 presents separate counts for protocols and conventions. These international agreement statistics, the most accurate ones available, are drawn from the State Department's series, *Treaties and Other International Agreements of the United States of America*.[3] According to the State Department's system of classification, "international agreements" include executive agreements, treaties, protocols, and conventions.

As Table 3.1 shows, both treaties and executive agreements increased dramatically at about the turn of this century. Theodore Roosevelt's "stewardship approach" is usually credited with the expansion of the executive's role in foreign policy (see, for example, Schlesinger 1973, 87-88). Roosevelt maintained that presidents should "do anything that the needs of the Nation demanded" as long as nothing in the Constitution or in the statutes prohibited it (1913, 389). This statement emphasized the singular role of presidents in both foreign and domestic affairs. The data here reveal, however, that the McKinley administration, not Roosevelt's, marked the beginning of modern presidential diplomacy.

A closer look is provided in Table 3.3, which summarizes American international agreements since the Civil War. President McKinley entered into more treaties and executive agreements than had his predecessors. These increases were timed to coincide with world events, specifically the Spanish-American War, which was concluded by executive agreement, although final settlement was made by treaty. The end of the war in 1898 gave the United States a large Asian dependency—the Philippines—which subsequently afforded the United States and American presidents more active interests in Asia, including understandings with Japan about Korea and the Open Door Policy with China. Thereafter Theodore Roosevelt continued the expansion of international agreements, not dramatically in his first term, but significantly in his second.

This discussion of the origins of contemporary presidential diplomacy shows how casual observation can mislead. The enormous attention paid to specific actions of individual incumbents in the study of the American presidency has made Theodore Roosevelt seem to have been an isolated political actor who advocated and achieved independence in presidential policy. Systematic analysis, however, suggests that the environment was the critical "political actor" in this important development. McKinley did not set about expanding the presidency; he simply confronted the exigencies of the Spanish-American War. The increasing complexity of the policy environment placed greater demands on the presidency for international agreements before Roosevelt espoused the theory. Ironically, Roosevelt's approach promoted the *image* of presidents as singular voices in international affairs. Yet the *workload* confronting presidents with the proliferation of international agreements makes it difficult for chief executives to speak with one voice while managing foreign policy decisions that impinge on many policy areas, countries, and regimes.

The second sharp rise in the level of international agreements, which accompanied U.S. involvement in World War II and the postwar emergence of the United States as a superpower, also resulted from a major environmental shock rather than from any president's isolated decisions. The war years brought a dramatic increase in executive foreign policy activity as agreements were signed on all war fronts from Africa to the Soviet Union. To be sure, the foreign policy strategies of Roosevelt and Truman were contributing factors (Schlesinger 1973). Setting the stage for American involvement in the war, Roosevelt sold American destroyers to the British by executive agreement and without congressional approval. Foreign policy activity grew still more in Truman's second term with U.S. involvement in the Korean War and the Marshall Plan (Table 3.2). The number of international agreements did not decline thereafter. Presidents since Truman have made, on average, more than nine hundred agreements over the course of their terms in office. Figure 3.1 more conveniently summarizes the changes in the numbers of treaties and executive agreements negotiated since Truman's second term. New patterns of behavior established by one president become institutionalized, and future presidents are expected to exhibit them. The substance of these numerous proposals usually stays in place rather than being dismantled by successive White House occupants. As a result, any one president can change U.S. foreign policy only marginally.

Types of Foreign Policy Activity

When the relationship between executive agreements and treaties is explored, it is commonly believed that presidents use more executive agreements than treaties to bypass the Senate's constitutionally prescribed checks and balances (Margolis 1986). According to this view, executive agreements enable presidents to enhance their autonomy in international affairs and thereby to promote their ability to act as independent policy makers. This position also implies that presidents are more likely to resort to executive agreements when the president's party does not control the Senate. (Presumably the president does not need to avoid the Senate when his party is in control.) Similarly, presidents are said to engage in more executive agreements than treaties in their first year in office because they do not yet have the information, expertise, or liaison talent to move treaties through the Senate.

Our view of the plural presidency contrasts with these hypotheses by implying that executive agreements increase in tandem with treaties. Presidents and a growing executive branch engage generally in more activities to keep up with the constant expansion of foreign policy. In their attempts to supervise foreign policy, presidents use executive agreements as convenient devices that accommodate the intricacies and details of the foreign policy environment rather than as political devices to circumvent the Senate. Control of the Senate and presidents' newness on the job would thus have little or no effect on the number of agreements and treaties negotiated.

The data in Table 3.1 and 3.2 indicate that the identity of the party in control of the Senate has little to do with the increasing reliance on executive agreements. Executive agreements *and* treaties increase with Presidents McKinley and Roosevelt, both of whom enjoyed Senate majorities of their own (Republican) party. The number of executive agreements does not consistently exceed the number of treaties until President Coolidge, who also worked with a strongly Republican Senate. In the aftermath of World War II and during the beginning of the Marshall Plan, executive agreements increased again with President Truman, whose party also controlled the Senate (except during the Eightieth Congress, 1947-1949). More precisely, the column in the two tables reporting the ratios between executive agreements and other forms of international agreements reveals no higher ratios when presidents face an opposition Senate than when they face a Senate controlled by their own party.[4] Neither the ratios nor the raw numbers demonstrate that presidents engage in more executive agreements in the first year of their terms. The institutional pattern shows greater executive branch aggrandizement of foreign policy through executive agreements rather than treaties, but this pattern results mostly from a more complex foreign policy environment and less from the specific behaviors of individual incumbents or the partisan division of the Senate.

We further analyze these issues by classifying Senate action on all international agreements submitted for ratification in the postwar period (Table 3.4). These statistics demonstrate that treaties, protocols, or conventions are rejected by the Senate only in very rare instances. In the thirty years studied, only two agreements were rejected. One protocol for the compulsory settlement of disputes incident to the Law of the Sea Convention was rejected in May 1960; the other negative vote in March 1983 pertained to two related protocols to the Convention for Unified Rules on International Air Carriage. Both rejections in 1960 and 1983 were followed by motions to reconsider. Technically, therefore, the measures are still pending before the Senate. During the twenty-seven years since the 1960 vote, however, no further action has been taken, nor has any subsequent action been taken on the 1983 measures. With these two exceptions, treaties, protocols, and conventions that are submitted for Senate consideration have typically been ratified. When treaties are in danger of rejection, presidents tend to withdraw them from consideration. The Senate may also leave an agreement pending, as it did with the two above, at the end of a session. Typically ratification is thereby delayed for a session or more. The infrequency of presidential defeat does not imply that the treaty ratification process is moribund. Although executive agreements have replaced treaties as "the official instrument of foreign policy commitment" (Johnson 1984, 12), the number of treaties, protocols, and conventions has also increased since Franklin Roosevelt (Table 3.3). In addition, treaties and other agreements often involve important and controversial topics, including the creation of NATO, strategic arms limitations, cooperation in the Middle East, and numerous trade and tariff understandings. These tend to be negotiated, at least informally, with the Senate, a fact that perhaps accounts for the very low rejection rate. Both institutions appear to be responding in very practical ways to an expanded policy environment: incumbent presidents have not consistently maneuvered around Congress as a constitutionally prescribed check on their diplomatic powers; also, the Senate has not abdicated its consent role.

Outside this broad pattern of practicality, however, two exceptions exist and reveal strategic efforts of presidents to build autonomy or the appearance of autonomy from Congress. First, secret executive agreements entered into on behalf of presidents and not published in the State Department's compilation of treaties and executive agreements are not recorded in these tables. Various secret agreements for covert paramilitary operations, for instance, have been reached with "Ukrainian guerrillas (1949-1953); Polish resistance groups (1950-1952); Albanian rebels (1949-1952); Tibetan insurgents (1953-1959); splinter groups in mainland China and North Korea (1950-1954); and factions in Guatemala (1954), Cuba (1961-1964), Laos (throughout the 1960s), and Vietnam (1955-1974)" (Johnson 1984, 76-78). Other political actions have been taken to boost pro-American groups in Greece, the Philippines, Iran, Ecuador, and Chile (Johnson 1984, 76-78). Researchers have not been able to determine how many of these secret agreements have been made in the past or how many currently exist. These decisions represent policy strategies designed to evade the Senate.

Congress has responded to these types of efforts by implementing mandatory reporting requirements and with certain applications of the legislative veto. In 1972, the Case Act was passed; it required that the State Department report all executive agreements to Congress within sixty days. Agreements that the executive wishes to keep secret under the guise of national security are to be submitted to the House and Senate committees on foreign affairs. These mandatory reporting requirements have been only partly successful. The executive branch does respond but often well after the sixty-day period (Johnson 1984, 122-123). As a frustrated Senate foreign policy staff aide commented: "The reports come up here so late, we have to rely on contacts and leaks in the executive branch to find out when really important negotiations are under way" (Johnson 1984, 123). Another tool is the legislative veto. Certain statutes, including the Atomic Energy Act of 1954, the Trade Act of 1975, and amendments to the Foreign Assistance Act of 1974, carry provisos that allow Congress to disapprove any executive agreement made under these statutes within sixty days. Attempts to apply such vetoes to all executive agreements have failed. Also, given the Supreme Court's 1983 ruling against the legislative veto in *Immigration and Naturalization Service* v. *Chadha* (103 S.Ct. 2764), the status of this type of oversight is unclear (Cooper 1985).

A second exceptional case in which presidents build autonomy from Congress involves the use of executive agreements in devising election strategies. The results given in Table 3.2 indicate that, of the seven presidents since 1949 who were in office during an election year, five had higher agreement/treaty ratios than in the previous three years. In other words, in election years, but not in other years, presidents are much more likely to enter into executive agreements rather than treaties. (This statement contrasts with the findings of Chapter 2, which indicate that presidents take fewer positions on congressional legislation prior to elections.) Nixon in 1972 and Carter in 1980 do not fit the pattern. The electoral trend noted here is a very recent phenomenon, however, and did not exist prior to Truman's second term. The election year findings would seem to make sense in light of the concept of the plural presidency. As presidents busy themselves for reelection or as they aid the election of their party's standard-bearer, they can advance the image of the presidency as a valuable policy maker by using executive agreements instead of treaties. Although the control they exercise is limited, they can appear to be making unilateral strides in foreign policy.

In sum, the level of executive agreements seems predicated more on the exigencies of U.S. involvement in foreign affairs than on presidents' attempts to circumvent the shared powers outlined in the Constitution. Although it is tempting to avoid the Senate, presidents in fact do so only in limited instances of secret negotiations and electoral image building. The concept of the plural presidency suggests that publicly recorded executive agreements are convenient tools that can accommodate the policy complexity created by both routine and important foreign matters, regardless of who controls the Senate or the White House.

The Multiplicity of Foreign Policies

The policy complexity shaping the presidency in foreign affairs not only encompasses the sheer number and types of activities but is heightened by the several types of policies that these activities target. Treaties and executive agreements may cover everything from nuclear defense systems to sewer systems. As we argued in the preceding chapter, the notion of the two presidencies is too simplistic to illuminate the legislative policy-making role of this institution. One might think, however, that, in examining international agreements, one of the two presidencies—the foreign policy presidency—would be especially relevant. The two presidencies model, however, also oversimplifies the various types of categories of international agreements. To study the variety of international agreements, we have categorized each agreement by policy type. Our classification includes matters well beyond those of trade, diplomacy, foreign aid, and defense, which are typically associated with general notions of foreign policy. The eight policy categories adopted are comparable to those used in Chapter 2 for legislative behaviors. The foreign trade and diplomacy category encompasses immigration, tariffs, customs, passports, territorial waters, and navigation rights. Defense matters include Strategic Arms Limitation Treaties (SALT), space or aeronautics programs for military purposes, and mutual defense assistance. Social welfare/civil rights agreements include education, health, medical care, housing, crime, the status of prisoners, and technical cooperation among nations. The government and economic management category encompasses such matters as banking, postal services, labor, and business issues. The resource category includes matters of energy, the environment, transportation, communication, weather and navigation stations, land transfers, and space and aeronautics programs unrelated to defense. Agriculture encompasses farming, food, and fishing. International agreements classified by policy area are presented in Table 3.5.

As Table 3.5 shows, the trade/diplomacy category of agreements is relatively important and the number of such agreements increases beginning with Kennedy. Defense agreements are less frequent overall after reaching a peak during the first Eisenhower term (because of Korean War agreements). Foreign aid agreements have remained relatively small in numbers and relatively stable over time, except for an increase under Kennedy that most likely reflected his commitment to Central America during the Alliance for Progress program. Together, these three "foreign policy" categories of international agreements account for an average of only 36 percent of the total number of international agreements made by presidents since 1949.

Most international agreements pertain to the domestic problems of the nations involved. Agreements in the area of agriculture and natural resources have increased significantly since President Truman. All presidents, notably since Eisenhower's second term, establish ongoing commitments to provide for U.S. support for road building, telephone lines, farm programs, commodity sales, and the construction of utility plants in the recipient country. Increases in social welfare and civil rights international agreements—such as those dealing with health care, education, housing, and job programs—began with President Ford. With more basic commitments to energy, communications, and agriculture established and maintained, policies in these other areas could and did begin to emerge. In addition, commitments on issues of economic management, including banking and taxing of U.S. citizens and corporations abroad, were negotiated in modest numbers.

As might be expected, individual presidents vary in these policy emphases, but not dramatically. Through the Marshall Plan, the Truman administration expressed considerable interest in social welfare and civil rights agreements (accounting for 27.7 percent of the total number of agreements made during Truman's second term). In contrast, Eisenhower focused on defense during and after Korea (30.2 percent of his first-term total and 24.1 percent of agreements in his second term). Under the Foreign Assistance Act of 1961, the Kennedy administration signed more foreign aid agreements than were signed under any other president. Differences found here are due in part to individual interests of the presidents but also to prominent environmental factors in the international sphere. Truman and Eisenhower, especially, were responding to war and its aftermath. Some of these variations are also systematically related to the president's party (as shown at the bottom of Table 3.5). Republican presidents are more likely than Democratic presidents to sponsor military agreements: 20.1 percent of all Republican agreements involve defense matters, compared with only 13.8 percent of agreements made during Democratic administrations. Democrats conclude more agreements in the social welfare and civil rights areas. The key result here is that attention given to many issue areas follows fairly stable patterns regardless of the occupant of the White House or his political party affiliations.

Nations as Political Actors

International diversity across a legion of countries intensifies the policy complexity that the presidency faces in foreign affairs. The plural presidency results in part from this interplay of international policy complexity and the diversity among nations. Table 3.6 displays the regions of the globe involved in U.S. international agreements. The agreements are most likely to involve three regions: Western Europe, Asia, and Central America. Greatest attention is paid to defense issues in Western Europe, whereas agriculture is the key topic of agreements with Asia and Central America. The institutional preoccupation with these three regions remains when the occupant of the Oval Office changes (see Table 3.7). Some variations, however, do occur over time. Although both Western Europe and Central America receive considerable attention from presidents, the number of executive agreements with both regions has declined. Of the U.S. international agreements signed during Truman's second term, 28.4 percent targeted Western Europe and 32.8 percent involved Central America. For Carter, agreements with Europe accounted for only 12.8 percent of the total agreements signed; Central American agreements composed only 11.2 percent of the total. The percentages increased somewhat under Reagan but did not return to their pre-1964 levels. These relative declines seem to reflect increases in agreements made with Asian nations. The Carter and Reagan administrations were also responsible for more frequent agreements with Middle Eastern countries. Because of the long-standing military tensions of this area, one might expect defense agreements to predominate in the Middle East. Although defense commitments are made, agricultural, social welfare/civil rights, and natural resource agreements are more numerous (Table 3.6). These agreements may direct attention away from a difficult military situation yet may show U.S. concern for the region.

Overall, U.S. commitments have been fairly stable and predictable. The attention to Western Europe, Asia, and Central America shifts among the three, but these changes do not reflect new commitments to other regions. The contrast between agreements in these regions and the minimal commitments undertaken with Eastern Europe, the Soviet Union, and Africa highlights these patterns even more. As the Cold War subsided after the early 1960s, the number of agreements with the Soviet Union and Eastern Europe did not substantially increase. Agreements with Eastern Europe have remained modest, and agreements with the Soviet Union increased only slightly during Nixon's efforts at détente but did not continue thereafter. The agreements negotiated with the Soviet Union do, however, involve substantive trade, agricultural, resource, and defense matters instead of symbolic overtures on cultural affairs. Agreements with Africa have increased, as the relative importance of Third World nations has grown in U.S. world outlooks, but the increase has not been steady.

Table 3.8 lists the top twenty-five nations with which the United States has signed international agreements since 1949. These agreements account for 47 percent, or nearly half, of all U.S. agreements with foreign nations. North American neighbors, Mexico and Canada, head the list, followed by Japan and Great Britain. A significant number of agreements are made with other members of the North Atlantic Treaty Organization, or NATO (West Germany, Spain, France, Italy, Turkey, and Greece), a finding consistent with the results of our regional analysis. Other leading partners in international agreements are countries from Asia (South Korea, the Philippines, Pakistan, Taiwan, Indonesia, South Vietnam) and Central America (Brazil, Colombia, Chile), which also parallels our earlier regional findings. Only two Communist nations, the Soviet Union and Yugoslavia, are among the top U.S. international partners.

Each international agreement was also classified by the regime type of the foreign partner.[5] When competitive elections create a legislature with two or more parties, the regime is *republican*, as in Austria, Great Britain, and the Netherlands. *Totalitarian* regimes, such as Bulgaria, Poland, and East Germany, lack competitive elections and have one-party legislatures in communist or socialist states. Regimes controlled by army generals or other members of the military are *military authoritarian* types. They include Chad since April 1975, Colombia between 1953 and 1957, and the Dominican Republic from 1949 to 1961. Nations ruled by hereditary monarchies or other autocratic elites have *nonmilitary authoritarian* regimes and include Jordan, Morocco, and Saudi Arabia. Finally, *colonial* regimes, like those of St. Lucia, Antigua, and the Solomon Islands, are semi-independent countries that are possessions of other states. Because we code the regime type at the time of the executive agreement, we can accurately accommodate changes in types that have occurred for any country during the 1949-1983 period. Chile, for example, was coded as a republican regime from 1949 to August 1973 and as a military regime thereafter.

We present these data in Table 3.9 for the postwar period. Not unexpectedly, democratic regimes are the predominant U.S. partners for every presidential administration. This is true for treaties, protocols, conventions, and executive agreements. The actions taken jointly between the executive and Congress, as well as the agreements entered into unilaterally by presidents, target primarily republican regimes. Agreements with totalitarian regimes increase beginning with Johnson but for all presidents represent a small portion of the total number of agreements promulgated. Nonmilitary authoritarian regimes are frequent partners. Although the number of commitments made to these regimes remained relatively stable during the period, commitments to military authoritarian regimes have grown. The reason is partly an increasing number of authoritarian regimes that have become dominated by the military during the last decade; we witness again a systematic pattern resulting more from the dynamics of the international environment than from the specific decisions made by particular incumbents.

The results by party reveal little difference between the agreements sponsored by Democratic and Republican presidents. Presidents of both parties support agreements with republican and nonmilitary authoritarian regimes. This group represents a reasonable pool of known allies and dependents of the United States. Presidential diplomacy does little to build up regions that are less friendly (Eastern Europe or totalitarian regimes) or are less well known (Africa). Furthermore, presidents do not seem to be bothered by the possible dictatorial, restrictive qualities of authoritarian regimes.

Presidents, as singular political figures, have only limited control of international agreements. For most of these agreements, incumbent strategies and actions appear less important than institutionalized commitments to various regimes across specific policy areas. Within the range of policy areas, presidential foreign policy is increasingly decentralized. Decisions made by the White House originate in various parts of the executive branch that specialize in these policy fields. In addition, the bureaucracies of the White House, the State Department, and other agencies monitor the countries involved. The more decentralized, varied, complex, and expansive foreign policy becomes, the less individual presidents can control. Thus foreign policy decisions for the most part reflect the connection of the presidency with the rest of the executive branch. The resulting mix of policy complexity and international diversity hampers presidents' efforts at independent action and clouds the popular image of the president as the sole organ of foreign relations.

Executive Orders

Perhaps presidents are afforded greater autonomy in their use of executive orders. Like executive agreements, executive orders do not require presidents to secure the approval of Congress to invoke them in making numerous types of policy decisions. Also like executive agreements, the orders may be issued by claiming authority from powers granted presidents in the Constitution or in acts of Congress. In issuing executive orders, however, unlike executive agreements, presidents are not as often confounded by the politics of foreign nations, ongoing commitments of the State Department, or congressional requirements. The image of presidents as autonomous policy actors appears to be more meaningful where executive orders are concerned. Yet as we demonstrate below, this image is no more relevant to executive orders than to international agreements. Presidents' use of executive orders is also very much influenced by the expansion of policy activities, the multiplicity of policy areas, the diversity of groups, and the organizational difficulties faced within the plural presidency.

We recorded each executive order since 1789 and classified those issued since 1949 by policy area, president, and the group to which the order was addressed.[6] The policy areas are comparable to those used for congressional roll call votes, executive agreements, and treaties.

Table 3.10 shows the total number of known executive orders since George Washington. Washington issued the first executive order on June 8, 1789, asking the heads of the original departments—State, War, Treasury, and the Attorney General—to make "a clear account" of affairs connected with their Departments (Lord 1979, 1). As might be expected, early executive orders were infrequent; they began to see significant use only after the Civil War. During the nineteenth century, executive orders had two primary administrative purposes. The earliest was for external administration: the disposition of public lands, especially the withdrawal of land for Indian, military, naval, and lighthouse reservations. In the 1870s executive orders were used for internal administration. Numerous orders were issued concerning Civil Service rules, the status of government employees and their work hours, salaries, pension requirements, and federal holidays. These two administrative forms are no longer the only types of executive orders, but they have remained a significant portion of the total number.

A relatively large increase in the number of executive orders occurred in Theodore Roosevelt's first term and an even greater increase in his second term. One might suspect this expansion of executive orders of reflecting Roosevelt's notion of presidential stewardship—presidents doing all they can in the best interest of the nation. Although Roosevelt was more active than his predecessors, his executive orders fit the nineteenth-century administrative mode. They did not advance major policy initiatives. As the federal government grew after the turn of the century, Roosevelt ordered greater numbers of internal regulations. In addition, his executive orders continued to deal with the management of public lands and energy sources. These orders complemented Roosevelt's interest in national parks and natural resources but only coincidentally. The orders themselves did not systematically establish national land policy; rather, they set aside and transferred land in the manner established by Roosevelt's predecessors. Yet the increase in executive orders during Roosevelt's administration did not represent an isolated flurry of presidential activity. Instead, presidents who succeeded Roosevelt—including those who advocated stewardship, such as Wilson, and those who did not, such as Taft, Harding, Coolidge, and Hoover—issued executive orders at roughly the same levels as Roosevelt had. These orders also continued to address internal and external administrative matters. The new level of executive activity begun under Roosevelt became institutionalized for subsequent chief executives and reflected a firmly expanded federal government.

Only with Franklin Roosevelt did the use of executive orders extend beyond administrative matters to include major presidential policy initiatives. Executive orders rose sharply between 1932 and 1933 (see Table 3.10). Herbert Hoover issued numerous administrative orders, but Roosevelt introduced important policies through executive orders. He closed banks during the banking emergency of 1933, wrote rules under the authority of the National Industrial Recovery Act, and established the Civilian Conservation Corps. In addition, Roosevelt issued orders for defense and national security. By executive order, Roosevelt established the Office of Price Administration and the Office of Economic Stabilization and provided for the internment of American citizens of Japanese ancestry living in the Pacific coastal states. The Japanese order, along with Truman's order to seize the steel industry, was later declared unconstitutional by the Supreme Court. However, the Court has usually upheld presidential executive orders as having the same force in law as statutes.

Substantive policy making through executive orders has also focused on civil liberties since Franklin Roosevelt's time. Roosevelt established the Fair Employment Practices Commission in 1943 to prevent discrimination in hiring by government agencies and military suppliers. Harry Truman ended segregation in the armed forces. Dwight Eisenhower, as noted at the beginning of the chapter, and John F. Kennedy issued executive orders to enforce desegregation of schools in Arkansas, Mississippi, and Alabama, planned by previous court decisions. Lyndon Johnson created equal employment opportunity in federal hiring and also in hiring by government contractors through an executive order in 1965. Indeed, the whole concept of affirmative action in federal employment stems from Johnson's order, not from provisions of the Civil Rights Act of 1964. The Reagan administration, which opposes affirmative action, proposed the issuance of an executive order that would amount to a "repeal" of Johnson's equal opportunity order but has not so far pursued this proposal (for general discussions of executive orders, see Watson and Thomas 1983; also see Fisher 1978).

Franklin Roosevelt's contribution to presidential power in this area was substantial, but this was not an isolated incident. His actions institutionalized presidents' assumption that they could use executive orders as policy-making devices rather than merely as administrative devices. Presidents after Roosevelt followed his lead. Indeed, future presidents had little choice. In Table 3.11, executive orders are categorized by policy area in order to observe some of these policy developments in more detail. Apart from executive orders on federal government personnel and interagency and congressional requests, presidents use these orders in five principal policy areas: defense, foreign trade, economic management, natural resources, and social welfare/civil rights. Relatively few executive orders are issued in the areas of agriculture, federalism, and foreign aid. The limited number of executive orders in agriculture is consistent with the meager attention paid agriculture in presidents' legislative stands (see Chapter 2). Agricultural executive orders and legislation deal principally with farming problems, which, as noted in the last chapter, do not provide presidents with abundant advantages for building broad constituency support. When international agreements are used, agriculture is much more prominent because it represents an easy, economical, and broad-based way to aid nations and also to facilitate the distribution of American farm surpluses.

Table 3.12 further analyzes the policy emphases of executive orders by individual presidents and by party. Social welfare and civil rights issues are especially prominent under Carter. Eisenhower issued fewer executive orders on social welfare/civil rights matters than any other president. The economy receives the most attention from Nixon, Truman, and Reagan. Executive orders in defense and natural resources have declined since Truman, whereas those on foreign trade increased markedly under Carter and Reagan. Democratic presidents are generally more likely to issue executive orders in the areas of resources and social welfare/civil rights than are Republican presidents. Although variations in policy emphasis on the part of incumbents are evident, the policy complexity within which these variations occur is even more plain. The presidency is not free to ignore any policy area and must ultimately juggle the interrelationships and inconsistencies across the several types of issues.

Table 3.13 examines the diverse groups affected by executive orders. Farmers, the poor, the handicapped, women, veterans, and the aged received surprisingly little attention from presidents since Truman— less than might have been thought, given presidents' verbal statements of concern for such groups. Table 3.14 summarizes the attention accorded different groups by individual presidents and by presidents' party affiliations. The differences here mirror differences in the policy interests of the presidents. Democratic presidents are more likely to issue executive orders affecting labor, minorities, and environmentalists. Republican presidents target business, farmers, and consumers.

Executive orders thus represent the interests of incumbents as they are combined with programmatic priorities that attach to the institution of the presidency. The intricacies inherent in these orders are heightened by the complexity across policy areas and the diversity among groups. Furthermore there are problems of coordination and coherence for recent presidents who rely on the Executive Office of the President and on departments and agencies to propose and draft executive orders. The occupant of the Oval Office is not personally issuing each executive order; instead, the institution turns this abundance of work into new standard operating procedures, patterns, and expectations. The type and frequency of executive orders issued by any new president is thus predominantly a function of the plural institution of the presidency already in place. Presidents do influence the direction of executive policy making but only in incremental ways.

Presidential Discretion?

In addition to executive agreements and executive orders into which the presidency enters without approval by Congress and treaties negotiated by the presidency and typically approved by the Senate, presidents have been granted specific types of discretion by Congress in foreign and domestic spending. Presidents have also exercised their own discretion through the impoundment of funds. Presidents' personal discretion strongly tests the concept of the plural presidency. Most of the constraints we have examined thus far do not seem to pertain to presidents' discretion in the use of foreign and domestic policy tools. Here presidents should be able to enact policies relatively free from obstacles created by the executive branch or the legislature. In this instance, the image of a singular policy maker may match political reality. As the reader will not be surprised to learn, we demonstrate below that this idea is again false.

Special Funding Authority in Foreign Affairs

Congress granted presidents apparently independent discretion for the funding of various military operations and foreign assistance projects. The Foreign Assistance Act of 1961 provides that presidents may use special funding authorities without prior congressional approval when a president determines that the effort "is vital to the security of the United States" (for full details, see U.S. General Accounting Office 1985). Three types of funding authority are granted presidents in this act: *waiver* authority, *transfer* authority, and *drawdown* authority.

The most frequently used funding authority is the waiver, granted presidents to meet emergencies or respond to situations in which formal foreign assistance agreements are not possible. The waiver provides for funds "without regard to any conditions as to eligibility contained in this [Foreign Assistance] Act, when the President determines that such use is important to the security of the United States" (U.S. General Accounting Office 1985, 29). The conditions being waived are time limits, usage limits, currency requirements, and war status limitations on the funds. Waiver authority, for instance, was used to undertake military operations in Laos, Vietnam, and Cambodia, even though these efforts would have been prohibited by the Foreign Assistance Act if waivers had not been invoked. Table 3.15 reports the total number and dollar amounts of waivers. More than $1.5 billion have been spent by presidents through the waiver authority.

A second form of special funding authority is the transfer, which allows presidents, again without approval from Congress, to transfer up to 10 percent of the funds under one provision of several foreign assistance acts to another provision of any other assistance act "whenever the President determines it to be necessary" (U.S. General Accounting Office 1985, 24). As Table 3.16 shows, these transfers have amounted to at least $437.5 million between various foreign assistance accounts; about half of these transfers involved U.S. efforts in Southeast Asia.

Finally, presidents have what is known as "drawdown authority" to provide Department of Defense equipment to a foreign government without congressional or other budgetary authorization or appropriations. A president may draw down U.S. military stock or equipment once he has determined that the vital security of the United States is at stake. After the equipment has been sent, presidents are authorized to replace or reimburse the Defense Department for the stocks and services that have been drawn down. Subsequent foreign assistance appropriations provide for replacements and reimbursements. As Table 3.17 makes plain, much of this money was used to give materiel to Vietnam and Cambodia, but the drawdown procedure has also been used to fund more recent operations in El Salvador. One of the most recent uses of the drawdown authority, not reflected in the table, was the shipment of arms to Iran by the Reagan administration.

By establishing these provisions, Congress in effect encourages the public to regard presidents as singular policy actors free to exercise personal discretion as to when the special funding authorities should be invoked. Presidents' own discretion, however, meets with ongoing institutional procedures that leave less room for individual flexibility than might be imagined. Each of the three funding authorities is implemented by an administrative measure known as a *presidential determination* (PD). Prior to 1968, overall responsibility for administering PDs was held by the Agency for International Development. Since then, the State Department has assumed control of the process, which primarily involves drafting a PD package (memorandum to the president, justification for the PD, and notification letters to Congress). The State Department has been less effective in establishing procedures to maintain an ongoing inventory of presidential determinations once they have been invoked. As a result both the executive and Congress have found themselves with erroneous information on the amounts of money being spent and the justification for spending it (U.S. General Accounting Office 1985, 3). The role of the State Department in drafting the presidential determinations and in overseeing their use reveals that the discretion of individual presidents is combined with and limited by an institutional arrangement between the presidency and the executive branch of government.

Other Budgetary Discretion

In addition to the discretion that Congress gives chief executives in foreign assistance, presidents may exercise two other types of discretionary actions in domestic policy making. First, a budget line is specifically designated as "funds under direct control of presidents." Presidents have expressly spent these monies, or have designated officials or agencies to do so, on such activities as flood and disaster relief, economic assistance abroad, military assistance to friendly nations, expansion of defense production through loans and contracts, drug prevention programs, and Appalachian development. Presidents thus obtain a large sum that they may spend or choose not to spend, according to their own priorities. Recommendations are made by the White House staff, however, and through the Executive Office of the President, so that the discretion is defined within institutional constraints. Table 3.18 shows the total sums made available by Congress to presidents since Truman and the monies spent by presidents.

Second, presidents have used budget impoundments to redirect and curb existing programs they dislike. Through impoundment, which began in earnest with Franklin Roosevelt, presidents effectively refuse to spend money that has already been appropriated by Congress. Presidents from Roosevelt through Kennedy primarily used impoundment to curb military programs. Johnson and Nixon broadened the scope of this policy tool by targeting domestic appropriations. No publicly available figures exist on the total amount of funds that have been impounded.

Congress decided to place restrictions on such funding decisions in the Budget and Impoundment Control Act of 1974.[7] Presidents are now required to send special messages to Congress specifying the reasons for and the estimated effects of each proposed rescission of funds. The "rescission requests" must be approved by both houses within forty-five days (P.L. 93-844). If either house passes a resolution disapproving the rescission, the funds must be spent. Table 3.19 shows the total rescission of funds requested since 1977. As would be expected, the rescissions are much greater during the Reagan years than during the Carter years. The Reagan administration requested substantial cuts in already appropriated funds, particularly in education, housing and urban development, and interior. Readily available data on the number of rescissions that have been disallowed by Congress also do not exist. In addition, it is not yet clear how the Supreme Court's decision, which struck down the legislative veto, will affect the provisions of the act.

127

In general, the phrase "personal presidential discretion" is not especially accurate when it is used to describe the control of foreign or domestic funds. Instead, these policy tools are more aptly characterized as methods for granting greater degrees of "institutional flexibility" than exist in other areas. Yet even this flexibility is exercised within a system of interinstitutional constraints placed upon the presidency and its incumbents by the Executive Office of the President, departments and agencies in the executive branch, and the Congress.

Conclusion: Institutional Policy Making

The dominant model of policy making in American presidential politics stresses the roles of key political actors, especially presidents, as policy makers. The result is that less attention is paid to the institutions within which these actors behave. We have concentrated in the last two chapters on how the plural institution of the presidency establishes a different set of premises for policy making, on the factors important in this process, and on the roles of individual actors. For the presidency, the plural institutional approach transcends presidents' specific actions as policy makers to emphasize the intricacies of the institution and the complexities of the environment within which it acts. Although presidency watchers detail the individual idiosyncrasies of presidential officeholders, the contemporary institution is a much more complicated, but much more predictable, policy maker. It is elaborate, decentralized, and organizationally stable, with key ongoing units that have well-established practices and norms. The institution accommodates numerous policy areas that place different demands, create different incentives, and allow presidents different degrees of success. The institution encompasses numerous groups and regimes that also express distinct demands and incentives and operate with varying degrees of success.

Institutional policy making occurs at the point where the predictable institution encounters the complex and unpredictable policy environment. Only within the arena defined by the institution, policy areas, and target groups are the actions of individual presidents relevant. Single executives play out their strategies and interests within this plural institutional setting. The notion that presidents are singular policy actors who can act with dispatch and decisiveness is merely an illusion. Singularity does not exist because there are too many executive orders, executive agreements, treaties, and pieces of legislation for presidents to make all of their decisions independently. Figures 3.2—3.4 show presidents' executive orders and, from Chapter 2, their legislative positions and vetoes on domestic, foreign, and defense policy since 1957. Presidents issue some sixty executive orders per year, take positions on seventy-seven pieces of legislation annually, and veto at least eleven of the bills passed by Congress in any given year. These are just three of the activities for which the presidency is responsible. We do not include in this comparison the 234 international agreements into which the executive enters annually because presidents have even less control over these decisions. The figures provide a startling view of the many policy demands placed on the presidency and the many policy techniques available to presidents through executive and legislative avenues. The complexity of policy types, the conflicts among techniques, and the diversity among targeted groups promote a reliance on institutional rather than personal decision making and encourage the institution of the presidency to become a diffused, less than coherent body—in short, a plural body.

Notes

1. Legally, presidents are officially responsible, but they routinely give their official signatory powers to personnel of the State Department and other agencies of the federal government.
2. Historically, the names have been chosen more or less at random. Recently, slightly more specific usage has been attached to the word "convention." There is a tendency to refer to multilateral agreements on general subjects as conventions. These agreements do not outline specific policy programs or arrangements but express the mutual concerns of the nations involved. In addition the term *protocol* has recently also been more consistently attached to documents that amend conventions, but there are no hard and fast rules about the names to use, and even these most recent tendencies are often violated.
3. Table 3.2 and several other tables in this chapter take Truman's second term as a convenient beginning. Truman's first term is marked by activities tied to the end of World War II and is therefore somewhat anomalous. Data acquired from State Department publications are not yet available for 1984 and succeeding years.
4. In Table 3.1, the ratio denotes the relationship of executive agreements to treaties. In Table 3.2, the ratio denotes the number of executive agreements relative to all other forms of international agreements—treaties, protocols, and conventions.
5. The regime types for countries were specified after a thorough analysis of several sources that provide political background for the nations of the world. These include Banks (1986), *The International Yearbook and Statesmen's Who's Who* (1986), Delury (1983), Taylor and Jodice (1983), and Clements (1986).
6. Collation and numbering of executive orders did not begin until 1907. Certain orders occurring before that date were entered into the numbered

series, but most orders in the nineteenth century were unnumbered. Some unnumbered orders exist as late as 1941. In a project conducted during 1935-1936 as part of the Works Projects Administration, the unnumbered orders were collected and analyzed from historical materials. This was the first and only time any attempt was made to establish a list of unnumbered orders. Generally, a list of unnumbered orders is difficult to compile because there is often little agreement as to whether a document was an order, a proclamation, a land order, or some other executive communication. Those presented here are drawn from the 1935 project, which is the most accurate account available of the unnumbered series (see Lord 1979).

7. Efforts by the Nixon administration to impound funds appropriated under the Federal Water Pollution Control Act Amendments of 1972 provided impetus for the act. Nixon instructed the administrator of the Environmental Protection Agency to withhold from the states $9 billion, more than one-half of the total appropriations. In *Train* v. *The City of New York* (1975), the U.S. Supreme Court held that the impoundment was unconstitutional.

Table 3.1   Treaties and Executive Agreements, 1789-1948

	Senate majority party same as president's?	Agreements	Treatiesa	Ratio agreements: treatiesb
Washington, I				
1789	Yes	0	0	—
1790	Yes	0	0	—
1791	Yes	0	0	—
1792	Yes	0	0	—
Total	—	0	0	—
Washington, II				
1793	Yes	0	0	—
1794	Yes	0	1	—
1795	Yes	0	2	—
1796	Yes	0	2	—
Total	—	0	5	—
Adams				
1797	Yes	0	1	—
1798	Yes	0	1	—
1799	Yes	0	1	—
1800	Yes	0	1	—
Total	—	0	4	—
Jefferson, I				
1801	Yes	0	1	—
1802	Yes	0	1	—
1803	Yes	0	3	—
1804	Yes	0	0	—
Total	—	0	5	—
Jefferson, II				
1805	Yes	0	1	—
1806	Yes	0	0	—
1807	Yes	0	0	—
1808	Yes	0	0	—
Total	—	0	1	—
Madison, I				
1809	Yes	0	0	—
1810	Yes	0	0	—
1811	Yes	0	0	—
1812	Yes	0	0	—
Total	—	0	0	—

(Table continues)

Table 3.1 (continued)

	Senate majority party same as president's?	Agreements	Treaties[a]	Ratio agreements: treaties[b]
Madison, II				
1813	Yes	0	0	—
1814	Yes	0	0	—
1815	Yes	0	1	—
1816	Yes	0	2	—
Total	—	0	3	—
Monroe, I				
1817	Yes	1	2	0.5
1818	Yes	0	0	—
1819	Yes	0	2	—
1820	Yes	0	0	—
Total	—	1	4	0.3
Monroe, II				
1821	Yes	0	0	—
1822	Yes	0	2	—
1823	Yes	0	1	—
1824	Yes	0	2	—
Total	—	0	5	—
J. Q. Adams				
1825	Yes	1	1	1.0
1826	Yes	1	2	0.5
1827	No	0	6	—
1828	No	0	3	—
Total	—	2	12	0.2
Jackson, I				
1829	Yes	0	1	—
1830	Yes	0	2	—
1831	Yes	0	2	—
1832	Yes	0	3	—
Total	—	0	8	—
Jackson, II				
1833	Yes	0	4	—
1834	Yes	0	0	—
1835	Yes	0	2	—
1836	Yes	0	2	—
Total	—	0	8	—

Table 3.1 (continued)

	Senate majority party same as president's?	Agreements	Treaties[a]	Ratio agreements: treaties[b]
Van Buren				
1837	Yes	0	1	—
1838	Yes	0	4	—
1839	Yes	1	2	0.5
1840	Yes	1	2	0.5
Total	—	2	9	0.2
W. Harrison				
1841	Yes	0	1	—
Tyler				
1841	Yes	0	0	—
1842	Yes	0	2	—
1843	Yes	1	2	0.5
1844	Yes	0	6	—
Total	—	1	10	0.1
Polk				
1845	Yes	1	3	0.3
1846	Yes	2	4	0.5
1847	Yes	1	5	0.2
1848	Yes	1	4	0.3
Total	—	5	16	0.3
Taylor				
1849	No	3	2	1.5
1850	No	0	2	—
Total	—	3	4	0.8
Fillmore				
1850	No	1	2	0.5
1851	No	0	2	—
1852	No	3	5	0.6
Total	—	4	9	0.4
Pierce				
1853	Yes	5	5	1.0
1854	Yes	4	9	0.4
1855	Yes	3	1	3.0
1856	Yes	0	5	—
Total	—	12	20	0.6

(Table continues)

Table 3.1 (continued)

	Senate majority party same as president's?	Agreements	Treaties[a]	Ratio agreements: treaties[b]
Buchanan				
1857	Yes	3	5	0.6
1858	Yes	1	9	0.1
1859	Yes	2	0	2.0
1860	Yes	2	2	1.0
Total	—	8	16	0.5
Lincoln, I				
1861	Yes	0	8	—
1862	Yes	1	6	0.2
1863	Yes	2	5	0.4
1864	Yes	0	3	—
Total	—	3	22	0.1
Lincoln, II				
1865	Yes	0	0	—
Johnson				
1865	Yes	0	0	—
1866	Yes	0	5	—
1867	Yes	0	7	—
1868	Yes	0	14	—
Total	—	0	26	—
Grant, I				
1869	Yes	1	2	0.5
1870	Yes	1	11	0.1
1871	Yes	0	5	—
1872	Yes	0	5	—
Total	—	2	23	0.1
Grant, II				
1873	Yes	2	2	1.0
1874	Yes	5	4	1.3
1875	Yes	0	1	—
1876	Yes	2	2	1.0
Total	—	9	9	1.0

Table 3.1 (continued)

	Senate majority party same as president's?	Agreements	Treatiesa	Ratio agreements: treatiesb
Hayes				
1877	Yes	1	1	1.0
1878	Yes	1	5	0.2
1879	No	1	1	1.0
1880	No	2	7	0.3
Total	—	5	14	0.4
Garfield				
1881	Yes	1	2	0.5
Arthur				
1881	Yes	0	2	—
1882	Yes	4	10	0.4
1883	Yes	4	2	2.0
1884	Yes	3	8	0.4
Total	—	11	22	0.5
Cleveland				
1885	No	5	2	2.5
1886	No	1	7	0.1
1887	No	3	4	0.8
1888	No	2	6	0.3
Total	—	11	19	0.6
B. Harrison				
1889	Yes	1	2	0.5
1890	Yes	2	2	1.0
1891	Yes	6	5	1.2
1892	Yes	2	7	0.3
Total	—	11	16	0.7
Cleveland				
1893	Yes	0	2	—
1894	Yes	2	3	0.7
1895	No	2	2	1.0
1896	No	2	4	0.5
Total	—	6	11	0.5

(Table continues)

Table 3.1 (continued)

	Senate majority party same as president's?	Agreements	Treaties[a]	Ratio agreements: treaties[b]
McKinley, I				
1897	Yes	2	3	0.7
1898	Yes	7	4	1.8
1899	Yes	9	9	1.0
1900	Yes	7	8	0.9
Total	—	25	24	1.0
McKinley, II				
1901	Yes	2	2	1.0
T. Roosevelt, I				
1901	Yes	4	7	0.5
1902	Yes	9	11	0.8
1903	Yes	1	11	0.1
1904	Yes	7	13	0.5
Total	—	21	42	0.5
T. Roosevelt, II				
1905	Yes	10	7	1.4
1906	Yes	7	13	0.5
1907	Yes	15	10	1.5
1908	Yes	4	35	0.1
Total	—	36	65	0.6
Taft				
1909	Yes	7	4	1.8
1910	Yes	5	12	0.4
1911	Yes	2	8	0.3
1912	Yes	3	4	0.8
Total	—	17	28	0.6
Wilson, I				
1913	Yes	4	15	0.3
1914	Yes	7	23	0.3
1915	Yes	13	1	13.0
1916	Yes	7	2	3.5
Total	—	31	41	0.8

Table 3.1 (continued)

	Senate majority party same as president's?	Agreements	Treaties[a]	Ratio agreements: treaties[b]
Wilson, II				
1917	Yes	4	1	4.0
1918	Yes	9	12	0.8
1919	No	7	11	0.6
1920	No	3	3	1.0
Total	—	23	27	0.9
Harding				
1921	Yes	14	13	1.1
1922	Yes	10	8	1.3
1923	Yes	7	7	1.0
Total	—	31	28	1.1
Coolidge, I				
1923	Yes	6	13	0.5
1924	Yes	18	28	0.6
Total	—	24	41	0.6
Coolidge, II				
1925	Yes	38	13	2.9
1926	Yes	21	7	3.0
1927	Yes	14	10	1.4
1928	Yes	23	41	0.6
Total	—	96	71	1.4
Hoover				
1929	Yes	26	21	1.2
1930	Yes	19	17	1.1
1931	Yes	22	7	3.1
1932	Yes	38	8	4.8
Total	—	105	53	2.0
F. Roosevelt, I				
1933	Yes	19	7	2.7
1934	Yes	21	16	1.3
1935	Yes	21	11	1.9
1936	Yes	26	25	1.0
Total	—	87	59	1.5

(Table continues)

Table 3.1 (continued)

	Senate majority party same as president's?	Agreements	Treatiesa	Ratio agreements: treatiesb
F. Roosevelt, II				
1937	Yes	23	13	1.8
1938	Yes	38	9	4.2
1939	Yes	30	10	3.0
1940	Yes	29	13	2.2
Total	—	120	45	2.7
F..Roosevelt, III				
1941	Yes	56	4	14.0
1942	Yes	130	4	32.5
1943	Yes	98	1	98.0
1944	Yes	83	6	13.8
Total	—	367	15	24.5
F. Roosevelt, IV				
1945	Yes	35	0	35.0
Truman				
1945	Yes	85	5	17.0
1946	Yes	144	19	7.6
1947	No	174	18	9.7
1948	No	202	21	9.6
Total	—	605	63	9.6

aTreaties include protocols and conventions.
bThe ratio is expressed as the number of executive agreements issued versus the number of treaties. In 1948, for example, 9.6 agreements were issued for every one treaty.

Source: Adapted from Margolis (1986).

Table 3.2 Treaties, Executive Agreements, Protocols, and Conventions, 1949-1983

	Senate majority party same as president's?	Agreements	Treaties	Protocols, conventions	Ratio agreements: others [a]
Truman					
1949	Yes	131	1	14	8.7
1950	Yes	144	1	14	9.6
1951	Yes	206	6	21	7.6
1952	Yes	285	4	21	11.4
Total	—	766	12	70	9.3
Eisenhower, I					
1953	Yes	154	3	21	6.4
1954	Yes	178	6	16	8.1
1955	No	300	4	39	7.0
1956	No	225	2	14	14.1
Total	—	857	15	90	8.2
Eisenhower, II					
1957	No	202	5	30	5.8
1958	No	183	4	20	7.6
1959	No	215	11	14	8.6
1960	No	248	6	20	9.5
Total	—	848	26	84	7.7
Kennedy					
1961	Yes	247	4	16	12.4
1962	Yes	296	21	3	12.3
1963	Yes	220	5	19	9.2
Total	—	763	30	38	11.2
Johnson					
1964	Yes	210	2	14	13.1
1965	Yes	197	1	20	9.4
1966	Yes	216	3	23	8.3
1967	Yes	203	2	27	7.0
1968	Yes	182	1	11	15.2
Total	—	1,008	9	95	9.7

(Table continues)

139

Table 3.2 (continued)

	Senate majority party same as president's?	Agreements	Treaties	Protocols, conventions	Ratio agreements: others [a]
Nixon, I					
1969	No	151	1	17	8.4
1970	No	190	6	27	5.8
1971	No	207	1	27	7.4
1972	No	249	7	32	6.4
Total	—	797	15	103	6.8
Nixon, II					
1973	No	189	3	37	4.7
1974	No	130	2	20	5.9
Total	—	319	5	57	5.1
Ford					
1974	No	70	0	26	2.7
1975	No	255	3	36	6.5
1976	No	352	4	30	10.4
Total	—	677	7	92	6.8
Carter					
1977	Yes	340	4	26	11.3
1978	Yes	304	4	36	7.6
1979	Yes	238	5	43	5.0
1980	Yes	139	4	26	4.6
Total	—	1,021	17	131	6.9
Reagan					
1981	Yes	194	3	52	3.5
1982	Yes	214	0	41	5.2
1983	Yes	113	0	21	5.4
Total	—	521	3	114	4.5

[a] The "Others" category refers to the total number of treaties, protocols, and conventions issued in a year. The ratio is expressed as the number of executive agreements issued to the number of commitments from the "Others" category. In 1983, for example, 5.4 agreements were issued for every one of the other commitments.

Sources: 1949-1980 calculated by the authors from U.S. Department of State, *Treaties and Other International Agreements* (1950-1980); 1981-1983 calculated from *Current Treaty Index* (1984).

Table 3.3 Total and Average Number of International Agreements since the Civil War

President	International agreements [a]		Executive agreements		Treaties [b]	
	Total	Average per year	Total	Average per year	Total	Average per year
A. Johnson	26	6.5	0	0.0	26	7.0
Grant, I	25	6.3	2	0.5	23	3.3
Grant, II	18	4.5	9	2.3	9	2.3
Hayes	19	4.8	5	1.3	14	3.5
Garfield/Arthur	36	9.0	12	3.0	24	6.0
Cleveland	30	7.5	19	4.8	11	2.8
B. Harrison	27	6.8	11	2.8	16	4.0
Cleveland	17	4.3	6	1.5	11	2.8
McKinley	53	13.3	27	6.8	26	6.5
T. Roosevelt, I	63	15.8	21	5.3	42	10.5
T. Roosevelt, II	101	25.3	31	7.8	70	17.5
Taft	45	11.3	17	4.3	28	7.0
Wilson, I	72	18.0	31	7.8	41	10.3
Wilson, II	50	12.5	23	5.8	27	6.8
Harding	59	19.7	31	10.3	28	9.3
Coolidge	232	38.7	120	20.0	112	18.7
Hoover	158	39.5	105	26.3	53	13.3
F. Roosevelt, I	146	36.5	87	21.8	59	14.8
F. Roosevelt, II	105	41.3	120	30.0	45	11.3
F. Roosevelt, III/IV	417	104.3	402	100.5	15	3.8
Truman, I	668	167.0	605	151.3	63	15.8
Truman, II	848	212.0	766	191.5	82	20.5
Eisenhower, I	962	240.5	857	214.3	105	26.3
Eisenhower, II	958	239.5	848	212.0	110	27.5

(Table continues)

Table 3.3 (continued)

President	International agreements[a]		Executive agreements		Treaties[b]	
	Total	Average per year	Total	Average per year	Total	Average per year
Kennedy	831	277.0	763	254.3	68	22.7
L. Johnson	1,112	222.4	1,008	201.6	104	20.8
Nixon, I	915	228.8	797	199.3	118	29.5
Nixon, II	381	224.1	319	187.6	62	36.5
Ford	776	337.4	677	294.3	99	43.0
Carter	1,169	292.3	1,021	255.3	148	37.0
Reagan	638	212.7	521	173.7	117	39.0

[a] Includes all treaties, executive agreements, protocols, and conventions.
[b] Includes treaties, protocols, and conventions.

Sources: 1865-1948 adapted from Margolis (1986); 1949-1980 calculated by the authors from U.S. Department of State, *Treaties and Other International Agreements* (1950-1980); for 1981-1983, *Current Treaty Index* (1984).

Figure 3.1 Treaties and Executive Agreements by Presidents, 1949-1983 (yearly averages)

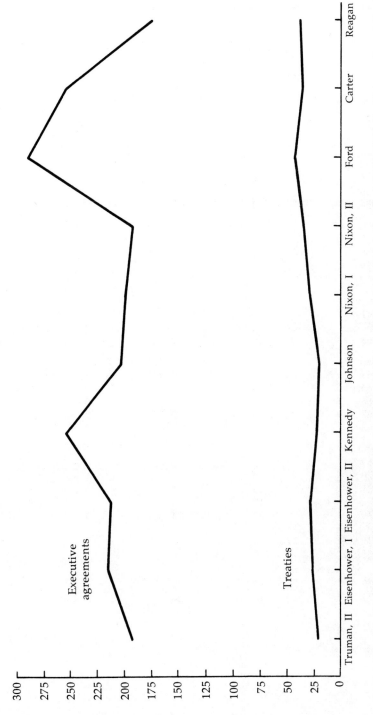

Source: Calculated by the authors from U.S. Department of State, *Treaties and Other International Agreements* (1950-1980). For Reagan, *Current Treaty Index* (1984).

Table 3.4 Senate Action on Treaties, Protocols, and Conventions, 1949-1984

	Ratified	Pending	Withdrawn	Rejected
Truman				
1949	9	19	7	0
1950	14	11	0	0
1951	15	39	1	0
1952	25	7	3	0
Eisenhower, I				
1953	25	15	0	0
1954	6	24	1	0
1955	20	16	1	0
1956	12	14	0	0
Eisenhower, II				
1957	12	15	1	0
1958	3	7	7	0
1959	8	15	0	0
1960	13	13	0	1
Kennedy				
1961	9	18	0	0
1962	8	17	1	0
1963	8	27	0	0
Johnson				
1964	14	14	3	0
1965	6	17	0	0
1966	9	29	0	0
1967	25	17	2	0
1968	15	14	0	0
Nixon				
1969	7	16	0	0
1970	10	18	1	0
1971	13	18	0	0
1972	18	23	0	0
1973	22	24	0	0
Nixon/Ford				
1974	9	27	0	0
Ford				
1975	15	23	0	0
1976	14	24	0	0

Table 3.4   (continued)

	Ratified	Pending	Withdrawn	Rejected
Carter				
1977	5	34	0	0
1978	10	31	0	0
1979	16	45	0	0
1980	19	55	0	0
Reagan				
1981	33	37	6	0
1982	7	9	0	0
1983	14	9	0	1
1984	20	40	0	0

Source: U.S. Congress, *Executive Proceedings of the Senate* (1949-1984).

Table 3.5 International Agreements by Policy Types, 1949-1983

	Foreign trade/ diplomacy	Foreign aid	Defense	Social welfare/ civil rights	Government/ economic management	Natural resources/ environment	Agriculture	Ceremonial/ cultural	Total
Truman									
1949	21	7	39	33	15	16	11	4	
1950	18	3	35	39	27	20	8	9	
1951	13	9	51	76	44	24	13	3	
1952	18	17	84	87	44	36	24	0	
Total	70	36	209	235	130	96	56	16	848
%	8.3	4.2	24.6	27.7	15.3	11.3	6.6	1.9	
Eisenhower, I									
1953	19	7	57	42	28	15	8	2	
1954	16	21	68	48	22	18	5	2	
1955	31	18	105	59	35	40	54	1	
1956	19	11	61	23	18	40	68	1	
Total	85	57	291	172	103	113	135	6	962
%	8.8	5.9	30.2	17.9	10.7	11.7	14.0	0.6	
Eisenhower, II									
1957	23	11	53	18	32	37	61	2	
1958	20	12	45	13	12	33	66	6	
1959	20	18	62	15	22	40	61	2	
1960	10	16	71	28	22	52	72	3	
Total	73	57	231	74	88	162	260	13	958
%	7.6	5.9	24.1	7.7	9.2	16.9	27.1	1.4	

	C1	C2	C3	C4	C5	C6	C7	C8	Total
Kennedy									
1961	21	34	40	18	18	37	95	4	
1962	54	41	36	22	17	39	107	4	
1963	36	10	28	31	28	41	68	2	
Total	111	85	104	71	63	117	270	10	831
%	13.4	10.2	12.5	8.5	7.6	14.1	32.5	1.2	
Johnson									
1964	24	5	29	18	23	43	80	4	
1965	29	6	38	16	21	48	58	2	
1966	37	6	25	15	15	58	81	5	
1967	50	8	31	20	19	48	54	2	
1968	21	6	26	11	23	50	53	4	
Total	161	31	149	80	101	247	326	17	1,112
%	14.5	2.8	13.4	7.2	9.1	22.2	29.3	1.5	
Nixon, I									
1969	16	1	27	10	10	47	55	3	
1970	65	10	30	7	14	37	55	5	
1971	47	11	40	15	16	29	77	0	
1972	47	7	65	23	17	47	77	5	
Total	175	29	162	55	57	160	264	13	915
%	19.1	3.2	17.7	6.0	6.2	17.5	28.9	1.4	
Nixon, II									
1973	43	8	35	12	17	46	66	2	
1974	25	6	28	12	13	42	26	0	
Total	68	14	63	24	30	88	92	2	381
%	17.8	3.7	16.5	6.3	7.9	23.1	24.1	0.5	

(Table continues)

Table 3.5 (continued)

	Foreign trade/ diplomacy	Foreign aid	Defense	Social welfare/ civil rights	Government/ economic management	Natural resources/ environment	Agriculture	Ceremonial/ cultural	Total
Ford									
1974	14	4	18	13	7	19	20	1	
1975	38	15	36	37	34	57	73	4	
1976	39	16	34	65	36	89	105	2	
Total	91	35	88	115	77	165	198	7	776
%	11.7	4.5	11.3	14.8	9.9	21.3	25.5	0.9	
Carter									
1977	43	12	29	53	29	111	89	4	
1978	64	8	15	62	32	88	71	4	
1979	66	7	26	42	18	79	42	6	
1980	36	1	16	25	18	34	37	2	
Total	209	28	86	182	97	312	239	16	1,169
%	17.9	2.4	7.4	15.6	8.3	26.7	20.4	1.4	
Reagan									
1981	29	15	40	33	22	63	42	5	
1982	35	18	38	29	22	63	47	3	
1983	16	8	19	13	10	45	23	0	
Total	80	41	97	75	54	171	112	8	638
%	12.4	6.4	15.2	11.8	8.5	26.8	17.5	1.2	

Democratic presidents									
Total	551	180	548	568	391	772	891	59	3,960
%	13.9	4.5	13.8	14.3	9.9	19.5	22.5	1.5	
Republican presidents									
Total	572	233	932	515	409	859	1,061	49	4,630
%	12.4	5.0	20.1	11.1	8.8	18.6	22.9	1.1	

Note: Includes treaties, executive agreements, protocols, and conventions.

Sources: Coded and calculated by the authors from U.S. Department of State, *Treaties and Other International Agreements* (1950-1980) for 1949-1980; for 1981-1983, *Current Treaty Index* (1984).

Table 3.6 U.S. International Agreements by Region and Policy Type, 1949-1983

	Foreign trade, diplomacy	Foreign aid	Defense	Social welfare/ civil rights	Government economic management	Natural resources/ environment	Agriculture	Ceremonial/ cultural	No. of agreements	Percentage of total agreements
W. Europe/ Britain	197	40	514	163	202	428	225	15	1,784	20.8
E. Europe	75	10	13	18	26	43	82	28	295	3.4
Africa	24	62	53	65	68	58	211	3	544	6.3
Asia	302	83	323	162	163	240	576	19	1,868	21.7
Middle East	60	104	117	157	82	129	272	15	936	10.9
Central America	174	91	268	321	111	250	385	7	1,607	18.7
Canada	20	0	92	12	16	141	17	0	298	3.5
U.S.S.R.	31	0	20	7	3	24	42	9	136	1.6
Mexico	40	5	14	108	32	100	30	4	333	3.9
Multilateral	200	18	66	70	97	218	112	8	789	9.2
No. of agreements	1,123	413	1,480	1,083	800	1,631	1,952	108	8,590	

Note: Includes treaties, executive agreements, protocols, and conventions.

Sources: Coded and calculated by the authors from U.S. Department of State, *Treaties and Other International Agreements* (1950-1980) for 1949-1980; for 1981-1983, *Current Treaty Index* (1984).

Table 3.7 U.S. International Agreements by Region, 1949-1983

	W. Europe/ Britain	E. Europe	Africa	Asia	Middle East	Central America	Canada	U.S.S.R.	Mexico	Multilateral	Total
Truman											
1949	45	1	3	19	3	41	6	1	9	18	
1950	48	6	2	27	5	56	5	0	2	8	
1951	67	3	7	23	15	87	7	0	5	19	
1952	81	4	13	34	45	94	9	0	9	21	
Total	241	14	25	103	68	278	27	1	25	66	848
%	28.4	1.7	2.9	12.1	8.0	32.8	3.2	0.1	2.9	7.8	
Eisenhower, I											
1953	51	2	14	23	18	43	5	0	3	19	
1954	63	3	6	34	21	45	5	2	10	11	
1955	92	9	3	58	23	107	12	2	3	34	
1956	82	5	4	54	12	53	6	0	5	20	
Total	288	19	27	169	74	248	28	4	21	84	962
%	30.0	2.0	2.8	17.6	7.7	25.8	2.9	0.4	2.2	8.8	
Eisenhower, II											
1957	74	5	7	37	26	54	5	0	9	20	
1958	65	13	5	46	18	33	3	2	4	18	
1959	68	7	6	51	18	49	7	1	8	25	
1960	81	8	5	69	22	59	5	0	6	19	
Total	288	33	23	203	84	195	20	3	27	82	958
%	30.0	3.4	2.4	21.2	8.8	22.7	2.1	0.3	2.8	8.6	

(Table continues)

Table 3.7 (continued)

	W. Europe/ Britain	E. Europe	Africa	Asia	Middle East	Central America	Canada	U.S.S.R.	Mexico	Multilateral	Total
Kennedy											
1961	70	9	23	55	26	48	9	0	8	19	
1962	72	8	35	62	29	76	7	1	6	24	
1963	48	5	20	60	27	47	7	1	6	23	
Total	190	22	78	177	82	171	23	2	20	66	831
%	23.4	2.7	9.6	21.8	10.1	21.1	2.8	0.2	2.4	8.1	
Johnson											
1964	47	13	26	47	24	23	10	3	6	27	
1965	36	8	27	52	16	30	13	1	6	29	
1966	51	3	21	62	28	30	10	3	7	27	
1967	34	8	25	56	17	27	13	4	9	39	
1968	31	3	13	52	21	39	4	8	3	20	
Total	199	35	112	269	106	149	50	19	31	142	1,112
%	17.9	3.1	10.1	24.2	9.5	13.4	4.5	1.7	2.8	12.8	
Nixon, I											
1969	33	6	10	48	15	14	9	6	2	26	
1970	41	9	13	62	14	39	8	4	12	21	
1971	34	5	16	70	22	42	9	7	7	23	
1972	37	12	8	84	22	61	6	17	13	28	
Total	145	32	47	264	73	156	32	34	34	98	915
%	15.8	3.5	5.1	28.9	8.0	17.0	3.5	3.7	3.7	10.7	

Nixon, II											
1973	33	15	3	62	19	28	10	23	10	26	
1974	24	5	6	45	17	14	8	5	6	22	
Total	57	20	9	107	36	42	18	28	16	48	381
%	15.0	5.2	2.4	28.0	9.4	11.0	4.7	7.3	4.2	12.6	
Ford											
1974	15	6	1	23	10	15	2	3	8	13	
1975	45	11	14	66	43	48	11	13	12	31	
1976	49	14	28	78	65	78	16	5	19	34	
Total	109	31	43	167	118	141	29	21	39	78	776
%	14.0	4.0	5.5	21.5	15.2	18.1	3.7	2.7	5.0	10.1	
Carter											
1977	42	18	37	79	80	39	17	6	19	33	
1978	47	17	41	88	58	34	10	7	24	18	
1979	40	18	14	67	43	32	15	4	25	28	
1980	22	7	23	44	21	27	3	0	11	11	
Total	151	60	115	278	202	132	45	17	79	90	1,169
%	12.8	5.1	9.8	23.6	18.1	11.2	3.8	1.4	6.8	7.6	
Reagan											
1981	44	13	27	42	37	35	10	2	18	21	
1982	43	8	23	61	39	42	9	3	16	11	
1983	29	8	15	28	17	18	7	2	7	3	
Total	116	29	65	131	93	95	26	7	41	35	638
%	18.2	4.5	10.2	20.5	8.8	14.9	4.1	1.1	6.4	5.5	

(Table continues)

Table 3.7 (continued)

	W. Europe/Britain	E. Europe	Africa	Asia	Middle East	Central America	Canada	U.S.S.R.	Mexico	Multilateral	Total
Democratic presidents											
Total	781	131	330	827	458	730	145	39	155	364	3,960
%	19.7	3.3	8.3	20.9	11.6	18.4	3.7	0.1	3.9	9.2	
Republican presidents											
Total	1,003	164	214	1,041	478	877	153	97	178	425	4,630
%	21.6	3.5	4.6	22.5	10.3	18.9	3.3	2.1	3.8	9.2	

Note: Includes treaties, executive agreements, protocols, and conventions.

Sources: Coded and calculated by the authors from U.S. Department of State, *Treaties and Other International Agreements* (1950-1980) for 1949-1980; for 1981-1983, *Current Treaty Index* (1984).

Table 3.8 Most Frequent International Agreement Partners of the
United States, 1949-1983

Country	Total number of agreements
Mexico	333
Canada	298
Japan	259
Great Britain	228
Egypt	222
South Korea	191
West Germany	173
Brazil	173
Philippines	167
Pakistan	152
Israel	144
Taiwan	141
Colombia	138
U.S.S.R.	136
India	134
Indonesia	132
South Vietnam	127
France	122
Italy	122
Turkey	119
Spain	116
Peru	113
Yugoslavia	107
Greece	101
Chile	100

Note: Includes treaties, executive agreements, protocols, and conventions.

Sources: Coded and calculated by the authors from U.S. Department of State, *Treaties and Other International Agreements* (1950-1980) for 1949-1980; for 1981-1983, *Current Treaty Index* (1984).

Table 3.9 U.S. International Agreements by Regime Type, 1949-1983

	Republican	Totalitarian	Military authoritarian	Nonmilitary authoritarian	Colonial	Multiple regime[a]	Total
Truman							
1949	82	3	9	35	0	17	
1950	89	6	11	44	0	9	
1951	121	2	12	76	2	20	
1952	165	4	13	107	1	20	
Total	457	15	45	262	3	66	848
%	53.9	1.8	5.3	30.9	0.3	7.9	
Eisenhower, I							
1953	83	2	5	66	0	22	
1954	104	4	12	67	1	12	
1955	155	11	23	118	0	36	
1956	129	5	17	68	1	21	
Total	471	22	57	319	2	91	962
%	49.0	2.3	5.9	33.0	0.2	9.4	
Eisenhower, II							
1957	113	4	15	79	5	21	
1958	113	15	8	51	1	19	
1959	130	11	10	61	1	27	
1960	153	7	12	81	3	18	
Total	509	37	45	272	10	85	958
%	53.1	3.9	4.7	28.4	1.0	8.9	

Kennedy							
1961	133	9	18	83	2	22	
1962	146	14	26	103	1	30	
1963	117	8	8	85	2	24	
Total	396	31	52	271	5	76	831
%	47.7	3.7	6.3	32.6	0.6	9.1	
Johnson							
1964	103	25	6	65	1	26	
1965	98	15	18	54	4	29	
1966	109	10	12	82	1	28	
1967	95	16	23	53	4	41	
1968	84	12	21	51	6	20	
Total	489	78	80	305	16	144	1,112
%	44.0	7.0	7.2	27.4	1.4	12.9	
Nixon, I							
1969	68	16	13	45	1	26	
1970	89	18	25	65	2	24	
1971	85	20	24	84	0	22	
1972	86	35	34	98	4	31	
Total	328	89	96	292	7	103	915
%	35.8	9.7	10.5	31.9	0.8	11.3	
Nixon, II							
1973	77	45	15	63	3	26	
1974	54	15	8	49	2	24	
Total	131	60	23	112	5	50	381
%	34.4	15.7	6.0	29.4	1.3	13.1	

(Table continues)

Table 3.9 (continued)

	Republican	Totalitarian	Military authoritarian	Nonmilitary authoritarian	Colonial	Multiple regime [a]	Total
Ford							
1974	42	9	7	24	1	13	
1975	102	27	33	97	1	34	
1976	132	22	52	142	2	36	
Total	276	58	92	263	4	83	776
%	35.6	7.5	11.9	33.9	0.5	10.7	
Carter							
1977	123	29	38	139	6	35	
1978	129	27	41	126	2	19	
1979	126	31	21	76	3	29	
1980	76	14	16	50	1	12	
Total	454	101	116	391	12	95	1,169
%	38.8	8.6	9.9	33.4	0.1	8.1	
Reagan, I							
1981	109	24	25	66	3	22	
1982	116	16	32	73	2	16	
1983	65	12	19	31	3	4	
Total	290	52	76	170	8	42	638
%	45.5	8.2	11.9	26.6	1.3	6.6	

Democratic presidents							
Total	1,796	225	293	1,229	36	381	3,960
%	45.3	5.7	7.4	31.0	1.0	9.6	
Republican presidents							
Total	2,005	318	389	1,428	36	454	4,630
%	43.3	6.9	8.4	30.8	0.8	9.9	

Note: International agreements include treaties, executive agreements, protocols, and conventions. Regime types reflect coded information in *The Europa Year Book* (1986); Clements (1986). Republican regimes involve legislatures with two or more active political parties. Totalitarian states are one-party Communist or Socialist republics. Military authoritarian regimes are those led by military officers. Nonmilitary authoritarian states include monarchies, dictatorships, and states controlled by other autocratic elites. Colonial regimes are possessions of other nations.

[a] In multilateral agreements.

Sources: Coded and calculated by the authors from U.S. Department of State, *Treaties and Other International Agreements* (1950-1980) for 1949-1980; for 1981-1983, *Current Treaty Index* (1984).

Table 3.10 Executive Orders of Presidents Washington through Reagan

	Numbered orders [a]	Unnumbered orders [b]	Total for term	Average number per year
Washington, I				
1789	—	3		
1790	—	2		
1791	—	0		
1792	—	2	7	1.75
Washington, II				
1793	—	1		
1794	—	0		
1795	—	0		
1796	—	0	1	0.25
Adams				
1797	—	0		
1798	—	1		
1799	—	0		
1800	—	0	1	0.25
Jefferson, I				
1801	—	2		
1802	—	0		
1803	—	0		
1804	—	0	2	0.50
Jefferson, II				
1805	—	0		
1806	—	1		
1807	—	1		
1808	—	0	2	0.50
Madison, I				
1809	—	0		
1810	—	1		
1811	—	0		
1812	—	0	1	0.25
Madison, II				
1813	—	0		
1814	—	0		
1815	—	0		
1816	—	0	0	0.00

Table 3.10 (continued)

	Numbered orders[a]	Unnumbered orders[b]	Total for term	Average number per year
Monroe, I				
1817	—	0		
1818	—	0		
1819	—	0		
1820	—	1	1	0.25
Monroe, II				
1821	—	0		
1822	—	0		
1823	—	0		
1824	—	0	0	0.00
J. Q. Adams				
1825	—	0		
1826	—	0		
1827	—	1		
1828	—	2	3	0.75
Jackson, I				
1829	—	2		
1830	—	2		
1831	—	1		
1832	—	1	6	1.50
Jackson, II				
1833	—	1		
1834	—	0		
1835	—	3		
1836	—	2	6	1.50
Van Buren				
1837	—	2		
1838	—	6		
1839	—	0		
1840	—	2	10	2.50
W. Harrison				
1841	—	0	0	0.00
Tyler				
1841	—	0		
1842	—	14		
1843	—	0		
1844	—	3	17	4.25

(Table continues)

Table 3.10 (continued)

	Numbered orders[a]	Unnumbered orders[b]	Total for term	Average number per year
Polk				
1845	—	3		
1846	—	1		
1847	—	12		
1848	—	2	18	4.50
Taylor				
1849	—	4		
1850	—	1	5	3.33
Fillmore				
1850	—	1		
1851	—	4		
1852	—	7	12	5.00
Pierce				
1853	—	7		
1854	—	15		
1855	—	11		
1856	—	2	35	8.75
Buchanan				
1857	—	3		
1858	—	3		
1859	—	8		
1860	—	2	16	4.00
Lincoln, I				
1861	—	3		
1862	1	6		
1863	1	14		
1864	0	19	44	11.00
Lincoln, II				
1865	0	4	4	12.00
A. Johnson				
1865	3	17		
1866	1	14		
1867	0	23		
1868	2	19	79	19.75

Table 3.10 (continued)

	Numbered orders[a]	Unnumbered orders[b]	Total for term	Average number per year
Grant, I				
1869	0	29		
1870	0	27		
1871	0	18		
1872	1	15	90	22.50
Grant, II				
1873	5	31		
1874	6	27		
1875	2	36		
1876	1	19	127	31.75
Hayes				
1877	0	30		
1878	0	12		
1879	0	29		
1880	0	21	92	23.00
Garfield				
1881	0	6	6	8.00
Arthur				
1881	1	13		
1882	0	23		
1883	0	25		
1884	2	32	96	24.00
Cleveland				
1885	3	35		
1886	0	25		
1887	3	15		
1888	0	32	113	28.25
B. Harrison				
1889	0	42		
1890	1	38		
1891	1	35		
1892	1	25	143	35.75
Cleveland				
1893	4	30		
1894	15	22		
1895	29	17		
1896	9	14	140	35.00

(Table continues)

163

Table 3.10 (continued)

	Numbered orders [a]	Unnumbered orders [b]	Total for term	Average number per year
McKinley, I				
1897	10	9		
1898	10	19		
1899	12	33		
1900	16	41	150	37.50
McKinley, II				
1901	6	29	35	46.70
T. Roosevelt, I				
1901	13	13		
1902	44	39		
1903	47	25		
1904	47	23	251	77.23
T. Roosevelt, II				
1905	171	13		
1906	165	2		
1907	188	5		
1908	280	6	830	207.50
Taft				
1909	129	15		
1910	129	38		
1911	175	12		
1912	206	20	724	181.00
Wilson, I				
1913	206	20		
1914	243	6		
1915	188	12		
1916	211	10	848	212.00
Wilson, II				
1917	296	17		
1918	259	7		
1919	225	8		
1920	175	1	955	238.75
Harding				
1921	227	1		
1922	174	1		
1923	118	1	522	202.33

Table 3.10   (continued)

	Numbered orders[a]	Unnumbered orders[b]	Total for term	Average number per year
Coolidge, I				
1923	62	0		
1924	189	5	256	182.86
Coolidge, II				
1925	271	0		
1926	201	1		
1927	238	2		
1928	232	2	947	236.75
Hoover				
1929	239	0		
1930	268	0		
1931	247	0		
1932	214	0	968	242.00
F. Roosevelt, I				
1933	527	1		
1934	474	2		
1935	384	0		
1936	275	0	1,663	415.75
F. Roosevelt, II				
1937	257	0		
1938	249	0		
1939	287	0		
1940	258	6	1,057	264.25
F. Roosevelt, III				
1941	382	2		
1942	288	—		
1943	122	—		
1944	100	—	773	193.25
F. Roosevelt, IV				
1945	29	—	29	87.88
Truman, I				
1945	139	—		
1946	148	—		
1947	103	—		
1948	109	—	499	136.00

(Table continues)

Table 3.10 (continued)

	Numbered orders[a]	Unnumbered orders[b]	Total for term	Average number per year
Truman, II				
1949	69	—		
1950	105	—		
1951	119	—		
1952	105	—	398	99.50
Eisenhower, I				
1953	90	—		
1954	73	—		
1955	65	—		
1956	44	—	272	68.00
Eisenhower, II				
1957	54	—		
1958	50	—		
1959	60	—		
1960	42	—	206	51.50
Kennedy				
1961	84	—		
1962	89	—		
1963	55	—	228	76.00
L. Johnson, I				
1963	7	—		
1964	56	—	63	58.33
L. Johnson, II				
1965	74	—		
1966	57	—		
1967	66	—		
1968	56	—	253	63.25
Nixon, I				
1969	61	—		
1970	72	—		
1971	63	—		
1972	55	—	251	62.75
Nixon, II				
1973	64	—		
1974	40	—	104	65.82

Table 3.10   (continued)

	Numbered orders [a]	Unnumbered orders [b]	Total for term	Average number per year
Ford				
1974	29	—		
1975	67	—		
1976	56	—	152	63.33
Carter				
1977	83	—		
1978	78	—		
1979	77	—		
1980	73	—	311	77.75
Reagan, I				
1981	76	—		
1982	63	—		
1983	57	—		
1984	41	—	237	59.25

[a] Numbered series begins in 1862.
[b] Unnumbered series ends in 1941.

Sources: Unnumbered series from 1789 to 1941 adapted from Lord (1979). Numbered series for 1862-1935 adapted from Lord (1944). Numbered series for 1936 to present compiled from *Code of Federal Regulations* (1936-1984).

Table 3.11   Total Executive Orders by Policy Type, 1949-1984

Policy	Frequency	Percentage of total
Foreign trade, diplomacy	345	13.9
Foreign aid	21	0.8
Defense	377	15.2
Social welfare, civil rights	229	9.3
Government/economic management	366	14.8
Natural resources, environment	337	13.6
Agriculture	34	1.4
Ceremonial/cultural	120	4.8
Federalism	13	0.5
Personnel, agency requests	633	25.5

Note: Policy types were coded on the basis of title descriptions and, in some cases, the text of the executive orders.

Source: Coded and calculated by the authors from *Code of Federal Regulations* (1936-1984).

Table 3.12   Executive Orders by Policy Type, 1949-1984

	Foreign trade/ diplomacy	Foreign aid	Defense	Social welfare/ civil rights	Government/ economic management	Natural resources/ environment	Agriculture	Ceremonial/ cultural	Federalism	Personnel, agency requests	Total
Truman											
1949	10	0	4	1	16	15	0	2	0	21	
1950	9	0	23	6	27	15	1	5	0	19	
1951	10	0	32	11	18	17	0	3	0	28	
1952	12	0	19	5	11	25	0	5	0	28	
Total	41	0	78	23	72	72	1	15	0	96	398
%	10.3	0.0	19.6	5.8	18.1	18.1	0.2	3.8	0.0	24.1	
Eisenhower, I											
1953	10	3	27	4	13	8	3	7	0	15	
1954	3	1	9	5	15	11	2	3	0	24	
1955	7	1	26	3	3	9	2	1	0	13	
1956	1	0	19	2	4	5	1	1	0	11	
Total	21	5	81	14	35	33	8	12	0	63	272
%	7.7	1.8	29.8	5.1	12.9	12.1	2.9	4.4	0.0	23.2	
Eisenhower, II											
1957	6	1	9	3	11	6	2	3	0	13	
1958	5	0	13	3	6	11	0	1	0	11	
1959	5	0	11	1	9	12	3	6	1	12	
1960	3	0	7	0	15	3	1	2	1	10	
Total	19	1	40	7	41	32	6	12	2	46	206
%	9.2	0.1	19.4	3.4	19.9	15.5	2.9	5.8	0.1	22.3	

(Table continues)

Table 3.12 (continued)

	Foreign trade/diplomacy	Foreign aid	Defense	Social welfare/civil rights	Government/economic management	Natural resources/environment	Agriculture	Ceremonial/cultural	Federalism	Personnel, agency requests	Total
Kennedy											
1961	6	2	12	5	15	19	3	5	1	16	
1962	3	2	23	9	22	12	2	5	0	11	
1963	9	0	14	12	7	2	0	5	0	13	
Total	18	4	49	26	44	33	5	15	1	40	228
%	8.1	1.7	20.9	11.1	18.7	14.0	2.1	6.4	0.1	17.0	
Johnson											
1964	7	0	10	7	10	7	1	3	1	10	
1965	13	2	6	10	4	8	2	4	0	25	
1966	12	1	7	6	8	5	1	4	0	13	
1967	5	1	10	6	10	12	2	0	0	20	
1968	7	0	8	11	5	4	0	1	1	19	
Total	44	4	41	40	37	36	6	12	2	87	316
%	14.2	1.3	13.3	12.9	12.0	11.7	1.9	3.9	0.1	28.2	
Nixon, I											
1969	6	0	5	10	8	6	1	5	1	19	
1970	7	0	11	7	13	9	1	4	0	20	
1971	5	0	7	5	12	6	2	6	2	18	
1972	6	0	4	5	7	9	0	5	1	18	
Total	24	0	26	27	40	30	4	20	4	75	251
%	9.6	0.0	10.4	10.8	16.0	12.0	1.6	8.0	1.6	30.0	

Nixon, II											
1973	3	0	3	3	11	15	1	4	0	24	
1974	6	0	4	5	5	6	0	0	1	13	
Total	9	0	7	8	16	21	1	4	1	37	104
%	8.7	0.0	6.7	7.8	15.4	20.2	0.1	3.8	0.1	35.6	
Ford											
1974	7	0	2	3	4	2	0	2	0	9	
1975	8	1	11	4	7	9	0	4	0	23	
1976	11	0	3	4	3	9	0	5	0	22	
Total	26	1	16	11	14	20	0	11	0	54	152
%	17.0	0.1	10.5	7.2	9.2	13.1	0.0	7.2	0.0	35.3	
Carter											
1977	15	1	8	13	4	9	0	4	0	29	
1978	12	0	4	18	11	6	0	1	0	26	
1979	18	3	5	8	7	15	1	5	0	15	
1980	24	1	4	11	4	12	0	2	0	15	
Total	69	5	21	50	26	42	1	12	0	85	311
%	22.2	1.6	6.8	16.1	8.4	13.5	0.1	3.9	0.0	27.3	
Reagan											
1981	28	0	5	5	6	10	1	4	1	16	
1982	18	1	4	9	11	3	0	2	1	14	
1983	16	0	4	8	13	5	1	0	1	9	
1984	12	0	4	1	11	0	0	1	0	12	
Total	74	1	17	23	41	18	2	7	3	51	237
%	31.2	0.1	7.2	9.7	17.3	7.6	0.1	3.0	0.1	21.5	

(Table continues)

Table 3.12 (continued)

	Foreign trade/diplomacy	Foreign aid	Defense	Social welfare/civil rights	Government/economic management	Natural resources/environment	Agriculture	Ceremonial/cultural	Federalism	Personnel, agency requests	Total
Democratic presidents											
Total	172	13	189	139	179	183	13	54	3	308	1,253
%	13.7	1.0	15.1	11.1	14.3	14.6	1.0	4.3	0.2	24.6	
Republican presidents											
Total	173	8	187	90	187	154	21	66	10	326	1,222
%	14.1	0.7	15.3	7.4	15.3	12.6	1.7	5.4	0.8	26.7	

Note: Policy types were coded on the basis of title descriptions and, in some cases, the text of the orders.

Source: Calculated by the authors from successive volumes of *Code of Federal Regulations* (1936–1984).

Table 3.13   Groups Affected by Executive Orders, 1949-1984

Group	Number of orders	Percentage of total
Nonmilitary government personnel	425	17.17
Foreign countries, international organizations	346	13.98
Military personnel	282	11.39
Government departments	232	9.37
States, territories, localities	231	9.37
Labor-management (dispute resolution)	198	8.00
Nation as a whole	160	6.46
Congress, independent regulatory agencies	96	3.88
Industries	70	2.83
Minorities	58	2.34
Environmentalists, conservationists	53	2.14
Consumers	42	1.70
Business, government contractors	40	1.61
Professionals	37	1.49
Farmers	29	1.17
Immigrants	26	1.05
Labor	21	0.84
Youth	20	0.80
Poor, hungry	17	0.69
Students, teachers	16	0.65
Handicapped	15	0.60
Women	15	0.60
Veterans	10	0.40
Small businesses	7	0.28
Aged	6	0.24
President himself, vice president	23	0.93
Total	2,475	—

Note: Groups were classified on the basis of the title descriptions and, in some cases, the text of the executive orders.

Source: Calculated by the authors from successive volumes of *Code of Federal Regulations* (1936-1984).

Table 3.14 Administrations' Executive Orders by Affected Group, 1949-1984 (percent)

President	Nation/consumers	Labor	Business/industry	Minorities	Farmers	Environmentalists	States/localities	Foreign countries, citizens	Military personnel	Nonmilitary personnel	Federal agencies, Congress
Truman	9.0	14.9	2.2	1.5	0.5	1.0	16.9	10.0	15.6	17.6	10.8
Eisenhower, I	5.7	7.6	4.9	3.4	1.9	0.4	12.1	10.6	19.7	15.2	18.6
Eisenhower, II	7.8	11.5	6.4	3.7	2.8	0.5	11.0	9.6	12.8	15.1	18.8
Kennedy	6.1	19.6	1.9	9.8	2.3	0.0	8.9	11.7	7.9	7.0	24.8
Johnson	5.9	9.3	2.8	12.0	1.2	0.9	9.9	16.4	14.5	18.5	8.6
Nixon, I	13.4	5.7	2.4	7.3	0.8	4.5	8.1	8.9	10.9	23.5	14.6
Nixon, II	14.1	4.0	5.1	5.1	2.0	3.0	6.1	11.1	7.1	25.3	17.2
Ford	8.3	3.0	1.8	7.1	0.6	4.7	4.1	21.9	8.3	29.6	10.7
Carter	7.8	2.2	7.8	13.4	0.6	5.6	3.7	24.1	4.1	22.2	8.4
Reagan	7.1	7.1	11.1	10.9	0.0	1.9	4.7	27.0	10.9	11.4	7.1
Democratic presidents	7.4	11.0	3.7	8.6	1.0	2.0	10.4	15.5	11.1	17.2	12.0
Republican presidents	8.9	6.9	5.5	6.2	1.3	2.3	8.2	14.6	12.5	19.0	14.6

Note: Groups were classified on the basis of the title descriptions and, in some cases, the text of executive orders.

Source: Calculated by the authors from successive volumes of *Code of Federal Regulations* (1936-1984).

Table 3.15 Foreign Assistance Authorized by Presidential Waivers

Fiscal year	Number of waivers	Authorization ($ millions)
1962	10	54.3
1963	12	85.7
1964	12	128.2
1965	9	107.0
1966	8	114.6
1967	6	97.2
1968	4	11.7
1969	1	4.0
1970	5	62.9
1971	9	209.5
1972	8	198.6
1973	6	106.9
1974	11	194.6
1975	2	77.6
1976	1	0.9
1977	0	0.0
1978	0 [a]	0.0
1979	2 [a]	15.0
1980	2 [a]	45.1
1981	5 [a]	53.2
1982	2 [a]	26.9
1983	1 [a]	0.1
Total	117	1,594.0

[a] Minimum number of waivers for the year; others may not have been filed.

Source: U.S. General Accounting Office (1985).

Table 3.16 Presidents' Foreign Assistance Fund Transfers

Date	Region/country	Use	Authorized transfer ($ millions)
March 21, 1962	NATO	Administrative expenses	2.0
March 22, 1962	Southeast Asia	Administrative expenses	3.0
June 5, 1962	Africa	Contingency funds	30.5
June 5, 1962	Africa	International organization funds	9.5
June 5, 1962	Africa	International organization funds	15.0
May 21, 1963	Central America	Alliance for Progress	10.0
March 21, 1964	Poland	Project Hope	1.6
May 19, 1964 [a]	Not specified	Military assistance	50.0
June 26, 1964 [a]	Southeast Asia/ Congo/Turkey	Military assistance	25.0
June 26, 1964 [a]	Southeast Asia/ Congo/Turkey	Military assistance	15.0
June 29, 1964	Central America	Alliance for Progress	8.0
June 29, 1964	Central America	Alliance for Progress	6.0
June 22, 1965	Southeast Asia/ Central America	Support assistance	18.0 [b]
January 18, 1966 [a]	Vietnam	Support assistance	28.0
January 18, 1966 [a]	Vietnam	International organization funds	28.0
February 10, 1966 [a]	Vietnam	Support assistance	18.0
February 10, 1966 [a]	Vietnam	Support assistance	10.0
June 8, 1966	Vietnam	AID administrative expenses	1.4
November 19, 1966	Vietnam	Administrative expenses	5.0
May 16, 1968	Vietnam	Administrative expenses	7.2
May 13, 1969	Vietnam	Administrative expenses	6.4
April 14, 1970	Vietnam	Administrative expenses	5.5
June 30, 1970	Cambodia	Military assistance	1.0
July 18, 1970	Not specified	Project Hope	0.5
October 23, 1970 [a]	Cambodia	Military assistance	50.0
February 11, 1971	Cambodia	Military assistance	10.0
March 23, 1971	Vietnam	Administrative expenses	3.6
March 1, 1972	Vietnam	Administrative expenses	3.6
June 13, 1973	Vietnam	Administrative expenses	2.9
April 19, 1974 [a]	Egypt	Security support assistance	8.0
May 16, 1974	Egypt	Security support assistance	0.7
June 30, 1974	Egypt	Security support assistance	20.0

Table 3.16 (continued)

Date	Region/country	Use	Authorized transfer ($ millions)
September 13, 1979	Caribbean	Disaster relief	2.2
January 24, 1980	Sinai	Air transport services	3.9
July 8, 1980	Not specified	AID expenses	7.0
September 28, 1981	Lebanon	Peace-keeping operation account	9.0
December 5, 1981	Chad	Airlift services	12.0
Total			437.5

[a] Transfers also demanded a waiver of the 10 percent limitation, which required that the president be allowed to move no more than 10 percent of the funds from one category to another.
[b] $13.8 million earmarked for Southeast Asia.

Source: U.S. General Accounting Office (1985, appendix I).

Table 3.17 Presidential Use of Drawdown Authority

Date	Country	Authorized drawdown ($ millions)
January 3, 1963	India	55.0
May 15, 1965	Vietnam	75.0
October 21, 1965	Vietnam	300.0
December 24, 1973	Cambodia	200.0
May 13, 1974	Cambodia	50.0
January 10, 1975	Cambodia	75.0
July 1, 1980	Thailand	1.1
December 9, 1980	Liberia	1.0
January 16, 1981	El Salvador	5.0
March 5, 1981	El Salvador	20.0
February 2, 1982	El Salvador	55.0
July 19, 1983	Chad	10.0
August 5, 1983	Chad	15.0
Total		862.1

Source: U.S. General Accounting Office (1985, 8).

Table 3.18   Funds under Direct Control of Presidents ($ thousands)

	New appropriations [a]	Expenditures [a]
Truman		
1949	5,764,550	4,043,390
1950	5,893,979	3,626,994
1951	9,835,233	4,158,371
1952	8,601,118	4,982,628
Eisenhower, I		
1953	1,908,363	1,828,402
1954	4,729,625	5,282,220
1955	2,795,550	4,380,621
1956	2,752,842	4,473,177
Eisenhower, II		
1957	3,833,671	4,110,828
1958	2,805,351	4,081,422
1959	2,053,603	1,776,687
1960	1,906,191	1,756,607
Kennedy		
1961	2,727,182	1,881,988
1962	4,169,606	3,442,593
1963	5,663,312	2,247,497
Johnson		
1964	3,328,604	4,118,812
1965	5,834,929	4,307,263
1966	5,895,356	4,324,210
1967	5,406,894	4,850,809
1968	4,717,468	4,843,612
Nixon		
1969	4,872,340	4,966,798
1970	4,974,375	4,774,263
1971	2,160,338	1,458,981
1972	7,158,172	4,276,286
1973	6,593,265	3,732,921
Nixon/Ford		
1974	12,429,746	3,329,179
Ford		
1975	8,725,806	3,987,744
1976	10,565,865	3,524,691

Table 3.18 (continued)

	New appropriations [a]	Expenditures [a]
Carter		
1977	4,639,051	2,486,877
1978	7,527,523	4,449,788
1979	5,920,801	2,623,373
1980	12,457,062	7,523,314
Reagan		
1981	14,661,873	7,009,911
1982	8,549,881	6,073,109
1983	3,332,254	5,492,070
1984	15,603,410	8,479,952
1985	20,463,618	12,049,885

Note: Funds that presidents are given direct authority to spend on programs such as disaster relief, economic assistance abroad, military assistance to friendly nations, expansion of defense production, drug abuse prevention, Peace Corps.

[a] New appropriations are those funds approved and appropriated by Congress for presidential spending; expenditures are those monies from the total appropriations that are actually spent by a president.

Source: U.S. Executive Office of the President, *Budget of the United States* (1950-1987).

Table 3.19 Presidents' Budget Rescission Requests, 1977-1986
($ thousands)

Item	1977	1978	1979	1980
Funds appropriated to the president	−41,500	−40,200	—	—
Agriculture	—	—	—	—
Commerce	−2,025	—	—	—
Defense-military	−878,950	—	—	—
Defense-civil	−6,600	—	—	—
Education	—	—	—	—
Energy	—	—	−50,000	—
Health and Human services	—	—	−227,258	−104
Housing	—	—	−608,167	—
Interior	−47,500	—	−3,127	—
Justice	—	—	—	−18
Labor	—	—	—	—
State	−12,000	−5,000	—	—
Transportation	−6,803	—	—	—
Treasury	—	—	—	—
Independent agencies	−60,000	−10,055	−26,140	—
Total	−1,055,378	−55,255	−914,692	−122

Note: Rescissions are decisions by presidents not to spend funds already appropriated by Congress. Under the Budget and Impoundment Control Act of 1974, presidents must notify Congress by rescission requests. Congress can deny the request by a resolution passed by either house.

Source: U.S. Executive Office of the President, *Budget of the United States* (1978-1987).

1981	1982	1983	1984	1985	1986
—	−10,629	−15,133	—	−105,399	−39,760
—	−2,000	−77,301	—	−310,218	−1,062,681
−34,493	−19,000	—	—	−325,371	−196,632
—	—	—	—	—	—
—	—	—	—	−16,200	—
−321,729	−1,157,205	−1,230,381	—	−173,939	−1,080,200
−101,926	−20,000	−69,000	—	−21,112	—
−344,218	—	—	—	−26,838	−787,417
−10,000	−9,421,639	—	−331,431	−260,057	−4,625,677
—	—	−63,500	−30,000	−72,389	−116,104
—	—	—	—	−13,659	−122,109
—	−4,095	—	−1,700	−276,566	−416,037
−10,185	—	—	—	−2,432	—
—	−9,623	−28,200	—	−49,327	−356,051
—	—	—	—	−9,530	−788,395
−433,240	−10,877	—	−25,418	−55,338	−717,995
−1,255,791	−10,655,068	−1,483,615	−388,549	−1,718,375	−10,309,058

Figure 3.2 Presidential Behavior on Foreign Policy

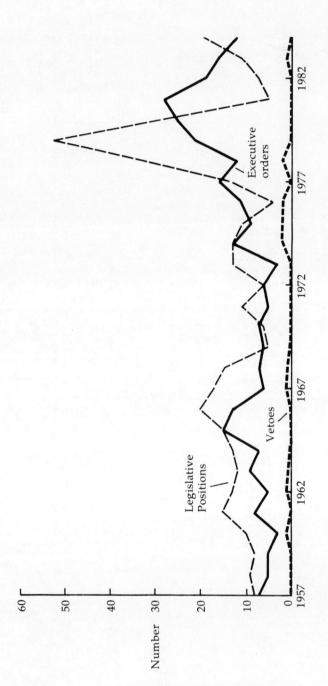

Source: Coded and calculated by the authors.

Figure 3.3 Presidential Behavior on Defense Policy

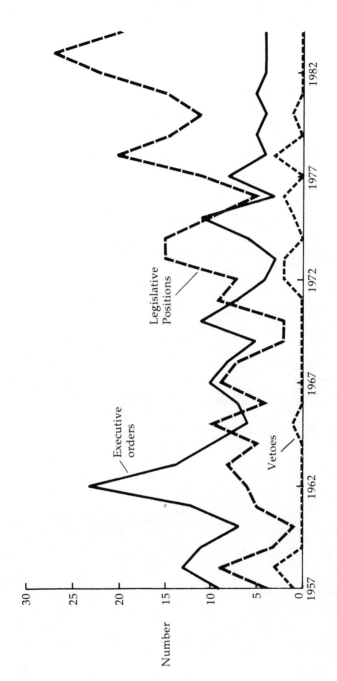

Source: Coded and calculated by the authors.

Figure 3.4 Presidential Behavior on Domestic Policy

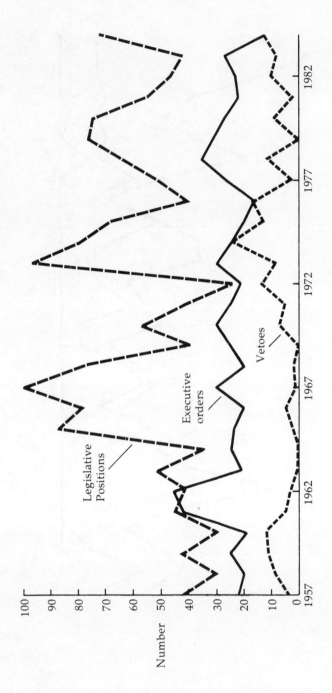

Source: Coded and calculated by the authors.

4

Administrative Directions

Imagine, if you will, an official body provided for by the Constitution and set up in Washington. It is composed of several hundred people who come from all over the United States. They have large powers. Although they are disciplined by some leadership, particularly expressed in one man, and must direct themselves therefore at certain given national ideals, most of them have their own jobs to think about and are reaching for their own way in life. Though sometimes they act in unseemly haste, they usually take a long time to resolve an issue. They are not necessarily responsive to the popular will, though they swear by it frequently. Individuals among them have often very little information of what others are up to; even the most powerful and best informed among them may be unaware of what is happening either in the group or in the government and outer world. (de Grazia 1969, 49)

If asked which part of American government is best described by the above passage, many people would respond, "The U.S. Congress." They would, in part, be right, but the same description aptly fits the American presidency. Indeed, de Grazia was describing the presidency. Although presidents have the image of being overworked, lonely figures who bear singular responsibility for tough decisions, they do not single-handedly identify and resolve national problems. Instead, many individuals participate, and at times presidents themselves may be the least important of the decision makers involved. As de Grazia observed,

On a normal issue that comes before the "President" some dozens of people are involved. It might be presumptuous to say that more of a collectivity is engaged than when the same type of issue would come before the Congress; but it would be equally presumptuous to say that fewer persons were taken up with the matter." (1969, 50)

The program complexity and group diversity associated with presidents' policy choices establish a large, ongoing, and decentralized organization. Because of its size and longevity, it exhibits considerable specialization and has many established rules and procedures. Two policy-related elements of the plural presidency—the program areas and groups involved in presidents' choices—thus contribute a third organizational component to the plural office.

Three Strategies of Presidential Decision Making

Presidents' responses to dual problems of organization and administration define the executive office. Presidents organize information and communication so that they can elicit the best advice possible for decision making. They also attempt to coordinate and control the activities of government and thereby to administer the decisions once they have been made. Three very different strategies have been used by presidents to address these two problems: (1) bureaucratic administration, (2) personal intimacy, and (3) political representativeness.

The first strategy involves, according to Max Weber, "the exercise of control on the basis of knowledge" (1947, 339). The key words are "control" and "knowledge." The advisory staff, put in place to obtain information, is also used to control subsequent decisions. In addition, the fundamental nature of "bureaucratic administration" is to gain objective, technical, and specialized information that is experiential as well as formal. Knowledge can come from the study of the problem at hand but may also "[grow] out of experience in the service" (1947, 339). "Official secrets" are learned about the best way of doing things and about identifying the other participants who can be instrumental in or detrimental to the process of control. This strategy suggests the need for a staff of experts who can act as both presidential advisers and administrative officers.

A second strategy for gaining knowledge and control involves personal intimacy—familiarity with the executives themselves. This strategy reflects a desire among all heads of state, not simply American presidents, to surround themselves with individuals who are personally loyal. As Aristotle wrote, "It is already the practice of kings to make themselves many eyes and ears and hands and feet. For they make colleagues of those who are friends of themselves and their governments" (1943, 165). Thus the knowledge is not expertise but intimacy. As Frederic Malek, an adviser on personnel for Richard Nixon, commented, "You don't get the best people. You get the people you know" (1978, 64). Adopting this approach, presidents invite people they trust to offer advice and help control the operation of government. These individuals' knowledge, then, depends not on their grasp of the affairs of government but on a personal understanding of their boss. Their retention hinges on unceasing loyalty to him during their tenure in office.

Presidents also pursue a third strategy: political representativeness. Through this approach, they respond most directly to the problem of group diversity that they confront in office. Individual staff members are chosen on the basis of their political backgrounds—their partisan affiliations, ties to specific social groups, or socioeconomic characteristics. These presidential loyalists are of a different sort from those gained through the intimacy strategy. Most obviously, presidents reward members of their own party with positions in the government, or presidents select other enthusiasts with a policy outlook similar to their own. George Washington began the practice of making party appointments; although he was opposed to the increasingly political climate that was emerging in the 1790s, he nonetheless recognized that presidents would have to keep that climate in mind:

> I shall not, while I have the honor to administer the government, bring a man into an office of consequence knowingly, whose political tenets are adverse to the measures which the general government are pursuing; for this, in my opinion, would be a sort of political suicide. (Fitzpatrick 1940, 315)

Because personal bonds between presidents and these partisan appointees do not necessarily exist, however, presidents sometimes find that these people espouse multiple goals and priorities within the broad commonality of the party that are not always consistent with presidential desires. Various wings and factions of the party make claims for representation in the advisory and administrative systems, thereby limiting their value to presidents.

In accordance with this third strategy of political representation, advisers are also selected as representatives from particular social groups, including women, racial and ethnic groups, and people from specific geographic regions. Presidents emphasize representation of groups traditionally underrepresented in presidential politics and thereby divert resources away from their goals of information and control. The appointment may thus be more important for political appearances than for political input. This third strategy also involves the choice of advisers from among social elites—wealthy business people, heads of corporations, lawyers, and academics—many of whom share outlooks, ideas, and upbringings. Presidents can rely on the information and the influence held by these elite appointees; they are, in miniature, the social and economic establishment of the nation. Taken together, the representation approach provides these solutions to the problems of organization and administration, which create their own problems of political balance among interests competing for access to the White House.

The three strategies—bureaucratic administration, personal intimacy, and political representation—are largely incompatible with one another. In the simplest terms, the bureaucratic strategy says, "Get the best people possible," the intimacy strategy says, "Get the people you know best," and the representation approach says, primarily, "Get people from the party and interest groups." The people who would be selected by each of the three strategies are rarely the same. Although presidents tend to pick individuals from their political party who fit within the bureaucratic and personal strategies, partisanship is not a requirement of either strategy but merely an incidental result. Taken together, the three strategies produce an administration diverse in ideological and policy positions, demographic balance, and political loyalties. They are likely to have differing levels of commitment to presidents as individuals and to the policy interests and programs that presidents wish to pursue.

The diversity and potential conflict within this plurality and the incompatibility of the strategies that produce it nonetheless prompt presidents to adopt all three strategies. One strategy checks the other, each accommodates needs in ways the others do not, and no single approach predominates. Even when presidents attempt to centralize control in the White House, they acknowledge that they are unable or unwilling to abandon their bureaucratic and partisan strategies. The central consequence of this plurality in administrative strategy is the increased size and scope of the presidential entourage. Moreover, its magnitude produces considerable institutional continuity across presidential administrations. Presidents find dismantling something entrenched from their predecessors quite difficult, and it is usually not worth the effort or not in their best interest to do so. We now examine each of the three strategies with the contradictory outlooks they produce.

The Bureaucratic Administration

According to the bureaucratic administrative strategy, a president's staff acts primarily on the basis of what Weber calls "rational-legal authority." Established, universal rules guide the behavior of individuals who occupy offices and gain their legitimized status from these official positions. More specifically, the rational-legal authority involves:

(1) A continuous organization of official functions bound by rules.
(2) A specified sphere of competence. This involves (a) a sphere of

obligations to perform functions which has been marked off as part of a systematic division of labour. (b) The provision of the incumbent with the necessary authority to carry out these functions. (c) That the necessary means of compulsion are clearly defined and their use is subject to definite conditions. A unit exercising authority which is organized in this way will be called an "administrative organ." (Weber 1947, 330)

Only the supreme chief of the organization occupies his position of authority by virtue of appropriation, of election, or of having been designated for the succession. But even *his* authority consists in a sphere of legal "competence." (Emphasis in the original; 1947, 333)

Presidents first adopted the bureaucratic administrative approach by seeking advice and using the administrative skills of their cabinet members, who had specific spheres of competence and who occupied offices established by law (Fenno 1959). The cabinet's role in this regard was always severely limited because of its dominant partisan character. Because of the problematic cabinet, the bureaucratic administrative strategy was permanently fixed in the White House in 1939 with the enactment of three important changes in the makeup of the presidency as a collective office: (1) the creation of the Executive Office of the President (EOP) as an official staff arm for presidents, (2) the transfer of the Bureau of the Budget from the Treasury Department to the executive office, and (3) the formal organization of the White House Office within the EOP.

Each of these changes led to the establishment of "rational-legal" authority on impersonal terms—the offices and spheres of competence were present regardless of who worked within them and who was president. During the ensuing years, the administrative organ of the executive office followed three central patterns of establishment (these are adapted from Polsby 1968, 144-168).[1] First, boundaries were defined between the executive office as an organization and other executive departments and agencies. Second, the complexity of the organization began to increase as more functions became internally separated (division of labor) and more functions were added to the office. Third, universalistic and automatic modes of decision making were implemented within the EOP, especially at the Bureau of the Budget, which was reorganized and renamed the Office of Management and Budget in 1970.

Organizational Boundaries. The organizational integrity of the executive office hinges on two key parameters: personnel size and budget resources. When an institution is small, it may overlap with other organizations. Indeed, such was the case with the early executive staff during Franklin Roosevelt's first terms. Employees were temporarily assigned to the White House from outside agencies to aid in specific tasks that Roosevelt wanted to accomplish (Cronin 1987, 347). No clear boundaries existed between the executive staff and agencies of the federal bureaucracy. As the executive office increased in size, however, outside employees were used less frequently because sufficient internal staff had been hired.

Tables 4.1 and 4.2 include data on the initial size of the executive staff, its expansion, and its eventual relative stability.[2] The growth of the executive office (or any office) adds an inertial feature to the institution, emphasizing its separateness from other already established organizations. The unit soon adopts rules and patterns of behavior that define the autonomy of the group and the regularity of its operation. As Moe has noted, "organizations have their own routines, their own agendas, their own norms, their own ways of coding and interpreting the world" (1985, 240).

Boundaries appear not haphazardly but because of the incentives and interests within the political institutions involved. Growth in the executive bureaucracy has five main sources.

1. Presidential initiative. One of the principal sources of growth in the executive bureaucracy has been presidential efforts in developing and coordinating programs from the executive office. In many instances, the executive office, and more narrowly the White House Office, have served as visible organizational centers for presidential efforts.

2. Congressional initiative. Despite its name, many units of the Executive Office of the President were the creation of Congress and were either not sought by presidents or were actually opposed by them. Congress contributed to the growth of the office because it desired policy coordination from a central agency.

3. Joint efforts of presidents and Congress. Presidents and Congresses have mandated the growth of units in the executive office by approving larger federal budgets each year.

4. Presidents' political strategy. Presidents have used the executive office not only as an administrative base but also as a political base. Administrative resources mobilize public support behind presidential proposals and also aid in reelection plans.

5. Federal budget growth. The large aggregate increases in the federal budget have increased the burden on the executive office to maintain policy coordination. Presidential participation in the budget process has placed greater burdens on the largest single unit of the EOP—the Bureau of the Budget/Office of Management and Budget (for an elaboration of these points, see Helmer 1981, 60).

Presidential initiative. Presidents' initiatives are apparent in the statistics shown in Table 4.1 on the growth of both the executive and White House offices. First, unevenness of growth over time, especially in the early period of these offices, stemmed partly from presidential responses to unpredictable change in the political and policy environments. Franklin Roosevelt sought to coordinate both domestic and military efforts of American involvement in World War II through the EOP, which totaled nearly 200,000 people in 1943 at the height of the war. Various war establishment units were also supervised from the White House, including the Office of War Mobilization, the Office for Emergency Management, the Board of Economic Warfare, the Office of Price Administration, and the Selective Service System.

Second, several other presidential initiatives more nearly derived from presidents' own interests and depended less on the vagaries of political events. Truman dismantled the wartime executive office but simultaneously increased the size of the White House Office in 1947 by nearly four times. This increase was meant to provide a base for policy interests that Truman wished to pursue in the form of an annual presidential legislative program (Moe 1985, 251; Hess 1976, 44-58). "Responsiveness, however, can breed dependency" (Helmer 1981, 63), and the size of the White House Office never decreased after Truman's early expansion. The next large increase in the size of the White House Office occurred in 1971, when Nixon attempted to control federal departments from the White House (Nathan 1983). Contrary to many popular beliefs about the dramatic growth of the office, Nixon's doubling of the White House staff was notably less than the fourfold increase by Truman. "It is [also] a common misconception to regard the current EOP as the legacy of the Nixon period" (Helmer 1981, 61). In fact, as the figures in the tables make clear, the greatest expansion of the executive office staff in the post-World II period occurred in 1958 under Eisenhower and in 1966 under Johnson. Eisenhower pursued some restructuring and additions to management responsibilities of the EOP (Berman 1979, 58-63), whereas Johnson tried to centralize programs of the Great Society in the White House (Moe 1985, 253-254).

The executive office under Nixon was, on the average, no larger than that under Johnson after 1966.

Third, the size of the executive office was reduced only once in the postwar period. In the aftermath of Watergate, Gerald Ford decreased the EOP by 67 percent, eliminating some of the agencies and councils established during the Nixon years. In the process, he did not reduce the size of the White House Office or the Office of Management and Budget. Indeed, both increased slightly by comparison with their counterparts under Nixon's administration.

Fourth, presidential initiatives need not be as dramatic as the large staff increases and decreases noted above. As Table 4.2 shows, increases in the Bureau of the Budget/Office of Management and Budget were consistently incremental after boosts by Franklin Roosevelt, who added 453 staff members to this office in the 1939-1943 period. Although presidential scholars often note that the OMB was reorganized and enlarged after 1970 (Moe 1985, 256), our analysis indicates that personnel increased only 17 percent from 1970 to 1971, considerably less than the largest increase of 96 percent from 1940 to 1941.

Congressional initiatives. Efforts by the Congress to enlarge and consolidate the executive office are evident from the data of Table 4.2. The Council of Economic Advisers (CEA) was created by the Employment Act of 1946. Congress gave the president the responsibility to "use all practicable means ... to promote maximum employment, production, and purchasing power" (60 U.S. Statute 24, February 20, 1946). The council was to advise presidents on fiscal and monetary measures designed to address inflation and unemployment. The CEA has remained roughly the same size since it was founded (thirty-seven people in 1949, thirty-three people in 1986), although there were small increases during the Johnson and Nixon administrations. The National Security Act of 1947, which gave presidents the responsibility for coordinating national defense and foreign policy, also gave presidents a committee of advisers—the National Security Council (NSC). Unlike the CEA, the NSC has increased in size as a result of presidential initiative. Most notably, for a short period under Eisenhower (1958-1960), policy formation and implementation were separated into two boards in the NSC staff system, and hence the council size increased. A second increase occurred in 1970 when Nixon instructed Henry Kissinger, his newly named head of the National Security Council, to reestablish an "Eisenhower NSC system" (Kissinger 1979). Presidents, however, have not appreciated all the initiatives that Congress has taken to enlarge the executive office. The Council on Environmental Quality, established by Congress in 1970, was actively resisted by

Nixon even though he later called it one of his accomplishments (Hess 1976, 124).

Congress, of course, is at a disadvantage in establishing presidential agencies. The bureaucratic administrative strategy favored by Congress gives presidents the ability to control policy and information in discretionary ways not envisioned by Congress. Congressional initiatives are ultimately translated by presidents as they see fit, and chief executives have considerable flexibility in making as much or as little as they desire from the offices provided. In addition, Congress is usually unable to reclaim authority in a policy area once it has established the executive apparatus.

Joint efforts of presidents and Congress. Presidents and Congress have also combined efforts to establish firmer boundaries for the executive office and units within this office. In addition to creating more units with more personnel, the two branches, working together, have increased the budgets for the existing organizational units. Table 4.3 shows the average expenditures of the executive office and selected units within it. Table 4.4 presents annual appropriation and expenditure figures for the White House Office and the total executive office. Table 4.5 lists similar figures for other key units of the EOP.[3]

A comparison of Table 4.2 with Table 4.4 shows that the number of personnel assigned to the executive offices and the amounts of money spent in running these offices are quite different. The staff of the Executive Office of the President has grown only 30 percent in the period since 1949, whereas expenditures for the EOP have increased nearly thirteen times during the same years. Even calculated in constant dollars, the executive office budget shows a 200 percent increase. This growth is explained by the dominant budget increases for just two units—the White House Office and the Bureau of the Budget/OMB. The budget of the former increased eighteen times in current dollars (and doubled in constant dollars) since 1949, whereas its staff size grew by a relatively moderate 63 percent. As Table 4.5 indicates, the budget of the latter grew eleven times in current dollars (and nearly doubled in constant dollars), with only a 7 percent increase in staff over the same period. The budget growth of these two units helps to illuminate some of the anomalies between the two sets of figures. Johnson's efforts to coordinate the Great Society, for instance, left the expenditures of the EOP virtually unchanged but increased the money spent by the Bureau of the Budget. Ford's personnel cutbacks in 1975 were countered by increases in expenditures during 1975 and 1976, with the largest increases observed in expenditures for the White House Office and the OMB. The budget figures presented in Table 4.5

also show that, although the reorganization of the OMB did not lead to personnel expansion, it was accompanied by budgetary expansion (a 58 percent increase from 1970 to 1972).

Perhaps most intriguing, these budgetary figures indicate that relatively few attempts were made by presidents since Johnson to work with less money. Figure 4.1 displays the budget growth in real dollars for the total executive office, the White House Office, and the Bureau of the Budget/Office of Management and Budget since 1949. Presidents may reduce the number of personnel for the total executive office, as Ford did, or for any one agency in the executive office, but they do not tamper with the overall budgets of these units. Carter and Reagan achieved decreases in the budgets for the three offices, but these decreases were relatively modest. Presidents and Congresses by and large accept the work of their predecessors, which enters the institutional history of the organization. The only case in which a president actually attempted to dismantle an organization occurred when Reagan attempted to curtail funds for the Council on Environmental Quality. Yet with pressures by Congress and citizens' groups, Reagan's efforts at budget cutting here were not fully successful. During his term of office, as Table 4.5 reveals, there was a tug-of-war between congressional appropriations and presidential expenditures for the council. The Congress from 1981 to 1984 authorized more money than the council actually spent. Ironically, in 1985, the council's expenditures more than quadrupled, although its budget authority was somewhat curtailed by President Reagan.

The president's political strategies. Few parts of the federal government are unaffected by presidential election campaigns and reelections, and the Executive Office of the President is no exception. Although all partisan activity should technically be independent of government, the White House Office has often coordinated certain aspects of presidential campaigns, including the dirty tricks that led to the break-in at the Democratic National Committee's headquarters in the Watergate Hotel. There is also a more subtle election cycle pattern inherent in the operating budgets for the White House Office: for ten of the twelve presidential election years since Franklin Roosevelt's second term, the White House Office budget has been larger than it was in one or more of the prior three years. Only 1960, when Eisenhower was not running for reelection, and 1984, when Reagan began his second term, do not fit this pattern. This observation does not reflect simply incremental budgeting, because expenditures in many of the nonelection years go down as well as up. Personnel increases, however, have not followed the same pattern as election-year budget increases. Thus to the extent that the campaign is run from the White House, it is run by existing staff.

Federal budget growth. The growth of the federal budget and the budget deficit have brought growing demands on presidents and their staffs to develop and coordinate budgeting and programs within the budget. Table 4.6 shows federal budget receipts, outlays, and surpluses or deficits. Since passage of the Budget and Accounting Act of 1921, presidents have become more and more involved in the budget process, so that, in the collective setting of the presidency, the Bureau of the Budget/OMB has become more involved than presidents in planning budget strategies. This trend helps account for the significant increases in appropriations to and expenditures by the OMB.

Organizational Complexity. Greater size typically means greater complexity. The larger an organization becomes, the more likely that internal differentiation occurs. In many ways, the internal complexity of an office reflects the complexity of the environment. Presidents attempt to satisfy disparate policy goals and policy groups by creating special offices or councils within the EOP. These special offices need not last long to allow presidents to exhibit their concern about a particular problem or group. Table 4.7 depicts every organizational unit of the executive office since its creation in 1939. Although a core of offices in the EOP is well established today, others have come and gone within and across presidential administrations. Figures 4.2 to 4.6 show the complexity of the EOP for selective years (one from each of the last five decades). Not surprisingly, every president wants to put his own stamp on the EOP by either adding units or modifying the hierarchy within which they are ordered. Presidents typically rearrange the EOP in their inaugural years. The reshuffling does little for presidents' overall control of the institution or its specific units, however. Even when the executive office was at its most complex, during the Nixon administration (Figure 4.5), executive control did not increase (Nathan 1975; Heclo 1977).

Table 4.8 analyzes the importance of specific White House units, as perceived by staff people in other units of the Carter and Reagan administration. The two administrations are roughly similar in their judgment of the relative importance of key units. The table also shows how important the White House staff considered the various actors in the external environment—the cabinet, Congress, press, and interest groups.

Automatic Decisions. Operating procedures within the Executive Office of the President have become more standardized in at least two ways. First, since Truman, procedures for hiring EOP personnel have become increasingly formalized and centralized. During the Truman and Eisenhower administrations, the White House served as a mere clearinghouse supervising appointments that were made by the national political party committees. Presidents Kennedy and Johnson adopted an in-house personnel system, supplanting party procedures. Their personnel staffs even identified potential vacancies and updated lists of available candidates. Nixon created an office to centralize these procedures further. Called the White House Personnel Operation, this office made rank-order evaluations of all candidates and recommended appointees on the basis of these rankings. Personnel staff also dramatically increased, from a dozen people in the Kennedy and Johnson administrations to sixty people in the latter part of Nixon's term in office. President Ford renamed the unit the President's Personnel Office, but the name change did not reflect any change in centralization or in the formalization of personnel decisions (MacKenzie 1981, chap. 2). Thus an office within an office took charge of hiring. The talent search was thus removed from the presidents' immediate control as a consequence of the bureaucratic administrative approach. Impersonal measures, not personal desires, were created to evaluate the qualifications and competence of staff members.

Second, the Office of Management and Budget guides federal departments and agencies in three separate ways involving *legislative clearance, enrolled bills,* and—a relatively recent innovation—*administrative clearance.* First, legislative clearance procedures require all departments and agencies of the federal government to submit their legislative proposals to OMB for approval. All program initiatives must be "in accord with the president's program" before they are sent to Capitol Hill. Second, the OMB has formal mechanisms for the examination of enrolled bills—legislation that has passed Congress and awaits the president's signature. Given that some nine hundred pieces of legislation are passed by Congress each year, presidents are unlikely to be familiar with very many of them. Departments in the executive branch make recommendations to the OMB, which in turn advises the White House as to whether the president should sign a given bill; presidents only involve themselves in the process when most of the work has already been done (see Figures 2.1 and 2.2, depicting the legislative clearance and enrolled bill processes). Third, on the basis of the precedents set by Nixon, Ford, and Carter, Ronald Reagan established, through Executive Order No. 12291, a system by which administrative rule making could be reviewed by OMB. The Office of Information and Regulatory Affairs in OMB screens various rules and regulations drafted by departments and agencies. Each agency must provide a "regulatory impact analysis" (RIA) of final regulations, justifying costs, benefits, and possible alternatives (West and Cooper, 1985). OMB then determines, on the basis of these RIAs, whether the rules are consistent with the White House criteria. If they are not, the rules are returned to the appropriate agency for modification. Table 4.9 summarizes OMB action on these administrative rules. Although most of the regulations are approved by OMB, any intervention by this office is significant. The increasing organizational diffusion and standard operating procedures of OMB are reflected in its budgeting, as well as its legislative and rule-making tasks.

The plural presidency clearly emerges from the confusion inherent in this processes as they take place in numerous departments, agencies, levels, and stages. The image of a single incumbent recasting the federal bureaucracy at his whim contrasts sharply with the various organizations and procedures that persist across administrations.

Presidents' Intimates

Apart from these broad organizational units, presidents have always relied on small groups of loyal advisers. This reliance in part reflects presidents' inability to interact easily with a large White House staff. In addition, however, it reflects the desires of presidents to seek advice on key decisions from a manageable group of loyalists. These personal advisers often reflect idiosyncracies associated with a given president, in contrast to the established procedures and organizations within the executive office that remain from one president to the next.

We compare presidents' closest political advisers in three ways, to see who they are, to see how they think, and to see how they view one another. The backgrounds of presidents' immediate advisers reveal their similarities and friendships with presidents. People nicknamed Kennedy's immediate advisers the "Irish mafia"; they included Kenneth O'Donnell, Lawrence O'Brien, and Robert Kennedy. Johnson brought Texans Walter Jenkins, Bill Moyers, and Jack Valenti to the White House. Nixon invited Californians H. R. Haldeman and John Ehrlichman and long-time friend John Mitchell. Ford relied on many former colleagues in Congress, including Sen. Robert Griffin of Michigan, former Wisconsin Rep. Melvin Laird, and Rep. Richard Cheney of Wyoming. Jimmy Carter was identified with a contingent of Georgians who came to Washington, including Bert Lance, Charles Kirbo, and Hamilton Jordan. Reagan relied on long-time friends and Californians such as William French Smith, William Clark, Edwin Meese, and Michael Deaver.

Table 4.10 measures the ideological closeness of White House staff advisers to Presidents Nixon, Carter, and Reagan. The staffs of these three presidents showed substantial differences in ideological consistency, ranging from the Carter group, which had little consistency, through the Nixon group, which had moderate consistency, to the Reagan group, which manifested relatively consistent beliefs across issue categories. Table 4.11 analyzes influence exerted by the top officials of the Carter and Reagan teams. This table gives the reader a sense of the importance of individuals and shows how they are distinct from the organizational units they head. Although, as noted in Table 4.8, the National Security Council and the Office of Management and Budget were viewed as very important offices in both the Carter and Reagan presidencies, the individuals in charge of these offices were nonetheless treated very differently. Zbigniew Brzezinski and James McIntyre, respective heads of the NSC and OMB during the Carter administration, did not exert influence nearly as great as that of William Clark and David Stockman in these positions in the Reagan administration.

In outlook and values these staff people are likely to differ significantly from members of the larger executive office. Presidents claim responsibility for numerous decisions of varying complexity and urgency. Presidents and their small groups of advisers often make decisions on long-range plans and more crisis-oriented issues concerning domestic, foreign, and military affairs. Still, an enormous apparatus that surrounds each president and his intimate advisers makes thousands of decisions that are attributed to the president although he and his advisers know little about them. The bureaucratic administration and personal intimacy strategies are conflicting avenues by which the presidency covers a vast range of decisions.

Political Appointments and Representation

Presidents have a third option in attempting to manage information and policy directions in the decisions of government—the appointment of people to key policy-making positions in the executive departments and agencies. Presidents are nominally "in charge" of the bureaucracy, but they have never really controlled it. Tables 4.12 and 4.13 make clear why contemporary presidents find it so difficult to wield any real clout over executive departments and why "infiltration" of departments with party supporters is not easily accomplished. Table

4.12 details the size of executive departments for select years. Table 4.13 gives employment figures for the independent agencies of the government.

Nevertheless, from the "spoils system" appointments by Andrew Jackson to the most recent subcabinet-level appointments by Ronald Reagan, presidents have appointed numerous individuals on the basis of partisan or ideological persuasion as a way of leaving their imprint "on the vast executive apparatus upon which the effective management of [their] programs depends" (Brown 1982, 282). Table 4.14 shows the full scope of appointments that presidents must make that require Senate approval. Most of them involve the commissioning of officers in the armed services, which are not only pro forma appointments but also pro forma confirmations. Of the approximately sixty thousand recommendations that presidents since Truman have sent to the Senate each year, only about two thousand are political appointments (MacKenzie 1981, 4-5). Of these two thousand appointments, the number that represents highly placed policy executives is smaller still. As Table 4.15 shows, presidents since Kennedy have, on the average, made fewer than seven hundred major appointments to such positions as department secretaries, undersecretaries, assistant secretaries, agency heads, ambassadors, and federal judges.[4]

Presidents do have considerable leeway in making appointments. The Senate rarely rejects a nomination. The rejection of Robert Bork, a Reagan nominee to the Supreme Court, marked the first time since G. Harrold Carswell in 1970 that a Supreme Court nominee was rejected. Table 4.16 displays the thirty rare instances in two hundred years in which presidents encountered difficulties with their nominees to the Supreme Court. A strategy that presidents adopt when their nominations run into trouble is to withdraw them from the Senate calendar. Soon after the Bork nomination was rejected, Reagan encountered problems with his next nominee, Judge Douglas Ginsburg, who subsequently withdrew. These cases receive considerable media attention, but they are an extremely small proportion of presidential appointments.

Presidential leeway in making appointments cannot be equated with presidential control of the appointment process. As part of an effort to manage the "vast executive apparatus," presidents have employed two distinctly partisan strategies in making appointments, both of which are inherently difficult to supervise. President Jackson used the *patronage approach*. He called for the "rotation in office" of executive personnel, replacing people at each inauguration. Although in principle the rotation idea was intended to democratize the aristocratic character of public service, in practice it established a spoils system, rewarding party workers with administrative posts. New York Senator William Marcy, a Jackson supporter, argued,

> When [politicians] are contending for victory, they avow their intention to enjoy the fruits of it. If they are defeated, they expect to retire from office. If they are successful, they claim, as a matter of right, the advantages of success. They see nothing wrong in the rule, that to the victor belongs the spoils of the enemy. (Quoted in Goldsmith 1974, 1: 177)

Under patronage, presidents made appointments to some 619 positions during the 1820s and 1830s, and this figure increased to 929 positions by 1849 (this number did not include another 8,000 deputy postmasters, whom presidents were also expected to appoint). Lincoln undertook the most thoroughgoing rotation of people from office; he removed 1,457 of the 1,639 governmental personnel he inherited, replacing incumbents with "loyal" Republicans (Goldsmith 1974, 2: 981-983). Nineteenth-century presidents thus made more appointments than do contemporary presidents. The merit system now used by the Selective Service in hiring federal bureaucrats has made it no longer possible for twentieth-century presidents to exercise patronage and retain personal control as broadly as their predecessors.

Patronage has continued on a smaller scale throughout the contemporary period, but it has been supplanted by a second, *partisan policy approach*. Presidents now use appointments as policy tools to choose individuals who, though still largely from the president's party, are deliberately selected for policy biases that fit with the president's program in departments and agencies. The beginnings of this approach were most clearly evident in the hiring practices of Kennedy, who selected individuals largely without input from national party professionals. In essence, he centered hiring decisions in the White House. Patronage continued to diminish in importance as efforts were made, most notably by Nixon and Reagan, to screen candidates for their policy commitments rather than for their service to the party.

Yet neither strategy has proved fully satisfactory in strengthening presidents' administrative control of the executive departments. Regardless of the approach taken, presidents cannot know whom to appoint to all positions. Think of the problem: you are elected president, and three months later you must fill two thousand offices. A reasonable strategy is to start with one's closest friends and perhaps also your business associates and political acquaintances. By this count, however, you would probably still have more than fifteen hundred positions left to fill. How is it possible to retain control of a bureaucracy if you have never met most of the people who are your appointees? Moreover, you will probably never meet a large proportion of these people once they are in office. No wonder neither presidential strategy has been overly successful. In the patronage approach, the president (actually one of his advisers) learns of possible appointees from members of Congress and from state and local politicians, who wish to reward party loyalists from their own locales. Once appointed, the partisans-turned-public-officers feel greater loyalty to those directly responsible for their appointments and frequently share a closer policy outlook with them than with the presidents who appointed them. In the policy approach, presidents who feel so inclined may directly select some of their White House personnel, thereby gaining slightly more control of the process. Ultimately, however, they probably exert only marginally more control over the appointees who eventually land the job.

Tables 4.17 and 4.18 trace the appointment of party people to departmental posts and judicial offices. Table 4.17 shows that presidential appointments to the so-called political departments—those with clientele groups, such as Agriculture, Commerce, Housing and Urban Development, and Labor—are quite partisan. Other departments, requiring more traditionally specialized backgrounds, such as Defense and State, have fewer partisan appointments. Reagan's attempt to place as many party stalwarts as possible in federal departments is also evidenced in this table: he has made more partisan appointments than any other president. Indeed, Reagan has the highest overall percentage of party appointments of any president since Franklin Roosevelt. An early study, using data somewhat different from those presented here, examined appointees by Presidents Roosevelt through Eisenhower and found that fully 89 percent of Roosevelt's, 84 percent of Truman's, and 76 percent of Eisenhower's appointees were partisan (Stanley, Mann, and Doig 1967). Beyond the problem of knowing the people hired, presidents face another difficulty in controlling their administrations: political executives, whether or not they come from the president's party, tend not to stay in government very long. MacKenzie (1981, 7-8) reports that, from 1945 through 1977, the median term of service for a cabinet secretary was only 2.1 years, with 40 percent staying less than 2 years. Turnover at the subcabinet level is comparable.

In contrast to their administrative appointments, presidents' appointments to the federal bench have a long-lasting impact because of the near-lifetime tenure of judges. For all presidents since Franklin Roosevelt, judicial appointments were more partisan than departmental appointments (see Table 4.18). Table 4.19 shows the legacy of these presidents' appointments to the federal courts. Even though Lyndon Johnson left office nearly twenty years ago, some 80 percent of his judicial appointees remain on the bench.

Presidents have also tried to "garner support from an enlarged collection of special interest groups in a fragmented political milieu" (Brown 1982, 280). In their appointments presidents have attempted to recognize various demographic groups traditionally underrepresented in American politics—blacks, Hispanics, women, Asians, American Indians. As Table 4.20 shows, neither Carter nor Reagan has done exceptionally well in breaking the "white male" mold for presidential appointees, but Carter comes considerably closer than Reagan. These hiring practices differ by departments (Table 4.21). Women are more likely to be appointed to the Departments of Education and Health and Human Services, whereas virtually no women are appointed to the Departments of Defense or Agriculture. Minorities are usually given positions in the Justice Department as U.S. attorneys. These same race and gender patterns are evident in appointments by Johnson through Reagan to the district courts (Table 4.22) and the circuit courts (Table 4.23). Among the five presidents considered, Carter has the strongest record of hiring women and minorities.

Except for truly "token" appointments of women and minorities to federal positions, most presidential appointments follow more traditional patterns of hiring. In effect, presidents take a third approach to appointments by selecting individuals of high socioeconomic status, creating a core of appointees with established careers and achievements who are touted as the "best" people possible (on the basis not of expertise but of social status). This pattern of recruitment has been very stable since the early years of the republic. Tables 4.24 to 4.27 reveal the backgrounds of major cabinet and diplomatic appointees since 1789. The profiles of these appointees throughout this period are quite similar: They are largely college-educated lawyers or business people with considerable prior government experience and are largely from the East Coast. As Table 4.28 shows, although the number of elite appointees has dropped since the nineteenth century, well over half of all presidential appointments during the latter twentieth century can still be classified as elitist. Although many modern presidents profess to be acting as representatives of groups locked out of the system, the overall profile of their appointees suggests otherwise. Presidential appointments reveal representation of a far different kind in selecting appointees when constituencies are powerful socioeconomic groups.

Conclusion

Three conflicting means are used by presidents in their efforts to tie all agencies and executive departments to the White House. The *bureaucratic administrative* approach attempts to select individuals with the expertise that will enable presidents to gain information in policy making. The *personal intimacy* approach is viewed as providing staff members who know presidents well enough to be able to give the best advise possible. The *political representation* approach is designed to gain presidential control by means of shared partisan, policy, and socioeconomic viewpoints. Each strategy aims to centralize appointments in the White House. Separately and together, however, the strategies result in wholly decentralized mechanisms for decision making. Appointees to departments and agencies are both physically and bureaucratically distant from presidents. Experts on the White House staff are not much closer. Even personal intimates of presidents sometimes feign ignorance of presidential involvement or their own involvement and give the impression that decisions were made elsewhere.

Chief executives are confronted with a keen dilemma. They seek *singular* control of information and policy decisions but are forced to work through a *collective* apparatus. The pastiche of staffs, interests, and loyalties makes it difficult for presidents to gain either the information or the control they seek. Presidents are faced with the problem that they do not control the collective organization, although the collectivity has considerable control over many of their decisions. "When those subject to bureaucratic control seek to escape the influence of the existing bureaucratic apparatus, this is normally possible only by creating an organization of their own which is equally subject to the process of bureaucratization" (Weber 1947, 338). The White House Office, as a specific unit within the larger executive office, thus symbolizes presidents' apparent power. It was established to give presidents immediate information and advice on pressing national problems that could not readily be obtained from the large executive office, but this immediacy has vanished with the emergence of a bureaucracy of some four hundred people. Thus presidents attempt to keep initiative in the White House but in so doing lose control of many of its central functions. Although presidents "have administrations," in common parlance, they in fact administer much less than does the broad organizational unit of the executive office. Through the organizational diffusion of the presidency, "the president" and "his administration" have become more independent from each other and less interdependent. In recent years, President Reagan has reportedly had some degree of success in controlling the federal bureaucracy, but a full assessment of his efforts awaits his departure from the White House.

The problem of control seems inherently unsolvable. Presidents could not control the cabinet departments, so they increased the size of the EOP. Because the EOP was itself too big and too diverse to control, succeeding presidents expanded the White House Office. Unfortunately, the single individual in the Oval Office can personally supervise only a limited number of people, organizations, offices, agencies, goals, desires, plans, and programs, and this number cannot be expanded by reorganization or reallocation of control. The image of a single executive in control of the executive branch or the White House is contradicted by these three rather flawed recruitment strategies.

Notes

1. Polsby uses the term *institutionalization* to denote the process of establishing fixed procedures for decision making, routines and sanctions for hiring and firing, and official positions within an organization. Because we are interested in describing the institution of the presidency and not just the institutionalization of its administrative component, we avoid use of the term here.
2. Tables 4.1.-4.4 begin with President Coolidge since his is the first full term with available data from the budget of the United States on presidential staff expenditures. Note also that, although the White House staff was formally designated the White House Office in 1939, Tables 4.2-4.4 use this term for all presidents listed.
3. Figures in Tables 4.4 and 4.5 are in current dollars; that is, they have not been adjusted for inflation. Amounts presented in Figure 4.1 have been calculated in constant (real) dollars using 1967 as the base. This procedure takes into account the inflation rate for the period, thereby discounting the budget figures. To obtain the constant dollar figures, the budget values are divided by the consumer price index for the period.
4. The data in Table 4.15 are not available for presidents prior to Kennedy.

Table 4.1 Expansion of White House Staff

President	Total executive staff: average number of full-time employees for term	White House staff: average number of full-time employees for term
Coolidge	137 [a]	37
Hoover	123 [a]	37
Roosevelt, I	103 [a]	47
Roosevelt, II	371	50
Roosevelt, III	121,318	51
Truman, I	78,389	188
Truman, II	1,269	256
Eisenhower, I	1,229	295
Eisenhower, II	2,357	408
Kennedy	2,058	422
Johnson	3,839	304
Nixon, I	5,227	478
Nixon, II	5,277	563
Ford	1,905	583
Carter	1,758	412
Reagan [b]	1,594	380

[a] Figures count the White House grounds staff and police force as part of the executive staff. The White House staff was the only policy unit during these years.
[b] 1981-1986.

Source: For Coolidge, Hoover, and Roosevelt's second term, U.S. Executive Office of the President, *Budget of the United States* (1924-1940); all others, U.S. Department of Commerce, *Statistical Abstract* (1933-1987).

Table 4.2 Size of Executive Office of President, 1924-1986

	Total executive staff	White House Office	Bureau of Budget/ OMB	National Security Council	Council of Economic Advisers	Council of Environmental Quality	All others
Coolidge							
1924	133	38	—	—	—	—	—
1925	133	38	—	—	—	—	—
1926	137	37	—	—	—	—	—
1927	141	37	—	—	—	—	—
1928	135	37	—	—	—	—	—
Hoover							
1929	131	36	—	—	—	—	—
1930	139	36	—	—	—	—	—
1931	114	37	—	—	—	—	—
1932	109	37	—	—	—	—	—
Roosevelt, I							
1933	110	50	—	—	—	—	60
1934	107	49	—	—	—	—	58
1935	97	44	—	—	—	—	53
1936	98	44	—	—	—	—	54
Roosevelt, II							
1937	100	45	—	—	—	—	55
1938	105	45	—	—	—	—	60
1939	631	45	103	—	—	—	483
1940	647	63	156	—	—	—	428

Roosevelt, III						
1941	21,428	53	305	—	—	21,070[a]
1942	86,817	49	459	—	—	86,309[a]
1943	194,194	51	556	—	—	193,587[a]
1944	182,833	50	546	—	—	182,237[a]
Roosevelt/Truman						
1945	174,138	61	565	—	—	173,512[a]
Truman, I						
1946	95,068	61	718	—	—	94,289[a]
1947	43,232	293	562	—	—	42,377[a]
1948	1,118	210	561	19	43	285
Truman, II						
1949	1,167	223	512	17	37	381
1950	1,256	295	520	17	36	388
1951	1,219	259	522	19	41	378
1952	1,434	245	498	23	34	634
Eisenhower, I						
1953	1,376	248	457	24	34	613
1954	1,175	266	419	28	26	436
1955	1,167	290	438	28	35	370
1956	1,196	374	430	27	31	334
Eisenhower, II						
1957	1,218	387	442	26	31	332
1958	2,660	394	440	64	28	1,734
1959	2,631	405	437	65	34	1,696
1960	2,919	446	434	65	32	1,942

(Table continues)

Table 4.2 (continued)

	Total executive staff	White House Office	Bureau of Budget/ OMB	National Security Council	Council of Economic Advisers	Council of Environmental Quality	All others
Kennedy							
1961	2,838	411	485	56	35	—	1,851
1962	1,676	467	497	44	44	—	626
1963	1,659	388	510	39	38	—	684
Johnson							
1964	1,542	349	520	43	42	—	588
1965	2,849	333	524	38	46	—	1,908
1966	4,683	295	583	37	53	—	3,672
1967	4,813	272	653	38	55	—	3,795
1968	5,306	273	594	35	78	—	4,326
Nixon							
1969	5,167	344	582	46	53	—	4,142
1970	4,742	311	633	75	59	32	3,632
1971	5,360	660	656	83	59	54	3,777
1972	5,639	596	703	81	70	57	4,132
1973	4,804	542	637	82	53	56	3,434
Nixon/Ford							
1974	5,751	583	688	85	42	61	4,292
Ford							
1975	1,910	625	699	89	40	61	422
1976	1,899	541	724	95	39	69	431

Carter							
1977	1,716	464	709	73	38	49	383
1978	1,613	371	602	74	33	49	484
1979	1,818	408	637	74	23	48	646
1980	1,886	406	616	69	35	49	711
Reagan							
1981	1,683	394	677	67	34	16	495
1982	1,596	366	612	60	40	12	506
1983	1,621	384	611	60	33	11	522
1984	1,595	374	603	64	29	13	512
1985	1,549	362	569	61	32	11	514
1986	1,519	363	543	67	33	11	502

Note: The Bureau of Budget moved to the executive office from the Treasury Department in 1939 and was reorganized and renamed the Office of Management and Budget in 1970. The National Security Council was created in 1947; the Council of Economic Advisers in 1946; the Council of Environmental Quality in 1969. The "All others" category includes personnel for Maintenance and Grounds, which ranges from sixty people in the 1930s to eighty people in the 1980s. Remaining employees have some tie to White House policy units.

[a]Includes war establishment units.

Sources: U.S. Department of Commerce, *Statistical Abstract* (1924-1987), U.S. Executive Office of the President, *Budget of the United States* (1924-1987), and U.S. Office of Personnel Management, *Federal Civilian Work Force Statistics* (1986).

Table 4.3 Average Expenditures for Selected Units in Executive Office of President, 1924-1986 (in thousands of current dollars)

President	Executive office total	White House Office	Bureau of Budget/OMB	National Security Council	Council of Economic Advisers	Council of Environmental Quality
Coolidge	501	391	—	—	—	—
Hoover	506	317	—	—	—	—
Roosevelt, I	403	264	—	—	—	—
Roosevelt, II	1,503	291	519	—	—	—
Roosevelt, III/IV	1,465,980	407	2,007	—	—	—
Truman, I	196,030	969	3,403	—	230	—
Truman, II	8,556	1,537	3,338	105	308	—
Eisenhower, I	9,226	2,121	3,398	203	277	—
Eisenhower, II	49,216	3,541	4,314	595	361	—
Kennedy	40,383	3,854	5,463	594	534	—
Johnson	26,120	3,882	7,888	619	693	—
Nixon, I	42,115	7,660	14,123	1,620	1,152	1,635
Nixon, II	57,614	11,458	19,491	2,485	1,462	2,334
Ford	86,024	15,792	23,457	2,907	1,522	2,958
Carter	80,733	17,309	29,632	3,246	1,956	3,750
Reagan [a]	99,737	20,863	35,973	3,860	2,124	699

Note: The Bureau of the Budget moved to the executive office from the Treasury Department in 1939 and was reorganized and renamed the Office of Management and Budget in 1970. The National Security Council was created in 1947, the Council of Economic Advisers in 1946, and the Council of Environmental Quality in 1969.

[a] 1981-1986.

Source: U.S. Executive Office of the President, *Budget of the United States* (1924-1987).

Table 4.4   Budget Allocations and Expenditures for White House Staff, 1924-1986 (in thousands of current dollars)

	Total executive office		White House Office	
	Appropriations	Expenditures	Appropriations	Expenditures
Coolidge				
1924	574	451	475	324
1925	657	412	558	311
1926	502	439	452	333
1927	819	613	709	496
1928	438	590	334	489
Hoover				
1929	437	487	335	360
1930	653	605	487	289
1931	425	507	290	331
1932	475	425	290	288
Roosevelt, I				
1933	392	369	267	255
1934	369	359	249	248
1935	442	458	268	279
1936	437	425	294	275
Roosevelt, II				
1937	515	502	294	278
1938	511	479	301	293
1939	2,531	2,371	304	287
1940	2,810	2,661	402	304
Roosevelt, III				
1941	3,896	10,219	396	343
1942	440,762	239,019	398	366
1943	1,722,539	1,646,903	399	416
1944	2,970,258	2,760,787	377	437
Roosevelt/Truman				
1945	1,223,701	2,672,974	429	473
Truman, I				
1946	657,022	446,364	418	507
1947	133,573	133,400	959	915
1948	6,692	8,327	1,028	1,486
Truman, II				
1949	9,948	7,997	1,245	1,271
1950	10,736	8,407	1,525	1,495
1951	9,339	8,710	1,736	1,587
1952	9,817	9,108	2,034	1,795

(Table continues)

211

Table 4.4 (continued)

	Total executive office		White House Office	
	Appropriations	Expenditures	Appropriations	Expenditures
Eisenhower, I				
1953	9,350	8,936	2,108	1,860
1954	9,395	9,493	1,950	1,780
1955	8,533	8,535	2,045	1,957
1956	10,395	9,938	3,283	2,885
Eisenhower, II				
1957	10,715	10,399	3,525	3,370
1958	51,029	75,074	3,583	3,535
1959	55,297	55,788	3,702	3,672
1960	63,140	55,604	2,521	3,585
Kennedy				
1961	71,780	69,042	3,906	3,864
1962	26,507	28,993	4,145	4,007
1963	23,601	23,113	4,195	3,691
Johnson				
1964	24,972	22,904	4,380	4,067
1965	26,444	24,018	4,380	4,112
1966	26,282	27,416	4,505	3,786
1967	29,307	27,767	4,605	3,671
1968	31,011	28,495	4,659	3,772
Nixon				
1969	32,066	30,889	4,924	4,577
1970	38,403	36,355	6,690	6,468
1971	49,958	47,127	10,109	8,623
1972	60,113	54,087	11,092	10,971
1973	93,369	49,164	11,517	11,635
Nixon/Ford				
1974	97,252	66,064	11,924	11,280
Ford				
1975	75,646	92,823	16,617	15,543
1976 [a]	69,258	79,224	17,013	16,041
Carter				
1977	78,149	73,387	17,412	17,236
1978	77,687	74,568	16,665	16,822
1979	81,763	79,590	17,413	16,159
1980	100,334	95,386	19,191	19,017

Table 4.4   (continued)

	Total executive office		White House Office	
	Appropriations	Expenditures	Appropriations	Expenditures
Reagan				
1981	103,121	95,635	21,528	21,078
1982	92,817	94,675	19,902	19,953
1983	101,371	94,186	22,115	20,766
1984	109,064	95,317	23,436	15,885
1985	115,715	111,261	25,439	24,306

Note: Figures for the White House Office include the salaries of the president and vice president. Figures for the total executive office include the budget for the White House mansion and grounds. All funds are those allocated and spent during the fiscal year ending June 30.

[a] Transition quarter excluded from figures for this year. In 1976 the beginning of the fiscal year was changed from July 1 to October 1. A transition quarter (July 1-September 30, 1976) was used. It belonged to neither fiscal 1976 nor fiscal 1977.

Source: U.S. Executive Office of the President, *Budget of the United States* (1924-1987).

Table 4.5 Budget Appropriations and Expenditures for Key Executive Office Units, 1939-1986 (in thousands of current dollars)

	Bureau of Budget/OMB		National Security Council		Council of Economic Advisers		Council of Environmental Quality	
	BA	E	BA	E	BA	E	BA	E
Roosevelt, II								
1939	481	397	—	—	—	—	—	—
1940	671	640	—	—	—	—	—	—
Roosevelt, III								
1941	836	945	—	—	—	—	—	—
1942	1,315	1,512	—	—	—	—	—	—
1943	1,982	2,126	—	—	—	—	—	—
1944	2,601	2,818	—	—	—	—	—	—
Roosevelt/Truman								
1945	2,956	2,633	—	—	—	—	—	—
Truman, I								
1946	3,037	3,278	—	—	—	—	—	—
1947	3,762	3,598	—	—	275	148	—	—
1948	3,377	3,334	—	52	350	311	—	—
Truman, II								
1949	3,281	3,261	200	113	310	319	—	—
1950	3,300	3,191	200	99	300	283	—	—
1951	3,377	3,225	160	121	300	286	—	—
1952	3,608	3,676	160	139	342	345	—	—
Eisenhower, I								
1953	3,461	3,442	155	154	225	243	—	—
1954	3,412	3,260	220	202	302	234	—	—
1955	3,889	3,310	215	204	341	304	—	—
1956	3,559	3,580	244	253	329	328	—	—
Eisenhower, II								
1957	3,935	3,853	248	252	366	340	—	—
1958	4,340	4,157	711	613	375	339	—	—
1959	4,551	4,615	759	767	393	383	—	—
1960	4,665	4,632	792	746	395	382	—	—
Kennedy								
1961	5,426	5,260	817	794	436	421	—	—
1962	5,517	5,304	554	503	584	506	—	—
1963	5,872	5,825	550	485	601	675	—	—
Johnson								
1964	6,500	6,636	575	515	615	613	—	—
1965	7,307	7,089	627	608	697	655	—	—
1966	8,104	7,627	738	731	675	613	—	—
1967	8,913	9,063	664	601	790	731	—	—
1968	9,500	9,024	664	639	858	854	—	—

Table 4.5 (continued)

	Bureau of Budget/OMB		National Security Council		Council of Economic Advisers		Council of Environmental Quality	
	BA	E	BA	E	BA	E	BA	E
Nixon								
1969	9,674	10,050	811	668	1,130	1,020	—	—
1970	11,676	12,141	1,860	1,418	1,187	1,188	350	—
1971	14,785	15,100	2,182	2,171	1,233	1,234	1,500	1,378
1972	18,311	19,200	2,424	2,221	2,112	1,166	2,300	1,891
1973	18,544	19,581	2,762	2,437	1,369	1,498	2,550	2,310
Nixon/Ford								
1974	18,271	19,400	2,802	2,532	1,414	1,425	2,466	2,358
Ford								
1975	21,735	21,910	2,900	2,621	1,600	1,468	2,500	2,735
1976 [a]	23,592	25,004	3,052	3,192	1,621	1,575	3,236	3,181
Carter								
1977	29,153	26,536	3,270	2,965	1,873	1,833	3,300	3,780
1978	30,371	29,299	3,315	3,039	2,018	2,024	2,854	1,267
1979	31,919	29,788	3,525	3,451	2,042	1,822	3,026	4,251
1980	33,431	32,907	3,645	3,527	2,102	2,145	3,126	5,702
Reagan								
1981	36,022	35,123	3,839	3,268	2,205	1,975	2,542	−906
1982	35,896	36,722	3,557	3,488	1,985	2,103	1,957	936
1983	34,987	32,531	4,064	3,852	2,177	2,048	926	827
1984	37,311	34,987	4,497	3,864	2,464	2,144	1,475	348
1985	38,852	39,754	4,605	4,454	2,560	2,170	700	1,830
1986	37,237	36,810	4,428	4,235	2,202	2,306	670	1,159

Note: The Bureau of the Budget was moved to the White House from the Treasury Department in 1939. It was reorganized and renamed the Office of Management and Budget in 1970. The Council of Economic Advisers was designated in 1946, with funding beginning in 1947. The National Security Council, authorized in 1947, did not expend funds until 1948. The Council of Environmental Quality began in 1970. BA = budget appropriations. E = expenditures.

[a] Transition quarter excluded from figures for the year. In 1976 the beginning of the fiscal year was changed from July 1 to October 1. A transition quarter (July 1-September 30, 1976) was used. It belonged to neither fiscal 1976 nor fiscal 1977.

Source: U.S. Executive Office of the President, *Budget of the United States* (1924-1987).

Figure 4.1 Expansion of Key White House Units by President (thousands of constant 1967 dollars)

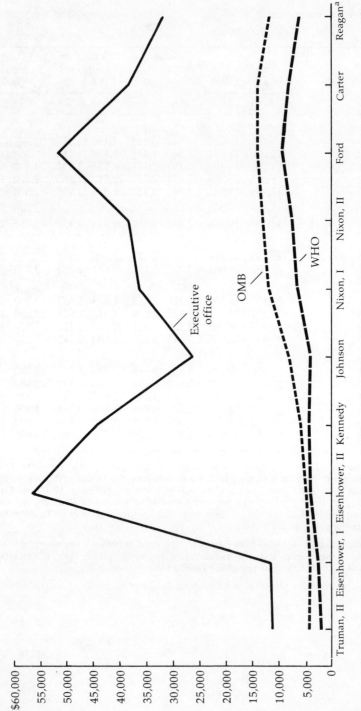

Note: OMB = Office of Management and Budget. WHO = White House Office.

[a] 1981-1986.

Source: Adapted from Table 4.3.

Table 4.6 Federal Budget Receipts and Outlays, 1924-1986 (in billions of current dollars)

Year	Receipts	Outlays	Surplus or deficit
1924	3.9	2.9	1.0
1925	3.6	2.9	0.7
1926	3.8	2.9	0.9
1927	4.0	2.8	1.2
1928	3.9	3.0	0.9
1929	3.8	2.9	0.9
1930	4.0	3.1	0.9
1931	3.2	4.1	−1.0
1932	2.0	4.8	−2.7
1933	2.1	4.7	−2.6
1934	3.1	6.5	−3.3
1935	3.8	6.3	−2.4
1936	4.2	7.6	−3.5
1937	5.6	8.4	−2.8
1938	7.0	7.2	−0.1
1939	6.6	9.4	−2.9
1940	6.9	9.6	−2.7
1941	9.2	14.0	−4.8
1942	15.1	34.5	−19.4
1943	25.1	78.9	−53.8
1944	47.8	94.0	−46.1
1945	50.2	95.2	−45.0
1946	43.5	61.7	−18.2
1947	43.5	36.9	6.6
1948	45.4	36.5	8.9
1949	41.6	40.6	1.0
1950	40.9	43.1	−2.2
1951	53.4	45.8	7.6
1952	68.0	68.0	a
1953	71.5	76.8	−5.3
1954	69.7	70.9	−1.2
1955	65.5	68.5	−3.0
1956	74.5	70.5	4.1
1957	80.0	76.7	3.2
1958	79.6	82.6	−2.9
1959	79.2	92.1	−12.9
1960	92.5	92.2	0.3
1961	94.4	97.8	−3.4
1962	99.7	106.8	−7.1
1963	106.6	111.3	−4.8
1964	112.7	118.6	−5.9
1965	116.8	118.4	−1.6
1966	130.9	134.7	−3.8

(Table continues)

217

Table 4.6 (continued)

Year	Receipts	Outlays	Surplus or deficit
1967	149.6	158.3	−8.7
1968	153.7	178.8	−25.2
1969	187.8	184.5	3.2
1970	193.7	196.6	−2.8
1971	187.1	210.2	−23.0
1972	207.3	230.7	−23.4
1973	230.8	245.7	−14.9
1974	263.2	269.4	−6.1
1975	279.2	332.3	−63.2
1976	298.1	371.8	−73.7
1976 [b]	81.2	96.0	−14.7
1977	355.6	409.2	−53.6
1978	399.7	458.7	−59.0
1979	463.3	503.5	−40.2
1980	517.1	590.9	−78.9
1981	599.3	678.2	−127.9
1982	617.8	745.7	−207.8
1983	600.6	808.3	−185.3
1984	666.5	851.8	−222.2
1985	734.1	946.3	−212.3
1986	769.1	989.8	−220.7

[a] Less than $50 million.

[b] Transition quarter. In 1976 the beginning of the fiscal year was changed from July 1 to October 1. A transition quarter (July 1-September 30, 1976) was used. It belonged to neither fiscal 1976 nor fiscal 1977.

Sources: 1929-1970, U.S. Department of Commerce, *U.S. Historical Statistics* (1971, pt. 2, 1105); 1971-1984, U.S. Department of Commerce, *Statistical Abstract* (1986, 305); 1985-1986, U.S. Executive Office of the President, *Budget of the United States* (1987).

Table 4.7   Units in the Executive Office of the President, 1939-Present

Unit	President	Duration
White House Office [a]	Roosevelt	1939-
Council on Personnel Administration	Roosevelt	1939-1940
Office of Government Reports	Roosevelt	1939-1942
Liaison Office for Personnel Management	Roosevelt	1939-1943
National Resources Planning Board	Roosevelt	1939-1943
Bureau of the Budget [a]	Roosevelt	1939-1970
Office of Emergency Management	Roosevelt	1940-1954
Committee for Congested Production Areas	Roosevelt	1943-1944
War Refugee Board	Roosevelt	1944-1945
Council of Economic Advisers	Truman	1946-
National Security Council	Truman	1947-
National Security Resources Board	Truman	1947-1953
Telecommunications Adviser to the President	Truman	1951-1953
Office of Director of Mutual Security	Truman	1951-1954
Office of Defense Mobilization	Truman	1952-1959
Permanent Advisory Committee on Government Organizations	Truman	1953-1961
Operations Coordinating Board	Truman	1953-1961
President's Board of Consultants on Foreign Intelligence Activities	Eisenhower	1956-1961
Office of Civil and Defense Mobilization	Eisenhower	1958-1962
National Aeronautics and Space Council	Eisenhower	1958-1973
President's Foreign Intelligence Advisory Board	Kennedy	1961-1977
Office of Emergency Planning	Kennedy	1962-1969
Office of Science and Technology	Kennedy	1962-1973
Office of Special Representative for Trade Negotiations	Kennedy	1963-
Office of Economic Opportunity	Johnson	1964-1975
Office of Emergency Preparedness	Johnson	1965-1973
National Council on Marine Resources and Engineering Development	Johnson	1966-1971
Council on Environmental Quality	Nixon	1969-
Council for Urban Affairs	Nixon	1969-1970
Office of Intergovernmental Relations	Nixon	1969-1973
Domestic Policy Council/Domestic Policy Staff [b]	Nixon	1970-1978
Office of Management and Budget	Nixon	1970-
Office of Telecommunications Policy	Nixon	1970-1977
Council on International Economic Policy	Nixon	1971-1977
Office of Consumer Affairs	Nixon	1971-1973
Special Action Office for Drug Abuse Prevention	Nixon	1971-1975
Federal Property Council	Nixon	1973-1977
Council on Economic Policy	Nixon	1973-1974
Energy Policy Office	Nixon	1973-1974
Council on Wage and Price Stability	Nixon	1974-1981

(Table continues)

Table 4.7 (continued)

Unit	President	Duration
Energy Resource Council	Nixon	1974-1977
Office of Science and Technology Policy	Ford	1976-
Intelligence Oversight Board	Ford	1976-
Office of Administration	Carter	1977-
Office of Drug Abuse Policy	Carter	1977-
Office of Policy Development	Carter	1978-
Office of Private Sector Initiatives	Reagan	1981-

Note: This list does not include short-term advisory commissions, study councils, and cabinet-level coordinating committees. Also excluded is the Central Intelligence Agency, which since 1947 has been formally part of the Executive Office of the President but in practice operates as an independent agency.

[a] Unit currently in operation as Office of Management and Budget.
[b] Unit currently in operation as Office of Policy Development.

Source: Adapted from Cronin (1980, 386), updated by the authors.

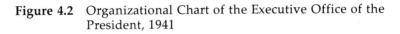

Figure 4.2   Organizational Chart of the Executive Office of the
President, 1941

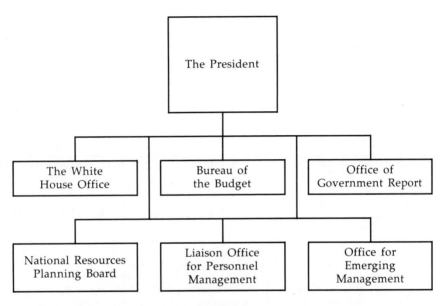

Source: United States Government Manual (1941, 592).

Figure 4.3   Organizational Chart of the Executive Office of the President, 1959

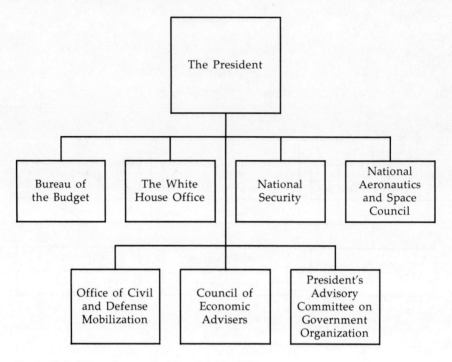

Source: *United States Government Manual* (1959, 593).

Figure 4.4   Organizational Chart of the Executive Office of the President, 1965

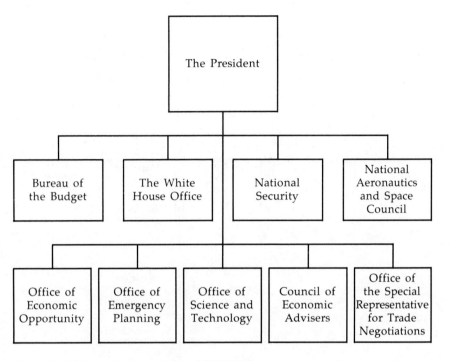

Source: United States Government Manual (1965, 595).

Figure 4.5 Organizational Chart of the Executive Office of the President, 1972

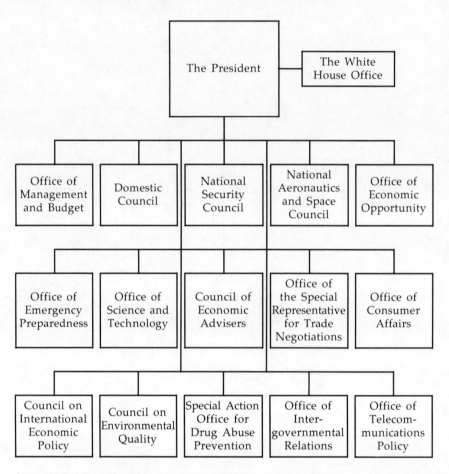

Source: United States Government Manual (1972, 68).

Figure 4.6 Organizational Chart of the Executive Office of the President, 1986

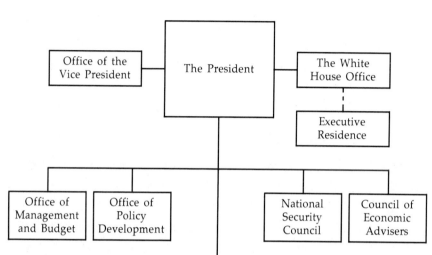

Source: *United States Government Manual* (1986, 847).

Table 4.8 Relative Importance of White House Units and External Groups, as Defined by White House Staff

	Grand mean of ratings by other units[a]	
Unit/group	Carter	Reagan
President	79.0	79.0
Office of Management and Budget	42.3	55.3
National Security Council	52.2	54.9
Legislation Liaison office	47.7	47.1
Domestic Policy Staff/OPD[b]	46.0	36.6
Council of Economic Advisers	34.5	26.1
Press Secretary's Office	29.9	25.8
Public Liaison Office	18.2	14.3
Cabinet	47.0	58.2
Members of Congress	42.6	33.8
Reporters	4.3	16.3
Interest groups	9.4	13.9

Note: Assessed by the importance of a hypothetical recommendation from the unit or group using a five-point scale ranging from "extremely important" to "no importance."

[a] Grand mean of the mean ratings given each unit by all other units. Excludes ratings by a unit of its own importance. Based on interviews of Carter's senior staff members who served from 1977 to 1980 and Reagan's senior staff members who served between 1981 and 1983.

[b] Domestic Policy Staff for Carter, until 1978, then renamed Office of Policy Development.

Sources: Kessel (1984b, 247, 248, 250; 1983, 456).

Table 4.9 Office of Management and Budget Review of Agency Rules, 1981-1985

OMB decision[a]	1981	1982	1983	1984	1985
Consistent without change					
Number	2,447	2,214	2,044	1,641	1,564
Percentage	87.1	84.1	82.3	78.0	70.7
Consistent with change					
Number	136	271	316	319	510
Percentage	4.9	10.3	12.7	15.2	23.1
Withdrawn by agency					
Number	50	32	40	52	69
Percentage	1.8	1.2	1.6	2.5	3.1
Returned for consideration					
Number	133	79	32	57	41
Percentage	4.7	3.0	1.3	2.7	1.8
Emergency, statutory, or judicial deadline					
Number	39	37	50	35	17
Percentage	1.4	1.4	2.0	1.7	1.2
Total regulations	2,803	2,633	2,482	2,104	2,211

[a] OMB decides whether a particular rule is consistent with Executive Order 12291. The order mandates that all agencies and departments must supply proper justification of the cost and necessity for their rules.

Source: U.S. Executive Office of the President, *Regulatory Programs* (1987).

Table 4.10 Ideological Closeness of Three White House Staffs

Policy area	Nixon	Carter	Reagan
International involvement	3.4	4.1	2.7
Economic management	2.0	3.1	1.3
Social welfare	3.3	3.6	1.9
Civil liberties	2.2	5.1	1.4
Agriculture	2.8	4.0	2.1

Note: Median issue positions were based on scores ranging from 1.0 (conservative position) to 7.0 (liberal position). Results were obtained from interviews of Nixon's domestic policy council, Carter's senior staff members serving from 1977 to 1980, and Reagan's senior staff members serving between 1981 and 1983.

Source: Kessel (1984b, 234).

Table 4.11 Influence Exerted by White House Aides, Carter and Reagan

Unit	Carter head	Overall influence score	Reagan head	Influence score
National Security Council	Brzezinski	136	Clark	268 [a]
Legislative Liaison	Moore	15 [a]	Duberstein	125
Domestic Policy Staff/OPD	Eizenstat	343	Harper	169
OMB	McIntyre	90	Stockman	262 [a]
Council of Economic Advisers	Schultze	102	Weidenbaum	1
Press Office	Powell	251	Gergen	84
Public Liaison	Wexler	138	Dole	0

Note: Influence evaluated in answers to questions regarding the respect, expertise, position, and sanctions that individuals have in the eyes of other staff. Drawn from interviews of Carter's senior staff members who served from 1977 to 1980 and Reagan's senior staff members who served between 1981 and 1983.

[a] Estimated values. Questions on influence were not asked of the individual, and so scores are based on the answers of others.

Source: Kessel (1984b, 250).

Table 4.12 Size of Federal Executive Bureaucracy for Selected Years

Executive department	Year established	Paid civilian employees		
		1980	1984	1986
Agriculture	1889	126,139	118,809	111,927
Commerce [a]	1913	48,563	35,217	35,408
Defense [b]	1947	960,116	1,043,784	1,087,893
Education	1980	7,364	5,343	4,680
Energy	1977	21,557	16,976	16,674
Health and Human Services [c]	1980	155,662	144,240	136,318
Housing and Urban Development	1965	16,964	12,393	11,545
Interior	1849	77,357	78,661	76,232
Justice	1870	56,327	61,398	65,285
Labor	1913	23,400	18,320	17,841
State	1789	23,497	24,706	25,482
Transportation	1966	72,361	62,781	61,348
Treasury	1789	124,663	130,654	140,669
Total	—	1,713,970	1,753,282	1,791,302

[a] Originally the Department of Commerce and Labor, established in 1903 and split in 1913.
[b] Originally the Department of War, established in 1789.
[c] Originally the Department of Health, Education, and Welfare, established in 1953.

Sources: For 1980 and 1984, U.S. Department of Commerce, *Statistical Abstract* (1987); for 1986, U.S. Office of Personnel Management, *Federal Civilian Work Force Statistics* (1986).

Table 4.13 Size of Independent Federal Agencies for Selected Years

Agency	Paid civilian employees		
	1980	1984	1986
ACTION	1,837	507	490
American Battle Monuments Commission	386	390	396
Board of Governors, Federal Reserve System	1,498	1,607	1,510
Civil Aeronautics Board	734	357	[a]
Commission on Civil Rights	304	257	204
Environmental Protection Agency	14,715	13,048	14,081
Equal Employment Opportunity Commission	3,515	3,168	3,156
Export-Import Bank	385	364	340
Farm Credit Administration	271	296	340
Federal Communications Commission	2,244	2,027	1,835
Federal Deposit Insurance Corporation	3,520	4,607	8,408
Federal Emergency Management Agency	3,427	2,691	2,537
Federal Home Loan Bank Board	1,470	1,497	786
Federal Labor Relations Authority	349	323	278
Federal Mediation and Conciliation Service	503	350	331
Federal Trade Commission	1,846	1,318	1,129
General Services Administration	37,654	29,681	24,842
International Trade Commission	424	458	520
Interstate Commerce Commission	1,998	1,071	809
National Aeronautics and Space Administration	23,714	22,085	21,911
National Endowment for the Arts	362	554	276
National Labor Relations Board	2,936	2,720	2,437
National Science Foundation	1,394	1,236	1,170
National Transportation Safety Board	384	348	344
Nuclear Regulatory Commission	3,283	3,678	3,587
Office of Personnel Management	8,280	6,553	6,120
Panama Canal Commission	8,700	8,078	8,292
Railroad Retirement Board	1,795	1,578	1,619
Securities and Exchange Commission	2,056	1,959	1,905
Selective Service System	97	338	290
Small Business Administration	5,804	5,093	5,092
Smithsonian Institution	4,403	4,690	4,797
Tennessee Valley Authority	51,714	33,589	30,680
U.S. Postal Service	660,014	682,653	791,685
Veterans Administration	228,285	239,923	243,833
All other	20,062	18,170	24,447
Total	1,100,363	1,097,262	1,210,477

[a] Board was disbanded December 31, 1984.

Sources: For 1980 and 1984, U.S. Department of Commerce, *Statistical Abstract* (1987); for 1986, U.S. Office of Personnel Management, *Federal Civilian Work Force Statistics* (1986).

Table 4.14 Total Executive Nominations Submitted for Senate Confirmation

	Presidential action			Senate action	
	Submitted	Rejected	Withdrawn	Unconfirmed [a]	Confirmed
Truman, II					
1949	55,311	2	39	401	54,869
1950	25,699	4	6	99	25,590
1951	20,636	0	5	196	20,435
1952	26,284	2	40	173	26,069
Eisenhower, I					
1953	23,542	0	31	92	23,419
1954	45,916	0	12	761	45,143
1955	40,686	3	15	771	39,897
1956	43,487	0	23	667	42,797
Eisenhower, II					
1957	45,114	0	33	416	44,620
1958	59,079	0	21	367	58,691
1959	46,934	1	6	556	46,371
1960	44,542	0	22	992	43,528
Kennedy					
1961	50,770	0	1,271	538	48,961
1962	52,079	0	8	291	51,780
1963	67,456	0	21	832	66,603
Johnson					
1964	54,734	0	15	1,121	53,598
1965	55,765	0	13	1,176	54,576
1966	67,254	0	160	805	66,289
1967	69,254	0	19	153	69,082
1968	50,977	0	15	1,813	49,149
Nixon					
1969	73,159	1	477	46	72,635
1970	61,305	1	10	132	61,162
1971	50,499	0	6	1,638	48,855
1972	66,554	0	5	495	66,054
1973	68,080	0	10	1,253	66,817
Nixon/Ford					
1974	66,304	0	4/46 [b]	1,816	64,437
Ford					
1975	75,039	0	6/236 [b]	3,521	71,276
1976	60,263	0	15	146	60,102

Table 4.14   (continued)

	Presidential action			Senate action	
	Submitted	Rejected	Withdrawn	Unconfirmed [a]	Confirmed
Carter					
1977	74,659	0	61	8,967	65,631
1978	62,850	0	5	3,746	59,099
1979	86,212	0	8	1,345	84,859
1980	69,929	0	10	113	69,806
Reagan					
1981	106,620	0	33	1,295/8 [b]	105,284
1982	79,648	0	22	47/7 [b]	79,562
1983	56,041	0	2	26/477 [b]	55,536
1984	41,852	0	2	107	41,743
1985	59,643	0	8	3,677/34 [b]	55,918
1986	39,971	0	8	70	39,893

[a] Those nominations not acted upon before Senate adjournment and carried over to the next session.
[b] Second figure indicates number of nominations that failed confirmation at adjournment under Senate rules. No final action was taken on the nominations, and they were not carried over to the next session.

Source: Successive volumes of U.S. Congress, *Executive Proceedings of the Senate.*

Table 4.15 Presidential Appointments Confirmed by Senate, 1961-1984

	Executive office	Cabinet departments	Ambassadors	Independent agencies	Federal judges[a]	Total
Kennedy						
1961	6	120	12	51	60	249
1962	8	49	12	30	54	153
1963	6	31	13	45	15	110
Total	20	200	37	126	129	512
Johnson						
1964	5	28	10	24	18	85
1965	11	69	20	40	29	169
1966	10	46	22	29	60	167
1967	5	56	21	30	36	148
1968	4	37	20	46	24	131
Total	35	236	93	169	167	700
Nixon						
1969	10	160	51	48	27	296
1970	7	28	8	27	65	135
1971	7	38	4	42	63	154
1972	2	36	8	20	25	91
1973	5	109	21	39	22	196
1974	1	38	9	18	17	83
Total	32	409	101	194	219	955
Ford						
1974	3	16	6	20	17	62
1975	4	73	18	55	17	167
1976	4	52	9	36	31	132
Total	11	141	33	111	65	361
Carter						
1977	16	177	37	63	26	319
1978	4	53	16	46	39	158
1979	7	59	29	35	128	258
1980	2	48	5	23	64	142
Total	29	337	87	167	257	877
Reagan						
1981	13	180	28	75	41	337
1982	4	31	9	56	37	137
1983	3	51	13	39	30	136
1984	3	40	6	24	37	110
Total	23	302	56	194	145	720

[a] Includes only appointments to Supreme Court, circuit courts, and district courts.

Source: Successive volumes of *Congressional Quarterly Almanac.*

Table 4.16   Supreme Court Nominees with Senate Problems

	Nominee	Action
Washington		
1793	William Paterson	Withdrawn
1795	John Rutledge	Rejected
Madison		
1811	Alexander Wolcott	Rejected
John Adams		
1828	John J. Critinden	Postponed
Jackson		
1835	Roger B. Taney	Postponed
Tyler		
1844	John C. Spencer	Rejected
1844	R. H. Walworth	Withdrawn
1844	Edward B. King	Withdrawn
1844	R. H. Walworth	Withdrawn
1845	John M. Read	Postponed
Polk		
1846	G. W. Woodward	Rejected
Fillmore		
1852	Edward A. Bradford	Postponed
1853	George E. Badger	Postponed
1853	William C. Micou	Postponed
Buchanan		
1861	Jeremiah S. Black	Rejected
A. Johnson		
1866	Henry Stanbery	Postponed
Grant		
1870	Ebenezer R. Hoar	Rejected
1874	George H. Williams	Withdrawn
1874	Caleb Cushing	Withdrawn
Hayes		
1881	Stanley Mattheys	Postponed
Cleveland		
1894	W. B. Hornblower	Rejected
1894	W. H. Peckham	Rejected
Hoover		
1930	John J. Parker	Rejected
L. Johnson		
1968	Abe Fortas[a]	Withdrawn
1968	Homer Thornberry	Withdrawn

(Table continues)

233

Table 4.16 (continued)

	Nominee	Action
Nixon		
1969	Clement F. Haynsworth	Rejected
1970	G. Harrold Carswell	Rejected
Reagan		
1987	Robert H. Bork	Rejected
1987	Douglas H. Ginsburg	Withdrawn

[a] Associate justice nominated for chief justice.

Source: Adapted from *Congressional Quarterly's Guide to the Supreme Court* (1979, 946-948).

Table 4.17 Presidential Appointees from President's Party (percent)

Department	Kennedy	Johnson	Nixon	Ford	Carter[a]	Reagan
Agriculture	77	80	81	100	92	94
Commerce	71	65	82	64	71	100
Defense	48	32	56	52	45	78
Education	—	—	—	—	—	82
Energy	—	—	—	—	59	94
Health, Education, Welfare/ Health and Human Services	73	53	66	45	56	88
Housing and Urban Development	—	86	78	100	92	94
Interior	54	50	86	100	45	93
Justice	68	65	68	80	38	100
Labor	100	75	80	50	62	53
Post Office	100	78	56	—	—	—
State[b]	64	34	51	31	39	69
Transportation	—	27	70	70	77	96
Treasury	55	67	79	43	72	90
Executive Office of the President	63	43	68	82	60	87

Note: Major appointments as listed by *Congressional Quarterly Almanac,* including cabinet, subcabinet, and lower-level policy positions.

[a] Carter figures for 1977-1978 only. *Congressional Quarterly Almanac* did not report the party affiliation for most of the appointees in 1979 and 1980.
[b] Includes ambassadors.

Sources: Kennedy-Carter adapted from Brown (1982). Reagan (1981-1984) calculated by the authors from *Congressional Quarterly Almanac.*

Table 4.18 Partisanship and Federal Judgeships

President	Appointees from president's party		Appointees from other party		Total appointees
	%	No.	%	No.	
Roosevelt	96.9	188	3.1	6	194
Truman	92.8	116	7.2	9	125
Eisenhower	94.8	165	5.2	9	174
Kennedy	91.0	111	9.0	11	122
Johnson	94.6	159	5.4	9	168
Nixon	93.0	198	7.0	15	213
Ford	81.3	52	18.7	12	64
Carter	95.2	240	4.8	12	252
Reagan [a]	96.7	118	3.3	4	122

Note: Includes U.S. Circuit Court and U.S. District Court posts only.

[a] 1981-1984.

Sources: For Roosevelt-Ford, *Congressional Quarterly Almanac* (1976). For Carter and Reagan, figures adapted from Goldman (1985, 319, 325).

Table 4.19 Legacy of Presidents' Judicial Appointments

President	Judges appointed [a]	Judges still serving	
		No.	%
Roosevelt	194	7	3.6
Truman	136	26	19.1
Eisenhower	170	68	40.0
Kennedy	129	72	55.8
Johnson	156	124	79.5
Nixon	226	164	72.6
Ford	60	48	80.0
Carter	258	238	92.2
Reagan [b]	201	175	87.0

[a] Figures for U.S. Supreme Court, Circuit Court, and District Court appointments.
[b] Appointments as of September 5, 1985.

Source: Congressional Quarterly Weekly Report (September 7, 1985, 1760).

Table 4.20 Sex, Race, and Ethnicity of Major Presidential Appointments by Carter and Reagan

Race/ethnicity	Carter				Reagan[a]			
	Female	Male	Total	%	Female	Male	Total	%
White	116	862	978	82.8	66	834	900	91.8
Black	22	122	144	12.2	6	34	40	4.1
Hispanic	4	45	49	4.1	5	32	37	3.8
American Indian	0	4	4	0.3	0	0	0	0.0
Asian	1	6	7	0.6	1	2	3	0.3
Total	143	1,039	1,182	—	78	902	980	—
Percentage	12.1	87.9	—	—	8.0	92.0	—	—

Note: All full-time appointments of department secretaries, undersecretaries, assistant secretaries, heads of other executive branch agencies, U.S. attorneys, judges, and ambassadors, including those who were appointed to but left positions to which they were appointed before the end of period. Data exclude White House staff appointments.

[a] January 20, 1981-April 20, 1983.

Source: U.S. Commission on Civil Rights (1983, 5-6).

Table 4.21 Appointments of Women and Minorities to Executive Departments by Carter and Reagan

Department	Carter					Reagan				
	Total	Women		Minorities		Total	Women		Minorities	
		No.	%	No.	%		No.	%	No.	%
Agriculture	12	1	8.3	1	8.3	16	1	6.3	0	0.0
Commerce	23	4	17.4	0	0.0	28	1	3.6	1	3.6
Defense	27	1	3.7	4	14.8	34	0	0.0	0	0.0
Education	18	8	44.4	4	22.2	26	3	11.5	6	23.1
Energy	17	3	17.6	3	17.6	22	2	9.1	1	4.5
Health and Human Services	18	3	16.7	4	22.2	28	5	27.8	3	16.7
Housing and Urban Development	10	1	10.0	3	30.0	13	1	7.7	2	15.4
Interior	17	2	11.8	4	23.5	18	1	5.6	2	11.1
Justice [a]	188	5	2.7	36	19.1	193	4	2.1	13	6.7
Labor	12	4	33.3	2	16.7	13	1	7.7	1	7.7
Transportation	14	2	14.3	3	21.4	16	2	12.5	1	6.3
Treasury	21	4	19.0	4	19.0	23	5	21.7	1	4.3
State	24	3	12.5	2	8.3	41	1	2.4	0	0.0
Ambassadors	159	12	7.5	14	8.8	125	7	5.6	10	8.0
Total	392	49	12.5	53	13.5 [b]	412	31	7.5	29	7.0 [c]

Note: All full-time appointments, including any pending appointments, incumbents, and appointees who have left their positions from January 20, 1977-April 20, 1983.

[a] Includes appointments of U.S. attorneys and U.S. marshals.

[b] For Carter five of the minority appointees were also women (all were black).

[c] Five of Reagan's minority appointees were also women (four black, one Asian).

Source: U.S. Commission on Civil Rights (1983, 8-9, 14-17).

Table 4.22 Characteristics of District Court Appointees (percent)

Characteristics	Johnson	Nixon	Ford	Carter	Reagan
Race					
White	93.4	95.5	88.5	78.7	93.0
Black	4.1	3.4	5.8	13.9	0.8
Hispanic	2.5	1.1	1.9	6.9	5.4
Asian	—	—	3.9	0.5	0.8
Sex					
Male	98.4	99.4	98.1	85.6	90.7
Female	1.6	0.6	1.9	14.4	9.3
Religious background					
Protestant	58.2	73.2	73.1	60.4	61.2
Catholic	31.1	18.4	17.3	27.2	31.8
Jewish	10.7	8.4	9.6	12.4	6.9
Party					
Democratic	94.3	7.2	21.2	94.1	3.3
Republican	5.7	92.8	78.8	4.5	96.9
Independent	—	—	—	1.5	—
Law school education					
Public institution	40.2	41.9	44.2	50.5	34.1
Private (non-Ivy)	36.9	36.9	38.5	32.2	49.6
Ivy League	21.3	21.2	17.3	17.3	16.3
Experience					
Judicial	34.3	35.1	42.3	54.5	50.4
Prosecutorial	45.8	41.9	50.0	38.6	43.4
Neither	33.6	36.3	30.8	28.2	28.7
Occupation					
Politics/government	21.3	10.6	21.2	4.4	7.8
Judiciary	31.1	28.5	34.6	44.6	40.3
Law firm	44.3	58.2	44.3	47.7	52.0
Professor of law	3.3	2.8	—	3.0	2.3
Other	—	—	—	0.5	1.6
Total appointees	122	179	52	202	129

Sources: Adapted from Goldman (1985, 318-319).

Table 4.23   Characteristics of Circuit Court Appointees (percent)

Characteristics	Johnson	Nixon	Ford	Carter	Reagan
Race					
White	95.0	97.8	100.0	78.6	93.5
Black	5.0	—	—	16.1	3.2
Hispanic	—	—	—	3.6	3.2
Asian	—	2.2	—	1.8	—
Sex					
Male	97.5	100.0	100.0	80.4	96.8
Female	2.5	—	—	19.6	3.2
Religious background					
Protestant	60.0	75.6	58.3	60.7	67.7
Catholic	25.0	15.6	33.3	23.7	22.6
Jewish	15.7	8.9	8.3	16.1	9.7
Party					
Democratic	95.0	6.7	8.3	89.3	—
Republican	5.0	93.3	91.7	5.4	100.0
Independent	—	—	—	5.4	—
Law school education					
Public institution	40.0	37.8	50.0	39.3	29.0
Private (non-Ivy)	32.5	26.7	25.0	19.6	45.2
Ivy League	27.5	35.6	25.0	41.1	25.8
Experience					
Judicial	65.0	57.8	75.0	53.6	70.9
Prosecutorial	47.5	46.7	25.0	32.1	19.3
Neither	20.0	17.8	25.0	37.5	25.8
Occupation					
Politics/government	10.0	4.4	8.3	5.4	3.2
Judiciary	57.5	53.3	75.0	46.4	61.3
Law firm	30.0	35.5	16.6	32.3	19.4
Professor of law	—	6.7	—	14.3	16.1
Other	—	—	—	1.8	—
Total appointees	40	45	12	56	31

Source: Adapted from Goldman (1985, 324-325).

Table 4.24 Educational Background of Major Cabinet and Diplomatic Appointees, 1789-1980 (percent)

Period	No college	Some college	Harvard, Yale, Princeton	Ivy League	Other private	Public	College abroad	Total who completed college
1789-1800	13.1	13.1	43.5	4.3	4.3	—	21.7	73.8
1801-1828	27.7	12.8	40.3	6.4	4.3	—	8.5	59.5
1829-1840	34.6	11.5	23.2	11.5	15.4	3.8	—	53.9
1841-1860	20.8	5.6	15.3	9.7	29.2	19.4	—	73.6
1861-1876	21.8	12.7	27.3	7.3	23.6	7.3	—	65.5
1877-1896	30.0	12.9	25.6	4.3	18.6	8.6	—	57.1
1897-1912	19.0	8.6	27.6	5.2	34.4	5.2	—	72.4
1913-1920	20.8	25.0	—	4.2	41.6	8.4	—	64.2
1921-1932	16.0	14.0	12.0	6.0	20.0	28.0	4.0	70.0
1933-1940	—	20.0	25.0	—	45.0	10.0	—	80.0
1941-1952	10.4	17.2	19.0	5.2	25.8	22.4	—	72.4
1953-1960	10.0	5.0	42.5	5.0	15.0	22.5	—	85.0
1961-1968	—	3.1	35.4	4.6	16.9	40.0	—	96.9
1969-1976	4.7	4.7	34.4	4.7	34.4	17.1	—	90.6
1977-1980	—	19.2	15.4	7.7	30.8	26.9	—	80.8

Source: Burch (1980, 3:366-367).

Table 4.25 Occupational Background of Major Cabinet and Diplomatic Appointees, 1789-1980

	Landowner, farmer, speculator	Lawyer and landowner	Lawyer	Big business	Small business	Government service	Other
Washington	2	5	4	2	—	—	1
J. Adams	—	3	3	2	—	—	1
Jefferson	2	3	5	1	—	—	1
Madison	2	3	6	3	—	—	2
Monroe	—	2	6	2	—	—	—
J. Q. Adams	—	2	5	2	1	—	—
Jackson	1	3	11	—	—	—	—
Van Buren	1	1	7	—	—	—	1
W. Harrison	—	—	5	—	—	—	—
Tyler	1	2	9	1	—	—	2
Polk	—	2	6	1	—	—	1
Taylor	—	1	6	1	—	—	—
Fillmore	1	1	8	1	—	—	1
Pierce	1	1	7	—	—	—	—
Buchanan	—	2	10	1	—	—	2
Lincoln	—	—	10	1	—	—	4
A. Johnson	—	—	9	1	—	4	4
Grant	—	—	17	4	—	1	2
Hayes	—	—	8	1	—	—	4
Garfield	—	—	5	—	—	1	—
Arthur	—	—	8	3	—	—	1
Cleveland	—	—	11	1	—	—	—
B. Harrison	—	—	6	5	1	1	1
Cleveland	—	—	9	2	—	—	2
McKinley	—	—	8	5	—	—	3

(Table continues)

Table 4.25 (continued)

	Landowner, farmer, speculator	Lawyer and landowner	Lawyer	Big business	Small business	Government service	Other
T. Roosevelt	—	—	10	8	—	3	5
Taft	—	—	7	5	—	—	3
Wilson	—	—	12	6	—	—	6
Harding	—	—	3	7	—	—	3
Coolidge	—	—	7	8	—	1	4
Hoover	—	—	5	8	—	—	4
F. Roosevelt	—	1	12	10	1	5	10
Truman	—	—	18	11	1	11	2
Eisenhower	—	—	5	20	4	4	7
Kennedy	—	—	11	4	—	9	3
L. Johnson	—	—	14	6	2	9	8
Nixon	—	—	10	13	1	8	7
Ford	1	—	5	5	1	4	8
Carter	1	—	5	5	1	8	6

Source: Burch (1980, 3:374-375).

Table 4.26 Geographic Background of Major Cabinet and Diplomatic Appointees, 1789-1980 (percent)

Period	Massachusetts	Other New England states	New Jersey	New York	Pennsylvania	Virginia	Other southern states	East, north, central	Midwest	Rocky Mountain	Pacific coast	District of Columbia
1789-1800	15.4	7.2	—	11.5	15.4	26.9	23.1	—	—	—	—	—
1801-1828	12.7	1.8	3.6	14.5	20.0	14.5	32.7	—	—	—	—	—
1829-1840	—	9.1	6.1	15.1	9.1	9.1	42.4	9.1	—	—	—	—
1841-1860	14.5	3.9	—	6.6	17.1	17.1	34.2	6.6	—	—	—	—
1861-1876	10.4	6.9	3.4	19.0	8.6	—	8.6	29.3	5.2	—	1.7	6.9
1877-1896	9.9	7.0	2.8	18.3	5.6	—	16.9	22.5	14.2	1.4	1.4	—
1897-1912	7.9	—	1.6	34.9	7.9	—	4.8	25.4	11.1	—	6.3	—
1913-1920	—	—	4.0	20.0	8.0	4.0	16.0	16.0	20.0	—	8.0	4.0
1921-1932	7.4	1.9	1.9	20.4	13.0	—	5.6	22.2	14.9	5.6	7.4	—
1933-1940	—	5.0	5.0	30.0	5.0	—	15.0	15.0	10.0	5.0	—	10.0
1941-1952	1.5	6.1	—	33.3	3.0	—	15.2	9.1	7.6	4.5	3.0	10.0
1953-1960	7.1	—	—	42.9	4.8	—	7.1	19.0	2.4	2.4	4.8	16.7
1961-1968	10.4	1.5	1.5	23.9	—	—	13.4	13.4	3.0	3.0	1.5	28.4
1969-1976	12.9	—	—	17.1	4.3	—	14.3	20.0	4.3	2.9	12.9	11.4
1977-1980	—	7.4	—	7.4	—	—	22.2	11.1	3.7	3.7	11.1	33.3

Source: Burch (1980, 3:360-361).

Table 4.27 Prior Governmental Experience of Major Cabinet and Diplomatic Appointees, 1789-1980 (percent)

Period	No experience	Relatively little experience	Considerable experience	Total officials
1789-1800	4.3	4.3	91.4	23
1801-1828	4.2	6.4	89.4	47
1829-1840	—	7.7	92.3	26
1841-1860	—	9.9	90.1	71
1861-1876	12.7	29.1	58.2	55
1877-1896	8.6	31.4	60.0	70
1897-1912	12.1	27.6	60.3	58
1913-1920	25.0	25.0	50.0	24
1921-1932	26.5	18.4	55.1	49
1933-1940	20.0	30.0	50.0	20
1941-1945	6.7	27.6	66.7	15
1946-1952	7.0	9.3	83.7	43
1953-1960	36.6	24.4	39.0	41
1961-1968	9.2	13.8	77.0	65
1969-1976	18.8	18.8	62.4	64
1977-1980	23.1	11.5	65.4	26

Note: "Considerable experience" is defined as having held any prominent federal or state post for four years or more. "Little experience" is defined as having held any other post or a major federal or state post for less than four years.

Source: Burch (1980, 3:370-371).

Table 4.28 Elite Status of Major Cabinet and Diplomatic Appointees, 1789-1980 (percent)

Period	Elite appointees	Period	Elite appointees
1789-1800	100.0	1921-1932	80.9
1801-1828	95.7	1933-1940	47.4
1829-1840	93.8	1941-1944	57.9
1841-1860	95.2	1945-1952	55.6
1861-1876	81.1	1953-1960	81.1
1877-1896	86.8	1961-1968	62.7
1897-1912	91.7	1969-1976	68.6
1913-1920	57.1	1977-1980	65.4

Note: Elite status is defined as holding an executive post in a major business or law firm and/or having considerable family wealth or family ties to a major business or firm.

Source: Burch (1980, 3:383).

5

Public Appearances of Presidents

What is the public presidency? One may be tempted to analyze chief executives' overtures to the public on a personal level and thereby to concentrate on the uniqueness of presidents—their specific contributions, styles of communication, speaking skills, mannerisms, likability, and personalities. Yet by doing so one misses the extent to which different incumbents' presentations reflect the presidency as an institution.

Eleven years after leaving office, Lyndon Johnson was asked by CBS News in his televised memoirs how politics had changed during his thirty years in political life as a member of Congress and as president of the United States. Johnson angrily replied:

> You guys. All you guys in the media. All of politics has changed be-
> cause of you. You've broken all the machines and the ties between
> us in Congress and the city machines. You've given us a new kind
> of people.... They're your creations, your puppets. No machine
> could ever create a Teddy Kennedy. Only you guys. They're all
> yours. Your product. (Quoted in Halberstam 1979, 15-16)

Although other politicians share Johnson's belief that American politics is increasingly image dominated and personalized, the burgeoning television news media were not alone in causing the erosion of brokered party politics. The change originated in the activities and approaches of several of Johnson's predecessors who, knowingly or not, established precedents for the public presidency well before television had been invented.

Nineteenth-century and early twentieth-century presidents regularly met the public at the White House. Theodore Roosevelt sporadically held news conferences structured around spontaneous exchanges with reporters rather than around written questions submitted in advance; Woodrow Wilson regularly did so. Calvin Coolidge used the radio for nationwide campaign addresses, and Franklin Roosevelt used it for fireside chats. The groundwork was thus laid for broad, personally based appeals by presidents, presidential candidates, and other politicians. Since Johnson, other technological advances—satellite hookups, closed-circuit cable television, and a direct, toll-free White House telephone number—have also helped connect the president in different ways with the American public.

Our expectations regarding what contemporary presidents should do in their dealings with the public and how they should do it show considerable continuity. Studies note the persistence of the connection between the public and the presidency, although it is typically not discussed in institutional terms (two of the most recent books are Edwards 1983, and Kernell 1986). As these and other works note, in maintaining the link, presidents are principally motivated by the need to gain public support in order to be more effective with other politicians (Neustadt 1960). The studies examine presidents' public appearances, press relations, congressional relations, and campaign efforts as means of securing public approval. Inasmuch as presidents have similar goals and adopt similar techniques to gain national attention, their efforts become regular, routine forms of behavior within the institution of the presidency. Although personal variations are apparent across presidents, they may be one of the least important (although most often highlighted) elements of these efforts at communication.

The public presidency can be understood as having two components. In this chapter we analyze the president's public to understand the ways in which presidents present themselves to the public to gain respect, support, and broader political influence. Important in this analysis is how presidents perceive their audiences. In Chapter 6, we discuss the public's president, emphasizing the popular support that individual presidents gain and lose from the population in general and from specific groups within this population. By identifying these two aspects of the public presidency, we again stress the plural nature of the American presidency, particularly in the types of opportunities presidents use to engage the public and the varied responses they receive from different segments of the American public.

The President's Public

Contemporary presidents' conceptions of and appeals to the American public appear to involve a tension among three different audiences. In approching these audiences, presidents invoke three distinct images as *common, constituent,* and *partisan* representatives. This tension is built into the plural presidency as presidents act out each image. Presidents first present the image of the single representative of the nation. In line with the constitutional mandate that the president is the only governmental official elected by the whole country, presidents going before the public as a whole express sentiments about the "public interest" and "common well-being." This image is reinforced by the president's designation as the "sole organ" of the nation in international affairs, so that he represents the nation to the world. Presidents thus focus on their office as a national one, with the entire country as their audience. The second image shows presidents appealing to specific groups within the broader national community. In this context, presidents act as constituent representatives of these particularized interests, which often cut across partisan lines. Their audience, in this case, is not "the public" but rather many "publics" within the larger population. Both of these links to the public are largely antiparty or nonpartisan. A third link between presidents and the public occurs through party. Party becomes the vehicle through which the "public interest" and "common well-being" are expressed. Rather than behaving as common or constituent representatives, presidents act as partisan representatives.

Each president since Washington has used slightly different combinations of these three types of representations—common, constituent, and partisan. The tension among the three types results when presidents attempt to accomplish partisan goals with nonpartisan rhetoric. As president of "all the people," chief executives attempt to go *above party,* directly to the people, to elicit support for their programs. By invoking this vertical referent presidents indicate that the American electorate is more important as a source of legitimation and support than Congress or political parties (Schwartz 1981). As constituent representatives, presidents attempt to go *around party* and speak to specially chosen political, demographic, geographic, or socioeconomic groups and other nonparty categorizations of the American public. By emphasizing interest group politics, presidents hope to increase support among chosen interests while not materially losing support from others. Some presidents also work *through party* by emphasizing partisan themes in campaigns and in office. Going through party is inconsistent with going above and around party, but presidents nonetheless attempt all three public strategies.

Lyndon Johnson's remarks, noted at the beginning of this chapter, illustrate the three strategies. Johnson operated most effectively as a

247

party leader (see Johnson 1979) and less so as a common or constituent leader. The plural office encompassed each, however: presidents as national public figures, presidents as conveyors of the needs and demands of certain groups at the expense of others, and presidents as party chiefs.

To measure these approaches to public appearances for contemporary presidents, we coded and aggregated all public appearances of presidents that were listed in the *Public Papers of the Presidents* from 1949 to 1984. These public activities were classified into seven categories: major national addresses, news conferences, foreign appearances, minor speeches, Washington appearances, U.S. appearances, and partisan appearances.

National Appearances

As might be expected, early presidents emphasized the common, national aspect of the public presidency. Presidential appearances, as undertaken by George Washington, were designed to gain respect, not support. There was no expectation that public favor once won would be, or should be, translated into political influence (Ketcham 1984). In addition, early presidents' antipathy toward parties and political factions heightened the emphasis on the chief executive as a representative of all the people.

In a letter sent by President Washington to Vice President John Adams, Chief Justice John Jay, and Treasury Secretary Alexander Hamilton, the president asked for advice on three important aspects of the early public office:

> Whether it would tend to prompt impertinent applications and involve disagreeable consequences to have it known, that the President will, every Morning at eight Oclock, be at leisure to give Audience to persons who may have business with him?
>
> Whether it would be satisfactory to the public for the President to make about four great entertainments in a year on such great occasions as . . . , The Anniversary of the Declaration of Independence . . . , The Alliance with France . . . , The Peace with Great Britain . . . , The Organization of the general Government: and whether arrangements of these . . . kinds could be in danger of diverting too much of the President's time from business, or of producing the evils which it was intended to avoid by his living more reclusive than the Presidts. [*sic*] of Congress have heretofore lived.
>
> Whether, during the recess of Congress, it would not be advantageous to the interests of the Union for the President to make the tour of the United States, in order to become better

acquainted with their principal Characters and internal Circumstances, as well as to be more accessible to numbers of well-
informed persons, who might give him useful information and
advices on political subjects? (Fitzpatrick 1940, 30: 310-311)

Following Washington's lead, presidents made grand tours
throughout the country one of the chief events of their terms in office.
James Monroe, "determined to quicken and symbolize national identity," embarked on a nationwide tour in the summer of 1817. After
triumphant visits to Baltimore, Philadelphia, and New York, the
Republican Monroe arrived in Boston on the Fourth of July and was
greeted by some forty thousand cheering people—Federalists and
Republicans alike (Ketcham 1984, 125-126). The *Columbia Centinel*, a
Boston newspaper, commented that Monroe's tour made us "one
people: for we have the sweet consolation ... to rest assured that the
president will be president not of a party, but of a great and powerful
nation" (quoted in Hofstadter 1969, 199).

In addition, presidents continually opened White House doors to
ordinary citizens. As late as the tenure of Herbert Hoover, presidents
held receptions and waited in receiving lines for people who literally
wanted only "to see" the chief executive. In his autobiography, Calvin
Coolidge commented on this part of his daily routine: "At twelve-
thirty the doors were opened, and a long line passed by who wished
merely to shake hands with the President. On one occasion I shook
hands with nineteen hundred in thirty-four minutes" (1929, 201).

In more contemporary instances, with the advent of radio and
especially television, presidents have given major speeches to the
nation, held news conferences before the Washington press corps, and
traveled abroad as envoys of the United States, all the time communi-
cating to their national audience. Eisenhower was the first president to
use television as an expressly presidential medium. Eisenhower's
advisers believed that television focused on the activities of a single
individual more effectively than the activities of larger groups. (They
believed that it was easier for the media to cover presidents than
Congress.) Television also appeared to highlight the drama and emo-
tion of a situation more than hard facts handled in depth (Halberstam
1979, 346). Although Franklin Roosevelt's fireside chats used radio
broadcasting with great success, they were important principally as
they brought the country together in times of hardship and fear.
Eisenhower, however, was the first president to accentuate the drama
and imagery of one-on-one speeches during ordinary, noncrisis times.
Television placed even more emphasis on the person in the office. He
introduced the cabinet during a broadcast as though the introductions

249

were part of that evening's entertainment; he often spoke upon his departure to and returns from travels abroad; he commented on the accomplishments of the administration and Congress.

The public activities of Eisenhower and his successors brought the presidency more attention and made its occupant appear to be more closely tied to the people than before. Such activities expand the constitutionally prescribed electoral consent of the governed to a continuous surrogate election for incumbents through their terms of office and thereby embody the crux of the nonpartisan public presidency. Whereas holding the energy of the executive in check was the original purpose of constitutionally prescribed electoral consent (see Chapter 1), the contemporary presidency expands both the office and support for presidential initiatives by coupling the energy of the office with a new focus on public approval and support. In addition, the public presidency places demands on all contemporary presidents to engage in public appearances and be evaluated by the public.

A more systematic exploration of presidents' appearances before national audiences begins with a compilation of national addresses delivered by presidents, provided in Table 5.1. Since Harry Truman, presidents have regularly delivered major addresses to the nation, preempting scheduled programming on radio and television. Although earlier presidents also made national addresses, Truman was the first to have access to both radio and television. These presidential speeches, which encompass inaugural addresses, State of the Union messages, other addresses before joint sessions of Congress, and addresses to the nation delivered during prime time, are heard by well over 50 million people (Ragsdale 1984).

Presidents have consistently asked and received permission from the three major television networks to preempt prime-time broadcasting when delivering a speech to the American people. From 1947 through 1975, there are only six instances in which a presidential request for air time was denied by one or more of the three television networks. From January 1964 through September 1965 Lyndon Johnson was denied air time five times; in October 1975 Gerald Ford was prevented from preempting prime-time programming (Rutkus 1976, 29).

As shown in Table 5.1, the number of major national speeches made by Presidents Truman through Reagan has been strikingly consistent. The eight presidents made major speeches infrequently. Counting all major speeches that have been delivered, including "obligatory" speeches that presidents have little choice about making—inaugural addresses and State of the Union messages—presidents have delivered roughly one national address every two months. When the State of the Union messages and inaugural message are excluded, the interval between major presidential speeches increases to three months. In addition, results in Table 5.1 demonstrate comparability across different incumbents in the Oval Office. The number of addresses that presidents give varies only modestly, regardless of who is president. Richard Nixon addressed the nation more than the other presidents, possibly because of Vietnam (Nixon gave twelve national addresses on Vietnam, typically announcing troop withdrawals). In contrast, Truman delivered speeches somewhat less frequently than the others. Formal broadcasts to the nation were relatively new activities at that time, and Truman apparently disliked them. He reportedly commented that he gave the speeches "so as not to disappoint all the nice folks who worked so hard on them, but I read them as fast as possible so the audience will not be bored" (Minow et al. 1973, 32-34). Thus the limited use of major addresses by each of the presidents maximizes their impact and minimizes problems of overexposure.

These presidential speeches are examined by general subject matter in Table 5.2 and by specific content in Table 5.3.[1] In Table 5.2, they are categorized according to whether the topic of the address involves foreign policy, economic policy (including energy), domestic policy, or general policy (encompassing at least two of the first three issue types). During the entire period from 1949 to 1984, presidents delivered slightly more foreign policy speeches than other types: 37 percent of all speeches involved matters of diplomacy, summitry, treaties, and war; 31 percent involved general issues. Beginning with Nixon in his second term, presidents began to deliver more economic addresses; this tendency reflects the inflation, high oil prices, and unemployment of the 1970s and 1980s. Few presidential speeches are made on domestic policy, largely because they typically discuss civil protests, riots, strikes, and other forms of internal dissent—events that presidents undoubtedly prefer not to emphasize.

In addition to major national addresses, presidents use news conferences as both forums of advocacy and devices to convey information. Although national in scope, news conferences are not as focused or dramatic as major addresses in which a president creates the appearance of intimacy with individual citizens. Although major speeches have the advantage of sharply drawing national attention to a president's remarks and perhaps winning support for a president's position on an issue or for the president, under certain circumstances this effect may not be wholly desirable. A president may wish to limit, rather than heighten, the national attention paid to an issue. To take one example, Lyndon Johnson's major announcement about the escalation of the Vietnam War in 1966 did not occur in a speech and was not made in prime time but instead took place at a news conference at midday. Presumably, Johnson wished to downplay the decision and thereby to defuse as much criticism as possible. Still, the confrontational format of the news conference can also work to a president's disadvantage if he is placed on the defensive by pointed questions.

Table 5.4 presents the 712 news conferences held by presidents from Truman through Reagan (see Table 5.5 for yearly tabulations of these data). These news conferences involve all formal exchanges with reporters during which a written transcript of the questions is kept. Interviews, call-ins, and informal remarks made to mark trip arrivals and departures have been excluded. The table shows that news conferences declined across three relatively distinct periods. President Truman held more press briefings than any of his successors (slightly more than three per month). In addition, although this fact is not evident from Table 5.4, the number of press conferences held by Franklin Roosevelt totaled nearly 7 per month—998 press conferences in all during his entire term (Grossman and Kumar 1981, 245). Presidents Eisenhower through Johnson gave only 2 conferences per month. Beginning with Nixon, the use of the press conference falls off even more, to an average of about 1 news conference per month. Although President Nixon was often accused of hiding from the press by infrequently holding news conferences, Ronald Reagan, often called "the great communicator," has been equally reluctant to hold official press briefings. Both Nixon and Reagan, and to a somewhat lesser degree Ford and Carter, seem to have adopted the strategy of going before the public in forums such as appearances in and out of Washington in which they have greater autonomy and control than is provided by the news conference medium. (These appearances are discussed in greater depth below.) Presidents may take the view that reporters at news conferences can shape the outcome of the questioning as much as the president. Such a possibility raises the cost of giving news conferences, a cost that presidents may be unwilling to pay.

As representatives of the nation, presidents also travel and make appearances outside the United States. Table 5.6 shows the number of days and appearances made by presidents during their foreign travels. These appearances involve all activities of a president that are recorded in *The Public Papers of the President* as he is touring a foreign country, including formal remarks and toasts to other heads of state, airport remarks, remarks to reporters, and remarks to American citizens who reside in the foreign country. Presidents' foreign appearances have remained stable at moderate levels during the time period from 1949 to 1984. Truman did not leave the country from 1949 to 1952, and Eisenhower stayed at home for all but three days of his first term. The other presidents traveled abroad, but the yearly averages indicate that they did so fairly infrequently. These presidents scheduled numerous appearances each day they traveled, as the table makes clear. One of the reasons for the moderate use of foreign appearances is that presidents are representing the United States abroad and hence are interested in capitalizing on these foreign appearances at home. The image of a single individual representing the entire nation before the world is an especially powerful one.

Foreign travel can also prompt criticism. When presidents spend too much time outside the country, they may be accused of paying inadequate attention to domestic problems—as if they were hiding out abroad. Many people accused Nixon of trying to disappear during the height of Watergate because he made a trip to the Soviet Union only a month before he resigned. In addition, the president may lose face abroad if he is always engaged in this kind of activity.

Major addresses, news conferences, and foreign travel are institutionalized forms of public behavior for contemporary presidents. The styles and skills of individual presidents are less critical than the link with the nation that the office demands. The public expects presidents to speak directly to the nation, to personify the nation abroad, and to hold exchanges, albeit increasingly pro forma ones, with the national press. All of these encounters permit presidents to make common appeals to the nation, but each rests on a different set of assumptions about the nature of the communication. Major addresses portray presidents as "in charge"—both in policy terms, as presidents discuss national problems and solutions, and in symbolic terms, as presidents develop a bond between themselves and the public through the language of their speeches (Hinckley 1988). News conferences display a confrontation between the president and the press that indirectly serves public awareness. Foreign travel also suggests a bond between presidents and the public. The association of the president with "the United States" may be more clear-cut here than with national addresses. In delivering a major address, presidents speak to the nation; traveling abroad, presidents speak as though they were the nation. In addition, each method of communication has very different effects on presidents' public support. Research indicates that major addresses improve presidents' public approval ratings, but neither news conferences nor foreign appearances affect—positively or negatively—the citizenry's perceptions of presidential performance (Ragsdale 1987a). The plural presidency thus reflects the intertwining of the three approaches and their outcomes.

Constituent Appearances

The plural nature of presidents' public encounters is more evident when we consider presidents' group appearances in conjunction with their national activities. Presidents conceive of the public as composed of various groups, showing greater and lesser degrees of organization, that make demands on the government. Although presidents' appeals to the nation as a whole and presidents' roles as party leaders receive much attention, little is known about the ways in which presidents act as group advocates.

At the most general level, presidents of both parties address groups that are tied to long-standing national interests. Presidents are bound politically and legally, for example, to promote economic prosperity—high employment and growth. As long as Americans take for granted a market-oriented, free-enterprise economy, presidents' policy actions must recognize certain groups that stand at the forefront of the political system. Successive presidents have made appeals to business and labor audiences in order to demonstrate a commitment to the strength and vitality of the nation's economy.

At a more specific level, constituent representation occurs when interest groups choose the presidency "as their best medium of expression when they found other pathways blocked" (Bentley 1908, 345). This point is perhaps most clearly illustrated by the efforts of blacks from the 1940s through the 1960s to win civil rights. Feeling that they were largely stymied in Congress and that court decisions lacked impact, the National Association for the Advancement of Colored People (NAACP) and other groups asked Franklin Roosevelt and his successors to promote the civil rights movement through executive action. Roosevelt responded after entreaties from his wife; Truman backed a civil rights bill; Eisenhower somewhat grudgingly sent troops to Little Rock, Arkansas, to protect the desegregation of a high school; and Kennedy, also with some reticence, reacted to turmoil in Alabama and Mississippi. Lyndon Johnson, attempting to secure passage of the Civil Rights Act of 1964, not only worked on behalf of civil rights groups but also mobilized them to lobby on behalf of this legislation. Johnson recounted that a "critical factor in holding the campaign together was the pressure applied by the major citizens' groups behind the bill—the religious groups, the unions, the troubled and concerned Southerners, and the civil rights organizations," especially on Republican members of Congress (Johnson 1979, 159). Thus presidents are not only sought by groups but may seek groups' assistance.

Other efforts are expressly designed to court these groups. The various means include appointments (see Chapter 4), advisory committees that make recommendations to presidents on topics of importance to constituent groups, and liaison offices in the White House. The Carter administration, for example, had seven assistants designated to take care of special constituencies—blacks, Jews, women, the aged, Hispanics, business people, and consumers (Page and Petracca 1983, 147).

Another important way of gaining the support and attention of these groups and, reciprocally, a way in which these groups gain the support and attention of presidents, is for the president to appear before constituent audiences. Presidents meet with groups at the White House, at other locations in Washington, D.C., and, at times, at locations throughout the country. Appearances before these more select audiences provide presidents with different strategies by which they can attempt to build popular support and influence other political elites. Tables 5.7-5.11 examine three types of group activities in which presidents engage. First, there are minor presidential speeches that involve substantive policy remarks made to a specific group or in a certain forum (Table 5.7). These speeches are usually as detailed in discussing a national problem as are major addresses, but they are shorter and not nationally broadcast.[2] Instead, they are used by a president to promote positions before groups that may be especially supportive of the president's ideas. Less often, presidents go before hostile groups to promote cooperation. Alternatively, in some instances, presidents may actually seek to antagonize hostile groups and thereby cause other groups to coalesce behind them. Because the success of presidents' policy efforts rests in part on their ability to form a coalition of active diverse groups, often with varying perspectives on national issues, these minor addresses are important in allowing presidents to tailor remarks to specific audiences. Compared with major national addresses, these targeted appeals are given with greater frequency and may work in ways that major addresses to the entire nation do not.

Some 431 such addresses were delivered by presidents from 1949 to 1984, as shown in Tables 5.7 and 5.8. Presidents Ford, Carter, and Reagan made more minor addresses than did their predecessors. The data in these tables do not indicate any particular patterns within the

255

terms of the presidents studied. Presidents do not give greater numbers of minor speeches during their first years or during election years. The tables, however, do indicate an increase in minor addresses, coupled with the decrease in news conferences since Nixon and especially Ford. Later presidents have defined policy discussions more on their own terms than did their predecessors.

The second group activity in which presidents engaged involves numerous appearances in and around Washington, D.C., to particular groups (Table 5.9). These Washington appearances involve brief public remarks before a group at the White House or at some other location in the capital. Such occasions are more ceremonial than they are policy events; examples include bill signings, the greeting of foreign guests, the honoring of a group or individual, and the commemoration of a historical or seasonal event. Although these appearances often border on the trivial, for example when a president greets high school students visiting the nation's capital or proclaims a local holiday, these instances nevertheless give presidents virtually cost-free "photo opportunities" that afford useful television and newspaper coverage.

Table 5.9 categorizes the 4,469 Washington appearances by presidents from 1949 to 1984 according to whether they took place in the White House or at some other spot in Washington, D.C. The data show that Presidents Truman and Eisenhower made fewer Washington appearances than any president since Kennedy. Although in the late 1940s and 1950s the White House was surely the focus of national political attention, it may not yet have become the focal point for visits by political groups and organized interests. Presidents Kennedy, Johnson, Ford, Carter, and Reagan made roughly comparable numbers of appearances in Washington, D.C. Nixon stands out as having made relatively few Washington appearances, especially outside the White House. During his tenure, Nixon seemed reticent to make speeches not only on the road but also in Washington. Nixon particularly minimized public exposure during the Vietnam War and during Watergate. Instead, he relied on major addresses to the nation in which he presented his case without confronting specific groups.

A third group strategy used by presidents involves appearances at various locations outside the District of Columbia. Like the Washington appearances, those made elsewhere are largely ceremonial. The president travels to a particular community to commemorate a local event, meets civic groups and local leaders, surveys damage caused by natural disasters, and speaks at a group's convention or at a university. Table 5.10 describes the 1,331 U.S. appearances made by presidents from Truman through Reagan; an annual breakdown appears in Table

5.11. The trend observed for Washington appearances repeats itself for U.S. public appearances. Truman and Eisenhower made far fewer appearances throughout the United States than did presidents beginning with Kennedy. Ford, Carter, and Reagan, in particular, appear to have made the most use of U.S. public appearances. (Carter's totals do not include the series of small "town meetings" he began early in his term; inclusion of these would make the Carter figures higher.) Together the three types of group appearances indicate that these last three presidents spent considerable time before specific groups and localities as constituent leaders.

This strategy of targeting specific group audiences conflicts, however, with a national strategy of statesmanship. Common appeals bring groups together, but constituent appeals pull groups apart. Attempts to gather influence through discrete channels essentially match the particularized politics of Congress and the bureaucracy, but presidents make universal appeals in addition to parochial ones. Using this combination, presidents may not be successful in gaining national public support because they also appeal to discrete group interests. Evidence suggests that presidents do not gain public support across the country from their minor speeches, Washington appearances, or U.S. appearances (Ragsdale 1987a). They may gain kudos from the groups or regions targeted in their appeals, but they are either disliked or ignored by other groups. Thus the appearances gain them nothing from the nation as a whole. Not only can the plural presidency be seen in the differences between these types of constituent appearances; it is also compounded by the discord between common and constituent efforts.

Partisan Appearances

The national and constituent approaches are supplemented by a third type of appeal in which presidents act as party leaders. They do so in ways that nonetheless maintain the popular conception of the office. The party becomes the vehicle through which presidents satisfy the public. Democracy is best served by a competitive exchange of ideas between the parties. The parties embody alternative conceptions of the public good, and they compete to translate these conceptions into law. John F. Kennedy asserted:

> No President, it seems to me, can escape politics. He has not only been chosen by the nation—he has been chosen by his Party. And if he insists that he is President of all the people and should, therefore, offend none of them—if he blurs the issues and differences between the parties—if he neglects the party machinery and

> avoids his party's leadership—then he has not only weakened the
> political party; . . . he has dealt a death blow to the democratic
> process itself. (Quoted in Ketcham 1984, 226)

Thus presidents pursue a course of public appearances that includes
meetings with party leaders, fund raisers and rallies for party candidates, and gatherings of party workers.

Although presidents make political appearances throughout their
terms in office, as Tables 5.12 and 5.13 show, they do so most
frequently during election years. Presidents make roughly three times
as many partisan appearances during midterm congressional election
years and presidential election years as they do in nonelection years.
Presidents Ford, Carter, and Reagan were again most likely to make
appearances as party leaders. This observation is especially interesting
for Jimmy Carter, who campaigned for the presidency as a candidate
largely outside the traditional structure of the Democratic party. These
greater partisan efforts since Ford may reflect efforts by parties to halt
some of the erosion of support during the 1960s and early 1970s.
Parties depend on the strong, visible figures of their incumbent
presidents to help unite an organization that can no longer as readily
depend on party machines and bosses to solidify support.

Partisan appearances are also in tension with common and constituent appearances. Presidents take these three mutually contradictory
steps to gain public support. They solicit support from their party, from
specific groups that may not be coincident with their party, and from
the country as a whole. These activities give rise to various images of
the single executive. Party appeals depict presidents as preeminently
partisan leaders who toe the party line and support party candidates.
The image is distinctly electoral. Nixon's grand tour across the country
on behalf of Republican congressional candidates in 1970 made him
appear as chiefly interested in narrow partisan advantages. Group
appeals make presidents seem like clientele advocates, representing the
desires of specific groups exclusively. In certain instances, presidents
also overtly oppose the concerns of others. Reagan's affiliation with
antiabortion groups is one example. In national appeals, presidents
seem to be the singular representative of the country. They bring
together all parties and groups. Presidents often characterize the
American collectivity broadly as the middle class. They appeal to
distinct group and partisan identities but attempt to create a larger
picture of groups working together for the common good. The following passage from Reagan's inaugural address illustrates the point nicely:

> Our concern must be for a special interest group that has been too
> long neglected. It knows no sectional boundaries or ethnic and

racial divisions, and it crosses party lines. It is made of men and women who raise our food, patrol our streets, man our mines and factories, teach our children, keep our homes and heal us when we're sick—professionals, industrialists, shopkeepers, clerks, cabbies, and truckdrivers. They are, in short, "We the people," this breed called Americans. (*Public Papers of the President* 1981, 2)

Presidents are expected to behave in each of these three ways, but they cannot usually overcome conflicts of imagery imposed by the different strategies. The plural presidency thus incorporates these conflicts as the single executive image is cast and recast along three separate dimensions.

The Mix of Public Activity

One final way of considering public appearances involves the presidents' total domestic public activity. Table 5.14 is a compilation of presidents' major speeches, news conferences, minor addresses, Washington appearances, and U.S. appearances. Partisan political appearances have been excluded because they involve presidents in activities of a nonofficial nature. Foreign appearances also do not figure in this tally because presidents often travel abroad for reasons other than public exposure back home (that is, matters of summitry, diplomacy, or war). The remaining items thus provide an overall measure of the level of presidents' official activity within the United States. As the figures indicate, public activities consume a considerable amount of a president's time. By one estimate, nearly one-third of a president's time in office is spent engaging in such public appearances (Kernell 1984, 243, referring to presidents since Nixon). The degree to which these activity levels are institutionally based is also apparent. Even Eisenhower, who was least active, made seven appearances per month. A sharp increase in the level of public activity begins with Kennedy. Presidents since Johnson reach an average of almost one public appearance per day.

Figure 5.1 depicts the growth in presidents' domestic appearances, showing the yearly rates by term in office. A central irony is made evident by examining these several types of appearances together. Table 5.14 shows an increase in total domestic appearances that reflects increases in minor speeches, Washington appearances, and U.S. appearances. News conferences decline, and major addresses remain steady. As noted above, however, presidents do not gain greater national public approval from this set of activities. Presidents work hard with these activities to gain greater public approval but do not attain it. Instead they can count only on well-timed but infrequently

259

used major addresses to the nation as a means of gaining broader public support (Ragsdale 1987a).

Conclusion

When most people are asked the question, "What do American presidents do on the job?" they think of critical decisions on such important matters of strategy, domestic legislation, budget allocations, and international diplomacy. Yet as the tables in this chapter reveal, presidents engage in much less grand, much more ceremonial tasks as part of their daily routine. Indeed, particularly since Kennedy, presidents have increased the amount of time they dedicate to ceremony. Presidents engage in these numerous public efforts presumably to increase or maintain their support within the public as a whole, among key groups within the public, and with key segments of their political parties. The premise of each appeal is unique. One promotes the image of presidents as singular political actors and symbols of the nation. Another effectively denies that presidents are such symbols and instead promotes the notion of group sponsorship. Such symbolism accentuates the parts, not the whole. The last appeal casts presidents as leaders of broad-based partisan collectivities. The plural institution of the presidency provides opportunities for presidents to engage in these contradictory forums frequently throughout their terms. The contradictions they create are likely to diminish, rather than improve, the support that presidents seek.

Notes

1. The speeches cannot be categorized in as much detail as the legislative positions, executive orders, and executive agreements of presidents. Presidents tend to address several topics within a broad subject area. In foreign policy speeches, for example, they speak of both defense and foreign policy issues, so that it is impossible to separate speeches about each of the two topics. Foreign speeches include those that discuss diplomacy, summitry, treaties, and war. Domestic speeches involve matters of civil rights, civil protests, riots, social welfare programs, education, and crime. Economic speeches deal with matters pertaining directly to the national economy and issues of energy, which have clear economic repercussions in the eyes of many observers. General speeches address more than one of the foreign, domestic, and economic topics. (The public impact of these several types of speeches is examined in Ragsdale 1987b.)
2. Minor speeches include any domestic public appearances by presidents, other than national addresses and news conferences, in which presidents

make moderately lengthy policy statements to a major group or forum. To be regarded as minor, the speech had to cover at least three pages of printed text in the *Public Papers*. Substantive policy statements include proposals for legislation, discussion of pending legislation, and announcements of positions. This coding differs from that of Lammers (1982) and Kernell (1984), who identify a category of "routine addresses" at least one thousand words long that were delivered outside the White House and involved "reasonably substantial statements before some group" (Lammers 1982, 149). Minor speeches, as classified here, can be delivered at or away from the White House, tend to be longer, and were coded in a more narrow fashion so that they encompass only specific policy remarks. The result is relatively fewer minor speeches than routine addresses.

Table 5.1 Major Presidential Speeches, 1949-1984

President	All speeches		Discretionary speeches [a]	
	Total	Average interval between speeches (months)	Total	Average interval between speeches (months)
Truman	15	3.2	11	4.4
Eisenhower, I	21	2.3	16	3.0
Eisenhower, II	20	2.5	16	3.0
Kennedy	15	2.3	11	3.2
Johnson [b]	23	2.7	15	4.2
Nixon, I	23	2.1	19	2.5
Nixon, II	13	1.5	11	1.8
Ford	12	2.4	8	3.5
Carter	17	2.8	13	3.7
Reagan	20	2.4	16	3.0
Total	179	$\bar{x} = 2.4$	136	$\bar{x} = 3.2$

Note: "Major speeches" are defined as live nationally televised and broadcast addresses to the country that preempt all major network programming. They include inaugural addresses, State of the Union messages, other addresses to joint sessions of Congress delivered during prime time, and prime time addresses to the nation.

[a] Excludes inaugural addresses and State of the Union messages.
[b] Includes full term from November 1963 to January 1969.

Source: Coded and calculated by the authors from successive volumes of *Public Papers of the Presidents.*

Table 5.2 Major Presidential Speeches by Subject Category, 1949-1984

President	General		Foreign		Economic		Domestic		Total
	No.	%	No.	%	No.	%	No.	%	
Truman	4	27	7	47	2	13	2	13	15
Eisenhower, I	10	25	8	38	1	5	2	10	21
Eisenhower, II	5	25	12	60	0	0	3	15	20
Kennedy	5	33	6	40	1	7	3	20	15
Johnson [a]	10	43	4	17	3	13	6	26	23
Nixon, I	4	17	13	54	4	17	2	9	23
Nixon, II	3	23	2	15	5	38	3	23	13
Ford	5	42	1	8	5	42	1	8	12
Carter	6	35	6	35	5	29	0	0	17
Reagan	4	20	8	40	8	40	0	0	20
Total	56		67		34		22		179
Average		31		37		19		12	

Note: Foreign policy subjects include diplomacy, summitry, treaties, and war. Economic policy includes the economy and energy. Domestic policy involves civil rights, civil protests, riots, social welfare, education, agriculture, and domestic political matters such as Watergate. General policy encompasses two or more of the three types.

[a] Includes full term from November 1963 to January 1969.

Source: Coded and calculated by the authors from successive volumes of *Public Papers of the Presidents.*

Table 5.3 Major Presidential Speeches by President, 1949-1984

President	Speech
Truman	
January 20, 1949	Inaugural address
July 13, 1949	National economy
January 4, 1950	State of the Union
July 19, 1950	Korean War
September 1, 1950	Korean War
September 9, 1950	Signing of the Defense Production Act
December 15, 1950	Declares national emergency (Korea)
January 8, 1951	State of the Union
April 11, 1951	Korean War: Relieves MacArthur of command
June 14, 1951	Need to extend inflation controls
November 7, 1951	International arms reduction
January 9, 1952	State of the Union
March 6, 1952	Mutual security program
April 8, 1952	Steel mills (nation)
June 10, 1952	Steel mills (Congress)
Eisenhower, I	
January 2, 1953	Inaugural address
February 2, 1953	State of the Union
April 16, 1953	World peace
May 19, 1953	National security costs
June 3, 1953	Report with the cabinet
July 26, 1953	Korean armistice signed
August 6, 1953	Achievements of the administration and the Eighty-third Congress
January 4, 1954	Administration purposes and accomplishments
January 7, 1954	State of the Union
March 15, 1954	Tax program
April 5, 1954	National goals and problems
August 23, 1954	Achievements of the Eighty-third Congress
January 6, 1955	State of the Union
July 15, 1955	Departure for the Geneva conference
July 25, 1955	Return from Geneva
February 29, 1956	Decision on second term
April 16, 1956	Farm bill veto
August 3, 1956	DDE and Dulles on Suez
October 31, 1956	Middle East, Eastern Europe
January 5, 1957	Middle East (Congress)
January 10, 1957	State of the Union
Eisenhower, II	
January 21, 1957	Inaugural address
February 20, 1957	Middle East and United Nations
May 14, 1957	Government costs
May 21, 1957	Mutual security programs
September 24, 1957	Desegregation in Little Rock

Table 5.3 (continued)

President	Speech
Eisenhower, II (continued)	
November 7, 1957	National security (advances in technology)
November 13, 1957	National security
December 23, 1957	Report on NATO conference in Paris
January 9, 1958	State of the Union
March 16, 1959	West Berlin and Soviet challenges to peace
August 6, 1959	Labor bill needed
September 10, 1959	Report on European trip
December 3, 1959	Departure on goodwill trip to Europe, Asia, Africa
January 7, 1960	State of the Union
February 21, 1960	South America departure
March 8, 1960	South America return
May 25, 1960	Events in Paris
January 17, 1960	Farewell address
Kennedy	
January 20, 1961	Inaugural address
January 30, 1961	State of the Union
May 25, 1961	National problems and needs
June 6, 1961	Return from Europe
July 25, 1961	Crisis in Berlin
January 11, 1962	State of the Union
March 2, 1962	Nuclear testing and disarmament
August 13, 1962	National economy
September 30, 1962	Situation at the University of Mississippi
October 22, 1962	Cuban missile crisis
January 14, 1963	State of the Union
May 12, 1963	Racial strife in Birmingham
June 11, 1963	Civil rights
July 26, 1963	Nuclear Test Ban Treaty
September 18, 1963	Nuclear Test Ban Treaty
Johnson	
November 27, 1963	Joint session
January 8, 1964	State of the Union
February 26, 1964	Tax bill signing
April 9, 1964	Moratorium on railroad labor dispute
July 2, 1964	Civil rights signing
October 18, 1964	Events in Russia, China, Great Britain
January 4, 1965	State of the Union
January 20, 1965	Inaugural address
March 15, 1965	American hopes and goals
May 2, 1965	Dominican Republic situation
August 30, 1965	Postponement of steel industry shutdown
September 3, 1965	Announcement of steel settlement
January 12, 1966	State of the Union

(Table continues)

265

Table 5.3 (continued)

President	Speech
Johnson (continued)	
January 10, 1967	State of the Union
July 24, 1967	Detroit riot (authorization of federal troops)
July 27, 1967	Civil disorder
January 17, 1968	State of the Union
January 26, 1968	North Korea
March 31, 1968	Vietnam; will not run
April 5, 1968	Martin Luther King assassination
June 5, 1968	Robert Kennedy assassination
October 31, 1968	Bombing halt
January 14, 1969	State of the Union
Nixon, I	
January 20, 1969	Inaugural address
May 14, 1969	Vietnam War
August 8, 1969	Domestic programs (family assistance plan, revenue sharing)
November 3, 1969	Vietnam War
December 15, 1969	Vietnam War (troop reductions)
January 22, 1970	State of the Union
April 20, 1970	Vietnam War (troop reductions)
April 30, 1970	Cambodian invasion
June 3, 1970	Report on Cambodian invasion
June 17, 1970	Economic Policy
October 10, 1970	Vietnam War (peace initiatives)
January 22, 1971	State of the Union
April 7, 1971	Vietnam War (general)
August 15, 1971	Economic policy (wage-price freeze)
September 9, 1971	Economic stabilization
October 7, 1971	Economic stabilization (postfreeze)
January 20, 1972	State of the Union
January 25, 1972	Peace plan
February 28, 1972	China
March 16, 1972	Busing
April 26, 1972	Vietnam
May 8, 1972	Vietnam
June 1, 1972	Return from Soviet Union
Nixon, II	
January 20, 1973	Inaugural address
January 23, 1973	Paris peace accord
March 29, 1973	Vietnam and domestic problems
April 30, 1973	Watergate
June 13, 1973	Price controls
August 15, 1973	Watergate
October 12, 1973	Ford as vice president
November 7, 1973	Energy shortage

Table 5.3 (continued)

President	Speech
Nixon, II (continued)	
November 25, 1973	Energy policy
January 30, 1974	State of the Union
April 29, 1974	Taxes
July 3, 1974	Return from Soviet Union
January 25, 1974	Inflation, economy
Ford	
August 9, 1974	Remarks on taking oath of office
August 12, 1974	Address to joint session of Congress
September 8, 1974	Nixon pardon
October 8, 1974	Economic policy (Whip Inflation Now program)
January 13, 1975	Energy and the economy
January 15, 1975	State of the Union
March 29, 1975	Signing of tax reduction bill
April 10, 1975	U.S. foreign policy
May 27, 1975	Energy programs
October 6, 1975	Federal tax and spending reductions
January 19, 1976	State of the Union
January 12, 1977	State of the Union
Carter	
January 20, 1977	Inaugural address
February 2, 1977	Report to the American people
April 18, 1977	Energy plan
April 20, 1977	Address to Congress on energy plan
November 8, 1977	Update on energy plan
January 19, 1978	State of the Union
February 1, 1978	Panama Canal treaties (benefits of)
September 18, 1978	Camp David Summit on Middle East
October 24, 1978	Anti-inflation program
January 23, 1979	State of the Union
April 5, 1979	Energy (decontrol of oil prices)
June 18, 1979	Report on Vienna Summit and SALT II
July 15, 1979	National goals
October 1, 1979	Soviet troops in Cuba and SALT II
January 4, 1980	Soviet invasion of Afghanistan
January 23, 1980	State of the Union
April 25, 1980	Hostage rescue attempt
Reagan	
January 20, 1981	Inaugural address
February 5, 1981	Economy
February 18, 1981	Program for economic recovery (Congress)
April 28, 1981	Economic recovery (Congress)
July 27, 1981	Tax reduction

(Table continues)

Table 5.3 (continued)

President	Speech
Reagan (continued)	
September 24, 1981	Economic recovery
January 26, 1982	State of the Union
April 29, 1982	Federal budget
August 16, 1982	Tax and budget legislation
September 1, 1982	Middle East
September 20, 1982	Lebanon
October 13, 1982	Economy
November 22, 1982	Arms reduction and deterrence
January 25, 1983	State of the Union
March 23, 1983	National security
April 27, 1983	Central America
September 5, 1983	Soviet attack on Korean airline
October 27, 1983	Lebanon, Grenada
January 25, 1984	State of the Union
May 9, 1984	Central America

Source: Coded and calculated by the authors from successive volumes of *Public Papers of the Presidents.*

Table 5.4 Presidential News Conferences, 1949-1984

President	Total conferences	Yearly average	Monthly average
Truman	160	40	3.3
Eisenhower, I	99	25	2.1
Eisenhower, II	94	24	2.0
Kennedy	65	22	1.9
Johnson[a]	132	26	2.1
Nixon, I	30	8	0.6
Nixon, II	9	5	0.5
Ford	41	19	1.4
Carter	59	15	1.2
Reagan	23	6	0.5

Note: News conferences are defined as formal exchanges with reporters. Excludes interviews and informal remarks at arrivals and departures.

[a] Includes full term from November 1963 to January 1969.

Source: Coded and calculated by the authors from successive volumes of *Public Papers of the Presidents.*

Table 5.5   Presidential News Conferences by Year, 1949-1984

Truman		Nixon, I	
1949	47	1969	8
1950	39	1970	6
1951	39	1971	9
1952	35	1972	7
Total	160	Total	30
Eisenhower, I		Nixon, II	
1953	23	1973	7
1954	33	1974	2
1955	19	Total	9
1956	24		
Total	99	Ford	
		1974	7
Eisenhower, II		1975	19
1957	26	1976	15
1958	21	Total	41
1959	31		
1960	16	Carter	
Total	94	1977	22
		1978	19
Kennedy		1979	12
1961	19	1980	6
1962	27	Total	59
1963	19		
Total	65	Reagan	
		1981	6
Johnson		1982	6
1963-64	33	1983	7
1965	17	1984	4
1966	41	Total	23
1967	22		
1968	19		
Total	132		

Source: Coded and calculated by the authors from successive volumes of *Public Papers of the Presidents.*

Table 5.6 Foreign Appearances by Presidents, 1949-1984

President	Days of travel	Number of appearances	Yearly average	
			Days	Appearances
Truman	0	0	0	0
Eisenhower, I	3	7	1	2
Eisenhower, II	50	115	13	29
Kennedy	28	77	9	26
Johnson [a]	29	55	6	11
Nixon, I	35	108	9	27
Nixon, II	17	25	9	14
Ford	30	63	14	29
Carter	52	69	13	17
Reagan	36	82	9	21

Note: Foreign appearances are defined as the total number of appearances made by a president during travel outside the United States.

[a] Includes full term from November 1963 to January 1969.

Source: Coded and calculated by the authors from successive volumes of *Public Papers of the Presidents.*

Table 5.7 Minor Presidential Speeches, 1949-1984

President	Total	Yearly average	Monthly average
Truman	39	10	0.8
Eisenhower, I	11	3	0.2
Eisenhower, II	18	5	0.4
Kennedy	30	10	0.9
Johnson [a]	49	10	0.8
Nixon, I	25	6	0.5
Nixon, II	22	12	1.1
Ford	77	35	2.7
Carter	82	21	1.7
Reagan	78	20	1.6

Note: Minor addresses are defined as any domestic public appearance other than major speeches and news conferences in which a president makes substantive, detailed policy statements to a major group or forum.

[a] Includes full term from November 1963 to January 1969.

Source: Coded and calculated by the authors from successive volumes of *Public Papers of the Presidents.*

Table 5.8   Minor Presidential Speeches by Year, 1949-1984

Truman			Nixon, I	
1949	8		1969	5
1950	13		1970	6
1951	9		1971	10
1952	9		1972	4
Total	39		Total	25
Eisenhower, I			Nixon, II	
1953	5		1973	12
1954	2		1974	10
1955	2		Total	22
1956	2			
Total	11		Ford	
			1974	5
Eisenhower, II			1975	36
1957	5		1976	36
1958	7		Total	77
1959	2			
1960	4		Carter	
Total	18		1977	21
			1978	15
Kennedy			1979	22
1961	6		1980	24
1962	7		Total	82
1963	17			
Total	30		Reagan	
			1981	11
Johnson			1982	27
1963-64	11		1983	19
1965	9		1984	21
1966	11		Total	78
1967	4			
1968	14			
Total	49			

Source: Coded and calculated by the authors from successive volumes of *Public Papers of the Presidents.*

Table 5.9 Washington Public Appearances by President, 1949-1984

President	Total Washington appearances			White House appearances			Other Washington appearances		
	Total	Yearly average	Monthly average	Total	Yearly average	Monthly average	Total	Yearly average	Monthly average
Truman	253	63	5.3	142	36	3.0	111	28	2.3
Eisenhower, I	124	31	2.6	54	14	1.1	70	18	1.5
Eisenhower, II	163	41	3.4	89	22	1.9	44	19	1.5
Kennedy	451	150	12.9	350	117	10.0	101	34	2.9
Johnson[a]	1,015	202	16.6	888	177	14.5	127	25	2.0
Nixon, I	368	92	7.7	289	72	6.0	79	20	1.6
Nixon, II	122	68	6.1	105	58	5.3	17	9	0.9
Ford	443	201	15.3	336	153	11.6	107	49	3.7
Carter	717	179	15.0	635	159	13.2	82	21	1.7
Reagan	813	203	17.0	720	180	15.0	93	23	1.9

Note: Washington public appearances are defined as appearances before a group at which remarks are made that do not include substantive detailed policy statements but instead involve ceremonial presentations to the groups or broad, idealistic comments.

[a] Includes full term from November 1963 to January 1969.

Source: Coded and calculated by the authors from successive volumes of *Public Papers of the Presidents.*

Table 5.10   U.S. Public Appearances by Presidents, 1949-1984

President	Total	Yearly average	Monthly average
Truman	53	13	1.1
Eisenhower, I	75	19	1.6
Eisenhower, II	43	11	0.9
Kennedy	97	32	2.8
Johnson [a]	244	49	3.9
Nixon, I	166	42	3.5
Nixon, II	38	21	1.9
Ford	183	83	6.3
Carter	172	43	3.6
Reagan	260	65	5.4

Note: Nonpartisan appearances by presidents before groups outside the vicinity of Washington, D.C., during which ceremonies take place and nonpolicy remarks are made.

[a] Includes full term from November 1963 to January 1969.

Source: Coded and calculated by the authors from successive volumes of *Public Papers of the Presidents.*

Table 5.11   Presidents' U.S. Public Appearances by Year, 1949-1984

Truman		Kennedy		Nixon, II	
1949	8	1961	15	1973	19
1950	26	1962	41	1974	19
1951	9	1963	41	Total	38
1952	10	Total	97		
Total	53			Ford	
		Johnson		1974	20
		1963-64	83	1975	77
Eisenhower, I		1965	31	1976	86
1953	16	1966	56	Total	183
1954	30	1967	32		
1955	22	1968	36	Carter	
1956	7	Total	244	1977	35
Total	75			1978	42
				1979	40
Eisenhower, II		Nixon, I		1980	55
1957	7	1969	39	Total	172
1958	10	1970	46		
1959	5	1971	61	Reagan	
1960	21	1972	20	1981	19
Total	43	Total	166	1982	65
				1983	103
				1984	73
				Total	260

Source: Coded and calculated by the authors from successive volumes of *Public Papers of the Presidents.*

Table 5.12 Political Appearances by Presidents, 1949-1984

President	Total	Election year average [a]	Nonelection year average
Truman	88	34	10
Eisenhower, I	66	27	7
Eisenhower, II	45	20	2
Kennedy	49	33	8
Johnson [b]	131	40	5
Nixon, I	102	43	9
Nixon, II	11	9	2
Ford	409	183	44
Carter	234	100	17
Reagan	206	81	23

Note: A political appearance is defined as any appearance before an expressly partisan political group or for an expressly partisan purpose.

[a] Average of midterm congressional election years and presidential election year.
[b] Includes full term from November 1963 to January 1969.

Source: Coded and calculated from successive volumes of *Public Papers of the Presidents.*

Table 5.13 Presidents' Political Appearances by Year, 1949-1984

Truman		Kennedy		Nixon, II	
1949	14	1961	7	1973	2
1950	6	1962	33	1974	9
1951	6	1963	9	Total	11
1952	62	Total	49		
Total	88			Ford	
		Johnson		1974	34
Eisenhower, I		1963-64	98	1975	44
1953	8	1965	4	1976	331
1954	17	1966	8	Total	409
1955	5	1967	7		
1956	36	1968	14	Carter	
Total	66	Total	131	1977	13
				1978	51
				1979	21
Eisenhower, II		Nixon, I		1980	149
1957	3	1969	12	Total	234
1958	16	1970	39		
1959	2	1971	5	Reagan	
1960	24	1972	46	1981	23
Total	45	Total	102	1982	35
				1983	22
				1984	126
				Total	206

Source: Coded and calculated by the authors from successive volumes of *Public Papers of the Presidents.*

Table 5.14   Level of Public Activities of Presidents, 1949-1984

President	Total activities	Yearly average	Monthly average
Truman	520	130	10.8
Eisenhower, I	330	83	6.9
Eisenhower, II	338	85	7.0
Kennedy	658	219	18.8
Johnson [a]	1,463	293	24.0
Nixon, I	634	159	13.2
Nixon, II	204	113	10.2
Ford	756	344	26.0
Carter	1,047	262	22.0
Reagan	1,194	299	24.9

Note: Public activities are defined as including all domestic public appearances by a president, including major speeches, news conferences, minor speeches, Washington appearances, and U.S. appearances but not political appearances.

[a] Includes full term from November 1963 to January 1969.

Source: Coded and calculated by the authors from successive volumes of *Public Papers of the Presidents.*

Figure 5.1 Domestic Public Appearances by President, 1949-1984 (yearly averages)

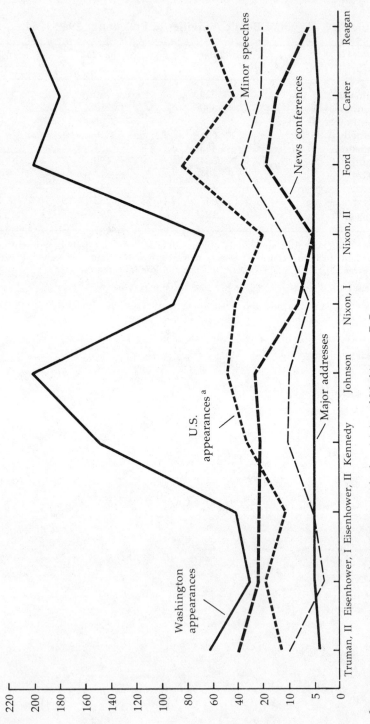

[a] Nonpartisan appearances before groups outside the vicinity of Washington, D.C.

Source: Coded and calculated by the authors from successive volumes of *Public Papers of the Presidents*.

6

Public Opinions

A study of the various publics that form opinions on American chief executives and on the institution within which they operate complements the study of the plural presidency. Indeed, as noted in Chapter 5, the plural nature of the institution reflects in part the various responses presidents make to the nation, to groups within the nation, and to their political parties. The concept of a plural institution makes it easy to imagine that public attitudes about it vary, depending on the group of American citizens consulted. Although presidents sometimes view themselves as representing "all the people," they may well represent some people some of the time and other people at other times.

Too often journalists, scholars, and even presidents have spoken of the public opinion as if "the public" were a proper noun. There are at least two reasons for this anthropomorphic tendency in public opinion analyses. The first is simplicity. Scholars can discuss a single public opinion more conveniently and concisely than they can the enormously diverse views of various groups in the American populace considered as a whole. Second, data on group attitudes are not readily available. Information does exist, but the data are not usually presented in a form that permits meaningful comparison.

What is gained in simplicity and efficiency by not collecting more data is lost in accuracy, however. For example, if 50 percent of the American public approves of the way Ronald Reagan is doing his job as president, then one-half of each demographic and political group in the country may support him. Equally plausible, however, is the alternative that wealthy citizens support the president and the unemployed and poor do not. The aggregate figure does not permit one to distinguish between the two very different interpretations.

This chapter provides systematic public opinion data that are comparable across administrations and extend over time and within regions, age groups, political parties, and categories defined on the basis of religion, employment, income, education, race, and gender. Although presidential approval polls provided the bulk of the material for this chapter, we have also compiled a variety of other public opinion data. We discuss here the most striking patterns and leave the critical task of providing more detailed analyses to future research.

Aggregate Approval and Disapproval

"Do you approve or disapprove of the way [the incumbent] is handling his job as president?" The Gallup Polling Organization has asked scientifically selected samples of American citizens this question monthly or bimonthly since Franklin Roosevelt's third presidential term. This time series is the longest and most valuable in public opinion history. News reporters, political scientists, and other presidency watchers commonly refer to the aggregate percentage of the public that approves of the president as his approval, or popularity, rating. These poll results are "very widely read," particularly in Washington, D.C., and are "widely taken to approximate reality" (Neustadt 1960, 205). All presidents pay considerable attention to public opinion, especially from this source. When his approval ratings were high, Lyndon Johnson routinely carried around newspaper clippings to show reporters and others. As a general measure of the president's personal prestige (Neustadt 1960), public approval has been shown to influence presidential election results (Sigelman 1980), presidents' public appearances (Ragsdale 1984, 1987a), their success in Congress (Ostrom and Simon 1985), and their actions in other policy areas (Ostrom and Job 1986).

Many scholarly studies have attempted to explain aggregate fluctuations in this series (Sigelman 1980). Some explanations rely on time: Mueller (1973) uses a "coalition of minorities" variable to explain the steady decline in a president's support following inauguration, whereas Stimson (1976) argues for an "expectation-disillusionment" hypothesis that has popularity dropping following the honeymoon period and then rising early in the fourth year. Others believe that relatively uncontrollable events such as the economy (Kenski 1977; Fassbender 1981; Hibbs, Rivers, and Vasilatos 1982), international crises and war (Kernell 1978), favorable events reported in the news (Brody and Page 1975), and symbolic events (MacKuen 1983) explain fluctuations in presidential approval. Still others argue that presidents have a degree of control over their approval ratings through speech making (Haight and Brody 1977; Ragsdale 1984).

The aggregate presidential approval data from 1949 to the present are shown in Tables 6.1 and 6.2 and in Figure 6.1. The data in Figure 6.1 provide a most useful comparison of presidents' aggregate approval ratings. Table 6.2 is more helpful for those intending to conduct detailed statistical analyses.

The widely held belief that Ronald Reagan is an enormously popular president is quickly dispelled by Figure 6.1: Reagan's 51 percent initial approval rating was the lowest postinauguration poll reading for any president since Truman. Indeed, the next lowest presidential approval score (Nixon, 59 percent) was a full eight percentage points higher than Reagan's at this point. For most of the rest of his presidency, the percentage approving of the way Ronald Reagan handled his job was the second lowest among all presidents since Truman. The lowest approval ratings went to Carter during the Iranian hostage crisis, to Ford after the Nixon pardon, or to Nixon during Watergate. Indeed, if one interpolates values for other presidents, during no month of Reagan's first term was his approval higher than that of other presidents. About five years into his presidency, Reagan began to be rated more highly than other presidents, but the reason is primarily that Reagan after reelection is being compared with Truman, Nixon, and Johnson when they were exceedingly unpopular presidents. Even Reagan's highest score (68 percent), after four months in office, is not very high relative to that of other presidents at other times. Kennedy or Eisenhower only rarely fell below this level. In fact, every president but Nixon bested Reagan's highest approval level at some time during their administrations (and Nixon tied it).

Given these observations, why did President Reagan have an impervious image, especially in his first term? Although the answer demands further research, we can speculate. Perhaps reporters have grown to expect a large drop in approval following the inauguration. Because Reagan's approval ratings started at a low level in relation to those for all previous presidents and increased after the assassination attempt, the drop was neither as large nor as quick as those of his predecessors. A low start may be the explanation for Reagan's apparent immunity to the standard range of failures associated with economic recessions and foreign policy that afflict many presidencies. Another possibility is suggested by the analyses of group support below. President Reagan polarized the American public more than any other president studied. His approval ratings may therefore have been relatively stable because polarized opinions tend to change more gradually.

Other trends and patterns can be observed in these figures. For example, every president experiences a general decline in approval after inauguration. Similarly, approval for all presidents but Kennedy tends to move upward near the end of the terms. One can also spot occasional sharp jumps in the figures at certain times, particularly following international crises.

Methods of Studying Group Public Opinions

Although some researchers pay attention to general breakdowns of public attitudes by treating party, income, occupation, race, age, and region separately, their analyses are hampered by reliance on group data published somewhat unevenly by Gallup (Hibbs, Rivers, and Vasilatos 1982; Monroe and Laughlin 1983; Ragsdale 1987b). Because of the limitations of Gallup opinion data, no consideration of how these or other personal, social, economic, or demographic attributes jointly influence individuals' evaluations of presidents could be given. Indeed, Hibbs, Rivers, and Vasilatos have written: "Ideally, analysis would be based on joint disaggregation along several dimensions. However, the presidential approval time-series data are not published in this form" (1982, 313).

Aggregation bias is a general problem that occurs when aggregate data are used to study opinion dynamics at the individual or group levels. Such serious methodological puzzles cannot always be solved (Achen 1982). Suppose, for example, that a person wants to know whether blacks are more likely to vote for Democrats, but the only information available is the proportion of blacks and the proportion of the population voting Democratic in each county. You might observe an aggregate correlation between these two variables, but you cannot determine whether black voters are the ones casting ballots for the Democrats. Indeed, whites who happen to live in black areas might be the ones more likely to vote for the Democrats. To distinguish between these and other possibilities, one needs information about individuals, not aggregates of individuals—hence the motivation for public opinion surveys. These surveys ask individuals about their behavior, and thus, when they are properly used, aggregation bias is less likely to occur. In the following discussion, we must also be aware of other methodological problems that are somewhat more likely to occur with public opinion data.

With few exceptions, every author studying presidential approval ratings has used the data published in the *Gallup Opinion Index*. Unfortunately, the *Gallup Opinion Index* is only a compilation of

Gallup's press releases. These releases were not meant to be a comprehensive guide to American public opinion, as the content of each press release was determined in part by its newsworthiness. Thus an unusual poll result or demographic breakdown is more likely to appear in the publication than one that is not as surprising. This approach is reasonable for the Gallup organization, which must sell its services to newspapers and other media organizations, but the approach is not optimal for scholars and students who come to use these data some thirty or forty years after they have been compiled. To help us adequately describe these problems, a brief discussion of the theory of sample surveys will be useful.

The goal of survey sampling is to obtain a reliable estimate of the "true" level of approval among the population of interest. A population may include all adult Americans, registered voters, probable voters, or some other similarly defined group. Time and financial constraints usually make it impossible to poll every person in the population of interest. Instead, poll takers use a random sample of Americans (usually about two thousand adults). Sampling theory helps us make inferences about the entire population of interest. Note that random sampling is not haphazard selection; the selection of only those people who are available or convenient could produce severe biases. Instead, a random sample is one in which each person in the population of interest is equally likely to be selected.[1]

If two surveys were conducted simultaneously, with two different randomly selected samples from the same population, the mean approval level for a president as estimated by these two surveys would not be identical. In theory, one could conduct a large number of simultaneous surveys, and there would be variation in the estimated mean approval ratings across these samples. *Sampling variance* indicates the amount of variation in these estimates. Sampling variation is a theoretical concept, as no one really takes more than one sample survey for one point in time from the same population, but it is the key concept in sampling theory. We hope, for example, that the average of these estimated approval ratings—each from a different simultaneous sample survey—equals the true approval rating from the entire population of interest. A survey for which this is true is said to be *unbiased*. If a survey's estimate is unbiased, the sampling variance in the approval estimate is equally dispersed around the true value. The single sample taken may not be near the mean of all the samples that could have been taken, but if the sampling procedure is unbiased, it will at least be correct on average, over the long run.

If researchers analyze only those presidential approval surveys that were interesting enough to be used as Gallup press releases and subsequently compiled in the *Gallup Opinion Index*, estimates of public approval would likely be biased. The particular type of bias that exists in this case is called *selection bias*. Statistical methods for coping with selection bias have been developed, but no better solution exists than collecting a more comprehensive set of available surveys. In the tables and figures below, we have supplemented the surveys reported in the *Gallup Opinion Index* with previously unpublished Gallup Polls. We obtained the electronic version of these polls from the Roper Center for Public Opinion Research, in Storrs, Connecticut, and corrected numerous errors in both previously published and unpublished data. We therefore reduced selection bias by including all available surveys. We also reduced other biases by correcting some of the polls that were previously reported in the *Gallup Opinion Index*.[2]

Even if the survey estimates are unbiased (that is, even if they are correct on average over the long run), large sample variances indicate that any one estimate (including ours) could still be far from the true population value. Thus, even if our sample is unbiased, we would prefer a smaller sampling variance. One way of decreasing sampling variance is by increasing the number of people interviewed in each survey. Intuitively we know that a random sample of only ten individuals from the U.S. population will not provide a very good estimate of aggregate presidential approval, but precisely why is this the case? The reason does not involve bias. A sample procedure that samples ten, one thousand, or ten thousand people would be right on average across samples in either case. The reason we prefer more interviews is that they reduce sampling variance, making it more likely that our one sample of individuals will produce estimates of approval closer to the true values in the population. The Gallup organization interviews roughly fifteen hundred to two thousand individuals, a sample that provides a reasonably small variance. It also uses a rather elaborate method of modified random selection designed to further reduce sampling variance. In the tables and figures for this chapter we present presidential approval scores for numerous demographic and socioeconomic groups. Within each group, there are fewer people than in the total sample, and so there is more sampling variance. We thus pay a price for moving from an anthropomorphic view that treats public opinion as if it had a life of its own to one that concentrates on the variations in different groups' opinions. To determine how much sampling variance there is in these groups, we list the number of people interviewed in each of these groups in many of the tables. This "sample size" gives us a sense of how confident we should be of any particular percentage. If the sample size is small, the probability that our particular sample is near the true value is smaller. In these situations, we would also find what appears to be more variation in presidential approval ratings over time, but whereas some of this time variation may be due to changes in the true population value, more of it may be due to the large sampling variance that one encounters with small sample sizes. It is, therefore, critical that we keep in mind the tradeoff between the contradictory goals of providing more detailed group breakdowns in our analyses and reducing sampling variance in our research.

A source of both bias and increased sampling variance may actually have been introduced by researchers who used only data in the *Gallup Opinion Index*. Because the data in the Gallup press releases, subsequently compiled in the index, were those that were generally more newsworthy and hence unique, a larger than usual portion of the observed variation in these data may be due to sampling variance rather than to true changes in opinion. In other words, even with as elaborate a sampling scheme as Gallup's, some samples or parts of samples will not be near the true value for the population. Because researchers have access to only those data published in the Gallup press releases, they may be using a large number of "unusual" samples. Our own reanalyses and more complete compilation of the original Gallup electronic data represent a significant effort to avoid this problem.[3]

Repeated cross-sectional analyses, such as the full complement of Gallup Polls, alleviate several problems involved in analyzing political opinions through single cross sections, individual-level time series data (that is, panels), or aggregate-level time series data. Single cross-section samples, which monitor attitudes at a single time point, obtain a "snapshot" of responses rather than the dynamic account of shifting attitudes that multiple cross-sectional surveys can offer. Unlike panel studies, multiple cross-sectional surveys are not hampered by the contaminated answers that respondents give when they are asked the same question several times in repeated interviews. The attrition of respondents that typically occurs in panel studies is not a problem with multiple cross sections. Indeed, the political science community has recently recognized the value of at least short-term multiple cross sections by completing weekly samples as part of the 1984 American National Elections Study. Finally, as we noted earlier, the aggregation bias that sometimes occurs when inferences about individual attitudes are being drawn from aggregate data can be avoided with properly analyzed multiple cross-sectional samples.

283

Group Public Opinions

Our first look at the subgroup variation that exists within public opinion toward presidents begins with an examination of the so-called gender gap. Sex differences are often a basis for variation in citizen attitudes and voter preferences. Table 6.3 indicates whether sex differences affect attitudes toward presidents. The results demonstrate no evidence of systematic trends across time in the split between male and female support for presidents, but they do show that a dramatic difference existed between the sexes regarding one president—Ronald Reagan. Men's approval of Reagan was on average nine percentage points higher than women's. This is fully three times as large as the next largest variation in female-male attitudes toward presidents.

Table 6.4 presents a more detailed quarterly breakdown of public approval by party identification, region, and income.[4] It has long been known that these political, demographic, and economic characteristics explain some attitude differences within the American public. Table 6.4 shows that citizens are more likely to support a president of their own party. Indeed, not only does this generalization hold on average for every quarter since 1965, but it does not weaken across time, unlike the public's general attachment to a party. Under President Reagan, the split in party support grew to a substantial difference of forty to fifty percentage points. It is also apparent that Republican presidents generally command more support among their partisans than Democratic presidents. The natural advantage that Democratic presidents have because of the large number of Democratic party identifiers may thus be partly canceled out by the greater support that Republicans show for their party's presidents.

Regional variations in presidential support are also evident in Table 6.4. The principle difference appears to be between the South and the other regions of the country for presidents Johnson through Carter. Nixon, Ford, and Carter typically received greater support from the South than from the rest of the nation as each developed his own "southern strategy," an approach originated by Nixon to gain Republican inroads in the predominantly Democratic South. Johnson received less support from this region perhaps because of his civil rights initiatives, which were intensely disliked by the South. The approval levels for President Reagan are roughly equal across the four regions.

Table 6.4 also reveals that Democratic presidents are supported more by the poor than by the wealthy, whereas Republican presidents have an advantage among the wealthy rather than among the poor. For most quarters and all presidencies, this difference is quite noticeable.

As with party identification and gender, the income gap is larger for Ronald Reagan than for any of his predecessors.

This preliminary look at the different publics to which presidents must pay attention suggests that the various groups' views depend predominantly on the intertwining of group characteristics with the parties of the presidents. This pattern is telling for presidents who wish to promote their images as central, singular leaders of the nation. Groups within the nation are likely to judge presidents on practical matters, such as the party the president represents and the socioeconomic groups he favors, thereby hampering attempts to build a singularly popular image.

We provide reanalyses of all the original Gallup polls taken during Jimmy Carter's presidency and Ronald Reagan's first term. Tables 6.5 through 6.14 present a complete set of these data; we offer a brief discussion in the text. These tables will permit the reader to do sophisticated analyses of fluctuations in group support for Carter and Reagan. In addition, these tables reveal the plurality of group opinions surrounding the president at any one time as well as the differences in opinion within these groups across time and in response to specific domestic and international events.

Analyses of public approval for presidents by party identification, education, race, sex, income, and region appear in Tables 6.5 and 6.6 (see also Figures 6.2 and 6.3). Particularly noteworthy is the very low support for Ronald Reagan among blacks. In September 1981, only 10 percent of black Americans supported Reagan; the figure was somewhat higher before and after this date, but it was always very low. It is also interesting that, in the middle of Carter's presidency, the effect of education on presidential approval shifted dramatically. Early in his term, college graduates approved of Carter more than did people with less education. By 1978, however, the effect had switched, and Carter was receiving more support from the less educated groups than from the educated (see Figure 6.3).

Table 6.7 presents analyses of presidential approval by religion and age (see Figure 6.4). Despite a common belief that Reagan has been very popular with the young, Carter actually had higher approval ratings from the lowest age category (twenty-six years old and younger). More interesting still is the high early-term approval for both Carter and Reagan among the young. Within a year or so, however, this early support dropped to a level below that of older citizens. Further analysis needs to be done, but the oft-noted tendency for public support to decline following the election may perhaps be due, fully or partly, to this early high support from the young. Currently, all

285

theories concerning this pattern emphasize factors that affect the nation as a whole. With our cross-sectional data, it is now possible to consider subgroup explanations of this phenomenon. The young, for example, may be especially impressed with the money spent, the fanfare created, and the attention given to the presidential nomination and election process, as well as with the symbolism and ceremony of the presidential inauguration. The young, perhaps in combination with certain other groups, may account for this seemingly more general phenomenon of declining support for the president after his first year in office.

The Gallup organization did not include survey questions about union membership, home ownership, and employment until December 1978. With these available data, Table 6.8 again demonstrates the sharp divisions in public approval for President Reagan. Whereas those with full- or part-time employment and the unemployed supported President Carter in roughly equal percentages, the employed supported Reagan about ten percentage points more than the unemployed. A similar effect can be seen for union membership: Carter had slightly more support from union members, but union members supported Reagan considerably less than nonunion members.

Tables 6.9, 6.10, and 6.11 present a joint disaggregation of presidential approval by both party and region identification. This format permits southern Democrats and northern Democrats, for example, to be studied and compared. Tables 6.12, 6.13, and 6.14 show presidential approval by Republican, Democratic, and independent poor and nonpoor Americans. Although there are relatively few poor Republicans in these samples (resulting in increased sampling variance and thus greater apparent volatility over time), the differences in income groups reported earlier for Reagan do not appear to be attributable solely to the fact that the poor tend to be Democratic. This point is evident from the large differences in approval between the poor and nonpoor for both Republicans (Table 6.12) and Democrats (Table 6.13). Although the Democratic poor are less sanguine about Reagan than the Republican poor, for instance, both groups favor him considerably less than the higher-income groups in either party. In the case of independents (Table 6.14), for whom partisan preferences play less of a role, the differences between poor and nonpoor Americans are even larger.

These analyses add to the complex picture of the various publics that presidents attempt to influence and present a truer picture of how public attitudes are likely to vary. The explanation is not simply that people within a party hold certain attitudes about the president but that, within the party, large differences can be found across income groups and regions. Presidents attempting to satisfy as many people as possible will have a difficult time juggling the demands of these different constituencies.

Other Approval Indicators

In addition to the Gallup data on presidential approval, many other indicators can be used to measure the popularity of the incumbent president. In recent years, a policy focus has been added to the standard question on presidential approval. Table 6.15, for example, summarizes the responses of the public when asked whether they approved or disapproved of the way Presidents Carter and Reagan handled the economy and foreign affairs. Although the question wording differs across presidencies, two generalizations seem to hold. First, Americans are generally happier with both presidents' handling of foreign policy than with their handling of the economy. Indeed, this result is evident across several levels of economic wealth and various types of international crises. Second, the magnitude of this result increases with time after the inauguration. More research needs to be done to determine the reason. One explanation could be a "two presidencies" effect—where the foreign policy presidency enjoys more support than the domestic policy presidency across time (see Chapter 2)—or presidents may simply spend more time working on foreign policy than on domestic policy as their terms progress. Further analysis is offered by Table 6.16, which reports survey results about Reagan's handling of the situation in Central America from Gallup, Harris, and ABC/*Washington Post*. This table, together with the others, points to another dimension of the various publics. There is an interconnection between group characteristics and policy areas. Not only do groups hold different opinions of different presidents at different times, but their opinions also may vary by the policy areas within which presidents work.

Table 6.17 presents a very different indicator of presidential approval. Once a year (usually in December), the Gallup organization has asked the following question of a sample of Americans: "What man that you have heard or read about living today in any part of the world do you admire the most?" [5] Since 1946 the incumbent president has always been one of the top four people mentioned by the public in this poll (see the boldface entries in Table 6.17). The ranking of the incumbent president varies somewhat, however. Truman, for example, was ranked first in only two of the seven polls conducted during his presidency. The current improvement in Truman's reputation makes it difficult to remember that he was a relatively unpopular president in his time. On the other hand, Eisenhower, Kennedy, and Reagan were the men most admired every year of their tenure. The admiration for the presidency even extends to (living) former presidents (see the italicized entries in the table).

A final indicator of presidential approval that we consider is the opinions of the British concerning American presidents. Richard Neustadt comments, "The public standing of a President of the United States may be quite different from his standing with constituents abroad" (1960, 88). The data in Table 6.18 indicate that the British public liked Carter somewhat more and Reagan considerably less than did Americans. British citizen forecasts of the effects of the elections of Richard Nixon, Jimmy Carter, and Ronald Reagan appear in Table 6.19.

Other Opinions

In Table 6.20, we present a measure of public confidence in the White House, Congress, the Supreme Court, and other institutions in American society. Confidence in the White House, which was comparable to confidence in the Supreme Court prior to the Watergate scandal, since then has dropped and has stayed at about half the level of that of the Court. Although Gerald Ford is widely credited with having restored credibility and confidence to the presidency, these data tell a different story. The percentage of the population having a great deal of confidence in the White House dropped precipitously during Watergate, but it also remained low during most of Ford's tenure. Indeed, the percentage of the public having a great deal of confidence in the White House did not rise above 20 percent until the election of Carter. Public confidence dropped again during the latter part of President Carter's term, but rose during Reagan's presidency. Compared with other institutions in American society, the White House typically enjoys less of the public's confidence than the Supreme Court but usually more than Congress.

Another question used to compare American institutions relates to the ethical and moral practices of these institutions. The data in Table 6.21 indicate that public judgments of the president as a moral and ethical leader improved from 1981 to 1985, with a moderate drop in the intervening years.

Table 6.22 presents the sometimes suprising results of a survey that asked Americans whether they would object strongly if a president behaved in certain ways. More than one-fifth of the sampled individuals (and one of every four women), for example, reported that they would object strongly if the president wore jeans in the Oval Office. In addition, 33 percent of the sample objected to the president using profane language in private (see Wayne 1986, for a more detailed study of these data).

Table 6.23 summarizes feelings of political tolerance in the selection of presidents for selected years over the last five decades. A majority of Americans would now support a "generally well-qualified" person for president who happened to be black, female, Catholic, or Jewish. For each of these groups, except Catholics, only a minority of Americans in past decades supported such a candidacy. For every group in the table, however, political tolerance has increased over time. Nevertheless, only 42 percent would support an atheist for president and only 29 percent would support a homosexual. These stated opinions also may not necessarily translate into votes because, apart from John Kennedy, who was Catholic, individuals who represent one or more of these groups have not as yet attained a nomination for the office.

Surveys have also monitored opinions on institutional change in the office. Approximately two-thirds of Americans support line-item veto power for presidents (see Table 6.24), and this level of support has changed little in the last four decades. The proportion who favor a single six-year presidential term has increased slightly over the years, but consistently fewer than one-third of Americans support this proposal even today.

More general indicators of public opinions, although not directly related to presidents, include feelings about political parties. Because the president is closely identified with a political party, an insight into patterns of support for the parties is critical for an understanding of the presidency. Table 6.25 indicates trends in opinions as to which party is best for prosperity and peace. At the escalation of the war in Vietnam (1964), for example, people felt more confident that the Democratic party would maintain peace, but by 1968 this partisan effect had been reversed. Citizens have also identified in survey answers what they believe to be the most important national problem for each year since 1935 (see Table 6.26). These national problems, which primarily involve war and economic difficulties of inflation and unemployment, are usually ones that presidents are expected to solve. Since 1945, citizens have also been asked which political party they believe is best able to handle the national problem they identified in these surveys. These patterns of party preferences, as shown in Table 6.27, are closely related to partisan control of the White House.

289

Conclusion

The data presented in this chapter reveal the wide variation in opinion that exists across groups, policy areas, and other aspects of the presidency as an institution. Presidents devote much of their energy to preserving and increasing public support across these groups and policy areas. To achieve this goal, presidents participate in several forms of public appearances mentioned in Chapter 5, numerous policy-relevant activities described in Chapters 2 and 3, and various appointment decisions outlined in Chapter 4. Yet despite the flurry of activities associated with contemporary presidents, they have difficulty achieving high levels of approval.

At a very basic level, citizens are often very inattentive to presidential activity. Although a president is more visible than any other politician in the nation, nonetheless "presidential standing outside Washington is actually a jumble of imprecise impressions held by relatively inattentive [people]" (Neustadt 1960, 87). On a more complex level, the results presented in this chapter demonstrate how the opinions formed of presidential performances in office depend on the economic, political, and demographic backgrounds of the citizenry. Our results in earlier chapters show that presidents attempt to accommodate groups within the nation when they make decisions on executive orders and appointments. The results in this chapter stress some of the reactions presidents elicit from these groups. On yet another level, presidents attempt to cope with events and policy matters to which citizens may pay attention. The complexity of the national and international environment adds to the variety of responses presidents must make. At each level, the plural nature of institutional patterns in public opinion expands as presidents attempt to solve group problems and to heighten awareness of these solutions among the groups involved. In advancing any of these solutions, presidents must understand how opinion is diffused among the several publics in the American citizenry.

Solutions provided for any one group in the electorate may alienate other groups or even broaden public support for the presidency. Presidents, in seeking to lead the nation and to have the highest possible approval ratings, always confront the paradoxes and dilemmas of the plural presidency: they must listen to myriad groups' views on the issues, many of which are contradictory, while attempting to devise solutions to the problems in such a way as to maintain the nation's unity and to retain their presidential images as national leaders of all the people.

Notes

1. Techniques such as random dialing of telephone numbers only approximate the idea, because many people (particularly the poor) do not have telephones. In addition, some large families may have only one number, so that each individual in the house is less likely to be selected.
2. Thus far, only those nearly two hundred Gallup Polls for Jimmy Carter and for Ronald Reagan's first presidential term have been checked, verified, corrected, and compiled. The polls for other presidents will appear in future editions of this volume. The data not from these terms have been collected from the *Gallup Opinion Index* and other sources as noted.
3. Even our more complete compilation may of course suffer from a similar problem: bias in the selection of a time to administer a poll. Presumably the Gallup organization was somewhat more likely to conduct a survey if it expected something interesting or unusual to be found. This method overemphasizes change in public opinion, and the results may therefore appear more volatile than they truly are.
4. The *Gallup Opinion Index* began reporting presidential approval by group only in 1965, although, as previous tables make clear, the data go back much farther.
5. In 1946 and 1947, Gallup asked about the "most admired person." Since 1969, Gallup has also asked, "Who is your second choice?"

Table 6.1 Presidential Approval by Time since Inauguration (percent)

				Percentage approving [a]				
Time	Truman	Eisenhower	Kennedy	Johnson	Nixon	Ford	Carter	Reagan
Month took office	—	—	—	—	59	71	—	51
After 1st month	—	68	—	79	61	50	71	55
After 2nd month	—	59	73	80	63	55	72	60
After 3rd month	87	74	83	75	61	48	63	67
After 4th month	—	74	76	73	65	42	64	68
After 5th month	—	—	74	77	63	39	63	58
After 6th month	—	71	71	75	65	39	67	60
After 7th month	75	—	73	74	62	37	66	60
After 8th month	—	75	75	—	58	39	59	52
After 9th month	—	65	76	—	56	51	51	56
After 10th month	63	—	77	—	68	52	56	54
After 11th month	—	60	78	—	59	—	57	49
After 12th month	50	68	77	69	61	46	52	47
After 13th month	—	71	78	69	56	47	50	47
After 14th month	—	68	79	71	53	44	48	46
After 15th month	43	—	77	—	56	41	41	44
After 16th month	—	64	73	69	59	39	43	45
After 17th month	—	61	71	67	55	46	42	44
After 18th month	32	—	69	64	55	48	39	41
After 19th month	—	71	66	70	56	50	43	42
After 20th month	—	65	67	69	—	48	48	42
After 21st month	35	64	62	65	58	47	49	42
After 22nd month	48	57	—	65	57	45	50	43
After 23rd month	60	63	74	63	52	—	51	41
After 24th month	—	69	76	64	56	—	43	35
After 25th month	—	71	70	63	50	—	37	40

After 26th month	54	66	67	61	50	—	42	41
After 27th month	—	68	66	56	50	—	40	41
After 28th month	55	69	64	57	49	53	32	46
After 29th month	—	—	61	54	48	—	29	47
After 30th month	—	72	61	51	50	—	29	42
After 31st month	—	71	63	48	49	—	32	43
After 32nd month	—	—	56	56	—	—	30	48
After 33rd month	36	77	58	47	52	—	31	46
After 34th month	—	75	58	46	49	—	38	53
After 35th month	39	77	—	44	50	—	54	54
After 36th month	—	76	—	49	50	—	58	55
After 37th month	—	72	—	44	52	—	55	55
After 38th month	—	69	—	46	53	—	39	54
After 39th month	—	—	—	45	—	—	39	52
After 40th month	—	69	—	45	62	—	38	54
After 41st month	69	67	—	49	57	—	31	54
After 42nd month	67	—	—	45	—	—	21	52
After 43rd month	—	69	—	51	—	—	32	54
After 44th month	69	67	—	47	—	—	—	57
After 45th month	57	—	—	39	—	—	—	58
After 46th month	—	75	—	38	62	—	—	61
After 47th month	57	79	—	38	59	—	34	59
After 48th month	—	73	—	42	67	—	—	64
After 49th month	51	72	—	46	65	—	—	60
After 50th month	—	72	—	49	—	—	—	56
After 51st month	—	67	—	41	48	—	—	52
After 52nd month	—	62	—	—	44	—	—	55
After 53rd month	51	—	—	50	44	—	—	58
After 54th month	—	63	—	41	39	—	—	58
After 55th month	—	—	—	43	36	—	—	63
After 56th month	—	59	—	40	33	—	—	60

(Table continues)

Table 6.1 (continued)

Time	Percentage approving[a]							
	Truman	Eisenhower	Kennedy	Johnson	Nixon	Ford	Carter	Reagan
After 57th month	45	57	—	35	27	—	—	63
After 58th month	—	—	—	—	27	—	—	65
After 59th month	—	58	—	42	29	—	—	63
After 60th month	37	54	—	43	26	—	—	64
After 61st month	37	50	—	44	27	—	—	—
After 62nd month				49	26			63

Note: The question was: "Do you approve or disapprove of the way [the incumbent] is handling his job as president?"

[a] In months in which more than one approval poll was conducted, the last results of the month are presented.

Source: Adapted from *Public Opinion*, February/March 1986, 37-38.

Table 6.2 Aggregate Public Approval from Truman to Reagan (percent)

Date	Approve	Disapprove	No opinion	Interviews
Truman				
January 7, 1949	69	17	14	—
March 6, 1949	57	24	19	—
June 11, 1949	57	26	17	—
September 25, 1949	51	31	18	—
January 8, 1950	45	40	15	—
February 26, 1950	37	44	19	—
Late April 1950	37	44	19	—
June 1950	37	45	18	—
July 1950	46	37	17	—
Late July 1950	40	40	20	—
August 20, 1950	43	32	25	—
October 1950	39	42	19	—
January 8, 1951	36	49	1	—
February 4, 1951	26	57	17	—
March 26, 1951	28	57	15	—
May 19, 1951	24	61	15	—
June 16, 1951	25	59	16	—
July 8, 1951	29	54	17	—
August 3, 1951	31	57	12	—
September 21, 1951	32	54	14	—
October 14, 1951	29	55	16	—
November 11, 1951	23	58	19	—
January 20, 1952	26	62	13	—
February 9, 1952	25	62	13	—
April 13, 1952	28	59	13	—
May 1952	28	59	13	—
June 15, 1952	32	58	10	—
October 9, 1952	32	55	13	—
December 6, 1952	31	56	13	—
Eisenhower, I				
January 11, 1953	78	4	18	—
February 1, 1953	68	7	25	—
February 22, 1953	67	8	25	—
March 28, 1953	74	8	18	—
April 1953	74	10	16	—
May 9, 1953	74	10	16	—
July 4, 1953	71	15	14	—
Late July 1953	73	13	14	—
August 1953	74	14	12	—
September 12, 1953	75	14	12	—
October 9, 1953	66	20	14	—
Early November 1953	61	26	13	—
Late November 1953	58	25	17	—
December 11, 1953	66	20	14	—
January 9, 1954	71	19	10	—
January 1954	70	17	13	—

(Table continues)

The Elusive Executive

Table 6.2 (continued)

Date	Approve	Disapprove	No opinion	Interviews
Eisenhower, I (continued)				
February 25, 1954	68	19	13	—
March 1954	65	22	13	—
April 1954	68	21	11	—
May 2, 1954	60	22	18	—
Late May 1954	61	23	16	—
June 12, 1954	62	24	14	—
Early July 1954	64	22	14	—
Late July 1954	75	11	14	—
August 5, 1954	68	20	12	—
August 26, 1954	62	23	15	—
September 1954	66	21	13	—
October 1954	61	26	13	—
November 1954	57	23	20	—
December 2, 1954	68	23	9	—
January 1, 1955	70	18	12	—
Late January 1955	70	17	13	—
February 10, 1955	71	16	13	—
Early March 1955	70	19	11	—
Late March 1955	66	21	13	—
April 14, 1955	68	18	14	—
May 12, 1955	69	16	15	—
July 1955	72	18	10	—
August 3, 1955	76	11	13	—
August 25, 1955	71	16	13	—
November 1955	77	13	10	—
December 8, 1955	75	13	12	—
Early January 1956	76	12	12	—
Late January 1956	77	14	9	—
February 16, 1956	76	14	10	—
March 1956	72	18	10	—
March 1956	73	18	9	—
April 19, 1956	69	19	12	—
July 12, 1956	69	21	12	—
August 3, 1956	67	20	13	—
November 22, 1956	75	15	10	—
December 1956	79	11	10	—
Eisenhower, II				
January 17, 1957	73	14	13	—
February 1957	72	16	12	—
February 28, 1957	72	18	10	—
Early April 1957	66	21	13	—
April 25, 1957	67	21	12	—
May 1957	62	23	15	—
June 6, 1957	62	23	15	—
June 27, 1957	63	23	15	—
Late August 1957	59	23	18	—
September 1957	59	26	15	—

Table 6.2 (continued)

Date	Approve	Disapprove	No opinion	Interviews
Eisenhower, II (continued)				
October 10, 1957	57	27	16	—
January 3, 1958	60	30	10	—
Late January 1958	58	27	15	—
February 14, 1958	54	32	14	—
March 6, 1958	50	34	16	—
Late March 1958	48	36	16	—
April 16, 1958	54	31	15	—
May 1958	53	32	15	—
Late May 1958	54	31	15	—
July 1958	52	32	16	—
July 1958	58	27	15	—
August 1958	56	27	15	—
September 10, 1958	56	29	15	—
October 1958	58	25	17	—
November 7, 1958	52	30	18	—
December 3, 1958	57	32	11	—
January 7, 1959	57	27	16	—
February 4, 1959	59	26	15	—
March 1959	58	26	16	—
April 2, 1959	62	22	16	—
April 29, 1959	60	24	16	—
May 29, 1959	64	21	15	—
June 25, 1959	60	24	16	—
July 23, 1959	61	26	13	—
August 20, 1959	66	20	14	—
September 18, 1959	66	19	15	—
October 16, 1959	66	19	15	—
November 1959	64	22	14	—
Middle December 1959	76	15	9	—
January 6, 1960	66	18	16	—
February 1960	64	21	15	—
March 1960	64	22	14	—
March 30, 1960	65	22	13	—
Late April 1960	62	22	16	—
May 26, 1960	65	22	13	—
June 1960	61	24	15	—
Late June 1960	57	26	17	—
July 1960	49	33	18	—
Late July 1960	63	26	11	—
Early August 1960	63	24	13	—
Late August 1960	61	28	11	—
September 1960	58	28	14	—
October 18, 1960	58	31	11	—
November 1960	59	26	15	—
December 1960	59	27	14	—

(Table continues)

Table 6.2 (continued)

Date	Approve	Disapprove	No opinion	Interviews
Kennedy				
February 10, 1961	72	6	22	—
March 10, 1961	73	7	20	—
April 1961	78	6	16	—
April 28, 1961	83	5	12	—
Early May 1961	77	9	14	—
Middle May 1961	75	10	15	—
May 28, 1961	74	11	15	—
June 23, 1961	71	14	15	—
July 27, 1961	74	12	14	—
August 1961	75	12	13	—
September 21, 1961	79	10	11	—
October 17, 1961	77	12	11	—
November 1961	79	9	12	—
December 1961	77	11	12	—
January 11, 1962	78	9	13	—
February 18, 1962	78	11	11	—
March 8, 1962	79	12	9	—
April 1962	77	13	10	—
May 3, 1962	74	16	10	—
May 31, 1962	71	19	10	—
Late June 1962	69	19	12	—
July 26, 1962	66	23	11	—
August 23, 1962	67	20	13	—
September 20, 1962	62	22	16	—
October 1962	61	24	15	—
November 16, 1962	73	14	13	—
December 1962	76	13	11	—
January 11, 1963	74	14	12	—
February 7, 1963	70	18	12	—
March 8, 1963	67	20	13	—
April 4, 1963	66	21	13	—
May 8, 1963	64	25	11	—
Middle May 1963	65	23	12	—
Late May 1963	64	24	12	—
June 21, 1963	61	26	13	—
July 1963	61	27	12	—
August 15, 1963	62	26	13	—
September 12, 1963	56	29	15	—
October 11, 1963	58	29	13	—
November 1963	58	30	12	—
Johnson				
Early December 1963	78	2	20	—
December 12, 1963	79	3	18	—
January 2, 1964	80	5	15	—
February 1, 1964	75	8	17	—
Middle February 1964	73	9	18	—
February 28, 1964	79	9	12	—

Table 6.2 (continued)

Date	Approve	Disapprove	No opinion	Interviews
Johnson (continued)				
Middle March 1964	77	9	14	—
March 27, 1964	75	12	13	—
April 1964	75	11	15	—
May 6, 1964	75	11	14	—
Late May 1964	74	13	13	—
June 4, 1964	74	12	14	—
Middle June 1964	74	14	12	—
Late June 1964	74	15	11	—
Late June 1964	74	15	11	—
November 1964	69	18	13	—
December 11, 1964	69	18	13	—
January 7, 1965	71	15	14	—
Late January 1965	71	16	13	—
February 1965	68	18	14	—
Early March 1965	69	21	10	—
Late March 1965	69	21	10	—
Early April 1965	67	22	11	—
April 23, 1965	64	22	14	—
May 13, 1965	70	18	12	—
June 4, 1965	69	19	12	—
June 24, 1965	65	21	14	—
July 16, 1965	65	20	15	—
Early August 1965	65	22	13	—
August 27, 1965	64	25	13	—
September 16, 1965	63	24	13	—
October 1965	66	21	13	—
October 19, 1965	64	22	14	—
November 18, 1965	62	22	16	—
December 11, 1965	63	26	11	—
Early January 1966	59	24	17	—
January 21, 1966	61	27	12	—
February 10, 1966	56	34	10	—
March 3, 1966	58	28	14	—
March 24, 1966	57	28	15	—
April 1966	54	33	13	—
May 5, 1966	46	34	20	—
May 19, 1966	50	33	17	—
June 1966	48	39	13	—
July 8, 1966	56	30	14	—
July 29, 1966	51	38	11	—
August 1966	48	38	14	—
September 8, 1966	46	39	15	—
Early October 1966	44	42	14	—
Late October 1966	44	41	15	—
November 10, 1966	48	37	15	—
December 1966	44	47	9	—

(Table continues)

Table 6.2 (continued)

Date	Approve	Disapprove	No opinion	Interviews
Johnson (continued)				
Early January 1967	47	37	16	—
January 26, 1967	46	38	16	—
February 1967	45	42	13	—
March 1967	45	41	14	—
Late March 1967	46	38	16	—
April 19, 1967	48	37	15	—
May 1967	45	39	16	—
June 2, 1967	44	40	16	—
June 22, 1967	52	35	13	—
July 1967	47	39	14	—
Early August 1967	40	48	12	—
August 24, 167	39	48	13	—
September 1967	38	47	15	—
October 1967	38	50	12	—
October 27, 1967	41	49	10	—
December 7, 1967	46	41	13	—
January 4, 1968	48	39	13	—
February 1, 1968	41	47	12	—
Late February 1968	41	48	11	—
March 15, 1968	36	52	12	—
April 4, 1968	42	47	11	—
Early May 1968	46	43	11	—
Late May 1968	41	45	14	—
Early June 1968	42	45	13	—
Late June 1968	40	47	13	—
July 1968	40	47	13	—
August 7, 1968	35	52	13	—
September 26, 1968	42	51	7	—
November 9, 1968	43	44	13	—
December 1968	44	43	13	—
January 1, 1969	49	37	14	—
Nixon, I				
January 23, 1969	59	5	36	—
February 20, 1969	60	6	34	—
March 12, 1969	65	9	26	—
Late March 1969	63	10	27	—
April 10, 1969	61	12	27	—
Early May 1969	62	15	23	—
May 15, 1969	65	12	23	—
Late May 1969	62	15	23	—
June 1969	63	16	21	—
July 19, 1969	58	22	20	—
August 14, 1969	65	20	15	—
September 11, 1969	60	24	16	—
September 19, 1969	58	23	19	—
October 3, 1969	57	24	19	—
Late October 1969	56	29	15	—

Table 6.2 (continued)

Date	Approve	Disapprove	No opinion	Interviews
Nixon, I (continued)				
November 12, 1969	67	19	14	—
December 1969	59	23	18	—
January 2, 1970	61	22	17	—
Middle January 1970	63	23	14	—
January 30, 1970	64	24	12	—
Late February 1970	56	27	17	—
March 18, 1970	53	30	17	—
March 27, 1970	54	34	12	—
April 17, 1970	56	31	13	—
April 29, 1970	57	32	11	—
May 21, 1970	59	29	12	—
June 13, 1970	55	31	14	—
July 9, 1970	61	28	11	—
July 31, 1970	55	32	13	—
August 25, 1970	55	31	14	—
Early September 1970	57	30	13	—
Late September 1970	51	31	18	—
October 9, 1970	58	27	15	—
November 13, 1970	57	30	13	—
December 3, 1970	52	34	14	—
January 1971	56	33	11	—
February 19, 1971	49	37	14	—
March 3, 1971	56	32	12	—
March 11, 1971	50	37	13	—
Early April 1971	49	38	13	—
April 23, 1971	50	38	12	—
May 1971	50	35	15	—
June 4, 1971	48	37	15	—
Middle June 1971	48	37	15	—
June 25, 1971	48	39	13	—
July 1971	50	37	13	—
Middle August 1971	50	38	12	—
October 8, 1971	52	37	11	—
October 29, 1971	49	37	14	—
November 19, 1971	50	37	13	—
December 16, 1971	49	37	14	—
January 7, 1972	49	39	12	—
February 4, 1972	52	36	12	—
March 3, 1972	56	32	12	—
March 24, 1972	53	36	11	—
May 26, 1972	62	30	8	—
June 16, 1972	59	30	11	—
June 23, 1972	56	33	11	—
November 1972	62	28	10	—
December 8, 1972	59	30	11	—

(Table continues)

Table 6.2 (continued)

Date	Approve	Disapprove	No opinion	Interviews
Nixon, II				
January 12, 1973	51	37	12	—
January 26, 1973	67	25	8	—
February 26, 1973	67	25	10	—
March 30, 1973	57	33	10	—
April 6, 1973	54	36	10	—
April 27, 1973	48	40	12	—
May 4, 1973	45	42	13	—
May 11, 1973	44	45	11	—
June 1, 1973	44	44	12	—
June 22, 1973	44	45	11	—
July 6, 1973	39	49	12	—
August 3, 1973	31	58	11	—
August 17, 1973	36	54	10	—
September 7, 1973	34	56	10	—
September 21, 1973	33	59	8	—
October 5, 1973	30	57	13	—
October 19, 1973	27	60	13	—
November 2, 1973	27	63	10	—
November 30, 1973	31	59	10	—
December 7, 1973	29	60	11	—
January 4, 1974	27	63	10	—
January 18, 1974	26	64	10	—
February 1, 1974	28	59	13	—
February 8, 1974	27	63	10	—
February 22, 1974	25	64	11	—
March 8, 1974	26	62	12	—
March 29, 1974	26	65	9	—
April 12, 1974	25	62	13	—
Late April 1974	26	60	14	—
May 10, 1974	25	61	14	—
May 31, 1974	28	61	11	—
June 21, 1974	26	61	13	—
July 12, 1974	24	63	13	—
August 12, 1974	23	66	10	—
Ford				
August 16, 1974	71	3	26	—
Early September 1974	66	13	21	—
September 27, 1974	50	28	22	—
Early October 1974	52	29	19	—
October 18, 1974	55	28	17	—
November 8, 1974	47	33	20	—
November 15, 1974	48	32	20	—
December 6, 1974	42	41	17	—
January 10, 1975	37	39	24	—
January 31, 1975	39	43	18	—
February 28, 1975	39	45	16	—
March 28, 1975	37	43	20	—

Table 6.2   (continued)

Date	Approve	Disapprove	No opinion	Interviews
Ford (continued)				
April 4, 1975	44	37	19	—
April 18, 1975	39	46	15	—
May 2, 1975	40	43	17	—
May 30, 1975	51	33	16	—
June 27, 1975	52	33	15	—
August 1, 1975	45	37	18	—
August 15, 1975	46	37	17	—
September 12, 1975	47	36	17	—
October 3, 1975	47	37	16	—
October 17, 1975	47	40	13	—
October 31, 1975	44	44	12	—
November 21, 1975	41	46	13	—
December 5, 1975	46	37	17	—
December 12, 1975	39	46	15	—
January 2, 1976	46	42	12	—
January 23, 1976	45	45	10	—
January 30, 1976	46	40	14	—
February 27, 1976	48	38	14	—
March 19, 1976	50	36	14	—
April 9, 1976	48	41	11	—
May 21, 1976	47	38	15	—
June 11, 1976	45	40	15	—
December 10, 1976	53	32	15	—
Carter				
January 1, 1977	65.53	8.23	26.14	2,831
March 1, 1977	70.19	9.32	20.48	2,617
March 15, 1977	74.70	8.98	16.32	2,727
March 22, 1977	71.60	10.20	18.20	2,736
March 29, 1977	67.38	14.11	18.51	2,679
April 12, 1977	63.20	17.55	19.26	2,747
April 26, 1977	63.45	18.09	18.46	2,681
May 3, 1977	65.71	18.76	15.53	2,692
May 17, 1977	63.71	18.69	17.60	2,761
May 31, 1977	62.37	19.46	18.17	2,708
June 14, 1977	63.08	17.98	18.94	2,703
July 5, 1977	62.07	22.02	15.91	2,734
July 19, 1977	66.59	17.30	16.11	2,700
August 2, 1977	59.95	22.75	17.30	2,694
August 16, 1977	66.10	15.82	18.07	2,667
September 6, 1977	53.79	29.02	17.19	2,729
September 27, 1977	59.44	23.40	17.16	2,675
October 11, 1977	54.78	29.03	16.19	2,680
October 18, 1977	54.29	29.50	16.22	2,658
October 25, 1977	51.34	30.42	18.23	2,715
November 1, 1977	54.87	30.05	15.08	2,692
November 15, 1977	55.87	29.65	14.49	2,651

(Table continues)

Table 6.2   (continued)

Date	Approve	Disapprove	No opinion	Interviews
Carter (continued)				
December 16, 1977	56.60	27.40	16.00	2,719
January 3, 1978	54.86	26.87	18.27	2,758
January 17, 1978	51.87	28.54	19.59	2,726
February 8, 1978	46.54	34.52	18.94	2,688
February 21, 1978	50.27	33.31	16.42	2,759
March 1, 1978	48.52	33.27	18.21	2,768
March 7, 19788	49.62	34.75	15.63	2,751
March 28, 1978	47.48	39.28	13.24	2,803
April 11, 1978	40.42	43.84	15.74	2,719
April 25, 1978	41.01	41.90	17.09	2,802
May 3, 1978	41.45	42.89	15.66	2,765
May 16, 1978	42.52	43.23	14.25	2,681
May 30, 1978	43.83	40.60	15.57	2,697
June 13, 1978	42.34	42.27	15.38	2,704
July 5, 1978	40.09	41.26	18.65	2,746
July 18, 1978	38.61	44.09	17.30	2,792
August 1, 1978	39.08	43.85	17.06	2,684
August 8, 1978	40.03	43.22	16.75	5,491
August 15, 1978	42.71	40.81	16.49	2,845
September 5, 1978	42.08	41.61	16.31	2,740
September 11, 1978	44.99	40.06	15.45	2,776
September 19, 1978	47.76	34.16	18.08	2,705
October 29, 1978	49.29	36.17	14.54	2,676
December 5, 1978	51.16	33.41	15.44	2,727
January 2, 1979	50.19	35.91	13.90	2,662
January 16, 1979	43.27	41.12	15.62	2,651
January 30, 1979	42.22	42.00	15.78	2,700
February 20, 1979	37.15	46.38	16.47	2,751
February 27, 1979	39.29	47.97	12.74	2,716
March 13, 1979	46.57	39.52	13.91	2,725
March 20, 1979	42.61	43.59	13.80	2,753
April 3, 1979	40.47	45.86	13.67	2,671
May 1, 1979	37.16	48.84	14.00	2,664
May 15, 1979	32.22	52.59	15.19	2,666
May 29, 1979	29.03	55.89	15.08	2,659
June 19, 1979	29.27	56.80	13.92	2,808
June 26, 1979	28.29	59.11	12.60	2,722
July 10, 1979	29.04	57.54	13.43	2,800
July 30, 1979	32.14	53.39	14.47	2,744
July 31, 1979	32.06	53.44	14.50	2,773
August 7, 1979	33.51	54.88	11.61	2,799
August 14, 1979	32.42	53.94	13.64	2,742
September 4, 1979	29.71	55.54	14.75	2,733
October 2, 1979	28.68	58.59	12.73	2,741
October 14, 1979	31.49	54.71	13.80	2,760
October 30, 1979	13.98	55.36	12.67	2,724
November 13, 1979	37.79	49.50	12.71	2,691

Table 6.2 (continued)

Date	Approve	Disapprove	No opinion	Interviews
Carter (continued)				
November 27, 1979	51.52	36.78	11.70	2,735
December 4, 1979	54.36	35.06	10.58	2,695
January 2, 1980	56.19	33.35	10.46	2,801
January 22, 1980	57.58	32.49	9.94	2,838
January 29, 1980	55.21	35.80	8.99	2,813
February 26, 1980	51.83	38.08	10.09	2,765
March 4, 1980	42.76	44.84	12.41	2,837
March 24, 1980	50.48	48.64	0.88	2,496
April 8, 1980	39.98	50.15	10.87	2,714
April 29, 1980	42.56	47.32	10.12	2,728
May 13, 1980	38.28	50.76	10.96	2,819
June 27, 1980	38.40	51.38	10.21	2,820
June 10, 1980	32.33	55.87	11.80	2,821
June 24, 1980	30.83	58.29	10.88	2,738
July 8, 1980	32.55	54.96	12.48	2,780
August 12, 1980	32.12	54.76	13.12	2,836
September 9, 1980	37.46	54.66	7.88	2,819
November 18, 1980	31.04	56.05	12.91	2,719
December 3, 1980	34.11	55.32	10.57	2,744
Reagan				
January 27, 1981	50.89	13.56	35.55	2,855
February 20, 1981	55.44	17.89	26.67	2,778
March 10, 1981	59.43	24.29	16.28	2,832
March 31, 1981	66.52	18.43	15.05	2,751
April 7, 1981	66.98	19.21	13.81	2,744
May 5, 1981	67.63	20.85	11.51	2,623
June 2, 1981	58.74	28.27	12.99	2,671
June 16, 1981	58.79	28.63	12.58	2,679
June 23, 1981	57.80	30.13	12.07	2,685
July 21, 1981	55.85	30.33	13.82	2,743
July 28, 1981	59.44	28.33	12.23	2,707
August 11, 1981	59.62	29.55	10.82	2,707
September 15, 1981	51.89	37.28	10.83	2,723
September 29, 1981	55.63	34.92	9.45	2,689
October 27, 1981	54.28	34.47	11.25	2,559
November 10, 1981	48.99	40.18	10.83	2,974
November 17, 1981	54.53	36.71	8.76	2,659
December 8, 1981	48.59	41.36	10.05	2,628
January 9, 1982	49.24	39.66	11.10	2,622
January 23, 1982	47.33	41.46	11.21	2,622
February 7, 1982	46.65	43.19	10.17	2,744
March 14, 1982	46.32	44.63	9.04	2,720
April 4, 1982	45.04	46.33	8.63	2,631
April 25, 1982	43.16	47.05	9.78	2,750
May 2, 1982	44.42	45.85	9.73	2,733
May 16, 1982	44.86	44.22	10.92	2,666

(Table continues)

Table 6.2 (continued)

Date	Approve	Disapprove	No opinion	Interviews
Reagan (continued)				
June 13, 1982	44.94	45.49	9.57	2,561
June 27, 1982	44.33	45.56	10.11	2,671
July 25, 1982	42.47	46.10	11.43	2,703
August 1, 1982	40.96	46.85	12.18	2,717
August 15, 1982	40.70	48.87	10.43	2,656
August 29, 1982	41.99	45.62	12.40	2,670
September 19, 1982	42.45	47.84	9.91	2,594
October 17, 1982	41.81	47.88	10.32	2,753
November 7, 1982	42.68	47.03	10.28	2,713
November 21, 1982	43.29	46.82	9.89	2,721
December 21, 1982	41.18	50.34	8.48	2,664
January 16, 1983	36.81	54.19	9.00	2,768
January 25, 1983	37.27	52.82	9.91	2,664
January 30, 1983	35.09	56.03	8.87	2,727
February 27, 1983	40.04	50.09	9.87	2,665
March 13, 1983	40.87	49.13	10.00	2,711
April 17, 1983	40.51	49.40	10.09	2,666
May 1, 1983	42.81	46.39	10.80	2,712
May 15, 1983	43.07	45.08	11.85	2,693
May 22, 1983	45.67	42.72	11.60	2,680
June 12, 1983	43.32	45.21	11.47	2,599
June 26, 1983	46.99	43.79	9.23	2,720
July 24, 1983	42.28	46.83	10.90	2,725
August 1, 1983	44.30	42.07	13.62	2,738
August 7, 1983	43.34	46.91	9.75	2,635
August 14, 1983	43.21	44.89	11.89	2,682
August 21, 1983	42.51	46.18	11.31	2,618
September 11, 1983	47.33	41.68	10.99	2,320
September 18, 1983	46.90	43.08	10.03	2,224
October 10, 1983	45.32	43.73	10.94	2,202
October 23, 1983	49.25	40.90	9.84	2,479
November 20, 1983	52.57	36.82	10.61	2,178
December 11, 1983	53.78	37.93	8.29	2,196
January 15, 1984	52.33	37.63	10.04	2,232
January 28, 1984	55.36	36.28	8.36	2,332
February 11, 1984	55.63	35.87	8.49	2,378
March 17, 1984	53.61	38.81	7.58	2,216
April 7, 1984	54.03	36.80	9.17	2,258
May 19, 1984	53.42	38.19	8.39	2,252
June 23, 1984	54.20	35.93	9.87	2,249
July 1, 1984	53.04	36.67	10.28	2,217
July 7, 1978	53.46	35.82	10.73	2,228
July 14, 1984	55.63	34.60	9.77	2,283
July 28, 1984	51.69	36.92	11.39	2,335
September 4, 1984	56.57	35.94	7.49	2,390
September 18, 1984	56.54	36.56	6.89	2,292
September 25, 1984	53.88	35.20	10.93	2,361

Table 6.2   (continued)

Date	Approve	Disapprove	No opinion	Interviews
Reagan (continued)				
October 27, 1984	58.06	32.99	8.95	2,301
November 19, 1984	60.78	31.01	8.21	2,193
December 1, 1984	61.54	30.35	8.11	2,231
December 9, 1984	59.26	31.53	9.21	2,204
January 13, 1985	61.63	29.50	8.87	1,522

Sources: 1977-1984 coded and calculated by the authors from their analysis of the original Gallup survey data. 1949-1976 adapted by the authors from *The Gallup Opinion Index,* Report 182, October-November 1980, 13-59.

Table 6.3   The Gender Gap in Presidential Approval, Eisenhower to Reagan (percent)

President	Men[a]	Women	Difference
Eisenhower	63	65	2
Kennedy	70	70	0
Johnson	56	54	2
Nixon	50	47	3
Ford	45	46	1
Carter	46	47	1
Reagan	54	45	9

[a] Figures reported are the average percentage approving.

Source: *Gallup Report,* March 1983, 15.

Figure 6.1 Aggregate Presidential Approval, Truman through Reagan

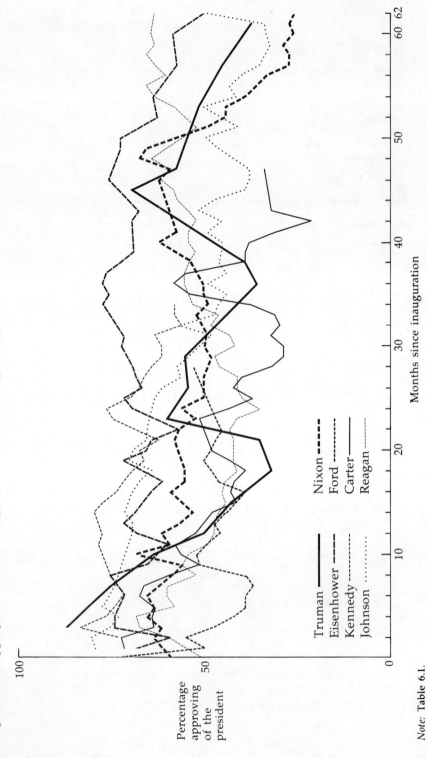

Truman ——
Eisenhower —— ——
Kennedy — — —
Johnson ··········

Nixon ■■ ■■
Ford —·—·—
Carter ············
Reagan ————

100

50

Percentage
approving
of the
president

0   10   20   30   40   50   60 62

Months since inauguration

Note: Table 6.1.

Table 6.4 Quarterly Presidential Approval by Party, Region, and Income, 1965-1984 (percent)

	Party			Region				Income		
Year/quarter	Rep.	Dem.	Ind.	East	Midwest	South	West	High	Middle	Low
Johnson										
1965/1	60	79	72	76	74	64	68	68	76	70
1965/2	51	77	62	79	70	52	63	65	71	67
1965/3	50	77	57	71	67	60	66	64	68	67
1965/4	46	76	60	75	64	51	59	65	66	64
1966/1	40	73	47	66	59	45	61	58	59	53
1966/2	33	65	44	59	51	43	48	48	54	52
1966/3	32	67	47	61	51	43	50	52	54	49
1966/4	28	66	40	62	46	40	43	47	48	53
1967/1	25	62	40	55	46	40	42	43	46	49
1967/2	29	61	41	52	46	39	49	46	46	47
1967/3	25	56	37	48	42	34	43	41	42	41
1967/4	25	60	35	49	39	35	44	41	42	41
1968/1	26	57	31	46	39	38	44	38	45	46
1968/2	32	61	39	55	46	39	43	46	49	44
1968/3	24	51	31	43	37	32	36	34	38	45
1968/4	29	59	35	50	43	33	43	41	45	42
Nixon										
1969/1	80	51	60	56	64	63	63	67	62	57
1969/2	83	49	58	63	60	63	64	66	64	58
1969/3	82	49	61	60	62	64	62	63	63	57
1969/4	83	49	63	59	64	66	60	67	60	59
1970/1	84	42	62	56	59	64	58	67	60	56
1970/2	81	42	61	55	55	63	59	64	56	53
1970/3	82	40	56	53	55	55	58	58	53	52
1970/4	82	39	55	55	52	61	55	60	55	49
1971/1	80	37	54	52	51	54	49	59	52	43

(Table continues)

Table 6.4 (continued)

Year/quarter	Party			Region				Income		
	Rep.	Dem.	Ind.	East	Midwest	South	West	High	Middle	Low
1971/2	80	34	48	48	48	53	46	52	50	43
1971/3	81	38	49	52	51	54	47	58	53	46
1971/4	85	34	45	52	45	52	47	54	48	43
1972/1	81	35	53	50	50	57	49	56	51	45
1972/2	88	43	62	59	56	68	51	63	59	53
1972/3	88	43	61	58	58	66	50	64	58	59
1972/4	88	44	60	57	60	65	50	66	58	56
1973/1	90	49	70	64	65	71	62	71	66	58
1973/2	75	29	47	41	45	51	42	52	42	39
1973/3	63	20	36	36	35	39	33	52	46	39
1973/4	54	17	27	24	29	36	28	31	27	27
1974/1	54	13	26	21	28	32	23	27	25	25
1974/2	51	14	26	22	26	31	27	30	24	25
1974/3	50	13	22	20	21	30	25	27	23	23
Ford										
1974/3	71	56	61	67	76	68	72	76	69	65
1974/4	68	37	49	46	50	47	48	53	47	42
1975/1	61	29	37	35	40	39	38	42	38	33
1975/2	66	37	51	47	47	48	48	54	47	33
1975/3	65	37	46	44	48	45	47	54	42	40
1975/4	63	31	43	39	47	42	41	46	41	35
1976/1	66	35	50	40	47	47	51	51	44	38
1976/2	68	35	49	41	49	50	49	52	42	42
1976/3	74	37	52	45	54	52	50	—	—	—
1976/4	80	40	54	49	58	54	51	—	—	—
Carter										
1977/1	56	81	70	67	67	72	63	73	72	66
1977/2	48	72	62	65	62	63	65	64	62	62

1977/3	47	73	61	63	64	63	60	64	62	60
1977/4	40	66	53	55	54	58	56	56	56	56
1978/1	34	60	53	53	55	55	47	48	51	54
1978/2	25	53	38	43	39	44	37	33	43	44
1978/3	20	52	36	40	38	40	44	40	47	52
1978/4	31	63	52	52	53	54	50	51	51	60
1979/1	24	55	43	47	38	46	42	44	43	41
1979/2	20	43	33	33	33	38	34	30	36	38
1979/3	19	36	24	25	25	34	26	25	28	31
1980/1	42	65	50	56	55	63	47	54	55	57
1980/2	28	57	35	42	43	53	36	52	44	48
1980/3	14	48	20	28	30	42	25	50	33	38
1980/4	14	49	30	28	35	38	36	33	31	43
Reagan										
1981/1	80	39	57	52	56	57	55	65	54	39
1981/2	89	49	66	62	66	66	64	74	64	47
1981/3	85	42	60	55	60	60	60	72	58	40
1981/4	84	33	53	50	53	52	51	61	47	31
1982/1	82	27	50	45	48	48	49	57	45	32
1982/2	79	24	47	44	46	44	45	56	43	30
1982/3	76	21	44	42	44	39	42	55	41	28
1982/4	79	22	44	39	44	40	48	55	41	29
1983/1	67	19	41	37	39	35	38	48	37	27
1983/2	78	26	49	45	44	45	50	57	46	29
1983/3	83	30	52	48	50	50	50	61	54	37
1983/4	87	33	54	50	55	55	51	64	61	44
1984/1	86	33	56	52	54	61	53	70	66	43
1984/2	85	32	58	52	51	54	59	71	58	45
1984/4	92	32	63	56	60	65	62	70	62	43

Note: Each number is the average of all Gallup Polls for which group breakdowns were reported for that quarter.

Sources: Compiled from *The Gallup Public Opinion Index*, periodic volumes, and from the authors' analysis of the original Gallup surveys.

Table 6.5 Presidential Approval by Party, Education, and Sex, 1977-1984 (percent)

	N	Party			Education			Sex	
		Rep.	Dem.	Ind.	<12	High school	College	M	F
Carter									
January 1, 1977	2,831	48.68	76.96	59.85	66.44	64.82	66.94	67.11	64.29
March 1, 1977	2,617	53.32	79.75	69.15	69.69	70.66	69.28	69.72	70.64
March 15, 1977	2,727	59.79	84.27	72.01	70.90	76.67	75.07	75.02	74.42
March 22, 1977	2,736	56.17	81.03	68.98	71.23	71.02	75.00	71.21	71.95
March 29, 1977	2,679	54.08	78.49	62.31	62.54	68.69	73.13	67.53	67.24
April 12, 1977	2,747	46.11	73.25	58.80	59.82	63.35	70.97	63.20	63.19
April 26, 1977	2,681	48.07	72.92	61.40	59.98	64.00	70.75	63.36	63.52
May 3, 1977	2,692	53.83	74.49	61.41	61.01	65.91	77.09	64.96	66.39
May 17, 1977	2,761	46.24	70.96	65.07	60.36	62.89	75.22	62.65	64.68
May 31, 1977	2,708	44.44	72.97	58.27	58.90	62.42	69.82	64.22	60.70
June 14, 1977	2,703	51.47	72.52	58.58	60.22	63.69	67.58	63.22	62.96
July 5, 1977	2,734	42.86	73.11	58.39	59.47	60.49	76.29	61.25	62.80
July 19, 1977	2,700	46.77	76.98	64.74	61.88	68.11	71.16	69.70	63.77
August 2, 1977	2,694	46.34	69.41	56.00	54.84	60.97	67.93	61.21	58.82
August 16, 1977	2,667	51.46	76.19	63.25	60.02	67.84	73.75	65.86	66.33
September 6, 1977	2,729	36.47	64.01	50.16	50.68	53.77	60.73	56.68	51.04
September 27, 1977	2,675	41.35	69.22	56.43	54.48	60.56	66.67	60.06	58.87
October 11, 1977	2,680	36.38	64.31	53.73	53.20	54.25	61.45	55.86	53.80
October 18, 1977	2,658	35.14	66.27	50.24	53.83	53.62	58.31	54.55	54.05
October 25, 1977	2,715	33.39	64.82	46.59	48.14	52.94	53.37	52.13	50.63
November 1, 1977	2,692	42.61	65.53	49.33	51.52	55.57	59.25	54.58	55.13
November 15, 1977	2,651	35.16	68.47	53.68	57.91	55.06	54.65	54.80	56.84
December 16, 1977	2,719	43.30	67.35	51.46	55.22	56.98	58.31	56.92	56.31
January 3, 1978	2,758	34.02	65.09	54.00	51.89	57.17	52.27	56.04	53.80
January 17, 1978	2,726	34.18	59.79	51.50	54.17	50.06	54.25	52.93	50.93
February 8, 1978	2,688	28.13	55.12	47.45	45.01	46.08	51.34	48.74	44.56
February 21, 1978	2,759	32.14	63.11	46.32	50.52	51.22	45.03	51.29	49.34
March 1, 1978	2,768	32.10	63.98	41.07	48.62	48.18	50.00	49.12	47.98
March 7, 1978	2,751	31.43	62.39	45.62	50.94	50.00	44.38	48.64	50.48
March 28, 1978	2,803	30.50	59.37	43.64	48.81	47.02	46.47	46.02	48.81
April 11, 1978	2,719	25.08	51.06	36.32	43.29	40.22	34.73	40.42	40.42
April 25, 1978	2,802	21.18	55.77	34.12	42.94	39.47	43.24	41.02	40.99
May 3, 1978	2,765	26.99	50.80	36.65	41.77	42.34	37.53	42.18	40.78
May 16, 1978	2,681	24.52	54.98	37.63	45.87	41.37	38.78	43.61	41.52
May 30, 1978	2,697	28.29	54.20	39.21	45.39	43.28	43.17	45.36	42.46
June 13, 1978	2,704	23.31	55.52	38.10	43.31	41.73	42.65	42.05	42.61
July 5, 1978	2,746	20.37	51.61	35.53	44.44	39.95	31.01	41.80	38.51
July 18, 1978	2,792	22.92	49.49	34.53	38.29	38.14	40.99	39.23	38.06
August 1, 1978	2,684	25.54	49.29	34.25	39.34	39.48	36.62	38.28	39.79
August 8, 1978	5,491	26.32	50.87	34.07	46.37	37.09	36.90	41.58	38.64
August 15, 1978	2,845	27.94	51.58	40.89	47.30	41.70	36.10	41.03	44.24
September 5, 1978	2,740	25.85	51.96	36.63	48.04	39.88	37.23	45.91	38.57
September 11, 1978	2,776	23.27	54.29	46.87	43.70	45.99	40.15	44.61	44.37
September 19, 1978	2,705	30.75	60.21	43.84	50.49	45.81	50.31	46.26	49.12

Table 6.5 (continued)

	N	Party			Education			Sex	
		Rep.	Dem.	Ind.	<12	High school	College	M	F
Carter (continued)									
October 29, 1978	2,676	33.03	62.36	44.17	53.66	47.30	47.09	47.17	51.21
December 5, 1978	2,727	—	—	—	54.89	48.24	55.15	48.59	53.53
January 2, 1979	2,662	32.37	59.21	49.23	48.19	50.29	53.65	49.24	51.03
January 16, 1979	2,651	23.65	54.77	41.80	41.17	45.00	41.65	42.82	43.67
January 30, 1979	2,700	23.97	54.65	38.20	41.68	40.45	50.13	44.00	40.60
February 20, 1979	2,751	21.49	47.53	33.26	40.58	36.09	34.31	37.46	36.86
February 27, 1979	2,716	26.77	48.27	35.29	39.26	39.95	36.97	39.80	38.83
March 13, 1979	2,725	30.16	56.00	44.69	54.06	42.21	47.15	46.93	46.24
March 20, 1979	2,753	28.77	53.08	37.37	40.07	42.15	50.13	43.10	42.16
April 3, 1979	2,671	21.64	51.74	37.18	36.96	40.66	47.66	39.08	41.72
May 1, 1979	2,664	28.40	46.72	30.93	40.50	34.57	40.26	34.67	39.43
May 15, 1979	2,666	23.51	36.69	31.11	30.18	32.19	36.54	31.22	33.16
May 29, 1979	2,659	20.26	35.88	25.96	27.47	30.50	26.54	27.22	30.71
June 19, 1979	2,808	33.02	21.52	26.83	32.67	27.55	28.83	26.93	31.42
June 26, 1979	2,722	18.70	34.17	28.37	32.40	27.47	22.38	28.27	28.30
July 10, 1979	2,800	17.98	37.24	27.16	29.18	28.92	29.27	27.04	30.83
July 30, 1979	2,744	15.81	42.47	27.77	32.14	32.43	31.04	32.90	31.45
July 31, 1979	2,773	19.06	40.21	28.85	35.99	31.13	26.85	31.30	32.76
August 7, 1979	2,799	22.44	42.71	29.61	38.05	31.32	32.71	32.49	34.45
August 14, 1979	2,742	21.87	42.17	27.32	36.06	31.02	30.00	33.61	31.34
September 4, 1979	2,733	14.67	37.28	28.47	34.15	27.30	29.37	29.26	30.12
October 2, 1979	2,741	19.69	33.94	27.45	28.42	29.01	27.88	29.70	27.75
October 14, 1979	2,760	23.93	39.42	25.85	31.50	31.00	33.51	32.90	30.19
October 30, 1979	2,724	17.73	39.92	30.94	35.40	31.70	25.26	29.76	34.02
November 13, 1979	2,691	26.53	47.44	29.42	38.26	38.14	35.56	37.20	38.33
November 27, 1979	2,735	38.72	62.20	47.30	54.20	51.58	45.26	48.81	53.98
December 4, 1979	2,695	41.58	61.85	54.60	57.77	51.75	56.93	53.16	55.45
January 2, 1980	2,801	40.42	65.28	53.15	56.32	54.73	61.34	56.09	56.29
January 22, 1980	2,838	40.95	67.22	54.66	57.40	59.07	51.61	57.43	57.71
January 29, 1980	2,813	53.63	55.02	56.54	55.00	56.06	52.77	54.65	55.77
February 26, 1980	2,765	38.72	62.22	46.69	53.33	52.20	47.15	52.04	51.63
March 4, 1980	2,837	25.17	54.52	37.40	43.85	43.33	37.96	43.34	42.22
March 24, 1980	2,496	57.71	48.55	48.09	58.52	47.83	43.77	53.28	47.81
April 8, 1980	2,714	28.37	47.72	36.09	40.27	38.56	37.82	37.07	40.79
April 29, 1980	2,728	25.13	55.25	36.00	47.33	43.01	29.89	41.34	43.67
May 13, 1980	2,819	30.73	47.03	31.03	40.72	38.25	32.99	35.47	40.83
May 27, 1980	2,820	21.43	50.70	31.94	42.22	37.76	32.98	35.71	40.92
June 10, 1980	2,821	14.61	43.39	28.61	33.06	32.86	28.50	29.82	34.62
June 24, 1980	2,738	20.09	41.56	24.31	32.99	29.47	31.90	31.49	30.17
July 8, 1980	2,780	15.38	47.80	23.59	34.61	34.24	21.29	28.52	36.18
August 12, 1980	2,836	13.88	47.81	19.57	37.01	30.32	28.69	31.44	32.75
September 9, 1980	2,819	11.86	61.28	21.52	46.31	33.69	33.76	35.34	39.34
November 18, 1980	2,719	12.10	49.77	22.70	35.74	30.57	23.89	27.94	34.00
December 3, 1980	2,744	14.27	49.15	30.63	39.68	32.57	28.07	29.73	38.03

(Table continues)

Table 6.5 (continued)

	N	Party			Education			Sex	
		Rep.	Dem.	Ind.	<12	High school	College	M	F
Reagan									
January 27, 1981	2,855	73.50	38.32	51.92	37.87	55.36	58.98	54.01	48.01
February 20, 1981	2,778	78.09	38.77	56.26	40.26	61.90	63.04	57.98	53.15
March 10, 1981	2,832	86.78	41.21	59.35	44.99	64.99	68.13	64.63	54.62
March 31, 1981	2,751	87.14	51.89	67.12	55.77	69.69	77.01	70.23	63.20
April 7, 1981	2,744	90.36	45.62	71.31	51.61	73.09	77.70	70.60	63.70
May 5, 1981	2,623	91.78	51.22	69.44	56.94	71.76	74.16	70.33	65.12
June 2, 1981	2,671	86.88	43.98	57.13	44.31	62.66	70.84	61.33	56.38
June 16, 1981	2,679	85.23	40.61	61.43	42.89	64.78	69.10	66.06	52.24
June 23, 1981	2,685	87.96	40.60	54.87	41.83	64.35	64.38	63.44	52.72
July 21, 1981	2,743	79.67	37.84	59.60	40.44	61.60	66.31	63.13	49.09
July 28, 1981	2,707	86.80	45.06	55.98	45.80	65.16	62.76	62.48	56.64
August 11, 1981	2,707	84.75	41.56	59.76	43.91	66.58	67.21	65.71	54.14
September 15, 1981	2,723	81.91	33.31	55.01	36.94	56.25	64.46	60.42	44.15
September 29, 1981	2,689	87.47	36.44	53.79	42.29	61.65	59.06	60.60	51.20
October 27, 1981	2,559	88.70	30.46	59.57	38.26	59.92	64.82	60.81	48.14
November 10, 1981	2,974	81.60	30.37	47.48	35.76	53.20	61.40	52.58	45.65
November 17, 1981	2,659	85.16	37.34	55.26	42.84	57.82	64.53	59.97	49.64
December 8, 1981	2,628	81.20	29.17	49.72	35.72	54.24	53.90	51.15	46.22
January 9, 1982	2,622	79.89	30.08	48.37	38.51	52.10	60.28	53.27	45.55
January 23, 1982	2,622	82.25	28.87	43.65	32.06	54.24	51.01	49.22	45.55
February 7, 1982	2,744	83.23	25.77	49.45	31.58	51.46	59.25	51.68	41.84
March 14, 1982	2,720	83.49	25.84	45.33	31.52	50.94	56.82	51.61	41.47
April 4, 1982	2,631	79.67	23.31	50.79	32.68	49.65	53.97	49.88	40.86
April 25, 1982	2,750	82.77	19.54	42.63	30.25	46.62	54.08	49.15	37.79
May 2, 1982	2,733	81.17	23.71	44.37	31.23	47.55	60.55	49.58	39.71
May 16, 1982	2,666	79.58	22.36	49.62	31.51	48.58	56.32	47.20	42.68
June 13, 1982	2,561	77.31	25.11	45.06	36.47	47.00	52.91	51.56	38.96
June 27, 1982	2,671	79.55	24.34	45.35	39.14	44.95	53.10	48.55	40.46
July 25, 1982	2,703	73.55	24.67	41.96	33.91	46.55	44.99	47.60	37.79
August 1, 1982	2,717	74.82	20.93	43.48	33.76	42.76	48.48	45.01	37.29
August 15, 1982	2,656	75.89	22.44	35.22	35.26	41.41	48.15	43.88	37.77
August 29, 1982	2,670	76.92	19.38	45.29	27.50	46.28	52.70	46.96	37.39
September 19, 1982	2,594	77.34	21.14	43.17	31.24	42.83	59.14	47.58	37.39
October 17, 1982	2,753	79.14	19.40	43.46	29.21	46.10	50.60	45.77	38.21
November 7, 1982	2,713	82.18	22.48	39.76	30.05	47.55	47.67	45.22	40.43
November 21, 1982	2,721	81.37	22.33	44.68	33.58	46.71	49.60	48.19	38.99
December 21, 1982	2,664	75.90	21.04	41.00	26.79	47.01	50.61	46.51	36.38
January 16, 1983	2,768	67.81	17.77	40.73	24.82	40.73	46.15	41.93	32.19
January 23, 1983	2,664	67.04	19.20	40.34	23.12	42.90	43.78	39.32	35.41
January 30, 1983	2,727	68.52	18.72	31.94	20.49	41.10	42.18	38.56	31.96
February 27, 1983	2,665	78.47	17.47	45.12	28.74	43.53	48.05	42.64	37.66
March 13, 1983	2,711	78.48	22.73	38.46	32.04	43.02	49.88	46.95	35.29
April 17, 1983	2,666	76.85	23.49	40.79	28.04	45.22	49.07	42.16	39.01
May 1, 1983	2,712	78.26	25.16	44.39	33.14	46.30	50.73	48.26	37.83

Table 6.5 (continued)

	N	Party			Education			Sex	
		Rep.	Dem.	Ind.	<12	High school	College	M	F
Reagan (continued)									
May 15, 1983	2,693	79.28	21.73	43.51	34.34	44.33	54.50	50.35	36.40
May 22, 1983	2,680	77.52	26.46	47.97	34.40	49.87	51.05	48.93	42.75
June 12, 1983	2,599	79.08	21.01	49.19	32.50	47.69	48.46	47.02	39.87
June 26, 1983	2,720	82.21	27.65	48.49	34.05	51.93	53.77	52.32	42.00
July 24, 1983	2,725	77.48	19.63	47.13	26.88	46.08	54.61	0.96	34.34
August 7, 1983	2,635	78.26	21.64	46.15	31.36	46.42	54.92	50.00	37.24
August 14, 1983	2,682	81.15	20.42	43.92	31.57	46.82	50.72	48.59	38.35
August 21, 1983	2,618	77.43	20.68	44.82	29.71	46.48	52.64	46.62	38.82
September 11, 1983	2,320	84.30	25.89	46.48	38.63	48.62	55.64	52.94	41.75
September 18, 1983	2,224	80.85	24.48	45.88	35.93	49.01	53.36	12.88	52.99
October 10, 1983	2,202	77.55	25.50	44.24	38.28	45.80	53.46	49.27	41.43
October 23, 1983	2,479	81.36	28.25	49.62	38.33	52.60	53.61	54.06	44.60
November 20, 1983	2,178	91.04	32.77	48.66	41.71	55.98	57.11	56.83	48.30
December 11, 1983	2,196	82.43	32.79	56.15	41.51	59.97	53.10	59.35	48.39
January 15, 1984	2,232	84.48	30.48	51.98	39.71	55.65	59.05	56.68	48.10
January 28, 1984	2,332	90.87	31.30	56.35	43.54	57.75	64.93	60.19	50.71
February 11, 1984	2,378	86.87	32.35	55.06	38.90	60.15	65.16	60.29	51.23
March 17, 1984	2,216	87.61	31.86	54.88	39.74	56.94	61.86	57.50	50.13
April 7, 1984	2,258	86.85	29.03	59.01	41.70	55.10	66.75	56.79	51.49
May 19, 1984	2,252	84.59	32.18	56.91	38.12	56.91	62.19	57.25	49.74
June 23, 1984	2,249	88.96	25.40	56.88	39.81	58.42	59.32	59.95	48.74
July 1, 1984	2,217	88.17	27.78	54.69	36.89	56.14	64.08	56.29	49.91
July 7, 1984	2,228	86.77	28.47	53.76	42.97	56.36	58.25	58.49	48.54
July 14, 1984	2,283	86.95	34.53	54.87	40.54	59.04	65.21	63.12	48.55
July 28, 1984	2,335	87.23	23.94	52.54	41.90	53.71	57.18	52.87	50.58
September 4, 1984	2,390	—	—	—	45.85	60.82	57.59	60.12	53.13
September 18, 1984	2,292	92.23	25.63	54.19	45.01	60.36	59.36	58.03	55.18
September 25, 1984	2,361	92.54	22.85	48.45	41.78	57.16	57.21	57.56	50.45
October 27, 1984	2,301	57.66	62.87	48.36	47.57	60.81	60.86	59.62	56.62
November 19, 1984	2,193	93.56	33.04	57.43	47.92	65.97	60.81	63.86	57.79
December 1, 1984	2,231	93.97	29.48	64.52	50.19	65.60	63.21	67.28	56.02
December 9, 1984	2,204	89.35	32.37	60.08	43.57	63.53	64.80	63.62	55.12
January 13, 1985	1,522	88.37	38.26	60.14	52.28	64.13	64.19	66.10	57.09

[a] Poor = less than $5,000 in total annual income.

Source: Authors' analysis of original Gallup Poll data.

Table 6.6   Presidential Approval by Race, Income, and Region, 1977-
1984 (percent)

		Race		Income [a]		Region	
	N	White	Non-white	Poor	Non-poor	Non-South	South
Carter							
January 1, 1977	2,831	66.09	62.36	64.22	65.91	64.19	71.51
March 1, 1977	2,617	68.89	78.89	66.41	71.00	70.44	69.25
March 15, 1977	2,727	73.14	84.59	71.40	75.36	73.76	78.72
March 22, 1977	2,736	70.80	78.07	66.59	72.57	72.33	68.56
March 29, 1977	2,679	66.91	70.69	61.01	68.61	67.08	68.51
April 12, 1977	2,747	62.13	71.21	58.75	64.22	62.93	64.29
April 26, 1977	2,681	62.30	71.65	59.96	64.20	62.80	65.89
May 3, 1977	2,692	66.39	60.14	64.87	66.10	63.57	73.65
May 17, 1977	2,761	64.66	56.17	64.32	63.61	63.46	64.75
May 31, 1977	2,708	61.49	69.62	54.07	63.89	61.98	64.00
June 14, 1977	2,703	62.95	63.95	60.36	63.62	63.59	60.95
July 5, 1977	2,734	61.30	67.79	62.00	62.08	60.68	67.71
July 19, 1977	2,700	65.64	72.83	58.39	68.38	66.48	67.04
August 2, 1977	2,694	58.87	67.67	60.65	59.81	59.96	59.89
August 16, 1977	2,667	65.77	68.21	58.71	67.48	65.65	67.76
September 6, 1977	2,729	53.13	57.50	59.91	52.62	54.22	52.19
September 27, 1977	2,675	59.35	60.06	58.77	59.58	58.47	63.16
October 11, 1977	2,680	53.93	61.39	51.66	55.31	54.68	55.15
October 18, 1977	2,658	54.17	55.24	53.85	54.56	53.05	59.12
October 25, 1977	2,715	50.60	57.48	51.57	51.31	50.83	53.33
November 1, 1977	2,692	53.75	63.21	53.06	55.19	54.54	56.11
November 15, 1977	2,651	53.90	70.35	55.88	55.86	54.60	60.45
December 16, 1977	2,719	55.74	64.44	65.12	55.09	55.16	62.04
January 3, 1978	2,758	53.54	63.34	55.02	54.83	54.47	56.42
January 17, 1978	2,726	51.63	53.61	51.40	51.97	50.91	55.48
February 8, 1978	2,688	45.33	55.42	39.67	47.82	45.32	51.27
February 21, 1978	2,759	49.61	55.52	49.35	50.46	49.69	52.71
March 1, 1978	2,768	47.18	59.28	54.59	47.45	48.42	48.92
March 7, 1978	2,751	48.12	62.68	50.72	49.42	48.80	52.92
March 28, 1978	2,803	46.60	54.82	48.38	47.32	47.15	48.84
April 11, 1978	2,719	39.14	52.49	41.89	40.13	40.73	39.27
April 25, 1978	2,802	40.39	45.71	42.89	40.66	39.27	48.41
May 3, 1978	2,765	40.09	53.60	46.09	40.70	40.96	43.30
May 16, 1978	2,681	41.05	53.90	48.03	41.68	40.39	50.72
May 30, 1978	2,697	42.80	52.00	43.82	43.83	43.42	45.41
June 13, 1978	2,704	39.47	64.13	45.61	41.74	41.63	45.16
July 5, 1978	2,746	38.85	47.19	37.69	40.58	39.68	41.86
July 18, 1978	2,792	36.84	53.33	38.56	38.62	37.92	41.37
August 1, 1978	2,684	38.00	48.24	35.19	39.83	37.57	45.77
August 8, 1978	5,491	38.17	52.20	43.48	39.29	38.23	47.48
August 15, 1978	2,845	41.50	53.76	48.97	41.56	42.66	42.91
September 5, 1978	2,740	39.87	55.79	49.33	40.66	41.09	46.11
September 11, 1978	2,776	43.84	48.77	42.93	44.76	44.35	45.08
September 19, 1978	2,705	46.39	58.92	47.86	47.72	45.97	55.08
October 29, 1978	2,676	48.28	55.50	52.61	48.67	49.72	47.56

Table 6.6 (continued)

	N	Race		Income[a]		Region	
		White	Non-white	Poor	Non-poor	Non-South	South
Carter (continued)							
December 5, 1978	2,727	49.22	64.29	53.01	50.87	50.64	53.20
January 2, 1979	2,662	48.66	61.97	39.67	51.85	47.83	58.56
January 16, 1979	2,651	42.72	47.99	39.21	43.95	42.03	48.28
January 30, 1979	2,700	41.86	44.57	42.42	42.19	40.48	49.00
February 20, 1979	2,751	36.80	41.58	43.61	36.18	36.97	37.92
February 27, 1979	2,716	37.71	52.20	42.71	38.72	39.22	53.85
March 13, 1979	2,725	45.05	60.45	53.10	45.43	46.20	48.02
March 20, 1979	2,753	41.49	50.75	44.86	42.23	41.39	47.34
April 3, 1979	2,671	38.87	52.56	41.82	40.29	39.43	44.79
May 1, 1979	2,664	36.41	42.51	35.40	37.46	36.39	40.35
May 15, 1979	2,666	31.91	34.46	35.55	31.60	31.00	37.24
May 29, 1979	2,659	28.21	34.81	31.48	28.65	27.42	35.51
June 19, 1979	2,808	28.26	35.32	36.96	27.94	29.02	30.29
June 26, 1979	2,722	26.45	42.58	33.54	27.57	28.03	29.31
July 10, 1979	2,800	28.86	30.19	29.82	28.91	28.56	30.92
July 30, 1979	2,744	31.11	39.04	32.04	32.16	31.05	36.45
July 31, 1979	2,773	29.99	46.78	37.57	31.19	30.86	36.65
August 7, 1979	2,799	32.63	40.06	38.21	32.80	31.21	43.20
August 14, 1979	2,742	30.69	44.91	34.42	32.14	29.94	41.81
September 4, 1979	2,733	29.43	31.61	28.76	29.87	29.47	30.70
October 2, 1979	2,741	28.15	32.52	29.31	28.58	26.47	37.85
October 14, 1979	2,760	29.86	45.08	34.63	30.97	31.05	33.27
October 30, 1979	2,724	31.45	35.74	35.67	31.42	30.51	38.04
November 13, 1979	2,691	36.19	47.96	44.78	36.80	36.37	43.74
November 27, 1979	2,735	51.37	52.49	59.44	50.34	49.98	57.61
December 4, 1979	2,695	54.13	56.23	54.47	54.34	53.57	57.54
January 2, 1980	2,801	55.56	60.91	58.43	55.88	54.54	63.05
January 22, 1980	2,838	57.30	59.81	59.03	57.37	56.90	60.32
January 29, 1980	2,813	55.59	51.65	45.75	56.36	54.24	58.96
February 26, 1980	2,765	51.21	56.95	50.56	52.01	52.01	51.04
March 4, 1980	2,837	41.53	50.52	41.46	42.95	41.99	45.89
March 24, 1980	2,496	50.25	52.38	58.36	49.53	49.85	53.02
April 8, 1980	2,714	39.48	35.50	44.61	38.19	38.76	39.86
April 29, 1980	2,728	41.57	48.47	45.25	42.22	40.01	51.88
May 13, 1980	2,819	39.11	33.41	40.91	37.93	37.17	42.83
May 27, 1980	2,820	37.33	45.36	43.28	37.89	37.02	43.60
June 10, 1980	2,821	32.17	33.54	38.29	31.45	30.08	40.53
June 24, 1980	2,738	29.82	37.00	42.19	29.32	29.99	34.11
July 8, 1980	2,780	31.38	39.65	37.40	31.83	31.01	38.38
August 12, 1980	2,836	29.93	45.69	46.13	30.16	29.83	41.23
September 9, 1980	2,819	32.68	65.93	50.76	35.71	37.36	37.84
November 18, 1980	2,719	27.56	54.91	41.72	29.77	28.77	39.45
December 3, 1980	2,744	31.23	54.76	43.69	32.90	33.55	35.97

(Table continues)

317

Table 6.6   (continued)

		Race		Income[a]		Region	
	N	White	Non-white	Poor	Non-poor	Non-South	South
Reagan							
January 27, 1981	2,855	54.42	25.22	31.25	53.37	50.33	53.04
February 20, 1981	2,778	62.07	24.59	37.21	57.65	54.86	57.58
March 10, 1981	2,832	64.99	21.33	36.13	61.92	58.49	62.96
March 31, 1981	2,751	72.98	25.07	53.33	68.14	65.71	69.70
April 7, 1981	2,744	73.77	22.74	37.88	70.08	66.64	68.46
May 5, 1981	2,623	73.19	31.32	43.01	70.48	67.11	69.65
June 2, 1981	2,671	64.71	19.55	39.00	61.24	58.33	60.33
June 16, 1981	2,679	64.61	19.01	33.58	61.59	57.86	62.32
June 23, 1981	2,685	63.73	20.97	39.84	59.70	57.79	57.86
July 21, 1981	2,743	60.86	26.91	32.07	58.66	56.23	54.43
July 28, 1981	2,707	65.87	19.84	47.00	60.89	60.58	54.88
August 11, 1981	2,707	66.58	18.04	33.88	62.19	60.30	57.09
September 15, 1981	2,723	58.49	10.43	28.89	54.42	52.20	50.64
September 29, 1981	2,689	62.28	12.08	30.43	58.25	55.45	56.32
October 27, 1981	2,559	61.60	19.23	26.02	57.28	56.01	47.50
November 10, 1981	2,974	56.01	18.75	28.01	51.63	49.79	46.07
November 17, 1981	2,659	59.39	25.91	40.00	56.07	53.46	58.48
December 8, 1981	2,628	54.65	17.18	28.32	51.00	48.72	48.10
January 9, 1982	2,622	55.23	13.33	32.96	51.11	49.21	49.34
January 23, 1982	2,622	51.99	15.73	25.82	49.54	48.62	42.23
February 7, 1982	2,744	52.42	11.40	28.98	48.38	46.92	45.51
March 14, 1982	2,720	50.79	12.81	33.33	47.86	45.99	47.63
April 4, 1982	2,631	50.40	14.50	29.60	46.86	45.25	44.22
April 25, 1982	2,750	48.98	16.87	26.71	45.12	—	—
May 2, 1982	2,733	48.65	16.99	25.87	47.09	42.97	50.09
May 16, 1982	2,666	50.69	13.95	25.20	46.90	47.57	34.25
June 13, 1982	2,561	49.84	12.05	26.27	46.84	44.53	46.64
June 27, 1982	2,671	49.34	16.13	31.67	46.18	43.97	45.78
July 25, 1982	2,703	46.15	19.84	26.56	44.61	43.55	38.31
August 1, 1982	2,717	45.42	14.54	30.10	42.31	41.11	40.43
August 15, 1982	2,656	45.59	13.03	30.15	41.85	41.72	36.49
August 29, 1982	2,670	47.04	9.47	23.71	44.22	42.13	41.44
September 19, 1982	2,594	47.16	13.10	28.43	44.15	43.87	36.20
October 17, 1982	2,753	47.23	12.38	20.07	44.31	42.73	38.38
November 7, 1982	2,713	47.61	15.25	23.10	44.91	44.03	37.78
November 21, 1982	2,721	47.30	20.44	28.81	45.05	44.96	36.97
December 21, 1982	2,664	45.99	8.96	26.95	42.86	42.60	36.32
January 16, 1983	2,768	40.73	17.17	20.34	38.35	37.37	34.79
January 23, 1983	2,664	41.61	9.24	29.61	38.01	39.08	30.65
January 30, 1983	2,727	38.75	12.60	24.09	36.47	35.55	33.39
February 27, 1983	2,665	44.71	13.78	34.81	40.68	39.81	41.12
March 13, 1983	2,711	45.03	13.45	37.22	41.97	41.51	38.45
April 17, 1983	2,666	45.08	13.12	23.13	42.66	42.25	34.09
May 1, 1983	2,712	47.47	17.54	27.11	44.65	43.03	42.00

Table 6.6   (continued)

	N	Race		Income [a]		Region	
		White	Non-white	Poor	Non-poor	Non-South	South
Reagan (continued)							
May 15, 1983	2,693	47.28	16.89	27.56	44.69	41.89	47.59
May 22, 1983	2,680	49.65	20.81	26.26	47.92	46.06	44.14
June 12, 1983	2,599	48.39	14.62	35.78	44.06	42.62	46.18
June 26, 1983	2,720	51.22	21.88	32.25	48.65	46.86	47.50
July 24, 1983	2,725	47.93	13.91	23.16	44.39	42.80	40.18
August 1, 1983	2,738	50.22	12.90	25.77	46.25	44.75	42.58
August 7, 1983	2,635	49.03	12.25	24.09	45.57	43.95	40.93
August 14, 1983	2,682	48.89	12.97	26.05	44.89	43.98	40.29
August 21, 1983	2,618	48.29	10.72	19.15	44.32	42.72	41.71
September 11, 1983	2,320	51.46	18.98	30.30	48.92	47.02	48.43
September 18, 1983	2,224	52.74	12.88	34.36	48.10	46.53	48.28
October 10, 1983	2,202	49.84	17.95	39.67	46.02	45.27	45.51
October 23, 1983	2,479	53.62	20.12	32.81	51.12	48.92	50.46
November 20, 1983	2,178	58.03	14.34	33.33	54.46	50.20	61.19
December 11, 1983	2,196	58.33	21.19	36.78	55.24	54.03	52.89
January 15, 1984	2,232	57.19	15.12	31.07	54.49	50.99	56.86
January 28, 1984	2,332	59.70	19.20	32.56	57.68	55.09	56.32
February 11, 1984	2,378	60.00	24.57	40.10	57.12	54.24	60.70
March 17, 1984	2,216	59.15	14.80	50.59	53.86	52.98	56.47
April 7, 1984	2,258	59.11	15.00	31.87	55.97	52.62	60.09
May 19, 1984	2,252	58.21	18.68	35.38	55.29	54.25	50.22
June 23, 1984	2,249	58.91	19.40	45.45	55.05	54.23	54.10
July 1, 1984	2,217	58.26	17.08	42.62	53.98	52.70	54.44
July 7, 1984	2,228	58.18	18.73	41.04	54.50	54.98	46.90
July 14, 1984	2,283	60.11	20.77	44.51	56.59	54.88	58.8
July 28, 1984	2,335	54.34	20.33	44.33	52.39	51.13	53.86
September 4, 1984	2,390	61.88	17.99	36.63	58.41	55.02	62.96
September 18, 1984	2,292	62.27	17.18	42.52	57.99	55.97	58.80
September 25, 1984	2,361	58.85	17.08	44.85	54.55	52.01	60.93
October 27, 1984	2,301	63.15	24.25	59.81	57.89	57.10	61.90
November 19, 1984	2,193	65.99	25.53	43.17	62.39	59.07	67.32
December 1, 1984	2,231	67.68	21.55	44.44	63.04	61.94	59.86
December 9, 1984	2,204	64.56	22.38	41.61	60.43	59.46	58.45
January 13, 1985	1,522						

[a] Poor = less than $5,000 in total annual income.

Source: Authors' analysis of original Gallup Poll data.

Figure 6.2 Approval Ratings of Carter and Reagan, by Race

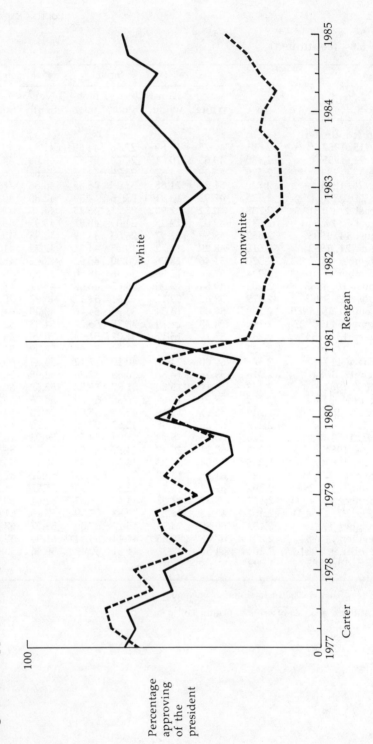

Note: Plotted using data from last survey in January, April, July, and October of each year.

Source: Table 6.6.

Figure 6.3 Approval Ratings of Carter and Reagan, by Education

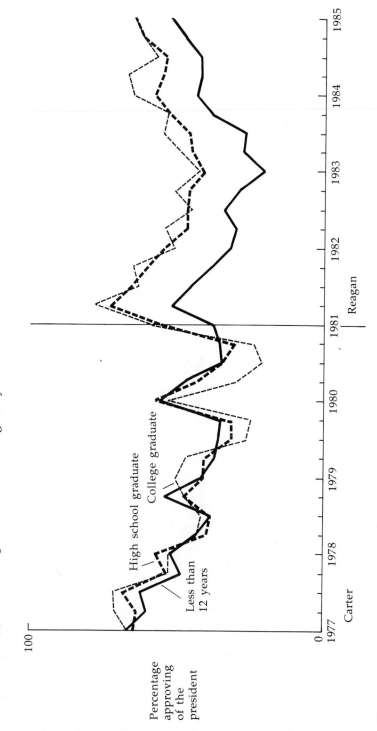

Note: Plotted using data from last survey in January, April, July, and October of each year.

Source: Table 6.5.

Table 6.7 Presidential Approval by Religion and Age, 1977-1984 (percent)

		Religion				Age			
	N	Protestant	Catholic	Jew	Other	<26	26-40	41-60	>60
Carter									
January 1, 1977	2,831	67.41	63.06	64.81	63.38	70.31	65.16	68.13	57.75
March 1, 1977	2,617	69.61	70.34	67.31	75.62	76.17	72.24	66.67	67.10
March 15, 1977	2,727	74.37	77.90	81.69	63.78	78.27	75.51	76.54	67.59
March 22, 1977	2,736	70.98	74.20	67.61	69.40	76.06	72.32	71.68	65.95
March 29, 1977	2,679	63.92	73.80	68.92	73.39	73.48	71.34	66.83	56.38
April 12, 1977	2,747	62.68	65.41	69.23	54.50	71.22	64.02	59.46	59.89
April 26, 1977	2,681	61.57	64.61	84.93	66.37	66.54	68.49	57.71	61.97
May 3, 1977	2,692	63.87	69.10	76.81	64.25	69.37	66.36	65.08	62.21
May 17, 1977	2,761	62.92	67.03	55.56	58.85	66.97	66.21	62.08	59.31
May 31, 1977	2,708	62.44	61.89	60.78	63.72	64.76	70.10	58.25	56.57
June 14, 1977	2,703	62.78	62.60	73.85	64.22	63.40	68.03	64.33	54.62
July 5, 1977	2,734	59.63	64.30	73.24	68.78	67.44	62.66	61.30	57.04
July 19, 1977	2,700	64.17	71.53	53.06	71.86	71.82	71.98	63.01	59.20
August 2, 1977	2,694	59.34	65.75	41.79	56.76	67.99	64.50	54.64	52.82
August 18, 1977	2,667	63.99	73.21	54.67	65.99	76.86	68.31	64.11	55.58
September 6, 1977	2,729	—	—	—	—	62.59	57.50	47.43	49.09
September 27, 1977	2,675	—	—	—	—	60.29	64.95	56.30	55.30
October 11, 1977	2,680	—	—	—	—	58.29	60.44	51.12	48.74
October 18, 1977	2,658	—	—	—	—	56.04	56.94	52.22	51.75
October 25, 1977	2,715	—	—	—	—	62.68	54.36	45.85	43.97
November 1, 1977	2,692	54.56	57.59	18.60	55.20	63.49	56.65	49.35	51.87
November 15, 1977	2,651	54.70	59.83	56.14	52.79	58.78	62.06	49.64	53.74
December 16, 1977	2,719	55.56	61.20	46.77	51.15	61.72	59.02	51.55	55.20
January 3, 1978	2,758	58.47	51.35	39.39	48.25	60.89	57.32	53.53	47.03
January 17, 1978	2,726	49.82	56.52	54.10	51.21	55.36	52.53	53.64	44.91

Date									
February 8, 1978	2,688	47.37	46.98	50.70	41.73	45.86	53.58	42.24	43.65
February 21, 1978	2,759	49.88	54.14	45.16	41.73	57.87	50.06	47.18	47.80
March 1, 1978	2,768	46.23	53.72	40.00	49.61	52.35	53.21	43.88	45.17
March 7, 1978	2,751	47.41	54.80	60.38	46.48	57.64	50.19	45.74	46.72
March 28, 1978	2,803	45.57	51.27	56.00	46.64	54.64	51.60	41.32	44.46
April 11, 1978	2,719	40.90	39.16	18.60	45.76	45.52	43.16	37.16	36.54
April 25, 1978	2,802	—	—	—	—	49.75	42.45	35.29	37.99
May 3, 1978	2,765	41.41	42.76	20.00	42.04	47.28	41.47	37.74	40.89
May 16, 1978	2,681	42.03	46.73	14.58	36.41	45.63	44.34	39.37	41.64
May 30, 1978	2,697	43.97	45.74	31.88	40.54	49.12	48.09	39.11	39.52
June 13, 1978	2,704	42.40	42.51	30.16	43.68	47.24	42.99	40.65	38.65
July 5, 1978	2,746	39.68	44.05	26.67	34.39	46.17	40.53	37.30	37.52
July 18, 1978	2,792	38.87	38.82	37.29	37.08	44.78	37.45	33.83	41.59
August 1, 1978	2,684	38.98	44.20	28.21	25.78	44.12	42.58	34.81	35.57
August 8, 1978	5,491	39.58	43.00	23.39	35.92	42.68	42.72	35.23	41.28
August 18, 1978	2,845	42.56	45.38	22.06	41.00	48.53	42.70	38.81	42.55
September 5, 1978	2,740	41.52	43.92	17.54	45.79	41.37	42.51	39.83	45.55
September 11, 1978	2,776	44.31	48.75	43.33	33.49	53.78	45.78	38.87	41.44
September 19, 1978	2,705	46.49	51.24	40.00	48.89	47.26	48.45	45.64	50.26
October 29, 1978	2,676	48.17	50.98	54.17	55.00	52.24	47.50	48.77	49.47
December 5, 1978	2,727	52.71	51.45	38.78	43.72	54.46	50.48	45.96	56.20
January 2, 1979	2,662	49.25	52.77	34.78	50.97	54.38	53.74	47.62	44.95
January 16, 1979	2,651	41.42	45.45	39.71	48.89	47.82	47.10	36.71	43.16
January 30, 1979	2,700	42.51	40.55	25.42	51.39	45.64	44.34	37.96	42.32
February 20, 1979	2,751	37.62	40.40	16.39	30.24	42.40	35.76	35.71	36.01
February 27, 1979	2,716	40.11	40.38	27.27	33.33	41.95	40.60	37.03	38.22
March 13, 1979	2,725	—	—	—	—	54.23	44.78	41.26	49.00
March 20, 1979	2,753	—	—	—	—	46.01	44.31	40.09	40.76
April 3, 1979	2,671	41.41	39.62	24.19	40.51	45.92	41.46	38.45	36.87
May 1, 1979	2,664	34.04	43.70	36.76	39.17	46.68	36.98	32.25	35.42
May 15, 1979	2,666	33.91	30.39	12.70	31.14	38.73	30.76	28.26	33.62
May 29, 1979	2,659	28.80	30.13	25.81	29.51	32.46	30.73	24.88	29.64

(Table continues)

Table 6.7 (continued)

		Religion				Age			
	N	Protestant	Catholic	Jew	Other	<26	26-40	41-60	>60
June 19, 1979	2,808	28.94	31.73	12.90	27.92	28.34	26.67	26.98	37.09
June 26, 1979	2,722	28.41	28.12	19.05	31.16	32.19	28.44	24.41	29.68
July 10, 1979	2,800	29.34	28.48	35.38	27.13	29.40	29.55	26.11	32.56
July 30, 1979	2,744	31.97	31.54	35.48	34.02	33.10	31.61	31.53	32.85
July 31, 1979	2,773	33.25	29.66	33.33	31.16	36.73	27.93	31.32	34.40
August 7, 1979	2,799	35.00	31.52	18.92	32.61	33.27	35.10	30.83	35.78
August 14, 1979	2,742	33.12	30.93	24.32	33.68	37.17	31.01	29.74	33.51
September 4, 1979	2,733	30.61	29.71	13.79	29.21	27.91	31.02	28.80	30.94
October 2, 1979	2,741	28.73	28.53	28.85	27.69	27.37	31.27	27.99	27.44
October 14, 1979	2,760	32.57	28.95	40.62	30.08	37.40	30.49	27.18	32.53
October 30, 1979	2,724	33.97	28.80	11.54	33.91	32.15	32.18	27.45	38.14
November 13, 1979	2,691	38.84	37.42	33.33	33.96	37.87	37.52	34.53	43.12
November 27, 1979	2,735	51.96	52.85	28.30	49.42	59.29	45.87	48.58	55.83
December 4, 1979	2,695	53.84	55.43	33.96	58.41	51.87	52.68	52.57	61.46
January 2, 1980	2,801	57.10	53.98	53.03	61.58	57.96	54.39	55.75	57.75
January 22, 1980	2,838	58.52	58.91	38.46	52.55	54.12	59.42	57.80	57.84
January 29, 1980	2,813	53.34	57.73	54.55	59.84	54.68	56.62	57.02	51.47
February 26, 1980	2,765	51.72	53.54	40.62	49.39	55.08	49.11	51.17	53.45
March 4, 1980	2,837	45.25	40.20	20.00	38.11	40.21	47.84	36.36	47.41
March 24, 1980	2,496	51.51	45.73	63.64	54.03	43.48	43.47	55.89	59.29
April 8, 1980	2,714	37.22	44.69	27.45	35.34	40.82	37.94	37.64	40.73
April 29, 1980	2,728	43.89	43.71	23.73	33.62	42.45	44.59	37.44	47.19
May 13, 1980	2,819	37.23	42.68	23.91	34.82	44.14	36.96	35.91	37.71
May 27, 1980	2,820	38.84	40.41	19.70	34.54	43.16	36.35	34.04	43.08
June 10, 1980	2,821	31.94	37.19	22.95	21.17	34.57	34.45	29.21	31.77
June 24, 1980	2,738	31.95	30.80	16.67	26.71	31.14	30.78	27.82	34.72

July 8, 1980	2,780	35.83	28.84	6.82	25.61	37.65	29.13	32.20	32.62
August 12, 1980	2,836	35.05	31.20	15.00	17.52	35.60	28.62	30.41	35.93
September 9, 1980	2,819	38.18	39.82	18.33	29.26	40.07	33.78	36.99	40.61
November 18, 1980	2,719	32.11	29.96	33.33	25.31	32.85	28.07	31.41	33.02
December 3, 1980	2,744	35.47	34.13	25.76	28.30	46.03	34.09	25.98	33.92
Reagan									
January 27, 1981	2,855	52.38	51.94	46.27	39.66	47.52	54.59	51.95	47.45
February 20, 1981	2,778	57.55	57.03	53.19	35.48	51.71	58.92	56.26	52.62
March 10, 1981	2,832	61.67	57.54	51.72	53.52	56.29	62.30	62.42	53.99
March 31, 1981	2,751	68.92	69.47	28.07	52.52	60.25	70.63	68.33	64.46
April 7, 1981	2,744	66.87	70.26	47.27	62.24	64.95	66.43	68.52	67.47
May 5, 1981	2,623	68.82	69.34	45.28	62.03	61.93	71.98	70.09	63.06
June 2, 1981	2,671	61.13	58.27	70.00	47.52	56.88	64.30	58.31	53.81
June 16, 1981	2,679	59.94	61.39	44.19	47.84	62.77	59.56	61.18	51.01
June 23, 1981	2,685	61.26	54.62	34.78	53.61	58.39	57.67	60.00	54.40
July 21, 1981	2,743	55.87	58.58	43.75	50.72	59.27	59.76	56.25	47.16
July 28, 1981	2,707	59.00	62.62	39.53	56.29	57.25	57.75	58.88	64.80
August 11, 1981	2,707	59.03	63.32	32.35	56.08	60.18	58.72	61.80	57.38
September 15, 1981	2,723	53.12	52.79	30.61	44.31	46.55	57.99	51.57	49.12
September 29, 1981	2,689	55.92	57.61	48.98	49.69	55.22	57.53	54.17	55.40
October 27, 1981	2,559	54.66	59.63	41.38	44.58	55.44	55.42	55.08	50.70
November 10, 1981	2,974	—	—	—	—	47.66	50.54	50.46	46.23
November 17, 1981	2,659	57.32	53.29	41.51	48.08	48.24	57.39	56.45	53.93
December 8, 1981	2,628	52.65	43.19	38.89	45.54	46.51	48.12	50.07	49.13
January 9, 1982	2,622	53.12	47.13	29.17	38.95	44.74	46.68	52.11	53.15
January 23, 1982	2,622	48.40	50.13	18.18	39.06	45.58	47.95	52.85	41.10
February 7, 1982	2,744	47.25	45.44	46.34	46.71	51.28	48.91	45.72	40.67
March 14, 1982	2,720	48.26	46.07	24.07	40.22	46.07	47.88	48.66	41.73
April 4, 1982	2,631	46.71	46.23	40.35	35.00	54.17	42.80	42.47	43.32

(Table continues)

Table 6.7 (continued)

		Religion				Age			
	N	Protestant	Catholic	Jew	Other	<26	26-40	41-60	>60
April 25, 1982	2,750	—	—	—	—	42.78	41.31	45.08	43.09
May 2, 1982	2,733	45.87	43.83	38.78	39.57	42.07	47.23	46.77	39.24
May 16, 1982	2,666	46.05	45.04	34.04	37.50	40.75	46.78	45.39	45.39
June 13, 1982	2,561	47.35	45.30	19.05	36.63	41.63	45.53	43.60	48.94
June 27, 1982	2,671	47.44	42.54	30.77	35.51	42.12	44.23	45.42	44.98
July 23, 1982	2,703	44.31	40.19	34.29	38.49	46.49	42.60	40.80	40.91
August 1, 1982	2,717	43.36	45.64	20.00	23.10	39.34	43.89	38.57	41.88
August 15, 1982	2,656	41.45	41.07	38.71	36.27	36.72	43.94	41.04	39.65
August 29, 1982	2,670	43.18	40.90	30.56	39.41	47.98	38.71	41.13	42.14
September 19, 1982	2,594	45.74	42.17	18.18	28.21	42.66	42.26	42.46	41.58
October 17, 1982	2,753	46.18	37.48	19.64	33.11	34.03	45.96	44.32	39.74
November 7, 1982	2,713	44.25	43.09	25.40	39.59	37.70	41.62	46.51	43.74
November 21, 1982	2,721	46.04	43.00	27.66	33.13	41.42	41.72	44.90	45.09
December 21, 1982	2,664	41.94	40.55	47.83	37.11	43.25	40.87	39.00	42.35
January 16, 1983	2,768	38.72	38.34	18.64	25.40	39.03	41.78	35.80	30.33
January 23, 1983	2,664	40.00	35.66	25.49	28.21	44.57	34.02	35.57	37.50
January 30, 1983	2,727	36.39	36.71	20.31	30.16	38.71	36.00	34.99	30.77
February 27, 1983	2,665	42.72	39.40	15.38	32.31	37.62	43.39	41.07	36.58
March 13, 1983	2,711	44.64	38.36	23.38	34.34	35.86	43.71	44.90	36.80
April 17, 1983	2,666	41.96	42.88	35.14	30.14	36.51	42.65	40.76	40.71
May 1, 1983	2,712	45.79	42.67	27.87	31.82	37.64	44.21	44.74	43.05
May 19, 1983	2,693	45.47	42.27	44.71	36.05	43.50	38.76	48.26	41.72
May 22, 1983	2,680	47.85	45.77	42.37	35.02	41.39	48.23	45.53	46.41
June 12, 1983	2,599	44.08	43.91	18.64	36.36	44.40	44.36	44.69	38.94
June 26, 1983	2,720	48.29	49.23	35.71	36.63	45.20	47.04	48.07	47.12
July 24, 1983	2,725	43.05	43.52	16.00	38.58	40.27	44.21	45.25	37.96

Date										
August 1, 1983	2,738	45.05	47.54	11.43	38.02		52.06	43.98	45.42	36.29
August 7, 1983	2,635	45.22	45.30	39.13	30.55		46.59	41.44	42.50	44.02
August 14, 1983	2,682	45.41	45.43	21.15	32.30		44.38	42.73	42.73	43.48
August 21, 1983	2,618	44.44	42.51	32.84	38.87		42.97	40.68	48.59	37.01
September 11, 1983	2,320	49.69	48.17	40.00	34.83		42.40	49.21	45.61	50.90
September 16, 1983	2,224	50.77	44.33	33.33	34.27		39.43	50.07	50.67	44.52
October 10, 1983	2,202	47.74	45.65	28.26	35.82		37.03	46.87	48.29	46.09
October 28, 1983	2,479	53.49	50.36	22.50	34.86		51.56	51.72	49.25	43.19
November 20, 1983	2,178	55.31	52.91	40.00	42.01		46.15	53.22	59.31	48.71
December 11, 1983	2,196	57.28	53.41	30.00	41.28		49.26	54.61	56.87	52.75
January 15, 1983	2,232	54.57	56.53	39.29	36.89		51.98	53.67	52.88	50.10
January 28, 1984	2,332	58.61	54.68	40.00	43.92		61.85	53.88	57.47	49.12
February 11, 1984	2,378	58.68	54.45	36.36	47.01		57.24	60.83	57.40	44.51
March 17, 1984	2,216	56.48	54.53	36.54	39.65		55.69	53.98	52.80	52.38
April 7, 1984	2,258	55.72	54.75	42.37	47.83		54.39	57.05	56.87	45.80
May 19, 1984	2,252	52.17	60.31	45.24	43.33		53.41	53.90	53.42	52.71
June 23, 1984	2,249	58.42	48.58	40.35	50.51		55.61	57.52	52.31	50.10
July 1, 1984	2,217	54.89	50.56	39.73	53.96		54.65	56.22	51.95	48.37
July 7, 1984	2,228	55.51	53.17	42.42	50.00		51.30	53.48	54.87	53.66
July 14, 1984	2,283	58.81	56.29	44.23	36.74		58.54	56.91	58.83	47.19
July 28, 1984	2,335	54.87	50.74	32.79	42.57		49.20	53.76	55.75	46.40
September 4, 1984	2,390	61.95	53.89	43.40	39.72		58.47	62.17	52.56	51.32
September 18, 1984	2,292	59.65	55.61	40.28	45.25		55.64	54.50	60.13	55.93
September 25, 1984	2,361	57.88	49.23	25.45	48.40		58.56	54.41	53.91	48.91
October 27, 1984	2,301	57.85	62.87	36.96	47.93		60.66	58.50	55.99	57.83
November 19, 1984	2,193	62.65	60.60	36.36	56.59		65.88	62.39	58.69	57.05
December 1, 1984	2,231	61.67	66.50	35.29	56.47		60.77	53.66	69.79	60.20
December 9, 1984	2,204	60.70	61.79	60.38	43.38		56.04	62.27	61.82	54.46
January 13, 1985	1,522	64.10	59.26	47.50	55.56		71.07	61.02	59.91	59.52

Source: Authors' analysis of original Gallup Poll data.

Figure 6.4 Approval Ratings of Carter and Reagan, by Age

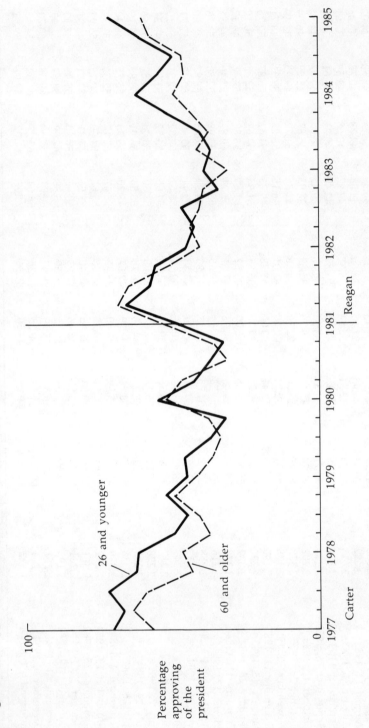

Note: Plotted using data from last survey in January, April, July, and October of each year.

Source: Table 6.7.

Table 6.8 Presidential Approval by Union Membership, Home Ownership, and Employment (percent)

	N	Union member?		Housing status			Employed? [a]	
		Yes	No	Own	Rent	Other	Yes	No
Carter								
March 28, 1978	2,803	53.55	46.10	45.98	52.65	41.96	46.26	49.03
October 29, 1978	2,676	44.86	50.40	—	—	—	—	—
December 5, 1978	2,727	48.42	52.00	—	—	—	—	—
January 2, 1979	2,662	50.08	51.00	48.80	53.00	54.76	—	—
January 16, 1979	2,651	43.52	43.46	42.46	46.79	35.54	—	—
January 30, 1979	2,700	36.53	43.93	41.06	44.48	40.43	—	—
February 20, 1979	2,751	38.16	37.00	36.36	38.82	38.00	35.56	39.16
February 27, 1979	2,716	42.25	38.47	38.93	36.54	42.68	41.61	36.14
March 13, 1979	2,725	45.49	46.86	43.62	52.50	50.70	46.43	46.68
March 20, 1979	2,753	42.91	42.33	42.36	43.30	42.95	40.75	45.00
April 3, 1979	2,671	41.11	40.75	38.65	43.97	44.32	38.67	42.64
May 1, 1979	2,664	37.52	36.96	34.01	42.54	41.61	34.75	40.64
May 15, 1979	2,666	28.60	32.93	30.46	36.29	31.36	31.04	34.08
May 29, 1979	2,659	27.12	29.22	28.83	28.88	36.00	27.22	31.33
June 19, 1979	2,808	29.73	29.15	29.16	29.43	29.84	25.19	34.78
June 26, 1979	2,722	26.79	28.36	25.26	35.91	31.54	26.63	30.39
July 10, 1979	2,800	24.41	31.00	28.26	31.50	27.74	29.28	28.78
July 20, 1979	2,744	31.55	31.79	32.36	32.16	29.90	32.80	31.29
July 31, 1979	2,773	30.29	32.30	31.28	33.70	24.32	31.71	32.29
August 7, 1979	2,799	30.23	34.73	32.02	34.19	46.15	32.21	35.13
August 14, 1979	2,742	29.43	32.25	32.76	32.43	28.08	31.36	34.22
September 4, 1979	2,733	28.30	30.53	29.42	30.73	30.16	29.09	30.60
October 2, 1979	2,741	28.75	28.82	27.86	30.22	31.25	30.23	26.30
October 14, 1979	2,760	32.51	31.24	30.90	31.73	35.97	31.92	30.91
October 30, 1979	2,724	34.53	31.13	30.35	35.23	39.17	31.75	32.48
November 13, 1979	2,691	39.55	37.22	39.02	35.47	31.25	35.75	40.43
November 27, 1979	2,735	53.86	51.05	51.58	51.77	45.92	50.27	53.29
December 4, 1979	2,695	55.12	54.75	54.08	55.45	50.75	51.93	57.80
January 2, 1980	2,801	51.26	57.56	55.45	58.21	55.93	55.78	56.61
January 22, 1980	2,838	58.97	57.27	57.41	57.27	62.82	57.05	58.43
January 29, 1980	2,813	59.06	54.04	57.26	50.55	46.67	56.89	53.13
February 26, 1980	2,765	52.96	51.51	51.34	52.63	58.02	52.78	50.44
March 4, 1980	2,837	47.57	41.51	43.41	41.74	40.87	42.68	42.60
March 24, 1980	2,496	49.57	50.43	50.29	50.00	57.30	48.54	52.40
April 8, 1980	2,714	39.31	38.28	37.54	43.35	36.36	36.78	42.15
April 29, 1980	2,728	46.41	41.09	44.19	39.17	37.90	41.22	44.25
May 13, 1980	2,819	41.27	37.18	37.20	41.65	36.36	39.06	37.75
May 27, 1980	2,820	33.97	39.95	36.96	41.15	44.68	37.41	40.18
June 10, 1980	2,821	30.24	32.94	32.28	31.84	35.64	31.28	33.72
June 24, 1980	2,738	28.02	31.61	30.75	32.56	18.48	28.74	33.53
July 8, 1980	2,780	32.11	32.79	30.56	39.23	28.57	30.83	35.28
August 12, 1980	2,836	30.99	32.40	32.06	32.45	30.70	29.35	35.85
September 9, 1980	2,819	38.06	37.35	35.21	42.16	40.62	35.45	40.43
November 18, 1980	2,719	28.80	31.80	28.50	38.49	24.74	28.08	35.23
December 3, 1980	2,744	31.69	34.60	31.40	40.33	38.40	31.59	37.52

(Table continues)

329

Table 6.8 (continued)

	N	Union member?		Housing status			Employed?[a]	
		Yes	No	Own	Rent	Other	Yes	No
Reagan								
January 27, 1981	2,855	49.92	51.38	54.44	44.24	35.71	53.35	47.72
February 20, 1981	2,778	—	—	59.68	46.73	44.95	—	—
March 10, 1981	2,832	60.20	59.17	64.19	46.40	61.36	64.30	52.48
March 31, 1981	2,751	61.67	68.01	70.06	57.43	66.22	69.77	62.61
April 7, 1981	2,744	63.44	67.89	71.43	57.40	60.00	73.48	59.92
May 5, 1981	2,623	65.93	68.17	71.39	54.79	77.88	—	—
June 2, 1981	2,671	56.02	59.28	60.79	52.37	66.67	62.52	54.21
June 16, 1981	2,679	56.99	59.53	62.53	48.65	59.37	63.66	54.12
June 23, 1981	2,685	52.90	59.09	62.08	45.99	53.64	64.50	49.62
July 21, 1981	2,743	52.08	56.47	59.27	48.46	49.23	61.52	48.42
July 28, 1981	2,707	53.95	60.86	64.73	46.46	54.55	59.01	60.73
August 11, 1981	2,707	46.73	62.52	62.57	51.40	72.07	65.85	51.62
September 15, 1981	2,723	48.92	53.10	57.24	38.84	58.40	55.97	45.76
September 29, 1981	2,689	47.32	57.48	60.14	44.97	48.45	58.54	50.93
October 27, 1981	2,559	52.63	54.79	58.88	42.86	52.68	58.54	48.87
November 10, 1981	2,974	—	—	53.86	39.30	44.72	52.62	43.88
November 17, 1981	2,659	50.74	55.75	58.98	42.49	62.86	59.97	47.45
December 8, 1981	2,628	47.57	49.18	53.58	36.80	61.05	52.12	43.20
January 9, 1982	2,622	38.75	52.29	53.89	39.42	44.32	50.61	47.66
January 23, 1982	2,622	43.65	48.42	52.16	35.87	44.09	54.02	39.31
February 7, 1982	2,744	41.11	48.24	50.53	38.49	45.95	51.43	40.58
March 14, 1982	2,720	39.83	48.61	48.93	37.52	53.91	52.14	40.12
April 4, 1982	2,631	37.28	47.46	49.39	35.51	45.08	50.04	39.21
April 25, 1982	2,750	—	—	45.68	37.61	41.83	47.08	38.16
May 2, 1982	2,733	34.48	47.10	48.78	33.84	50.00	—	—
May 16, 1982	2,666	35.89	47.11	47.63	37.55	47.41	47.12	42.26
June 13, 1982	2,561	33.33	48.02	48.33	36.40	42.11	47.60	41.87
June 22, 1982	2,671	37.29	46.11	50.78	28.59	41.36	47.75	40.42
July 25, 1982	2,703	35.10	44.19	45.14	34.15	45.13	44.21	40.14
August 1, 1982	2,717	31.96	42.92	44.43	32.34	39.94	42.93	38.38
August 15, 1982	2,656	32.03	42.77	44.23	31.48	43.24	43.82	36.95
August 29, 1982	2,670	33.57	44.20	44.85	33.57	50.83	45.95	37.47
September 19, 1982	2,594	36.11	43.73	46.07	34.08	40.74	45.33	38.91
October 17, 1982	2,753	36.77	43.31	45.48	30.56	51.45	—	—
November 7, 1982	2,713	36.19	44.28	46.50	33.86	47.86	44.90	40.17
November 21, 1982	2,721	32.93	46.06	45.96	37.11	43.40	45.70	40.37
December 21, 1982	2,664	37.40	42.05	44.28	34.06	47.31	46.74	34.62
January 16, 1983	2,768	27.05	39.10	38.67	32.35	36.46	39.08	34.58
January 23, 1983	2,664	35.85	37.67	38.90	33.13	41.12	41.21	32.99
January 30, 1983	2,727	25.37	37.52	37.88	28.05	38.21	38.97	31.20
February 27, 1983	2,665	38.88	40.45	42.02	33.01	55.21	44.53	35.39
March 13, 1983	2,711	37.58	41.61	46.28	28.61	46.74	45.26	36.32
April 17, 1983	2,666	31.78	42.60	46.09	29.66	29.03	43.75	36.83
May 1, 1983	2,712	40.69	43.46	46.66	33.51	36.89	47.87	37.53

Table 6.8 (continued)

	N	Union member?		Housing status			Employed?[a]	
		Yes	No	Own	Rent	Other	Yes	No
Reagan (continued)								
May 15, 1983	2,693	36.03	44.86	45.61	35.65	47.11	48.74	36.30
May 22, 1983	2,680	44.85	45.87	49.65	37.71	30.89	—	—
June 12, 1983	2,599	38.53	44.76	47.29	34.73	38.61	46.25	39.85
June 26, 1983	2,720	40.35	48.74	51.59	36.34	40.46	50.23	43.04
July 24, 1983	2,725	33.91	44.51	45.39	35.20	36.36	47.51	35.77
August 1, 1983	2,738	37.23	46.07	48.09	32.92	47.01	50.59	37.34
August 7, 1983	2,635	38.17	44.56	47.24	33.90	42.25	46.20	39.56
August 14, 1983	2,682	36.57	44.68	47.61	32.45	31.01	45.49	40.38
August 21, 1983	2,618	35.18	44.34	47.54	29.04	42.94	47.11	37.20
September 11, 1983	2,320	43.25	48.18	52.76	36.35	39.02	50.94	42.53
September 18, 1983	2,224	40.49	48.00	51.25	38.63	32.95	51.63	41.06
October 10, 1983	2,202	36.63	47.10	48.05	40.83	35.90	50.04	39.41
October 23, 1983	2,479	46.58	49.88	52.29	40.51	44.86	54.49	42.18
November 20, 1983	2,178	—	—	57.48	40.96	54.12	57.63	46.59
December 11, 1983	2,196	42.49	56.24	58.58	45.97	34.52	57.89	48.36
January 15, 1984	2,232	45.85	53.89	56.40	42.16	50.88	57.12	46.39
January 28, 1984	2,332	50.99	56.42	57.88	49.66	46.07	61.76	47.40
February 11, 1984	2,378	56.25	55.47	60.65	44.26	47.06	61.52	47.68
March 17, 1984	2,216	43.91	56.15	57.15	44.97	43.94	55.56	50.96
April 7, 1984	2,258	45.53	56.20	58.22	45.81	34.74	59.25	46.91
May 19, 1984	2,252	44.00	56.11	57.52	44.57	44.44	57.48	47.11
June 23, 1984	2,249	46.52	55.66	57.60	46.23	55.32	58.03	49.18
July 1, 1984	2,217	46.30	54.68	56.29	44.61	57.69	57.96	45.48
July 7, 1984	2,228	37.09	57.33	57.29	47.10	46.76	55.62	50.28
July 11, 1984	2,283	46.52	57.83	58.68	46.90	69.74	61.36	47.51
July 28, 1984	2,335	43.85	53.47	54.99	45.67	38.33	54.69	47.63
September 4, 1984	2,390	51.89	57.73	61.65	45.72	36.78	60.42	50.49
September 18, 1984	2,292	48.66	58.27	60.40	46.06	50.00	59.50	52.25
September 25, 1984	2,361	42.34	56.36	57.76	41.72	62.35	57.55	48.85
October 27, 1984	2,301	43.00	61.37	59.32	52.85	68.75	61.79	52.74
November 19, 1984	2,193	57.01	61.74	65.45	50.25	48.33	62.25	58.77
December 1, 1984	2,231	53.10	63.40	65.83	50.93	62.50	66.12	54.78
December 9, 1984	2,204	53.90	60.53	61.99	53.74	52.05	62.87	54.04
January 13, 1985	1,522	54.33	63.42	64.53	54.16	50.00	66.35	55.85

[a] Full- or part-time employment.

Source: Authors' analysis of original Gallup Poll data.

Table 6.9   Republican Approval of the President by Region, 1977-1984

	Non-South (%)	South (%)	N
Carter			
January 1, 1977	47.28	56.52	606
March 1, 1977	54.70	46.00	632
March 15, 1977	60.48	55.81	582
March 22, 1977	56.11	56.47	543
March 29, 1977	52.12	61.74	564
April 12, 1977	46.89	42.71	514
April 26, 1977	46.19	57.14	570
May 3, 1977	51.15	67.44	522
May 17, 1977	47.75	38.46	558
May 31, 1977	42.92	52.22	549
June 14, 1977	56.01	31.18	509
July 5, 1977	42.22	46.75	546
July 19, 1977	45.53	53.66	541
August 2, 1977	44.44	54.55	587
August 16, 1977	50.52	55.77	581
September 6, 1977	36.54	36.21	521
September 27, 1977	42.01	38.04	549
October 11, 1977	37.17	31.71	569
October 18, 1977	34.16	40.00	535
October 25, 1977	33.55	32.63	563
November 1, 1977	41.73	46.15	521
November 15, 1977	37.39	26.32	566
December 16, 1977	44.17	37.50	552
January 3, 1978	33.88	34.78	582
January 17, 1978	32.18	44.00	591
February 8, 1978	28.17	27.91	583
February 21, 1978	32.04	32.54	669
March 1, 1978	32.66	29.13	648
March 7, 1978	31.79	29.41	665
March 28, 1978	30.26	31.50	636
April 11, 1978	23.90	30.17	618
April 25, 1978	21.02	21.98	543
May 3, 1978	27.16	26.09	578
May 16, 1978	24.06	26.88	571
May 30, 1978	25.68	37.50	615
June 13, 1978	22.70	26.05	652
July 5, 1978	20.83	18.49	599
July 18, 1978	21.47	27.52	624
August 1, 1978	25.58	25.27	650
August 8, 1978	23.39	40.36	1,292
August 15, 1978	28.46	25.45	637
September 5, 1978	27.48	15.58	561
September 11, 1978	22.29	26.87	623
September 19, 1978	27.67	42.86	657
October 29, 1978	34.32	27.42	666

Table 6.9 (continued)

	Non-South (%)	South (%)	N
Carter (continued)			
January 2, 1979	29.65	44.68	519
January 16, 1979	25.74	11.90	554
January 30, 1979	24.59	21.60	609
February 20, 1979	20.82	24.14	577
February 27, 1979	26.31	80.00	579
March 13, 1979	31.52	24.79	577
March 20, 1979	30.28	22.12	563
April 3, 1979	20.78	26.14	550
May 1, 1979	27.11	33.96	567
May 15, 1979	22.25	28.97	570
May 29, 1979	18.79	27.91	533
June 19, 1979	32.18	36.34	1,817
June 26, 1979	18.54	19.75	615
July 10, 1979	18.88	13.13	634
July 30, 1979	13.81	25.97	468
July 31, 1979	21.01	9.37	572
August 7, 1979	22.61	21.33	557
August 14, 1979	19.42	31.09	567
September 4, 1979	12.07	27.91	525
October 2, 1979	20.12	17.24	579
October 14, 1979	23.29	26.79	610
October 30, 1979	17.19	20.00	626
November 13, 1979	27.17	23.08	505
November 27, 1979	39.19	36.63	545
December 4, 1979	40.30	47.52	570
January 2, 1980	39.24	46.91	527
January 22, 1980	41.24	39.24	547
January 29, 1980	52.14	60.95	619
February 26, 1980	40.72	29.41	674
March 4, 1980	25.64	23.08	572
March 24, 1980	58.68	53.12	551
April 8, 1980	29.55	23.88	645
April 29, 1980	22.85	36.73	597
May 15, 1980	30.69	30.93	602
May 27, 1980	23.44	14.18	616
June 10, 1980	12.93	20.55	664
June 28, 1980	20.20	19.71	642
July 8, 1980	16.12	12.40	650
August 12, 1980	12.66	18.80	670
September 9, 1980	14.21	4.00	759
November 18, 1980	9.83	20.90	653
December 3, 1980	15.14	11.11	708

(Table continues)

Table 6.9 (continued)

	Non-South (%)	South (%)	N
Reagan			
January 27, 1981	73.45	73.73	683
February 20, 1981	76.78	83.23	794
March 10, 1981	86.53	87.65	764
March 31, 1981	85.36	93.79	762
April 7, 1981	90.28	90.77	778
May 5, 1981	91.39	93.15	657
June 2, 1981	86.45	88.57	686
June 16, 1981	84.88	86.50	745
June 23, 1981	87.89	88.20	756
July 21, 1981	78.63	84.21	718
July 28, 1981	88.02	80.18	712
August 11, 1981	85.06	83.45	754
September 15, 1981	81.55	83.61	691
September 29, 1981	86.35	92.54	742
October 27, 1981	88.87	87.97	690
November 10, 1981	83.28	73.64	739
November 17, 1981	85.74	83.22	640
December 8, 1981	80.94	82.26	633
January 9, 1982	80.68	76.47	726
January 23, 1982	82.44	81.36	676
February 7, 1982	82.20	87.31	662
March 14, 1982	82.34	88.10	630
April 4, 1982	78.93	83.04	615
May 2, 1982	79.50	87.07	669
May 16, 1982	79.86	78.10	671
June 13, 1982	76.50	81.20	683
June 29, 1982	80.35	76.71	660
July 25, 1982	76.77	60.84	707
August 1, 1982	76.77	67.59	683
August 15, 1982	77.64	67.97	705
August 29, 1982	75.98	80.58	676
September 19, 1982	77.76	75.42	653
October 17, 1982	78.72	81.48	700
November 7, 1982	82.93	78.81	651
November 21, 1982	82.64	76.03	628
December 21, 1982	75.22	78.79	693
January 16, 1983	66.67	73.79	640
January 23, 1983	67.73	64.17	622
January 30, 1983	69.80	63.77	648
February 27, 1983	76.41	87.72	627
March 13, 1983	79.32	75.00	618
April 12, 1983	77.68	73.33	553
May 1, 1983	77.39	83.53	598
May 15, 1983	77.69	84.31	637
May 22, 1983	77.69	76.60	614

Table 6.9 (continued)

	Non-South (%)	South (%)	N
Reagan (continued)			
June 12, 1983	77.87	84.55	607
June 26, 1983	82.48	80.95	596
July 24, 1983	78.11	74.56	644
August 7, 1983	80.75	66.67	644
August 14, 1983	80.74	83.19	679
August 21, 1983	77.08	79.09	638
September 11, 1983	84.42	83.87	586
September 18, 1983	79.80	86.32	590
October 10, 1983	76.71	82.72	579
October 23, 1983	81.41	81.15	660
November 20, 1983	89.86	95.08	536
December 11, 1983	81.07	90.36	569
January 15, 1984	81.14	94.23	612
January 28, 1984	89.33	97.46	624
February 11, 1984	84.67	94.59	670
March 17, 1984	87.84	86.46	581
April 7, 1984	85.01	96.15	631
May 19, 1984	86.40	77.39	571
June 23, 1984	90.18	83.33	670
July 1, 1984	87.65	90.35	600
July 7, 1984	85.97	90.35	620
July 14, 1984	86.25	90.48	636
July 28, 1984	86.04	92.44	642
September 18, 1984	91.12	97.24	798
September 25, 1984	91.30	96.70	791
October 27, 1984	56.70	60.10	1,358
November 19, 1984	92.92	95.78	745
December 1, 1984	93.67	95.65	763
December 9, 1984	89.03	90.65	695
January 13, 1985	88.57	87.50	516

Source: Authors' analysis of original Gallup Poll data.

Table 6.10 Democratic Approval of the President by Region, 1977-1984

	Non-South (%)	South (%)	N
Carter			
January 1, 1977	75.26	82.79	1,367
March 1, 1977	81.29	75.08	1,215
March 15, 1977	84.03	85.03	1,252
March 22, 1977	81.33	80.07	1,297
March 29, 1977	79.06	76.68	1,176
April 12, 1977	72.15	77.00	1,271
April 26, 1977	73.58	70.83	1,204
May 3, 1977	72.51	81.07	1,215
May 17, 1977	69.90	75.29	1,312
May 31, 1977	73.06	72.63	1,328
June 14, 1977	73.11	70.34	1,241
July 5, 1977	70.33	82.68	1,361
July 19, 1977	76.82	77.54	1,225
August 2, 1977	69.42	69.37	1,190
August 16, 1977	76.61	74.92	1,201
September 6, 1977	63.98	64.15	1,231
September 27, 1977	66.60	77.60	1,332
October 11, 1977	63.35	67.47	1,258
October 18, 1977	63.85	74.15	1,251
October 25, 1977	64.75	65.08	1,157
November 1, 1977	65.59	65.33	1,169
November 15, 1977	64.02	81.69	1,129
December 16, 1977	65.22	74.11	1,179
January 3, 1978	64.83	65.94	1,355
January 17, 1978	58.26	64.67	1,328
February 8, 1978	53.76	59.66	1,279
February 21, 1978	61.69	68.70	1,293
March 1, 1978	63.36	66.27	1,155
March 7, 1978	60.22	70.29	1,279
March 28, 1978	59.42	59.20	1,216
April 11, 1978	51.91	48.24	1,228
April 25, 1978	54.17	61.42	1,214
May 3, 1978	51.49	48.64	1,372
May 16, 1978	53.37	60.66	1,235
May 30, 1978	53.78	55.63	1,262
June 13, 1978	55.12	56.93	1,214
July 5, 1978	51.05	53.66	1,335
July 18, 1978	47.78	56.63	1,285
August 1, 1978	47.16	57.59	1,260
August 8, 1978	49.23	56.98	2,542
August 15, 1978	50.72	54.46	1,359
September 5, 1978	51.31	53.92	1,276
September 11, 1978	52.46	62.67	1,260
September 19, 1978	58.63	65.92	1,234

Table 6.10 (continued)

	Non-South (%)	South (%)	N
Carter (continued)			
October 29, 1978	63.03	60.08	1,161
January 2, 1979	56.89	66.11	1,194
January 16, 1979	52.65	61.60	1,112
January 30, 1979	49.89	72.24	1,151
February 20, 1979	48.13	45.04	1,233
February 27, 1979	48.31	33.33	1,216
March 13, 1979	54.68	60.70	1,166
March 20, 1979	51.21	59.36	1,232
April 3, 1979	50.27	57.56	1,175
May 1, 1979	45.16	52.56	1,113
May 15, 1979	33.78	47.84	1,123
May 29, 1979	33.26	44.57	1,193
June 19, 1979	22.21	18.79	827
June 26, 1979	32.78	38.37	1,042
July 10, 1979	35.31	43.17	1,136
July 30, 1979	40.33	50.38	1,241
July 31, 1979	38.30	47.64	1,241
August 7, 1979	39.83	52.59	1,194
August 14, 1979	38.03	55.56	1,181
September 4, 1979	37.88	35.14	1,183
October 2, 1979	30.89	43.75	1,214
October 14, 1979	39.36	39.63	1,233
October 30, 1979	36.81	52.32	1,185
November 13, 1979	46.36	50.96	1,330
November 27, 1979	58.55	74.37	1,201
December 4, 1979	61.10	64.45	1,143
January 2, 1980	64.17	69.49	1,302
January 22, 1980	66.06	71.28	1,263
January 29, 1980	54.26	57.48	1,276
February 26, 1980	61.51	64.66	1,260
March 4, 1980	53.12	59.55	1,227
March 24, 1980	47.93	50.86	1,102
April 8, 1980	46.20	54.22	1,186
April 29, 1980	52.11	65.63	1,238
May 13, 1980	44.59	55.56	1,295
May 27, 1980	47.31	61.87	1,284
June 10, 1980	39.77	55.27	1,339
June 24, 1980	39.26	50.20	1,191
July 8, 1980	46.49	52.03	1,251
August 12, 1980	45.21	56.96	1,395
September 9, 1980	59.90	66.54	1,312
November 18, 1980	46.97	57.59	1,099
December 3, 1980	48.10	52.01	1,115

(Table continues)

Table 6.10   (continued)

	Non-South (%)	South (%)	N
Reagan			
January 27, 1981	38.34	38.26	1,169
February 20, 1981	38.32	40.32	1,122
March 10, 1981	40.97	42.06	1,143
March 31, 1981	51.16	54.44	1,110
April 7, 1981	45.53	45.95	1,039
May 5, 1981	50.72	53.02	1,066
June 2, 1981	44.21	43.21	1,046
June 16, 1981	39.78	43.67	1,155
June 23, 1981	41.61	36.80	1,101
July 21, 1981	39.76	31.09	1,073
July 29, 1981	45.65	43.45	1,094
August 11, 1981	40.58	45.02	1,054
September 15, 1981	33.78	31.65	1,243
September 29, 1981	34.78	41.08	1,128
October 27, 1981	33.72	18.85	1,113
November 10, 1981	29.90	31.79	1,225
November 17, 1981	35.84	42.62	1,074
December 8, 1981	29.56	28.09	1,018
January 9, 1982	29.35	32.45	1,127
January 23, 1982	29.72	26.14	1,112
February 7, 1982	26.90	21.79	1,269
March 14, 1982	24.52	29.96	1,095
April 4, 1982	22.01	27.78	1,197
May 2, 1982	23.41	24.81	1,185
May 16, 1982	24.84	14.53	1,203
June 13, 1982	23.71	30.00	1,119
June 27, 1982	24.84	22.52	1,204
July 25, 1982	24.21	26.34	1,212
August 1, 1982	20.22	23.51	1,252
August 15, 1982	23.06	20.25	1,105
August 29, 1982	19.61	18.66	1,166
September 19, 1982	22.32	17.81	1,121
October 17, 1982	18.45	21.78	1,227
November 7, 1982	23.02	20.98	1,139
November 23, 1982	23.88	17.31	1,200
December 21, 1982	21.71	19.17	1,188
January 16, 1983	18.13	16.67	1,227
January 23, 1983	19.64	17.87	1,172
January 30, 1983	18.14	20.92	1,143
February 27, 1983	17.26	18.15	1,242
March 13, 1983	23.90	18.89	1,157
April 17, 1983	24.52	20.46	1,196
May 1, 1983	23.55	29.79	1,276
May 15, 1983	21.31	23.35	1,100
May 22, 1983	25.32	30.04	1,130

Table 6.10   (continued)

	Non-South (%)	South (%)	N
Reagan (continued)			
June 12, 1983	19.64	26.21	1,185
June 26, 1983	27.02	30.17	1,161
July 24, 1983	19.66	19.54	1,192
August 7, 1983	20.77	24.53	1,146
August 14, 1983	19.89	22.10	1,156
August 21, 1983	19.38	24.64	1,112
September 11, 1983	24.36	30.67	981
September 18, 1983	23.22	28.30	858
October 10, 1983	23.87	30.00	902
October 23, 1983	27.15	31.52	1,023
November 20, 1983	29.39	43.81	894
December 11, 1983	32.21	34.30	863
January 15, 1984	30.50	30.43	889
January 28, 1984	30.89	32.51	952
February 11, 1984	30.25	39.13	878
March 17, 1984	30.54	37.30	948
April 7, 1984	28.16	32.47	961
May 19, 1984	32.73	30.47	957
June 23, 1984	24.96	26.94	874
July 1, 1984	26.80	31.38	882
July 7, 1984	29.53	25.00	836
July 14, 1984	33.79	37.31	918
July 28, 1984	22.14	29.38	848
September 18, 1984	24.02	31.55	874
September 25, 1984	20.95	30.91	862
October 27, 1984	62.46	68.00	668
November 19, 1984	30.43	41.24	802
December 1, 1984	27.88	34.92	831
December 9, 1984	31.36	36.00	800
January 13, 1985	37.04	42.31	562

Source: Authors' analysis of original Gallup Poll data.

Table 6.11 Independent Approval of the President by Region, 1977-1984

	Non-South (%)	South (%)	N
Carter			
January 1, 1977	59.64	60.81	807
March 1, 1977	68.01	75.00	739
March 15, 1977	70.31	81.54	861
March 22, 1977	72.48	51.06	864
March 29, 1977	62.92	59.51	902
April 12, 1977	60.10	51.45	920
April 26, 1977	60.71	64.38	860
May 3, 1977	59.66	67.68	907
May 12, 1977	64.90	65.73	856
May 31, 1977	58.76	56.03	786
June 14, 1977	57.45	63.80	915
July 5, 1977	60.39	49.26	757
July 19, 1977	66.48	57.14	865
August 2, 1977	57.75	48.08	859
August 16, 1977	63.40	62.58	819
September 6, 1977	51.77	43.50	911
September 27, 1977	57.00	53.45	723
October 11, 1977	56.41	42.68	804
October 18, 1977	51.86	42.95	822
October 25, 1977	45.83	49.48	938
November 1, 1977	49.12	50.31	900
November 15, 1977	55.41	46.30	855
December 16, 1977	50.36	55.61	890
January 3, 1978	55.36	47.20	750
January 17, 1978	53.34	44.16	767
February 8, 1978	46.45	51.25	765
February 21, 1978	46.95	43.57	747
March 1, 1978	42.36	36.17	901
March 7, 1978	47.45	39.13	730
March 28, 1978	42.89	46.74	951
April 11, 1978	37.85	30.12	837
April 25, 1978	32.46	42.20	1,014
May 3, 1978	35.14	43.06	753
May 16, 1978	34.50	48.90	837
May 30, 1978	40.89	31.01	760
June 13, 1978	37.82	39.22	777
July 5, 1978	35.17	37.50	774
July 18, 1978	35.23	31.33	837
August 1, 1978	32.99	39.44	727
August 8, 1978	33.33	37.28	1,529
August 15, 1978	43.06	29.51	763
September 5, 1978	35.76	41.74	789
September 11, 1978	48.81	38.46	830
September 19, 1978	43.06	47.93	755

Table 6.11 (continued)

	Non-South (%)	South (%)	N
Carter (continued)			
October 29, 1978	44.60	42.07	849
January 2, 1979	48.07	53.76	910
January 16, 1979	40.59	47.09	921
January 30, 1979	38.37	37.50	877
February 20, 1979	32.77	35.44	869
February 27, 1979	35.26	40.00	921
March 13, 1979	44.11	47.13	913
March 20, 1979	36.43	41.57	899
April 3, 1979	36.61	39.34	885
May 1, 1979	31.60	27.85	889
May 15, 1979	32.32	26.14	900
May 29, 1979	25.99	25.79	863
June 19, 1979	28.47	18.52	164
June 26, 1979	29.98	21.39	1,001
July 10, 1979	28.08	23.08	994
July 30, 1979	28.76	24.00	965
July 31, 1979	27.12	34.27	884
August 7, 1979	27.52	38.62	1,003
August 14, 1979	27.08	28.40	937
September 4, 1979	29.60	23.46	973
October 2, 1979	25.14	38.56	889
October 14, 1979	25.56	27.16	917
October 30, 1979	30.88	31.18	863
November 13, 1979	27.80	38.52	809
November 27, 1979	48.63	41.25	890
December 2, 1979	54.55	54.86	934
January 2, 1980	50.81	62.64	922
January 22, 1980	55.73	50.26	966
January 29, 1980	55.67	60.36	918
February 26, 1980	47.73	40.94	831
March 4, 1980	37.70	36.00	968
March 24, 1980	46.09	56.25	813
April 8, 1980	36.49	34.74	845
April 29, 1980	34.78	40.10	864
May 13, 1980	31.32	29.68	867
May 27, 1980	32.01	31.58	883
June 10, 1980	28.51	29.05	818
June 24, 1980	24.86	21.89	905
July 8, 1980	21.08	34.87	835
August 12, 1980	18.33	25.81	746
September 9, 1980	20.73	25.00	711
November 18, 1980	22.71	22.66	881
December 3, 1980	30.13	32.73	852

(Table continues)

341

The Elusive Executive

Table 6.11   (continued)

	Non-South (%)	South (%)	N
Reagan			
January 27, 1981	48.72	64.10	936
February 20, 1981	55.59	58.96	862
March 10, 1981	57.10	69.19	925
March 31, 1981	66.71	69.08	879
April 7, 1981	69.17	80.95	927
May 5, 1981	68.83	72.33	900
June 2, 1981	55.97	62.35	891
June 16, 1981	58.95	72.39	726
June 23, 1981	53.68	59.73	760
July 21, 1981	57.58	67.58	901
July 28, 1981	55.71	57.35	836
August 11, 1981	62.39	50.27	845
September 15, 1981	53.87	60.00	729
September 29, 1981	53.42	55.56	792
October 27, 1981	59.89	58.27	705
November 10, 1981	46.78	50.28	893
November 17, 1981	54.08	60.00	874
December 8, 1981	47.77	60.43	903
January 9, 1982	46.95	55.38	769
January 23, 1982	44.48	39.73	834
February 7, 1982	48.63	54.17	813
March 14, 1982	45.36	45.16	995
April 4, 1982	52.18	44.81	819
May 2, 1982	41.68	57.24	879
May 16, 1982	51.48	41.61	792
June 13, 1982	44.52	47.48	759
June 27, 1982	42.96	58.40	807
July 25, 1982	42.97	37.75	784
August 1, 1982	43.26	44.37	782
August 15, 1982	35.10	35.81	846
August 29, 1982	44.54	49.24	828
September 19, 1982	43.48	41.61	820
October 17, 1982	42.74	47.58	826
November 7, 1982	39.82	39.51	923
November 21, 1982	45.27	42.07	893
December 21, 1982	42.56	34.81	783
January 16, 1983	40.14	43.01	901
January 23, 1983	42.96	28.75	870
January 30, 1983	33.20	27.27	936
February 27, 1983	43.96	49.69	800
March 13, 1983	37.29	43.50	936
April 17, 1983	42.20	34.16	917
May 1, 1983	44.26	44.91	838
May 15, 1983	42.71	46.96	956
May 22, 1983	47.82	48.60	936

Table 6.11 (continued)

	Non-South (%)	South (%)	N
Reagan (continued)			
June 12, 1983	48.78	50.98	807
June 26, 1983	48.09	50.00	963
July 24, 1983	46.78	48.57	889
August 1, 1983	45.81	42.82	1,542
August 7, 1983	45.28	50.00	845
August 14, 1983	44.56	41.32	847
August 21, 1983	44.63	45.70	868
September 11, 1983	46.28	47.30	753
September 18, 1983	44.25	52.20	776
October 10, 1983	42.68	50.34	721
October 23, 1983	47.63	57.32	796
November 20, 1983	46.64	57.66	748
December 11, 1983	54.71	61.64	764
January 15, 1984	51.37	54.42	731
January 28, 1984	54.83	62.76	756
February 11, 1984	54.55	57.23	830
March 17, 1984	53.36	61.98	687
April 7, 1984	55.76	72.66	666
May 19, 1984	55.76	62.93	724
June 23, 1984	54.48	69.30	705
July 1, 1984	54.35	56.20	735
July 7, 1984	55.89	40.91	772
July 14, 1984	52.60	65.15	729
July 28, 1984	51.44	57.72	845
September 18, 1984	53.91	55.22	620
September 25, 1984	47.95	50.34	708
October 27, 1984	45.08	74.19	275
November 19, 1984	55.09	70.83	646
December 1, 1984	64.51	64.57	637
December 9, 1984	61.37	54.03	709
January 13, 1985	58.92	66.22	444

Source: Authors' analysis of original Gallup Poll data.

Table 6.12 Republican Approval of the President by Income, 1977-1984

	Poor (%)	Nonpoor (%)	N
Carter			
January 1, 1977	28.92	51.82	606
March 1, 1977	51.11	53.70	617
March 15, 1977	60.00	59.75	582
March 22, 1977	48.72	57.42	543
March 29, 1977	38.30	57.23	564
April 12, 1977	52.46	45.25	514
April 26, 1977	32.88	50.30	570
May 3, 1977	54.19	53.68	522
May 17, 1977	52.46	45.47	558
May 31, 1977	33.33	46.45	549
June 14, 1977	50.00	51.72	509
July 5, 1977	47.44	42.09	546
July 19, 1977	38.82	48.25	541
August 2, 1977	52.94	45.22	587
August 16, 1977	43.08	52.52	581
September 6, 1977	58.44	32.66	521
September 27, 1977	57.58	39.13	549
October 11, 1977	33.66	36.97	569
October 18, 1977	34.91	35.31	535
October 25, 1977	22.39	34.88	563
November 1, 1977	50.00	41.65	521
November 15, 1977	34.25	35.29	566
December 16, 1977	53.85	41.89	552
January 3, 1978	35.71	33.79	582
January 17, 1978	22.86	35.70	591
February 8, 1978	14.06	29.87	583
February 21, 1978	28.12	32.81	669
March 1, 1978	43.66	30.68	648
March 7, 1978	32.99	31.16	665
March 28, 1978	19.72	31.86	636
April 11, 1978	25.25	25.05	618
April 25, 1978	17.65	21.83	543
May 3, 1978	14.29	28.35	578
May 16, 1978	20.90	25.00	571
May 30, 1978	23.23	29.26	615
June 13, 1978	38.46	20.86	652
July 5, 1978	19.74	20.46	599
July 18, 1978	28.87	21.82	624
August 1, 1978	26.53	25.36	650
August 8, 1978	37.05	24.06	1,292
August 15, 1978	29.73	27.71	637
September 5, 1978	21.43	26.34	561
September 11, 1978	25.00	23.05	623
September 19, 1978	32.67	29.89	657

Table 6.12 (continued)

	Poor (%)	Nonpoor (%)	N
Carter (continued)			
October 29, 1978	34.12	32.87	666
January 2, 1979	2.13	35.38	519
January 16, 1979	19.70	24.18	554
January 30, 1979	9.41	26.34	609
February 20, 1979	22.81	21.35	577
February 27, 1979	31.25	26.21	579
March 13, 1979	42.31	28.26	577
March 20, 1979	25.81	29.14	563
April 3, 1979	17.50	21.96	550
May 1, 1979	33.87	27.72	567
May 15, 1979	18.52	24.34	570
May 29, 1979	13.33	21.14	533
June 19, 1979	45.17	30.71	1,817
June 26, 1979	20.41	18.55	615
July 10, 1979	24.44	16.91	634
July 30, 1979	19.05	15.49	468
July 31, 1979	25.71	18.13	572
August 7, 1979	35.42	21.22	557
August 14, 1979	26.09	21.50	567
September 4, 1979	12.66	15.02	525
October 2, 1979	20.69	19.58	579
October 14, 1979	32.18	22.56	610
October 30, 1979	32.43	15.76	626
November 13, 1979	53.33	23.91	505
November 27, 1979	41.82	38.37	545
December 4, 1979	48.89	40.95	570
January 2, 1980	31.67	41.54	527
January 22, 1980	46.67	40.44	547
January 29, 1980	50.94	53.89	619
February 26, 1980	21.54	40.56	674
March 4, 1980	35.09	24.08	572
March 24, 1980	55.22	58.06	551
April 8, 1980	31.25	28.06	645
April 29, 1980	33.33	24.21	597
May 13, 1980	30.00	30.81	602
May 27, 1980	21.95	21.39	616
June 10, 1980	17.39	14.29	664
June 24, 1980	36.07	18.42	642
July 8, 1980	27.63	13.76	650
August 12, 1980	34.43	11.82	670
September 9, 1980	17.02	11.52	759
November 18, 1980	39.58	9.92	653
December 3, 1980	29.82	12.90	708

(Table continues)

345

Table 6.12 (continued)

	Poor (%)	Nonpoor (%)	N
Reagan			
January 27, 1981	69.77	73.75	683
February 20, 1981	53.73	80.33	794
March 10, 1981	77.27	87.36	764
March 31, 1981	93.51	86.42	762
April 7, 1981	79.55	91.01	778
May 5, 1981	76.92	92.72	657
June 2, 1981	71.43	87.89	686
June 16, 1981	48.15	88.13	745
June 23, 1981	84.62	88.28	756
July 21, 1981	44.23	82.43	718
July 28, 1981	84.29	87.07	712
August 11, 1981	60.42	86.40	754
September 15, 1981	59.09	83.46	691
September 29, 1981	85.00	87.61	742
October 27, 1981	65.12	90.26	690
November 10, 1981	65.63	83.11	739
November 17, 1981	79.55	85.57	640
December 8, 1981	68.75	82.22	633
January 9, 1982	60.78	81.33	726
January 23, 1982	53.33	84.31	676
February 7, 1982	69.70	83.94	662
March 14, 1982	71.74	84.42	630
April 4, 1982	63.41	80.84	615
April 25, 1982	57.89	84.95	708
May 2, 1982	61.67	83.09	669
May 16, 1982	80.00	79.56	671
June 13, 1982	60.98	78.35	683
June 27, 1982	72.00	80.16	660
July 25, 1982	39.58	76.02	707
August 1, 1982	61.11	75.99	683
August 15, 1982	63.38	77.29	705
August 29, 1982	66.67	77.60	676
September 19, 1982	66.67	78.30	653
October 17, 1982	48.84	81.13	700
November 7, 1982	71.88	82.71	651
November 21, 1982	63.04	82.82	628
December 21, 1982	53.66	77.30	693
January 16, 1983	38.46	69.72	640
January 23, 1983	76.32	66.44	622
January 30, 1983	73.58	68.07	648
February 27, 1983	70.59	79.17	627
March 13, 1983	79.71	78.13	618
April 17, 1983	65.22	77.91	553
May 1, 1983	60.00	79.75	598
May 15, 1983	50.00	81.99	637

Table 6.12 (continued)

	Poor (%)	Nonpoor (%)	N
Reagan (continued)			
May 22, 1983	50.98	79.93	614
June 12, 1983	48.08	81.98	607
June 26, 1983	55.10	84.64	596
July 24, 1983	48.00	79.97	644
August 7, 1983	42.86	80.30	644
August 14, 1983	72.50	81.69	679
August 21, 1983	34.62	79.25	638
September 11, 1983	78.13	84.66	586
September 18, 1983	77.78	81.05	590
October 10, 1983	72.31	78.21	579
October 23, 1983	74.42	81.85	660
November 20, 1983	73.91	91.81	536
December 11, 1983	51.85	83.95	569
January 15, 1984	81.82	84.63	612
January 28, 1984	75.68	91.82	624
February 11, 1984	82.93	87.12	670
March 17, 1984	83.33	87.84	581
April 7, 1984	76.92	87.27	631
May 19, 1984	57.89	86.49	571
June 23, 1984	72.55	90.31	670
July 1, 1984	85.71	88.35	600
July 7, 1984	90.00	86.55	620
July 14, 1984	82.05	87.27	636
July 28, 1984	83.67	87.52	642
September 18, 1984	98.33	91.73	798
September 25, 1984	94.12	92.47	791
October 27, 1984	57.50	57.67	1,358
November 19, 1984	85.19	93.87	745
December 1, 1984	80.00	94.85	763
December 9, 1984	80.00	89.92	695
January 13, 1985	72.22	89.58	516

Note: Poor = less than $5,000 in total annual income.

Source: Authors' analysis of original Gallup Poll data.

Table 6.13 Democratic Approval of the President by Income, 1977-1984

	Poor (%)	Nonpoor (%)	N
Carter			
January 1, 1977	75.57	77.29	1,367
March 1, 1977	73.36	81.26	1,201
March 15, 1977	79.25	85.46	1,252
March 22, 1977	74.06	82.61	1,297
March 29, 1977	73.61	79.58	1,176
April 12, 1977	63.95	76.05	1,271
April 26, 1977	71.30	73.31	1,204
May 3, 1977	75.47	74.05	1,215
May 17, 1977	67.42	71.68	1,312
May 31, 1977	63.46	75.28	1,328
June 14, 1977	66.39	74.00	1,241
July 5, 1977	69.80	74.04	1,361
July 19, 1977	69.14	79.05	1,225
August 2, 1977	66.05	70.15	1,190
August 16, 1977	69.01	77.73	1,201
September 6, 1977	59.52	65.17	1,231
September 27, 1977	61.37	71.28	1,332
October 11, 1977	67.18	63.78	1,258
October 18, 1977	65.58	66.67	1,251
October 25, 1977	64.85	64.82	1,157
November 1, 1977	62.56	66.18	1,169
November 15, 1977	60.75	69.99	1,129
December 16, 1977	71.93	66.25	1,179
January 3, 1978	63.90	65.35	1,355
January 17, 1978	57.82	60.30	1,328
February 8, 1978	48.94	56.51	1,279
February 21, 1978	61.22	63.59	1,293
March 1, 1978	64.19	63.94	1,155
March 7, 1978	63.48	62.15	1,279
March 28, 1978	60.00	59.25	1,216
April 11, 1978	49.43	51.50	1,228
April 25, 1978	55.74	55.77	1,214
May 3, 1978	59.05	49.12	1,372
May 16, 1978	60.73	53.93	1,235
May 30, 1978	52.77	54.53	1,262
June 13, 1978	51.98	56.33	1,214
July 5, 1978	46.61	52.68	1,335
July 18, 1978	50.80	49.18	1,285
August 1, 1978	40.72	51.11	1,260
August 8, 1978	51.88	50.61	2,542
August 15, 1978	58.89	49.91	1,359
September 5, 1978	54.03	51.46	1,276
September 11, 1978	51.15	54.94	1,260
September 19, 1978	58.63	60.95	1,234

Table 6.13 (continued)

	Poor (%)	Nonpoor (%)	N
Carter (continued)			
October 29, 1978	66.99	61.34	1,161
January 2, 1979	54.59	60.12	1,194
January 16, 1979	48.45	56.10	1,112
January 30, 1979	61.20	53.41	1,151
February 20, 1979	50.00	47.02	1,233
February 27, 1979	50.49	47.82	1,216
March 13, 1979	62.84	54.73	1,166
March 20, 1979	58.33	51.89	1,232
April 3, 1979	52.63	51.59	1,175
May 1, 1979	39.81	48.34	1,113
May 15, 1979	49.51	33.84	1,123
May 29, 1979	34.13	36.24	1,193
June 19, 1979	17.44	22.00	827
June 26, 1979	37.74	33.52	1,042
July 10, 1979	41.04	36.55	1,136
July 30, 1979	43.35	42.32	1,241
July 31, 1979	43.75	39.56	1,241
August 7, 1979	49.75	41.32	1,194
August 14, 1979	42.71	42.06	1,181
September 4, 1979	36.84	37.36	1,183
October 2, 1979	36.81	33.43	1,214
October 14, 1979	40.34	39.26	1,233
October 30, 1979	37.78	40.42	1,185
November 13, 1979	51.24	46.77	1,330
November 27, 1979	66.51	61.29	1,201
December 4, 1979	62.10	61.80	1,143
January 2, 1980	70.33	64.32	1,302
January 22, 1980	64.25	67.76	1,263
January 29, 1980	41.57	57.03	1,276
February 26, 1980	62.43	62.18	1,260
March 4, 1980	52.36	54.92	1,227
March 24, 1980	59.32	47.26	1,102
April 8, 1980	48.17	47.64	1,186
April 29, 1980	51.52	55.82	1,238
May 13, 1980	51.08	46.35	1,295
May 27, 1980	53.12	50.43	1,284
June 10, 1980	54.42	41.28	1,339
June 24, 1980	54.78	39.56	1,191
July 8, 1980	50.00	47.46	1,251
August 12, 1980	63.83	45.32	1,395
September 9, 1980	73.16	59.27	1,312
November 18, 1980	56.86	48.63	1,099
December 3, 1980	57.04	48.00	1,115

(Table continues)

Table 6.13 (continued)

	Poor (%)	Nonpoor (%)	N
Reagan			
January 27, 1981	20.25	41.25	1,169
February 20, 1981	32.28	39.83	1,122
March 10, 1981	25.36	43.38	1,143
March 31, 1981	34.97	54.40	1,110
April 7, 1981	21.29	49.89	1,039
May 5, 1981	28.40	55.31	1,066
June 2, 1981	32.09	45.72	1,046
June 16, 1981	28.37	42.31	1,155
June 23, 1981	15.08	43.90	1,101
July 21, 1981	21.62	40.43	1,073
July 28, 1981	32.80	46.65	1,094
August 11, 1981	22.70	44.47	1,054
September 15, 1981	21.30	35.20	1,243
September 29, 1981	16.90	39.25	1,128
October 27, 1981	13.92	33.19	1,113
November 10, 1981	19.11	32.02	1,225
November 17, 1981	26.89	38.64	1,074
December 8, 1981	17.12	31.19	1,018
January 9, 1982	22.56	31.09	1,127
January 23, 1982	17.19	30.39	1,112
February 7, 1982	20.39	26.50	1,269
March 14, 1982	26.24	25.79	1,095
April 4, 1982	18.60	24.10	1,197
April 25, 1982	14.18	20.27	1,167
May 2, 1982	16.84	25.08	1,185
May 16, 1982	9.70	24.37	1,203
June 13, 1982	16.26	26.20	1,119
June 27, 1982	17.91	25.62	1,204
July 25, 1982	18.28	25.83	1,212
August 1, 1982	17.05	21.56	1,252
August 15, 1982	12.78	23.77	1,105
August 29, 1982	11.63	20.72	1,166
September 19, 1982	14.84	22.15	1,121
October 17, 1982	6.43	21.50	1,227
November 7, 1982	7.59	24.87	1,139
November 21, 1982	12.31	23.55	1,200
December 21, 1982	20.26	21.16	1,188
January 16, 1983	12.03	18.46	1,227
January 23, 1983	16.39	19.52	1,172
January 30, 1983	10.47	20.19	1,143
February 27, 1983	14.08	17.91	1,242
March 13, 1983	18.09	24.23	1,157
April 17, 1983	11.84	25.19	1,196
May 1, 1983	23.88	25.31	1,276
May 15, 1983	16.51	22.30	1,100

Table 6.13 (continued)

	Poor (%)	Nonpoor (%)	N
Reagan (continued)			
May 22, 1983	17.61	27.73	1,130
June 12, 1983	28.57	20.22	1,185
June 26, 1983	24.65	28.07	1,161
July 24, 1983	11.27	20.76	1,192
August 1, 1983	20.25	45.45	1,078
August 7, 1983	12.33	23.00	1,146
August 14, 1983	10.42	21.84	1,156
August 21, 1983	9.30	21.64	1,112
September 11, 1983	12.15	27.57	981
September 18, 1983	17.20	25.36	858
October 10, 1983	26.89	25.29	902
October 23, 1983	24.81	28.75	1,023
November 20, 1983	22.22	34.09	894
December 11, 1983	23.08	33.94	863
January 15, 1984	13.00	32.70	889
January 28, 1984	18.49	33.13	952
February 11, 1984	23.66	33.38	878
March 17, 1984	36.59	31.41	948
April 7, 1984	11.71	31.29	961
May 19, 1984	32.20	32.18	957
June 23, 1984	22.22	25.81	874
July 1, 1984	16.46	28.89	882
July 7, 1984	17.81	29.49	836
July 14, 1984	27.18	35.46	918
July 28, 1984	22.47	24.11	848
September 18, 1984	15.05	26.89	874
September 25, 1984	14.71	23.55	862
October 27, 1984	65.71	62.54	668
November 19, 1984	20.95	34.86	802
December 1, 1984	17.98	30.86	831
December 9, 1984	18.87	33.33	800
January 13, 1985	26.83	39.16	562

Note: Poor = less than $5,000 in total annual income.

Source: Authors' analysis of original Gallup Poll data.

Table 6.14 Independent Approval of the President by Income, 1977-1984

	Poor (%)	Nonpoor (%)	N
Carter			
January 1, 1977	67.27	58.68	807
March 1, 1977	67.95	69.53	731
March 15, 1977	65.49	72.99	861
March 22, 1977	61.98	70.12	864
March 29, 1977	56.41	63.18	902
April 12, 1977	47.41	60.76	920
April 26, 1977	56.77	62.41	860
May 3, 1977	56.86	63.65	907
May 17, 1977	64.49	65.15	856
May 31, 1977	46.77	59.25	786
June 14, 1977	56.49	58.93	915
July 5, 1977	53.41	59.04	757
July 19, 1977	47.06	67.56	865
August 2, 1977	56.78	55.87	859
August 16, 1977	52.42	65.18	819
September 6, 1977	61.62	48.77	911
September 27, 1977	57.61	56.26	723
October 11, 1977	39.33	55.52	804
October 18, 1977	53.12	48.69	822
October 25, 1977	50.96	46.04	938
November 1, 1977	37.72	51.02	900
November 15, 1977	60.94	52.41	855
December 16, 1977	56.31	50.83	890
January 3, 1978	51.96	54.32	750
January 17, 1978	53.51	51.15	767
February 8, 1978	36.27	49.17	765
February 21, 1978	38.27	47.30	747
March 1, 1978	42.73	40.83	901
March 7, 1978	39.02	46.45	730
March 28, 1978	46.58	43.04	951
April 11, 1978	37.04	36.24	837
April 25, 1978	36.27	33.88	1,014
May 3, 1978	32.91	37.09	753
May 16, 1978	39.56	37.40	837
May 30, 1978	44.32	38.54	760
June 13, 1978	40.86	37.72	777
July 5, 1978	33.33	36.01	774
July 18, 1978	19.57	36.38	837
August 1, 1978	32.32	34.55	727
August 8, 1978	31.53	34.46	1,529
August 15, 1978	40.00	41.02	763
September 5, 1978	50.86	34.18	789
September 11, 1978	40.78	47.73	830
September 19, 1978	47.27	42.43	755

Table 6.14 (continued)

	Poor (%)	Nonpoor (%)	N
Carter (continued)			
October 29, 1978	41.41	44.66	849
January 2, 1979	30.09	51.94	910
January 16, 1979	35.85	42.58	921
January 30, 1979	33.33	38.69	877
February 20, 1979	42.86	32.23	869
February 27, 1979	35.09	35.32	921
March 13, 1979	39.82	45.37	913
March 20, 1979	23.71	39.03	899
April 3, 1979	36.17	37.29	885
May 1, 1979	26.97	31.37	889
May 15, 1979	22.81	32.32	900
May 29, 1979	37.65	24.68	863
June 19, 1979	18.42	29.37	164
June 26, 1979	34.86	27.58	1,001
July 10, 1979	20.18	28.07	994
July 30, 1979	24.44	28.11	965
July 31, 1979	29.29	28.79	884
August 7, 1979	22.12	30.56	1,003
August 14, 1979	22.83	27.81	937
September 4, 1979	28.44	28.47	973
October 2, 1979	19.39	28.45	889
October 14, 1979	28.23	25.47	917
October 30, 1979	27.45	31.16	863
November 13, 1979	29.49	29.41	809
November 27, 1979	52.44	46.78	890
December 4, 1979	41.33	55.76	934
January 2, 1980	46.77	53.60	922
January 22, 1980	52.48	54.91	966
January 29, 1980	50.57	57.16	918
February 26, 1980	47.06	46.64	831
March 4, 1980	22.43	39.26	968
March 24, 1980	61.04	46.74	813
April 8, 1980	55.22	34.45	845
April 29, 1980	42.31	35.37	864
May 13, 1980	30.99	31.03	867
May 27, 1980	36.96	31.35	883
June 10, 1980	12.66	30.31	818
June 24, 1980	26.47	24.03	905
July 8, 1980	25.23	23.35	835
August 12, 1980	19.35	19.60	746
September 9, 1980	19.74	21.73	711
November 18, 1980	18.84	23.03	881
December 3, 1980	33.00	30.32	852

(Table continues)

Table 6.14   (continued)

	Poor (%)	Nonpoor (%)	N
Reagan			
January 27, 1981	34.07	53.85	936
February 20, 1981	32.89	58.52	862
March 10, 1981	32.61	62.30	925
March 31, 1981	47.50	69.09	879
April 7, 1981	49.23	72.97	927
May 5, 1981	57.75	70.45	900
June 2, 1981	40.00	59.54	891
June 16, 1981	35.00	63.81	726
June 23, 1981	41.07	55.97	760
July 21, 1981	42.50	61.27	901
July 28, 1981	35.62	57.93	836
August 11, 1981	42.86	60.80	845
September 15, 1981	21.28	57.33	729
September 29, 1981	30.65	55.75	792
October 27, 1981	32.43	61.08	705
November 10, 1981	12.50	51.30	893
November 17, 1981	38.36	56.80	874
December 8, 1981	22.22	51.79	903
January 9, 1982	32.56	50.37	769
January 23, 1982	23.94	45.48	834
February 7, 1982	28.33	51.13	813
March 14, 1982	25.74	47.54	995
April 4, 1982	37.50	51.92	819
April 25, 1982	26.60	44.56	875
May 2, 1982	21.59	46.90	879
May 16, 1982	38.00	50.40	792
June 13, 1982	23.61	47.31	759
June 27, 1982	40.00	46.03	807
July 25, 1982	37.21	42.55	784
August 1, 1982	39.13	43.90	782
August 15, 1982	29.31	35.66	846
August 29, 1982	27.27	47.14	828
September 19, 1982	28.85	45.25	820
October 17, 1982	35.71	44.18	826
November 7, 1982	33.33	40.43	923
November 21, 1982	33.61	46.38	893
December 21, 1982	26.14	42.88	783
January 16, 1983	26.56	41.82	901
January 23, 1983	27.40	41.53	870
January 30, 1983	20.51	32.98	936
February 27, 1983	49.35	44.67	800
March 13, 1983	34.95	39.45	936
April 17, 1983	20.83	43.12	917
May 1, 1983	17.14	48.29	838
May 15, 1983	27.47	45.20	956

Table 6.14 (continued)

	Poor (%)	Nonpoor (%)	N
Reagan (continued)			
May 22, 1983	25.88	50.18	936
June 12, 1983	38.24	50.20	807
June 26, 1983	31.76	50.11	963
July 24, 1983	28.75	48.95	889
August 1, 1983	29.14	47.18	1,542
August 7, 1983	35.48	47.47	845
August 14, 1983	33.33	44.64	847
August 21, 1983	25.00	46.72	868
September 11, 1983	37.29	47.26	753
September 18, 1983	34.85	46.90	776
October 10, 1983	29.31	45.55	721
October 23, 1983	23.46	52.59	796
November 20, 1983	35.62	50.07	748
December 11, 1983	51.79	56.50	764
January 15, 1984	32.88	54.10	731
January 28, 1984	33.90	58.25	756
February 11, 1984	36.99	56.80	830
March 17, 1984	53.45	55.01	687
April 7, 1984	55.56	59.26	666
May 19, 1984	26.79	59.43	724
June 23, 1984	64.58	56.32	705
July 1, 1984	46.77	55.42	735
July 7, 1984	36.67	55.20	772
July 14, 1984	52.50	55.01	729
July 28, 1984	44.62	53.21	845
September 18, 1984	29.51	56.89	620
September 25, 1984	50.79	48.22	708
October 27, 1984	52.63	48.05	275
November 19, 1984	66.67	56.64	646
December 1, 1984	60.87	64.81	637
December 9, 1984	34.09	61.80	709
January 13, 1985	51.85	60.67	444

Note: Poor = less than $5,000 in total annual income.

Source: Authors' analysis of original Gallup Poll data.

Table 6.15 Carter and Reagan on the Economy and Foreign Policy (percent)

	Economy[a]			Foreign policy[b]		
	Approve	Disapprove	DK/no opinion	Approve	Disapprove	DK/no opinion
Carter[c]						
May 1977	47	53	—	—	—	—
June 1977	44	56	—	—	—	—
July 1977	41	59	—	48	52	—
August 1977	39	61	—	—	—	—
September 1977	35	65	—	32	68	—
October 1977	32	68	—	38	62	—
November 1977	33	67	—	38	62	—
December 1977	34	66	—	42	58	—
January 1978	28	72	—	43	57	—
February 1978	27	73	—	38	62	—
April 1978	22	78	—	29	71	—
June 1978	21	79	—	25	75	—
July 1978	16	84	—	22	78	—
August 1978	16	84	—	22	78	—
September 1978	22	78	—	56	44	—
November 1978	23	77	—	47	53	—
December 1978	27	73	—	46	54	—
February 1979	22	78	—	37	63	—
March 1979	16	84	—	45	55	—

Reagan						
September 25-26, 1981	59	34	7	—	—	—
October 1-5, 1981	53	37	9	—	—	—
October 9-11, 1981	—	—	—	63	30	7
October 14-18, 1981	54	39	7	61	26	13
November 17-22, 1981	46	46	8	54	35	10
January 22-30, 1982	46	46	8	52	33	15
February 17-18, 1982	38	57	5	40	41	19
March 3-8, 1982	42	53	5	45	43	12
March 18-21, 1982	43	52	5	43	45	12
April 21-25, 1982	44	51	5	53	34	14
May 24-28, 1982	40	53	7	46	35	19
August 17, 1982	40	55	5	—	—	—
September 9-13, 1982	41	52	7	50	35	15
September 24-26, 1982	40	55	5	43	45	13
October 5-11, 1982	41	51	9	44	39	17
December 7-18, 1982	38	57	6	40	41	19
January 18-22, 1983	38	58	5	45	33	22
February 25-March 2, 1983	43	54	3	—	—	—
April 8-12, 1983	42	54	4	—	—	—

Note: DK = don't know.

a Carter question: "How would you rate (Carter) on his handling of the economy—excellent, pretty good, only fair, or poor?"
Reagan question: "Do you approve or disapprove of the way (the president) is handling the nation's economy?"
b Carter question: "How would you rate (Carter) on his handling of foreign policy—excellent, pretty good, only fair, or poor?"
Reagan question: "Do you approve or disapprove of the way (the president) is handling foreign affairs?"
c Approval for Carter is the percentage who rated him as excellent or pretty good in each policy area.

Sources: Adapted from *Public Opinion*, March/May 1979, 29; April/May 1983, 36.

Table 6.16 Approval of Reagan's Handling of the Situation in Central America (percent)

Month	Year	ABC News/Washington Post			Gallup			Harris		
		Approve	Disapprove	No opinion	Approve	Disapprove	No opinion	Excellent/ good	Fair/ good	Not sure
February	1983	29	47	25	—	—	—	—	—	—
April		27	50	22	21	50	30	—	—	—
May		30	39	31	—	—	—	—	—	—
June		—	—	—	25	46	29	—	—	—
July		33	48	19	—	—	—	—	—	—
August		—	—	—	24	51	25	33	58	9
October		—	—	—	26	50	24	40	52	8
November		—	—	—	36	44	20	34	59	7
December		—	—	—	—	—	—	—	—	—
January	1984	—	—	—	28	49	23	30	64	6
February		42	46	12	29	48	23	30	61	9
March		—	—	—	—	—	—	29	61	10
April		—	—	—	29	48	23	—	—	—
May		37	51	12	28	49	23	31	62	7
June		—	—	—	—	—	—	33	63	4
July		—	—	—	27	45	28	31	66	3
September		—	—	—	—	—	—	41	57	2
October		—	—	—	—	—	—	42	53	5
November		—	—	—	34	43	23	—	—	—

March	1985	—	—	—	—	—	—	34	59	7
May		40	47	14	29	50	21	32	63	5
June		43	45	12	—	—	—	36	57	6
July		44	45	11	—	—	—	36	57	6
September		—	—	—	—	—	—	32	64	4
November		—	—	—	—	—	—	38	57	4
January	1986	—	—	—	—	—	—	39	58	3
March		47	34	19	—	—	—	—	—	—
April		—	—	—	—	—	—	40	54	6

Source: Adapted from *Public Opinion,* Summer 1986, 28.

Table 6.17   The Most Admired Man, 1946-1984

Year	Man	Year	Man
1946	1. Gen. Douglas MacArthur 2. Dwight Eisenhower 3. **Harry Truman** 4. Eleanor Roosevelt [a] 5. Sir Winston Churchill 6. *Herbert Hoover* 7. Henry Wallace 8. Thomas Dewey 9. Harold Stassen 10. James Byrnes	1947	1. Gen. Douglas MacArthur 2. Dwight Eisenhower 3. Sir Winston Churchill 4. **Harry Truman** 5. George Marshall 6. Eleanor Roosevelt [a] 7. James Byrnes 8. Pope Pius XII 9. Sister Kenny [a] 10. Thomas Dewey
1948	1. **Harry Truman** 2. Dwight Eisenhower 3. Gen. Douglas MacArthur 4. Sir Winston Churchill 5. George Marshall 6. *Herbert Hoover* 7. Thomas Dewey 8. Pope Pius XII 9. Harold Stassen 10. Albert Einstein	1949	1. **Harry Truman** 2. Dwight Eisenhower 3. Sir Winston Churchill 4. Gen. Douglas MacArthur 5. *Herbert Hoover* 6. Pope Pius XII 7. Sen. Robert Taft 8. Bernard Baruch 9. Alben Barkley 10. Thomas Dewey
1950	1. Dwight Eisenhower 2. Gen. Douglas MacArthur 3. **Harry Truman** 4. Sir Winston Churchill 5. *Herbert Hoover* 6. Sen. Robert Taft 7. Bernard Baruch 8. Pope Pius XII 9. Dr. Ralph Bunche 10. Earl Warren	1951	1. Gen. Douglas MacArthur 2. Dwight Eisenhower 3. **Harry Truman** 4. Sir Winston Churchill 5. Sen. Robert Taft 6. *Herbert Hoover* 7. Pope Pius XII 8. Estes Kefauver 9. Albert Einstein 10. Thomas Dewey
1952	1. Dwight Eisenhower 2. Gen. Douglas MacArthur 3. Sir Winston Churchill 4. **Harry Truman** 5. Adlai Stevenson 6. Pope Pius XII 7. *Herbert Hoover* 8. Bishop Fulton Sheen 9. Albert Einstein 10. Sen. Robert Taft	1953	1. **Dwight Eisenhower** 2. Sir Winston Churchill 3. Gen. Douglas MacArthur 4. *Harry Truman* 5. Adlai Stevenson 6. Bishop Fulton Sheen 7. Sen. Joseph McCarthy 8. Bernard Baruch 9. Pope Pius XII 10. *Herbert Hoover*

Table 6.17   (continued)

Year	Man	Year	Man
1954	1. **Dwight Eisenhower** 2. Sir Winston Churchill 3. Adlai Stevenson 4. Sen. Joseph McCarthy 5. *Harry Truman* 6. Gen. Douglas MacArthur 7. Pope Pius XII 8. Bishop Fulton Sheen 9. *Herbert Hoover* 10. Dr. Albert Schweitzer	1955	1. **Dwight Eisenhower** 2. Sir Winston Churchill 3. Gen. Douglas MacArthur 4. *Harry Truman* 5. Dr. Albert Schweitzer 6. Pope Pius XII 7. *Herbert Hoover* 8. Bishop Fulton Sheen 9. Rev. Billy Graham 10. Adlai Stevenson
1956	1. **Dwight Eisenhower** 2. Sir Winston Churchill 3. Bishop Fulton Sheen 4. Dr. Albert Schweitzer 5. Adlai Stevenson 6. Gen. Douglas MacArthur 7. Pope Pius XII 8. Dag Hammarskjold 9. Rev. Billy Graham 10. Dr. Jonas Salk	1957	1. **Dwight Eisenhower** 2. Sir Winston Churchill 3. *Harry Truman* 4. Rev. Billy Graham 5. Dr. Albert Schweitzer 6. Dr. Jonas Salk 7. Gen. Douglas MacArthur 8. Bishop Fulton Sheen 9. Adlai Stevenson 10. Pope Pius XII
1958	1. **Dwight Eisenhower** 2. Sir Winston Churchill 3. Dr. Albert Schweitzer 4. Rev. Billy Graham 5. *Harry Truman* 6. Gen. Douglas MacArthur 7. Richard Nixon 8. Dr. Jonas Salk 9. Bernard Baruch 10. Gov. Orval Faubus	1959	1. **Dwight Eisenhower** 2. Sir Winston Churchill 3. Dr. Albert Schweitzer 4. *Harry Truman* 5. Pope John XXIII 6. Rev. Billy Graham 7. Dr. Thomas Dooley 8. *Herbert Hoover* 9. Richard Nixon 10. Gen. Douglas MacArthur
1960	1. **Dwight Eisenhower** 2. Sir Winston Churchill 3. Dr. Albert Schweitzer 4. John Kennedy 5. Richard Nixon 6. Rev. Billy Graham 7. Adlai Stevenson 8. *Harry Truman* 9. Henry Cabot Lodge, Jr. 10. Gen. Douglas MacArthur	1961	1. **John Kennedy** 2. *Dwight Eisenhower* 3. Sir Winston Churchill 4. Adlai Stevenson 5. Dr. Albert Schweitzer 6. *Harry Truman* 7. Rev. Billy Graham 8. Richard Nixon 9. Pope John XXIII 10. Gen. Douglas MacArthur

(Table continues)

Table 6.17 (continued)

Year	Man	Year	Man
1962	1. **John Kennedy** 2. *Dwight Eisenhower* 3. Sir Winston Churchill 4. Dr. Albert Schweitzer 5. *Herbert Hoover* 6. Gen. Douglas MacArthur 7. *Harry Truman* 8. Pope John XXIII 9. Adlai Stevenson 10. Richard Nixon	1963	1. **Lyndon Johnson** 2. *Dwight Eisenhower* 3. Sir Winston Churchill 4. Dr. Albert Schweitzer 5. Robert Kennedy 6. Rev. Billy Graham 7. Adlai Stevenson 8. Pope John VI 9. Charles de Gaulle 10. Richard Nixon
1964	1. **Lyndon Johnson** 2. Sir Winston Churchill 3. *Dwight Eisenhower* 4. Rev. Martin Luther King 5. Robert Kennedy 6. Barry Goldwater 7. Rev. Billy Graham 8. Adlai Stevenson 9. Dr. Albert Schweitzer 10. Pope John VI	1965	1. **Lyndon Johnson** 2. *Dwight Eisenhower* 3. Robert Kennedy 4. Rev. Billy Graham 5. Pope John VI 6. Rev. Martin Luther King 7. Richard Nixon 8. Hubert Humphrey 9. Barry Goldwater 10. *Harry Truman*
1966	1. **Lyndon Johnson** 2. *Dwight Eisenhower* 3. Robert Kennedy 4. Rev. Billy Graham 5. Pope Paul VI 6. U Thant 7. Everett Dirksen 8. George Romney 9. Richard Nixon 10. Ronald Reagan	1967	1. *Dwight Eisenhower* 2. **Lyndon Johnson** 3. Rev. Billy Graham 4. Robert Kennedy 5. Pope John VI 6. Everett Dirksen 7. Richard Nixon 8. George Wallace 9. Ronald Reagan 10. *Harry Truman*
1968	1. *Dwight Eisenhower* 2. **Lyndon Johnson** 3. Edward Kennedy 4. Rev. Billy Graham 5. Richard Nixon 6. Hubert Humphrey 7. George Wallace 8. Pope Paul VI 9. *Harry Truman* 10. Eugene McCarthy	1969	1. **Richard Nixon** 2. Rev. Billy Graham 3. Spiro Agnew 4. *Lyndon Johnson* 5. Edward Kennedy 6. Hubert Humphrey 7. *Harry Truman* 8. George Wallace 9. Pope Paul VI 10. Edmund Muskie

Table 6.17 (continued)

Year	Man	Year	Man
1970	1. **Richard Nixon**	1971	1. **Richard Nixon**
	2. Rev. Billy Graham		2. Rev. Billy Graham
	3. Edward Kennedy		3. Edward Kennedy
	4. Spiro Agnew		4. *Lyndon Johnson*
	5. Pope Paul VI		5. Hubert Humphrey
	6. Edmund Muskie		6. Spiro Agnew
	7. *Lyndon Johnson*		7. Ralph Nader
	8. Ronald Reagan		8. Pope Paul VI
	9. Hubert Humphrey		9. Bob Hope
	10. *Harry Truman*		10. George Wallace
1972	1. **Richard Nixon**	1973	1. Henry Kissinger
	2. Rev. Billy Graham		2. Rev. Billy Graham
	3. *Harry Truman*		3. **Richard Nixon**
	4. Henry Kissinger		4. Edward Kennedy
	5. Edward Kennedy		5. **Gerald Ford**
	6. George Wallace		6. George Wallace
	7. Spiro Agnew		7. Ralph Nader
	8. Pope Paul VI		8. Henry Jackson
	9. George McGovern		9. Pope Paul VI
	10. Willy Brandt		10. Barry Goldwater
1974	1. Henry Kissinger	1977	1. **Jimmy Carter**
	2. Rev. Billy Graham		2. Anwar Sadat
	3. **Gerald Ford**		3. Hubert Humphrey
	4. Edward Kennedy		4. Rev. Billy Graham
	5. George Wallace		5. *Gerald Ford*
	6. Nelson Rockefeller		6. Henry Kissinger
	7. *Richard Nixon*		7. Menachem Begin
	8. Barry Goldwater		8. Ronald Reagan
	9. Ronald Reagan		9. Pope Paul VI
	10. Henry Jackson		10. *Richard Nixon* and Bob Hope
1978	1. **Jimmy Carter**	1979	1. **Jimmy Carter**
	2. Pope John Paul II		2. Pope John Paul II
	3. Rev. Billy Graham		3. Edward Kennedy
	4. Anwar Sadat		4. Anwar Sadat
	5. *Gerald Ford*		5. Ronald Reagan
	6. Ronald Reagan		6. Rev. Billy Graham
	7. Edward Kennedy		7. *Gerald Ford*
	8. *Richard Nixon*		8. Henry Kissinger
	9. Menachem Begin		9. *Richard Nixon*
	10. Henry Kissinger		10. Menachem Begin

(Table continues)

Table 6.17 (continued)

Year	Man	Year	Man
1980	1. Pope John Paul II 2. **Jimmy Carter** 3. Anwar Sadat 4. Rev. Billy Graham 5. Ronald Reagan 6. Henry Kissinger 7. *Richard Nixon* 8. *Gerald Ford* 9. Edward Kennedy 10. Menachem Begin	1981	1. **Ronald Reagan** 2. Pope John Paul II 3. *Jimmy Carter* 4. Rev. Billy Graham 5. Edward Kennedy 6. Menachem Begin 7. Bob Hope 8. *Gerald Ford* 9. Henry Kissinger 10. Rev. Jesse Jackson
1982	1. **Ronald Reagan** 2. Pope John Paul II 3. Rev. Billy Graham 4. *Jimmy Carter* 5. Edward Kennedy 6. Lech Walesa 7. Menachem Begin 8. Henry Kissinger 9. Rev. Jesse Jackson 10. *Gerald Ford*	1983	1. **Ronald Reagan** 2. Pope John Paul II 3. Lech Walesa 4. Rev. Billy Graham 5. Edward Kennedy 6. *Jimmy Carter* and Rev. Jesse Jackson 8. John Glenn 9. Henry Kissinger 10. Walter Mondale
1984	1. **Ronald Reagan** 2. Pope John Paul II 3. Jesse Jackson 4. Rev. Billy Graham 5. Walter Mondale 6. Edward Kennedy 7. *Jimmy Carter* 8. Henry Kissinger 9. Lee Iacocca 10. George Bush		

Note: Boldface indicates the president during the current year; italics indicate former presidents. In 1975 and 1976 the question was not asked.

[a]In 1946 and 1947, the question referred to the "most admired person."

Source: Adapted from the *Gallup Report*, December 1984, 4-5.

Table 6.18   The British Public's Rating of Reagan and Carter (percent)

	Is	Is not	Don't know	Rating [a]
Carter				
1977 (2) [b]	61	11	28	50
1978 (2)	45	33	22	12
1979 (4)	38	44	18	−6
1980 (3)	50	35	15	15
1977-1980 (11)	47	33	20	14
Reagan				
1981 (2)	30	34	37	−4
1982 (4)	27	58	15	−31
1983 (4)	27	60	13	−33
1984 (4)	32	55	13	−23
1981-1984 (14)	29	54	17	−25

Note: The question was: "Do you think Mr. Reagan (Carter) is or is not proving a good president of the United States?" Sample sizes ranged from 900 to 1,100.

[a] "Rating" is the difference between "Is" and "Is not."
[b] The number of monthly polls asking the question each year appears in parentheses.

Source: Adapted from *Public Opinion*, October/November 1984, 48.

Table 6.19   The British Public's Appraisal of the Elections of Nixon, Carter, and Reagan (percent)

Version	Good thing	Bad thing	Don't know	Rating [a]
...America?				
Nixon	60	7	33	53
Carter	42	19	39	23
Reagan	30	40	31	−10
...America's standing in the world?				
Nixon	57	7	36	50
Carter	40	18	42	22
Reagan	32	35	34	−3
...peace in the world?				
Nixon	—	—	—	—
Carter	—	—	—	—
Reagan	26	37	37	−11
...America's relations with Britain?				
Nixon	59	4	37	55
Carter	44	16	39	28
Reagan	46	22	32	24

Note: The question was: "As you may know, Richard Nixon (Jimmy Carter, Ronald Reagan) has been elected president of the United States. Do you think this will be a good thing or a bad thing for..." Sample sizes ranged from 900 to 1,100.

[a] "Rating" is the difference between "Good thing" and "Bad thing."

Source: Adapted from *Public Opinion*, October/November 1984, 49.

Table 6.20 Confidence in Leaders of Major Institutions, 1966-1984 (percent)

Date	Survey organization	Major institution										
		White House[a]	Congress	Supreme Court	Medicine	Education	Military	Org. religion	Companies	Press	Org. labor	Average
February 1966	Harris	41	42	50	72	61	62	41	55	29	22	48
January 1967[b]	Harris	37	41	40	60	56	56	40	47	26	20	42
August 1971	Harris	23	19	23	61	37	27	27	27	18	14	28
October 1972[b]	Harris	27	21	28	48	33	36	29	27	18	15	28
March 1973	NORC	29	24	32	54	37	32	35	29	23	16	31
September 1973	Harris	19	30	33	58	44	40	36	30	30	20	34
December 1973	Harris	13	17	—	60	46	—	29	28	28	16	31
March 1974	NORC	14	17	33	60	49	40	44	31	26	18	33
August 1974	Harris	28	18	40	49	39	34	32	22	25	17	30
September 1974	Harris	18	16	35	48	39	31	32	16	26	18	28
March 1975	NORC	13	13	31	50	31	35	24	19	24	10	25
April 1975	Harris	13	14	29	43	36	24	32	20	26	14	25
August 1975	Harris	16	12	28	54	37	30	36	20	28	18	28
March 1976	Harris	16	18	32	—	—	36	—	22	21	—	28
March 1976	NORC	14	14	35	54	38	39	31	22	28	12	29
January 1977	Harris	23	16	29	42	37	28	29	20	18	14	26
March 1977	NORC	28	19	36	52	41	36	40	27	25	15	32
November 1977	Harris	23	15	31	55	41	31	34	23	19	15	29
March 1978	NORC	13	13	28	46	28	30	31	22	20	11	24
August 1978	Harris	14	10	29	42	41	29	34	22	23	15	26
February 1979	Harris	17	18	28	30	33	29	20	18	28	10	23
March 1980	NORC	12	9	25	52	30	28	35	27	22	15	26
November 1980	Harris	17	18	27	34	36	28	22	16	19	14	23
September 1981	Harris	24	16	29	37	34	28	22	16	16	12	23
March 1982	NORC	19	13	31	45	33	31	32	23	18	12	26

November 1982	Harris	20	13	25	32	30	31	20	18	14	8	21
March 1983	NORC	13	10	27	52	29	29	28	24	13	8	23
November 1983	Harris	23	20	33	35	36	35	22	18	19	10	25
March 1984	NORC	19	13	35	52	29	37	32	32	17	9	28
November 1984	Harris	42	28	35	43	40	45	24	19	18	12	31
Average		21	18	32	49	38	34	31	25	22	14	29

Note: NORC = National Opinion Research Center. The question was: "As far as the people *running* various institutions are concerned, would you say you have a great deal of confidence, only some confidence, or hardly any confidence at all in them?"

[a] "White House" (Harris) and "Executive Branch" (NORC).
[b] Electoral participants only.

Source: Adapted from *Public Opinion*, April/May 1985, 8.

Table 6.21   Judging Ethical and Moral Practices of the President and Other Occupational Groups (percent)

	Excellent/good		
Occupational group	1981	1983	1985
President	53	48	65
Supreme Court	56	49	57
Military leaders	55	47	48
U.S. senators and representatives	36	33	42
Federal government officials	23	25	33
State and local government officials	31	31	37
Labor union leaders	23	21	23
Average workers	72	72	74
Small business proprietors	75	68	76
Corporate executives	33	29	39
Corporate board members	28	27	35
Stockbrokers	31	34	34
Bankers	56	49	57
Advertising executives	31	35	38
Lawyers	45	44	43
Physicians	75	70	76
College professors	60	66	69
Scientists	69	64	75
Media news reporters	57	58	51
Average	48	46	51

Note: The question, asked in July 1985, was: "How would you rate the ethical and moral practices of (specific category) (1) Excellent, (2) Good, (3) Only Fair, (4) Poor, (5) No Opinion?"

Source: Adapted from Lipset (1986).

Table 6.22 Public Objections to Presidential Behavior (percent)

Behavior	Sex		Race		Education			Age			
	M	F	W	NW	GS	HS	C	18-34	35-49	50-65	65+
Smoked marijuana occasionally	65	75	71	64	78	71	66	50	80	86	84
Told ethnic or racial jokes in private	37	49	41	57	47	40	46	35	43	51	52
Was not a member of a church	31	45	38	41	48	30	33	24	43	48	51
Used tranquilizers occasionally	34	38	35	45	47	35	31	30	34	41	45
Used profane language in private	29	38	33	39	59	31	24	19	32	45	55
Had seen a psychiatrist	32	28	29	32	39	30	23	28	26	31	35
Wore jeans in the Oval Office	17	25	21	24	28	21	17	11	20	29	38
Were divorced	17	18	17	22	30	16	14	9	17	23	29
Had a cocktail before dinner each night	13	15	13	18	27	13	9	9	13	16	26

Note: The survey question was: "I am going to read a number of statements that could describe a person. Please tell me whether or not you would object strongly to each statement if it were true about a president." The figures reported are the percent of respondents who object strongly. M = male. F = female. W = white. NW = nonwhite. GS = grade school. HS = high school. C = college.

Source: Adapted from Wayne (1982b, 31).

Table 6.23 Tolerance in Presidential Choices (percent)

Year	Black[a]		Woman[b]		Catholic[c]		Jew[d]		Atheist[e]		Homosexual[f]	
	Yes	No	Yes	No	Yes	No	Yes	No	Yes	No	Yes	No
1937	—	—	31	65	64	28	46	46	—	—	—	—
1940	—	—	—	—	62	31	—	—	—	—	—	—
1949	—	—	48	48	—	—	—	—	—	—	—	—
1955	—	—	52	44	—	—	—	—	—	—	—	—
1958	38	53	52	43	68	25	62	28	18	75	—	—
1959	—	—	—	—	69	20	—	—	—	—	—	—
1960	—	—	—	—	71	20	—	—	—	—	—	—
1961	47	45	—	—	82	13	68	23	—	—	—	—
1963	59	34	—	—	84	13	77	17	—	—	—	—
1965	54	40	—	—	87	10	80	15	—	—	—	—
1967	67	23	57	39	89	9	82	13	—	—	—	—
1969	70	23	54	39	88	8	86	8	—	—	—	—
1971	—	—	66	29	—	—	—	—	—	—	—	—
1975	77	18	73	23	—	—	—	—	—	—	—	—
1978	77	16	76	19	91	4	82	12	40	53	26	66
1983	—	—	80	16	92	5	88	7	42	51	29	64
1984	—	—	78	17	—	—	—	—	—	—	—	—

[a] Question: "If your party nominated a generally well-qualified man for president and he happened to be black, would you vote for him?" 1958-1978 question: "There's always much discussion about the qualifications of presidential candidates—their education, age, race, religion and the like. If your party nominated a generally well-qualified man for president and he happened to be Negro, would you vote for him?"
[b] Question: "If your party nominated a woman for president, would you vote for her if she were qualified for the job?"
[c] Question: "If your party nominated a generally well-qualified man for president and he happened to be Catholic, would you vote for him?"

[d] Question: "Between now and the political conventions ... there will be discussion about the qualifications of presidential candidates—their education, age, religion, race, and so on. If your party nominated a generally well-qualified man for president and he happened to be a Jew, would you vote for him?"

[e] Question: "Between now and the political convention ... there will be discussion about the qualifications of presidential candidates—their education, age, religion, race, and so on. If your party nominated a generally well-qualified man for president and he happened to be an Athiest, would you vote for him?"

[f] Question: "Between now and the political convention ... there will be discussion about the qualifications of presidential candidates—their education, age, religion, race, and so on. If your party nominated a generally well-qualified man for president and he happened to be a homosexual, would you vote for him?"

Sources: Gallup Report, May 1983, 18, August/September 1984, 13; September 1983, 10, 11, 13, and 14.

Table 6.24 Public Attitudes toward Constitutional Changes in Presidential Power

	Line-item veto [a]		Six-year presidential term [b]	
Year	Favor	Oppose	Yes, favor	No, oppose
1936	—	—	26	74
1938	—	—	21	67
1943 [c]	—	—	29	59
1945 [d]	57	14	25	68
1969	—	—	18	75
1971	—	—	20	73
1973	—	—	28	64
1975	69	20	—	—
1978	70	19	—	—
1979	—	—	30	62
1981 (January) [e]	—	—	30	63
1981 (October)	—	—	31	61
1983	67	25	—	—

[a] Question: "At the present time, when Congress passes a bill, the president cannot veto parts of that bill, but must accept it in full or veto it. Do you think this should be changed so that the president can veto some items in a bill without vetoing the entire bill?"

[b] Question: "Some people feel that limiting a president to one term of six years would best serve the national interest because he could devote all his energies to solving national problems rather than spending a lot of time trying to get reelected. Others prefer the present system because they feel it takes a president a long time learning how to do his job and that knowing that he will have to seek reelection will make him answerable to the wishes of the people. Which point of view comes closer to the way you, yourself, feel? Do you favor or oppose changing the term of office of the president to one six-year term with no reelection?"

[c] Question: "Would you favor changing the term of office of the president hereafter to one six-year term with no reelection?"

[d] Question: "Would you favor changing the term of office of the president of the United States in the future to one six-year term with no reelection?"

[e] Question: "Would you favor changing the term of the president of the United States to one six-year term with no reelection?"

Sources: Adapted from Gallup Report, April 1984, 20; February 1983, 12.

Table 6.25 Party Best for Prosperity and Peace (percent)

Year	Month	Prosperity[a]			Peace[b]		
		Republican party	Democratic party	No difference, no opinion	Republican party	Democratic party	No difference, no opinion
1951	September	—	—	—	28	21	51
	November	29	37	34	—	—	—
1952	January	31	35	34	36	15	49
1956	October	39	39	22	46	16	38
1960	October	31	46	23	40	25	35
1964	October	21	53	26	22	45	33
1968	October	34	37	29	37	24	39
1972	September	38	35	27	32	28	40
1976	August	23	47	30	29	32	39
1980	September	35	36	29	25	42	33
1981	April	41	28	31	29	34	37
	October	40	31	29	—	—	—
1982	October	34	43	23	29	38	33
1983	September	33	40	27	26	39	35
1984	April	44	36	20	30	42	28

[a]Question: "Which political party—the Republican party or the Democratic party—do you think will do a better job of keeping the country prosperous?"
[b]Question: "Which political party do you think would be more likely to keep the United States out of World War III—the Republican party or the Democratic party?"

Source: Adapted from Gallup Report, April 1984, 18-19.

Table 6.26 The Public's Most Important Problem

Year	Problem
1935	Unemployment
1936	Unemployment
1937	Unemployment
1938	Keeping out of war
1939	Keeping out of war
1940	Keeping out of war
1941	Keeping out of war, winning war
1942	Winning war
1943	Winning war
1944	Winning war
1945	Winning war
1946	High cost of living
1947	High cost of living, labor unrest
1948	Keeping peace
1949	Labor unrest
1950	Labor unrest
1951	Korean War
1952	Korean War
1953	Keeping peace
1954	Keeping peace
1955	Keeping peace
1956	Keeping peace
1957	Race relations, keeping peace
1958	Unemployment, keeping peace
1959	Keeping peace
1960	Keeping peace
1961	Keeping peace
1962	Keeping peace
1963	Keeping peace, race relations
1964	Vietnam, race relations
1965	Vietnam, race relations
1966	Vietnam
1967	Vietnam, high cost of living
1968	Vietnam
1969	Vietnam
1970	Vietnam
1971	Vietnam, high cost of living
1972	Vietnam
1973	High cost of living, Watergate
1974	High cost of living, Watergate, energy crisis
1975	High cost of living, unemployment
1976	High cost of living, unemployment
1977	High cost of living, unemployment
1978	High cost of living, energy problems
1979	High cost of living, energy problems
1980	High cost of living, unemployment

Table 6.26   (continued)

Year	Problem
1981	High cost of living, unemployment
1982	Unemployment, high cost of living
1983	Unemployment, high cost of living
1984	Unemployment, fear of war

Source: Adapted from *Gallup Report*, October 1984, 22.

Table 6.27   The Party Best Able to Handle the Most Important Problem
(percent)

Year	Month	Republican	Democratic	Uncommitted
1945	August	23	48	29
1946	August	35	34	31
1948	April	32	28	40
1950	September	19	27	54
1956	October	33	25	42
1958	February	19	40	41
1958	March	23	39	38
1959	February	26	34	40
1959	March	26	41	33
1959	October	27	29	44
1960	March	24	32	44
1960	July	23	36	41
1960	August	35	36	29
1960	October	27	29	44
1962	April	16	40	44
1962	September	17	33	50
1963	April	17	36	47
1963	October	23	49	28
1964	March	16	39	45
1964	May	16	40	44
1964	July	25	38	37
1964	October	23	49	28
1965	June	16	37	47
1965	August	16	36	48
1965	October	17	34	49
1965	December	17	38	45
1966	May	22	29	49
1966	September	21	28	51
1967	November	30	28	42
1968	May	28	30	42
1968	July	31	27	42
1968	September	37	25	38
1968	October	34	29	37
1970	February	27	25	48
1970	August	19	31	50
1970	October	21	30	49
1971	June	20	30	50
1971	August	18	35	47
1971	December	22	32	46
1972	May	28	34	38
1972	October	39	29	32
1974	January	15	39	46
1974	June	16	38	46
1974	August	20	38	42
1974	September	13	39	48

Table 6.27 (continued)

Year	Month	Republican	Democratic	Uncommitted
1974	October	18	39	43
1975	February-March	14	42	44
1975	October	15	42	43
1976	January	18	40	42
1976	April	18	39	43
1976	October	23	43	34
1977	October	14	38	48
1978	February	19	35	46
1978	April	22	32	46
1978	July	19	33	48
1978	September	20	34	46
1978	October	21	31	48
1979	February	23	29	48
1979	March	23	29	48
1979	May	21	31	48
1979	August	20	30	50
1979	October	25	33	42
1980	January	21	34	45
1980	March	28	32	40
1980	July	30	27	43
1980	September	35	32	33
1980	October	40	31	29
1981	January-February	39	20	41
1981	May	36	21	43
1981	October	32	29	39
1982	January	30	34	36
1982	April	25	35	40
1982	June	28	35	37
1982	August	26	35	39
1982	October	29	41	30
1983	April	20	41	39
1983	July	24	38	38
1983	November	28	35	37
1984	February	30	32	38
1984	June	33	35	32

Source: Adapted from *Gallup Report*, July 1984, 21.

7
Elections and Reelections

Elections cast a long shadow over the presidency. The image of a single executive is fostered by presidential candidates who overestimate their ability to solve national problems and infrequently acknowledge the institutional constraints within which presidents are forced to operate. The office was intended by the framers of the Constitution to be republican in origin. Although the framers did not fully trust the citizenry to make the proper choice for chief executive and hence contrived the electoral college, they nevertheless considered popular consent an integral part of the office. Indeed, unlike many other democratic nations, the United States in its constitutional arrangement provides for a unique prize—a separately elected chief executive. In most countries, the legislature is the focus of republican government. There is competition in these countries among political parties that attempt to build successful electoral coalitions. In turn, this competition will decide the legislative coalitions in the legislative assembly and, ultimately, the executive branch of government. Although in the United States the legislative seats in Congress were also seen as prizes worthy of organizational campaign efforts—and provided the encouragement necessary for the development of early, albeit local, political parties—presidential elections advanced the cause of national political parties in America and created a truly national office for which the parties could compete. Richard McCormick (1975) argues that the first presidential elections created the central characteristics of the emerging *national* politics and the first truly national political parties:

> The rivalry between John Adams and Thomas Jefferson in 1796 and again in 1800 served not only to dramatize and polarize the emerging partisan cleavage: It also enlarged party strife beyond the bounds of congressional districts, bringing it to embrace entire

states and, by extension, the whole nation. . . . I would contend that it was the contest for the presidency that was to exert the determining influence on the structure of the American party system. (94)

That the presidency is more important than any legislative seat (by any measure) and can be controlled for four years by winning only one election makes it a political prize almost unequaled in the democratic world.

Elections and parties shape the presidency as an institution in three ways.[1] First, the presidential parties, and the electoral coalitions they form, increase the group diversity of the office. As noted in Chapter 6, the plural presidency is confronted with different publics that evaluate the incumbent and also hold different opinions about presidential candidates. These publics may form electoral coalitions through parties affiliated with the candidates. The institution of the presidency, moreover, manifests some continuity as a result of features that are shared over time by incumbents of the same party. Second, campaign issues and promises add to the complexity of policy making in office. Presidential candidates identify numerous problems that they will attempt to solve if they are elected. The presidency must work to accommodate this campaign baggage when it reaches the White House. Finally, the images constructed by candidates, stressing their personal qualities and their job competence, foster the image of a single executive. Public expectations of presidents stem in part from the institutional arrangement according to which the chief executive is separately elected.

Presidential Parties in Nomination Contests

Tremendous effort must be expended to win a party's presidential nomination (see, for example, Aldrich 1980). Enormous organizational and personal efforts of large numbers of campaign activists over nearly a two-year period are required. The data presented in the tables for this chapter document the enormous costs involved in presidential nominations and campaigns. Even the physical effect of the campaign on the candidates is dramatic. With all the money, time, and effort involved, the campaign should determine the outcome of the primary election vote, but such is usually not the case. Tables 7.1 and 7.2, for example, list apparent leaders in races for presidential nomination at various stages of their campaigns in presidential contests since 1936. Table 7.1 shows that only two nomination contests in the last fifty years featured a preprimary front-runner of the party controlling the presidency who did not eventually become the nominee: President Johnson (in 1968) and President Truman (in 1952) began as candidates but later decided to drop out of the race. For the party out of power, the situation is similar. All preprimary front-runners save one since 1932 have been nominated for president by their party. The exception was Edmund Muskie, who left the race in 1972. For the three elections without preprimary front-runners, the leading candidate going into the convention—if there was one—became the party's nominee in each case.[2] The campaign appears merely to reinforce early preferences.

Although this conclusion cannot be taken as universal, much of the campaign for the two major parties' nominations appears to be nothing more than a ratification of the precontest candidate standings. The current process thus favors candidates with already established national reputations. With well-developed reputations and corresponding visibility, front-runners can more easily overcome problems of building support coalitions among exceedingly diverse populations. This is not always the situation, as we see plainly in the case of Jimmy Carter in 1976, but it is the dominant tendency. Indeed, probably for this reason very few members of the U.S. House of Representatives have become presidential candidates. Table 7.3 lists every member of the House of Representatives in this century who competed in primaries in more than one state and who received at least one-half of 1 percent of the total primary vote or 5 percent of the delegate votes on the first ballot at their party's national convention. None of these twelve members of the House was ever nominated for the presidency by the relevant party.

The fact that nomination campaigns do not seem to influence voters' decisions does not mean that activists in presidential campaigns have no bearing on American politics. On the contrary, these coalitions of activists become the core of a president's governing coalition. They are important both during and between presidential elections. Although not as clearly defined as organized interest groups, what observers call "presidential parties" are unmistakable features of the American political landscape. Several presidential parties exist in varied forms at any point in the electoral cycle. A "Ronald Reagan party," composed of the White House staff and many top political appointees, may be said to exist. This "party" probably also includes many conservative members of Congress as well as officials of state and local government. Owing in large part to a residue of Reagan support from the 1980 and 1984 elections, a large group of citizens might be called "Reagan identifiers." These people were electoral supporters of Reagan and continue to back him as president. Reagan's supporters were known to exist long before 1980; many favored him in previous campaigns. Other parts of the "Reagan party" derived from past efforts for other presidential campaigns. Residual supporters from the Ford, Nixon, Goldwater, and even Eisenhower presidential parties are identifiable in the Reagan coalition. On the Democratic side, some semblance of a "Jimmy Carter party," mobilized in 1976 but fading thereafter, still remains. For some time there has also been an "Edward Kennedy party," and perhaps even a more generic party for the Kennedy family.

A poignant example of the emergence and disappearance of presidential parties appeared with the presidential candidacy of George McGovern in 1984. McGovern believed that he had some identifiable presidential party support in 1984 that could be resurrected from what remained of his 1972 campaign effort. Probably most of his previous supporters had faded into other presidential camps. During the campaign, the former senator said in an interview, "They come up to me wearing buttons for Mondale, Glenn, Hart, and all the others and tell me they are glad to see I haven't given up. They say I'm the reason they got back into politics back in 1972" (Gailey 1983, 16). Indeed, Gary Hart was George McGovern's campaign manager in 1972. Although this statement foreshadowed the eventual outcome of McGovern's candidacy, it also revealed the long-term importance of McGovern's 1972 campaign for presidential politics more than a decade later.

In a study of presidential activists, John Kessel (1980) found that "two thirds of the Republicans and 72 percent of the Democrats began" their careers in a presidential election year. Among county political leaders, "Four times as many began in presidential campaigns as in *any* other type." This reasoning leads Kessel to his observation that "a presidential party at any time is a residue of its past campaign" (61-62). Leon Epstein (1986) also notes:

> The presidential party is a more coherent *national* phenomenon than is any other kind of American party. Congressional parties are national too, but each is so diverse, given the considerable independence of its members in relating to their separate constituencies, that it unites only for limited purposes.... Long established, [the national Republican and Democratic party organizations] were until recently the principal structures through which presidential candidates conducted their general election campaigns and through which incumbent presidents maintained their partisan followings. But even when they exercised their traditional roles in presidential campaigns, the national committees acted primarily as agencies for presidential nominees (or incumbent presidents) rather than as independently powerful organizations. (85-86)

These semipermanent presidential coalitions obviously play a central role in modern-day presidential politics and will probably continue to do so. Political parties are an important factor of American politics, in part because national political party labels are often proxies for particular presidential parties; in only rare instances do presidential parties cross political party boundary lines. As such, the national political parties—whose labels and broad policy positions remain generally stable over time—represent, at any one point in time, the balance of power among many presidential parties. These presidential parties participate in constant battles that are most competitive prior to election time for control of the national party. Beck (1982) notes:

> Politics consists of a series of impermanent coalitions between various sectors of society with elections offering a choice between temporary alliances. Party label is a guide to what these alliances might look like. . . , but it is only an imperfect guide. (93)

Presidents may appeal to multiple groups and interests because of their initial electoral attention to these groups within their presidential parties. Just as the false image of a singular executive exists in other areas of presidential politics, it obviously also exists in party conflict. The president may appear as the "chief of party," but this party is far from uniform. Indeed, many individuals within the national political party, as distinct from the presidential party, have no more loyalty to the incumbent president than do members of the opposition political party. In order to study presidential nominations and elections appropriately, we should concentrate on the different aspects of presidential parties and their overlap with national political parties. By focusing on these parties we can identify meaningful political patterns within the complex, and sometimes chaotic jumble of presidential campaign politics.

To illuminate the role that presidential parties play both within and across campaigns, we present presidential primary election results from 1960 to 1984 in Tables 7.4 through 7.10.[3] As Aldrich (1980, 99) notes, "There is a dynamic, or time-related, pattern to the outcome of each campaign." He argues that the

> dynamics of a campaign ... do have a sense of inevitability. Preconvention campaigns are unstable.... Once the competitive balance is substantially tipped, candidates with momentum have an increasing probability of attaining the nomination, while candidates whose chances begin to decline substantially will see them continue to decline until they are forced to retire from active competition. (135)

The process by which presidential nomination campaigns winnow out contenders is quite evident in our tables.

The institution of the presidential primary election has also changed over time, with important consequences for presidential nomination politics. The number of presidential primaries has grown dramatically—from sixteen in 1960 to thirty-six in 1980. Moreover, until 1984, very few states with presidential primaries changed back to a party convention or caucus system. Serious contenders for the nomination were therefore forced to campaign in most of these primary states in the hopes of gaining enough delegate votes prior to the convention for a "first ballot" victory. In 1984, however, more than 36 percent of the presidential primaries were eliminated. The effects of this change were unclear in the 1984 election because of the existence of two dominant preprimary front-runners; this phenomenon must be watched in subsequent elections.

The data in these tables also indicate the decline in "favorite son" candidates who run only in their home states, hoping to act as brokers at the national convention, and the drop in successful slates of unpledged delegates. With so many primary election states, candidates have usually compiled sufficient delegate support to preclude any major brokering activity at the convention. Finally, the data in these tables emphasize again that the winners of the early primaries, particularly New Hampshire, are much more likely to become their party's nominees.

Just as the preprimary front-runner has become the eventual nominee in most campaigns over the last five decades, the official nomination has become much less controversial. Tables 7.11 and 7.12 indicate that the last convention in which more than one ballot was required to determine the nomination was the 1952 Democratic convention. Since then, both Democrats and Republicans have nominated their presidential candidates on the first ballot.

Tables 7.13 through 7.19 present more detailed information on how states vote in party conventions. These tables present the first-ballot votes for presidential candidates for each Democratic and Republican national convention. After these votes, in some conventions many delegates shifted to the winning candidate; in others the final nomination was made by acclamation. The format used in these tables more clearly shows intraparty conflict and disagreement than do statistics on the number of ballots cast or the final vote tally. For example, although the decision was made on the first ballot, the 1976 Republican nomination contest was won by only 117 in a total of 2,259 delegates. In addition, our tables make it possible to trace candidates' support across states and over time to reveal clues about the nature of political conflict within each of the national parties—conflicts their nominees must resolve in order to be successful and conflicts that they as presidents of the country will also face.

These tables also indicate the complex pattern of support from different states and regions for presidential nominees. These data demonstrate the plural nature of state support for a presidential nominee and the likely sources of support for a potential president. In fact, these data may be viewed as a political map. They outline the sources of the president's unique presidential party and also help to show how one of these presidential parties merges with others as one campaign ends and another begins.

Taking another perspective on national political parties, we may also consider how they represent their constituents. According to one form of representation, votes are allocated by state at the national political party convention. Most often, national parties use a (different) weighted average of the size of the state and the degree to which that state supported past candidates of that party. Population and demographic changes are often very rapid, however, so that some of these a priori decisions perhaps reflect underlying priorities different from those that parties originally had in mind. The data from these tables also suggest that the two national parties use different normative criteria in representing constituents. New York went Republican in six of the last ten presidential elections, for example, but in 1984 was allocated one percentage point *less* representation in the Republican party convention than in the Democratic (6.09 percent of the delegates to the Republican convention and 7.26 percent of the delegates to the Democratic convention came from New York). More analysis is needed to determine how each state is represented at the national conventions, what normative criteria are used by the parties, and how these factors affect the final vote results. An increasingly large number of scholars are studying the relationship of democratic representation and the degree of partisan bias found in legislative redistricting by focusing on the translation of citizen votes in general elections into legislative seats (Grofman and Lijphart 1986; King and Browning 1987). Some of the methods developed in this literature might profitably be used in the study of primary election results as they translate into party convention delegates allocated by states.

Political Parties and the Presidency

Table 7.20 lists the party affiliation of the winning and losing presidential candidates, as well as that of members of the House and Senate. Just as the emergence, consolidation, and decline of presidential parties may be seen to have exerted a powerful influence on American nomination politics, successful presidential parties probably play a role in defining the politics of U.S. general elections. Consider three groups of Americans during a period of stability in the White House. For those just coming of age and moving into the potential electorate, the constancy of Franklin Roosevelt's presidency, for example, probably substantially affected the structuring of attitudes and party affiliations. Many of those who came of voting age during FDR's tenure became Democrats. He shaped the political options, not only for the Democrats, but also for the opposition Republicans. For those already in the electorate, the choice was also defined. By making similar voting decisions for several successive elections (for or against FDR), these voters probably developed quite stable political preferences. The final group of Americans includes those moving out of the electorate (dying or "retiring" from political attentiveness). This group's perceptions were developed during an earlier political alignment; their movement out of the electorate means that the FDR alignment had a proportionately larger effect on the *current* electorate. This stability continued after FDR with Truman in the White House for seven years.

It may be partly coincidence, but the start of this long period of stability in the White House is often identified by scholars as marking a critical realignment of politics and political parties in the United States. Certainly the Depression, the war, FDR's personal appeal and leadership, and other factors greatly affected this realignment. At least some of the apparent aggregate electoral stability, however, may plausibly have been attributed to "rerunning" the same elections and having citizens again and again decide whether to vote for or against FDR.

Most scholars believe that the critical realignment that preceded the Roosevelt realignment occurred around 1896. Unlike the one that occurred in the Depression-ridden 1930s, this realignment favored the Republican party. As Table 7.20 indicates, the Republican candidate, William McKinley, was elected president in both 1896 and 1900. Also contributing to the postrealignment electoral stability at that time was the Democratic candidate, William Jennings Bryan, who ran (and lost) in *both* elections. Bryan also ran and lost again in 1908. If anything adds to the continuity of voting behavior across time, and in making several elections look similar to political analysts, it is offering the same candidate choices to the same voters. Even successive elections are usually marked by some difference in issues and in the demographic composition of the electorate, of course, but the existence of the same candidates across time may have a strong stabilizing influence.

If these periods of relatively infrequent changes in presidential incumbents produced more stable political alignments, then the current period of high presidential turnover, with each election appearing quite different from its predecessor, is likely to have contributed to higher party and electoral volatility. More people today identify as political independents; higher levels of split-ticket voting and lower levels of voter turnout occur concurrently. These may be associated with higher levels of incumbent turnover in the presidency. Scholars must do the necessary research to determine whether the patterns of presidential turnover in Table 7.20 are a cause of party realignments; they obviously show a strong association with such phenomena, but whether they are also a causal factor remains to be demonstrated.

Table 7.20 also makes it possible to trace the emergence of new controlling parties in Congress and the presidency and the decline of older ones. That political parties are truly national electoral forces is clear once we observe that presidents share party labels with a majority of members of at least one house, and usually both houses, of Congress. Throughout American history, this factor has been crucial in making national policy. Epstein (1986) states:

> The very idea of a party label common to a president and members of Congress suggests the possibility of a bridge over the separation of powers. Certainly the common party affiliation served in that way during much of American history, occasionally with striking success and more often with some success. The bridge, rather like a drawbridge, has not always been usable, and it has been difficult to maintain. But its existence has been significant. (86)

General Elections and Reelections

Tables 7.21 through 7.23 display each state's voter turnout history from 1824 to 1984; national turnout data appear at the bottom. Voter turnout has usually changed gradually across election years but has varied considerably across states within election years. Even in 1984, voter turnout ranged from a low of 40.6 percent in South Carolina to 68.5 percent in Minnesota.

National election results for the presidency appear in Table 7.24 by party for the period 1856 to 1984. From this table, one can observe general trends across history that favor one or the other of the two major parties. Electoral college votes clearly exaggerate the popular vote results for each party. Table 7.24 also reveals that third parties in American politics do poorly. Even though these parties do not usually fare well in electoral competition, however, Table 7.24 seems to show a cyclical pattern in the support that they do receive. Third parties tend to receive a modest percentage of the total electoral vote (5 percent or more) approximately every third to fifth election in our history as a nation.

Complementing these data, state-level voting returns by party appear in Tables 7.25 through 7.29. Except in the cases of George Wallace in 1968, Eugene McCarthy in 1976, and John Anderson in 1980, data for parties other than the Democrats and Republicans are aggregated in the "Other" column for each election year. A list of every minor party candidate since 1840 appears with the relevant percentage of the popular vote in Table 7.30. Important electoral patterns are also evident in the electoral college data presented in Tables 7.31 to 7.33.

By looking at these data differently, we may observe the extent of the electoral mandate produced by each president. Presidents, and others as well, have argued that electoral mandates should be interpreted as licenses to implement particular policy agendas. Whether electoral mandates should be interpreted as policy mandates is an important question that has been considered in a fair amount of political research (Goodin 1977; Harmon and Brauen 1979). For the case to be made, however, one must at a minimum use clear measures of the extent of presidents' electoral victories. Table 7.34 presents such information. For the last thirty presidential elections, three measures of the size of presidential electoral victories are presented. The rank for each presidential election victory also appears. These figures highlight the sometimes large differences between public perceptions of an electoral victory and the actual electoral result. The 1980 and 1984 election victories by Ronald Reagan, for example, have both been called "landslides." This perception is valid when percentages of the electoral college vote are used to measure election mandates. Electoral college votes, however, exaggerate voters' preferences. Because the concept of a policy mandate requires that voters cast their ballots for specific reasons, we need to examine measures more directly related to voters. These voter-based measures, shown in the "percentage of popular vote" and "popular vote advantage" columns in Table 7.34, indicate that Ronald Reagan's 1980 victory was slightly below average. According to these measures, too, 1984 was a bigger electoral victory for Ronald Reagan than 1980, but it was not the biggest presidential win in history. These data will help to place current elections within the proper perspective of U.S. electoral history.

The diverse composition of Democratic and Republican electoral coalitions for president can be traced over the last nine presidential elections from the survey data in Tables 7.35 and 7.36 (Axelrod 1986). Table 7.35 summarizes selected groups' voter support for the Democratic party as compared with the national support the party received. Since 1952, support among poor people for the Democratic party has grown (see column 1 in this table). In 1980, poor Americans gave the Democrats fully 30 percent more support than did the nation as a whole. Except in 1960, when John Kennedy attracted the Catholic vote, blacks have consistently supported the Democratic presidential nominee more than any other group in the party's electoral coalition. Partly because of blacks, central city support for the Democratic party has also grown steadily since the early 1950s. Labor union support for the party, however, has changed little in the last three decades, and support from the southern region of the country has dropped considerably. For three election years (1964, 1968, and 1972), the percentage vote from the South for the Democratic party was actually less than the percentage vote that the Democratic party received nationally. This reveals the success of the Republican party in breaking up the existing Democratic coalition.

Table 7.36 displays the same information for selected groups in the Republican electoral coalition. The most striking difference in group support between Democrats and Republicans is that the Republicans have only small percentage advantages from all the groups supporting them. Apparently the Republican party gains proportionately smaller support from much larger groups in the electorate. Whereas the Republicans have enjoyed only a 1 to 7 percent electoral advantage over Democrats among white citizens, these individuals make up 88 to 90 percent of the eligible electorate and an even larger percentage of the voting electorate. This proportion is often enough to make up for the 25 to 30 percent advantage that the Democrats exercise among the much smaller number of black citizens. The only clear temporal patterns for Republican groups in this table are the increase in white support and the decrease in nonunion support in the presidential vote. Both of these changes have been gradual, however.

The data in these two tables emphasize again that American chief executives must accommodate different publics and groups once they are in office. Presidents must be able to balance within their own electoral coalitions groups that often make less than obvious partners (such as blacks and southerners in the Democratic party). In addition, presidents must respond to some pressure from groups affiliated with the opposition party. The elections and parties surrounding the presidency thus establish it as an institution in which presidents must make intragroup, intergroup, intraparty, and interparty responses to a wide variety of constituencies with important electoral bases.

Survey data also allow us to examine how voters perceive the images of presidential candidates in elections such as those of 1980 and 1984. Research indicates that candidate image is a critical component of voters' decisions (Rusk 1987) and has two dimensions: the personal qualities that voters find important in presidential candidates and the job competence that they seek from candidates across a range of national problems. As presented in Figures 7.1 and 7.2, voters had distinct impressions concerning the positive and negative factors associated with particular candidates. Jimmy Carter, for example, was clearly perceived as a man of high moral principle, but few people felt he had strong leadership abilities. Figures 7.1 and 7.2 also permit a comparison of Ronald Reagan's qualities across elections. The perception of Ronald Reagan as a strong leader remained nearly as high in 1984 as it was in 1980. Perceptions of Reagan as likable, intelligent, and (to a lesser extent) morally upright did erode somewhat. Complementing this analysis, Figures 7.3 and 7.4 illustrate the policy competence of presidential candidates in 1980 and 1984 as perceived by the public on a wide range of issues. Voters not only evaluated presidential candidates' ability to perform on a wide variety of issues but made relatively sharp distinctions as to which candidate was better able to handle these matters. Combining the personal and competence elements of these presidential images, Americans focus attention on a single individual who supposedly has the strength, intelligence, honesty, and likability to cope with assorted policy problems.

During their campaigns, presidential candidates and the national parties that nominate them are also known for making numerous promises to solve varied national problems. Figure 7.5 displays the several kinds of promises made by winning presidential candidates, from John Kennedy to Ronald Reagan. The data presented in Figure 7.6 indicate that presidents, once elected, do reasonably well at keeping their promises. The majority of programs offered by incumbents are either fully or partly realized during their terms in office. The sheer breadth of the promises made by presidential candidates, however, leads them to formulate wide-ranging proposals that may not be fully coherent. Part of the policy complexity of the presidency is created by these many election promises.

Exceptions and Anomalies

Just as exceptions seem to exist for every rule in the English language, exceptions, anomalies, and other odd facts surface in stories about presidential elections. Perhaps these exceptions and anomalies can be viewed in a systematic fashion. Take the example of the "faithless electors," often considered an anomaly in American politics. In presidential elections, Americans vote for electors who, in turn, vote for a presidential candidate. Although this system was originally designed as a check on the masses, who would possibly vote incorrectly, it was soon seen as a political anachronism, and electors were thereafter expected to vote for the candidate that they originally supported. Electors who failed to do so have historically been called "faithless." Table 7.37 lists the eight faithless electors in our two-hundred-year history. The problem of faithless electors has never changed the outcome of a presidential election, but some observers warn that it could and have proposed making this second stage in presidential elections automatic. Indeed, Table 7.37 indicates that the empirical problem may be more serious now than in earlier times: six of the eight electors were faithless within the last forty years.

The electoral college usually operates as a winner-take-all system within states. At times in American history, however, electoral college votes within one state have been split. Table 7.38 provides information about these exceptions. Some of the splits were caused by the faithless elector problem, but others resulted from particular districting systems or close votes. Many of these exceptions occurred early in American history when selection of presidential electors by masses of voters was not the norm. Table 7.39 lists the seventeen states in which electoral college votes were not counted in a state's final tally. Primarily a result of the Civil War, this particular anomaly seems unlikely to recur. Table 7.40 details states' early methods of selecting presidential electors. As the data in this table indicate, splits in a state's electoral college votes did not occur solely in the nineteenth century. Indeed, since 1969, Maine's four electors have been chosen by assigning one elector to the winning presidential candidate in each of Maine's two congressional districts and two electors to the candidate winning the aggregated statewide vote; this procedure has not, however, produced an outcome different from that which would have resulted from the winner-take-all system.

Although the electoral college does not require that a majority or even a plurality of voters nationwide support the winning presidential candidate, many observers feel that the victorious candidate should be the one who received a majority of the popular vote. Table 7.41 lists presidents who served without receiving a majority of the popular vote. Nine of these individuals succeeded presidents in the middle of a term, but the others won election with a minority of the popular vote, sometimes because third-party candidates attracted significant numbers of votes. Three presidents lost the contest for the popular vote but still received a majority of electors and hence were declared the winner: John Quincy Adams, Rutherford B. Hayes, and Benjamin Harrison.

Until the Twenty-fifth Amendment to the Constitution was enacted, no provision covered a disabled chief executive. No election was called, no acting president was appointed, and no other action was taken. The Twenty-fifth Amendment filled this gap by specifying certain procedures to be followed in the case of a disabled president, but since its enactment the procedures of this amendment have not been implemented. Table 7.42 documents the known cases in our history when presidents were incapacitated. Table 7.43 lists instances of incomplete terms of vice presidents.

Presidents and Money

The overall expenditures of Republican and Democratic presidential candidates in general elections, from 1860 to the present, appear in current dollars in Table 7.42. For most of these years, Republican expenditures were higher, but both parties showed increases in their campaign expenditures until 1964. At that point, the Republican party began spending more than twice the amount spent by Democrats. In 1972, during the Nixon-McGovern campaign, the Republicans spent nearly triple the amount spent by Democrats on the presidency. Partly in response, but also in reaction to Watergate and other factors, the U.S. Congress approved public funding of presidential campaigns in the Federal Election Campaign Act of 1974. Implementation of this law in 1976 brought about equality in expenditures for presidential campaigns by both parties.

Under this law, presidential candidates' expenditures are limited both nationally and within states. Table 7.45 outlines the limits for presidential primary elections and for the general election. Political parties are also given money to run their party conventions. Table 7.46 indicates limits that specifically apply to the parties. Table 7.47 describes official certifications of public funds expended in the last three presidential elections; Table 7.48 gives details of 1984 primary election funding; and Table 7.49 lists all minor-party expenditures from 1908 to 1984. Even with these expenditure limits, the money that presidents receive indicates the diversity of the groups that presidents represent once they have been elected.

A final topic to be mentioned is presidential compensation. Tables 7.50 and 7.51 detail the annual compensation of current and former presidents, respectively. Although the figures in both cases have increased over time, expenditures on former presidents have risen more dramatically.

Conclusion

This chapter has emphasized the plural nature of presidential coalitions in nominations and elections. Presidential candidates must respond to a broad set of groups within presidential parties. Presidential parties in one election often merge into other presidential parties in succeeding elections and at any one point in time reflect many past presidential campaigns. National political parties are an amalgam of changing and competing presidential parties; in a single election, their component parts join together in a more distinct and coherent fashion to achieve electoral victory. The national political parties field presidential candidates, and they are almost always the same political parties that nominate congressional candidates and win congressional seats. Presidential and congressional parties are clearly linked in both the nomination and electoral arenas. The links between the presidency and elections to the House of Representatives (Table 7.52) and the U.S. Senate (Table 7.53), for example, are evident. In part the reason is that members of Congress are some of the staunchest members of various presidential parties. As these tables show, the party of the president loses seats at midterm elections and wins them back at presidential elections. These electoral results affect presidents in office when they seek to exercise political influence over legislative outcomes (Chapter 2). Presidents who attempt to gain favorable legislative decisions mobilize members within the presidential party.

Institutional patterns found in presidential elections also shape other aspects of the presidency. Presidential election coalitions feed into more permanent presidential parties and form the core supporters of the president in the public (Chapter 6). In addition, presidents make numerous appearances before their presidential parties in the hopes of sustaining the support of their original electoral coalitions (Chapter 5). Presidential parties are also the key initial source of appointees for the incumbent president (Chapter 4).

Apart from the importance of presidential parties, promises and images advanced by the candidates and sought by the voters also determine the shape of the presidency. Some of the policy complexity of the presidency originates in the presidential campaign itself—in the charges and countercharges and promises and counterpromises that are made, in the rationales for why national problems often go unsolved,

393

and in the proposals to alleviate such problems. Presidential candidates suggest ways of addressing a wide variety of issues in the campaign and then feel impelled to act on their suggestions once they have been elected. During the campaign, too, presidential candidates are carefully building images for voters' consumption. They wish to construct images that stress their virtues in being able to handle the pressure and expectations of the "highest office in the land."

The interrelationships among group desires, policy promises, and candidate images help to create one of the essential ironies of the presidency—the image of a single executive who acts alone to meet the many policy and group demands in society. This coexists with the reality of the presidency as a plural institution that must attempt to accommodate these needs and demands. Individual presidents and presidential candidates at times add to this irony by alternately promoting the image of a single executive and catering to the demands of various constituencies.

Notes

1. The study of American presidential elections is irrevocably tied to the study of American political parties. The study of American national parties, in turn, can be fruitful only if we focus on presidents and on the American presidential system. In presenting a systematic view of the nomination and election of candidates for the presidency, this chapter thus also concentrates to a large extent on political parties.
2. These tables are also consistent with much recent scholarly literature on forecasting presidential elections; the best forecasting models have no need to take into account developments during the electoral campaign (see Rosenstone 1983).
3. For each primary, the votes of all candidates with at least 10 percent support appear in the tables or in footnotes to the tables. Note that the format we chose for these tables makes it considerably easier to see the rise and decline in support for each candidate. It also emphasizes that the field is reduced in size as time progresses.

Table 7.1 Party Front-runners and Nominees: The Party Controlling the Presidency

Year	Preprimary front-runner	Leader in final poll of party rank and file	Nominee	Election outcome
1936	Roosevelt	Roosevelt	Roosevelt	Won
1940	Roosevelt	Roosevelt	Roosevelt	Won
1944	Roosevelt	Roosevelt	Roosevelt	Won
1948	Truman	Truman	Truman	Won
1952	Truman	Kefauver	Stevenson	Lost
1956	Eisenhower	Eisenhower	Eisenhower	Won
1960	Nixon	Nixon	Nixon	Lost
1964	Johnson	Johnson	Johnson	Won
1968	Johnson	Humphrey	Humphrey	Lost
1972	Nixon	Nixon	Nixon	Won
1976	Ford	Ford	Ford	Lost
1980	Carter	Carter	Carter	Lost
1984	Reagan	Reagan	Reagan	Won

Source: Keech (1982, 32).

Table 7.2 Party Front-runners and Nominees: The Party Out of Power

Year	Preprimary front-runner	Leader in final poll of party rank and file	Nominee	Election outcome
1936	Landon	Landon	Landon	Lost
1940	Unknown	Willkie	Willkie	Lost
1944	Dewey	Dewey	Dewey	Lost
1948	Dewey-Taft	Dewey	Dewey	Lost
1952	Eisenhower-Taft	Eisenhower	Eisenhower	Won
1956	Stevenson	Stevenson	Stevenson	Lost
1960	Kennedy	Kennedy	Kennedy	Won
1964	Unknown	Goldwater-Nixon tie	Goldwater	Lost
1968	Nixon	Nixon	Nixon	Won
1972	Muskie	McGovern	McGovern	Lost
1976	Unknown	Carter	Carter	Won
1980	Reagan	Reagan	Reagan	Won
1984	Mondale	Mondale	Mondale	Lost

Source: Keech (1982, 32).

Table 7.3 House Members as Presidential Candidates, 1900-1986

Year	House member	Votes received
1904	William Randolph Hearst D-N.Y., 1903-1907	200 delegate votes (20%)
1908	Joseph G. Cannon R-Ill., 1873-1891, 1893-1913, 1915-1923 Speaker of the House, 1903-1911	58 delegate votes (6%)
1912	Oscar W. Underwood D-Ala., 1895-1896, 1897-1915	117.5 delegate votes (11%)
1912	James B. "Champ" Clark D-Mont., 1893-1895, 1897-1921 Speaker, 1911-1919	440.5 delegate votes (40%) 405,537 primary votes (42%)
1928	Cordell Hull D-Tenn., 1907-1921, 1923-1931	71.83 delegate votes (7%)
1932	John N. Garner D-Texas, 1903-1933 Speaker, 1931-1933	90 delegate votes (8%) 249,816 primary votes (9%)
1972	Paul N. "Pete" McCloskey, Jr. R-Calif., 1967-1983	132,731 primary votes (2%)
1972	John M. Ashbrook R-Ohio, 1961-1982	311,543 primary votes (5%)
1972	Shirley Chisholm D-N.Y., 1969-1983	151.95 delegate votes (5%) 430,703 primary votes (3%)
1976	Morris K. Udall D-Ariz., 1961-present	329.5 delegate votes (11%) 1,611,754 primary votes (10%)
1980	John B. Anderson[a] R-Ill., 1961-1981	1,572,174 primary votes (12%)
1980	Philip M. Crane R-Ill., 1969-present	97,793 primary votes (1%)

Note: The table shows twentieth-century members of the House who competed in primaries in more than one state and received at least 0.5 percent of the vote cast or received at least 5 percent of the first-ballot delegate votes at their party's national convention (figure in parentheses is percentage of total votes cast, rounded to nearest whole number).

[a] After dropping out of the Republican nomination contest, Anderson ran in the general election as an independent. He received 5,720,060 votes, almost 7 percent of the total.

Source: Adapted from *Congressional Quarterly Weekly Report*, May 10, 1986, 1027.

Table 7.4 Leading Candidates in Presidential Primaries, 1960 (percent)

Date	State	Democrats					Republicans		
		John Kennedy	Edmund Brown	Wayne Morse	Hubert Humphrey	Other[a]	Richard Nixon	Nelson Rockefeller	Other[b]
March 8	N.H.	85.2	—	—	—	14.8	89.3	3.8[c]	7.0
April 5	Wis.	56.5	—	—	43.5	—	100.0	—	—
April 12	Ill.	64.6[c]	—	—	8.1[c]	27.3[d]	99.9	—	0.1[c]
April 19	N.J.	—	—	—	—	100.0[e]	—	—	100.0[e]
April 26	Mass.	92.4[c]	—	—	0.8[c]	6.8	86.0[c]	6.6[c]	7.5
	Pa.	71.3[c]	—	—	5.4[c]	76.7	98.1	1.3[c]	0.5
May 3	D.C.	—	—	42.6	57.4	—	—	—	—
	Ind.	81.0	—	—	—	19.0	95.4	—	100.0[e]
	Ohio	—	—	—	—	100.0[f]	100.0	—	4.6
May 10	Neb.	88.7	—	—	3.5[c]	7.8	93.8[c]	2.6[c]	3.6[c]
	W.Va.	60.8	—	—	39.2	—	—	—	100.0[e]
May 17	Md.[g]	70.3	—	17.2	—	12.5	93.1	—	—
May 20	Ore.	51.0	—	31.9	5.7	11.5	93.1	4.1[c]	2.9[c]
May 24	Fla.	—	—	—	—	100.0[h]	100.0	—	—
June 7	Calif.	—	67.7	—	—	32.3[i]	100.0	—	—
	S.D.	—	—	—	100.0	—	—	—	100.0[e]

[a] In addition to scattered votes, "others" includes Paul C. Fisher, who received 19,677 votes in the Indiana primary.

[b] In addition to scattered votes, "others" includes Lar Daly, who received 40,853 votes in the Indiana primary, and 7,536 in the Maryland primary; Paul C. Fisher, who received 6,853 votes in the New Hampshire primary; John H. Latham, who received 42,084 votes in the Indiana primary; and Andrew J. Easter, who received 3,881 votes in the Maryland primary.

[c] Write-in.

[d] Adlai E. Stevenson (Illinois) received 15.1 percent of the vote, and Stuart Symington (Missouri) received 10.8 percent of the vote.

[e] Unpledged delegates at large.

[f] Michael V. DiSalle (Ohio) received 100.0 percent of the vote.

[g] No Republican primary in Maryland in 1960.

[h] George A. Smathers (Florida) received 100 percent of the vote.

[i] George H. McLain (California) received 32.3 percent of the vote.

Source: Adapted from *Congressional Quarterly's Guide to U.S. Elections* (1985).

Table 7.5 Leading Candidates in Presidential Primaries, 1964 (percent)

		Democrats			Republicans			
Date	State	Lyndon Johnson	George Wallace	Others	Barry Goldwater	Henry Lodge	Nelson Rockefeller	Others
March 10	N.H.	95.3	—	4.7	22.3	35.5	21.0	21.2
April 7	Wis.	—	—	100.0[a]	—	—	—	100.0[b]
April 14	Ill.	91.6	4.2	4.2	62.0	8.2[c]	0.2[c]	29.6[d]
April 21	N.J.	82.3	8.3	9.4	28.0[c]	41.7[c]	3.2[c]	27.0[e]
April 28	Mass.	73.4[a]	0.7[c]	25.9[f]	10.1[c]	76.9[c]	2.7[c]	10.3
	Pa.	82.8[c]	4.8[c]	12.4	8.5[c]	20.5[c]	2.0[c]	69.0[g]
May 2	Texas[h]	—	—	—	74.7	8.8	4.5	12.0
May 5	D.C.	—	—	100.0[i]	—	—	—	n.a.[j]
	Ind.	—	29.8	70.2[k]	67.0	—	—	33.0[l]
	Ohio	—	—	100.0[m]	—	—	—	100.0[n]
May 12	Neb.	89.3	1.7	9.0	49.1	16.3	1.7	32.8[o]
	W.Va.	—	—	100.0[i]	—	—	100.0	—
May 15	Ore.	99.5	0.5	—	17.6	27.7	33.0	21.7
May 19	Md.	—	42.7	57.3[p]	—	—	—	100.0[i]
May 26	Fla.	100.0	—	—	42.2	—	—	57.8[i]
June 2	Calif.	—	—	100.0[i]	51.6	—	48.4	—
	S.D.	—	—	100.0[i]	32.0	—	—	68.0[i]

[a] John W. Reynolds (Wisconsin) received 66.2 percent of the vote, and George C. Wallace (Alabama) received 33.8 percent of the vote.
[b] John W. Byrnes (Wisconsin) received 99.7 percent of the vote.
[c] Write-in.

[d] Margaret Chase Smith (Maine) received 25.3 percent of the vote.

[e] Richard Nixon received 22.1 percent of the vote.

[f] Robert F. Kennedy received 19.1 percent of the vote.

[g] William W. Scranton (Pennsylvania) received 51.9 percent of the vote.

[h] No Democratic primary authorized.

[i] Unpledged delegates.

[j] Source: District of Columbia Board of Elections. No figures are available for vote for delegates to Republican convention.

[k] Matthew E. Welsh (Indiana) received 64.9 percent of the vote; and Wallace (Alabama) received 29.8 percent of the vote.

[l] Harold E. Stassen (Pennsylvania) received 26.8 percent of the vote.

[m] Albert S. Porter (Ohio) received 100 percent of the vote.

[n] James A. Rhodes (Ohio) received 100 percent of the vote.

[o] Nixon received 31.5 percent of the vote.

[p] Daniel B. Brewster (Maryland) received 53.1 percent of the vote; and Wallace (Alabama) received 42.7 percent of the vote.

Source: Adapted from Congressional Quarterly's Guide to U.S. Elections (1985).

Table 7.6 Leading Candidates in Presidential Primaries, 1968 (percent)

Date	State	Democrats					Republicans			
		Eugene McCarthy	Robert Kennedy	Hubert Humphrey	Lyndon Johnson	Others	Ronald Reagan	Richard Nixon	Nelson Rockefeller	Others
March 12	N.H.	41.9	—	—	49.6	8.5	—	77.6	10.8	11.6
April 2	Wis.	56.2	6.3	0.5	34.6	2.8	10.4	79.7	1.6	8.3
April 23	Pa.	71.7	11.0[a]	8.7[a]	3.6[a]	5.0	2.8[a]	59.7[a]	18.4[a]	19.1[a]
April 30	Mass.	49.3	27.6[a]	17.7[a]	2.8	2.7	1.7[a]	25.8[a]	30.0[a]	42.5[b]
May 7	D.C.	—	62.5[c]	37.5[c]	—	—	—	90.1[d]	[d]	9.9[d]
	Ind.	27.0	42.3	—	—	30.7[e]	—	100.0	—	—
	Ohio	—	—	—	—	100.0[f]	—	—	—	100.0[f]
May 14	Neb.	31.2	51.7	7.4	5.6	4.1	21.3	70.0	5.1[a]	3.6
	W.Va.	—	—	—	—	100.0[e]	—	—	—	100.0[g]
May 28	Fla.	28.7	—	—	—	71.3[h]	—	—	—	100.0[g]
	Ore.	44.0	38.0	3.3[a]	12.1	2.7	20.4	65.0	11.6[a]	3.0
June 4	Calif.	41.8	46.3	—	—	12.0[g]	100.0	—	—	—
	N.J.	36.1[a]	31.3[a]	20.3[a]	—	12.3	3.1[a]	81.1[a]	13.0[a]	2.8
	S.D.	20.4	49.5	—	30.0	—	100.0	100.0	—	—
June 11	Ill.	38.6	—	17.1	—	44.3[i]	7.1[a]	78.1[a]	9.7[a]	5.1[a]

[a] Write-in.

[b] John A. Volpe (Massachusetts) received 29.5 percent of the vote.

[c] Source: District of Columbia Board of Elections. No figures are available for vote for delegates to Republican convention.

[d] Prior to the primary, the District Republican organization agreed to divide the nine delegate votes, with six going to Rockefeller, according to the 1968 *Congressional Quarterly Almanac*, vol. 24.

[e] Roger D. Branigin (Indiana) received 30.7 percent of the vote.

[f] One candidate in each party's primary received 100 percent of the vote: in the Democratic primary, Stephen M. Young (Ohio), and in the Republican primary, James A. Rhodes (Ohio).

[g] Unpledged delegates at large.

[h] George A. Smathers (Florida) received 46.1 percent of the vote, and 25.2 percent were unpledged delegates at large.

[i] Edward M. Kennedy (Massachusetts) received 33.7 percent of the vote.

Source: Adapted from *Congressional Quarterly's Guide to U.S. Elections* (1985).

Table 7.7 Leading Candidates in Presidential Primaries, 1972 (percent)

Date	State	Democrats					Republicans			
		Hubert Humphrey	George McGovern	Henry Wallace	Edmund Muskie	Others[a]	Richard Nixon	John Ashbrook	Paul McCloskey	Others[b]
March 7	N.H.	0.4[c]	37.1	0.2[c]	46.4	15.9	67.6	9.7	19.8	2.9
March 14	Fla.	18.6	6.2	41.6	8.9	24.8	87.0	8.8	4.2	—
March 21	Ill.	0.1[c]	0.3[c]	0.6[c]	62.6	36.4[d]	97.0[c]	0.5[c]	0.1[c]	2.4[c]
April 4	Wis.	20.7	29.6	22.0	10.3	17.4	96.9	0.9	1.3	0.8
April 25	Mass.	7.9	52.7	7.4	21.3	10.6	81.2	4.0	13.5	1.4
	Pa.	35.1	20.4	21.3	20.4	2.8	83.3[c]	—	—	16.8
May 2	D.C.[e]	—	—	—	—	100.0[f]	—	—	—	—
	Ind.	47.1	—	41.2	11.7	—	100.0	—	—	—
	Ohio	41.2	39.6	—	8.9	10.2	100.0	—	—	—
May 4	Tenn.	15.9	7.2	68.2	2.0	6.7	95.8	2.1	2.1	—
May 6	N.C.	—	—	50.3	3.7	45.9[g]	94.8	—	5.2	—
May 9	Neb.	34.3	41.3	12.4	3.6	8.3	92.4	2.6	4.6	0.4
	W.Va.	66.9	—	33.1	—	—	—	—	—	100.0[h]
May 16	Md.	26.8	22.4	38.7	2.4	9.8	86.2	5.8	8.0	1.6
	Mich.	15.7	26.8	51.0	2.4	4.1	95.5	—	2.9	1.7
May 23	Ore.	12.5	50.2	20.0	2.5	14.7	82.0	5.9	10.4	2.6
	R.I.	20.3	41.2	15.3	20.7	2.4	88.3	3.1	6.0	—
June 6	Calif.	38.6	43.5	7.5[c]	2.0	8.3	90.1	9.8	—	—
	N.J.	—	—	—	—	100.0[i]	—	—	—	100.0[h]
	N.M.	25.9	33.3	29.3	4.2	7.4	88.5	—	6.1	5.5
	S.D.	—	100.0	—	—	—	100.0	—	—	—

(Notes follow)

Table 7.7 (continued)

[a] In addition to scattered votes, "others" includes Patrick Paulsen, who received 1,211 votes in the New Hampshire primary.

[b] In addition to scattered votes, "others" includes Edward T. Coll, who received 280 votes in the New Hampshire primary and 589 votes in the Massachusetts primary.

[c] Write-in.

[d] Eugene McCarthy received 36.3 percent of the vote.

[e] No Republican primary was held in 1972.

[f] Walter E. Fauntroy (District of Columbia) received 71.8 percent of the vote.

[g] Terry Sanford (North Carolina) received 37.3 percent of the vote.

[h] Unpledged delegates at large.

[i] Shirley Chisholm (New York) received 66.9 percent of the vote; and Sanford (North Carolina) received 33.1 percent of the vote.

Source: Adapted from *Congressional Quarterly's Guide to U.S. Elections* (1985).

Table 7.8 Leading Candidates in Presidential Primaries, 1976 (percent)

		Democrats					Republicans		
Date	State	Jimmy Carter	Frank Church	Morris Udall	George Wallace	Others	Gerald Ford	Ronald Reagan	Others
February 24	N.H.	28.4	—	22.7	1.3 [a]	37.7 [b]	49.4	48.0	2.6
March 2	Mass.	13.9	—	17.7	16.7	49.6 [c]	61.2	33.7	5.0
	Vt.	42.2	—	—	—	48.8 [d]	84.0	15.2	—
March 9	Fla.	34.5	0.4	2.1	30.5	30.8 [e]	52.8	47.2	—
March 16	Ill.	48.1	—	—	27.6	23.8	58.9	40.1	1.0
March 23	N.C.	53.6	—	2.3	34.7	9.1	52.4	45.9	1.7
April 6	Wis.	36.6	—	35.6	12.5	13.1	55.2	44.3	0.3
April 27	Pa.	37.0	—	18.7	11.3	31.8 [f]	92.1	5.1	2.8
May 4	D.C.	39.7	—	26.0	—	1.6 [g]	100.0 [o]	—	—
	Ga.	83.4	0.5	1.9	11.5	1.4	37.1	68.3	—
	Ind.	68.0	—	—	15.2	16.9	48.7	51.3	—
May 11	Neb.	37.6	38.5	2.7	3.2	5.8	45.4	54.5	0.1
	W.Va.	—	—	—	11.0	h	56.8	43.2	—
May 18	Md.	37.1	—	5.5	4.1	53.3 [i]	58.0	42.0	—
	Mich.	43.4	—	43.1	6.9	6.2	64.9	34.3	0.8
May 25	Ariz.	62.6	—	7.5	16.5	13.3	35.1	63.4	1.5
	Idaho	11.9	78.7	1.3	1.5	4.4	24.9	74.3	0.8
	Ky.	59.4	—	10.9	16.8	12.2	50.9	46.9	2.1
	Nev.	23.3	9.0	3.0	3.3	61.3 [j]	28.8	66.3	5.0
	Ore.	26.7	33.6	2.7	1.3	27.3 [k]	50.3	45.8	3.9
	Tenn.	77.6	2.4	3.7	10.9	5.3	49.8	49.1	1.1
	Mont.	24.6	59.4	6.3	3.4	6.3	34.6	63.1	2.2
June 1	R.I.	30.2	27.2	4.2	0.8	37.5	65.3	31.2	3.5
	S.D.	41.2	—	33.3	2.4	23.2	44.0	51.2	4.8

(Table continues)

Table 7.8 (continued)

Date	State	Democrats					Republicans		
		Jimmy Carter	Frank Church	Morris Udall	George Wallace	Others	Gerald Ford	Ronald Reagan	Others
June 8	Calif.	20.5	7.4	5.0	3.0	64.1 [l]	34.5	65.5	—
	N.J.	58.4	13.6	—	8.6	14.8	100.0	—	—
	Ohio [m]	39.0	5.3	10.1	12.5	30.0 [n]	55.2	44.8	—

[a] Write-in votes.

[b] Birch Bayh received 15.2 percent of the vote; and Sargent Shriver received 8.2 percent of the vote.

[c] Henry M. Jackson received 22.3 percent of the vote.

[d] Shriver received 27.6 percent of the vote.

[e] Jackson received 23.9 percent of the vote.

[f] Jackson received 24.6 percent of the vote. Jackson suspended his campaign May 1.

[g] Uncommitted slate headed by delegate Walter E. Fauntroy received 21.6 percent of the vote; another uncommitted slate headed by Mayor Walter E. Washington received 11.1 percent.

[h] Sen. Robert C. Byrd received 89.0 percent of the vote. Byrd was also on the ballot in Florida, where he received 0.4 percent, and in Georgia, where he received 0.7 percent.

[i] Edmund G. Brown received 48.4 percent of the vote.

[j] Brown received 52.7 percent of the vote.

[k] Brown received 24.7 percent of the vote; these were write-in votes.

[l] Brown received 59.0 percent of the vote.

[m] State Treasurer Gertrude W. Donahey headed an at-large slate that received 4.0 percent.

[n] Brown received 15.2 percent of the vote.

[o] Ford unopposed; no primary held.

Source: Adapted from Congressional Quarterly's Guide to U.S. Elections (1985).

Table 7.9 Leading Candidates in Presidential Primaries, 1980 (percent)

Date	State	Democrats				Republicans				
		Jimmy Carter	Edward Kennedy	Edmund Brown	Others	Ronald Reagan	George Bush	John Anderson	Howard Baker	Others
February 17	P.R.	51.7	48.0	0.2	0.1	—	60.1	—	37.0	22.1
February 26	N.H.	47.1	37.3	9.6	6.0	49.6	22.7	9.8	12.1	5.8
March 4	Mass.	28.7	65.1	3.5	2.7	28.8	31.0	30.7	4.8	4.7
	Vt.	73.1	25.5	0.09	1.31	30.1	21.7	29.0	12.3	6.9
March 8	S.C.	—	—	—	—	54.7	14.8	—	0.5	30.0
March 11	Fla.	60.7	23.2	4.9	11.2	56.2	30.2	9.2	1.0	3.4
	Ga.	88.0	8.4	1.9	1.7	73.2	12.6	8.4	0.4	5.4
	Ala.	81.6	13.2	4.0	1.2	69.7	25.9	0.9	0.9	2.6
March 18	Ill.	65.0	30.0	3.0	2.0	48.4	11.0	36.7	1.0	2.9
March 25	N.Y.[a]	41.1	58.9	—	—	—	—	—	—	—
April 1	Conn.	41.5	46.9	2.6	9.0	33.9	38.6	22.1	1.3	4.1
	Wis.	56.2	30.1	11.8	1.9	40.2	30.4	27.4	0.4	1.6
	Kans.	56.6	31.6	4.9	6.9	63.0	12.6	18.2	1.3	4.9
April 5	La.	55.7	22.5	4.7	17.1	74.9	18.8	—	—	6.3
April 22	Pa.	45.4	45.7	2.3	6.6	42.5	50.5	2.1	2.5	2.4
May 3	Texas	55.9	22.8	2.6	18.7	51.0	47.4	—	—	1.6
May 6	Ind.	67.7	32.3	—	—	73.7	16.4	9.9	—	—
	N.C.	70.1	17.7	2.9	9.3	67.6	21.8	5.1	1.5	4.0
	D.C.	36.9	61.7	—	1.4	—	66.1	26.9	—	7.0
	Tenn.	75.2	18.1	1.9	4.8	74.1	18.1	4.5	—	3.3
May 13	Md.	47.5	38.0	3.0	11.5	48.2	40.9	9.7	—	1.2
	Neb.	46.9	37.6	3.6	11.9	76.0	15.3	5.8	—	2.9
May 20	Mich.	—	—	29.4	70.6	31.8	57.5	8.2	—	2.5
	Ore.	56.7	31.1	9.3	2.9	54.0	34.6	10.2	—	1.2

(Table continues)

Table 7.9 (continued)

Date	State	Democrats				Republicans				
		Jimmy Carter	Edward Kennedy	Edmund Brown	Others	Ronald Reagan	George Bush	John Anderson	Howard Baker	Others
May 27	Ark.[b]	60.1	17.5	—	22.4	—	—	—	—	—
	Idaho	62.0	22.0	4.0	12.0	82.3	4.0	9.7	—	4.0
	Ky.	66.9	23.0	—	10.1	82.4	7.2	5.1	—	5.3
	Nev.	37.6	28.8	—	33.6	83.0	6.5	—	—	10.5
June 3	Calif.	37.6	44.8	4.0	13.5	80.3	4.9	13.6	—	1.2
	Miss.	—	—	—	—	89.4	8.2	—	—	2.4
	Mont.	51.0	37.0	—	12.0	87.0	10.0	—	—	4.0
	N.J.	38.0	56.0	—	6.0	81.0	17.0	—	—	2.0
	N.M.	41.8	46.3	—	11.9	63.8	9.9	12.0	—	14.3
	Ohio	51.1	44.4	—	4.5	80.8	19.2	—	—	—
	R.I.	25.8	68.3	0.8	5.1	72.8	18.6	—	—	8.6
	S.D.	45.4	48.6	—	6.0	82.2	4.2	—	—	13.6
	W.V.	62.2	37.8	—	—	83.6	14.1	—	—	2.3

[a] No Republican primary was held in New York.
[b] No Republican primary was held in Arkansas.

Source: Adapted from Congressional Quarterly's Guide to U.S. Elections (1985).

Table 7.10 Leading Candidates in Presidential Primaries, 1984 (percent)

Date	State	Democrats				Republicans	
		Walter Mondale	Gary Hart	Jesse Jackson	Others [a]	Ronald Reagan [b]	Others [a]
February 28	N.H.	27.9	37.3	5.3	29.5 [c]	86.1	13.9
March 6	Vt.	20.0	70.0	7.8	2.2	98.7	1.3
March 13	Ala. [d]	34.6	20.7	19.6	24.1	—	—
	Fla.	33.4	39.2	12.2	15.2	100.0	0.0
	Ga.	30.5	27.3	21.0	20.8	100.0	0.0
	Mass.	25.5	39.0	5.0	30.5 [e]	89.5	10.5
	R.I.	34.5	45.0	8.7	11.8	90.7	9.3
March 18	P.R. [f]	99.1	0.6	—	0.3	—	—
March 20	Ill.	40.4	35.2	21.0	3.4	99.9	0.1
March 27	Conn. [d]	29.1	52.7	12.0	6.2	—	—
April 3	N.Y. [d]	44.8	27.4	25.6	2.2	—	—
	Wis.	41.1	44.4	9.8	4.7	95.2	4.8
April 10	Pa.	45.1	33.3	16.0	5.6	99.3	0.7
May 1	D.C.	25.6	7.1	67.3	—	100.0	—
	Tenn.	41.0	29.1	25.3	4.6	90.9	9.1
May 5	La.	22.3	25.0	42.9	9.8	89.7	10.3
	Texas [g]	—	—	—	—	96.5	3.5
May 8	Ind.	40.9	41.8	13.7	3.6	100.0	0.0
	Md.	42.5	24.3	25.5	7.7	100.0	0.0
	N.C. [d]	35.6	30.2	25.4	8.8	—	—
	Ohio	40.3	42.0	16.4	1.3	100.0	0.0
May 15	Neb.	26.6	58.2	9.1	6.1	99.0	1.0
	Ore.	27.3	58.5	9.3	4.9	98.0	2.0
May 22	Idaho	30.1	58.0	5.7	6.2	92.2	7.8
June 5	Calif.	35.3	38.9	18.4	7.4	100.0	0.0
	Mont.	5.9	9.0	1.1	84.0	92.4	7.6
	N.J.	45.1	29.7	23.6	1.6	100.0	0.0
	N.M.	36.1	46.7	11.8	5.4	94.9	5.1
	S.D. [d]	39.0	50.7	5.2	5.1	—	—
	W.Va.	53.8	37.3	6.7	2.2	91.8	8.2
	N.D.	2.8	85.1	0.2	11.9	100.0	0.0

[a] "Others" includes uncommitted voters.
[b] Reagan won all twenty-four primaries with at least 86 percent of the vote in each.
[c] John Glenn received 12 percent of the vote, and George McGovern received 5 percent of the vote.
[d] No Republican primary was held.
[e] McGovern received 21 percent of the vote.
[f] No Republican primary was held in Puerto Rico.
[g] No Democratic primary was held.

Source: Adapted from *Congressional Quarterly's Guide to U.S. Elections* (1985).

Table 7.11 Republican National Conventions, 1856-1984

Year	City	Date	Presidential nominee	Ballots[a]
1856	Philadelphia	June 17-19	John C. Fremont	2
1860	Chicago	May 16-19	Abraham Lincoln	3
1864	Baltimore	June 7-8	Abraham Lincoln	1
1868	Chicago	May 20-21	Ulysses S. Grant	1
1872	Philadelphia	June 5-6	Ulysses S. Grant	1
1876	Cincinnati	June 14-16	Rutherford B. Hayes	7
1880	Chicago	June 2-8	James A. Garfield	36
1884	Chicago	June 3-6	James G. Blaine	4
1888	Chicago	June 19-25	Benjamin Harrison	8
1892	Minneapolis	June 7-10	Benjamin Harrison	1
1896	St. Louis	June 16-18	William McKinley	1
1900	Philadelphia	June 19-21	William McKinley	1
1904	Chicago	June 21-23	Theodore Roosevelt	1
1908	Chicago	June 16-19	William H. Taft	1
1912	Chicago	June 18-22	William H. Taft	1
1916	Chicago	June 7-10	Charles E. Hughes	3
1920	Chicago	June 8-12	Warren G. Harding	10
1924	Cleveland	June 10-12	Calvin Coolidge	1
1928	Kansas City	June 12-15	Herbert Hoover	1
1932	Chicago	June 14-16	Herbert Hoover	1
1936	Cleveland	June 9-12	Alfred M. Landon	1
1940	Philadelphia	June 24-28	Wendell L. Willkie	6
1944	Chicago	June 24-28	Thomas E. Dewey	1
1948	Philadelphia	June 21-25	Thomas E. Dewey	3
1952	Chicago	July 7-11	Dwight D. Eisenhower	1
1956	San Francisco	August 20-23	Dwight D. Eisenhower	1
1960	Chicago	July 25-28	Richard M. Nixon	1
1964	San Francisco	July 13-16	Barry Goldwater	1
1968	Miami Beach	August 5-8	Richard M. Nixon	1
1972	Miami Beach	August 21-23	Richard M. Nixon	1
1976	Kansas City	August 16-19	Gerald R. Ford	1
1980	Detroit	July 14-17	Ronald Reagan	1
1984	Dallas	August 20-23	Ronald Reagan	1

[a] Number of ballots required to select nominee.

Source: Adapted from *Congressional Quarterly's Guide to U.S. Elections* (1985).

Table 7.12   Democratic National Conventions, 1832-1984

Year	City	Date	Presidential nominee	Ballots [a]
1832	Baltimore	May 21	Andrew Jackson	1
1835	Baltimore	May 20	Martin Van Buren	1
1840	Baltimore	May 5	Martin Van Buren	1
1844	Baltimore	May 27-29	James K. Polk	9
1848	Baltimore	May 22-26	Lewis Cass	4
1852	Baltimore	June 1-6	Franklin Pierce	49
1856	Cincinnati	June 2-6	James Buchanan	17
1860	Baltimore	June 18-23	Stephen A. Douglas	2
1864	Chicago	August 29	George B. McClellan	1
1868	New York	July 4-11	Horatio Seymour	22
1872	Baltimore	July 9	Horace Greeley	1
1876	St. Louis	June 27-29	Samuel J. Tilden	2
1880	Cincinnati	June 22-24	Winfield S. Hancock	2
1884	Chicago	July 8-11	Grover Cleveland	2
1888	St. Louis	June 5	Grover Cleveland	1
1892	Chicago	June 21	Grover Cleveland	1
1896	Chicago	July 7	William J. Bryan	5
1900	Kansas City	July 4-6	William J. Bryan	1
1904	St. Louis	July 6-9	Alton S. Parker	1
1908	Denver	July 7-10	William J. Bryan	1
1912	Baltimore	June 25-July 2	Woodrow Wilson	46
1916	St. Louis	June 14-16	Woodrow Wilson	1
1920	San Francisco	June 28-July 6	James M. Cox	43
1924	New York	June 24-July 9	John W. Davis	103
1928	Houston	June 26-29	Alfred E. Smith	1
1932	Chicago	June 27-July 2	Franklin D. Roosevelt	4
1936	Philadelphia	June 23-27	Franklin D. Roosevelt	[b]
1940	Chicago	July 15-18	Franklin D. Roosevelt	1
1944	Chicago	July 19-21	Franklin D. Roosevelt	1
1948	Philadelphia	July 12-14	Harry S Truman	1
1952	Chicago	July 21-26	Adlai E. Stevenson	3
1956	Chicago	August 13-17	Adlai E. Stevenson	1
1960	Los Angeles	July 11-15	John F. Kennedy	1
1964	Atlantic City	August 24-27	Lyndon B. Johnson	[b]
1968	Chicago	August 26-29	Hubert H. Humphrey	1
1972	Miami Beach	July 10-13	George McGovern	1
1976	New York	July 12-15	Jimmy Carter	1
1980	New York	August 11-14	Jimmy Carter	1
1984	San Francisco	July 16-19	Walter Mondale	1

[a] Number of ballots required to select nominee.
[b] Acclamation.

Source: Adapted from *Congressional Quarterly's Guide to U.S. Elections* (1985).

Table 7.13 The 1960 Political Party Conventions

| | Democratic first ballot [a] | | | | | Republican first ballot | | |
State	Total	Kennedy	Johnson	Stevenson	Symington	Total	Nixon	Goldwater
Alabama	29	3.5	20	0.5	3.5	22	22	—
Alaska	9	9	—	—	—	6	6	—
Arizona	17	17	—	—	—	14	14	—
Arkansas	27	—	27	—	—	16	16	—
California	81	33.5	7.5	31.5	8	70	70	—
Colorado	21	13.5	—	5.5	2	18	18	—
Connecticut	21	21	—	—	—	22	22	—
Delaware	11	—	11	—	—	12	12	—
Florida	29	—	—	—	—	26	26	—
Georgia	33	—	33	—	—	24	24	—
Hawaii	9	1.5	3	3.5	1	12	12	—
Idaho	13	6	4.5	0.5	2	14	14	—
Illinois	69	61.5	—	2	5.5	60	60	—
Indiana	34	34	—	—	—	32	32	—
Iowa	26	21.5	0.5	2	0.5	26	26	—
Kansas	21	21	—	—	—	22	22	—
Kentucky	31	3.5	25.5	1.5	0.5	26	26	—
Louisiana	26	—	26	—	—	26	16	10
Maine	15	15	—	—	—	16	16	—
Maryland	24	24	—	—	—	24	24	—
Massachusetts	41	41	—	—	—	38	38	—
Michigan	51	42.5	—	2.5	6	46	46	—
Minnesota	31	—	—	—	—	28	28	—
Mississippi	23	—	—	—	—	12	12	—
Missouri	39	—	—	—	39	26	26	—
Montana	17	10	2	2.5	2.5	14	14	—
Nebraska	16	11	0.5	—	4	18	18	—
Nevada	15	5.5	6.5	2.5	0.5	12	12	—

State							
New Hampshire	11	11	—	—	—	14	14	—
New Jersey	41	—	—	—	—	38	38	—
New Mexico	17	4	13	—	—	14	14	—
New York	114	104.5	3.5	3.5	2.5	96	96	—
North Carolina	37	6	27.5	3	0.5	28	28	—
North Dakota	11	11	—	—	—	14	14	—
Ohio	64	64	—	—	—	56	56	—
Oklahoma	29	—	29	—	—	22	22	—
Oregon	17	16.5	—	0.5	—	18	18	—
Pennsylvania	81	68	4	7.5	—	70	70	—
Rhode Island	17	17	—	—	—	14	14	—
South Carolina	21	—	21	1	—	13	13	—
South Dakota	11	4	2	—	2.5	14	14	—
Tennessee	33	—	33	—	—	28	28	—
Texas	61	—	61	—	—	54	54	—
Utah	13	8	3	—	1.5	14	14	—
Vermont	9	9	—	—	—	12	12	—
Virginia	33	—	33	—	—	30	30	—
Washington	27	14.5	2.5	6.5	3	24	24	—
West Virginia	25	15	5.5	3	1.5	22	22	—
Wisconsin	31	23	—	—	—	30	30	—
Wyoming	15	15	—	—	—	12	12	—
Canal Zone [b]	4	—	4	—	—	—	—	—
District of Columbia	9	9	—	—	—	8	8	—
Puerto Rico	7	7	—	—	—	3	3	—
Virgin Islands	4	4	—	—	—	1	1	—
Total	1,521	806	409	79.5	86	1,331	1,321	10

[a] Other candidates: Barnett, 23 (Mississippi); Smathers, 30 (29 in Florida, 0.5 in Alabama, 0.5 in North Carolina); Humphrey, 41.5 (31 in Minnesota, 8 in Wisconsin, 1.5 in South Dakota, 0.5 in Nebraska, 0.5 in Utah); Meyner, 43 (41 in New Jersey, 1.5 in Pennsylvania, 0.5 in Pennsylvania); Loveless, 1.5 (Iowa); Faubus, 0.5 (Alabama); Brown, 0.5 (California); Rosellini, 0.5 (Washington).

[b] There were no Republican delegates from the Canal Zone.

Source: Adapted from *Congressional Quarterly's Guide to U.S. Elections* (1985).

Table 7.14 The 1964 Republican Party Convention

State	Total votes	Goldwater	Rockefeller	Scranton
		First *ballot* [a]		
Alabama	20	20	—	—
Alaska	12	—	—	8
Arizona	16	16	—	—
Arkansas	12	9	1	2
California	86	86	—	—
Colorado	18	15	—	3
Connecticut	16	4	—	12
Delaware	12	7	—	5
Florida	34	32	—	2
Georgia	24	22	—	2
Hawaii	8	4	—	—
Idaho	14	14	—	—
Illinois	58	56	2	—
Indiana	32	32	—	—
Iowa	24	14	—	10
Kansas	20	18	—	1
Kentucky	24	21	—	3
Louisiana	20	20	—	—
Maine	14	—	—	—
Maryland	20	6	1	13
Massachusetts	34	5	—	26
Michigan	48	8	—	—
Minnesota	26	8	—	—
Mississippi	13	13	—	—
Missouri	24	23	—	1
Montana	14	14	—	—
Nebraska	16	16	—	—
Nevada	6	6	—	—
New Hampshire	14	—	—	14
New Jersey	40	20	—	20
New Mexico	14	14	—	—
New York	92	5	87	—
North Carolina	26	26	—	—
North Dakota	14	7	1	—
Ohio	58	57	—	—
Oklahoma	22	22	—	—
Oregon	18	—	18	—
Pennsylvania	64	4	—	60
Rhode Island	14	3	—	11
South Carolina	16	16	—	—
South Dakota	14	12	—	2
Tennessee	28	28	—	—
Texas	56	56	—	—

Table 7.14   (continued)

State	Total votes	First ballot [a] Goldwater	Rockefeller	Scranton
Utah	14	14	—	—
Vermont	12	3	2	2
Virginia	30	29	—	1
Washington	24	22	—	1
West Virginia	14	10	2	2
Wisconsin	30	30	—	—
Wyoming	12	12	—	—
District of Columbia	9	4	—	5
Puerto Rico	5	—	—	5
Virgin Islands	3	—	—	3
Total	1,308	883	114	214

Note: The Democratic nomination was won by acclamation.

[a] Other candidates: George Romney, 41 (40 in Michigan, 1 in Kansas); Margaret C. Smith, 27 (14 in Maine, 5 in Vermont, 3 in North Dakota, 2 in Alaska, 1 in Massachusetts, 1 in Ohio, 1 in Washington); Walter H. Judd, 22 (18 in Minnesota, 3 in North Dakota, 1 in Alaska); Hiram L. Fong, 5 (4 in Hawaii, 1 in Alaska); Henry C. Lodge, 2 (Massachusetts).

Source: Adapted from *Congressional Quarterly's Guide to U.S. Elections* (1985).

Table 7.15 The 1968 Political Party Conventions

	Democratic first ballot [a]					Republican first ballot [b]			
State	Total	Humphrey	McCarthy	McGovern	Phillips	Total	Nixon	Rockefeller	Reagan
Alabama	32	23	—	—	—	26	14	—	12
Alaska	22	17	2	3	—	12	11	1	—
Arizona	19	14.5	2.5	2	—	16	16	—	—
Arkansas	33	30	2	—	—	18	—	—	—
California	174	14	91	51	17	86	—	—	86
Colorado	35	16.5	10	5.5	3	18	14	3	1
Connecticut	44	35	8	—	1	16	4	12	—
Delaware	22	21	—	—	—	12	9	3	—
Florida	63	58	5	—	—	34	32	1	1
Georgia	43	19.5	13.5	1	3	30	21	2	7
Hawaii	26	26	—	—	—	14	—	—	—
Idaho	25	21	3.5	0.5	—	14	9	—	5
Illinois	118	112	3	3	—	58	50	5	3
Indiana	63	49	11	2	1	26	26	—	—
Iowa	46	18.5	19.5	5	—	24	13	8	3
Kansas	38	34	1	3	—	20	—	—	—
Kentucky	46	41	5	—	—	24	22	2	—
Louisiana	36	35	—	—	—	26	19	—	7
Maine	27	23	4	—	—	14	7	7	—
Maryland	49	45	2	2	—	26	18	8	—
Massachusetts	72	2	70	—	—	34	—	34	—
Michigan	96	72.5	9.5	7.5	6.5	48	4	—	—
Minnesota	52	38	11.5	—	2.5	26	9	15	—
Mississippi	24	9.5	6.5	4	2	20	20	—	—
Missouri	60	56	3.5	—	0.5	24	16	5	3
Montana	26	23.5	2.5	—	—	14	11	—	3
Nebraska	30	15	6	9	—	16	16	—	—
Nevada	22	18.5	2.5	1	—	12	9	3	—
New Hampshire	26	6	20	—	—	8	8	—	—

New Jersey	82	62	19	—	1	40	18	—	—
New Mexico	26	15	11	—	—	14	8	1	5
New York	190	96.5	87	1.5	2	92	4	88	—
North Carolina	59	44.5	2	0.5	—	26	9	1	16
North Dakota	25	18	7	—	—	8	5	2	1
Ohio	115	94	18	2	1	58	2	—	—
Oklahoma	41	37.5	2.5	0.5	0.5	22	14	1	7
Oregon	35	—	35	—	—	18	18	—	—
Pennsylvania	130	103.75	21.5	2.5	1.5	64	22	41	1
Rhode Island	27	23.5	2.5	—	—	14	—	14	—
South Carolina	28	28	—	—	—	22	22	—	—
South Dakota	26	2	—	24	—	14	14	—	—
Tennessee	51	49.5	0.5	1	—	28	28	—	—
Texas	104	100.5	2.5	—	1	56	41	—	15
Utah	26	23	2	—	1	8	2	—	—
Vermont	22	8	6	7	—	12	9	3	—
Virginia	54	42.5	5.5	—	2	24	22	2	—
Washington	47	32.5	8.5	6	—	24	15	3	6
West Virginia	38	34	3	—	1	14	11	3	—
Wisconsin	59	8	49	1	1	30	30	—	—
Wyoming	22	18.5	3.5	—	—	12	12	—	—
Canal Zone[c]	5	4	—	1	—	—	—	—	—
District of Columbia	23	2	—	—	21	9	6	3	—
Guam	5	5	—	—	—	—	—	—	—
Puerto Rico	8	8	—	—	—	5	—	5	—
Virgin Islands	5	5	—	—	—	3	2	1	—
Total	2,622	1,759.25	601	146.5	67.5	1,333	692	277	182

[a] Other candidates: Dan K. Moore, 17.5 (12 in North Carolina, 3 in Virginia, 2 in Georgia, 0.5 in Alabama); Edward M. Kennedy, 12.75 (proceedings record, 12.5 (3.5 in Alabama, 3 in Iowa, 3 in New York, 1 in Ohio, 1 in West Virginia, 0.75 in Pennsylvania, 0.5 in Georgia); Paul Bryant, 1.5 (Alabama); George Wallace, 0.5 (Alabama); James H. Gray, 0.5 (Georgia). Not voting, 15 (3 in Alabama, 3 in Georgia, 2 in Mississippi, 1 in Arkansas, 1 in California, 1 in Delaware, 1 in Louisiana, 1 in Rhode Island, 1 in Vermont, 1 in Virginia).

[b] Other candidates: James A. Rhodes, 55 (Ohio); George Romney, 50 (44 in Michigan, 6 in Utah); Clifford P. Case, 22 (New Jersey); Frank Carlson, 20 (Kansas); Winthrop Rockefeller, 18 (Arkansas); Hiram L. Fong, 14 (Hawaii); Harold Stassen, 2 (1 in Minnesota, 1 in Ohio); John V. Lindsay, 11 (Minnesota).

[c] There were no Republican delegates from the Canal Zone.

Source: Adapted from Congressional Quarterly's Guide to U.S. Elections (1985).

Table 7.16 The 1972 Political Party Conventions

State	Democratic first ballot[a]						Republican first ballot		
	Total	McGovern	Jackson	Wallace	Chisholm	Sanford	Total	Nixon	McCloskey
Alabama	37	9	1	24	—	1	18	18	—
Alaska	10	6.50	3.25	—	—	—	12	12	—
Arizona	25	21	3	—	—	1	18	18	—
Arkansas	27	1	1	—	—	—	18	18	—
California	271	—	—	—	—	—	96	96	—
Colorado	36	27	—	—	7	—	20	20	—
Connecticut	51	30	20	—	—	1	22	22	—
Delaware	13	5.85	6.50	—	0.65	—	12	12	—
Florida	81	2	—	75	2	—	40	40	—
Georgia	53	14.50	14.50	11	12	1	24	24	—
Hawaii	17	6.50	8.50	—	1	—	14	14	—
Idaho	17	12.50	2.50	—	2	—	14	14	—
Illinois	170	119	30.50	0.50	4.50	2	58	58	—
Indiana	76	26	20	26	1	—	32	32	—
Iowa	46	35	—	—	3	4	22	22	—
Kansas	35	20	10	—	2	1	20	20	—
Kentucky	47	10	35	—	—	2	24	24	—
Louisiana	44	10.25	10.25	3	18.50	2	20	20	—
Maine	20	5	—	—	—	—	8	8	—
Maryland	53	13	—	38	2	—	26	26	—
Massachusetts	102	102	—	—	—	—	34	34	—
Michigan	132	50.50	7	67.50	3	1	48	48	—
Minnesota	64	11	—	—	6	—	26	26	—
Mississippi	25	10	—	—	12	3	14	14	—
Missouri	73	24.50	48.50	—	1	—	30	30	—
Montana	17	16	—	—	1	—	14	14	—
Nebraska	24	21	3	—	—	—	16	16	—
Nevada	11	5.75	5.25	—	—	—	12	12	—
New Hampshire	18	10.80	5.40	—	—	—	14	14	—

New Jersey	109	89	11.50	—	4	1.50	40	40	—
New Mexico	18	10	—	8	—	—	14	13	1
New York	278	263	9	37	6	27	88	88	—
North Carolina	64	—	—	—	—	—	32	32	—
North Dakota	14	8.40	2.80	0.70	0.70	3	12	12	—
Ohio	153	77	39	—	23	3	56	56	—
Oklahoma	39	10.50	23.50	—	1	4	22	22	—
Oregon	34	34	—	—	—	—	18	18	—
Pennsylvania	182	81	86.50	2	9.50	1	60	60	—
Rhode Island	22	22	—	—	—	—	8	8	—
South Carolina	32	6	10	6	4	6	22	22	—
South Dakota	17	17	—	—	—	—	14	14	—
Tennessee	49	—	—	33	10	—	26	26	—
Texas	130	54	23	48	4	3	52	52	—
Utah	19	14	1	—	—	—	14	14	—
Vermont	12	12	—	—	—	—	12	12	—
Virginia	53	33.50	4	1	5.50	9	30	30	—
Washington	52	—	52	—	—	—	24	24	—
West Virginia	35	16	14	1	—	4	18	18	—
Wisconsin	67	55	3	—	5	—	28	28	—
Wyoming	11	3.30	6.05	—	1.10	—	12	12	—
District of Columbia	15	13.50	1.50	—	—	—	9	9	—
Puerto Rico	7	7	—	—	—	—	5	5	—
Virgin Islands	3	1	1.50	—	0.50	—	3	3	—
Canal Zone	3	3	—	—	—	—	—	—	—
Guam	3	1.50	1.50	—	—	—	3	3	—
Total	3,016	1,728.35	525.00	381.70	151.95	77.50	1,348	1,347	1

[a] Other candidates: Humphrey, 66.70 (46 in Minnesota, 4 in Ohio, 4 in Wisconsin, 3 in Michigan, 2 in Indiana, 2 in Pennsylvania, 2 in Florida, 1 in Utah, 1 in Colorado, 1 in Hawaii, 0.70 in North Dakota); Mills, 33.80 (25 in Arkansas, 3 in Illinois, 3 in New Jersey, 2 in Alabama, 0.55 in Wyoming, 0.25 in Alaska); Muskie, 24.30 (15 in Maine, 5.50 in Illinois, 1.80 in New Hampshire, 1 in Texas, 1 in Colorado); Kennedy, 12.70 (4 in Iowa, 3 in Illinois, 2 in Ohio, 1 in Kansas, 1 in Indiana, 1 in Tennessee, 0.70 in North Dakota); Hays, 5 (Ohio); McCarthy, 2 (Illinois); Mondale, 1 (Kansas); Clark, 1 (Minnesota); not voting, 5 (Tennessee).

Source: Adapted from Congressional Quarterly's Guide to U.S. Elections (1985).

Table 7.17 The 1976 Political Party Conventions

	Democrats first ballot						Republicans first ballot		
State	Total votes	Carter	Udall	Brown	McCormack	Others[a]	Total votes	Ford	Reagan
Alabama	35	30	—	—	—	5	37	—	37
Alaska	10	10	—	—	—	—	19	17	2
Arizona	25	6	19	—	—	—	29	2	27
Arkansas	26	25	1	—	—	—	27	10	17
California	280	73	2	205	—	—	167	—	167
Colorado	35	15	6	11	—	3	31	5	26
Connecticut	51	35	16	—	—	—	35	35	—
Delaware	12	10.5	—	1.5	—	—	17	15	2
Florida	81	70	—	1	—	10	66	43	23
Georgia	50	50	—	—	—	—	48	—	48
Hawaii	17	17	—	—	—	—	19	18	1
Idaho	16	16	—	—	—	—	21	4	17
Illinois	169	164	1	2	1	1	101	86	14
Indiana	75	72	—	—	—	3	54	9	45
Iowa	47	25	20	1	—	1	36	19	17
Kansas	34	32	2	—	—	—	34	30	4
Kentucky	46	39	2	—	—	5	37	19	18
Louisiana	41	18	—	18	—	5	41	5	36
Maine	20	15	5	—	—	—	20	15	5
Maryland	53	44	6	3	—	—	43	43	—
Massachusetts[b]	104	65	21	—	2	16	43	28	15
Michigan	133	75	58	—	—	—	84	55	29
Minnesota	65	37	2	1	11	14	42	32	10
Mississippi[c]	24	23	—	—	—	—	30	16	14
Missouri	71	58	4	2	7	—	49	18	31
Montana	17	11	2	—	—	4	20	—	20
Nebraska	23	20	—	3	—	—	25	7	18

Nevada	11	3	—	6.5	1.5	—	18	5	13
New Hampshire	17	15	2	—	—	—	21	18	3
New Jersey	108	108	—	—	67	—	63	4	21
New Mexico	18	14	4	—	—	—	21	—	20
New York	274	209.5	56.5	4	4	—	154	133	29
North Carolina [d]	61	56	—	—	3	—	54	25	7
North Dakota	13	13	—	—	—	—	18	11	6
Ohio	152	132	20	—	—	—	97	91	36
Oklahoma	37	32	1	—	4	—	36	—	14
Oregon	34	16	—	10	8	—	30	16	10
Pennsylvania	178	151	21	6	—	—	103	93	—
Rhode Island	22	14	—	8	—	—	19	19	27
South Carolina	31	28	—	1	2	—	36	9	11
South Dakota	17	11	5	—	1	—	20	9	22
Tennessee	46	45	—	—	1	—	43	21	—
Texas	130	124	—	4	2	—	100	—	100
Utah	18	10	—	5	3	—	20	—	20
Vermont	12	5	4	3	—	—	18	18	—
Virginia	54	48	6	—	—	—	51	16	35
Washington	53	36	11	3	3	—	38	7	31
West Virginia	33	30	1	—	2	—	28	20	8
Wisconsin	68	29	25	1	13	1	45	45	—
Wyoming	10	8	1	—	—	—	17	7	10
District of Columbia	17	12	5	—	—	—	14	14	—
Guam	3	3	—	—	—	—	4	4	—
Puerto Rico	22	22	—	—	—	—	8	8	—
Virgin Islands	3	3	—	—	—	—	4	4	—
Canal Zone [e]	3	3	—	0.5	—	—	—	—	—
Democrats abroad	3	2.5	—	—	—	—	—	—	—
Total	3,008	2,238.5	329.5	300.5	114.5	22.0	2,259	1,187	1,070

(Notes follow)

Table 7.17 (continued)

[a] Other votes: George Wallace, 57 (Alabama 5, Florida 10, Illinois 1, Indiana 3, Kentucky 5, Louisiana 5, Massachusetts 11, North Carolina 3, South Carolina 2, Tennessee 1, Texas 1, Wisconsin 10); Frank Church, 19 (Colorado 3, Montana 4, Nevada 1, Oregon 8, Utah 1, Washington 2); Hubert Humphrey, 10 (Minnesota 9, South Dakota 1); Henry M. Jackson, 10 (Massachusetts 2, New York 4, Washington 1, Wisconsin 3); Fred Harris, 9 (Massachusetts 2, Minnesota 4, Oklahoma 3); Milton J. Shapp, 2 (Massachusetts 1, Utah 1). Receiving one vote each: Robert C. Byrd (West Virginia); Cesar Chavez (Utah); Leon Jaworski (Texas); Barbara C. Jordan (Oklahoma); Edward M. Kennedy (Iowa); Jennings Randolph (West Virginia); Fred Stover (Minnesota). In addition, a Nevada delegate cast one-half vote for nobody.

[b] Massachusetts passed when it was first called and cast its vote at the end of the ballot.

[c] One abstention.

[d] Two abstentions.

[e] There were no Republican delegates from the Canal Zone.

Source: Adapted from *Congressional Quarterly's Guide to U.S. Elections* (1985).

Table 7.18 The 1980 Political Party Conventions

State	Democrat first ballot[a]				Republican first ballot				
	Total	Carter	Kennedy	Other[b]	Total	Reagan	Anderson	Bush	Other[c]
Alabama	45	43	2	0	27	27	0	0	0
Alaska	11	8.4	2.6	0	19	19	0	0	0
Arizona	29	13	16	0	28	28	0	0	0
Arkansas	33	25	6	2	19	19	0	0	0
California	306	140	166	0	168	168	0	0	0
Colorado	40	27	10	3	31	31	0	0	0
Connecticut	54	26	28	0	35	35	0	0	0
Delaware	14	10	4	0	12	12	0	0	0
Florida	100	75	25	0	51	51	0	0	0
Georgia	63	62	0	1	36	36	0	0	0
Hawaii	19	16	2	1	14	14	0	0	0
Idaho	17	9	7	1	21	21	0	0	0
Illinois	179	163	16	0	102	81	21	0	0
Indiana	80	53	27	0	54	54	0	0	0
Iowa	50	31	17	2	37	37	0	0	0
Kansas	37	23	14	0	32	32	0	0	0
Kentucky	50	45	5	0	27	27	0	0	0
Louisiana	51	50	1	0	31	31	0	0	0
Maine	22	11	11	0	21	21	0	0	0
Maryland	59	34	24	1	30	30	0	0	0
Massachusetts	111	34	77	0	42	33	9	0	0
Michigan	141	102	38	1	82	67	0	13	1[d]
Minnesota	75	41	14	20	34[d]	33	0	0	1
Mississippi	32	32	0	0	22	22	0	0	0
Missouri	77	58	19	0	37	37	0	0	0

(Table continues)

Table 7.18 (continued)

	Democrat first ballot[a]				Republican first ballot				
State	Total	Carter	Kennedy	Other[b]	Total	Reagan	Anderson	Bush	Other[c]
Montana	19	13	6	0	20	20	0	0	0
Nebraska	24	14	10	0	25	25	0	0	0
Nevada	12	8.12	3.88	0	17	17	0	0	0
New Hampshire	19	10	9	0	22	22	0	0	0
New Jersey	113	45	68	0	66	66	0	0	0
New Mexico	20	10	10	0	22	22	0	0	0
New York	282	129	151	2	123	121	0	0	0
North Carolina	69	66	3	0	40	40	0	0	0
North Dakota	14	5	7	2	17	17	0	0	0
Ohio	161	89	72	0	77	77	0	0	0
Oklahoma	42	36	3	2	34	34	0	0	0
Oregon	39	26	13	0	29	29	0	0	0
Pennsylvania	185	95	90	0	83	83	0	0	0
Rhode Island	23	6	17	0	13	13	0	0	0
South Carolina	37	37	0	0	25	25	0	0	0
South Dakota	19	9	10	0	22	22	0	0	0
Tennessee	55	51	4	0	32	32	0	0	0
Texas	152	108	38	6	80	80	0	0	0
Utah	20	11	4	5	21	21	0	0	0
Vermont	12	5	7	0	19	19	0	0	0
Virginia	64	59	5	0	51	51	0	0	0
Washington	58	36	22	0	37	36	1	0	0
West Virginia	35	21	10	4	18	18	0	0	0
Wisconsin	75	48	26	1	34	28	6	0	0
Wyoming	11	8	3	0	19	19	0	0	0

District of Columbia	19	12	5	2	14	14	0	0	0
Guam	4	4	0	0	4	4	0	0	0
Puerto Rico	41	21	20	0	14	14	0	0	0
Virgin Islands	4	4	0	0	4	4	0	0	0
Democrats Abroad	4	1.5	2	.5	4	4	0	0	0
Total	3,331	2,123.02	1,150.48	54.5[e]	1,994	1,939	37	13	1

[a] Other votes: uncommitted, 10 (3 in Texas, 2 in North Dakota, 2 in Colorado, 2 in Arkansas, 1 in Maryland, and 1 in Idaho): William Proxmire, 10 (Minnesota); Scott M. Matheson 5 (Utah); Koryne Horbal, 5 (Minnesota); abstentions, 4 (2 in the District of Columbia, 1 in Hawaii, 1 in Michigan); Ronald V. Dellums, 2.5 (2 in New York, 0.5 from Democrats abroad). Receiving 2 votes each were: John C. Culver (Iowa); Warren Spannaus (Minnesota); Alice Tripp (Minnesota); Kent Hance (Texas); Robert C. Byrd (West Virginia); Jennings Randolph (West Virginia). Receiving 1 vote each were: Dale Bumpers (Arkansas); Edmund S. Muskie (Colorado); Walter F. Mondale (Minnesota); Hugh L. Carey (Oklahoma); Tom Steed (Oklahoma); Edmund G. Brown, Jr. (Wisconsin).

[b] At the conclusion of the roll call, Delaware switched to 14 for Carter and none for Kennedy. Iowa switched to 33 for Carter and 17 for Kennedy. Totals after switches: Carter, 2,129; Kennedy, 1,146.5. The votes received by other candidates did not change. After the switches, Carter was nominated by acclamation following a motion to that effect by the Massachusetts delegation.

[c] Other votes: Alabama, 1 for Philip Crane; Alaska, 1 for Henry Hyde, 4 abstentions; Colorado, 2 abstentions, 1 for Eugene Schroeder; Florida, 3 abstentions, 1 opposed; Georgia, 11 for Jack Kemp, 1 for Donald Rumsfeld, 2 abstentions; Idaho, 2 for Crane, 1 for Kemp; Illinois, 8 for Crane, 6 for Kemp, 5 for Jim Thompson, 4 abstentions; Kansas, 4 abstentions; Kentucky, 2 for Crane; Massachusetts, 1 for Kemp; New Mexico, 1 for Kemp, 1 abstention; New York, 1 for Crane; North Dakota, 1 for Crane; Ohio, 13 for Kemp, 1 for Crane; Oklahoma, 1 abstention; Oregon, 1 for Crane; Pennsylvania, 1 for Howard Baker; Rhode Island, 5 for Crane; South Carolina, 2 abstentions; Virginia, 6 for Kemp; Washington, 2 for Crane, 3 for Kemp, 1 for William Simon, 1 abstention; Wisconsin, 4 abstentions; Wyoming, 1 abstention. Totals: 42 for Kemp, 30 abstentions, 23 for Crane, 5 for Thompson; 1 for Hyde, 1 for Schroeder, 1 for Rumsfeld, 1 for Simon, 1 for Ashbrook, 1 for Vander Jagt, 1 for Baker, and 1 opposed.

[d] One vote for Anne Armstrong. Four not voting.

[e] This figure does not include: 2 absent (1 in Georgia, 1 in Oklahoma) and 1 not voting (Texas).

Source: Adapted from Congressional Quarterly's Guide to U.S. Elections (1985).

Table 7.19 The 1984 Political Party Conventions

| State | Total votes | Democrat first ballot | | | | | Republican first ballot: Reagan (total votes) |
		Mondale	Hart	Jackson	Other[a]	Abstained[b]	
Alabama	62	39	13	9	1	0	38
Alaska	14	9	4	1	0	0	18
Arizona	40	20	16	2	0	2	32
Arkansas	42	26	9	7	0	0	29
California	345	95	190	33	0	27	176
Colorado	51	1	42	1	0	7	35
Connecticut	60	23	36	1	0	0	35
Delaware	18	13	5	0	0	0	19
Florida	143	82	55	3	0	2	82
Georgia	84	40	24	20	0	0	37
Hawaii	27	27	0	0	0	0	14
Idaho	22	10	12	0	0	0	21
Illinois	194	114	41	39	0	0	93 c
Indiana	88	42	38	8	0	0	52
Iowa	58	37	18	2	1	0	37
Kansas	44	25	16	3	0	0	32
Kentucky	63	51	5	7	0	0	37
Louisiana	69	26	19	24	0	0	41
Maine	27	13	13	0	1	0	20
Maryland	74	54	3	17	0	0	31
Massachusetts	116	59	49	5	3	0	52
Michigan	155	96	49	10	0	0	77
Minnesota	86	63	3	4	16	0	32
Mississippi	43	26	4	13	0	0	30
Missouri	86	55	14	16	0	0	47
Montana	25	11	13	1	0	0	20
Nebraska	30	12	17	1	0	0	24
Nevada	20	9	10	1	0	0	22
New Hampshire	22	12	10	0	0	0	22
New Jersey	122	115	0	7	0	0	64

New Mexico	28	13	13	2	0	0	24
New York	285	156	75	52	0	0	136
North Carolina	88	53	19	16	0	0	53
North Dakota	18	10	5	1	2	0	18
Ohio	175	84	80	11	0	0	89
Oklahoma	53	24	26	3	0	0	35
Oregon	50	16	31	2	0	0	32
Pennsylvania	195	177	0	18	0	0	98 [c]
Rhode Island	27	14	12	0	0	0	14
South Carolina	48	16	13	19	0	0	35
South Dakota	19	9	10	0	0	0	19
Tennessee	76	39	20	17	0	0	46
Texas	200	119	40	36	2	0	109
Utah	27	8	19	0	0	0	26
Vermont	17	5	8	3	0	1	19
Virginia	78	34	18	25	0	0	50
Washington	70	31	36	3	0	0	44
West Virginia	44	30	14	0	0	0	19
Wisconsin	89	58	25	6	0	0	46
Wyoming	15	7	7	0	0	1	18
American Samoa [d]	6	6	0	0	0	0	—
Democrats Abroad	5	3	1.5	0.5	0	0	—
District of Columbia	19	5	0	14	0	0	14
Guam	7	7	0	0	0	0	4
Latin America [d]	5	5	0	0	0	0	—
Puerto Rico	53	53	—	—	—	—	14
Virgin Islands	6	4	0	2	0	0	4
Total	3,923	2,191	1,200.5	465.5	26	40	2,235 [e]

[a] Other votes: Alabama, 1 for Martha Kirkland; Iowa, 1 for George McGovern; Maine, 1 for Joseph R. Biden, Jr.; Massachusetts, 3 for McGovern; Minnesota, 16 for Thomas F. Eagleton; North Dakota, 2 for Eagleton; Texas, 2 for John Glenn.

[b] This figure does not include the following absences: Florida, 1; Missouri, 1; New York, 2; Oregon, 1; Rhode Island, 1; Texas, 3; and Virginia, 1.

[c] One delegate in Illinois and one in Pennsylvania abstained; there were 92 votes for Reagan in Illinois and 97 for Reagan in Pennsylvania.

[d] American Samoa and Latin America did not have any Republican delegates.

[e] This is the total number of ballots. Reagan received 2,233 because of two abstentions—one in Pennsylvania and one in Illinois.

Source: Adapted from Congressional Quarterly's Guide to U.S. Elections (1985).

Table 7.20 Political Parties in Congress and the Presidency, 1789-1988

Year	Presidential candidate			House			Senate		
	Winner	Loser	Congress	Majority	Opposition	Other	Majority	Opposition	Other
1789-1791	F (Washington)	F (Adams)	1st	Ad-38	Op-26	—	Ad-17	Op-9	—
1791-1793	F (Washington)	—	2nd	F-37	DR-33	—	F-16	DR-13	—
1793-1795	F (Washington)	F (Adams)	3rd	DR-57	F-48	—	F-17	DR-13	—
1795-1797	F (Washington)	—	4th	F-54	DR-52	—	F-19	DR-13	—
1797-1799	F (J. Adams)	DR (Jefferson)	5th	F-58	DR-48	—	F-20	DR-12	—
1799-1801	F (J. Adams)	—	6th	F-64	DR-42	—	F-19	DR-13	—
1801-1803	DR (Jefferson)	F (Adams)	7th	DR-69	F-36	—	DR-18	F-13	—
1803-1805	DR (Jefferson)	—	8th	DR-102	F-39	—	DR-25	F-9	—
1805-1807	DR (Jefferson)	F (Pinckney)	9th	DR-116	F-25	—	DR-27	F-7	—
1807-1809	DR (Jefferson)	—	10th	DR-118	F-24	—	DR-28	F-6	—
1809-1811	DR (Madison)	F (Pinckney)	11th	DR-94	F-48	—	DR-28	F-6	—
1811-1813	DR (Madison)	—	12th	DR-108	F-36	—	DR-30	F-6	—
1813-1815	DR (Madison)	F, I, DR (Clinton)	13th	DR-112	F-68	—	DR-27	F-9	—
1815-1817	DR (Madison)	—	14th	DR-117	F-65	—	DR-25	F-11	—
1817-1819	DR (Monroe)	F (King)	15th	DR-141	F-42	—	DR-34	F-10	—
1819-1821	DR (Monroe)	—	16th	DR-156	F-27	—	DR-35	F-7	—
1821-1823	DR (Monroe)	I, DR (Adams)	17th	DR-158	F-25	—	DR-44	F-4	—
1823-1825	DR (Monroe)	—	18th	DR-187	F-26	—	DR-44	F-4	—
1825-1827	C (J.Q. Adams)	DR (Jackson)	19th	Ad-105	J-97	—	Ad-26	J-20	—
1827-1829	C (J.Q. Adams)	—	20th	J-119	Ad-94	—	J-28	Ad-20	—
1829-1831	D (Jackson)	NR (Adams)	21st	D-139	NR-74	—	D-26	NR-22	—
1831-1833	D (Jackson)	—	22nd	D-141	NR-58	14	D-25	NR-21	2
1833-1835	D (Jackson)	NR (Clay)	23rd	D-147	AM-53	60	D-20	NR-20	8
1835-1837	D (Jackson)	—	24th	D-145	W-98	—	D-27	W-25	—
1837-1839	D (Van Buren)	W (Harrison)	25th	D-108	W-107	24	D-30	W-18	—
1839-1841	D (Van Buren)	—	26th	D-124	W-118	—	D-28	W-22	—

Years			Congress						
1841-1843	W (Tyler) [a]	D (Van Buren)	27th	W-133	D-102	6	W-28	D-22	2
1843-1845	W (Tyler)	—	28th	D-142	W-79	1	W-28	D-25	1
1845-1847	D (Polk)	W (Clay)	29th	D-143	W-77	6	D-31	W-25	—
1847-1849	D (Polk)	—	30th	W-115	D-108	4	D-36	W-21	1
1849-1851	W (Fillmore)	D (Cass)	31st	D-112	W-109	9	D-35	W-25	2
1851-1853	W (Fillmore)	—	32nd	D-140	W-88	5	D-35	W-24	3
1853-1855	D (Pierce)	W (Scott)	33rd	D-159	W-71	4	D-38	W-22	2
1855-1857	D (Pierce)	—	34th	R-108	D-83	43	D-40	R-15	5
1857-1859	D (Buchanan)	R (Fremont)	35th	D-118	R-92	26	D-36	R-20	8
1859-1861	D (Buchanan)	—	36th	R-114	D-92	31	D-36	R-26	4
1861-1863	R (Lincoln)	SD (Breckinridge)	37th	R-105	D-43	30	R-31	D-10	8
1863-1865	R (Lincoln)	—	38th	R-102	D-75	9	R-36	D-9	5
1865-1867	R (A. Johnson) [b]	D (McClellan)	39th	U-149	D-42	—	U-42	D-10	—
1867-1869	R (A. Johnson)	—	40th	R-143	D-49	—	R-42	D-11	—
1869-1871	R (Grant)	D (Seymour)	41st	R-149	D-63	—	R-56	D-11	—
1871-1873	R (Grant)	—	42nd	R-134	D-104	5	R-52	D-17	5
1873-1875	R (Grant)	D, LR (Greeley)	43rd	R-194	D-92	14	R-49	D-19	—
1875-1877	R (Grant)	—	44th	D-169	R-109	14	R-45	D-29	2
1877-1879	R (Hayes)	D (Tilden)	45th	D-153	R-140	—	R-39	D-36	1
1879-1881	R (Hayes)	—	46th	D-149	R-130	14	D-42	R-33	1
1881-1883	R (Arthur) [c]	D (Hancock)	47th	R-147	D-135	11	R-37	D-37	1
1883-1885	R (Arthur)	—	48th	D-197	R-118	10	R-38	D-36	2
1885-1887	D (Cleveland)	R (Blaine)	49th	D-183	R-140	2	R-43	D-34	—
1887-1889	D (Cleveland)	—	50th	D-169	R-152	4	R-39	D-37	—
1889-1891	R (B. Harrison)	D (Cleveland)	51st	R-166	D-159	—	R-39	D-37	—
1891-1893	R (B. Harrison)	—	52nd	D-235	R-88	9	R-47	D-39	2
1893-1895	D (Cleveland)	R (Harrison)	53rd	D-218	R-127	11	D-44	R-38	3
1895-1897	D (Cleveland)	—	54th	R-244	D-105	7	R-43	D-39	6
1897-1899	R (McKinley)	D, P (Bryan)	55th	R-204	D-113	40	R-47	D-34	7
1899-1901	R (McKinley)	—	56th	R-185	D-163	9	R-53	D-26	8
1901-1903	R (T. Roosevelt) [d]	D (Bryan)	57th	R-197	D-151	9	R-55	D-31	4
1903-1905	R (T. Roosevelt)	—	58th	R-208	D-178	—	R-57	D-33	—

(Table continues)

Table 7.20 (continued)

Year	Presidential candidate Winner	Presidential candidate Loser	Congress	House Majority	House Opposition	House Other	Senate Majority	Senate Opposition	Senate Other
1905-1907	R (T. Roosevelt)	D (Parker)	59th	R-250	D-136	—	R-57	D-33	—
1907-1909	R (T. Roosevelt)	—	60th	R-222	D-164	—	R-61	D-31	—
1909-1911	R (Taft)	D (Bryan)	61st	R-219	D-172	—	R-61	D-32	—
1911-1913	R (Taft)	—	62nd	D-228	R-161	1	R-51	D-41	—
1913-1915	D (Wilson)	PR (Roosevelt)	63rd	D-291	R-127	17	D-51	R-44	1
1915-1917	D (Wilson)	—	64th	D-230	R-196	9	D-56	R-40	—
1917-1919	D (Wilson)	R (Hughes)	65th	D-216	R-210	6	D-53	R-42	—
1919-1921	D (Wilson)	—	66th	R-240	D-190	3	R-49	D-47	—
1921-1923	R (Harding)	D (Cox)	67th	R-301	D-131	1	R-59	D-37	—
1923-1925	R (Coolidge)	—	68th	R-225	D-205	5	R-51	D-43	2
1925-1927	R (Coolidge)	D (Davis)	69th	R-247	D-183	4	R-56	D-39	1
1927-1929	R (Coolidge)	—	70th	R-237	D-195	3	R-49	D-46	1
1929-1931	R (Hoover)	D (Smith)	71st	R-267	D-167	1	R-56	D-39	1
1931-1933	R (Hoover)	—	72nd	D-220	R-214	1	R-48	D-47	1
1933-1934	D (F. Roosevelt)	R (Hoover)	73rd	D-310	R-117	5	D-60	R-35	1
1935-1936	D (F. Roosevelt)	—	74th	D-319	R-103	10	D-69	R-25	2
1937-1938	D (F. Roosevelt)	R (Landon)	75th	D-331	R-89	13	D-76	R-16	4
1939-1940	D (F. Roosevelt)	—	76th	D-261	R-164	4	D-69	R-23	4
1941-1942	D (F. Roosevelt)	R (Willkie)	77th	D-268	R-162	5	D-66	R-28	2
1943-1944	D (F. Roosevelt)	—	78th	D-218	R-208	4	D-58	R-37	1
1945-1946	D (Truman)[e]	R (Dewey)	79th	D-242	R-190	2	D-56	R-38	1
1947-1948	D (Truman)	—	80th	R-245	D-188	1	R-51	D-45	—
1949-1950	D (Truman)	R (Dewey)	81st	D-263	R-171	1	D-54	R-42	—
1951-1952	D (Truman)	—	82nd	D-234	R-199	1	D-49	R-47	—
1953-1954	R (Eisenhower)	D (Stevenson)	83rd	R-221	D-211	1	R-48	D-47	1
1955-1956	R (Eisenhower)	—	84th	D-232	R-203	—	D-48	R-47	1

	President	Opponent	House	House	House	Senate	Senate	Senate
1957-1958	R (Eisenhower)	D (Stevenson)	D-233	R-200	—	D-49	R-47	—
1959-1960	R (Eisenhower)	—	D-283	R-153	f	D-64	R-34	—
1961-1962	D (Kennedy)	R (Nixon)	D-263	R-174	—	D-65	R-35	—
1963-1964	D (L. Johnson) g	—	D-258	R-177	—	D-67	R-33	—
1965-1966	D (L. Johnson)	R (Goldwater)	D-295	R-140	—	D-68	R-32	—
1967-1968	D (L. Johnson)	—	D-246	R-187	—	D-64	R-36	—
1969-1970	R (Nixon)	D (Humphrey)	D-245	R-189	—	D-57	R-43	—
1971-1972	R (Nixon)	—	D-254	R-180	—	D-54	R-44	2
1973-1974	R (Nixon)	D (McGovern)	D-239	R-192	1	D-56	R-42	2
1975-1976	R (Ford)	—	D-291	R-144	—	D-60	R-37	2
1977-1978	D (Carter)	R (Ford)	D-292	R-143	—	D-61	R-38	1
1979-1980	D (Carter)	—	D-276	R-157	—	D-58	R-41	1
1981-1982	R (Reagan)	D (Carter)	D-243	R-192	—	R-53	D-46	1
1983-1984	R (Reagan)	—	D-269	R-165	—	R-54	D-46	—
1985-1986	R (Reagan)	D (Mondale)	D-252	R-182	—	R-53	D-47	—
1987-1988	R (Reagan)	—	D-259	R-176	—	D-55	R-45	—

(Congresses: 85th, 86th, 87th, 88th, 89th, 90th, 91st, 92nd, 93rd, 94th, 95th, 96th, 97th, 98th, 99th, 100th)

Note: Ad = Administration. AM = Anti-Masonic. C = Coalition. D = Democratic. DR = Democratic-Republican. F = Federalist. I = Independent. J = Jacksonian. L = Liberal Republican. NR = National Republican. Op = Opposition. P = Populist. PR = Progressive. R = Republican. U = Unionist. W = Whig.

a And W (W. Harrison).
b And R (Lincoln).
c And R (Garfield).
d And R (McKinley).
e And D (F. Roosevelt)
f Excludes Hawaii; two senators (one Republican, one Democrat) and one representative (Democrat) seated in August.
g And D (Kennedy).

Sources: Adapted and updated from U.S. Department of Commerce, *Historical Statistics* (1971, Y 204-210); and U.S. Department of Commerce, *Statistical Abstract,* (1987, 247).

Table 7.21 State Voter Turnout in Presidential Elections, 1824-1876

State	1824	1828	1832	1836	1840	1844	1848	1852	1856	1860	1864	1868	1872	1876
Alabama	49.1	54.6	31.5	64.9	89.7	80.3	69.7	45.3	71.0	78.7	b	77.9	79.6	72.8
Arkansas	—	—	—	28.9	67.6	63.5	55.9	48.6	60.2	79.5	b	49.0	67.6	64.7
California	—	—	—	—	—	—	—	75.7	81.6	71.2	64.6	72.3	57.9	75.9
Colorado	—	—	—	—	—	—	—	—	—	—	—	—	—	c
Connecticut	14.9	27.2	46.0	52.3	75.7	80.0	72.3	72.3	81.8	73.3	76.3	80.1	71.3	82.0
Delaware	—	—	67.1	69.5	82.8	85.8	80.4	75.0	78.5	79.5	79.8	84.3	73.3	73.4
Florida	—	—	—	—	—	—	64.0	56.9	77.6	79.5	b	c	77.0	93.5
Georgia	—	31.8	29.0	61.8	88.8	92.6	86.0	54.8	82.8	85.1	b	73.2	55.2	63.5
Illinois	24.3	52.4	46.0	43.5	86.0	76.0	70.5	64.7	72.4	80.5	69.2	76.7	75.0	87.5
Indiana	37.1	68.7	71.9	69.2	84.4	84.7	78.5	80.3	88.3	89.4	82.9	92.5	85.3	94.6
Iowa	—	—	—	—	—	—	90.7	80.2	87.0	94.2	95.4	97.7	79.0	99.1
Kansas	—	—	—	—	—	—	—	—	—	—	31.8	51.3	77.8	65.7
Kentucky	25.4	70.7	74.0	61.1	74.3	80.7	73.9	64.2	76.7	74.1	44.0	69.9	66.2	80.9
Louisiana	—	36.2	22.3	19.2	39.4	47.1	51.1	48.7	53.6	58.6	b	75.9	76.4	77.9
Maine	19.1	42.7	66.2	37.7	83.7	71.3	68.4	61.2	78.1	68.9	73.2	74.4	57.9	71.5
Maryland	53.7	70.3	55.7	67.6	84.5	81.4	76.0	72.8	80.0	81.1	57.7	72.6	75.0	82.7
Massachusetts	29.0	25.7	39.4	43.4	66.7	65.8	64.6	57.8	69.8	65.8	63.8	66.9	62.0	72.3
Michigan	—	—	—	35.0	84.9	79.8	74.5	71.3	81.1	80.0	66.2	77.4	64.0	78.0
Minnesota	—	—	—	—	—	—	—	—	—	74.9	57.5	71.1	67.5	71.3
Mississippi	41.3	56.6	28.0	64.4	88.2	86.1	80.7	61.7	78.3	89.5	b	a	71.1	79.7
Missouri	19.8	54.0	41.0	36.1	75.1	77.8	62.5	46.3	54.7	69.1	36.3	43.0	66.6	76.6
Nebraska	—	—	—	—	—	—	—	—	—	—	—	46.1	43.7	53.0
Nevada	—	—	—	—	—	—	—	—	—	—	57.5	73.7	74.4	90.0
New Hampshire	18.0	74.3	70.1	38.2	86.3	68.9	67.4	65.7	87.9	80.7	84.3	82.3	80.9	92.0
New Jersey	35.6	71.0	68.8	69.2	80.4	87.2	82.7	79.8	83.1	89.4	81.0	89.5	81.4	94.8
New York	—	80.2	84.2	70.5	91.9	92.1	79.6	84.7	89.9	95.5	89.3	91.7	80.5	89.6
North Carolina	41.8	56.9	31.3	53.0	82.4	78.8	71.4	65.8	66.7	70.9	b	91.2	71.9	90.1

Ohio	34.8	75.9	73.9	75.5	84.5	83.6	77.5	80.6	82.3	88.3	87.6	90.4	84.4	94.4
Oregon	—	—	—	—	—	—	—	—	—	97.8	91.8	85.8	60.5	70.4
Pennsylvania	18.8	56.5	52.3	53.1	77.5	77.3	76.3	72.6	80.8	78.4	85.0	88.3	68.6	83.5
Rhode Island	12.0	17.1	26.3	23.8	33.2	45.1	41.1	57.8	62.9	59.4	58.8	46.6	40.2	49.4
South Carolina	—	—	—	—	d	d	d	d	d	d	b	79.6	60.4	e
Tennessee	28.3	55.0	31.3	57.3	89.7	89.8	83.4	72.9	82.9	80.9	b	39.7	66.2	74.6
Texas	—	—	—	—	—	—	69.6	42.6	58.1	67.4	b	a	56.3	54.6
Vermont	—	54.5	50.0	52.5	73.8	70.8	70.5	63.5	72.5	63.0	77.0	75.9	69.1	83.3
Virginia	11.6	27.7	31.1	35.2	54.7	54.2	47.3	63.3	67.8	71.5	b	a	66.2	77.6
West Virginia	—	—	—	—	—	—	—	—	—	—	51.6	58.0	61.2	83.6
Wisconsin	—	—	—	—	—	—	58.3	59.6	80.8	79.0	66.8	79.8	70.6	83.9
United States	26.9	57.6	55.4	57.8	80.2	78.9	72.7	69.6	78.9	81.2	73.8	78.1	71.3	81.8

[a] Mississippi, Texas, and Virginia did not participate in the 1868 election.
[b] Confederate states did not participate in the 1864 election.
[c] Florida (in 1868) and Colorado (in 1876) cast three Republican electoral votes through its legislature rather than by popular vote.
[d] South Carolina chose its electors through its legislature until 1868.
[e] Information not available.

Source: Adapted from U.S. Department of Commerce, *Historical Statistics* (1971, Y 27-78).

Table 7.22 State Voter Turnout in Presidential Elections, 1880-1932

State	1880	1884	1888	1892	1896	1900	1904	1908	1912	1916	1920	1924	1928	1932
Alabama	58.8	54.2	56.6	68.5	51.9	38.9	24.2	21.5	22.6	24.3	20.6	13.5	19.1	17.5
Arizona	—	—	—	—	—	—	—	—	38.6	48.7	46.8	44.4	47.9	55.1
Arkansas	59.5	59.1	68.9	55.0	48.2	40.8	33.8	40.2	30.7	40.0	20.9	15.3	21.4	22.1
California	67.1	68.8	76.5	73.8	75.0	69.9	61.7	60.2	46.9	58.0	47.2	50.8	59.0	64.0
Colorado	57.4	52.4	57.4	54.6	65.2	71.2	71.0	65.4	59.1	60.5	56.0	62.5	68.4	75.3
Connecticut	81.4	79.9	85.5	85.4	83.3	79.7	80.5	76.3	71.5	73.8	58.7	57.9	72.6	70.8
Delaware	81.9	76.0	68.8	80.4	64.6	81.9	82.0	86.2	84.1	86.1	75.1	68.1	75.3	76.3
Florida	85.9	83.1	85.0	35.3	40.0	29.9	24.4	26.2	24.2	33.8	30.3	17.0	33.0	30.5
Georgia	49.4	41.0	37.6	53.1	34.3	24.4	23.8	22.0	18.9	23.7	10.5	11.5	15.7	16.5
Idaho	—	—	—	63.1	76.1	77.8	65.3	65.8	59.8	67.4	61.1	65.2	66.0	74.4
Illinois	89.9	84.4	82.9	86.0	95.7	89.9	80.5	81.6	74.7	66.8	60.5	64.1	73.4	74.6
Indiana	94.4	92.2	93.3	89.0	95.1	92.1	89.7	89.9	77.8	81.9	71.0	70.7	74.9	78.9
Iowa	93.7	90.0	87.9	88.5	96.1	91.0	79.7	77.6	74.2	75.0	64.5	68.4	68.9	69.1
Kansas	80.8	85.1	88.2	80.7	85.5	91.2	78.1	82.5	76.3	65.8	58.0	64.1	65.9	71.1
Kentucky	75.5	70.8	81.1	73.8	89.2	87.0	77.7	84.0	74.6	82.8	71.8	61.0	67.7	67.4
Louisiana	50.3	49.8	50.0	45.1	35.8	21.7	15.6	19.8	19.3	21.6	14.1	12.4	20.1	23.4
Maine	85.0	75.0	71.7	63.5	63.0	56.0	49.5	53.2	63.4	65.1	46.9	44.9	60.2	66.3
Maryland	79.8	79.9	84.8	79.9	87.3	85.9	69.6	70.9	64.8	68.1	52.3	41.0	56.8	51.2
Massachusetts	71.2	69.3	71.7	74.6	70.6	67.4	67.6	65.1	63.4	62.8	53.3	56.6	74.0	69.5
Michigan	75.5	76.0	80.9	73.2	95.3	89.0	78.9	75.9	69.8	72.9	55.1	53.7	56.3	62.0
Minnesota	68.9	68.2	76.3	66.6	75.2	76.7	64.3	66.1	61.2	65.0	59.5	62.0	68.5	66.2
Mississippi	50.1	49.2	43.8	18.8	22.1	16.9	15.6	16.5	15.1	20.0	9.4	12.0	15.2	13.8
Missouri	78.0	77.0	81.8	77.4	88.5	83.1	74.9	79.7	74.9	81.5	67.6	63.3	69.1	70.9
Montana	—	—	—	74.2	73.8	75.3	65.8	61.9	63.3	68.0	61.4	59.2	65.3	70.3
Nebraska	67.7	67.8	75.9	66.2	74.1	80.2	70.1	77.8	77.1	84.5	55.7	63.8	71.5	72.1
Nevada	76.5	61.6	71.4	70.1	69.2	71.4	59.2	92.1	68.1	73.6	61.0	56.1	63.0	73.2
New Hampshire	93.3	87.4	90.2	85.8	78.1	83.9	81.6	80.8	78.2	77.3	67.5	67.4	77.8	77.5

New Jersey	95.4	88.6	91.9	90.3	88.4	85.9	83.6	82.4	69.1	70.7	59.1	60.7	75.6	72.0
New Mexico	—	—	—	—	—	—	—	—	59.6	77.8	62.3	61.8	60.3	69.7
New York	89.3	87.5	92.3	86.3	84.3	84.6	83.3	79.7	72.1	71.6	56.4	56.3	68.3	66.1
North Carolina	83.0	86.3	85.2	78.0	85.3	70.2	46.1	52.0	46.1	49.8	44.6	35.9	43.1	44.0
North Dakota	—	—	—	56.6	63.1	65.2	61.4	73.2	60.8	77.7	67.4	63.8	72.4	74.5
Ohio	94.4	93.4	91.9	86.2	95.5	91.5	83.1	87.5	74.8	76.5	62.6	57.8	66.9	65.5
Oklahoma	—	—	—	—	—	—	—	71.5	57.4	60.4	48.6	47.4	50.5	54.4
Oregon	79.1	63.0	53.5	58.4	69.9	58.3	47.6	47.3	51.8	54.2	52.3	55.3	57.7	60.7
Pennsylvania	88.8	82.3	83.0	75.7	81.8	75.0	74.3	71.8	64.4	63.4	42.8	45.8	62.7	53.1
Rhode Island	48.7	48.1	53.4	63.0	59.2	56.2	63.4	62.4	62.7	65.8	57.9	66.3	68.9	71.7
South Carolina	83.9	43.0	35.0	29.1	25.2	18.0	18.4	20.6	14.6	17.5	8.6	6.4	8.5	12.3
South Dakota	—	—	—	70.7	78.0	85.4	73.0	69.5	61.9	60.9	56.6	59.4	72.0	76.5
Tennessee	75.1	73.1	77.6	64.0	70.8	56.6	47.7	48.1	45.1	46.6	35.4	23.3	25.7	26.5
Texas	68.8	80.2	78.3	79.4	88.3	61.4	29.6	33.6	30.8	35.0	21.7	25.8	24.8	27.2
Utah	—	—	—	—	79.4	84.5	78.4	73.0	66.4	79.5	69.6	69.7	73.4	80.0
Vermont	81.6	70.5	71.4	60.4	67.5	57.9	50.7	48.9	56.8	58.2	45.3	51.3	66.8	66.6
Virginia	64.1	81.7	83.2	75.3	71.0	59.6	27.7	27.4	25.7	27.1	19.4	18.1	24.0	22.1
Washington	—	—	—	67.3	63.1	64.9	60.9	59.0	50.8	54.7	52.4	51.2	56.6	64.2
West Virginia	82.6	86.7	94.5	90.3	93.6	91.3	89.2	86.9	81.9	83.6	71.7	75.2	76.4	81.9
Wisconsin	82.4	82.2	81.1	76.8	84.9	77.5	72.0	68.7	68.7	70.2	52.3	57.3	65.9	65.1
Wyoming	—	—	—	47.7	50.7	51.1	50.8	49.2	50.3	54.9	52.3	71.0	68.7	74.9
United States	79.4	77.5	79.3	74.7	79.3	73.2	65.2	65.4	58.8	61.6	49.2	48.9	56.9	56.9

Source: Adapted from U.S. Department of Commerce, *Historical Statistics* (1971, Y 27-78).

Table 7.23 State Voter Turnout in Presidential Elections, 1936-1984

State	1936	1940	1944	1948	1952	1956	1960	1964	1968	1972	1976	1980	1984
Alabama	18.8	18.9	15.0	12.6	24.2	27.6	31.2	36.1	52.8	43.3	46.3	48.7	50.2
Alaska	—	—	—	—	—	—	59.2	48.0	53.0	46.9	48.1	57.2	60.3
Arizona	52.0	57.0	42.2	45.4	53.9	47.8	53.8	56.8	50.6	47.4	46.1	44.5	46.6
Arkansas	17.3	18.2	19.3	21.9	36.9	38.0	41.1	51.2	54.1	48.1	51.1	51.5	52.2
California	66.0	73.4	65.1	63.2	69.4	64.0	67.9	66.1	62.0	59.5	50.4	49.0	49.9
Colorado	75.5	79.7	67.9	64.5	76.2	69.2	71.7	67.6	64.0	59.5	58.8	55.8	54.8
Connecticut	74.6	77.2	73.9	71.2	80.9	75.8	77.1	71.3	68.8	66.2	62.8	61.0	61.0
Delaware	79.8	79.4	66.9	68.5	78.4	72.7	74.5	69.5	68.7	62.1	57.2	54.8	55.8
District of Columbia	—	—	—	—	—	—	—	39.4	34.7	30.4	32.2	35.4	43.8
Florida	31.3	40.9	33.5	34.1	47.6	43.6	50.0	51.9	53.8	48.6	49.2	48.7	49.0
Georgia	17.7	17.7	17.6	21.4	31.9	31.3	32.9	45.3	44.7	37.3	42.0	41.2	42.2
Hawaii	—	—	—	—	—	—	58.9	52.4	53.3	49.4	46.7	43.5	44.5
Idaho	71.8	77.0	64.5	63.1	78.2	75.2	80.6	75.2	71.9	63.3	60.7	67.8	60.4
Illinois	81.6	82.2	74.8	70.3	76.0	72.4	76.5	72.6	69.3	62.3	59.4	57.7	57.3
Indiana	78.7	81.1	71.7	67.2	75.7	73.7	76.9	71.7	69.5	60.8	60.1	57.6	56.3
Iowa	73.5	75.5	64.3	62.4	75.8	74.0	76.8	70.0	67.9	64.0	63.1	62.9	62.3
Kansas	76.6	75.1	62.2	65.0	71.7	67.4	71.8	63.6	63.4	59.5	58.8	56.7	57.0
Kentucky	59.9	59.5	51.9	47.9	57.0	60.5	60.5	54.8	51.3	48.0	48.0	49.9	50.7
Louisiana	27.3	29.4	25.1	27.5	40.2	36.0	45.1	47.1	54.9	44.0	48.7	53.1	54.2
Maine	64.4	65.0	57.3	49.0	63.1	61.8	74.0	65.0	66.4	60.3	63.7	64.6	65.2
Maryland	58.1	57.2	46.7	41.7	57.5	54.6	58.3	54.7	55.2	49.8	49.3	50.0	51.4
Massachusetts	75.9	78.7	71.0	71.5	75.0	72.0	76.9	68.4	66.4	62.0	61.7	59.0	57.9
Michigan	62.1	66.6	63.7	55.6	68.5	71.1	72.7	66.2	64.9	59.4	58.8	59.9	58.2
Minnesota	69.7	72.3	63.0	65.7	72.6	68.7	77.1	73.7	71.7	68.6	71.5	70.0	68.5
Mississippi	14.4	14.7	15.0	16.0	23.8	21.0	25.7	34.1	53.3	44.2	48.0	51.9	52.0
Missouri	77.3	74.4	62.2	61.0	71.8	68.8	72.6	65.2	64.9	57.3	57.3	58.7	57.7
Montana	70.8	72.2	59.0	62.3	71.8	71.6	71.7	70.6	68.4	67.6	63.3	65.0	65.0
Nebraska	75.6	75.4	67.9	58.2	71.9	67.6	72.1	66.6	60.0	56.4	56.2	56.7	56.1

State												
Nevada	69.1	75.7	64.8	64.0	69.7	65.9	61.0	60.0	55.9	49.5	44.2	41.2	41.7
New Hampshire	77.8	79.6	73.5	70.3	79.2	74.4	80.2	71.4	68.5	63.6	57.3	57.2	53.9
New Jersey	75.0	76.1	69.1	63.0	72.3	68.9	71.8	69.2	65.8	59.8	57.7	54.9	56.9
New Mexico	68.7	66.6	48.8	53.4	60.5	56.8	64.5	62.8	60.0	57.7	53.4	50.8	51.6
New York	72.6	75.7	70.9	65.0	71.2	67.9	66.9	64.4	59.7	56.3	50.7	48.0	51.1
North Carolina	47.4	42.7	38.0	35.4	51.3	47.4	54.1	51.9	54.1	42.8	43.0	43.4	47.7
North Dakota	78.0	78.4	61.5	61.6	75.5	71.3	79.1	72.9	70.0	68.3	67.2	64.8	62.9
Ohio	71.8	75.4	66.9	58.4	69.7	66.4	71.3	65.3	62.7	57.3	55.1	55.4	58.0
Oklahoma	56.4	60.5	52.8	52.5	68.6	61.4	64.3	62.4	60.0	56.7	54.9	52.2	51.2
Oregon	62.5	67.1	58.4	56.5	69.6	71.1	72.4	67.2	64.6	62.1	61.3	61.3	62.6
Pennsylvania	72.5	67.6	59.8	56.0	66.5	65.5	70.7	66.6	64.3	56.0	54.2	51.9	53.9
Rhode Island	78.0	75.6	65.0	66.0	79.8	73.2	77.3	69.3	65.6	61.0	59.7	58.7	55.9
South Carolina	12.5	10.1	9.8	12.8	29.1	24.7	31.4	38.7	46.0	38.2	40.3	40.4	40.6
South Dakota	77.5	79.5	59.3	63.3	74.4	74.7	78.8	75.4	72.8	69.4	64.1	67.4	63.9
Tennessee	30.0	30.6	28.2	28.7	44.7	45.9	50.4	51.5	53.2	43.5	48.7	48.7	49.3
Texas	24.8	30.1	28.2	26.0	43.5	37.9	42.4	44.1	48.2	45.0	46.3	44.9	47.0
Utah	77.9	83.1	75.0	76.0	82.9	77.2	78.9	78.0	75.2	69.4	68.4	64.4	60.6
Vermont	68.5	66.8	56.9	54.5	66.8	66.5	72.9	67.0	62.9	60.7	55.7	57.6	60.1
Virginia	23.0	22.1	22.3	21.6	29.9	31.8	34.4	41.6	50.5	44.7	47.0	47.6	51.1
Washington	66.5	70.6	67.0	63.2	71.2	70.4	74.1	67.2	64.3	63.1	59.8	57.4	58.8
West Virginia	84.9	83.0	65.5	65.8	76.3	74.6	77.9	73.0	69.3	62.5	57.2	52.8	51.4
Wisconsin	68.9	72.4	65.7	59.8	72.5	67.8	73.5	68.6	65.6	62.5	66.5	67.3	63.4
Wyoming	74.0	74.8	63.3	59.6	72.5	67.4	73.9	74.1	65.3	64.4	58.6	53.3	51.8
United States	61.0	62.5	55.9	53.0	63.3	60.6	64.0	61.7	60.6	55.2	53.5	52.6	53.3

Sources: Adapted from U.S. Department of Commerce, Historical Statistics (1971, Y 27–78); and U.S. Department of Commerce, Statistical Abstract (1985, 254, 1986, 255).

Table 7.24 Aggregate Presidential Election Outcomes (percent)

Year	Popular votes			Electoral votes		
	Republican	Democrat	Other	Republican	Democrat	Other
1856	33.11	45.28	21.61	38.51	58.78	2.70
1860	39.82	29.46	30.72	59.41	3.96	36.63
1864	55.02	44.96	0.02	90.99	9.01	0.00
1868	52.66	47.34	0.00	72.79	27.21	0.00
1872	55.63	43.83	0.54	81.95	12.03	6.02
1876	47.95	50.97	1.08	50.14	49.86	0.00
1880	48.27	48.25	3.48	57.99	42.01	0.00
1884	48.25	48.50	3.25	45.39	54.61	0.00
1888	47.82	48.62	3.56	58.10	41.90	0.00
1892	42.96	46.05	10.99	32.66	62.39	4.95
1896	51.01	46.73[a]	2.26	60.63	39.37	0.00
1900	51.67	45.51	2.82	65.32	34.68	0.00
1904	56.41	37.60	5.99	70.59	29.41	0.00
1908	51.58	43.05	5.37	66.46	33.54	0.00
1912	23.18	41.84	34.98	1.51	81.92	16.57
1916	46.11	49.24	4.65	47.83	52.17	0.00
1920	60.30	34.17	5.53	76.08	23.92	0.00
1924	54.06	28.84	17.10	71.94	25.61	2.45
1928	58.20	40.77	1.03	83.62	16.38	0.00
1932	39.64	57.42	2.94	11.11	88.89	0.00
1936	36.54	60.79	2.67	1.51	98.49	0.00
1940	44.82	54.70	0.48	15.44	84.56	0.00
1944	45.89	53.39	0.72	18.64	81.36	0.00
1948	45.12	49.51	5.37	35.59	57.07	7.34
1952	55.13	44.38	0.49	83.24	16.76	0.00
1956	57.37	41.97	0.66	86.06	13.94	0.00
1960	49.55	49.72	0.73	40.79	56.42	2.79
1964	38.47	61.05	0.48	9.67	90.33	0.00
1968	43.42	42.72	13.86	55.95	35.50	8.55
1972	60.69	37.53	1.78	96.65	3.16	0.19
1976	48.00	50.06	1.94	44.61	55.20	0.19
1980	50.75	41.01	8.24	90.89	9.11	0.00
1984	58.80	40.60	0.60	97.58	2.42	0.00

[a] Democrat, Populist.

Source: Adapted from *Congressional Quarterly's Guide to U.S. Elections* (1985).

Table 7.25 Percentage of Popular Votes for President by State, 1948 and 1952

	1948			1952		
State	Harry S Truman (D)	Thomas E. Dewey (R)	Other	Dwight D. Eisenhower (R)	Adlai E. Stevenson (D)	Other
Alabama	0.0	19.0	81.0	35.0	64.6	0.4
Arizona	53.8	43.8	2.4	58.4	41.7	0.0
Arkansas	61.7	21.0	17.3	43.8	55.9	0.3
California	-47.6	47.1	5.3	56.3	42.7	1.0
Colorado	51.9	46.5	1.6	60.3	39.0	0.7
Connecticut	47.9	49.6	2.5	55.7	43.9	0.4
Delaware	48.8	50.0	1.2	51.8	47.9	0.3
Florida	48.8	33.6	17.6	55.0	45.0	0.0
Georgia	60.8	18.3	20.9	30.3	69.7	0.0
Idaho	50.0	47.3	2.7	65.4	34.4	0.2
Illinois	50.1	49.2	0.7	54.8	44.9	0.3
Indiana	48.8	49.6	01.6	58.1	41.0	0.9
Iowa	50.3	47.6	2.1	63.8	35.6	0.6
Kansas	44.6	53.6	1.8	68.8	30.5	0.7
Kentucky	56.7	41.5	1.8	49.8	49.9	0.3
Louisiana	32.8	17.5	49.7	47.1	52.9	0.0
Maine	42.4	56.9	0.7	66.2	33.8	0.0
Maryland	47.8	49.2	3.0	55.4	43.8	0.8
Massachusetts	54.7	43.2	2.1	54.2	45.5	0.3
Michigan	47.6	49.2	3.2	55.4	44.0	0.6
Minnesota	57.2	39.9	2.9	55.3	44.1	0.6
Mississippi	10.1	2.5	87.4	39.6	60.4	0.0
Missouri	58.1	41.5	0.4	50.7	49.1	0.2
Montana	53.1	43.2	3.7	59.4	40.1	0.5
Nebraska	45.9	54.2	0.0	69.2	30.9	0.0
Nevada	50.4	47.3	2.0	61.5	38.6	0.0

(Table continues)

Table 7.25 (continued)

State	1948			1952		
	Harry S Truman (D)	Thomas E. Dewey (R)	Other	Dwight D. Eisenhower (R)	Adlai E. Stevenson (D)	Other
New Hampshire	46.7	52.4	0.9	60.9	39.1	0.0
New Jersey	45.9	50.3	3.8	56.8	42.0	1.2
New Mexico	56.3	43.0	0.7	55.5	44.2	0.3
New York	45.0	46.0	9.0	55.5	43.6	0.9
North Carolina	58.0	32.7	9.3	46.1	53.9	0.0
North Dakota	43.4	52.2	4.4	71.0	28.4	0.6
Ohio	49.5	49.2	1.3	56.8	43.2	0.0
Oklahoma	62.8	37.3	0.0	54.6	45.4	0.0
Oregon	46.4	49.8	3.8	60.5	38.9	0.6
Pennsylvania	46.9	50.9	2.2	52.7	46.9	0.4
Rhode Island	57.6	41.4	1.0	50.9	49.1	0.0
South Carolina	24.1	3.8	72.1	49.3	50.7	0.0
South Dakota	47.0	51.8	1.2	69.3	30.7	0.0
Tennessee	49.1	36.9	14.0	50.0	49.7	0.3
Texas	65.4	24.6	10.0	53.1	46.7	0.2
Utah	54.0	45.0	1.0	58.9	41.1	0.0
Vermont	36.9	61.5	1.6	71.5	28.2	0.3
Virginia	47.9	41.0	11.1	56.3	43.4	0.3
Washington	52.6	42.7	4.7	54.3	44.7	1.0
West Virginia	57.3	42.2	0.5	48.1	51.9	0.0
Wisconsin	50.7	46.3	3.0	61.0	38.7	0.3
Wyoming	51.6	47.3	1.1	62.7	37.1	0.2
Total	49.5	45.1	5.4	55.1	44.4	0.5

Source: Adapted from *Congressional Quarterly's Guide to U.S. Elections* (1985).

Table 7.26 Percentage of Popular Votes for President by State, 1956 and 1960

	1956			1960		
State	Dwight D. Eisenhower (R)	Adlai E. Stevenson (D)	Other	John F. Kennedy (D)	Richard M. Nixon (R)	Other
Alabama	39.5	56.4	4.1	56.8	42.1	1.1
Alaska	0.0	0.0	0.0	49.1	50.9	0.0
Arizona	61.0	38.9	0.1	44.4	55.5	0.1
Arkansas	45.8	52.5	1.7	50.2	43.1	6.7
California	55.4	44.3	0.3	49.6	50.1	0.3
Colorado	59.5	39.8	0.7	44.9	54.6	0.5
Connecticut	63.7	36.3	0.0	53.7	46.3	0.0
Delaware	55.1	44.6	0.3	50.6	49.0	0.4
Florida	57.2	42.7	0.1	48.5	51.5	0.0
Georgia	33.3	66.4	0.3	62.5	37.4	0.1
Hawaii	0.0	0.0	0.0	50.0[a]	50.0	0.0
Idaho	61.2	38.8	0.0	46.2	53.8	0.0
Illinois	59.5	40.3	0.2	50.0	49.8	0.2
Indiana	59.9	39.7	0.4	44.6	55.0	0.4
Iowa	59.1	40.7	0.2	43.2	56.7	0.1
Kansas	65.4	34.2	0.4	39.1	60.5	0.4
Kentucky	54.3	45.2	0.5	46.4	53.6	0.0
Louisiana	53.3	39.5	7.2	50.4	28.6	21.0
Maine	70.9	29.1	0.0	43.0	57.1	0.0
Maryland	60.0	40.0	0.0	53.6	46.4	0.0
Massachusetts	59.3	40.4	0.3	60.1	39.6	0.3
Michigan	55.6	44.2	0.2	50.9	48.8	0.3
Minnesota	53.7	46.1	0.2	50.6	49.2	0.3
Mississippi	24.5	58.2	17.3	36.3	24.7	39.0
Missouri	49.9	50.1	0.0	50.3	49.7	0.0
Montana	57.1	42.9	0.0	48.6	51.1	0.3
Nebraska	65.5	34.5	0.0	37.9	62.1	0.0

(Table continues)

Table 7.26 (continued)

State	1956			1960		
	Dwight D. Eisenhower (R)	Adlai E. Stevenson (D)	Other	John F. Kennedy (D)	Richard M. Nixon (R)	Other
Nevada	58.0	42.0	0.0	51.2	48.8	0.0
New Hampshire	66.1	33.8	0.1	46.6	53.4	0.0
New Jersey	64.7	34.2	1.1	50.0	49.2	0.8
New Mexico	57.8	41.8	0.4	50.2	49.4	0.4
New York	61.2	38.8	0.0	52.5	47.3	0.2
North Carolina	49.3	50.7	0.0	52.1	47.9	0.0
North Dakota	61.7	38.1	0.2	44.5	55.4	0.1
Ohio	61.1	38.9	0.0	46.7	53.3	0.0
Oklahoma	55.1	44.9	0.0	41.0	59.0	0.0
Oregon	55.3	44.8	0.0	47.3	52.6	0.1
Pennsylvania	56.5	43.3	0.2	51.1	48.7	0.2
Rhode Island	58.3	41.7	0.0	63.6	36.4	0.0
South Carolina	25.2	45.4	29.4	51.2	48.8	0.0
South Dakota	58.4	41.6	0.0	41.8	58.2	0.0
Tennessee	49.2	48.6	2.2	45.8	52.9	1.3
Texas	55.3	44.0	0.7	50.5	48.5	1.0
Utah	64.6	35.4	0.0	45.2	54.8	0.0
Vermont	72.2	27.8	0.0	41.4	58.7	0.0
Virginia	55.4	38.4	6.2	47.0	52.4	0.6
Washington	53.9	45.4	0.7	48.3	50.7	1.0
West Virginia	54.1	45.9	0.0	52.7	47.3	0.0
Wisconsin	61.6	37.8	0.6	48.1	51.8	0.1
Wyoming	60.1	39.9	0.0	45.0	55.0	0.0
Total	57.4	42.0	0.7	49.7	49.6	0.7

[a] Kennedy won by 115 votes.

Source: Adapted from *Congressional Quarterly's Guide to U.S. Elections* (1985).

Table 7.27 Percentage of Popular Votes for President by State, 1964 and 1968

State	1964			1968			
	Lyndon B. Johnson (D)	Barry M. Goldwater (R)	Other	Richard M. Nixon (R)	Hubert H. Humphrey (D)	George C. Wallace (AI)	Other
Alabama	0.0	69.5	30.6	14.0	18.8	65.8	1.4
Alaska	65.9	34.1	0.0	45.3	42.7	12.1	0.0
Arizona	49.5	50.5	0.1	54.8	35.0	9.6	0.6
Arkansas	56.1	43.4	0.5	30.8	30.4	38.9	0.0
California	59.1	40.8	0.1	47.8	44.7	6.7	0.7
Colorado	61.3	38.2	0.5	50.5	41.3	7.5	0.7
Connecticut	67.8	32.1	0.1	44.3	49.5	6.1	0.1
Delaware	61.0	38.8	0.3	45.1	41.6	13.3	0.0
Florida	51.2	48.9	0.0	40.5	30.9	28.5	0.0
Georgia	45.9	54.1	0.0	30.4	26.8	42.8	0.0
Hawaii	78.8	21.2	0.0	38.7	59.8	1.5	0.0
Idaho	50.9	49.1	0.0	56.8	30.7	12.6	0.0
Illinois	59.5	40.5	0.0	47.1	44.2	8.5	0.3
Indiana	56.0	43.6	0.5	50.3	38.0	11.5	0.3
Iowa	61.9	37.9	0.2	53.0	40.8	5.7	0.5
Kansas	54.1	45.1	0.8	54.8	34.7	10.2	0.3
Kentucky	64.0	35.7	0.3	43.8	37.7	18.3	0.3
Louisiana	43.2	56.8	0.0	23.5	28.2	48.3	0.0
Maine	68.8	31.2	0.0	43.1	55.3	1.6	0.0
Maryland	65.5	34.5	0.0	41.9	43.6	14.5	0.0
Massachusetts	76.2	23.4	0.4	32.9	63.0	3.7	0.4
Michigan	66.7	33.1	0.2	41.5	48.2	10.0	0.4
Minnesota	63.8	36.0	0.3	41.5	54.0	4.3	0.2
Mississippi	12.9	87.1	0.0	13.5	23.0	63.5	0.0
Missouri	64.1	36.0	0.0	44.9	43.7	11.4	0.0
Montana	59.0	40.6	0.5	50.6	41.6	7.3	0.5
Nebraska	52.6	47.4	0.0	59.8	31.8	8.4	0.0
Nevada	58.6	41.4	0.0	47.5	39.3	13.3	0.0

(*Table continues*)

Table 7.27 (continued)

	1964			1968			
State	Lyndon B. Johnson (D)	Barry M. Goldwater (R)	Other	Richard M. Nixon (R)	Hubert H. Humphrey (D)	George C. Wallace (AI)	Other
New Hampshire	63.6	36.4	0.0	52.1	43.9	3.8	0.2
New Jersey	65.6	33.9	0.6	46.1	44.0	9.1	0.8
New Mexico	59.0	40.4	0.6	51.9	39.8	7.9	0.5
New York	68.6	31.3	0.1	44.3	49.8	5.3	0.6
North Carolina	56.2	43.9	0.0	39.5	29.2	31.3	0.0
North Dakota	58.0	41.9	0.2	55.9	38.2	5.8	0.1
Ohio	62.9	37.1	0.0	45.2	43.0	11.8	0.0
Oklahoma	55.8	44.3	0.0	47.7	32.0	20.3	0.0
Oregon	63.7	36.0	0.3	49.8	43.8	6.1	0.3
Pennsylvania	64.9	34.7	0.4	44.0	47.6	8.0	0.4
Rhode Island	80.9	19.1	0.0	31.8	64.0	4.1	0.0
South Carolina	41.1	58.9	0.0	38.1	29.6	32.3	0.0
South Dakota	55.6	44.4	0.0	53.3	42.0	4.8	0.0
Tennessee	55.5	44.5	0.0	37.9	28.1	34.0	0.0
Texas	63.3	36.5	0.2	39.9	41.1	19.0	0.0
Utah	54.7	45.3	0.0	56.5	37.1	6.4	0.1
Vermont	66.3	33.7	0.0	52.8	43.5	3.2	0.6
Virginia	53.5	46.2	0.3	43.4	32.5	23.6	0.5
Washington	62.0	37.4	0.6	45.2	47.3	7.4	0.2
West Virginia	67.9	32.1	0.0	40.8	49.6	9.6	0.0
Wisconsin	62.1	37.7	0.2	47.9	44.3	7.6	0.3
Wyoming	56.6	43.4	0.0	55.8	35.5	8.7	0.0
District of Columbia	85.5	14.5	0.0	18.2	81.8	0.0	0.0
Total	61.1	38.5	0.5	43.4	42.7	13.5	0.3

Note: AI = American Independent.

Source: Adapted from *Congressional Quarterly's Guide to U.S. Elections* (1985).

Table 7.28 Percentage of Popular Votes for President by State, 1972 and 1976

| State | 1972 | | | 1976 | | | |
	Richard M. Nixon (R)	George S. McGovern (D)	Other	Jimmy Carter (D)	Gerald R. Ford (R)	Eugene J. McCarthy (I)	Other
Alabama	48.8	47.5	3.7	55.7	42.6	0.0	1.6
Alaska	58.1	34.6	7.3	35.7	57.9	0.0	6.5
Arizona	61.6	30.4	8.0	39.8	56.4	2.6	1.2
Arkansas	68.9	30.7	0.4	65.0	34.9	0.1	0.1
California	55.0	41.5	3.5	47.6	49.3	0.7	2.3
Colorado	62.6	34.6	2.9	42.6	54.0	2.4	1.0
Connecticut	58.6	40.1	1.4	46.9	52.1	0.3	0.8
Delaware	59.6	39.2	1.2	52.0	46.6	1.0	0.4
Florida	71.9	27.8	0.3	51.9	46.6	0.8	0.7
Georgia	75.3	24.7	0.0	66.7	33.0	0.1	0.2
Hawaii	62.5	37.5	0.0	50.6	48.1	0.0	1.3
Idaho	64.2	26.0	9.7	36.8	59.3	0.3	3.5
Illinois	59.0	40.5	0.5	48.1	50.1	1.2	0.6
Indiana	66.1	33.3	0.5	45.7	53.3	0.0	1.0
Iowa	57.6	40.5	1.9	48.5	49.5	1.6	0.5
Kansas	67.7	29.5	2.9	44.9	52.5	1.4	1.2
Kentucky	63.4	34.8	1.9	52.8	45.6	0.6	1.1
Louisiana	66.0	28.6	5.4	51.7	46.0	0.5	1.8
Maine	61.5	38.5	0.0	48.1	48.9	2.3	0.8
Maryland	61.3	37.4	1.4	52.8	46.7	0.3	0.2
Massachusetts	45.2	54.2	0.6	56.1	40.4	2.6	0.9
Michigan	56.2	41.8	2.0	46.4	51.8	1.3	0.4
Minnesota	51.6	46.1	2.4	54.9	42.0	1.8	1.3
Mississippi	78.2	19.6	2.2	49.6	47.7	0.5	2.3
Missouri	62.3	37.7	0.0	51.1	47.5	1.2	0.2
Montana	57.9	37.9	4.2	45.4	52.8	0.0	1.8
Nebraska	70.5	29.5	0.0	38.5	59.2	1.5	0.8

(Table continues)

Table 7.28 (continued)

	1972			1976			
State	Richard M. Nixon (R)	George S. McGovern (D)	Other	Jimmy Carter (D)	Gerald R. Ford (R)	Eugene J. McCarthy (I)	Other
Nevada	63.7	36.3	0.0	45.8	50.2	0.0	4.1
New Hampshire	64.0	34.9	1.2	43.5	54.7	1.2	0.6
New Jersey	61.6	36.8	1.7	47.9	50.1	1.1	0.9
New Mexico	61.1	36.6	2.4	48.1	50.5	0.3	1.2
New York	57.3	40.3	0.3	51.9	47.5	0.1	0.6
North Carolina	69.5	28.9	1.7	55.2	44.2	0.0	0.5
North Dakota	62.1	35.8	2.1	45.8	51.6	1.0	1.6
Ohio	59.6	38.1	2.3	48.9	48.7	1.4	1.0
Oklahoma	73.7	24.0	2.3	48.7	50.0	1.3	0.0
Oregon	52.5	42.3	5.3	47.6	47.8	3.9	0.7
Pennsylvania	59.1	39.1	1.7	50.4	47.7	1.1	0.8
Rhode Island	53.0	46.8	0.2	55.4	44.1	0.1	0.5
South Carolina	70.8	27.7	1.5	56.2	43.1	0.0	0.7
South Dakota	54.2	45.5	0.3	48.9	50.4	0.0	0.7
Tennessee	67.7	29.8	2.5	55.9	42.9	0.3	0.8
Texas	66.2	33.3	0.6	51.1	48.0	0.5	0.4
Utah	67.6	26.4	6.0	33.6	62.4	0.7	3.2
Vermont	62.9	36.6	0.5	43.1	54.4	2.1	0.4
Virginia	67.8	30.1	2.1	48.0	49.3	0.0	2.8
Washington	56.9	38.6	4.5	46.1	50.0	2.4	1.5
West Virginia	63.6	36.4	0.0	58.0	41.9	0.0	0.0
Wisconsin	53.4	43.7	2.9	49.4	47.8	1.7	1.2
Wyoming	69.0	30.5	0.5	39.8	59.3	0.4	0.5
District of Columbia	21.6	78.1	0.3	81.6	16.5	0.0	1.9
Total	60.7	37.5	1.8	50.1	48.0	0.9	1.0

Source: Adapted from *Congressional Quarterly's Guide to U.S. Elections* (1985).

Table 7.29 Percentage of Popular Votes for President by State, 1980 and 1984

State	1980				1984		
	Ronald Reagan (R)	Jimmy Carter (D)	John Anderson (I)	Other	Ronald Reagan (R)	Walter Mondale (D)	Other
Alabama	48.8	47.5	1.2	2.5	60.5	38.3	1.2
Alaska	54.3	26.4	7.0	12.3	66.6	29.9	3.5
Arizona	60.6	28.2	8.8	2.4	66.4	32.5	1.1
Arkansas	48.1	47.5	2.7	1.7	60.5	38.3	1.2
California	52.7	35.9	8.6	2.8	57.5	41.3	1.2
Colorado	55.1	31.1	11.0	2.8	63.4	35.1	1.5
Connecticut	48.2	38.5	12.2	1.1	60.7	38.8	0.5
Delaware	47.2	44.8	6.9	1.1	59.8	39.9	0.3
Florida	55.5	38.5	5.2	0.8	65.3	34.7	0.0
Georgia	41.0	55.8	2.2	1.0	60.2	39.8	0.0
Hawaii	42.9	44.8	10.6	1.7	55.1	43.8	1.1
Idaho	66.4	25.2	6.2	2.2	72.4	26.4	1.2
Illinois	49.7	41.7	7.3	1.3	56.2	43.3	0.5
Indiana	56.0	37.7	5.0	1.3	61.7	37.7	0.6
Iowa	51.3	38.6	8.8	1.3	53.3	45.9	0.8
Kansas	57.8	33.3	7.0	1.9	66.3	32.6	1.1
Kentucky	49.1	47.6	2.4	0.9	60.0	39.4	0.6
Louisiana	51.2	45.8	1.7	1.3	60.8	38.2	1.0
Maine	45.6	42.3	10.2	1.9	60.8	38.8	0.4
Maryland	44.2	47.1	7.8	0.9	52.5	47.0	0.5
Massachusetts	41.9	41.7	15.2	1.2	51.2	48.4	0.4
Michigan	49.0	42.5	7.0	1.5	59.2	40.2	0.6
Minnesota	42.6	46.5	8.5	2.4	49.5	49.7	0.8
Mississippi	49.4	48.1	1.3	1.2	61.9	37.4	0.7
Missouri	51.2	44.3	3.7	0.8	60.0	40.0	0.0
Montana	56.8	32.4	8.1	2.7	60.5	38.2	1.3
Nebraska	65.9	26.0	7.0	1.1	70.6	28.8	0.6

(Table continues)

Table 7.29 (continued)

State	1980 Ronald Reagan (R)	Jimmy Carter (D)	John Anderson (I)	Other	1984 Ronald Reagan (R)	Walter Mondale (D)	Other
Nevada	62.5	26.9	7.1	3.5	65.8	32.0	2.2
New Hampshire	57.7	28.4	12.9	1.0	68.6	30.9	0.5
New Jersey	52.0	38.6	7.9	1.5	60.1	39.2	0.7
New Mexico	54.9	36.7	6.5	1.9	59.7	39.2	1.1
New York	46.7	44.0	7.5	1.8	53.8	45.8	0.4
North Carolina	49.3	47.2	2.9	0.6	61.9	37.9	0.2
North Dakota	64.2	26.3	7.8	1.7	64.8	33.8	1.4
Ohio	51.5	40.9	5.9	1.7	58.9	40.1	1.0
Oklahoma	60.5	35.0	3.3	1.2	68.6	30.7	0.7
Oregon	48.3	38.7	9.5	3.5	55.9	43.7	0.4
Pennsylvania	49.6	42.5	6.4	1.5	53.3	46.0	0.7
Rhode Island	37.2	47.7	14.4	0.7	51.8	47.9	0.3
South Carolina	49.4	48.2	1.6	0.8	63.6	35.6	0.8
South Dakota	60.5	31.7	6.5	1.3	63.0	36.5	0.5
Tennessee	48.7	48.4	2.2	0.7	57.8	41.6	0.6
Texas	55.3	41.4	2.5	0.8	63.6	36.1	0.3
Utah	72.8	20.6	5.0	1.6	74.5	24.7	0.8
Vermont	44.4	38.4	14.9	2.3	57.9	40.8	1.3
Virginia	53.0	40.3	5.1	1.6	62.3	37.1	0.6
Washington	49.7	37.3	10.6	2.4	56.2	42.9	0.9
West Virginia	45.3	49.8	4.3	0.6	54.7	44.3	1.0
Wisconsin	47.9	43.2	7.1	1.8	54.3	45.1	0.6
Wyoming	62.6	28.0	6.8	2.6	69.1	27.7	3.2
District of Columbia	—	—	—	—	13.7	85.4	0.9
Total	50.7	41.0	6.6	1.7	58.8	40.6	0.6

Source: Adapted from Congressional Quarterly's Guide to U.S. Elections (1985).

Table 7.30 Minor Party Presidential Candidates, 1840-1984

Year	Candidate[a]	Party	Popular vote (%)	Total popular vote by year (%)
1840	James G. Birney	Liberty	0.28	0.28
1844	James G. Birney	Liberty	2.30	2.30
1848	Martin Van Buren	Free Soil	10.12	10.12
1852	John P. Hale	Free Soil	4.91	4.99
	Jacob Broom	Native American	0.08	
1856	Millard Fillmore	Whig-American	21.53	21.53
1860	John C. Breckinridge	Southern Democrat	18.09	30.70
	John Bell	Constitutional Union	12.61	
1864	—	—	—	—
1868	—	—	—	—
1872	Charles O'Conor	Straight-out Democrat	0.29	0.34
	James Black	Prohibition	0.05	
1876	Peter Cooper	Greenback	0.90	0.99
	Green Clay Smith	Prohibition	0.08	
	James B. Walker	American	0.01	
1880	James B. Weaver	Greenback	3.32	3.44
	Neal Dow	Prohibition	0.11	
	John W. Phelps	American	0.01	
1884	Benjamin F. Butler	Greenback	1.74	3.21
	John P. St. John	Prohibition	1.47	
1888	Clinton B. Fisk	Prohibition	2.19	3.50
	Alston J. Streeter	Union Labor	1.29	
	Robert H. Cowdrey	United Labor	0.01	
	James Langdon Curtis	American	0.01	

(Table continues)

Table 7.30 (continued)

Year	Candidate[a]	Party	Popular vote (%)	Total popular vote by year (%)
1892	James B. Weaver	Populist	8.50	10.93
	John Bidwell	Prohibition	2.25	
	Simon Wing	Socialist Labor	0.18	
1896	John M. Palmer	National Democrat	0.96	2.26
	Joshua Levering	Prohibition	0.90	
	Charles H. Matchett	Socialist Labor	0.26	
	Charles E. Bentley	National Prohibition	0.14	
1900	John G. Woolley	Prohibition	1.50	2.81
	Eugene V. Debs	Socialist	0.62	
	Wharton Barker	Populist	0.36	
	Joseph F. Malloney	Socialist Labor	0.29	
	Seth H. Ellis	Union Reform	0.04	
	Jonah F. R. Leonard	United Christian	b	
1904	Eugene V. Debs	Socialist	2.98	5.98
	Sillas C. Swallow	Prohibition	1.91	
	Thomas E. Watson	Populist	0.84	
	Charles H. Corregan	Socialist Labor	0.25	
1908	Eugene V. Debs	Socialist	2.82	5.35
	Eugene F. Chafin	Prohibition	1.70	
	Thomas L. Hisgen	Independence	0.55	
	Thomas E. Watson	Populist	0.19	
	August Gillhaus	Socialist Labor	0.09	
	Daniel B. Turney	United Christian	b	

Year	Candidate	Party		
1912	Theodore Roosevelt	Progressive	27.39	34.96
	Eugene V. Debs	Socialist	5.99	
	Eugene W. Chafin	Prohibition	1.38	
	Arthur E. Reimer	Socialist Labor	.20	
1916	Allan L. Benson	Socialist	3.18	4.64
	James Franklin Hanly [c]	Prohibition	1.19	
		Progressive	0.19	
	Arthur E. Reimer	Socialist Labor	0.08	
1920	Eugene V. Debs	Socialist	3.42	5.24
	Parley P. Christensen	Farmer Labor	0.99	
	Aaron S. Watkins	Prohibition	0.70	
	William W. Cox	Socialist Labor	0.11	
	Robert C. Macauly	Single Tax	0.02	
1924	Robert M. LaFollette	Progressive	16.56	17.07
	Herman P. Faris	Prohibition	0.19	
	Frank T. Johns	Socialist Labor	0.10	
	William Z. Foster	Communist	0.13	
	Gilbert O. Nations	American	0.08	
	William J. Wallace	Commonwealth Land	0.01	
1928	Norman M. Thomas	Socialist	0.72	1.02
	William Z. Foster	Communist	0.13	
	William F. Varney	Prohibition	0.09	
	Verne L. Reynolds	Socialist Labor	0.06	
	Frank E. Webb	Farmer Labor	0.02	
1932	Norman M. Thomas	Socialist	2.22	2.93
	William Z. Foster	Communist	0.26	
	William D. Upshaw	Prohibition	0.21	
	William H. Harvey	Liberty	0.13	
	Verne L. Reynolds	Socialist Labor	0.09	
	Jacob S. Coxey	Farmer Labor	0.02	
	James R. Cox	Jobless	b	

(Table continues)

Table 7.30 (continued)

Year	Candidate[a]	Party	Popular vote (%)	Total popular vote by year (%)
1936	William Lemke	Union	1.96	2.65
	Norman M. Thomas	Socialist	0.41	
	Earl R. Browder	Communist	0.17	
	David L. Colvin	Prohibition	0.08	
	John W. Aiken	Socialist Labor	0.03	
1940	Norman M. Thomas	Socialist	0.23	0.48
	Roger W. Babson	Prohibition	0.12	
	Earle R. Browder	Communist	0.10	
	John W. Aiken	Socialist Labor	0.03	
1944	Norman M. Thomas	Socialist	0.16	0.41
	Claude W. Watson	Prohibition	0.16	
	Edward A. Teichert	Socialist Labor	0.09	
	Gerald L. K. Smith	America First	[b]	
1948	J. Strom Thurmond	States' Rights Democrat	2.40	5.37
	Henry A. Wallace	Progressive	2.38	
	Norman M. Thomas	Socialist	0.29	
	Claude A. Watson	Prohibition	0.21	
	Edward A. Teichert	Socialist Labor	0.06	
	Farrell Dobbs	Socialist Workers	0.03	
1952	Vincent Hallinan	Progressive	0.23	0.45
	Stuart Hamblen	Prohibition	0.12	
	Eric Hass	Socialist Labor	0.05	
	Darlington Hoopes	Socialist	0.03	
	Farrell Dobbs	Socialist Workers	0.02	

Year	Candidate	Party		Total
1956	T. Coleman Andrews	Constitution	0.17	0.32
	Eric Hass	Socialist Labor	0.07	
	Enoch A. Haltwick	Prohibition	0.07	
	Farrell Dobbs	Socialist Workers	0.01	
	Darlington Hoopes	Socialist	b	
1960	Eric Hass	Socialist Labor	0.07	0.19
	Rutherford L. Decker	Prohibition	0.06	
	Farrell Dobbs	Socialist Workers	0.06	
1964	Eric Hass	Socialist Labor	0.06	0.15
	Clifton Deberry	Socialist Workers	0.05	
	E. Harold Munn	Prohibition	0.03	
	John Kasper	National States' Rights	0.01	
1968	George C. Wallace	American Independent	13.53	13.73
	Henning A. Blomen	Socialist Labor	0.07	
	Fred Halsted	Socialist Workers	0.06	
	Dick Gregory [c]	Peace and Freedom	0.06	
		Peace and Freedom	0.04	
	E. Harold Munn	Prohibition	0.02	
	Eldridge Cleaver	Peace and Freedom	0.01	
	Charlene Mitchell	Communist	b	
1972	John G. Schmitz	American	1.40	1.69
	Benjamin Spock	People's	0.10	
	Louis Fisher	Socialist Labor	0.07	
	Linda Jenness	Socialist Workers	0.05	
	Gus Hall	Communist	0.03	
	Evelyn Reed	Socialist Workers	0.02	
	E. Harold Munn	Prohibition	0.02	
	John Hospers	Libertarian	b	
	Gabriel Green	Universal	b	

(Table continues)

Table 7.30 (continued)

Year	Candidate[a]	Party	Popular vote (%)	Total popular vote by year (%)
1976	Eugene J. McCarthy	Independent	0.93	1.88
	Roger MacBride	Libertarian	0.21	
	Lester Maddox	American Independent	0.21	
	Thomas J. Anderson	American	0.20	
	Peter Camejo	Socialist Workers	0.11	
	Gus Hall	Communist	0.07	
	Margaret Wright	People's Party	0.06	
	Lyndon H. LaRouche	U.S. Labor	0.05	
	Benjamin C. Bubar	Prohibition	0.02	
	Jules Levin	Socialist Labor	0.01	
	Frank P. Zeidler	Socialist	0.01	
1980	John B. Anderson	Independent	6.61	8.14
	Ed Clark	Libertarian	1.06	
	Barry Commoner	Citizens	0.27	
	Gus Hall	Communist	0.05	
	John R. Rarick	American Independent	0.05	
	Ellen McCormick	Right to Life	0.04	
	Deirdre Griswold	Workers' World	0.02	
	Percy L. Greaves, Jr.	American	0.01	
	Benjamin C. Bubar	Statesman	0.01	
	David McReynolds	Socialist	0.01	
	Andrew Pulley	Socialist Workers	0.01	

1984			0.65
David Bergland	Libertarian	0.25	
Lyndon H. LaRouche, Jr.	Independent	0.09	
Sonia Johnson	Citizens	0.08	
Bob Richards	Populist	0.07	
Dennis L. Serrette	Independent Alliance	0.05	
Gus Hall	Communist	0.04	
Mel Mason	Socialist Workers	0.03	
Larry Holmes	Workers World	0.02	
Delmar Dennis	American	0.01	
Ed Winn	Workers League	0.01	
Earl F. Dodge	Prohibition	b	
Gavrielle Holmes	Workers World	b	
John B. Anderson	National Unity Party of Kentucky	b	
Gerald Baker	Big Deal	b	
Arthur J. Lowery	United Sovereign Citizens	b	

[a] Only candidates and parties that received popular votes in more than one state are listed. Candidates who received votes but declined the nomination of a party (for example, Orval Faubus in 1960) are also excluded.
[b] Less than 0.01 percent of the vote.
[c] No candidate recorded.

Sources: Congressional Quarterly's Guide to U.S. Elections (1985); *Congressional Quarterly's Guide to the 1976 Elections* (1977); *Congressional Quarterly Weekly Report*, January 17, 1981, 138. Adapted and amended from Rosenstone, Behr, and Lazarus (1984); updated to 1984 with data from U.S. Federal Election Commission (1985b).

Table 7.31 Electoral Votes by State, 1948-1960

State	Electoral votes	1948 winner	Electoral votes	1952 winner	1956 winner	1960 winner
Alabama	11	TH	11	S	S [a]	K [b]
Alaska	—	—	3	—	—	N
Arizona	4	T	4	E	E	N
Arkansas	9	T	8	S	S	K
California	25	T	32	E	E	N
Colorado	6	T	6	E	E	N
Connecticut	8	D	8	E	E	K
Delaware	3	D	3	E	E	K
Florida	8	T	10	E	E	N
Georgia	12	T	12	S	S	K
Idaho	4	T	4	E	E	N
Illinois	28	T	27	E	E	K
Indiana	13	D	13	E	E	N
Iowa	10	T	10	E	E	N
Kansas	8	D	8	E	E	N
Kentucky	11	T	10	S	E	N
Louisiana	10	TH	10	S	E	K
Maine	5	D	5	E	E	N
Maryland	8	D	9	E	E	K
Massachusetts	16	T	16	E	E	K
Michigan	19	D	20	E	E	K
Minnesota	11	T	11	E	E	K
Mississippi	9	TH	8	S	S	B
Missouri	15	T	13	E	S	K
Montana	4	T	4	E	E	N
Nebraska	6	D	6	E	E	N
Nevada	3	T	3	E	E	K
New Hampshire	4	D	4	E	E	N
New Jersey	16	D	16	E	E	K
New Mexico	4	T	4	E	E	K
New York	47	D	45	E	E	K
North Carolina	14	T	14	S	S	K
North Dakota	4	D	4	E	E	N
Ohio	25	T	25	E	E	N
Oklahoma	10	T	8	E	E	N [c]
Oregon	6	D	6	E	E	N
Pennsylvania	35	D	32	E	E	K
Rhode Island	4	T	4	E	E	K
South Carolina	8	TH	8	S	S	K
South Dakota	4	D	4	E	E	N
Tennessee	12	T [d]	11	E	E	N
Texas	23	T	24	E	E	K

Table 7.31 (continued)

State	Electoral votes	1948 winner	Electoral votes	1952 winner	1956 winner	1960 winner
Utah	4	T	4	E	E	N
Vermont	3	D	3	E	E	N
Virginia	11	T	12	E	E	N
Washington	8	T	9	E	E	N
West Virginia	8	T	8	S	E	K
Wisconsin	12	T	12	E	E	N
Wyoming	3	T	3	E	E	N
Total	531		531			
Winner						
(votes)		T (303)		E (442)	E (457)	K (303)

Note: B = Byrd. D = Dewey. E = Eisenhower. K = Kennedy. N = Nixon. S = Stevenson. T = Truman. TH = Thurmond.

[a] One electoral vote went to Jones.
[b] Six electoral votes went to Byrd.
[c] One electoral vote went to Byrd.
[d] Thurmond received one electoral vote.

Source: Adapted from *Congressional Quarterly's Guide to U.S. Elections* (1985).

Table 7.32 Electoral Votes by State, 1964-1976

State	Electoral votes	1964 winner	1968 winner	Electoral votes	1972 winner	1976 winner
Alabama	10	G	W	9	N	C
Alaska	3	J	N	3	N	F
Arizona	5	G	N	6	N	F
Arkansas	6	J	W	6	N	C
California	40	J	N	45	N	F
Colorado	6	J	N	7	N	F
Connecticut	8	J	H	8	N	F
Delaware	3	J	N	3	N	C
District of Columbia	3	J	H	3	M	C
Florida	14	J	N	17	N	C
Georgia	12	G	W	12	N	C
Hawaii	4	J	H	4	N	C
Idaho	4	J	N	4	N	F
Illinois	26	J	N	26	N	F
Indiana	13	J	N	13	N	F
Iowa	9	J	N	8	N	F
Kansas	7	J	N	7	N	F
Kentucky	9	J	N	9	N	C
Louisiana	10	G	W	10	N	C
Maine	4	J	H	4	N	F
Maryland	10	J	H	10	N	C
Massachusetts	14	J	H	14	M	C
Michigan	21	J	H	21	N	F
Minnesota	10	J	H	10	N	C
Mississippi	7	G	W	7	N	C
Missouri	12	J	N	12	N	C
Montana	4	J	N	4	N	F
Nebraska	5	J	N	5	N	F
Nevada	3	J	N	3	N	F
New Hampshire	4	J	N	4	N	F
New Jersey	17	J	N	17	N	F
New Mexico	4	J	N	4	N	F
New York	43	J	H	41	N	C
North Carolina	13	J	N [a]	13	N	C
North Dakota	4	J	N	3	N	F
Ohio	26	J	N	25	N	C
Oklahoma	8	J	N	8	N	F
Oregon	6	J	N	6	N	F
Pennsylvania	29	J	H	27	N	C
Rhode Island	4	J	H	4	N	C
South Carolina	8	G	N	8	N	C
South Dakota	4	J	N	4	N	F

Table 7.32 (continued)

State	Electoral votes	1964 winner	1968 winner	Electoral votes	1972 winner	1976 winner
Tennessee	11	J	N	10	N	C
Texas	25	J	H	26	N	C
Utah	4	J	N	4	N	F
Vermont	3	J	N	3	N	F
Virginia	12	J	N	12	N [b]	F
Washington	9	J	H	9	N	F [c]
West Virginia	7	J	H	6	N	C
Wisconsin	12	J	N	11	N	C
Wyoming	3	J	N	3	N	F
Total	538			538		
Winner (votes)		J (486)	N (301)		N (520)	C (297)

Note: C = Carter. F = Ford. G = Goldwater. H = Humphrey. J = Johnson. M = McGovern. N = Nixon. W = Wallace.

[a] One electoral vote went to Wallace.
[b] One electoral vote went to Hospers.
[c] One electoral vote went to Reagan.

Source: Adapted from *Congressional Quarterly's Guide to U.S. Elections* (1985).

Table 7.33   Electoral Votes by State, 1980 and 1984

State	1980 Electoral votes	1980 Winner	1984 Electoral votes	1984 Winner
Alabama	9	R	9	R
Alaska	3	R	3	R
Arizona	6	R	7	R
Arkansas	6	R	6	R
California	45	R	47	R
Colorado	7	R	8	R
Connecticut	8	R	8	R
Delaware	3	R	3	R
District of Columbia	3	C	3	M
Florida	17	R	21	R
Georgia	12	C	12	R
Hawaii	4	C	4	R
Idaho	4	R	4	R
Illinois	26	R	24	R
Indiana	13	R	12	R
Iowa	8	R	8	R
Kansas	7	R	7	R
Kentucky	9	R	9	R
Louisiana	10	R	10	R
Maine	4	R	4	R
Maryland	10	C	10	R
Massachusetts	14	R	13	R
Michigan	21	R	20	R
Minnesota	10	C	10	M
Mississippi	7	R	7	R
Missouri	12	R	11	R
Montana	4	R	4	R
Nebraska	5	R	5	R
Nevada	3	R	4	R
New Hampshire	4	R	4	R
New Jersey	17	R	16	R
New Mexico	4	R	5	R
New York	41	R	36	R
North Carolina	13	R	13	R
North Dakota	3	R	3	R
Ohio	25	R	23	R
Oklahoma	8	R	8	R
Oregon	6	R	7	R
Pennsylvania	27	R	25	R
Rhode Island	4	C	4	R
South Carolina	8	R	8	R
South Dakota	4	R	3	R
Tennessee	10	R	11	R

Table 7.33 (continued)

State	1980 Electoral votes	1980 Winner	1984 Electoral votes	1984 Winner
Texas	26	R	29	R
Utah	4	R	5	R
Vermont	3	R	3	R
Virginia	12	R	12	R
Washington	9	R	10	R
West Virginia	6	C	6	R
Wisconsin	11	R	11	R
Wyoming	3	R	3	R
Total	538		538	
Winner (votes)		R (489)		R (525)

Note: C = Carter. M = Mondale. R = Reagan.

Source: Adapted from *Congressional Quarterly's Guide to U.S. Elections* (1985).

Table 7.34 Electoral Mandates

Year	Winning candidate	Percentage of popular vote	Rank	Popular vote advantage (%)[a]	Rank	Percentage of electoral vote	Rank
1868	Ulysses S. Grant	52.66	15	5.32	19	72.79	15
1872	Ulysses S. Grant	55.63	10	11.80	11	78.14	13
1876	Rutherford B. Hayes	47.95	26	−3.02	30	50.14	30
1880	James A. Garfield	48.27	25	0.02	28	57.99	22
1884	Grover Cleveland	48.50	24	0.25	26	54.61	27
1888	Benjamin Harrison	47.82	27	−0.80	29	58.10	21
1892	Grover Cleveland	46.05	28	3.09	23	52.35	28
1896	William McKinley	51.01	18	4.28	21	60.63	20
1900	William McKinley	51.67	16	6.16	18	65.32	19
1904	Theodore Roosevelt	56.41	9	8.81	15	70.58	17
1908	William H. Taft	51.58	17	8.53	16	66.45	18
1912	Woodrow Wilson	41.84	30	14.45	10	81.92	11
1916	Woodrow Wilson	49.24	23	3.13	22	52.16	29
1920	Warren G. Harding	60.30	4	26.13	1	76.08	14
1924	Calvin Coolidge	54.06	13	25.22	2	71.94	16
1928	Herbert C. Hoover	58.20	6	17.43	8	83.62	9
1932	Franklin D. Roosevelt	57.42	7	17.78	7	88.89	6
1936	Franklin D. Roosevelt	60.79	2	24.25	3	98.49	1
1940	Franklin D. Roosevelt	54.70	12	9.88	13	84.55	8
1944	Franklin D. Roosevelt	53.39	14	7.50	17.	81.36	12
1948	Harry S Truman	49.51	22	4.39	20	57.06	23
1952	Dwight D. Eisenhower	55.13	11	10.75	12	83.24	10
1956	Dwight D. Eisenhower	57.37	8	15.40	9	86.06	7

Year	Name						
1960	John F. Kennedy	49.72	21	0.17	27	56.42	24
1964	Lyndon B. Johnson	61.05	1	22.58	5	90.33	5
1968	Richard M. Nixon	43.42	29	0.70	25	55.95	25
1972	Richard M. Nixon	60.69	3	23.16	4	96.65	3
1976	Jimmy Carter	50.10	20	2.10	24	55.20	26
1980	Ronald Reagan	50.70	19	9.70	14	90.89	4
1984	Ronald Reagan	58.80	5	18.20	6	97.58	2
	Average	52.80	—	9.91	—	72.52	—

[a] Percentage point difference between winner and nearest rival.

Source: Calculated by the authors.

Table 7.35 The Democratic Presidential Coalition, 1952-1984

Year	Percentage deviation in loyalty to Democrats					
	Poor	Blacks	Union	Catholic	South	Cities
1952	2	38	14	12	10	6
1956	5	26	13	11	10	13
1960	−2	22	16	32	2	15
1964	8	38	19	14	−3	13
1968	1	49	8	18	−4	15
1972	8	49	8	8	−2	24
1976	17	38	13	7	3	10
1980	30	47	9	3	6	28
1984	25	40	14	6	3	29

Note: Table entries are the percentage advantage in loyalty each group has to the Democrats over the nation as a whole. Poor = income under $3,000 per year before 1980; $5,000 per year since 1980. Blacks = all nonwhites. Union = member or union member in family. Catholic = Catholic and other non-Protestant. South = from southern or border state. Cities = central cities of twelve largest metropolitan areas.

Source: Axelrod (1986, 282).

Table 7.36 The Republican Presidential Coalition, 1952-1984

Year	Percentage deviation in loyalty to Republicans					
	Nonpoor	White	Nonunion	Protestant	Northern	Noncentral cities
1952	1	2	6	6	6	2
1956	1	1	5	4	2	2
1960	0	1	5	13	0	2
1964	1	3	6	5	−1	1
1968	0	3	2	5	3	1
1972	1	5	3	4	−1	2
1976	1	5	4	5	1	1
1980	1	5	4	5	1	1
1984	2	7	4	3	1	2

Note: Table entries are the percentage advantage in loyalty each group has to the Republicans over the nation as a whole. Nonpoor = income over $3,000 per year before 1980; $5,000 per year since 1980. Nonunion = no union members in family. Northern = all states other than southern and border states. Noncentral cities = not from one of the twelve largest metropolitan areas.

Source: Axelrod (1986, 283).

Figure 7.1 Candidates' Public Images, 1980, Reagan and Carter

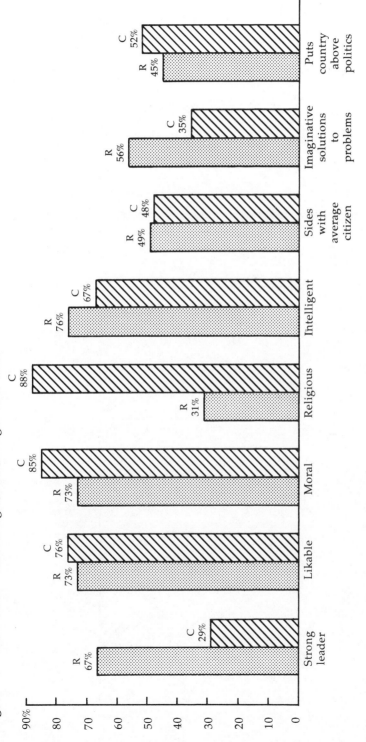

Note: Entries are percentage of respondents ascribing the characteristic to the candidate.

Source: Adapted by the authors from *The Gallup Poll: Public Opinion 1980* (1985, 154-155).

Figure 7.2 Candidates' Public Images, 1984, Reagan and Mondale

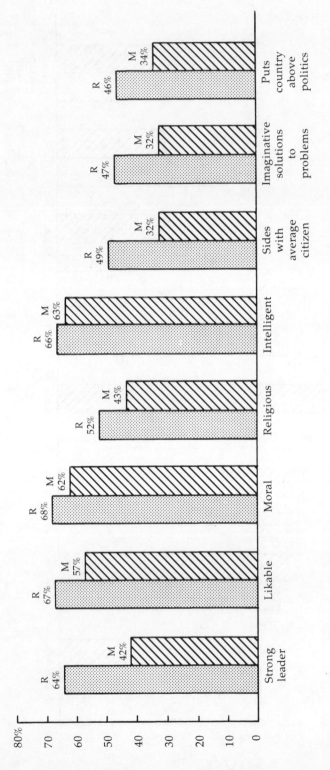

Note: Entries are percentage of respondents ascribing the characteristic to the candidate.

Source: Adapted by the authors from *The Gallup Poll: Public Opinion 1980* (1985, 149).

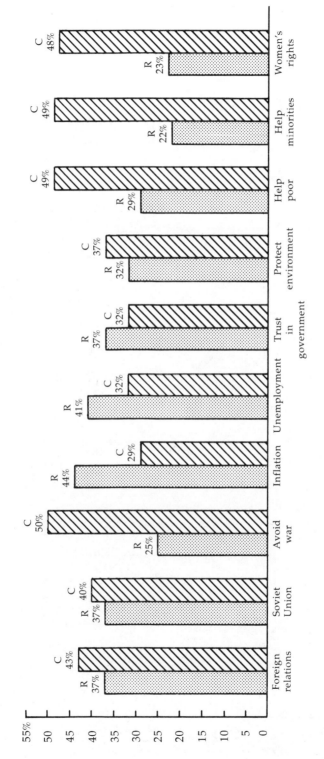

Figure 7.3 Candidates' Ability to Handle Problems, 1980, Reagan and Carter

Note: Entries are percentage of respondents who say the candidate is the person best able to handle the problem.

Source: Adapted by the authors from *The Gallup Opinion Index*, Report 181, September 1980, 19.

Figure 7.4 Candidates' Ability to Handle Problems, 1984, Reagan and Mondale

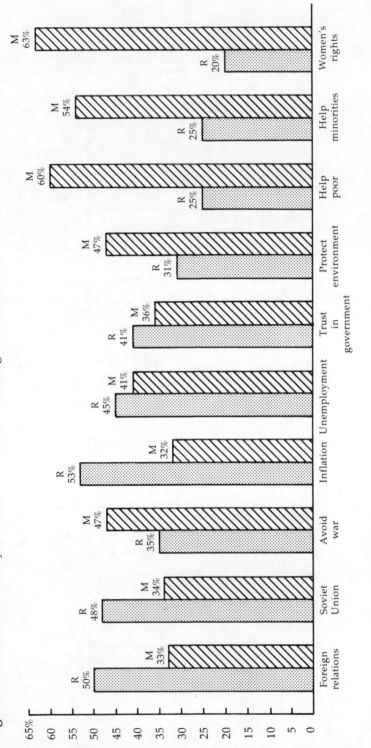

Note: Entries are percentage of respondents who say the candidate is the person best able to handle the problem.

Source: Adapted by the authors from *The Gallup Report,* Reports 227-228, August/September 1984, 17.

Figure 7.5 Presidential Campaign Promises, Kennedy to Reagan

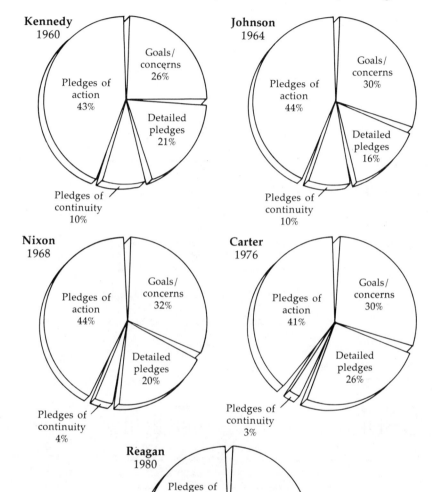

Note: Johnson and Nixon include foreign and domestic commitments; Kennedy, Carter, and Reagan involve domestic commitments only.

Source: Adapted by the authors from Fishel (1986).

Figure 7.6 Percentage of Presidential Campaign Promises Kept, Kennedy to Reagan

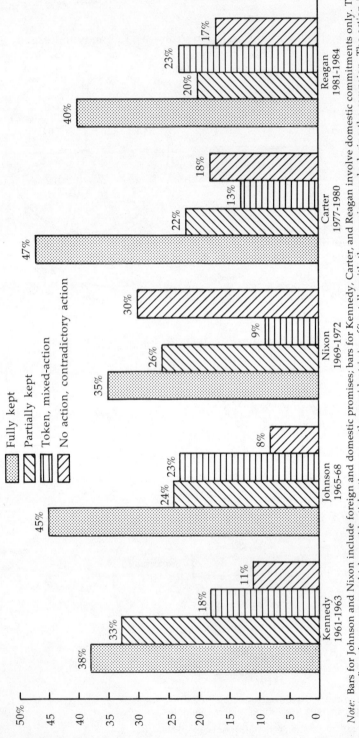

Note: Bars for Johnson and Nixon include foreign and domestic promises; bars for Kennedy, Carter, and Reagan involve domestic commitments only. The entries reflect the extent to which presidential actions once the president is in office tally with the promises made during the campaign. The action includes executive orders and proposed legislation.

Source: Adapted by the authors from Fishel (1986, 39).

Table 7.37 Faithless Electors

Year	Elector	State	Elected to vote for	Voted for
1796	Unknown	Pennsylvania	John Adams	Thomas Jefferson
1820	Unknown	New Hampshire	James Monroe	John Quincy Adams
1948	Preston Parks	Tennessee	Harry Truman	Strom Thurmond
1956	W. F. Turner	Alabama	Adlai Stevenson	Walter E. Jones
1960	Henry D. Irwin	Oklahoma	Richard Nixon	Harry F. Byrd
1968	Dr. Lloyd W. Bailey	North Carolina	Richard Nixon	George C. Wallace
1972	Roger L. McBride	Virginia	Richard Nixon	John Hospers
1976	Mike Padden	Washington	Gerald Ford	Ronald Reagan

Source: Adapted from *Congressional Quarterly's Guide to U.S. Elections* (1985).

Table 7.38 Splitting States' Electoral College Votes, 1836-1984

Year	State	Split electors[a]
1860	New Jersey	4 Republicans, 4 Douglas Democrats
1880	California	4 Democrats, 1 Republican
1892	California	8 Democrats, 1 Republican
1892	Michigan	9 Republicans, 1 Democrat[b]
1892	North Dakota	2 Fusionists, 1 Republican[c]
1892	Ohio	22 Republicans, 1 Democrat
1892	Oregon	3 Republicans, 1 Populist[d]
1896	California	8 Republicans, 1 Democrat
1896	Kentucky	12 Republicans, 1 Democrat
1904	Maryland	7 Democrats, 1 Republican
1908	Maryland	6 Democrats, 2 Republicans
1912	California	11 Progressives, 2 Democrats
1916	West Virginia	7 Republicans, 1 Democrat

[a] These electoral vote splits occurred because of close votes. Other cases have occurred because of the faithless elector problem (see Table 7.37).
[b] Split was due to a districting system.
[c] Fusionists were Democrats and Populists. The two Fusionists also split, one voting for Democrat Grover Cleveland and one for Populist James B. Weaver.
[d] The Populist won with Democratic support.

Source: Adapted from *Congressional Quarterly's Guide to U.S. Elections* (1985).

Table 7.39 Uncast Electoral Votes

Year	State	Explanation
1789	New York	Legislature failed to agree on electors
1864	Confederate states[a]	Civil War
1868	Mississippi	Not yet readmitted to the Union
1868	Texas	Not yet readmitted to the Union
1868	Virginia	Not yet readmitted to the Union
1872	Arkansas	Vote rejected by Congress
1872	Louisiana	Vote rejected by Congress

[a] Confederate states included Alabama, Arkansas, Florida, Georgia, Louisiana, Mississippi, North Carolina, South Carolina, Tennessee, Texas, and Virginia.

Source: Adapted from *Congressional Quarterly's Guide to U.S. Elections* (1985).

Table 7.40 Early Methods of Selecting Presidential Electors

State	1788–1789	1792	1796	1800	1804	1808	1812	1816	1820	1824	1828	1832	1836
New Hampshire	T,L[a]	T[b]	T,L[a]	L	T	T	T	T	T	T	T	T	T
Massachusetts	D8,L[f]	D4,L[e]	D14,L[d]	L	D17,A2	L	D6[c]	L	D13,A2	T	T	T	T
Connecticut	L	L	L	L	L	L	L	L	T	T	T	T	T
New Jersey	L	L	L	L	T	T	L	T	T	T	T	T	T
Pennsylvania	T	T	T	L	T	T	T	T	T	T	T	T	T
Delaware	D3[h]	L	L	L	L	L	L	L	L	L	L	T	T
Maryland	T	T	D10	D10	D9[j]	D9[j]	D9[j]	D9[j]	D9[j]	D9[j]	D9[j]	D4[i]	T
Virginia	D12	D21	D21	T	T	T	T	T	T	T	T	T	T
South Carolina	L	L	L	L	L	L	L	L	L	L	L	L	L
Georgia	L	L	T	L	L	L	L	L	L	L	T	T	T
New York	—	L[k]	L	L	L	L	L	L	L	L	D30,E[g]	T	T
Vermont	—	L	L	L	L	L	L	L	L	L	T	T	T
North Carolina	—	L	D12	D12	D14	D14	T	T	T	T	T	T	T
Rhode Island	—	L	L	T	T	T	T	T	T	T	T	T	T
Kentucky	—	D4	D4	D4	D2[m]	D2	D3[m]	D3[m]	D3[m]	D3[l]	T	T	T
Tennessee	—	—	E[n]	E[n]	D5	D5	D8	D8	D8	D11	D11	T	T
Ohio	—	—	—	—	T	T	T	T	T	T	T	T	T
Louisiana	—	—	—	—	—	—	L	L	L	L	T	T	T
Indiana	—	—	—	—	—	—	—	L	L	T	T	T	T
Mississippi	—	—	—	—	—	—	—	—	T	T	T	T	T
Illinois	—	—	—	—	—	—	—	—	D3	D3	T	T	T
Alabama	—	—	—	—	—	—	—	—	L	T	T	T	T
Maine[o]	—	—	—	—	—	—	—	—	D7,A2	D7,A2	D7,A2	T	T
Missouri	—	—	—	—	—	—	—	—	—	D3	T	T	T
Arkansas	—	—	—	—	—	—	—	—	—	—	—	—	T
Michigan	—	—	—	—	—	—	—	—	—	—	—	—	T

(Notes follow)

Table 7.40 (continued)

Note: T = by people on general ticket. D = by people in districts. L = by legislature. A = by people at large. E = by electors.

[a] A majority of the popular vote was necessary for a vote choice. In case of a failure to elect, the legislature supplied the deficiency.

[b] A majority of votes was necessary for a choice. In case of a failure to elect one or more electors, a second election was held by the people, at which a choice was made from the candidates in the first election who had the most votes. The number of candidates in the second election was limited to twice the number of electors wanted.

[c] One district chose six electors; one, five electors; two, three electors each; and one, one elector.

[d] A majority of votes was necessary for a popular choice. Deficiencies were filled by the General Court, as in 1792. It also chose two electors at large. In 1796 it chose nine electors, and the people, seven.

[e] Two of the districts voted for five members each, and two for three members each. A majority of votes was necessary for a choice. In case of a failure to elect by popular vote, the General Court supplied the deficiency. In the election of 1792, the people chose five electors and the General Court, eleven.

[f] Each of the eight districts chose two electors, from which the General Court (that is, the legislature) selected one. It also elected two electors at large.

[g] One district elected three electors; two, two electors each; and twenty-seven, one elector each. The thirty-four electors thus elected chose two presidential electors.

[h] Each qualified voter voted for one elector. The three electors who received most votes in the state were elected.

[i] One district chose four electors; one, three electors; one, two electors; one, one elector.

[j] During the years 1804-1828, Maryland chose eleven electors in nine districts: two of the districts elected two members each.

[k] The state was divided into four districts, and the members of the legislature residing in each district chose three electors.

[l] Two districts chose five electors each, and one chose four electors.

[m] Each district elected four electors.

[n] In 1796 and 1800, Tennessee chose three presidential electors—one each for the districts of Washington, Hamilton, and Mero. Three "electors" for each county in the state were appointed by the legislature, and the "electors" residing in each of the three districts chose one of the three presidential electors.

[o] Maine is the only remaining state without a winner-take-all popular vote system. Since 1969, Maine has selected two of its electors by congressional districts and another two by the winner of the statewide vote total.

Source: Adapted and amended from U.S. Department of Commerce, *Historical Statistics* (1971, Y 1-47).

Table 7.41   Presidents without Majorities

Years	President	Percentage of the vote	Succeeded president [a]	Date
1825-1829	Adams [b]	30.5	—	—
1841-1845	Tyler	—	Harrison	April 4, 1841
1845-1849	Polk	49.6	—	—
1849-1850	Taylor	47.3	—	—
1850-1853	Fillmore	—	Taylor	July 9, 1850
1857-1861	Buchanan	45.3	—	—
1861-1865	Lincoln	39.8	—	—
1865-1869	Johnson	—	Lincoln	April 15, 1885
1877-1881	Hayes [b]	48.0	—	—
1881-1881	Garfield	48.3	—	—
1881-1885	Arthur	—	Garfield	September 19, 1881
1885-1889	Cleveland	48.5	—	—
1889-1893	Harrison [b]	47.9	—	—
1893-1897	Cleveland	46.0	—	—
1901-1905	Roosevelt	—	McKinley	September 14, 1901
1913-1917	Wilson	41.8	—	—
1917-1921	Wilson	49.3	—	—
1923-1925	Coolidge	—	Harding	August 2, 1923
1945-1949	Truman	—	Roosevelt	April 12, 1945
1949-1953	Truman	49.5	—	—
1961-1963	Kennedy	49.7	—	—
1963-1965	Johnson	—	Kennedy	November 22, 1963
1969-1973	Nixon	43.4	—	—
1974-1977	Ford	—	Nixon	August 14, 1974

[a] Presidents succeeded by other presidents after death or resignation.
[b] Presidents John Quincy Adams, Rutherford B. Hayes, and Benjamin Harrison received neither a majority nor a plurality. Candidates Jackson (with 43.1%), Tilden (with 51.0%), and Cleveland (with 48.66%) were the aggregate popular choices over Adams, Hayes, and Harrison, respectively.

Source: Adapted from *Congressional Quarterly's Guide to U.S. Elections* (1985).

Table 7.42 Instances of Presidents' Disabilities

President	Extent of disability
William Henry Harrison	Bedridden for 7 days before his death
Zachary Taylor	Bedridden for 5 days before his death
Abraham Lincoln	Unconscious for 9.5 hours before his death
James A. Garfield	Bedridden for 80 days before his death
William McKinley	Bedridden for 8 days before his death
Woodrow Wilson	Incapacitated for 280 days from his stroke until he resumed cabinet meetings
Warren G. Harding	Semi-invalid for 4 days before his death
Dwight D. Eisenhower	Incapacitated for 143 days from heart attack until announced recovery
Ronald Reagan	Incapacitated for 20 hours after the attempt on his life
Ronald Reagan	Incapacitated for 8 hours while under anesthesia during colon surgery

Source: Amended, updated, and expanded version of Hansen (1962, 1).

Table 7.43 Incomplete Terms of Vice Presidents

Vice president	Term	President at time
George Clinton	March 4, 1809-April 20, 1812 [a]	James Madison
Elbridge Gerry	March 4, 1813-November 23, 1814	James Madison
William R. King	March 4, 1853-April 18, 1853	Franklin Pierce
Henry Wilson	March 4, 1873-November 22, 1875	Ulysses S. Grant
Thomas A. Hendricks	March 4, 1885-November 25, 1885	Grover Cleveland
Garret A. Hobart	March 4, 1897-November 21, 1899	William McKinley
James S. Sherman	March 4, 1909-October 30, 1912	William H. Taft
Spiro T. Agnew	January 20, 1973-October 10, 1973	Richard M. Nixon

Note: This list does not include vice presidents who succeeded to the presidency.

[a] Second term.

Source: Adapted and updated from *CQ Guide to Current American Government* (1986, 72).

Table 7.44 Financing Presidential General Elections, 1860-1984
(current dollars)

Year	Republicans	Democrats
1860	100,000	50,000
1864	125,000	50,000
1868	150,000	75,000
1872	250,000	50,000
1876	950,000	900,000
1880	1,100,000	355,000
1884	1,300,000	1,400,000
1888	1,350,000	855,000
1892	1,700,000	2,350,000
1896	3,350,000	675,000
1900	3,000,000	425,000
1904	2,096,000	700,000
1908	1,665,518	629,341
1912 [a]	1,071,549	1,134,848
1916	2,441,565	2,284,590
1920	5,417,501	1,470,371
1924 [b]	4,020,478	1,108,836
1928	6,256,111	5,342,350
1932	2,900,052	2,245,975
1936	8,892,972	5,194,741
1940	3,451,310	2,783,654
1944	2,828,652	2,169,077
1948 [c]	2,127,296	2,736,334
1952	6,608,623	5,032,926
1956	7,778,702	5,106,651
1960	10,128,000	9,797,000
1964	16,026,000	8,757,000
1968 [d]	25,402,000	11,594,000
1972	37,624,278	13,041,661
1976	21,820,000	21,820,000
1980	29,400,000	29,400,000
1984	40,400,000	40,400,000

Note: Beginning in 1976, the major parties' presidential election campaigns were financed by the federal government. The parties' expenditures were also limited.

[a] Progressive party, with T. Roosevelt as candidate, spent $665,420.

[b] Progressive party, with R. M. LaFollette as candidate, spent $236,963.

[c] Progressive party, with Henry Wallace as candidate, spent $1,133,863; States' Rights, with Strom Thurmond as candidate, spent $163,442.

[d] American Independent party, with George Wallace as candidate, spent $7,223,000.

Sources: Adapted and updated from U.S. Department of Commerce, *Historical Statistics* (1971, Y 187-188); and *Congressional Quarterly Weekly Report*, July 31, 1976, 2036; August 4, 1984, 1924. See Table 7.49 for expenditures of minor candidates.

Table 7.45   Public Financing of Presidential Campaigns, 1976-1984

Year	COLA[a] (%)	Primary election limit[b] ($ millions)	General election limit ($ millions)	Party convention limit ($ millions)
1976	9.1	10.9	21.8	2.2
1980	47.2	14.7	29.4	4.4
1984	102.0	20.2	40.4	8.1

[a] COLA = Cost-of-living adjustment; calculated by the Department of Labor using 1974 as the base year.

[b] Primary candidates receiving matching funds must comply with two types of spending limits: a national limit (listed in the above table) and a separate limit for each state. The state limit is $200,000 or sixteen cents multiplied by the state's voting age population, whichever is greater. (Both amounts are adjusted for increases in the cost of living.) The maximum amount of primary matching funds a candidate may receive is half of the national spending limit.

Source: U.S. Federal Election Commission (1985a, 8).

Table 7.46   National Party Spending Limit for the Nominee, 1976-1984

Year	VAP (millions)	COLA (%)	General election limit[a] ($ millions)
1976	146.8	9.1	3.2
1980	157.5	47.2	4.6
1984	171.4	102.0	6.9

Note: VAP = voting age population of United States. COLA = cost-of-living adjustment.

[a] Limit applies to expenditures made by the national committee of a political party on behalf of its nominee in the general election, regardless of whether the nominee receives public funding. The expenditures are sometimes called "coordinated party expenditures" or "441a(d) expenditures." They are not considered contributions and do not count against a publicly funded candidate's expenditure limit. The general election limit is calculated as two cents times the VAP and adjusted by the COLA.

Source: U.S. Federal Election Commission (1985a, 9).

Table 7.47 Public Funding Certifications in Presidential Elections ($ millions)

Recipient	1976	1980	1984
Primary candidates [a]	24.8	31.3	36.5
Party convention committees	4.1	8.8	16.2
General election candidates	43.6	63.1 [b]	80.8
Total	72.5	103.2	133.5

[a] There were fifteen primary matching fund recipients in 1976, ten in 1980, and eleven in 1984.
[b] Three nominees received public funding in 1980—the two major party nominees and John Anderson, who qualified as a third-party candidate eligible to receive partial public funding.

Source: U.S. Federal Election Commission (1986).

Table 7.48 1984 Primary Matching Funds (dollars)

Candidate	Matching funds requested	Donors of matchable contributions	Matching funds certified [a]
Reubin Askew	986,655	6,013	975,901
Alan Cranston	2,157,879	40,647	2,113,736
John Glenn	3,347,866	34,987	3,325,383
Gary Hart	5,546,708	123,380	5,328,467
Ernest Hollings	833,735	6,486	821,600
Jesse Jackson	3,128,176	87,144	3,053,185
Sonia Johnson	197,022	5,672	193,735
Lyndon LaRouche	501,215	5,297	494,146
George McGovern	634,829	17,314	612,735
Walter Mondale	9,819,910	203,772	9,494,921
Ronald Reagan	10,421,010	255,465	10,100,000
Total	37,575,006	786,177	36,513,809

[a] If matching fund requests contained the proper documentation, they were certified. The difference between "matching funds requested" and "matching funds certified" is the amount that was not matched because of the lack of proper documentation.

Source: U.S. Federal Election Commission (1985a, 6).

Table 7.49   Minor Party Presidential Campaign Expenditures,
1908-1984

Year	Minor party	Minor party expenditures (dollars)	Average of major party expenditures (dollars)	Minor party expenditures as percentage of major party expenditures
1908	Socialist	95,504	1,147,430	8.3
1912	Progressive	665,420	1,103,199	60.3
	Socialist	71,598		6.5
1924	Progressive	236,963	2,564,659	9.2
1948	Progressive	1,133,863	2,431,815	46.6
	States' Rights	163,442		6.7
1952	Socialist Labor	88,018	5,820,775	1.5
1956	Socialist Labor	22,727	6,442,677	0.4
1960	Socialist Labor	66,170	9,962,500	0.7
	National States' Rights	4,269		a
1964	Socialist Labor	59,344	12,391,500	0.5
	National States' Rights	41,964		0.3
	Socialist Workers	2,570		a
1968	American Independent	7,223,000	18,498,000	39.0
	National States' Rights	24,727		a
	Socialist Labor	80,130		a
	Socialist Workers	40,481		a
1972	American Independent	710,000	41,289,000	1.7
	Communist	173,600		0.4
	Socialist Workers	118,000		0.3
	Socialist Labor	114,000		0.3
	Christian National Crusade	93,000		0.2
	People's	40,539		0.1
	Prohibition	37,000		0.1
	Libertarian	17,000		a
	Conservative	6,000		a
	Flying Tigers	977		a
1976	Communist	504,710	21,973,856	2.3
	Eugene McCarthy	442,491		2.0
	Libertarian	387,429		1.8
	American	187,815		0.9
	U.S. Labor	180,653		0.8
	Socialist Workers	151,648		0.7
	Socialist Labor	59,820		0.3
	American Independent	44,488		0.2
1980	John B. Anderson	15,040,669	29,040,183	51.7
	Libertarian	3,210,758		11.1
	Communist	194,774		0.07
	Socialist Workers	186,252		0.6
	Right to Life	83,412		0.3

Table 7.49   (continued)

Year	Minor party	Minor party expenditures (dollars)	Average of major party expenditures (dollars)	Minor party expenditures as percentage of major party expenditures
1980 (continued)				
	Workers' World	40,310		0.1
	Socialist	36,059		0.1
	Citizens	23,408		0.1
	American Independent	13,931		a
	American	13,716		a
	Statesman	812		a
1984	Libertarian	635,918	40,400,000	0.02
	Independent	6,895,896		0.17
	Citizens	441,681		0.01
	Populist	231,868		0.01
	Independent Alliance	190,146		a
	Communist	310,728		0.01
	Socialist Workers	171,976		a
	Workers World	14,254		a
	American	16,080		a
	Workers League	0		a
	Prohibition	0		a
	National Unity Party of Kentucky	621,809		0.02
	Big Deal	0		a
	United Sovereign Citizens	0		a

[a]Less than 0.1 percent.

Sources: U.S. Department of Commerce, *Historical Statistics* (1971, 1081); Heard (1960, 54); Alexander (1962, 1966, 1971, 1976, 1979); the 1980 statistics are provided by the Federal Election Commission, reprinted in Rosenstone, Behr, and Lazarus (1984), updated to 1984 with data from the Federal Election Commission.

Table 7.50 Compensating the President

Category	Dates	Amount (dollars)	Description
Salary	Before 1949	75,000	
	1949-68	100,000	
	since 1969	200,000	
Expense account	Before 1951	50,000	Tax-free expense account, with no record-keeping requirement
	Since 1951	50,000	Taxable expense account
Travel expenses	Before 1978	40,000	"To be expended in the discretion of the President and accounted for on his certificate solely" (U.S. Code, 347)
	Since 1978	100,000	
Miscellaneous	Since 1978	1,000,000	Fund; "in his discretion, to meet unanticipated needs for the furtherance of the national interest, security, or defense, including personnel needs and needs for services" (U.S. Code, 352)

Source: Created by the authors from information in the *U.S. Code.*

Table 7.51   The Cost to Taxpayers of Former Presidents,
1955-1987 (current dollars)

Year	Libraries	Office allowances	Secret Service protection	Total
1955	63,745	—	—	63,745
1956	64,853	—	—	64,853
1957	74,836	—	—	74,836
1958	142,536	—	—	142,536
1959	168,057	160,000	—	328,057
1960	180,140	200,000	—	380,140
1961	219,223	250,000	—	469,223
1962	294,297	300,000	—	594,297
1963	325,520	310,000	—	635,520
1964	380,251	300,000	49,507	729,758
1965	559,485	310,000	100,790	970,275
1966	611,966	235,000	289,022	1,135,988
1967	613,745	235,000	346,633	1,195,378
1968	676,000 312,000 [a]	251,000	390,298	1,629,298
1969	1,406,808 1,074,000 [b]	253,000	527,552	3,261,360
1970	1,980,855	335,000	727,617	3,043,472
1971	2,252,289 1,610,000 [c]	343,000	1,002,355	5,207,644
1972	2,513,559 882,000 [d]	418,000	1,275,120	5,088,679
1973	2,722,116	408,000	1,241,117	4,371,233
1974	2,863,457	60,000	979,789	3,903,246
1975	4,542,447	160,000	1,530,144	6,232,591
1976	6,409,380	364,168	2,294,887	9,698,435
1977	6,297,611	390,000	4,679,489	11,367,100
1978	7,230,486	671,000	6,252,190	14,153,676
1979	7,523,783 2,667,000 [e]	771,000	7,187,582	18,149,365
1980	10,171,000	740,394	7,563,432	18,474,826
1981	12,295,000	718,325	9,741,663	22,754,958
1982	11,532,000	1,025,000	11,750,238	23,384,738
1983	12,972,000	1,029,000	10,941,419	24,942,419
1984	14,350,000	1,068,000	10,741,124	26,159,124
1985	14,636,000	1,151,000	11,416,329	27,203,329
1986 [f]	14,612,000	1,100,000	9,387,497	25,099,497
1987 [f]	16,202,000	1,234,000	9,843,965	27,279,965

[a] Truman Library addition.
[b] Hoover Library addition.
[c] Eisenhower Library addition.
[d] Roosevelt Library addition.
[e] Truman Library addition.
[f] Estimated.

Sources: Adapted and amended from information provided by the General Services Administration, the Office of Presidential Libraries, and the office of Sen. Lawton Chiles (D-Fla.); reprinted in *Congressional Quarterly Weekly Report,* April 5, 1986, 771.

Table 7.52 Effects of Midterm Elections on the House

		Incumbents lost by		Open seats lost by	
Year	President	Dem.	Rep.	Dem.	Rep.
1954	Rep.	3	18	2	3
1956	Rep.	7	7	2	4
1958	Rep.	1	35	0	14
1960	Rep.	23	2	6	6
1962	Dem.	9	5	2	3
1964	Dem.	5	39	5	8
1966	Dem.	39	1	4	3
1968	Dem.	5	0	2	4
1970	Rep.	2	9	6	8
1972	Rep.	6	3	9	5
1974	Rep.	4	36	2	13
1976	Rep.	7	5	3	7
1978	Dem.	14	5	8	6
1980	Dem.	27	3	10	1
1982	Rep.	1	22	4	6
1984	Rep.	13	3	5	1
1986	Rep.	1	6	7	8

Note: Midterm elections appear in italics.

Source: National Journal, November 8, 1986, 2677.

Table 7.53 Effects of Midterm Elections on the Senate

		Incumbents lost by		Open seats lost by	
Year	President	Dem.	Rep.	Dem.	Rep.
1954	Rep.	2	4	1	1
1956	Rep.	1	3	3	1
1958	Rep.	0	11	0	2
1960	Rep.	1	0	1	0
1962	Dem.	2	3	0	3
1964	Dem.	1	3	0	0
1966	Dem.	1	0	2	0
1968	Dem.	4	0	3	2
1970	Rep.	3	2	1	0
1972	Rep.	1	4	3	2
1974	Rep.	0	2	1	3
1976	Rep.	5	4	2	3
1978	Dem.	5	2	3	3
1980	Dem.	9	0	3	0
1982	Rep.	1	1	1	1
1984	Rep.	1	2	0	1
1986	Rep.	0	7	1	2

Note: Midterm elections appear in italics.

Source: National Journal, November 8, 1986, 2677.

8

Toward a New Agenda for Research on the Presidency

We have sought to make two major points in this book, one methodological and the other theoretical. We intend both to fundamentally change the way in which the American presidency is studied and analyzed.

First, we believe that research into the presidency should be conducted in a more rigorous, systematic, and, when possible, quantitative manner. More detailed and anecdotal information exists on presidents and the presidency than on any other person or office in history. This material is of tremendous popular interest and, together with more systematic data, has served as evidence for an enormous number of trenchant books and articles (for example, see Corwin 1957; Koenig 1986; Rossiter 1960; Neustadt 1980; Barber 1980). Worthwhile data on the presidency are emerging, covering a long period of time and making comparisons across presidents more precise and generalizations about the institution more clear-cut. In addition, systematic data on the presidency are increasingly being analyzed with more sophisticated and vigorous methodologies. We hope that the nascent quantitative study of the presidency can build on the well-developed tradition of classical scholarship and can use this wealth of existing data.

Second, we want to alter the subject of analysis. We believe that more emphasis should fall on the presidency as an institution. We defined this institution quite broadly, encompassing not just the set of public laws and the White House organizational structures but also standard operating procedures, predictable patterns of behavior, basic role orientations, and guiding rules of interaction. Our definition even embraces patterns that presidents themselves, as actors within the institution, might not recognize but that are decipherable during their terms and from their policy efforts and outputs. For the analyst, discovering such patterns is a critical part of systematic description and scientific explanation.

We have shown that the institutional presidency is neither monolithic nor unified. As Alfred de Grazia wrote, "The President is a Congress with a skin thrown over him. . . . [He] operates under all the fictions of a single person . . . , [but this] defies the truth of the normalcy of the typical President and the collectivity of his behavior" (1969, 51-52). The more powers presidents have been given through legislation and have taken through their own initiatives, the less presidents can do personally. The more entrenched the stewardship role of presidents becomes—the role that portrays them as doing all they can in the best interest of the nation—the larger and more complex the presidency must grow to handle the tasks. Consequently, contemporary presidents choose among various possible ways of acting, at least some of which may be inconsistent across the many policy areas upon which they impinge. As we saw at the end of Chapter 3, the positions taken by presidents on congressional legislation show patterns that contrast with those exhibited by executive orders promulgated by presidents. For these and other activities, including international agreements and national speech making, we have found variety across policy areas, with foreign policy distinct from domestic policy, and even with some types of foreign policy differing from others.

We have also found that the strategies of individual presidents increase the complexity of the picture. Presidents establish their own precedents in different policy fields and across types of actions. In so doing, however, they also enlarge the institution of the presidency and set new institutional standards for their successors. For example, President Harry S Truman's efforts to fashion a legislative program enlarged demands on the executive office to monitor the various proposals both separately and as a package and put pressure on Truman's successors to follow suit.

These two general points about what we study and the way we study it deserve further clarification.

The Methodology of Presidential Research

Presidential research is at a stage analogous to that at which the discipline of economics found itself in the 1950s and the study of the U.S. Congress found itself in the 1960s. Anecdotes and unsystematic information abound. The key questions of measurement and systematic description have not been answered, and explanation has been attempted with only uneven success.

General theories of the presidency are far too often explicitly or implicitly tied to the current incumbent. Studies of presidential power in particular have erred by emphasizing an impressive office (under Roosevelt), an imperial presidency (during the Nixon and Johnson administrations), and an imperiled executive (for Ford and Carter), depending primarily on the incumbent chief executive. If the presidency does indeed have a general aspect that transcends the person, this approach must change. We believe that systematic description and explanation will facilitate systematic analysis and will lead toward more general theorizing.

As recently as 1973 John Mueller wrote that regression analysis was used "sparingly in political science" (97). Things have obviously changed in many fields of the discipline, particularly in American politics. However, many areas of presidency research stand out more generally as an exception. In large part, the general paucity of systematic studies may reflect the common misperception that, because only one person is president at a time, statistical analyses are not possible. We have shown that this "$N = 1$ problem," as it is sometimes called, is due to theoretical emphasis, not data availability. We no longer need, for example, to rely only on comparisons of successive presidents to understand how the institution of the presidency operates. An institutional approach continues to treat the behavior of individual presidents as important but defines it within the context of more meaningful institutional patterns. Once we refocus theoretical attention on the plural presidency, the $N = 1$ problem vanishes, and a wealth of meaningful data appears.

The Plural Presidency and the Individual President

At least four general patterns exist in the American presidency. First, in some instances, the institution provides continuity between administrations and remains constant in important respects. Second, at other times, presidents display general similarities that transcend their specific differences. Third, the institution offers individual officeholders the opportunity to take unique actions that may not be perpetuated by any successive incumbents. Finally, some of the most striking patterns stem from exogenous events in the national and international environment. These patterns illuminate the office and its occupants generally and help us view their individual qualities in context.

Institutionalized Continuity

The transition between administrations provides one of the strongest tests for the first set of institutional patterns. How can the presidency truly exist as an ongoing institution when, on January 20 following the election of a new president, virtually every important White House office changes occupants? The turnover remains largely the same, whether or not the successive executives belong to different political parties, and it inevitably exerts dramatic effects on the presidency. A new chief establishes a new direction.

Still, the compositions and outlook of current presidential parties reflect past campaigns and past administrations and thereby provide some continuity. In addition, as broad new themes shape specific relationships among (new) individuals in (old) organizations, many arrangements and procedures persist from previous administrations. This process produces many of the shared features emphasized earlier. When one individual incumbent replaces another, the newcomer may well perpetuate established practices out of a need to respond quickly in a context of limited information and expertise. Even presidents who innovate are often reacting against a predecessor of the opposition party. President Kennedy, for example, adopted a more collegial National Security Council system in direct response to the hierarchy associated with Eisenhower's. Nixon later explicitly reinstituted Eisenhower's approach.

The executive apparatus shows even more systematic continuity. Although members of the White House staff change with some frequency, the broader institution of the presidency is hardly recreated each time a new administration enters office. Many, if not all, top staff people change during a transition, but the career staff stay, especially those at the Office of Management and Budget. The State Department often processes executive agreements after one president has left office and the other has just come on board.

As an example, on January 6, 1977, the International Trade Commission recommended to President Ford that tariffs be placed on shoes imported from abroad. Ford decided not to act on the matter but instead left it to his successor. The day after Jimmy Carter took office, he received a memo from the National Security Council on shoe import quotas. On February 4, the Office of the United States Trade Representative—a unit within the Executive Office of the president charged with advising presidents on trade—also provided Carter with a background memo. In both instances, the National Security Council and the Office of the United States Trade Representative were acting on material inherited from the Ford administration (see DiClerico 1985, 248-249). This item on the national policy agenda continued to be addressed, regardless of who was president and indeed regardless of whether there was a president.

Such coherence and continuity, moreover, are not simply functions of the established units within the large Executive Office of the President but also reflect institutional forms of behavior. National speech making by presidents, for example, varies little across incumbents because presidents need to use vivid public appearances in order to maximize the political support gained from them. Because of the fairly stable pattern of speech making established by the presidents since 1949, we can venture a prediction that President Reagan's successor will deliver roughly five major prime-time addresses annually during his term.

Noninstitutionalized Similarities and Differences

General patterns take on recognizable forms in different administrations, but individual incumbents give these patterns slightly different characters. Public opinion is a case in point. Although certain similarities are evident for all modern presidents—for example, public support for the president tends to begin high and erode steadily—interesting differences remain. For example, public approval in Ronald Reagan's case started out lower than usual, and, although it too fell, it did so at a much slower rate. To take another example, executive agreements have been signed with the Soviet Union infrequently by all presidents since Truman, but, as we saw in Chapter 3, Nixon entered into somewhat more agreements than the other presidents, especially in his second term, because of his efforts at détente.

President-Specific Patterns

In a third set of patterns, our data reveal exclusively president-specific dynamics. For most of the history of recorded public opinion, for example, the majority of socioeconomic and political groups differed only moderately in their approval of any incumbent president. However, the pattern changed dramatically in 1981. Under Reagan, most population groups are (and have remained) more polarized than at any other time. An astute observer might have been able to forecast this tendency before Reagan's first term, but the data on public approval of previous presidents could not have helped in the forecast. A full understanding of this complex, plural institution thus requires a detailed understanding of the successive individual presidents as well as of the institution.

The Institution, the Individual, and the Environment

The overall environment also plays an important role (see Rockman 1984). Some of the most striking patterns in the presidency derive from the way national politics depends on exogenous events, such as wars or international economic conditions. These events are not wholly or even principally under presidents' control, although they are sometimes mistakenly assumed to be so. Herbert Hoover made this point when he said, "Once upon a time my political opponents honored me as possessing the fabulous intellectual and economic power by which I created a world-wide depression all by myself." Sharing Hoover's sentiments, William Howard Taft observed,

> There is a class of people that . . . visit the President with responsibility for everything that is done and that is not done. If poverty prevails where, in their judgement, it should not prevail, then the President is responsible. If other people are richer than they ought to be, the President is responsible. While the President's powers are broad, he cannot do everything. . . . This would be ludicrous if it did not sometimes take serious results. The President cannot make clouds to rain, he cannot make the corn to grow, he cannot make business to be good. (1916, 47-50)

Whether or not presidents are falsely credited with or blamed for the effects of dynamics beyond their control, these powerful environmental patterns are undeniable.

One area of the growing quantitative literature, on "presidential greatness," takes a perspective that sharply contrasts with the last category of patterns in the presidency. In this approach, presidents are evaluated and compared on the basis of their accomplishments in office. Scholars then compare individual presidents and rate their overall "greatness." The central assumption upon which the approach rests is that the qualities and abilities associated with certain presidents set them apart from other presidents. This line of inquiry might be viewed as suggesting a possible objection to our emphasis on the institutional aspects of the plural presidency. If the person determines the success of the presidency, after all, then perhaps it might be argued that we should focus exclusively on the individual rather than our emphasis on the institution.

The evidence seems to indicate that presidents are judged "great" because of factors that have little to do with the individual's qualifications. Demonstrating this point in the format of a public lecture is usually easiest: the speaker walks into a crowded lecture hall and writes on a blackboard from left to right: "Great," "Near Great," "Average," "Below Average," and "Failure." Together, the audience and the speaker place past presidents in what they believe to be the appropriate categories. The only rule governing the discussion is that no one is permitted to give a reason for his or her choice. Decisions are made by taking a vote when necessary. In our experience, the result is virtually always the same. Washington, Lincoln, Franklin Roosevelt, and Kennedy fall in the "Great" category, and Nixon, Hoover, and sometimes Carter land in the "Failure" category. Wilson, Theodore Roosevelt, Jefferson, and Jackson usually appear in the "Near Great" category. These results are similar to those of the surveys taken of historians by Schlesinger (1949, 1962), Maranell (1970), and Murray and Blessing (1983). (See Table 8.1 for standardized versions of these and other ratings; Tables 8.2 and 8.3 report on the general public's more specific comparisons of recent presidents. Tables 8.4 through 8.7 provide lists of objective differences among the presidents and presidencies.)

The audience next considers what the presidents in the "Great" category have in common and eventually realizes that presidents who happened to die in office (particularly if they were assassinated) or who were in office during a major war or international crisis are much more likely to be considered "Great." Those in the "Failure" category have either scandal (Nixon) or economic problems (Hoover and Carter) to blame (see Simonton 1986). We therefore conclude that whereas presidents may be perceived as great because of their character, integrity, honesty, family background, personality, ability, or qualification, the circumstances surrounding their administrations have a significant influence on these perceptions. Shakespeare once wrote: "Some men are born great, some achieve greatness and some have greatness thrust upon 'em." If he had been writing about American presidents, he might have omitted his first two categories.

Thus patterns in the presidency may emerge that are the result of institutional constraints, noninstitutional continuities, and differences across the various presidents; they may also be due to external environmental factors beyond presidents' immediate control. Some more modest patterns may even result from the characteristics and decisions of individual presidents. In all cases, scholars should focus on these patterns rather than on idiosyncratic anecdotes and unsystematic observations.

Conclusion

Americans electing a president in 1988 will spend some $40 million, just during the general election campaign period, for the most expensive executive election in the world. They will spend hours watching the campaign unfold on the television news, in commercials, and in televised debates. Weekly they will hear of the latest polls reporting who is ahead. They will watch as the final vote results are announced on election night with great drama and celebration and will endure analyses the next day explaining why the victor won. The newly elected president will speak to the country on inauguration day as the omnipotent and benevolent champion of the people. Yet while the country is engrossed in this ritual exchange of power and is captivated by the image of a single executive boldly proclaiming the vision for a new generation, the institution of the presidency persists in ways that the country and even the new president know little about. De Grazia writes:

> In part the President is an office, the presidency, whose head knows what is going on in government and has something to say about it. Secondly, the President is an office whose head knows what is going on but has nothing to say about it. Thirdly, the President is an office whose head does not know what is going on and has nothing to say about it. There is a little of the first in the presidency, a good deal of the second, and a great amount of the third. (1969, 53)

One might ask of the presidency, "How could the institution be plural and still be defined as an institution? Isn't the notion of a plural institution a contradiction in terms?" Yet observers of other institutions, like the U.S. Congress and the bureaucracy, are accustomed to regarding institutions as collective bodies in which mixed signals are common; policy areas are handled by specialists; diverse groups make unequivocal demands that, when taken together, elicit disparate responses; and the policy environment is sufficiently complex that worries of institutional paralysis abound.

The presidency, like these other institutions, is a collective body. It faces the same challenges of coordination, needs for specialization, demands from groups, and environmental strains. By viewing the presidency as a collective, fragmented, segmented, and plural body, scholars can identify systematic patterns and provide a better understanding of presidents and the office they hold.

Table 8.1 Assessments of Former Presidents

President	Schlesinger [a]		Maranell [b]										Murray-Blessing [c]			
	1948	1962	B	R	SO	PR	ST	ACT	ID	F	ACC	IN	PO	CH	RA	CO
Washington	1.53	1.54	1.65	1.22	0.60	1.78	0.89	0.44	-0.41	0.57	1.72	0.86	1.57	1.57	1.87	-1.38
J. Adams	0.70	0.66	-0.55	0.50	0.60	0.61	0.41	0.34	-0.20	-0.85	0.37	0.26	0.81	0.33	0.59	0.31
Jefferson	1.17	1.21	1.21	1.22	1.44	1.47	1.18	0.91	0.81	1.35	1.31	1.11	1.38	1.28	1.52	0.11
Madison	0.12	0.44	-0.66	-0.93	-0.23	0.23	0.05	0.03	0.55	0.58	0.10	0.02	0.52	0.14	0.23	0.52
Monroe	0.35	-0.22	0.88	-0.93	-0.23	0.17	-0.02	-0.06	0.40	1.03	0.13	-0.31	0.14	0.24	0.19	-0.57
J.Q. Adams	0.47	0.33	-1.54	-0.22	-0.23	0.16	-0.22	0.01	1.18	-1.15	-0.24	-0.14	.05	-0.05	0.13	1.19
Jackson	1.06	1.10	0.99	1.22	1.44	0.87	1.37	1.51	-0.74	-1.40	0.83	1.08	1.09	1.09	1.02	1.33
Van Buren	0.00	-0.11	0.55	-0.22	-0.23	-0.37	-0.34	-0.24	-0.47	0.19	-0.46	-0.56	-0.05	0.05	-0.32	-0.84
W. Harrison	—	—	—	—	—	—	—	—	—	—	—	—	—	—	—	—
Tyler	-0.82	-0.99	-0.22	-0.23	-0.78	-0.72	-0.56	0.09	-1.09	-0.80	-1.29	-0.90	-0.90	-0.83	-0.36	0.99
Polk	0.59	0.88	-0.11	0.50	0.60	0.30	0.55	0.59	-1.44	-0.19	0.50	-0.26	0.90	0.81	0.42	-0.70
Taylor	-1.17	-0.88	-0.77	—	-1.07	-0.96	-0.72	-0.86	0.01	-0.76	-0.99	-1.38	-0.81	-0.71	-0.70	-0.36
Fillmore	-1.06	-1.10	-0.33	-0.93	-1.07	-1.19	-1.22	-1.22	0.36	0.27	-1.14	-1.72	-1.00	-1.19	-0.86	-0.77
Pierce	-1.41	-1.32	-1.10	-1.65	-1.07	-1.29	-1.33	-1.29	-0.17	0.16	-1.25	-1.73	-1.38	-1.38	-1.11	-0.23
Buchanan	-1.29	-1.43	-1.21	-1.65	-1.07	-1.28	-1.19	-1.26	-0.02	0.01	-1.14	-0.98	-1.57	-1.47	-1.27	-2.40
Lincoln	1.64	1.65	1.54	1.22	1.44	2.10	1.74	0.93	-0.61	1.50	2.07	1.42	1.66	1.66	1.99	1.12
A. Johnson	-0.47	-0.77	-1.65	0.50	-0.23	-0.30	-0.40	0.12	0.66	-2.18	-0.40	0.03	-1.19	-1.09	-1.23	0.11
Grant	-1.53	-1.54	-0.88	-1.65	-1.90	-1.50	-1.36	-1.37	-0.55	0.59	-1.38	-0.05	-1.28	-1.28	-1.35	-1.04
Hayes	0.23	0.22	0.77	0.50	-0.23	0.59	-0.69	-0.74	-0.29	0.14	-0.64	-1.06	-0.14	-0.33	-0.38	
Garfield	—	—	—	—	—	—	—	—	—	—	—	—	—	—	—	—
Arthur	-0.23	-0.55	0.22	-0.23	-0.52	-0.68	-0.69	-0.45	0.18	-0.52	-1.32	-0.52	-0.52	-0.53	-0.57	0.18
Cleveland	0.82	0.55	0.11	0.50	0.60	0.25	0.18	0.20	0.08	-0.88	0.11	-0.29	0.33	0.52	0.12	-1.04
B. Harrison	-0.70	-0.44	-0.44	-0.93	-1.07	-0.89	-0.97	-0.95	-0.33	0.19	-0.86	-1.52	-0.62	-0.62	-0.66	-0.50
McKinley	-0.35	0.11	0.66	-0.22	-0.23	-0.39	-0.30	-0.34	-0.25	0.49	-0.21	-0.33	0.24	0.71	-0.16	-0.36
T. Roosevelt	0.94	0.99	1.32	1.22	1.44	1.18	1.36	1.61	-0.57	0.19	1.26	1.20	1.28	1.38	1.34	-0.50
Taft	-0.12	0.00	0.00	-0.22	-0.23	-0.05	-0.17	-0.16	-0.04	0.01	-0.01	0.09	-0.24	-0.14	-0.23	

(Table continues)

Table 8.1 (continued)

President	Schlesinger [a]					Maranell [b]							Murray-Blessing [c]			
	1948	1962	B	R	SO	PR	ST	ACT	ID	F	ACC	IN	PO	CH	RA	CO
Wilson	1.29	1.32	1.10	1.22	1.44	1.01	1.35	1.05	4.23	-2.23	1.11	1.42	1.19	1.19	1.22	0.99
Harding	-1.64	-1.65	-1.43	-1.65	-1.90	-1.84	-1.66	-1.66	-0.81	1.71	-1.61	-0.15	-1.66	-1.66	-1.60	-0.64
Coolidge	-0.94	-1.21	-0.99	-0.93	-1.07	-0.99	-1.17	-1.37	-1.41	-0.83	-1.20	-0.37	-1.09	-1.00	-0.87	-0.43
Hoover	-0.59	-0.33	-1.32	-0.22	-0.23	-0.09	-0.23	-0.14	1.00	-1.01	-0.29	0.24	-0.33	-0.24	-0.36	1.53
F. Roosevelt	1.41	1.43	1.43	1.22	1.44	1.57	1.98	2.06	-0.62	1.31	1.91	1.52	1.47	1.47	1.91	-1.65
Truman	—	0.77	0.44	1.22	0.60	0.94	1.06	1.25	-0.44	0.31	1.12	1.08	1.00	1.00	0.92	1.06
Eisenhower	—	-0.66	0.33	0.50	-0.23	-0.29	-0.43	-0.59	0.13	1.21	-0.32	0.82	0.62	0.90	0.48	0.24
Kennedy	—	—	—	—	1.44	0.63	0.68	1.06	1.14	1.61	0.36	1.18	0.43	0.43	0.36	0.58
L. Johnson	—	—	—	—	—	0.06	1.00	1.39	-1.01	-0.47	0.53	1.12	0.71	0.62	0.58	1.60
Nixon	—	—	—	—	—	—	—	—	—	—	—	—	-1.47	-1.57	-1.30	2.00
Ford	—	—	—	—	—	—	—	—	—	—	—	—	-0.71	-0.43	-0.60	-0.50
Carter	—	—	—	—	—	—	—	—	—	—	—	—	-0.43	-0.81	-0.63	0.99

Note: B = Bailey. R = Rossiter. SO = Sokolsky. PR = Prestige. ST = strength. ACT = activeness. ID = idealism. F = flexibility. ACC = accomplishments. IN = information. PO = Porter's unpublished rating, reported by Murray-Blessing. CH = *Chicago Tribune*, reported in Murray-Blessing. RA = Murray-Blessing rating. CO = rating the degree to which presidents were controversial. For comparability cross-studies and measures, each is standardized (by subtracting out its mean and dividing by its standard deviation). Thus "a positive score [for an incumbent] signifies that the president is above the mean, and a score near zero indicates relative mediocrity" (Simonton 1986, 280-282).

[a] Schlesinger (1949, 1962) polled experts in 1948 and 1962 concerning the greatness of past presidents.
[b] Maranell (1970) surveyed 571 historians on seven distinct presidential dimensions: general prestige, strength of action, activeness, idealism, flexibility, administration accomplishments, and the amount of information the respondents had about the president.
[c] Murray and Blessing (1983) surveyed 846 historians and compared their rating with Porter (1981) and one published in the *Chicago Tribune Magazine* in 1982. They also provide a measure of how controversial each president was.

Source: Adapted from Simonton (1986, 281).

Table 8.2 Comparison of Presidents in 1977 (percent)

President	Did the best job in the White House	Most inspired confidence	Was most personally appealing	Was best administrator	Was best in domestic affairs	Was best in foreign affairs	Set the highest moral standards
F. Roosevelt	23	29	9	19	25	15	10
Truman	17	12	5	14	11	12	16
Eisenhower	8	11	6	9	5	12	12
Kennedy	23	36	67	26	25	20	24
Johnson	2	1	1	4	7	2	2
Nixon	2	1	1	2	2	20	1
Ford	8	4	5	6	8	3	18

Note: The question was: "I'd like to ask you about the ... presidents of the United States. Please keep in mind Roosevelt, Truman, Eisenhower, Kennedy, Johnson, Nixon, and Ford. If you had to choose one, which president do you think ...." "Don't know" and "no opinion" responses are not recorded.

Source: Adapted from *Public Opinion*, October/November 1979, 24.

Table 8.3 Comparison of Presidents in 1981 (percent)

President	Was best on domestic affairs	Was best in foreign affairs	Was least able to get things done
Roosevelt	24	11	1
Truman	10	11	1
Eisenhower	9	10	5
Kennedy	23	20	4
Johnson	10	2	9
Nixon	5	30	12
Ford	5	3	13
Carter	2	5	44

Note: The question was: "I'd like to ask you about the . . . presidents of the United States. Please keep in mind Roosevelt, Truman, Eisenhower, Kennedy, Johnson, Nixon, Ford, and Carter. If you had to choose one, which president do you think . . ." "Don't know" and "no opinion" responses are not recorded.

Source: Adapted from *Public Opinion*, February/March 1981, 38.

Table 8.4 Physical Characteristics and Personal Backgrounds of Presidents

President	Dates [a]	Height in inches [b]	Number of siblings [c]	Age at death of father [d]	Age at death of mother [d]	Father's class	Spouse's father's class
Washington	1789-1796	2.0	8	11	8	Upper	Upper
J. Adams	1797-1800	-5.0	2	26	61	Middle	Middle
Jefferson	1801-1808	2.5	7	14	33	Upper	Upper
Madison	1809-1816	-8.0	6	50	78	Upper	Upper
Monroe	1817-1824	0.0	4	16	68	Upper	Upper
J. Q. Adams	1825-1828	-5.0	4	60	51	Upper	Upper
Jackson	1829-1836	1.0	2	0	14	Working	Middle
Van Buren	1837-1840	-6.0	7	34	34	Middle	Middle
Tyler [e]	1841-1844	0.0	7	23	7	Upper	Upper
Polk	1845-1848	-4.0	7	32	54	Upper	Upper
Taylor	1849-1850	-4.0	8	41	38	Middle	Upper
Fillmore	1851-1852	-3.0	7	63	31	Middle	Middle
Pierce	1853-1856	-2.0	8	34	34	Upper	Middle
Buchanan [f]	1857-1860	0.0	6	30	42	Middle	—
Lincoln	1861-1864	4.0	2	42	10	Work./middle	Upper
A. Johnson	1865-1868	-2.0	1	3	47	Working	Working
Grant	1869-1876	-3.5	4	51	61	Middle	Upper
Hayes	1877-1880	-3.5	2	0	44	Middle	Upper
Arthur	1881-1884	2.0	8	46	39	Middle	Upper
Cleveland [f]	1885-1888	-1.0	8	17	45	Middle	—
B. Harrison	1889-1892	-6.0	8	45	17	Upper	Middle
Cleveland [f]	1893-1896	-1.0	8	17	45	Middle	—
McKinley	1897-1901	-5.0	8	50	55	Middle	Upper
T. Roosevelt	1902-1908	-2.0	3	19	25	Upper	Upper
Taft	1909-1912	0.0	5	34	50	Upper	Upper
Wilson [e]	1913-1920	-1.0	3	46	31	Middle	Middle

(Table continues)

Table 8.4 (continued)

President	Dates[a]	Height in inches[b]	Number of siblings[c]	Age at death of father[d]	Age at death of mother[d]	Father's class	Spouse's father's class
Harding	1921-1923	0.0	7	58	45	Middle	Upper
Coolidge	1924-1928	-2.0	1	54	13	Middle	Middle
Hoover	1929-1932	-1.0	2	6	10	Middle	Upper
F. Roosevelt	1933-1944	2.0	0	19	60	Upper	Upper
Truman	1945-1952	-3.0	2	30	63	Middle	Middle
Eisenhower	1953-1960	-1.5	5	51	56	Middle	Working
Kennedy	1961-1963	0.0	8	46	46	Upper	Upper
L. Johnson	1964-1968	3.0	4	29	50	Upper	Upper
Nixon	1969-1974	-0.5	4	44	55	Working	Working
Ford	1975-1976	0.0	3	49	54	Middle	Middle
Carter	1977-1980	-2.5	3	29	59	Middle	Middle

Note: Presidents W. H. Harrison and J. Garfield are excluded due to short tenure in office.

[a] The president with at least one year in office and who serves the most days in the calendar year is credited with that year.

[b] Greater than or less than (−) six feet.

[c] Siblings include all brothers and sisters who lived with the president for a full year prior to either the president's or the sibling's eighteenth birthday. Figures are rounded off to the nearest year. For any president dying before one or both parents, his own age is given at death of father and mother.

[d] Age at death of father and mother. Figures are rounded off to the nearest year. For any president dying before one or both parents, his own age is given at death. Because Gerald Ford adopted the name of his stepfather, his stepfather is used in determining the age at death of the father.

[e] For Presidents Wilson and Tyler, entries for wife's father's class were determined using the first wife.

[f] Because Presidents Cleveland and Buchanan were bachelors upon entering the White House, no socioeconomic indicator for the wife's father's class is provided.

Source: Adapted from Holmes and Elder (1986).

Table 8.5   Foreign Policy Activity, Washington to Carter

President	Reelected	Introvert (I)/ extrovert (E)[a]	Number of war years[b]	Territorial expansion	Troop commitment (1798-1968)[c]
Washington	Yes	I	0	0	—
J. Adams	No	E	0	0	2
Jefferson	Yes	E	0	1	3
Madison	Yes	E	3	0	6
Monroe	Yes	E	0	2	8
J. Q. Adams	No	I	0	0	3
Jackson	Yes	I	0	0	6
Van Buren	No	I	0	0	4
Tyler	No	I	0	0	5
Polk	No	E	2	3	2
Taylor	No	E	0	0	2
Fillmore	No	E	0	0	1
Pierce	No	E	0	1	8
Buchanan	No	E	0	0	11
Lincoln	Yes	E	4	0	3
A. Johnson	No	E	0	1	8
Grant	Yes	I	0	0	8
Hayes	No	I	0	0	—
Arthur	No	I	0	0	2
Cleveland	Yes	I/E	0	0	10
B. Harrison	No	I	0	0	5
McKinley	No	E	1	5	6
T. Roosevelt	Yes	E	1	1	14
Taft	No	E	0	0	7
Wilson	Yes	E	2	2	22
Harding	No	I	0	0	3
Coolidge	Yes	I	0	0	6
Hoover	No	I	0	0	1
F. Roosevelt	Yes	I/E	3	0	9
Truman	Yes	E	4	1	6
Eisenhower	Yes	E	1	0	8
Kennedy	No	E	0	0	4
L. Johnson	Yes	E	4	0	5
Nixon	Yes	I	4	0	—
Ford	No	I	0	0	—
Carter	No	I	0	0	—
Reagan	Yes	E	0	0	—

(Notes follow)

Table 8.5 (continued)

Note: Presidents W. H. Harrison and J. Garfield are excluded due to short tenure in office.

[a] As judged by Holmes and Elder (1986).

[b] Major wars, those classified as "interstate" or "extrasystemic" wars in Singer and Small (1982) are given a count of one year plus an additional war year for each year beyond the first in which the United States was involved for four months or longer. In addition to the "interstate" and "extrasystemic" wars covered in Singer and Small, one war outside the time span of that study was classified as a major war, the War of 1812 (1812-1814). (Criteria for inclusion and data on major wars are in Singer and Small [1974, 17-39 and 59-75].) The Civil War is not included in the Singer and Small study, but because of its magnitude it is included in this count and is given four war years (1861-1864).

[c] Troop commitment is calculated from "A Chronological List of 199 U.S. Military Hostilities Abroad without a Declaration of War, 1798-1972." Actions listed under a single entry receive one count, credited to the president in office when the action was first initiated. The one exception to this rule is the listing for "1816-1818: Spanish Florida." Because actions were taken against both the Spanish and the Seminole Indians, two counts were given, one to President Madison and one to President Monroe. The Vietnam and Korean wars are excluded (as are the declared wars) from the count because of their listing in the "War Years" column.

Source: Adapted from Holmes and Elder (1986).

Table 8.6 Education and High-Level Government Experience of Presidents

President	Educational background, college[a]	Books published[b]	Years in House[c]	Years in Senate[c]	Years as governor[c]	Years as vice president[c]	Years in cabinet[c]	General in U.S. military[d]
Washington	None	0	0	2[e]	0	0	0	9
J. Adams	Harvard	5	0	5[d]	0	4	0	0
Jefferson	William and Mary	3	8	5[d]	3	4	7	0
Madison	Princeton	2	8	7[d]	0	0	8	0
Monroe	William and Mary	1	0	7[f]	4	0	6	0
J. Q. Adams	Harvard	6	0	6	0	0	8	0
Jackson	None	0	0	4	0	0	0	10
Van Buren	None	0	0	8	2	4	3	0
Tyler	William and Mary	0	3	9	3	0	0	0
Polk	U. of North Carolina	0	14	0	2	0	0	0
Taylor	None	0	0	0	0	0	0	12
Fillmore	None	0	8	0	0	1	0	0
Pierce	Bowdoin	0	4	5	0	0	0	1
Buchanan	Dickinson	0	10	10	0	0	4	0
Lincoln	None	0	2	0	0	0	0	0
A. Johnson	None	0	10	4	4	0	0	0
Grant	U.S. Military Academy	0	0	0	0	0	1	6
Hayes	Kenyon	0	3	0	6	0	0	3
Arthur	Union	0	0	0	0	1	0	0
Cleveland	None	0	0	0	2	0	0	0
B. Harrison	Miami of Ohio	0	0	6	0	0	0	0
McKinley	Allegheny	0	14	0	4	0	0	0
T. Roosevelt	Harvard	14	0	0	2	1	0	0
Taft	Yale	1	0	0	0	0	5	0
Wilson	Princeton	9	0	0	2	0	0	0

(Table continues)

Table 8.6 (continued)

President	Educational background, college[a]	Books published[b]	Years in House[c]	Years in Senate[c]	Years as governor[c]	Years as vice president[c]	Years in cabinet[c]	General in U.S. military[d]
Harding	Ohio Central	0	0	6	0	0	0	0
Coolidge	Amherst	1	0	0	2	3	0	0
Hoover	Stanford	2	0	0	0	0	9	0
F. Roosevelt	Harvard	3	0	0	4	0	0	0
Truman	None	0	0	10	0	0	0	0
Eisenhower	U.S. Military Academy	1	0	0	0	0	0	7
Kennedy	Harvard	5	6	8	0	0	0	0
L. Johnson	Southwest Texas State Teacher's College	0	12	12	0	3	0	0
Nixon	Whittier	1	4	2	0	8	0	0
Ford	U. of Michigan	1	25	0	0	2	0	0
Carter	U.S. Naval Academy	1	0	0	4	0	0	0
Reagan	Eureka	2	0	0	8	0	0	0

Note: Public office held after a president is out of the White House is not included. N/E = northeastern. Presidents W. H. Harrison and J. Garfield are excluded due to short tenure in office.

[a] Refers to undergraduate education.

[b] The number of books published prior to year elected or assuming office, whatever is first.

[c] Number of years in which a president served six or more months.

[d] The military experience indicator is based on how many years they had the rank of general officer and were on active duty. Temporary administrative posts during a war are not included.

[e] These years were spent in the Continental Congress.

[f] Four of these years were spent in the Continental Congress.

Source: Adapted from Holmes and Elder (1986).

Table 8.7 Political and Economic Environment during Presidency

President	Van Duijn international economic classification [a]	Majority support in election	Elected in realigning election [b]	One-party dominance [c]	Assassination attempts [d]
Washington	Prosperity	Yes	No	6/8	No
J. Adams	Prosperity	Yes	No	4/4	No
Jefferson	Prosperity/War	Yes	Yes	8/8	No
Madison	Prosperity/War	Yes	No	8/8	No
Monroe	Recession	Yes	No	8/8	No
J.Q. Adams	Depression	No	No	2/8	No
Jackson	Depression	Yes	Yes	8/8	Yes
Van Buren	Recovery	Yes	No	4/4	No
Tyler	Recovery	No	No	2/4	No
Polk	Prosperity	No	No	2/4	No
Taylor	Prosperity	No	No	0/2	No
Fillmore	Prosperity	No	No	0/3	No
Pierce	Prosperity	Yes	No	2/4	No
Buchanan	Prosperity	No	No	2/4	No
Lincoln	Prosperity	No	Yes	4/4	Yes
A. Johnson	Recession	No	No	2/4	No
Grant	Recession/Depression	Yes	No	6/8	No
Hayes	Depression	No	No	0/4	No
Arthur	Depression	No	No	2/4	No
Cleveland	Recovery/Prosperity	No	No	2/8	No
B. Harrison	Recovery	No	No	2/4	No
McKinley	Prosperity	Yes	Yes	5/5	Yes
T. Roosevelt	Prosperity	Yes	No	7/7	Yes
Taft	Prosperity	Yes	No	2/4	No
Wilson	Prosperity/War	No	No	6/8	No
Harding	Recession	Yes	No	3/3	No
Coolidge	Recession	Yes	No	5/5	No
Hoover	Depression	Yes	No	2/4	No
F. Roosevelt	Depression/Recovery	Yes	Yes	12/12	Yes
Truman	Recovery/Prosperity	No	No	6/8	Yes
Eisenhower	Prosperity	Yes	No	2/8	No
Kennedy	Prosperity	No	No	3/3	Yes
L. Johnson	Prosperity/Recovery	Yes	No	5/5	No
Nixon	Recession	No	No	0/6	No
Ford	Depression/Recovery	No	No	0/2	Yes
Carter	—	Yes	No	4/4	No
Reagan	—	Yes	No	0/8	Yes

(Notes follow)

Table 8.7 (continued)

Note: Presidents W. H. Harrison and J. Garfield are excluded due to short tenure in office.

[a] Presidents who spend two full terms or more in office must spend more than three years in a Van Duijn period to be put in that period. Presidents spending more than one full term but less than two full terms must spend more than two years in a period to be so classified. A president with one term or less is placed in the period where he spent most of his time in office; a president who served equal time in two periods is included in the period during which he was elected.
[b] The concept developed by Key (1955) is used with Crittenden (1982) to classify elections.
[c] Number of years with one-party dominance/number of years in the White House. A president has one-party dominance any year that his party has a majority in both houses in Congress. Because Andrew Johnson was a Democrat who ran on the Unionist ticket in 1864 with a Republican (Lincoln), he is considered to have consensus for the two years the Unionists controlled Congress, the Thirty-ninth Congress, and not the two years when the Republicans controlled Congress. This coding rule generally conforms to voting patterns in the Fortieth Congress, 1867-1869.
[d] Assassination attempt figures are for all known attempts on the president's life while he was in office or while he was president-elect.

Source: Adapted from Holmes and Elder (1986).

Bibliography

Achen, Christopher H. 1982. "Toward Theories of Data." In *Political Science: State of the Discipline,* ed. Ada Finifter. Washington, D.C.: American Political Science Association.

___. 1986. *Statistical Analysis of Quasi-Experiments.* Berkeley: University of California Press.

Aldrich, John. 1980. *Before the Convention.* Chicago: University of Chicago Press.

Alexander, Herbert. 1962. *Financing the 1960 Election.* Princeton, N.J.: Citizens' Research Foundation.

___. 1966. *Financing the 1964 Election.* Princeton: Citizens' Research Foundation.

___. 1971. *Financing the 1968 Election.* Lexington, Mass.: D.C. Heath.

___. 1976. *Financing the 1972 Election.* Lexington, Mass.: D.C. Heath.

___. 1979. *Financing the 1976 Election.* Washington, D.C.: Congressional Quarterly.

Aristotle. 1943. *Politics.* New York: Modern Library.

Axelrod, Robert. 1986. "Presidential Election Coalitions in 1984." *American Political Science Review* 80 (March):281-290.

Banks, Arthur, ed. 1986. *Political Handbook of the World, 1984-1985.* Binghamton, N.Y.: CSA Publications.

Barber, James David. 1977. *The Presidential Character: Predicting Presidential Performance.* Englewood Cliffs, N.J.: Prentice-Hall.

Bax, Frans R. 1977. "Legislative-Executive Relations in Foreign Policy: New Partisanship or New Competition?" *Orbis* 20, 4 (Winter):881-904.

Beck, Nathaniel. 1982. "Parties, Administrations, and American Macroeconomic Outcomes." *American Political Science Review* 76 (March):83-93.

Bensel, Richard F. 1980. "Creating the Statutory State: The Implications of a Rule of Law Standard in American Politics." *American Political Science Review* 74 (September):734-744.

Bentley, Arthur. 1908. *The Process of Government.* Chicago: University of Chicago Press.

Berman, Larry. 1979. *The Office of Management and Budget and the Presidency.* Princeton: Princeton University Press.

Bliss, Howard, and M. Glen Johnson. 1975. *Beyond the Water's Edge: America's Foreign Policies.* Philadelphia: J. B. Lippincott.

Brody, Richard, and Benjamin Page. 1975. "The Impact of Events on Presidential Popularity: The Johnson and Nixon Administrations." In *Perspectives on the Presidency,* ed. A. Wildavsky. Boston: Little, Brown.

Brown, Roger. 1982. "Party and Bureaucracy: From Kennedy to Reagan." *Political Science Quarterly* 97 (Summer):279-294.

Browning, Robert. 1986. *Politics and Social Welfare in the United States.* Knoxville: University of Tennessee Press.

Brunk, Gregory, and Thomas Mineheart. 1984. "How Important Is Elite Turnover to Policy Change?" *American Journal of Political Science* 28 (August):559-569.

Bunce, Valerie. 1981. *Do New Leaders Make a Difference? Executive Succession and Public Policy under Capitalism and Socialism.* Princeton: Princeton University Press.

Bunce, Valerie, and Philip Roeder. 1986. "The Effects of Leadership Succession in the Soviet Union." *American Political Science Review* 80 (March):215-224.

Burch, Philip. 1980. *Elites in American History.* 3 vols. New York: Holmes and Meier.

Burnham, Walter Dean. 1982. *The Current Crisis in American Politics.* Oxford: Oxford University Press.

Chamberlain, Lawrence. 1946. *The President, Congress, and Legislation.* New York: Columbia University Press.

Clausen, Aage R. 1973. *How Congressmen Decide.* New York: St. Martin's.

Clements, John. 1986. *Clements' Encyclopedia of World Governments.* Dallas: Political Research.

Code of Federal Regulations, Title 3: The President. 1936-1984. Washington, D.C.: U.S. Government Printing Office.

Congressional Quarterly. 1979. *The Washington Lobby.* 3d ed. Washington, D.C.: Congressional Quarterly.

Congressional Quarterly Almanac. 1957-1985. Washington, D.C.: Congressional Quarterly.

Congressional Quarterly Weekly Report. Successive vols. Washington, D.C.: Congressional Quarterly.

Congressional Quarterly's Guide to the 1976 Elections. 1977. Washington, D.C.: Congressional Quarterly.

Congressional Quarterly's Guide to U.S. Elections. 1985. 2d ed. Washington, D.C.: Congressional Quarterly.

Congressional Quarterly's Guide to the U.S. Supreme Court. 1979. Washington, D.C.: Congressional Quarterly.

Coolidge, Calvin. 1929. *The Autobiography of Calvin Coolidge.* Rutland, Vt.: Academy Books.

Cooper, Joseph. 1985. "The Legislative Veto in the 1980s." In *Congress Reconsidered,* ed. L. Dodd and B. Oppenheimer. 3d ed. Washington, D.C.: Congressional Quarterly.

Corwin, Edward S. 1940. *The President: Office and Powers, 1787-1957.* New York: New York University Press.

CQ Guide to Current American Government. 1986. Washington, D.C.: Congressional Quarterly.

Cronin, Thomas. 1980. *The State of the Presidency.* 2d ed. Boston: Little, Brown.

——. 1987. "The Swelling of the Presidency." In *American Government: Readings and Cases,* ed. P. Woll. 9th ed. Boston: Little, Brown.

Current Treaty Index. 1984. Buffalo: William Hein.

Dahl, Robert. 1956. *A Preface to Democratic Theory.* Chicago: University of Chicago Press.

——. 1961. *Who Governs?* New Haven: Yale University Press.

Davis, Eric L. 1979. "Legislative Reform and the Decline of Presidential Influence on Capitol Hill." *British Journal of Political Science* 9 (October):465-479.

De Grazia, Alfred. 1965. *Republic in Crisis: Congress against the Executive Force.* New York: Federal Legal Publication.

——. 1969. "The Myth of the President." In *The Presidency,* ed. A. Wildavsky. Boston: Little, Brown.

Delury, George, ed. 1983. *World Encyclopedia of Political Systems and Parties.* 2 vols. New York: Facts on File.

Destler, I. M. 1974. *Presidents, Bureaucrats, and Foreign Policy.* Princeton: Princeton University Press.

DiClerico, Robert. 1983. *The American President.* Englewood Cliffs, N.J.: Prentice-Hall.

——. 1985. *The American President.* 2d ed. Englewood Cliffs, N.J.: Prentice-Hall.

Edelman, Murray. 1971. *Politics as Symbolic Action.* Champaign: University of Illinois Press.

Edwards, George. 1980. *Presidential Influence in Congress*. San Francisco: W. H. Freeman.

___. 1983. *The Public Presidency*. New York: St. Martin's.

___. 1985. "Measuring Presidential Influence in Congress." *Journal of Politics* 47 (May):632-645.

Edwards, George, Steven Shull, and Norman Thomas, eds. 1985. *The Presidency and Public Policy Making*. Pittsburgh: University of Pittsburgh Press.

Epstein, Leon. 1986. *Political Parties in the American Mold*. Madison: University of Wisconsin Press.

Europa Year Book. 1986. 2 vols. London: Europa Publications.

Farrand, Max, ed. 1913. *The Records of the Federal Convention of 1787*. New Haven: Yale University Press.

Fenno, Richard. 1959. *The President's Cabinet*. New York: Vintage.

Fishel, Jeff. 1986. *Presidents and Promises*. Washington, D.C.: Congressional Quarterly.

Fisher, Louis. 1978. *The Constitution between Friends*. New York: St. Martin's.

Fitzpatrick, John, ed. 1940. *Writings of George Washington*. Washington, D.C.: U.S. Government Printing Office.

Ford, Paul, ed. 1892-1899. *The Writings of Thomas Jefferson*. New York: G. P. Putnam.

Friedrich, Carl. 1937. *Constitutional Government and Politics*. New York: Harper Brothers.

Frye, Altou, and William D. Rogers. 1979. "Linkages Begin at Home." *Foreign Policy* 35 (Summer):49-67.

Gailey, Phil. 1983. "For McGovern, the Second Time Around Is Good." *New York Times*, November 3, 16.

Gallup Opinion Index. Nos. 1-184 (June 1965-Jan. 1981). Wilmington, Del.: Scholarly Resources.

Gallup Poll. 1972-1986. Wilmington, Del.: Scholarly Resources.

Gallup Poll: Public Opinion, 1935-1971. 3 vols. New York: Random House, 1972.

The Gallup Report. Nos. 185-255 (Feb. 1981-Dec. 1986). Wilmington, Del.: Scholarly Resources.

George, Alexander, and Juliette George. 1964. *Woodrow Wilson and Colonel House*. New York: Dover.

Goehlert, Robert, and Fenton Martin. 1985. *The Presidency: A Research Guide*. Santa Barbara: ABC-CLIO Information Services.

Goldman, Sheldon. 1985. "Reaganizing the Judiciary: The First Term Appointments." *Judicature* 68 (April-May):313-329.

Goldsmith, William. 1974. *The Growth of Presidential Power*. 3 vols. New York: Chelsea House.

Goodin, R. E. 1977. "The Importance of Winning Big." *Legislative Studies Quarterly* 2 (November):399-407.

Graber, Doris, ed. 1982. *The President and the Public*. Philadelphia: Institute for the Study of Human Issues.

Greenstein, Fred. 1974. "What the President Means to Americans: Presidential 'Choice' between Elections." In *Choosing the President*, ed. J. Barber. Englewood Cliffs, N.J.: Prentice-Hall.

——. 1982. *The Hidden-Hand Presidency: Eisenhower as Leader*. New York: Basic Books.

Greenstein, Fred, Larry Berman, and Alvin S. Felzenberg. 1977. *Evolution of the Modern Presidency: A Bibliography Survey*. Washington, D.C.: American Enterprise Institute.

Grofman, Bernard, and Arend Lijphart. 1986. *Electoral Laws and Their Political Consequences*. New York: Agathon Press.

Grossman, Michael, and Martha Kumar. 1981. *Portraying the President*. Baltimore: Johns Hopkins University Press.

Haight, Timothy, and Richard A. Brody. 1977. "The Mass Media and Presidential Broadcasting and News in the Nixon Administration." *Communications Research* 4 (January):41-60.

Halberstam, David. 1979. *The Powers That Be*. New York: Dell.

Hamilton, Alexander, James Madison, and John Jay. 1961. *The Federalist Papers*. New York: Mentor. (First published in 1788.)

Hamilton, Lee H., et al. 1978. "Making the Separation of Powers Work." *Foreign Affairs* 57 (Fall):17-39.

Hammond, Thomas, and Jane Fraser. 1984. "Studying Presidential Performance in Congress." *Political Methodology* 10 (2):211-244.

Hansen, Richard. 1962. *The Year We Had No President*. Lincoln: University of Nebraska Press.

Harmon, Kathryn Newcomer, and Marsha L. Brauen. 1979. "Joint Electoral Outcomes as Cues for Congressional Support of U.S. Presidents." *Legislative Studies Quarterly* 4 (May):281-300.

Hayek, Friedrich. 1944. *The Road to Serfdom*. Chicago: University of Chicago Press.

——. 1960. *The Constitution of Liberty*. Chicago: University of Chicago Press.

Heard, Alexander. 1960. *The Costs of Democracy*. Chapel Hill: University of North Carolina Press.

Heclo, Hugh. 1977. *A Government of Strangers*. Washington, D.C.: Brookings Institution.

___. 1981. "Introduction: The Presidential Illusion." In *The Illusion of Presidential Government*, ed. H. Heclo and L. Salamon. Boulder, Colo: Westview Press.

Heclo, Hugh, and Lester Salamon, eds. 1981. *The Illusion of Presidential Government*. Boulder, Colo.: Westview Press.

Helmer, John. 1981. "The Presidential Office: Velvet Fist in an Iron Glove." In *The Illusion of Presidential Government*, ed. H. Heclo and L. Salamon. Boulder, Colo.: Westview Press.

Hess, Stephen. 1976. *Organizing the Presidency*. Washington, D.C.: Brookings Institution.

Hibbs, Douglas A., and Heino Fassbender. 1981. *Contemporary Political Economy*. Amsterdam: North Holland.

Hibbs, Douglas A., Douglas Rivers, and Nicholas Vasilatos. 1982. "On the Demand for Economic Outcomes: Macroeconomic Performance and Mass Political Support in the United States, Great Britain, and Germany." *Journal of Politics* 44:426-462.

Hinckley, Barbara. 1978. *Stability and Change in Congress*. New York: Harper and Row.

___. 1983. *Stability and Change in Congress*. 3d ed. New York: Harper and Row.

___. 1988. *The Presidency as Symbolic Office*. Chatham, N.J.: Chatham House.

Hofstadter, Richard. 1969. *The Idea of a Party System: The Rise of Legitimate Opposition in the United States, 1780-1840*. Berkeley: University of California Press.

Holmes, Jack E., and Robert E. Elder, Jr. 1986. "Our Best and Worst Presidents: Some Possible Reasons for Perceived Performance." Paper presented at the annual meeting of the American Political Science Association.

Holsti, Ole, and David Rosenau. 1984. *American Leadership in World Affairs: Vietnam and the Breakdown in Consensus*. Boston: Allen and Unwin.

Holtzman, Abraham. 1970. *Legislative Liaison: Executive Leadership in Congress*. New York: Crowell and Readers Digest Press.

Hughes, Barry B. 1978. *The Domestic Context of American Foreign Policy*. San Francisco: W. H. Freeman.

Huntington, Samuel P. 1965. "Congressional Responses in the Twentieth Century." In *The Congress and America's Future*, ed. D. Truman. Englewood Cliffs, N.J.: Prentice-Hall.

Hutchinson, William, and William Rachal, eds. 1962. *The Papers of James Madison*. 13 vols. Chicago: University of Chicago Press.

International Yearbook and Statesmen's Who's Who, 1986. 1986. London: Information Services.

Jackson, John. 1974. *Constituencies and Leaders in Congress.* Cambridge, Mass.: Harvard University Press.

Johnson, Loch. 1984. *The Making of International Agreements: Congress Confronts the Executive.* New York: New York University Press.

Johnson, Lyndon. 1979. *Vantage Point.* New York: Popular Library.

Jordan, Amos A., and William J. Taylor. 1981. *American National Security: Policy and Process.* Baltimore: Johns Hopkins University Press.

Kaufman, Herbert. 1956. "Emerging Conflicts in the Doctrines of Public Administration." *American Political Science Review* 50 (December):1057-1073.

Keech, William. 1982. "Selecting and Electing Presidents, 1936-1980." In *Rethinking the Presidency,* ed. T. Cronin. Boston: Little, Brown.

Kenski, Henry. 1977. "The Impact of Economic Conditions on Presidential Popularity." *Journal of Politics* 39 (August):764-773.

Kernell, Samuel. 1978. "Explaining Presidential Popularity." *American Political Science Review* 72 (June):506-522.

———. 1984. "The Presidency and the People." In *The Presidency and the Political System,* ed. M. Nelson. Washington, D.C.: Congressional Quarterly.

———. 1986. *Going Public.* Washington, D.C.: Congressional Quarterly.

Kessell, John H. 1974. "The Parameters of Presidential Politics." *Social Science Quarterly* (June):8-24.

———. 1977. "The Seasons of Presidential Politics." *Social Science Quarterly* 58 (March):418-435.

———. 1980. *Presidential Campaign Politics.* Homewood, Ill.: Dorsey Press.

———. 1983. "The Structures of the Carter White House." *American Journal of Political Science* 27 (August):431-463.

———. 1984a. *Presidential Parties.* Homewood, Ill.: Dorsey Press.

———. 1984b. "The Structures of the Reagan White House." *American Journal of Political Science* 28 (May):231-258.

Kesselman, Mark. 1961. "Presidential Leadership in Congress on Foreign Policy." *Midwest Journal of Political Science* 5 (August):184-189.

———. 1965. "Presidential Leadership in Congress on Foreign Policy: A Replication of a Hypothesis." *Midwest Journal of Political Science* 9 (November):401-406.

Ketcham, Ralph. 1984. *Presidents above Party: The First American Presidency, 1789-1829.* Chapel Hill: University of North Carolina Press.

King, Gary. 1986a. "How Not to Lie with Statistics: Avoiding Common Mistakes in Quantitative Political Science." *American Journal of Political Science* 30 (August):666-687.

———. 1986b. "Political Parties and Foreign Policy: A Structuralist Approach." *Political Psychology* 7 (March):83-101.

_____. 1986c. "The Significance of Roll Calls in Voting Bodies: A Model and Statistical Estimation." *Social Science Research* 15 (June):135-152.

King, Gary, and Robert X. Browning. 1987. "Democratic Representation and Partisan Bias: A Model of Seats and Votes for American Congressional Elections." *American Political Science Review* 81 (December):1251-1276.

King, Gary, and Lyn Ragsdale. 1986a. "Guns, Butter, and Presidential Vetoes." Mimeo.

_____. 1986b. "President of Which People? Toward a Study of Executive Representation." Paper presented at the annual meeting of the American Political Science Association, Washington, D.C., August 28-31.

Kingdon, John. 1984. *Agendas, Alternatives, and Public Policies.* Boston: Little, Brown.

Kissinger, Henry. 1979. *The White House Years.* Boston: Little, Brown.

Koenig, Louis W. 1986. *The Chief Executive.* 5th ed. New York: Harcourt Brace Jovanovich.

Kumar, Martha Joynt. 1983. "Presidential Libraries: Gold Mine, Booby Trap, or Both?" In *Studying the Presidency,* ed. G. Edwards and S. Wayne. Knoxville: University of Tennessee Press.

Lammers, William. 1982. "Presidential Attention-Focusing Activities." In *The President and the Public,* ed. D. Graber. Philadelphia: Institute for the Study of Human Issues.

LeLoup, Lance, and Steven A. Shull. 1979. "Congress versus the Executive: The Two Presidencies Reconsidered." *Social Science Quarterly* 59 (March):704-719.

Light, Paul. 1982. *The President's Agenda.* Baltimore: Johns Hopkins University Press.

Lindblom, Charles. 1968. *The Policy-making Process.* Englewood Cliffs: Prentice-Hall.

Lipset, Seymour Martin. 1986. "Unions in Transition." *Public Opinion* 9 (September-October):54.

Lord, Clifford, ed. 1944. *Presidential Executive Orders.* 2 vols. 1862-1935. New York: Hastings House.

_____. 1979. *List and Index of Presidential Executive Orders, Unnumbered Series, 1789-1941.* Wilmington, Del.: Michael Glazier.

Lowi, Theodore, 1979. *The End of Liberalism.* 2d ed. New York: W. W. Norton.

_____. 1985. *The Personal President: Power Invested, Promise Unfulfilled.* Ithaca: Cornell University Press.

McCormick, Richard P. 1975. "Political Development in the Second

Party System." In *The American Party Systems,* ed. W. N. Chambers and W. D. Burnham. 2d ed. New York: Oxford University Press.

MacKenzie, G. Calvin. 1981. *The Politics of Presidential Appointments.* New York: Free Press.

MacKuen, Michael. 1983. "Political Drama, Economic Conditions, and the Dynamics of Presidential Popularity." *American Journal of Political Science* 27 (February):165-192.

Malek, Frederic. 1978. *Washington's Hidden Tragedy.* New York: Free Press.

Manning, B. 1977. "The Congress, the Executive, and Intermestic Affairs: Three Proposals." *Foreign Affairs* 52 (January):306-324.

Maranell, G. M. 1970. "The Evaluation of Presidents: An Extension of the Schlesinger Polls." *Journal of American History* 57:104-113.

March, James, and Johan Olsen. 1984. "The New Institutionalism: Organizational Factors in Political Life." *American Political Science Review* 78 (September):735-736.

Margolis, Lawrence. 1986. *Executive Agreements and Presidential Power in Foreign Policy.* New York: Praeger.

Mayhew, David. 1974. *Congress: The Electoral Connection.* New Haven: Yale University Press.

Minow, N., et al. 1973. *Presidential Television.* New York: Basic Books.

Moe, Ronald, and Steven Teel. 1970. "Congress as Policy-Maker: A Necessary Reappraisal." *Political Science Quarterly* 85 (September):468-470.

Moe, Terry. 1985. "The Politicized Presidency." In *The New Direction in American Politics,* ed. J. Chubb and P. Peterson. Washington, D.C.: Brookings Institution.

Monroe, Kristen, and Dona Laughlin. 1983. "Economic Influences on Presidential Popularity." *Political Behavior* 5 (September):309-345.

Mueller, John. 1973. *War, Presidents, and Public Opinion.* New York: John Wiley.

Murphy, Walter F., and Michael N. Danielson. 1977. *Carr and Bernstein's "American Democracy."* 8th ed. Hinsdale, Ill.: Dryden Press.

Murray, R. K., and T. H. Blessing. 1983. "The Presidential Performance Study: A Progress Report." *Journal of American History* 70:535-555.

Nathan, Richard. 1975. *The Plot That Failed: Nixon and the Administrative Presidency.* New York: John Wiley.

____. 1983. *The Administrative Presidency.* New York: John Wiley.

Nelson, Michael, ed. 1985. *The Presidency and the Political System.* Washington, D.C.: Congressional Quarterly.

Neustadt, Richard. 1960. *Presidential Power.* New York: John Wiley.

____. 1976. *Presidential Power.* New York: John Wiley.

___. 1980. *Presidential Power*. New York: John Wiley.

Ornstein, Norman J., Thomas E. Mann, Michael J. Malbin, Allen Schick, and John F. Bibby. 1984. *Vital Statistics on Congress, 1984-1985 Edition*. Washington, D.C.: American Enterprise Institute.

Ostrom, Charles, and Brian Job. 1986. "The President and the Political Use of Force." *American Political Science Review* 80 (June):541-566.

Ostrom, Charles, and Dennis Simon. 1985. "Promise and Performance: A Dynamic Model of Presidential Popularity." *American Political Science Review* 79 (June):334-358.

Page, Benjamin, and Richard A. Brody. 1972. "Policy Voting and the Electoral Process: The Vietnam War Issue." *American Political Science Review* 66 (September):979-995.

Page, Benjamin, and Mark Petracca. 1983. *The American Presidency*. New York: McGraw-Hill.

Peterson, Mark. 1985. "Domestic Policy and Legislative Decision Making: Congressional Responses to Presidential Initiatives, 1953-1981." Paper presented at the annual meeting of the Midwest Political Science Association, Chicago, Illinois, April 19.

Pika, Joseph. 1979. "White House Boundary Rules: Linking Advisory Systems and Presidential Publics." Paper presented at the annual meeting of the American Political Science Association.

Polsby, Nelson. 1968. "The Institutionalization of the U.S. House of Representatives." *American Political Science Review* 62 (March):144-168.

___. 1983. "Some Landmarks in Modern Presidential-Congressional Relations." In *Both Ends of the Avenue*, ed. A. King. Washington, D.C.: American Enterprise Institute.

Presidential Elections since 1789. 1983. Washington, D.C.: Congressional Quarterly.

Presidential Vetoes, 1789-1976. 1978. Washington, D.C.: U.S. Government Printing Office.

Presidential Vetoes, 1977-1984. 1985. Washington, D.C.: U.S. Government Printing Office.

Public Papers of the Presidents of the United States. 1949-1984. Washington, D.C.: U.S. Government Printing Office.

Ragsdale, Lyn. 1984. "The Politics of Presidential Speechmaking, 1949-80." *American Political Science Review* 78 (December):971-984.

___. 1987a. "A Political Capital Model of Presidents' Public Appearances." Mimeo, University of Arizona, Tucson.

___. 1987b. "Presidential Speechmaking and the Public Audience: Individual Presidents and Group Attitudes." *Journal of Politics* 49 (August):704-727.

Ragsdale, Lyn, and Gary King. 1987. "Presidential Policy Responsiveness to Citizen Preferences." Paper presented at the annual meeting of the Midwest Political Science Association, Chicago, Illinois.

Report of the President's Committee on Administrative Management. 1937. Washington, D.C.: U.S. Government Printing Office.

Rivers, Douglas, and Nancy Rose. 1985. "Passing the President's Program." *American Journal of Political Science* 29 (May):183-196.

Rockman, Bert. 1984. *The Leadership Question: The Presidency and the American System.* New York: Praeger.

Rohde, David, and Dennis Simon. 1985. "Presidential Vetoes and Congressional Response: A Study of Institutional Conflict." *American Journal of Political Science* 29 (August):397-427.

Roosevelt, Theodore. 1913. *Theodore Roosevelt: An Autobiography.* New York: Macmillan.

Rosenstone, Steven. 1983. *Forecasting Presidential Elections.* New Haven: Yale University Press.

Rosenstone, Steven, Roy Behr, and Edward Lazarus. 1984. *Third Parties in America.* Princeton: Princeton University Press.

Rossiter, Clinton. 1960. *The American Presidency.* New York: Mentor Books.

Rourke, John T. 1977. "Congress and the Cold War." *World Affairs* 139 (Spring):259-277.

Rubin, Richard. 1981. *Press, Party, and Presidency.* New York: Norton.

Rusk, Jerrold. 1987. "Issues and Voting." In *Research in Micropolitics: Voting Behavior,* ed. S. Long. Vol. 2. Greenwich, Conn.: JAI Press.

Rutkus, D. 1976. "A Report on Simultaneous Television Network Coverage of Presidental Addresses to the Nation." In *Hearings on Federal Communication Commission Oversight,* U.S. Congress, House, Committee on Interstate and Foreign Commerce, March 2-3.

Schattschneider, E. E. 1975. *The Semi-Sovereign People.* Hinsdale, Ill.: Dryden Press.

Schlesinger, Arthur, Jr. 1973. *The Imperial Presidency.* Boston: Houghton Mifflin.

Schlesinger, Arthur, Sr. 1949. *Paths to the Present.* New York: Macmillan.

___. 1962. "Our Presidents: A Rating by Seventy-five Historians." *New York Times Magazine,* July 29, 12-13.

Schlesinger, Joseph. 1985. "The New American Political Party." *American Political Science Review* 79 (December):1152-1169.

Schwartz, Barry. 1981. *Vertical Classification: A Study in Structuralism and the Sociology of Knowledge.* Chicago: University of Chicago Press.

Shull, Steven A. 1983. *Domestic Policy Formation: Presidential-Congressional Partnership?* Westport, Conn.: Greenwood Press.

Sigal, Leon. 1973. *Reporters and Officials: The Organization and Politics of Newsmaking.* Lexington, Mass.: D.C. Heath.

Sigel, Roberta. 1966. "Image of the American Presidency: Part II of an Exploration into Popular Views of Presidential Power." *Midwest Journal of Political Science* 10 (February):123-137.

Sigelman, Lee. 1979. "A Reassessment of the Two Presidencies Thesis." *Journal of Politics* 41 (November):1195-1205.

———. 1980. "Gauging the Public Response to Presidential Leadership." *Presidential Studies Quarterly* 10 (Summer):427-433.

Simonton, Dean. 1986. "Presidential Greatness: The Historical Consensus and Its Psychological Significance." *Political Psychology* 7 (June):259-283.

Singer, J. David, and Melvin Small. 1974. *Wages of War: Eighteen Sixteen to Nineteen Sixty-Five.* Ann Arbor, Mich.: ICPSR.

Small, Melvin, and J. David Singer. 1982. *Resort to Arms: International and Civil Wars, 1816-1980.* Beverly Hills: Sage.

Smith, Steven, and Christopher Deering. 1984. *Committees in Congress.* Washington, D.C.: Congressional Quarterly.

Stanley, David, Dean Mann, and Jameson Doig. 1967. *Men Who Govern.* Washington, D.C.: Brookings Institution.

Stimson, James A. 1976. "Public Support for American Presidents: A Cyclical Model." *Public Opinion Quarterly* 40 (Spring):1-21.

Sundquist, James. 1968. *Politics and Policy: The Eisenhower, Kennedy, and Johnson Years.* Washington, D.C.: Brookings Institution.

Taft, William Howard. 1916. *The Presidency.* New York: Charles Scribner.

Tannenhaus, Joseph, and Mary Ann Foley. 1981. "Separating Objects of Specific and Diffuse Support: Experiments on Presidents and the Presidency." *Micropolitics* 1 (December):345-367.

Taylor, Charles, and David Jodice. 1983. *World Handbook of Political and Social Indicators.* 3d ed. 2 vols. New Haven, Conn.: Yale University Press.

Tourtellot, Arthur. 1964. *The Presidents on the Presidency.* New York: Doubleday.

Truman, David. 1951. *The Governmental Process.* New York: Alfred A. Knopf.

———. 1959. *The Congressional Party.* New York: John Wiley.

U.S. Commission on Civil Rights. 1983. *Equal Opportunity in Presidential Appointments.* Washington, D.C.: U.S. Government Printing Office.

U.S. Congress. Clerk of the House of Representatives. 1981. *Statistics of *the Presidential and Congressional Election of November 4, 1980.* Washington, D.C.: U.S. Government Printing Office.

U.S. Congress. Senate. 1949-1984. *Executive Proceedings of the Senate.* Washington, D.C.: U.S. Government Printing Office.

U.S. Department of Commerce. 1900-1986. *Statistical Abstract of the United States.* Washington, D.C.: U.S. Government Printing Office.

___. 1971. *U.S. Historical Statistics: Colonial Times to 1970.* 2 vols. Washington, D.C.: U.S. Government Printing Office.

U.S. Department of State. 1950-1980. *Treaties and Other International Agreements.* Washington, D.C.: U.S. Government Printing Office.

U.S. Executive Office of the President. Office of Management and Budget. 1924-1987. *The Budget of the United States.* Washington, D.C.: U.S. Government Printing Office.

___. Office of Management and Budget. 1987. *Regulatory Programs of the United States, April 1, 1986-March 31, 1978.* Washington, D.C.: U.S. Government Printing Office.

U.S. Federal Election Commission. 1985a. *Federal Election Commission Annual Report, 1984.* Washington, D.C.: U.S. Government Printing Office.

___. 1985b. *Federal Elections '84.* Washington, D.C.: U.S. Government Printing Office.

___. 1986. *Federal Election Commission Annual Report, 1985.* Washington, D.C.: U.S. Government Printing Office.

U.S. General Accounting Office. 1985. *Use of Special Presidential Authority for Foreign Assistance.* Washington, D.C.: U.S. Government Printing Office.

U.S. Office of Personnel Management. 1986. *Federal Civilian Work Force Statistics, May 1986.* Washington, D.C.: U.S. Government Printing Office.

University Microfilms International. 1983. *Dissertations on Presidents.* Ann Arbor, Mich.: University Microfilms.

Watson, Richard, and Norman Thomas. 1983. *The Politics of the Presidency.* New York: John Wiley.

Wayne, Stephen. 1978. *The Legislative Presidency.* New York: Harper and Row.

___. 1982a. "Congressional Liaison in the Reagan White House: A Preliminary Assessment of the First Year." In *President and Congress,* ed. N. Ornstein. Washington, D.C.: American Enterprise Institute.

___. 1982b. "Expectations of the President." In *The President and the Public,* ed. D. Graber. Philadelphia: Institute for the Study of Human Issues.

Wayne, Stephen, Richard Cole, and James Hyde. 1979. "Advising the President on Enrolled Legislation: Patterns of Executive Influence." *Political Science Quarterly* 94 (Summer):303-317.

Weber, Max. 1947. *The Theory of Social and Economic Organization*. Glencoe, Ill.: Free Press.

West, William, and Joseph Cooper. 1985. "The Rise of Administrative Clearance." In *The Presidency and Public Policy Making*, ed. G. Edwards, S. Shull, and N. Thomas. Pittsburgh: University of Pittsburgh Press.

Wildavsky, Aaron. 1966. "The Two Presidencies." *Trans-Action* 4 (December):7-14.

Wilson, Woodrow. 1973. *Congressional Government*. Cleveland: World Publishing.

—. 1908. *Constitutional Government in the United States*. New York: Columbia University Press.

Index

Note: Entries in italic refer to tables and figures.

Branch of the Government, 22-23
House of Representatives
  effect of midterm elections, 393, *482*
  members as presidential candidates,
    381, *396*
  role call votes, 42, *69-70*
House role call votes
  data on, 42-44, *69-70*
  evaluating presidential priorities
    in, 42
  presidential success judged by, 49
  support for president by issue area,
    53-55, 75-80
  support for president by region, 55,
    81-82
Huntington, Samuel P., 47

*Immigration and Naturalization Service
v. Chadha*, 115
Inauguration, public approval after,
  280
Income level, presidential support by,
  284-285, *309-311, 316-319*
Incumbent strategy, plural presidency
  and, 15-16
Independent agencies of the
  government, 199, *229*
Independent approval of Carter and
  Reagan, *352-355*
Information vs. meaning, 2
In-party support for president, 54-57,
  77-78
Institutional continuity, 486-487
Institutional vs. political actor
  perspective, 10
Institutional policy making, 128-129.
  See also Presidential policy
Institutionalization, 204*n*
Interest groups
  presidential appearances before,
    254-255
  presidential ratings by, 56-57, *86-87*
International agreements. *See also*
  Conventions; Executive agreements;
  Foreign policy; Protocols; Treaties
  limited control of presidents on,
    120-121
  by policy type, 116-118, *146-149*
  by regime type, *156-159*
  by region, 118-120, *150-155*

International policy. *See* Foreign
  policy
International Trade Commission, 486
Iran-contra affair, 32

Japan, international agreements with,
  119
Jefferson, Thomas, on the presidency,
  17, 19
Johnson, Lyndon B., 24
  and the civil rights movement, 254-
    255
  congressional support for, 51
  interest group ratings, 57
  positions taken by, 43, 46, *69, 71*
  on public presidency, 245
Judicial appointments, 201-202, *235*

Kennedy, John F.
  political appointment approach of,
    200
  positions taken by, 43, 46, *69, 71*
  on presidents as party leaders, 257-
    258
Kesselman, Mark, 40-41

Law of the Sea Convention, 113-114
Legislation. *See* Congressional
  legislation
Legislation requests, 39-40, *66*
Legislative management
  processes involved in, 37-38, *64*
  staff, 37, *63*
Legislative positions
  and interest groups, 56-57
  organization of relations with
    Congress and, 36-44
  partisan connections and, 50-51
  policy complexity and, 44-46, 51-56
  presidential vs. congressional
    dominance in, 46-50
  veto power and, 57-59
Legislative veto applications, 115
Lincoln, Abraham, use of patronage
  system by, 200
Lobbyists, 37, *63*
Lowi, Theodore, 15

McCormick, Richard P., 50, 379-380
McKinley, William, 111, 386